Human Societies

Human Societies

An Introductory Reader in Sociology

Edited by Anthony Giddens

Polity Press

This collection and introductory material copyright © Anthony Giddens 1992

First published in 1992 by Polity Press in association with Blackwell Publishers

Reprinted 1992, 1995

Editorial office:
Polity Press
65 Bridge Street
Cambridge CB2 1UR, UK

Marketing and production:
Blackwell Publishers, the publishing imprint of Basil Blackwell Ltd
108 Cowley Road
Oxford OX4 1JF, UK

ISBN 0 7456 0957 0
ISBN 0 7456 0958 9 (pbk)

A CIP catalogue record for this book is available from the British Library.

Typeset in Times by Graphicraft Typesetters Ltd., Hong Kong
Printed in Great Britain by T.J. Press (Padstow) Ltd, Padstow, Cornwall

This book is printed on acid-free paper.

Contents

Sources and Acknowledgements

The author and publisher are grateful to the following for permission to reprint copyright material as readings in the book:

1 Abridged from *The Sociological Imagination* by C. Wright Mills (Oxford University Press, New York, 1959). Copyright © 1959 by Oxford University Press, Inc.; renewed 1987 by Yaraslava Mills. Reprinted by permission of the publisher.

2 Abridged from *Thinking Sociologically* by Zygmunt Bauman (Basil Blackwell, Oxford, 1990). Copyright © Zygmunt Bauman 1990.

3 Reprinted by permission of Macmillan Publishing Company from *Encounters: Two Studies in the Sociology of Interaction* by Erving Goffman (The Bobbs-Merrill Company, Inc., Indianapolis and New York, 1961). Copyright © 1961 Bobbs-Merrill.

4 From *Behavior in Public Places: Notes on the Social Organization of Gatherings* by Erving Goffman (The Free Press, New York/Collier-Macmillan Ltd., London).

5 From *Relating to Others* by Steve Duck (Open University Press, Milton Keynes, 1988).

6 From *The Metronomic Society: Natural Rhythms and Human Timetables* by Michael Young (Thames and Hudson Ltd., 1988). Copyright © Michael Young 1988.

7 From *Museums of Madness: The Social Organization of Insanity in Nineteenth-Century England* by Andrew T. Scull (Allen Lane, London, 1979). Copyright © Andrew Scull 1979.

8 From *The Islington Crime Survey: Crime, Victimization and Policing in Inner-City London* by Trevor Jones, Brian MacLean and Jock Young (Gower Publishing Company Ltd.).

9 From 'Irregular Work, Irregular Pleasures: Heroin in the 1980s' by John Auld, Nicholas Dorn and Nigel South in *Confronting Crime* edited by Roger Matthews and Jock Young (Sage Publications Ltd., London, 1986). Copyright © the authors.

10 From *Business Crime: Its Nature and Control* by Michael Clarke (Polity Press, 1990). Copyright © Michael Clarke.

11 From *Criminal Women: Autobiographical Accounts* edited by Pat Carlen (Polity Press, 1985). Copyright © Josie O'Dwyer and Pat Carlen.

12 From *Women: A World Report* by Debbie Taylor (Methuen, London, 1985).

13 From *'Just like a Girl': How Girls Learn to be Women* by Sue Sharpe (Penguin Books, Harmondsworth 1976). Copyright © Sue Sharpe 1976.

14 From *Equal at Work? Women in Men's Jobs* by Anna Coote (William Collins Sons & Company Ltd, Glasgow & London, 1979). Copyright © Anna Coote. Reproduced by permission of Rogers, Coleridge and White Ltd.

15 From 'The Embodiment of Masculinity: Cultural, Psychological and Behavioural Dimensions' by Marc E. Mishkind, Judith Rodin, Lisa R. Silberstein and Ruth H. Striegel-Moore in *Changing Men: New Directions in Research on Men and Masculinity* edited by Michael S. Kimmel (Sage Publications, London 1987). Copyright © Sage Publications, Inc. 1987. Reprinted by permission of Sage Publications, Inc.

16 From *Women on Rape* by Jane Dowdeswell (Thorsons, Wellingborough, 1986). Copyright © Jane Dowdeswell.

17 From 'Dangerous Liaisons' by C. Sanders, *New Statesman and Society*, 6 July 1990.

18 From *The Class Structure of the Advanced Societies*, 2nd edn, by Anthony Giddens (Unwin Hyman Ltd., 1980). Copyright © Anthony Giddens, 1980.

19 From *Contemporary British Society* edited by Nicholas Abercrombie and Alan Warde, with Keith Soothill, John Urry and Sylvia Walby (Polity Press, Cambridge, 1988). Copyright © the authors.

20 From *The Upper Classes: Property and Privilege in Britain* by John Scott (Macmillan, London and Basingstoke, 1982).

21 From 'What about the Workers?', by Robert Waller, *New Statesman and Society*, 13 July 1990.

22 From 'Women at Class Crossroads: Repudiating Conventional Theories of Family Class' by Hakon Leiulsfrud and Alison Woodward, *Sociology*, vol. 21, no. 3.
23 From *Political Parties: A Genuine Case for Discontent?* by Jean Blondel (Wildwood House, London, 1978). Copyright © Jean Blondel 1978. Reprinted by permission of the author.
24 From *Politics against Markets: The Social Democratic Road to Power* by Gosta Esping-Andersen (Princeton University Press, Princeton, NJ, 1985). Copyright © 1985 Princeton University Press. Reprinted by permission of Princeton University Press.
25 From *Models of Democracy* by David Held (Polity Press, Cambridge, 1987). Copyright © David Held 1987.
26 Extract taken from *Soviet Society under Perestroika* by David Lane (Unwin Hyman, part of HarperCollins Publishers, London. Reproduced by kind permission of Unwin Hyman Ltd.
27 From *Nations and Nationalism* by Ernest Gellner (Basil Blackwell, Oxford, 1983). Copyright © Ernest Gellner 1983.
28 From *The Bureacratization of the World* by Henry Jacoby, translated by Eveline Kanes (University of California Press, Berkeley, Calif., 1973). Copyright © 1973 The Regents of the University of California.
29 From *Inside Organizations: Understanding the Human Dimension* by Michael Owen Jones, Michael Dane Moore and Richard Christopher Snyder, pp. 116–26. Copyright © 1988 by Sage Publications Inc. Reprinted by permission of Sage Publications, Inc.
30 From *Greedy Institutions: Patterns of Undivided Commitment* by Lewis A. Coser (The Free Press, Macmillan, New York, 1974). Copyright © The Free Press 1974.
31 From *The Imaginary War: Was there an East–West Conflict?* by Mary Kaldor (Basil Blackwell, Oxford, 1990). Copyright © Mary Kaldor 1990. First published by Basil Blackwell Ltd.. 1990.
32 From *The Military: More than just a Job?* edited by Charles C. Moskos and Frank R. Wood (Pergamon-Brassey's International Defence Publishers Inc.
33 From *Women and War* by Jean Bethke Elshtain (Harvester Wheatsheaf, Brighton, 1987).
34 From *Children and Prejudice* by Frances Aboud (Basil Blackwell, Oxford, 1988). Copyright © Frances Aboud 1988.
35 From *'There Ain't No Black in the Union Jack': The Cultural Politics of Race and Nation* by Paul Gilroy (Unwin Hyman, London, 1987). Copyright © Paul Gilroy 1987. Reproduced by kind permission of Unwin Hyman.
36 From 'Black Entrepreneurs' by E. Cashmore, *New Statesman and Society*, 17 August 1990.
37 From *The Family, Sex and Marriage in England 1500–1800* by Laurence Stone (Weidenfeld and Nicolson, London, 1977).
38 From *Grounds for Divorce* by Gwynn Davis and Mervyn Murch (Clarendon Press, Oxford, 1988). Copyright © Gwynn Davis and Mervyn Murch 1988. Reprinted by permission of Oxford University Press.
39 From 'Household Spending, Personal Spending and the Control of Money in Marriage' by Jan Pahl, *Sociology*, vol. 24, no. 1.
40 Extract taken from *Intimate Intrusions: Women's Experience of Male Violence* by Elizabeth A. Stanko (Routledge & Kegan Paul, London, 1985). Copyright © Elizabeth A. Stanko 1985. Reproduced by kind permission of Unwin Hyman Ltd.
41 *Reproductive Technologies: Gender, Motherhood and Medicine* edited by Michelle Stanworth (Polity Press, Cambridge, 1987).
42 From *Learning to Labour: How working class kids get working class jobs* by Paul E. Willis (Gower Publishing Group 1977)
43 From *The Sociology of School and Education* by Ivan Reid (Fontana, London, 1986). Copyright © Ivan Reid 1986.
44 From 'Finishing School' by Saeeda Khanum, *New Statesman and Society*, 25 May 1990.
45 From *Media, Myths and Narratives: Television and the Press* by James W. Carey, pp. 113–22 (Sage Publications Inc., 1988). Reprinted by permission ot Sage Publications.
46 *Ideology and Modern Culture: Critical Social Theory in the Era of Mass Communication* by John B. Thompson (Polity Press, Cambridge, 1990). Copyright © John B. Thompson 1990.
47 From *The Invisible Religion: The Problem of Religion in Modern Society* by Thomas Luckmann (Macmillan, New York, 1967). Copyright © Thomas Luckmann.
48 From 'Toward Desacralizing Secularization Theory' by Jeffrey K. Hadden, in *Social Forces*, vol. 65, no. 3, March 1987. Copyright © 1987 The University of North Carolina Press.
49 From *Radical Islam: Medieval Theology and Modern Politics* by Emmanuel Sivan (Yale University Press, New Haven, Conn., 1985). Copyright © 1985 Yale University.
50 From *Disorganized Capitalism: Contemporary Transformations of Work and Politics* by Claus Offe, edited by John Keane (Polity Press, Cambridge, 1985).
51 From 'Britain in the Decade of the Three Economies' by J. Gershuny and R. E. Pahl in *New Society*, 3 January 1980.
52 From 'House of the Rising Sun' by J. Seabrook in *New Statesman and Society*, 23 March 1990.
53 From *Case Studies in Organizational Behaviour* edited by Chris W. Clegg, Nigel J. Kemp and Karen Legge (Paul Chapman Publishing Ltd., 1985).

54   From 'From Fordism to Flexible Accumulation' by E. Schoenberger in *Environment and Planning D: Society and Space* (Pion Ltd., 1988).

55   'Female Workers in the First and Third Worlds: The 'Greening' of Women's Labour' by Ruth Pearson, in *On Work: Historical, Comparative and Theoretical Approaches* edited by R. E. Pahl (Basil Blackwell, Oxford, 1988).

56   From *The Information Society: Issues and Illusions* by David Lyon (Polity Press, Cambridge, 1988).

57   From *The Third World* by Peter Worsley (Weidenfeld and Nicolson, London, 1968).

58   From 'The New International Division of Labour' by Ankie Hoogvelt in *The World Order: Socialist Perspectives* edited by Ray Bush, Gordon Johnston and David Coates (Polity Press, Cambridge, 1987).

59   From *The Hunger Machine: The Politics of Food* by Jon Bennett (Polity Press in association with Channel Four Television and Yorkshire Television, 1987).

60   From *Electronic Colonialism: The Future of International Broadcasting and Communication* (2nd edn.) by Thomas L. McPhail (Sage Publications Inc., 1987). Reprinted by permission Sage Publications, Inc.

61   From *Problems and Planning in Third World Cities* edited by Michael Pacione (Croom Helm, London, 1981).

62   Excerpts from *Urban Fortunes: The Political Economy of Place* by John R. Logan and Harvey L. Molotch, excerpts from pp. 50–62 (The University of California Press, 1987). Copyright © 1987 The Regents of the University of California.

63   From 'Economic Restructuring and the Internationalization of the Los Angeles Region' by Edward W. Soja in *The Capitalist City: Global Restructuring and Community Politics* edited by Michael Peter Smith and Joe R. Feagin (Basil Blackwell, Oxford, 1987).

64   From *In Sickness and in Health: The British Experience 1650–1850*, edited by Roy Porter and Dorothy Porter (Fourth Estate, London, 1988). Copyright © Roy Porter and Dorothy Porter 1988.

65   From *Health and the Global Environment* by Ross Hume Hall (Polity Press, Cambridge, 1990). Copyright © Ross Hume Hall 1990.

66   Excerpts from *Reproductive Rights and Wrongs: The Global Politics of Population Control and Contraceptive Choice* by Betsy Hartmann (Harper & Row, New York, 1987). Copyright © 1987 by Betsy Hartmann. Reprinted by permission of HarperCollins Publishers.

67   From *Revolution: A Sociological Interpretation* by Michael S. Kimmel (Polity Press, Cambridge, 1990). Copyright © Michael S. Kimmel 1990.

68   From 'The Green Movement: A Socio-Historical Exploration' by Johan Galtung, in *International Sociology*, vol. 1, no. 1, 1986.

69   From 'Reinventing the Global Village', by Deirdre Boden (Dept. of Sociology, Washington University, 1990). Unpublished ms.

70   From *People Studying People: The Human Element in Fieldwork* by Robert A. Georges and Michael O. Jones (University of California Press, Berkeley, Calif., 1980). Copyright © 1980 The Regents of the University of California.

71   From 'Girls, Wives, Factory Lives' by A. Pollert, in *New Society*, 22 October 1981.

72   Extract from *The Survey Method: The Contribution of Surveys to Sociological Explanation* by Catherine Marsh (George Allen and Unwin, London, 1982). Reproduced by kind permission of Unwin Hyman Ltd. Copyright © Catherine Marsh 1982.

73   From *Poor Britain* by Joanna Mack and Stuart Lansley (George Allen & Unwin, 1985). Reproduced by kind permission of Unwin Hyman Ltd.

74   From *Garfinkel and Ethnomethodology* by John Heritage (Polity Press, Cambridge, 1984). Copyright © John Heritage 1984.

75   From Karl Marx and Fredrick Engels, *Selected Works in One Volume* (Lawrence & Wishart Ltd, London, 1968). Reprinted by permission of Lawrence & Wishart Ltd.

76   From 'The Field of Sociology' by Emile Durkheim, in *Emile Durkheim: Selected Writings* edited by Anthony Giddens (Cambridge University Press, Cambridge, 1972). Copyright © Cambridge University Press 1972.

77   From *Basic Concepts in Sociology* by Max Weber (Peter Owen Ltd, London). Copyright © Philosophical Library New York, 1962.

78   From *Essays on Sex Equality* by John Stuart Mill and Harriet Taylor Mill, ed. by Alice S. Rossi (University of Chicago Press, Chicago, 1970). Copyright © 1970 The University of Chicago.

79   From *Mind, Self and Society: From the Standpoint of a Social Behaviorist* by George H. Mead, ed. Charles W. Morris. (The University of Chicago Press, Chicago, 1934). Copyright © University of Chicago, 1934.

80   From *Function, Purpose and Powers: Some Concepts in the Study of Individuals and Societies*, 2nd edn. by Dorothy Emmet (Macmillan, London, 1972). Copyright © Dorothy Emmet 1972.

81   From *Structuralism and Since: From Levi-Strauss to Derrida* edited by John Sturrock. Copyright © Oxford University Press 1979. Reprinted by permission of Oxford University Press.

82   From *Social Theory and Modern Sociology* by Anthony Giddens (Polity Press, Cambridge, 1987). Copyright © Anthony Giddens 1987.

Introduction

This book has been designed to accompany my introductory text, *Sociology*,[1] but it can be read as a completely separate work. It is aimed at those who are approaching sociology for the first time and I have devoted considerable care to ensuring that all the sources included are clear and accessible for beginning students.

Although the selections are weighted towards the study of Britain, as in *Sociology* the emphasis throughout is upon the global nature of sociological thought today. Consequently the selections are not insular, but offer a broad coverage of developments affecting the industrialized societies in general. In the current era global processes impinge upon the most local and personal aspects of social life; conversely, individual actions and localized social interaction contribute to globally ordered systems. In choosing the selections represented here, therefore, I have ranged from small-scale studies of interaction right through to the analysis of the most extensive forms of social system now influencing our lives.

Many of the selections contain empirical material of a generalizing kind. But I have also incorporated a substantial range of sources based upon more qualitative materials, including many in which the individuals concerned speak for themselves rather than being spoken for by the sociological researcher. Such an emphasis is not only consonant with what I hold to be essential methodological presuppositions of social analysis; it also represents a claim that 'case studies' often reveal more of a general nature about social processes than do apparently more extensive empirical observations.

Globalizing influences do not work exclusively towards integration. Although there are some fundamental respects in which a planetary social order has been created, globalization also divides, marginalizes and excludes. From its earliest origins, modernity has intruded into geographical areas other than those which form its core regions of origin, and has corroded, or radically altered, other social orders or cultures with which it has come into contact. The economically advanced societies of the first world developed in conjunction with the emergence of third world systems. The acceleration of globalizing trends in the present century has certainly changed some of these pre-existing connections, but it is now more than ever true that the study of the industrialized countries must be related to an understanding of the less developed sectors of the world.

Accordingly I have included various selections which either focus directly upon the third world or trace out first world–third world relationships. The term 'third world', of course, was never a particularly happy one and has become distinctly threadbare with the virtual disappearance of the 'second world', coupled to the emergence of the 'newly industrializing countries'. New concepts and terminologies are needed to analyse these processes, as they are when we consider the restructuring of what were the second world countries.

The format and sequence of the different parts of the book more or less follow those set out in *Sociology*, save that discussions of cultural diversity and socialization, which figure as the first two chapters of that book, are not included here. An extensive number of selections is provided concerning research methods and theoretical perspectives in sociology. As in the textbook, these are placed at the end of the volume. The reason for this is my belief that abstract notions in sociology cannot readily be mastered until students have had the opportunity to become acquainted with more substantive studies and debates. However, students are encouraged to consult the two concluding sections of the book at any point for amplification of methodological or theoretical issues raised in earlier selections.

Each part of the book is preceded by a prefatory description of the selections included, but I have kept these short in order to give primacy to the source materials themselves. Although every effort has been made to concentrate upon sources that are immediately accessible, inevitably there are differences in style and complexity among the selections. Some involve rather more demanding arguments than others, and the fluency with which the authors express their findings or views varies. I hope, however, that these contrasts will help to give the reader a sense of the range and diversity of sociological writings at the present time.

Many of the selections come from books or articles which might be difficult for most readers to obtain, either because of the limited circulation of the source materials concerned or, conversely, because more popular works are in such demand that access to them, even in the best supplied of libraries, is limited. Nevertheless, I hope that readers will be sufficiently intrigued or stimulated by the readings included here to locate the original books or articles to pursue them further.

In order to maximize the readability of the selections, references and footnotes have been kept to a minimum. Those that are retained should provide ample opportunity for the reader to follow up lines of thought or investigation not directly analysed in the articles themselves.

Part 1

On the Nature of Sociology

More than most other intellectual endeavours, sociology presumes the use of disciplined imagination. Imagination, because the sociologist must distance her- or himself from the here and now in order to grasp how societies have changed in the past and what potential transformations lie in store; discipline, because the creative ability of the imagination has to be restrained by conceptual and empirical rigour.

C. Wright Mills's discussion of the sociological imagination (reading 1) has long been the classic discussion of these issues. We cannot understand ourselves as individuals, Mills emphasizes, unless we grasp the involvement of our own biography with the historical development of social institutions. On the other hand, we cannot comprehend the nature of those institutions unless we understand how they are organized in and through individual action. It is the business of sociology to analyse the social orders which constrain our behaviour, but at the same time to acknowledge that we actively make our own history.

These ideas are echoed by Zygmunt Bauman (reading 2). The focus of his discussion, however, is the similarities and differences between sociology and common-sense understandings of social life. Sociology, he agrees with Mills, teaches us to see our own individual experiences in relation to wider social systems, as well as to broad patterns of social change. As such, it is a distinctive way of thinking about the social world. Studying human social activity, Bauman says, is different from analysing objects or events in the natural world. We are all in some sense knowledgeable and skilful in respect of our participation in day-to-day social activity. Sociological knowledge builds upon the practical forms of knowing by means of which we organize our everyday lives. Sociological concepts, however, need to be more clearly formulated and precise than those of ordinary language.

Sociological investigation ranges over much broader arenas, in time as well as in space, than the immediate settings of interaction with which we are most familiar in the daily round. Moreover, sociologists focus attention upon unintended and unanticipated consequences of human activity, whereas in ordinary activities we concern ourselves mainly with the intentions and emotions of other people. As Mills also stresses, sociological thought must take an imaginative leap beyond the familiar, and the sociologist must be prepared to look behind the routine activities in which much of our mundane life is enmeshed.

1   C. Wright Mills

The Sociological Imagination and
the Promise of Sociology

The sociological imagination enables its possessor to understand the larger historical scene in terms of its meaning for the inner life and the external career of a variety of individuals. It enables [the sociologist] to take into account how individuals, in the welter of their daily experience, often become falsely conscious of their social positions. Within that welter, the framework of modern society is sought, and within that framework the psychologies of a variety of men and women are formulated. By such means the personal uneasiness of individuals is focused upon explicit troubles and the indifference of publics is transformed into involvement with public issues.

The first fruit of this imagination – and the first lesson of the social science that embodies it – is the idea that the individual can understand his* own experience and gauge his own fate only by locating himself within his period, that he can know his own chances in life only by becoming aware of those of all individuals in his circumstances. In many ways it is a terrible lesson; in many ways a magnificent one. We do not know the limits of man's capacities for supreme effort or willing degradation, for agony or glee, for pleasurable brutality or the sweetness of reason. But in our time we have come to know that the limits of 'human nature' are frighteningly broad. We have come to know that every individual lives, from one generation to the next, in some society; that he lives out a biography, and that he lives it out within some historical sequence. By the fact of his living he contributes, however minutely, to the shaping of this society and to the course of its history, even as he is made by society and by its historical push and shove.

The sociological imagination enables us to grasp history and biography and the relations between the two within society. That is its task and its promise...

No social study that does not come back to the problems of biography, of history and of their intersections within a society has completed its intellectual journey. Whatever the specific problems of the classic social analysts, however limited or however broad the features of social reality they have examined, those who have been imaginatively aware of the promise of their work have consistently asked three sorts of questions:

1   What is the structure of this particular society as a whole? What are its essential components, and how are they related to one another? How does it differ from other varieties of social order? Within it, what is the meaning of any particular feature for its continuance and for its change?

2   Where does this society stand in human history? What are the mechanics by which it is changing? What is its place within and its meaning for the development of humanity as a whole? How does any particular feature we are examining affect, and how is it affected by, the historical period in which it moves? And this period – what are its essential features? How does it differ from other periods? What are its characteristic ways of history-making?

* Mills uses language that now would be regarded as sexist. Such is also the case with a few of the other more 'classical' selections included in the volume. Virtually all authors today recognize that words like 'he' and 'his', when used to mean human beings as a whole, are an expression of implicit gender power – and that such usage should be avoided.

3   What varieties of men and women now prevail in this society and in this period? And what varieties are coming to prevail? In what ways are they selected and formed, liberated and repressed, made sensitive and blunted? What kinds of 'human nature' are revealed in the conduct and character we observe in this society in this period? And what is the meaning for 'human nature' of each and every feature of the society we are examining?

Whether the point of interest is a great power state or a minor literary mood, a family, a prison, a creed – these are the kinds of questions the best social analysts have asked. They are the intellectual pivots of classic studies of man in society – and they are the questions inevitably raised by any mind possessing the sociological imagination. For that imagination is the capacity to shift from one perspective to another – from the political to the psychological; from examination of a single family to comparative assessment of the national budgets of the world; from the theological school to the military establishment; from considerations of an oil industry to studies of contemporary poetry. It is the capacity to range from the most impersonal and remote transformations to the most intimate features of the human self – and to see the relations between the two. Back of its use there is always the urge to know the social and historical meaning of the individual in the society and in the period in which he has his quality and his being...

Perhaps the most fruitful distinction with which the sociological imagination works is between 'the personal troubles of milieu' and 'the public issues of social structure'. This distinction is an essential tool of the sociological imagination and a feature of all classic work in social science...

In these terms, consider unemployment. When, in a city of 100,000, only one man is unemployed, that is his personal trouble, and for its relief we properly look to the character of the man, his skills and his immediate opportunities. But when, in a nation of 50 million employees, 15 million men are unemployed, that is an issue, and we may not hope to find its solution within the range of opportunities open to any one individual. The very structure of opportunities has collapsed. Both the correct statement of the problem and the range of possible solutions require us to consider the economic and political institutions of the society, and not merely the personal situation and character of a scatter of individuals.

Consider war. The personal problem of war, when it occurs, may be how to survive it or how to die in it with honour; how to make money out of it; how to climb into the higher safety of the military apparatus; or how to contribute to the war's termination. In short, according to one's values, to find a set of milieux and within it to survive the war or make one's death in it meaningful. But the structural issues of war have to do with its causes; with what types of men it throws up into command; with its effects upon economic and political, family and religious institutions, with the unorganized irresponsibility of a world of nation states.

Consider marriage. Inside a marriage a man and a woman may experience personal troubles, but when the divorce rate during the first four years of marriage is 250 out of every 1,000 attempts, this is an indication of a structural issue having to do with the institutions of marriage and the family and other institutions that bear upon them.

Or consider the metropolis – the horrible, beautiful, ugly, magnificent sprawl of the great city. For many upper-class people, the personal solution to 'the problem of the city' is to have an apartment with private garage under it in the heart of the city, and forty miles out, a house by Henry Hill, garden by

Garrett Eckbo, on a hundred acres of private land. In these two controlled environments – with a small staff at each end and a private helicopter connection – most people could solve many of the problems of personal milieux caused by the facts of the city. But all this, however splendid, does not solve the public issues that the structural fact of the city poses. What should be done with this wonderful monstrosity? Break it all up into scattered units, combining residence and work? Refurbish it as it stands? Or, after evacuation, dynamite it and build new cities according to new plans in new places? What should those plans be? And who is to decide and to accomplish whatever choice is made? These are structural issues; to confront them and to solve them requires us to consider political and economic issues that affect innumerable milieux.

In so far as an economy is so arranged that slumps occur, the problem of unemployment becomes incapable of personal solution. In so far as war is inherent in the nation-state system and in the uneven industrialization of the world, the ordinary individual in his restricted milieu will be powerless – with or without psychiatric aid – to solve the troubles this system or lack of system imposes upon him. In so far as the family as an institution turns women into darling little slaves and men into their chief providers and unweaned dependants, the problem of a satisfactory marriage remains incapable of purely private solution. In so far as the overdeveloped megalopolis and the overdeveloped automobile are built-in features of the overdeveloped society, the issues of urban living will not be solved by personal ingenuity and private wealth.

What we experience in various and specific milieux, I have noted, is often caused by structural changes. Accordingly, to understand the changes of many personal milieux we are required to look beyond them. And the number and variety of such structural changes increase as the institutions within which we live become more embracing and more intricately connected with one another. To be aware of the idea of social structure and to use it with sensibility is to be capable of tracing such linkages among a great variety of milieux. To be able to do that is to possess the sociological imagination.

2 Zygmunt Bauman

Thinking Sociologically

The central question of sociology, one could say, is: in what sense does it matter that in whatever they do or may do people are dependent on other people; in what sense does it matter that they live always (and cannot but live) in the company of, in communication with, in an exchange with, in competition with, in co-operation with other human beings? It is this kind of question (and not a separate collection of people or events selected for the purpose of study, nor some set of human actions neglected by other lines of investigation) that constitutes the particular area of sociological discussion and defines sociology as a relatively autonomous branch of human and social sciences. Sociology, we may conclude, is first and foremost a *way of thinking* about the human world; in principle one can also think about the same world in different ways.

Among these other ways from which the sociological way of thinking is set apart, a special place is occupied by so-called *common sense*. Perhaps more than other branches of scholarship, sociology finds its relation with common sense (that rich yet disorganized, non-systematic, often inarticulate and ineffable knowledge we use to conduct our daily business of life) fraught with problems decisive for its standing and practice.

Indeed, few sciences are concerned with spelling out their relationship to common sense; most do not even notice that common sense exists, let alone that it presents a problem. Most sciences settle for defining themselves in terms of boundaries that separate them from or bridges that connect them with other sciences – respectable, systematic lines of inquiry like themselves. They do not feel they share enough ground with common sense to bother with drawing boundaries or building bridges. Their indifference is, one must admit, well justified. Common sense has next to nothing to say of the matters of which physics, or chemistry, or astronomy, or geology speak (and whatever it has to say on such matters comes courtesy of those sciences themselves, in so far as they manage to make their recondite findings graspable and intelligible for lay people). The subjects dealt with by physics or astronomy hardly ever appear within the sight of ordinary men and women: inside, so to speak, your and my daily experience. And so we, the non-experts, the ordinary people, cannot form opinions about such matters unless aided – indeed, instructed – by the scientists. The objects explored by sciences like the ones we have mentioned appear only under very special circumstances, to which lay people have no access: on the screen of a multi-million-dollar accelerator, in the lens of a gigantic telescope, at the bottom of a thousand-feet-deep shaft. Only the scientists can see them and experiment with them; these objects and events are a monopolistic possession of the given branch of science (or even of its selected practitioners), a property not shared with anybody who is not a member of the profession. Being the sole owners of the experience which provides the raw material for their study, the scientists are in full control over the way the material is processed, analysed, interpreted. Products of such processing would have to withstand the critical scrutiny of other scientists – but their scrutiny only. They will not have to compete with public opinion, common sense or any other form in which non-specialist views may appear, for the simple reason that there is no public opinion and no commonsensical point of view in the matters they study and pronounce upon.

With sociology it is quite different. In sociological study there are no equivalents of giant accelerators or radiotelescopes. All experience which provides raw material for sociological findings – the stuff of which sociological knowledge is made – is the experience of ordinary people in ordinary, daily life; an experience accessible in principle, though not always in practice, to everybody; and experience that, before it came under the magnifying glass of a sociologist, had already been lived by someone else – a non-sociologist, a person not trained in the use of sociological language and seeing things from a sociological point of view. All of us live in the company of other people, after all, and interact with each other. All of us have learned only too well that what we get depends on what other people do. All of us have gone more than once through the agonizing experience of a communication breakdown with friends and strangers. Anything sociology talks about was already there in our lives. And it must have been, otherwise we should be unable to conduct our business of life. To live in the company of other people, we need a lot of knowledge; and common sense is the name of that knowledge.

Deeply immersed in our daily routines, though, we hardly ever pause to think about the meaning of what we have gone through; even less often have we the opportunity to compare our private experience with the fate of others, to see the *social* in the *individual*, the *general* in the *particular*; this is precisely what sociologists can do for us. We would expect them to show us how our individual *biographies* intertwine with the *history* we share with fellow human beings. And yet whether or not the sociologists get that far, they have no other point to start from than the daily experience of life they share with you and me – from that raw knowledge that saturates the daily life of each one of us. For this reason alone the sociologists, however hard they might have tried to follow the example of the physicists and the biologists and stand aside from the object of their study (that is, look at your and my life experience as an object 'out there', as a detached and impartial observer would do), cannot break off completely from their insider's knowledge of the experience they try to comprehend. However hard they might try, sociologists are bound to remain on both sides of the experience they strive to interpret, inside and outside at the same time. (Note how often the sociologists use the personal pronoun 'we' when they report their findings and formulate their general propositions. That 'we' stands for an 'object' that includes those who study and those whom they study. Can you imagine a physicist using 'we' of themselves and the molecules? Or astronomers using 'we' to generalize about themselves and the stars?)

There is more still to the special relationship between sociology and common sense. The phenomena observed and theorized upon by modern physicists or astronomers come in an innocent and pristine form, unprocessed, free from labels, ready-made definitions and prior interpretations (that is, except such interpretations as had been given them in advance by the physicists who set the experiments that made them appear). They wait for the physicist or the astronomer to name them, to set them among other phenomena and combine them into an orderly whole: in short, to give them *meaning*. But there are few, if any, sociological equivalents of such clean and unused phenomena which have never been given meaning before. Those human actions and interactions that sociologists explore had all been given names and theorized about, in however diffuse, poorly articulated form, by the actors themselves. Before sociologists started looking at them, they were objects of commonsensical knowledge. Families, organizations, kinship networks, neighbourhoods, cities and villages, nations and churches and any other groupings held together by regular human interaction have already been given meaning and significance by the actors, so that the actors consciously address them in their actions as bearers of such meanings. Lay actors and professional sociologists would have to use the same names, the same language when speaking of them. Each term sociologists may use will already have been heavily burdened with meanings it was given by the commonsensical knowledge of 'ordinary' people like you and me.

For the reason explained above, sociology is much too intimately related to common sense to afford that lofty equanimity with which sciences like chemistry or geology can treat it. You and I are allowed to speak of human interdependence and human interaction, and to speak with authority. Don't we all practise them and experience them? Sociological discourse is wide open: no standing invitation to everybody to join, but no clearly marked borders or effective border guards either. With poorly defined borders whose security is not guaranteed in advance (unlike sciences that explore objects inaccessible to lay experience), the sovereignty of sociology over social knowledge, its right to make authoritative pronouncements on the subject, may always be contested. This is why drawing a boundary between sociological knowledge proper and the common sense that is always full of sociological ideas is such an important matter for the identity of sociology as a cohesive body of knowledge; and why sociologists pay this matter more attention than other scientists.

We can think of at least four quite seminal differences between the ways in which sociology and common sense – your and my 'raw' knowledge of the business of life – treat the topic they share: human experience.

To start with, sociology (unlike common sense) makes an effort to subordinate itself to the rigorous rules of *responsible speech*, which is assumed to be an attribute of science (as distinct from other, reputedly more relaxed and less vigilantly self-controlled, forms of knowledge). This means that the sociologists are expected to take great care to distinguish – in a fashion clear and visible to anybody – between the statements corroborated by available evidence and such propositions as can only claim the status of a provisional, untested guess. Sociologists would refrain from misrepresenting ideas that are grounded solely in their beliefs (even the most ardent and emotionally intense beliefs) as tested findings carrying the widely respected authority of science. The rules of responsible speech demand that one's 'workshop' – the whole procedure that has led to the final conclusions and is claimed to guarantee their credibility – be wide open to an unlimited public scrutiny; a standing invitation ought to be extended to everyone to reproduce the test and, be this the case, prove the findings wrong. Responsible speech must also relate to other statements made on its topic; it cannot simply dismiss or pass by in silence other views that have been voiced, however sharply they are opposed to it and hence inconvenient. It is hoped that once the rules of responsible speech are honestly and meticulously observed, the trustworthiness, reliability and eventually also the practical usefulness of the ensuing propositions will be greatly enhanced, even if not fully guaranteed. Our shared faith in the credibility of beliefs countersigned by science is to a great extent grounded in the hope that the scientists will indeed follow the rules of responsible speech, and that the scientific profession as a whole will see to it that every single member of the profession does so on every occasion. As to the scientists themselves, they point to the virtues of responsible speech as an argument in favour of the superiority of the knowledge they offer.

The second difference is related to the *size of the field* from which the material for judgement is drawn. For most of us, as non-professionals, such a field is confined to our own life-world: things we do, people we meet, purposes we set for our own pursuits and guess other people set for theirs. Rarely, if at all, do we make an effort to lift ourselves above the level of our daily concerns to broaden the horizon of experience, as this would require time and resources most of us can ill afford or do not feel like spending on such effort. And yet, given the tremendous variety of life-conditions, each experience based solely on an individual life-world is necessarily partial and most likely one-sided. Such shortcomings can be rectified only if one brings together and sets against each other experiences drawn from a multitude of life-worlds. Only then will the incompleteness of individual experience be revealed, as will be the complex network of dependencies and interconnections in which it is entangled – a network which reaches far beyond the realm which could be scanned from the vantage point of a singular biography. The overall result of such a broadening of horizons will be the discovery of the intimate link between individual biography and wide social processes the individual may be unaware of and surely unable to control. It is for this reason that the sociologists' pursuit of a perspective wider than the one offered by an individual life-world makes a great difference – not just a quantitative difference (more data, more facts, statistics instead of single cases), but a difference in the quality and the uses of knowledge. For people like you or me, who pursue our respective aims in life and struggle for more control over our plight, sociological knowledge has something to offer that common sense cannot.

The third difference between sociology and common sense pertains to the way in which each one goes about *making sense* of human reality; how each one goes about explaining to its own satisfaction why this rather than that happened or is the case. I imagine that you (much as myself) know from your own experience that you are 'the author' of your actions; you know that what you do (though not necessarily the results of your actions) is an effect of your intention, hope or purpose. You normally do as you do in order to achieve a state of affairs you desire, whether you wish to possess an object, to receive an accolade from your teachers or to put an end to your friends' teasing. Quite naturally, the way you think of your action serves you as a model for making sense of all other actions. You explain such actions to yourself by imputing to others intentions you know from your own experience. This is, to be sure, the only way we can make sense of the human world around us as long as we draw our tools of explanation solely from within our respective life-worlds. We tend to perceive everything that happens in the world at large as an outcome of somebody's intentional action. We look for the persons responsible for what has happened and, once we have found them, we believe our inquiry has been completed. We assume somebody's goodwill lies behind every event we like and somebody's ill intentions behind every event we dislike. We would find it difficult to accept that a situation was not an effect of intentional action of an identifiable 'somebody'; and we would not lightly give up our conviction that any unwelcome condition could be remedied if only someone, somewhere, wished to take the right action. Those who more than anyone else interpret the world for us – politicians, journalists, commercial advertisers – tune in to this tendency of ours and speak of the 'needs of the state' or 'demands of the economy', as if the state or the economy were made to the measure of individual persons like ourselves and could have needs or make demands. On the other hand, they portray the complex problems of nations, states and economic systems (deeply seated in the very structures of such figurations) as the effects of the thoughts and deeds of a few individuals one can name, put in front of a camera and interview. Sociology stands in opposition to such a personalized world-view.... When thinking sociologically, one attempts to make sense of the human condition through analysing the manifold webs of human interdependency – that toughest of realities which explains both our motives and the effects of their activation.

Finally, let us recall that the power of common sense over the way we understand the world and ourselves (the immunity of common sense to questioning, its capacity for self-confirmation) depends on the apparently self-evident character of its precepts. This in turn rests on the routine, monotonous nature of daily life, which informs our common sense while being simultaneously informed by it. As long as we go through the routine and habitualized motions which fill most of our daily business, we do not need much self-scrutiny and self-analysis. When repeated often enough, things tend to become familiar, and familiar things are self-explanatory; they present no problems and arouse no curiosity. In a way, they remain invisible. Questions are not asked, as people are satisfied that 'things are as they are', 'people are as they are', and there is precious little one can do about it. Familiarity is the staunchest enemy of inquisitiveness and criticism – and thus also of innovation and the courage to change. In an encounter with that familiar world ruled by habits and reciprocally reasserting beliefs, sociology acts as a meddlesome and often irritating stranger. It disturbs the comfortingly quiet way of life by asking questions no one among the 'locals' remembers being asked, let alone answered. Such questions make evident things into puzzles: they *defamiliarize* the familiar. Suddenly, the daily way of life must come under scrutiny. It now appears to be just one of the possible ways, not the one and only, not the 'natural', way of life....

One could say that the main service the art of thinking sociologically may render to each and every one of us is to make us more *sensitive*; it may sharpen up our senses, open our eyes wider so that we can explore human conditions which thus far had remained all but invisible. Once we understand better how the apparently natural, inevitable, eternal aspects of our lives have been brought into being through the exercise of human power and human resources, we will find it hard to accept once more that they are immune and impenetrable to human action – our own action included. Sociological thinking is, one may say, a power in its own right, an *anti-fixating* power. It renders flexible again the world hitherto oppressive in its apparent fixity; it shows it as a world which could be different from what it is now. It can be argued that the art of sociological thinking tends to widen the scope, the daring and the practical effectiveness of your and my *freedom*. Once the art has been learned and mastered, the individual may well become just a bit less manipulable, more resilient to oppression and regulation from outside, more likely to resist being fixed by forces that claim to be irresistible.

To think sociologically means to understand a little more fully the people around us, their cravings and dreams, their worries and their misery. We may then better appreciate the human individuals in them and perhaps even have more respect for their rights to do what we ourselves are doing and to cherish doing it: their rights to choose and practise the way of life they prefer, to select their life-projects, to define themselves and – last but not least – vehemently defend their dignity. We may realize that in doing all those things other people come across the same kind of obstacles as we do and know the bitterness of frustration as well as we do. Eventually, sociological thinking may well promote solidarity between us, a solidarity grounded in mutual understanding and respect, solidarity in our joint resistance to suffering and shared condemnation of the cruelty that causes it. If this effect is achieved, the cause of freedom will be strengthened by being elevated to the rank of a *common* cause.

Thinking sociologically may also help us to understand other forms of life, inaccessible to our direct experience and all too often entering the commonsensical knowledge only as stereotypes – one-sided, tendentious caricatures of the way people different from ourselves (distant people, or people kept at a distance by our distaste or suspicion) live. An insight into the inner logic and meaning of the forms of life other than our own may well prompt us to think again about the alleged toughness of the boundary that has been drawn between ourselves and others, between 'us' and 'them'. Above all, it may prompt us to doubt that boundary's natural, preordained character. This new understanding may well make our communication with the 'other' easier than before, and more likely to lead to mutual agreement. It may replace fear and antagonism with tolerance. This would also contribute to our freedom, as there are no guarantees of my freedom stronger than the freedom of all, and that means also of such people as may have chosen to use their freedom to embark on a life different from my own. Only under such conditions may our own freedom to choose be exercised.

Part 2

Social Interaction in Everyday Life

Erving Goffman was the pre-eminent analyst of day-to-day social interaction – above all of interaction in circumstances of 'co-presence': face-to-face social engagements between individuals present in a single physical setting. Investigating co-present interaction, Goffman points out, is distinct from the study of social groups or collectivities as such (reading 3). The analysis of interaction in situations of co-presence can be understood as a series of *encounters* into which individuals enter in the course of their daily activities. An encounter is a unit of focused interaction, in which a number of individuals directly address each other in some way. Unfocused interaction, by contrast, refers to those forms of mutual communication which occur simply because people are in the same setting – a room, a hallway, a street – as one another.

Civil inattention, discussed by Goffman in reading 4, is an important feature of unfocused interaction between strangers. When people pass one another in the street, or experience the multitude of fleeting social contacts which make up much of city life, they acknowledge each other in subtle, yet socially very important ways. Civil inattention, Goffman argues, is a fundamental part of orderly life in public social environments. The manipulation of the gaze – how individuals look at others, and for how long – he shows to be an essential, and again extraordinarily complex, feature of everyday social interaction.

Reading 5, by Steve Duck, considers how casual interaction turns into more stably established relationships. Such relationships, Duck shows, depend upon a process of self-change as individuals negotiate the forms of reciprocity which turn a series of encounters into a durable social involvement with another person. Repetition and habit form a key part of established relationships, as they do of many other contexts of social life. In reading 6 Michael Young investigates why habitual actions figure so prominently in our day-to-day activities. As in so many areas of sociology, what appears 'obvious', the significance of the 'force of habit', turns out when subjected to scrutiny to be puzzling.

3   Erving Goffman

Focused Interaction and Unfocused Interaction

The study of every unit of social organization must eventually lead to an analysis of the interaction of its elements. The analytical distinction between units of organization and processes of interaction is, therefore, not destined to divide up our work for us. A division of labour seems more likely to come from distinguishing among types of units, among types of elements, or among types of processes.

Sociologists have traditionally studied face-to-face interaction as part of the area of 'collective behaviour'; the units of social organization involved are those that can form by virtue of a breakdown in ordinary social intercourse: crowds, mobs, panics, riots. The other aspect of the problem of face-to-face interaction – the units of organization in which orderly and uneventful face-to-face interaction occurs – has been neglected until recently, although there is some early work on classroom interaction, topics of conversation, committee meetings and public assemblies.

Instead of dividing face-to-face interaction into the eventful and the routine, I propose a different division – into *unfocused interaction* and *focused interaction*. Unfocused interaction consists of those interpersonal communications that result solely by virtue of persons being in one another's presence, as when two strangers across the room from each other check up on each other's clothing, posture and general manner, while each modifies his own demeanour because he himself is under observation. Focused interaction occurs when people effectively agree to sustain for a time a single focus of cognitive and visual attention, as in a conversation, a board game or a joint task sustained by a close face-to-face circle of contributors. Those sustaining together a single focus of attention will, of course, engage one another in unfocused interaction, too. They will not do so in their capacity as participants in the focused activity, however, and persons present who are not in the focused activity will equally participate in this unfocused interaction.

... I call the natural unit of social organization in which focused interaction occurs a *focused gathering*, or an *encounter*, or a *situated activity system*. I assume that instances of this natural unit have enough in common to make it worthwhile to study them as a type....

Focused gatherings and groups do share some properties and even some that are requisites. If persons are to come together into a focused gathering and stay for a time, then certain 'system problems' will have to be solved: the participants will have to submit to rules of recruitment, to limits on overt hostility and to some division of labour. Such requisites are also found in social groups. Now if social groups and focused gatherings both exhibit the same set of properties, what is the use of distinguishing between these two units of social organization? And would not this distinction become especially unnecessary when all the members of the group are the only participants in the gathering?

Paradoxically, the easier it is to find similarities between these two units, the more mischief may be caused by not distinguishing between them. Let us address the problem, then: what is the difference between a group and a focused gathering?

A social group may be defined as a special type of social organization. Its elements are individuals: they perceive the organization as a distinct collective unit, a social entity, apart from the particular relationships the participants may have to one another; they perceive themselves as members who belong, identifying with the organization and receiving moral support from doing so; they sustain a sense of hostility to outgroups. A symbolization of the reality of the group and one's relation to it is also involved.

Small groups, according to this conception of groups, are distinguished by what their size makes possible (although not necessary), such as extensive personal knowledge of one another by the members, wide consensus and reliance on informal role differentiation. Small groups themselves – let me temporarily call them 'little groups' to distinguish them from all the other phenomena studied under the title of small-group research – differ in the degree to which they are formally or informally organized; long-standing or short-lived; multi-bonded or segmental; relatively independent, as in the case of some families and gangs, or pinned within a well-bounded organizational structure, as in the case of army platoons or office cliques.

Social groups, whether big or little, possess some general organizational properties. These properties include regulation of entering and leaving; capacity for collective action; division of labour, including leadership roles; socialization function, whether primary or adult; a means of satisfying personal ends; and latent and manifest social function in the environing society. These same properties, however, are also found in many other forms of social organization, such as a social relationship binding two persons, a network of relationships interlocking a set of friends, a complex organization or a set of businessmen or gamesters who abide by ground rules while openly concerned only with defeating the designs of their co-participants. It is possible, of course, to call any social relationship between two individuals a two-person group, but I think this is unwise. A group that is just beginning or dying may have only two members, but I feel that the conceptual framework with which this ill-manned group is to be studied ought to differ from the framework used in studying the many-sidedness of the social relationship between these two individuals. And to call any two individuals a 'two-person group' solely because there is a social relationship between them is to slight what is characteristic of groups and to fail to explore what is uniquely characteristic of relationships. . . .

Given these definitions, differences between groups and encounters become apparent. Some of the properties that are important to focused gatherings or encounters, taken as a class, seem much less important to little groups, taken as a class. Examples of such properties include embarrassment, maintenance of poise, capacity for non-distractive verbal communication, adherence to a code regarding giving up and taking over the speaker role and allocation of spatial position. Furthermore, a crucial attribute of focused gatherings – the participants' maintenance of continuous engrossment in the official focus of activity – is not a property of social groups in general, for most groups, unlike encounters, continue to exist apart from the occasions when members are physically together. A coming-together can be merely a phase of group life; a falling-away, on the other hand, is the end of a particular encounter, even when the same pattern of interaction and the same participants appear at a future meeting. Finally, there are many gatherings – for example, a set of strangers playing poker in a casino – where an extremely full array of interaction processes occurs with only the slightest development of a sense of group. All these qualifications can be made even though data for the study of little groups and for the study of focused gatherings are likely to be drawn from the same social occasion. In the same way, these qualifications can be made even though any social group can be partly described in terms of the character of the gatherings its members maintain together, just as any gathering can be described in terms of the overlapping group affiliations of its participants.

In the life of many little groups, occasions regularly arise when all the members and only the members come together and jointly sustain a situated activity system or encounter: they hold a meeting, play a game, discuss a movie, or take a cigarette break together. To call these gatherings 'meetings of the group' can easily entrap one into thinking that one is studying the group directly. Actually, these are meetings of persons who are members of a group, and, even though the meeting may have been called because of issues faced by the group, the initial data concern participants in a meeting, not members of a group.

It is true that on such occasions there is likely to be a correspondence between the realm of group life and the realm of face-to-face interaction processes. For example, leadership of a little group may be expressed during gatherings of members by the question of who is chairman, or who talks the most, or who is most frequently addressed. It is also likely that the leadership demonstrated in the gathering will both influence, and be influenced by, the leadership in the group. But group leadership is not made up exclusively of an 'averaging' of positions assumed during various gatherings. In fact, the group may face circumstances in which its leader is careful to let others take leadership during a meeting, his capacity to lead the group resting upon the tactful way in which he plays a minor role during gatherings of group members. The group leader can do this because 'taking the chair' is intrinsically a possibility of gatherings, not groups.

Similarly, the factions that occur in a little group may coincide with the coalitions formed during gatherings of group members. We know, however, that such 'open' expression of structural cleavage can be seen as dangerous to the group and destructive of the opportunity of accomplishing business during the gathering, so that this congruence will often specifically be avoided. Coalitions during the gathering will then cross-cut factions in the group.

Further, even when all the members of a group are the only participants in a gathering, and the gathering has been called in order to transact business pertaining to the group, we will inevitably find that the persons present are also members of other social groups and that each of these groups can claim only a subset – moreover, a different subset – of those present. Some of the positions in the gathering are likely to be allocated on the basis of these divisive group affiliations. Of course, other positions in the gathering are likely to be allocated on the basis of factors other than group affiliation, e.g. recognized experience, command of language, priority of appearance in the meeting-place or age.

Finally, while the morale of the group and the solidarity of its members may increase with an increasing number of meetings, there are strong groups that rarely have focused gatherings containing all their members and weak groups that have many.

There are issues apart from those that arise because of the difference between being a member of a group and being a participant in a gathering. Some of the properties that clearly belong both to groups and to gatherings turn out upon close examination to mean two different ranges of things, in part because of a difference in level of abstraction employed in the two cases. For example, one form of leadership that can be extremely important in gatherings is the maintenance of communication ground rules, i.e. 'order'; this aspect of leadership does not seem to have the same importance in group analysis, however. Similarly, tension management is a requirement in both groups and gatherings, but what is managed in each case seems different. Tension in encounters arises when the official focus of attention is threatened by distractions of various kinds; this state of uneasiness is managed by tactful acts, such as the open expression in a usable way of what is distracting attention. There will be circumstances, then, when tactfully expressed ranklings may ease interaction in a gathering while destroying the group to which the participants happen to belong.

The preceding arguments are meant to suggest that a frequent empirical congruence between the structure of a group and the structure of a gathering of its members does not imply any invariant analytical relation between the two realms. The concepts tailored to the study of groups and those tailored to the study of encounters may be analytically related, but these relations are by no means self-evident.

I want to say, finally, that distinguishing between little groups and focused gatherings allows one not only to see that a gathering may itself generate a fleeting little group but also to examine the relation between this group and long-standing groups from which the participants in the encounter may derive.

When all and only the members of a little group come together in a gathering, the effect of the gathering, depending on the outcome of its activity, will be to strengthen or weaken somewhat the little group. The potentiality of the encounter for generating its own group seems to be expended in what it does for and to the long-standing group. Often, there seems to be no chance for the fleeting circle of solidarity to develop much solidity of its own, for it fits too well in a pattern already established. However, when individuals come into a gathering who are not also members of the same little group, and especially if they are strangers possessing no prior relationships to one another, then the group formation that is fostered by the encounter will stand out as a contrast to all other groups of which the encounter's participants are members. It is under these circumstances – when the participants in a gathering have not been together in a group before and are not likely to be so again – that the locally generated group seems to cast its strongest shadow. It is under these circumstances, too, that the fates of these two units of organization seem most closely tied together, the effectiveness of the gathering rather directly affecting the solidarity of the group.

Paradoxically, then, if a gathering, on its own, is to generate a group and have group-formation mark the gathering as a memorable event, then a stranger or two may have to be invited – and this is sometimes carefully done on sociable occasions. These persons anchor the group-formation that occurs, preventing it from drifting back into the relationships and groups that existed previously among the participants.

4   Erving Goffman

Civil Inattention and Face Engagements in Social Interaction

Civil inattention

When persons are mutually present and not involved together in conversation or other focused interaction, it is possible for one person to stare openly and fixedly at others, gleaning what he can about them while frankly expressing on his face his response to what he sees – for example, the 'hate stare' that a Southern white sometimes gratuitously gives to Negroes walking past him. It is also possible for one person to treat others as if they were not there at all, as objects not worthy of a glance, let alone close scrutiny. Moreover, it is possible for the individual, by his staring or his 'not seeing', to alter his own appearance hardly at all in consequence of the presence of the others. Here we have 'non-person' treatment . . .

Currently, in our society, this kind of treatment is to be contrasted with the kind generally felt to be more proper in most situations, which will here be called 'civil inattention'. What seems to be involved is that one gives to another enough visual notice to demonstrate that one appreciates that the other is present (and that one admits openly to having seen him), while at the next moment withdrawing one's attention from him so as to express that he does not constitute a target of special curiosity or design.

In performing this courtesy the eyes of the looker may pass over the eyes of the other, but no 'recognition' is typically allowed. Where the courtesy is performed between two persons passing on the street, civil inattention may take the special form of eyeing the other up to approximately eight feet, during which time sides of the street are apportioned by gesture, and then casting the eyes down as the other passes – a kind of dimming of lights. In any case, we have here what is perhaps the slightest of interpersonal rituals, yet one that constantly regulates the social intercourse of persons in our society.

By according civil inattention, the individual implies that he has no reason to suspect the intentions of the others present and no reason to fear the others, be hostile to them or wish to avoid them. (At the same time, in extending this courtesy he automatically opens himself up to a like treatment from others present.) This demonstrates that he has nothing to fear or avoid in being seen and being seen seeing, and that he is not ashamed of himself or of the place and company in which he finds himself. It will therefore be necessary for him to have a certain 'directness' of eye expression. As one student suggests, the individual's gaze ought not to be guarded or averted or absent or defensively dramatic, as if 'something were going on'. Indeed, the exhibition of such deflected eye expressions may be taken as a symptom of some kind of mental disturbance.[1]

Civil inattention is so delicate an adjustment that we may expect constant evasion of the rules regarding it. Dark glasses, for example, allow the wearer to stare at another person without that other being sure that he is being stared at. One person can look at another out of the corner of his eyes. The fan and parasol once served as similar aids in stealing glances, and in polite Western society the decline in use of these instruments in the last fifty years has lessened the elasticity of communication arrangements. It should be added, too, that the closer the onlookers are to the individual who interests them, the more exposed his position (and theirs), and the more obligation they will feel to ensure him civil inattention. The further they are from him, the more licence they will feel to stare at him a little. . . .

In addition to these evasions of rules we also may expect frequent infractions of them. Here, of course, social class subculture and ethnic subculture introduce differences in patterns, and differences, too, in the age at which patterns are first employed.

The morale of a group in regard to this minimal courtesy of civil inattention – a courtesy that tends to treat those present merely as participants in the gathering and not in terms of other social characteristics – is tested whenever someone of very divergent social status or very divergent physical appearance is present.

English middle-class society, for example, prides itself in giving famous and infamous persons the privilege of being civilly disattended in public, as when the Royal children manage to walk through a park with few persons turning around to stare. And in our own American society, currently, we know that one of the great trials of the physically handicapped is that in public places they will be openly stared at, thereby having their privacy invaded, while, at the same time, the invasion exposes their undesirable attributes.

> The act of staring is a thing which one does not ordinarily do to another human being; it seems to put the object stared at in a class apart. One does not talk to a monkey in a zoo, or to a freak in a sideshow – one only stares.[2]

> An injury, as a characteristic and inseparable part of the body, may be felt to be a personal matter which the man would like to keep private. However, the fact of its visibility makes it known to anyone whom the injured man meets, including the stranger. A visible injury differs from most other personal matters in that anyone can deal with it regardless of the wish of the injured person; anyone can stare at the injury or ask questions about it, and in both cases communicate to and impose upon the injured person his feelings and evaluations. His action is then felt as an intrusion into privacy. It is the visibility of the injury which makes intrusion into privacy so easy. The men are likely to feel that they have to meet again and again people who will question and stare, and to feel powerless because they cannot change the general state of affairs...[3]

Perhaps the clearest illustration both of civil inattention and of the infraction of this ruling occurs when a person takes advantage of another's not looking to look at him, and then finds that the object of his gaze has suddenly turned and caught the illicit looker looking. The individual caught out may then shift his gaze, often with embarrassment and a little shame, or he may carefully act as if he had merely been seen in the moment of observation that is permissible; in either case we see evidence of the propriety that should have been maintained.

To behave properly and to have the *right* to civil inattention are related: propriety on the individual's part tends to ensure his being accorded civil inattention; extreme impropriety on his part is likely to result in his being stared at or studiously not seen. Improper conduct, however, does not automatically release others from the obligation of extending civil inattention to the offender, although it often weakens it. In any case, civil inattention may be extended in the face of offensiveness simply as an act of tactfulness, to keep an orderly appearance in the situation in spite of what is happening.

Ordinarily, in middle-class society, failure to extend civil inattention to others is not negatively sanctioned in a direct and open fashion, except in the social training of servants and children, the latter especially in connection with according civil inattention to the physically handicapped and deformed. For examples of such direct sanctions among adults one must turn to despotic societies where glancing at the emperor or his agents may be a punishable offence, or to the rather refined rules prevailing in some of our Southern states concerning how much of a look a coloured male can give to a white female, over how much distance, before it is interpreted as a punishable sexual advance.

Given the pain of being stared at, it is understandable that staring itself is widely used as a means of negative sanction, socially controlling all kinds of improper public conduct. Indeed, it often constitutes the first warning an individual receives that he is 'out of line' and the last warning that it is necessary to give him. In fact, in the case of those whose appearance tests to the limit the capacity of a gathering to proffer civil inattention, staring itself may become a sanction against staring. The autobiography of an ex-dwarf provides an illustration:

> There were the thick-skinned ones, who stared like hill people come down to see a traveling show. There were the paper-peekers, the furtive kind who would withdraw blushing if you caught them at it. There were the pitying ones, whose tongue clickings could almost be heard after they had passed you. But even worse, there were the chatterers, whose every remark might as well have been 'How do you do, poor boy?' They said it with their eyes and their manners and their tone of voice.
>
> I had a standard defense – a cold stare. Thus anesthetized against my fellow man, I could contend with the basic problem – getting in and out of the subway alive.[4]

The structure of face engagements

When two persons are mutually present and hence engaged together in some degree of unfocused interaction, the mutual proffering of civil inattention – a significant form of unfocused interaction – is not the only way they can relate to one another. They can proceed from there to engage one another in focused interaction, the unit of which I shall refer to as a *face engagement* or an *encounter*. Face engagements comprise all those instances of two or more participants in a situation joining each other openly in maintaining a single focus of cognitive and visual attention – what is sensed as a single *mutual activity*, entailing preferential communication rights. As a simple example – and one of the most common – when persons are present together in the same situation they may engage each other in a talk. This accreditation for mutual activity is one of the broadest of all statuses. Even persons of extremely disparate social positions can find themselves in circumstances where it is fitting to impute it to one another. Ordinarily the status does not have a 'latent phase' but obliges the incumbents to be engaged at that very moment in exercising their status.

Mutual activities and the face engagements in which they are embedded comprise instances of small talk, commensalism, lovemaking, gaming, formal discussion and personal servicing (treating, selling, waitressing and so forth). In some cases, as with sociable chats, the coming together does not seem to have a ready instrumental rationale. In other cases, as when a teacher pauses at a pupil's desk to help him for a moment with a problem he is involved in, and will be involved in after she moves on, the encounter is clearly a setting for a mutual instrumental activity, and this joint work is merely a phase of what is primarily an individual task. It should be noted that while many face engagements seem to be made up largely of the exchange of verbal statements, so that conversational encounters can in fact be used as the model, there are still other kinds of encounters where no word is spoken. This becomes very apparent, of course, in the study of engagements among children who have not yet mastered talk, and where, incidentally, it is possible to see the gradual transformation of a mere physical contacting of another into an act that establishes the social relationship of jointly accrediting a face-to-face encounter. Among adults, too, however, non-verbal encounters can be observed: the significant acts exchanged can be gestures or even, as in board and card games, moves. Also, there are certain close comings-together over work tasks which give rise to a single focus of visual and cognitive attention and to intimately co-ordinated contributions, the order and kind of contribution being determined by shared appreciation of what the task-at-the-moment requires as the next act. Here, while no word of direction or sociability may be spoken, it will be understood that lack of attention or co-ordinated response constitutes a breach in the mutual commitment of the participants.

Where there are only two participants in a situation, an encounter, if there is to be one, will *exhaust* the situation, giving us a *fully-focused gathering*. With more than two participants, there may be persons officially present in the situation who are officially excluded from the encounter and not themselves so engaged. These unengaged participants change the gathering into a *partly-focused* one. If more than three persons are present, there may be more than one encounter carried on in the same situation – a *multi-focused* gathering. I will use the term *participation unit* to refer both to encounters and to unengaged participants; the term *bystander* will be used to refer to any individual present who is not a ratified member of the particular encounter in question, whether or not he is currently a member of some other encounter.

In our society, face engagements seem to share a complex of properties, so that this class of social unit can be defined analytically, as well as by example.

An encounter is initiated by someone making an opening move, typically by means of a special expression of the eyes but sometimes by a statement or a special tone of voice at the beginning of a statement. The engagement proper begins when this overture is acknowledged by the other, who signals back with his eyes, voice or stance that he has placed himself at the disposal of the other for purposes of a mutual eye-to-eye activity – even if only to ask the initiator to postpone his request for an audience.

There is a tendency for the initial move and the responding 'clearance' sign to be exchanged almost simultaneously, with all participants employing both signs, perhaps in order to prevent an initiator from placing himself in a position of being denied by others. Glances, in particular, make possible this effective simultaneity. In fact, when eyes are joined, the initiator's first glance can be sufficiently tentative and ambiguous to allow him to act as if no initiation has been intended, if it appears that his overture is not desired.

Eye-to-eye looks, then, play a special role in the communication life of the community, ritually establishing an avowed openness to verbal statements and a rightfully heightened mutual relevance of acts. In Simmel's words:

> Of the special sense-organs, the eye has a uniquely sociological function. The union and interaction of individuals is based upon mutual glances. This is perhaps the most direct and purest reciprocity which exists any-where. This highest psychic reaction, however, in which the glances of eye to eye unite men, crystallizes into no objective structure; the unity which momentarily arises between two persons is present in the occasion and is dissolved in the function. So tenacious and subtle is this union that it can only be maintained by the shortest and straightest line between the eyes, and the smallest deviation from it, the slightest glance aside, completely destroys the unique character of this union. No objective trace of this relationship is left behind, as is universally found, directly or indirectly, in all other types of associations between men, as, for example, in inter-change of words. The interaction of eye and eye dies in the moment in which directness of the function is lost. But the totality of social relations of human beings, their self-assertion and self-abnegation, their intimacies and estrangements, would be changed in unpredictable ways if there

occurred no glance of eye to eye. This mutual glance between persons, in distinction from the simple sight or observation of the other, signifies a wholly new and unique union between them.[5]

It is understandable, then, that an individual who feels he has cause to be alienated from those around him will express this through some 'abnormality of the gaze', especially averting of the eyes. And it is understandable, too, that an individual who wants to control others' access to him and the information he receives may avoid looking toward the person who is seeking him out. A waitress, for example, may prevent a waiting customer from 'catching her eye' to prevent his initiating an order. Similarly, if a pedestrian wants to ensure a particular allocation of the street relative to a fellow pedestrian, or if a motorist wants to ensure priority of his line of proposed action over that of a fellow motorist or a pedestrian, one strategy is to avoid meeting the other's eyes and thus avoid co-operative claims. And where the initiator is in a social position requiring him to give the other the formal right to initiate all encounters, hostile and teasing possibilities may occur, of which Melville's *White Jacket* gives us an example:

> But sometimes the captain feels out of sorts, or in ill-humour, or is pleased to be somewhat capricious, or has a fancy to show a touch of his omnipotent supremacy; or, peradventure, it has so happened that the first lieutenant has, in some way, piqued or offended him, and he is not unwilling to show a slight specimen of his dominion over him, even before the eyes of all hands; at all events, only by some one of these suppositions can the singular circumstance be accounted for, that frequently Captain Claret would pertinaciously promenade up and down the poop, purposely averting his eye from the first lieutenant, who would stand below in the most awkward suspense, waiting the first wink from his superior's eye.
> 'Now I have him!' he must have said to himself, as the captain would turn toward him in his walk; 'now's my time!' and up would go his hand to his cap; but, alas! the captain was off again; and the men at the guns would cast sly winks at each other as the embarrassed lieutenant would bite his lips with suppressed vexation.
> Upon some occasions this scene would be repeated several times, till at last Captain Claret, thinking that in the eyes of all hands his dignity must by this time be pretty well bolstered, would stalk toward his subordinate, looking him full in the eyes; whereupon up goes his hand to the cap front, and the captain, nodding his acceptance of the report, descends from his perch to the quarter-deck.[6]

As these various examples suggest, mutual glances ordinarily must be withheld if an encounter is to be avoided, for eye contact opens one up for face engagement. I would like to add, finally, that there is a relationship between the use of eye-to-eye glances as a means of communicating a request for initiation of an encounter, and other communication practices. The more clearly individuals are obliged to refrain from staring directly at others, the more effectively will they be able to attach special significance to a stare, in this case, a request for an encounter. The rule of civil inattention thus makes possible, and 'fits' with, the clearance function given to looks into others' eyes. The rule similarly makes possible the giving of a special function to 'prolonged' holding of a stranger's glance, as when unacquainted persons who had arranged to meet each other manage to discover one another in this way.

5 Steve Duck

What are We Trying to Develop when We Develop a Relationship?

It is difficult to define what develops when a relationship develops, since a lot of what happens is 'all in the mind'. People certainly change their lives in major or minor ways to accommodate the new relationship, but the 'sense of being in the relationship' is what makes the real difference and couples often develop a story about where they first met. Such stories may be inaccurate or accurate, but that is less the point than is the fact that people regard the stories as meaningful and treat them *as if* they were true. It is partly the emergence of such stories that marks the time (often quite early on) when the partners realize that they are 'in a relationship' rather than just being two people who have met one another on a number of occasions and talked and done things together. It is therefore necessary to consider what a relationship might be, so that we can begin to reach an understanding of how it comes to be.

According to Hinde, the nature of relationships is determined by a set of features which change and intensify as the relationship proceeds.[1] He argues that we can achieve some understanding of relationships by looking at where they are located on the following eight dimensions of assessment.

1 *Content of interactions*. Relationships derive much of their essence from the things that the partners do together: customer–waiter relationships differ from father–daughter relationships in the nature of the activities that occur within the relationship. For a father to charge his daughter for every meal or cup of coffee in the home, for instance, or for customer and waiter to hug and tell one another secrets or play hide-and-seek would violate the norms for conducting their respective relationships. The types of activities typically engaged in help to define the relationship and differentiate it from others. Naturally, as relationships develop (from acquaintance to close friendship, for example) so the partners will alter their interactions to embrace different content. They may talk to one another about different subjects or go to different places: indeed, it is sometimes a quite significant escalation of a relationship for one person to invite another to visit his or her home or to talk about a previously taboo area – a sign of the breaking of a barrier and an indication of a desire to increase the intimacy.

2 *Diversity of interactions*. Some relationships do not involve a lot of variety of action. Student–instructor relationships, for example, are typified by interactions concerned with tasks that are focused on a rather limited range of topics to do with the relevant academic discipline and do not normally involve going on picnics or talking about holiday travel plans. On the other hand, parent–child relationships involve a lot of diversity – playing, instructing, comforting, protecting, educating, healing, feeding and so on. Hinde, adopting a distinction current in sociology, therefore draws a distinction between uniplex relationships (where the types of interactions are limited in scope) and multiplex relationships (where the varieties of interactions are far greater). One way to classify and differentiate relationships, therefore, is in terms of the diversity of interactions that comprise them: the more diverse the interactions, the deeper the relationship.

3 *Qualities of interactions*. Although the content of interactions is significant,

the 'adverbial properties' are important too: it's not what you do but the way that you do it. A significant means of understanding relationships, therefore, is in terms of the qualities of the interactions that occur. We can assess these qualities by examining the intensity and style of interactions, the non-verbal signals exchanged, and so on. Intensity could be measured simply – for example, by checking whether the partners shout at one another or whisper in each other's ear. Style could be assessed in terms of the 'immediacy' of the language they use; for example, whether one person includes the other in the content of the speech (by saying 'We went together,' for instance, or 'I went and X came along,' which convey different messages about the relationship between the speaker and X). Non-verbal signals are also important: they are the bodily cues that accompany speech in socially significant ways – such as whether we look directly at someone when we speak to them or look down sheepishly, or whether we smile or frown when they talk to us.

4 *Relative frequency and patterning of interactions.* One of the clearest signals of an increasingly deepening voluntary relationship is the increase in frequency of meetings between the persons. In the case of involuntary relationships, like close family ties, there are other and better indices of increasing closeness, such as the affection expressed verbally and non-verbally, the absence of conflict, and so on. We meet people more often out of choice because we like to or we want to enjoy their company more often. Thus friends increase the frequency of meetings as their relationship grows. Another signal is the way in which interactions are patterned according to societal norms or the preferences of partners: thus for a couple to make love more often than the social norm tells us something about their sense of duty to society's statistics, but does not tell us about their relationship or their sexual satisfaction unless we map it on to their expressed desires for sex. The answer to the question 'How is their sexual activity patterned relative to the wishes of each partner?' could reveal much more information about the nature of the relationship between the partners than is revealed by simple statistics about the absolute frequency of their sexual activity. Thus Blumstein and Schwartz show that even in happily married couples, frequency of intercourse varies between 'less than once per month' (about 6 per cent of couples happily married between two and ten years) to 'three or more times per week' (about 27 per cent of couples happily married for more than two years).[2]

5 *Reciprocity and complementarity.* In some relationships I do what you do. You say 'How are you?', and I say 'Fine, how are you?'; or you buy me a drink, and I feel obligated to buy you one. You invite me to dinner and I say 'No, you took me out last time, now it's my turn.' These are reciprocal actions and the sense of superficiality in a relationship is directly related to the degree to which you do feel obligated to reciprocate: the more superficial the relationship, the more people keep count of whose turn it is to do the behaviour next. On the other hand, when I ask you for help and you give it, or you try to dominate and I submit, or you look in need of a hug and I give you one, then our behaviour is complementary: it is different behaviour but it goes together to make a perfect whole. In complementary behaviours people take account of each other's needs to a greater extent, by definition. Thus relationships where reciprocity is greater than complementarity are on the whole less intimate and complementarity develops with the relationship.

6 *Intimacy.* There are two sorts of intimacy: physical and psychological. As we get to know someone better, so our access to their body and their soul increases. Friends, especially female same-sex friends, are permitted to touch one another more often and in a greater variety of parts of the body than are

casual acquaintances and the nature of a relationship can be seen in terms of a map of accessibility: the hands are available for almost anyone to touch, but knees, for instance, are parts reserved only for persons that we know quite well.

The same applies to psychological intimacy. The more you know someone, the more you are granted access to their inner feelings, fears and concerns. The more that individuals 'self-disclose' (that is, report their inner feelings), the more they are offering friendship and intimacy, as long as they do this appropriately and match it to their partner's disclosures.

7   *Interpersonal perception.* Individuals have views of themselves ('Myself as I am'), of other individuals ('X as I see her or him') and of such abstract entities as their ideal self ('Myself as I would like to be'). We can also hold views of 'Myself as my friend sees me'. One line of research argues that understanding between people is greater to the extent that there is a correspondence between A's 'Myself as I am' and B's 'A as I see her or him', for instance. In other words, if my perception of you matches your perception of yourself, the better the relationship will be. My understanding of you is also increased, of course, if we are actually similar. In exploring and developing this notion by means of interpersonal perception instruments, White showed that wives are consistently better at understanding their husbands, even when the two of them are not similar, than their husbands are at understanding their wives.[3] Wives tend, on the other hand, to see themselves as more in agreement with the husband's attitudes despite the degree to which they are really similar. They seem, therefore, to take a more positive view of their relationship than husbands do. Wives are also more accurate at predicting their husband's response to an item than husbands are at predicting their wife's response, a finding that is possibly due to the (undesirable, but real) power difference in the traditional marriage: it is generally more useful for a person low in power to be able to predict the actions of another who has greater power than the other way round, which perhaps helps to explain why students spend so much time trying to understand what teachers like to see written in answers to their favourite questions!

8   *Commitment.* As individuals grow closer together, so their commitment to one another increases. The degree of commitment can be used by researchers as a barometer or measure of the strength of their relationship. What 'commitment' essentially means is some sort of determination to continue and respect a relationship in the face of adversities or temptations. Examples are exclusivity, if the relationship is a sexual one, and a tendency to put the other person's interests on an equal or greater footing than one's own.

6   Michael Young

Time, Habit and Repetition in Day-to-Day Life

Why do people repeat themselves so much? Why do they do more or less the same thing every year at Christmas, or on their own birthdays, or every day as they go about their daily rounds, getting out of bed in the morning, washing, dressing, getting breakfast, reading the paper, opening the mail, walking to the garage or the station, talking to colleagues, telephoning the same people day after day, writing letters which are much like letters written on other days, stopping themselves going into the pub with a twinge of regret, as on other days? It cannot all be due to their biological clocks. People do not settle down to their Christmas dinner by measuring the day's length to the nearest few minutes: they are not birds compelled to fly to the dinner table (or into the oven) at just that precise moment.

Some additional force must be responsible for the regularity of Christmas, although it is one day in Western Europe and another in Eastern Europe, and for its absence in large parts of the world; and for keeping most people head-down at their daily tasks when it is not Christmas. I am in other words looking for a 'sociological clock' which is as powerful and omnipresent a synchronizer as the biological clock. I propose that this force is the force of habit and its extension, custom – the tendency we all have, in greater or lesser measure, to do again what we have done before. Habit is as intrinsic to the cyclic (including some of its irregularities) as conscious memory is to the linear. Habit and memory are each means of preserving the past to do service in the present, but in the main for different though complementary ends: the first to ensure continuity, and the second to open the way for change. . . .

Habits are always being created anew. As the Chinese proverb says, 'a habit begins the first time'. Habits are generated and locked into place by recurrences so that they become automatic, rather than deliberate. In his *Principles of Psychology* William James gives habit a central place as 'the enormous flywheel of society, its most precious conservative agent': 'any sequence of mental actions which has been frequently repeated tends to perpetuate itself; so that we find ourselves automatically prompted to *think*, *feel* or *do* what we have been before accustomed to think, feel or do, under like circumstances, without any consciously formed *purpose*, or anticipation of results.'[1] For James habit was even more than second nature. He agreed with the Duke of Wellington:

> 'Habit a second nature! Habit is ten times nature,' the Duke of Wellington is said to have exclaimed . . . 'There is a story, which is credible enough, though it may not be true, of a practical joker, who, seeing a discharged veteran carrying home his dinner, suddenly called out "Attention!", whereupon the man instantly brought his hands down, and lost his mutton and potatoes in the gutter. The drill had been thorough, and its effects had become embodied in the man's nervous structure.'[2]

This story also illustrates James's statement that 'in habit the only command is to start'. After that the actions are automatic. 'Second nature' is one term for it, despite the Duke. Another popular term, in a society fancying airplanes for transport, is the phrase 'to go on automatic'.

There are degrees of automation. When it is complete, there is no need for thinking at all; there may not even be any conscious recognition of the situation that produces the habitual behaviour. No proposition is more self-evident than that people take a great deal as self-evident. I just act, without having to reason why. Without thinking about it, I scratch my head, or wink, or open my mouth when I am puzzled, and at a particular corner on my ordinary route to work I go through the routine motions with my arms and feet, all without being aware of it, unless on one occasion I put my foot hard on the accelerator instead of the brake or do something else eccentric, in which case I may remember it for life (if there is any left); and I do not do these things because I am so very notably absentminded compared to others but because on such matters everyone is absentminded. We are all to a considerable extent like A. J. Cook, the miners' leader in the British General Strike of 1926: 'Before he gets up he has no idea what he is going to say; when he's on his feet he has no idea what he is saying; and when he sits down he has no idea what he has just said.'[3] . . .

Habits are not usually chosen with any deliberation; they just grow, wild flowers rather than cultivated ones. They would not do this so readily and constantly without a series of overlapping advantages which assure that their growth will not be stopped. I will mention four of them. The first advantage is that habit increases the skill with which actions can be performed. The multiplication table is tiresome to learn but, once it has become habitual, reproducing it is very accurate and very quick. Reading and writing are difficult to acquire in the first place but, once acquired, both can be very efficient. To master the piano is very difficult indeed for the beginner, whose convulsive movements of the body and mangling of the keyboard make it seem impossible that any euphony will ever be achieved; but a few years later the hands may caper over the notes as though to the manner born, and all as the result of unflagging repetition. In such cases an act of will (even if abetted by the cajoling of parents or teachers) can inaugurate a habit which the will does not thereafter have to be engaged in guiding.

The second advantage is that a habit diminishes fatigue. Driving a car, or thinking about existentialism, or speaking a foreign language, or saying our prayers, is tiring the first time it is done, and if a person does not persevere because it is tiring it will always remain so. But persevere, and before too long the same person will be rattling off talk about existentialism while watching a football match or the television, or even driving a car while shouting at his children in the back to be quiet, in the hope that quietness will become as much a habit for them as shouting is for him. If fatigue could not be reduced by such means – or (to put it another way) effort invested now with an immense rate of return in reduced effort in the future – a life of any complexity could be insupportable.

> If an act became no easier after being done several times, if the careful direction of consciousness were necessary to its accomplishment on each occasion, it is evident that the whole activity of a lifetime might be confined to one or two deeds – that no progress could take place in development. A man might be occupied all day in dressing and undressing himself; the attitude of his body would absorb all his attention and energy; the washing of his hands or the fastening of a button would be as difficult to him on each occasion as to the child on its first trial; and he would, furthermore, be completely exhausted by his exertions.[4]

The third advantage is still more significant: a habit not only economizes on the effort put into the humdrum and the foreseen but also spares attention for the unforeseen. A capacity for attention is held in permanent reserve, ready to be mobilized to deal with the unexpected – the truck which appears from nowhere directly in front of one's own car, or the shout for help, or the summons to appear before the boss. Habit, by allowing predictable events or features of an event to be managed with hardly any effort, enables people to concentrate most of their attention on the unpredictable. Habit is necessary to allow this concentration. Without it, people would not be able to cope with the changes in their environments which cannot be reduced to rule; they would be without the adaptability which has enabled them to survive countless threats to their existence. Habits are one of our chief tools for survival.

The fourth advantage – the economizing of memory – in a sense encompasses all the other advantages. If Mr Murgatroyd on any morning arrived at work to find he had left his habits behind him, and had only his memory to guide him, he might as well get back into his car and go home. The same is true for the whole workforce. Without their usual collection of habits they would be looking at each other almost as if for the first time, in bewilderment, like a regiment lost in a forest, or an assembly of people with severe Alzheimer's Disease for whom there was nothing in life except today, wondering what on earth to do with themselves while Mr M ransacked his memory about the organization of the factory and telephoned the head office for orders. Even if the head office were not stricken by the same disability – and if only one person was left with the capacity for habit he or she would soon rule the corporation, and perhaps the world – it would be a task indeed to translate their orders for axles into routines for everyone in the factory in time to get any made that day. Starting from scratch with only their conscious recollections to guide them, it would be miraculous if he and the other managers decided what exactly should be done, and by whom, in time for anyone else to do any work before the bell for the end of the shift. Without habit, every day would be more than fully absorbed in puzzling about what to do, with none of it available for anything else, until they all decided to give it up and stay at home for good – unless home too was similarly overtaken. It would be too much to have to rely on memory to reinvent the wheel, or the axle, even every year, let alone every day.

The head office might decide to send down for an inspection not another production manager but a psychiatrist. All of us know that some people are like the indecisive imaginary Mr M, who now does not know whether to put on sandals or boots when he arrives in his office, if he can find where it is. James was severe on such a condition:

> The more of the details of our daily life we can hand over to the effortless custody of automatism, the more our higher powers of mind will be set free for their own proper work. There is no more miserable human being than one in whom nothing is habitual but indecision, and for whom the lighting of every cigar, the drinking of every cup, the time of rising and going to bed every day, and the beginning of every bit of work, are subjects of express volitional deliberation. Full half the time of such a man goes to the deciding, or regretting, of matters which ought to be so ingrained in him as practically not to exist for his consciousness at all. If there be such daily duties not yet ingrained in any one of my readers, let him begin this very hour to set the matter right.[5]

... Mr Murgatroyd and his men have something which is in many circumstances better than memory. They do not have to make room in their consciousness for the past. They do not have to recall what they did; instead they can be guided by the habit of what they did do. Jerome Bruner said about selectivity:

> Selectivity is the rule and a nervous system, in Lord Adrian's phrase, is as much an editorial hierarchy as it is a system for carrying signals. We have learned too that the 'arts' of sensing and knowing consist in honoring our highly limited capacity for taking in and processing information. We honor that capacity by learning the methods of compacting vast ranges of experience in economical symbols – concepts, language, metaphor, myth, formulae. The price of failing at this art is either to be trapped in a confined world of experience or to be the victim of an overload of information.[6]

He might have added habits after formulae. A habit is a memory unconsciously edited for action.

Part 3

Conformity and Deviance

In every society, as well as in smaller communities, deviance from widely accepted standards of behaviour is punished in one way or another. With the rise of modern institutions, however, we find the development of specialized places of punishment and correction, most notably asylums and prisons. These are sometimes termed 'carceral' organizations, because in them individuals are 'incarcerated' – kept separate from the wider social world.

In reading 7, Andrew Scull traces the rise of the asylum in eighteenth- and nineteenth-century England. As he points out, before the eighteenth century the 'psychiatrically disturbed' were not treated as a distinct category of people, but were simply lumped together with others on the margins of the social order, such as the poor, vagrants and the handicapped. The separation of a distinct grouping of the 'mentally ill', he shows, cannot be understood simply as a process of social reform, but was closely connected with broad social changes affecting government and social control.

Reading 8 examines current attitudes towards crime on the part of those living in a particular area of London. Worries about crime, the authors indicate, are a significant feature of the outlook of many people in the neighbourhood. The inner city is perceived as a dangerous place, although residents tend to have a good understanding of differential vulnerability to crime – for example, those in older age groups correctly recognize that they are less likely than younger persons to be the victims of personal attack or property damage.

The consumption of illegal drugs is often thought by laypersons and social analysts alike to be a particularly pernicious problem in inner-city areas. John Auld et al. show in reading 9 that there is some basis for this assumption. Illegal drug-taking, particularly among teenagers and young adults, has increased substantially in recent years, and both the supply and the consumption of such drugs tend to be heavily clustered in the poorer city areas. The idea that rising drug use is directly related to crime, however, is placed in question. According to the authors, we should understand the nature of drug-taking in terms of its place in a wider 'irregular economy', centred in households, local neighbourhoods and informal groups.

It is easy to suppose that criminal activity is primarily a phenomenon of the underprivileged, and in fact most of the prison population are drawn from such a group. However, 'white-collar' or business crime in various guises is an exceedingly common phenomenon. As Clarke demonstrates (reading 10), business crimes – particularly those involving violations of trust – are relatively easy both to commit and to conceal. In contrast to other types of criminal activity, business crime is not immediately evident. A manager in an insurance company, for example, may be embezzling money for many years without the offence being detected, if indeed it ever is.

In the final reading in this part, reading 11, Josie O'Dwyer and Pat Carlen consider the experience of women in prison. Women currently make up only a very small proportion of the total prison population in Britain, and apart from some illegal activities which are predominantly female (for instance, prostitution), the majority of offenders in all types of crime are men. Women's prisons, however, by no means form a benign environment: as O'Dwyer and Carlen describe them, such prisons are characterized by a good deal of violence and intimidation.

7   **Andrew T. Scull**

The Social Control of the Mad

The typical response to the deranged underwent dramatic changes in English society between the mid-eighteenth and mid-nineteenth centuries. At the outset of this period, mad people for the most part were not treated even as a separate category or type of deviants. Rather, they were assimilated into the much larger, more amorphous class of the morally disreputable, the poor and the impotent, a group which also included vagrants, minor criminals and the physically handicapped. Furthermore, just as in the case of the indigent generally, the societal response to the problems posed by the presence of mentally disturbed individuals did not involve segregating them into separate receptacles designed to keep them apart from the rest of society. The overwhelming majority of the insane were still to be found at large in the community. By the mid-nineteenth century, however, virtually no aspect of this traditional response remained intact. The insane were clearly and sharply distinguished from other 'problem populations'. They found themselves incarcerated in a specialized, bureaucratically organized, state-supported asylum system which isolated them both physically and symbolically from the larger society. And within this segregated environment, now recognized as one of the major varieties of deviance in English society, their condition had been diagnosed as a uniquely and essentially medical problem. Accordingly, they had been delivered into the hands of a new group of professionals, the so-called 'mad-doctors'.

Conventionally, of course, this transformation process is known to historians as the 'reform' of the treatment of the 'mentally ill'. The very language that is used thus reflects the implicit assumptions which have hitherto marked most historians' treatment of the subject – a naïve Whiggish view of history as progress, and a failure to see key elements of the reform process as sociologically highly problematic. For those writing from this perspective, lunacy reform reflects two converging forces. On the one hand, the rise of an urbanized, industrial society is seen as producing a social order whose very complexity forced the adoption of some form of institutional response. On the other, the acceptance of state 'responsibility' for the insane, the advent of the asylum and the developing link between medicine and insanity are pictured as the 'natural' outcome of the growing civilization of social existence, the rise of humanitarian concern for one's fellow citizens and the advances of science and human understanding. The direction taken by lunacy reform is thus presented as at once inevitable and basically benign – both in intent and in consequences. . . .

Almost all aspects of this purported 'explanation' are false, or provide a grossly distorted and misleading picture of what lunacy reform was all about. Reform did indeed have deep structural roots in the changing nature of English society, but these roots were embedded to a far greater extent and in far more complex ways in the nature of capitalism as a social phenomenon than conventional simplistic references to urbanization and industrialization have managed to grasp. The reformers did indeed profess to be actuated by 'humane' concern with the well-being of the lunatic. (I have yet to meet a reformer who conceded that his designs on the objects of his attentions were malevolent.) But whatever the Victorian *haute bourgeoisie*'s degree of sympathy with the sufferings of the lower orders, and however convinced one may or may not be of the depth of

their interest in the latters' welfare, it remains the case that to present the outcome of reform as a triumphant and unproblematic expression of humanitarian concern is to adopt a perspective which is hopelessly biased and inaccurate:
one which relies, of necessity, on a systematic neglect and distortion of the
available evidence. It is time to transfer our attention away from the rhetoric of
intentions and to consider instead the actual facts about the establishment and
operation of the new apparatus for the social control of the mad. Similarly with
the notion that the medical capture of insanity reflected and was somehow
caused by some mysterious advance in scientific understanding: as an ideological
prop for the professional claims of psychiatry, this claim has obvious merits; as
an historical analysis of the process itself, it has none. Quite regardless of one's
opinions on the extent of scientifically-based psychiatric knowledge of mental
illness today, there would, I think, be a widespread consensus on the dearth of
almost any real knowledge base in early nineteenth-century medicine which
would have given the medical profession a rationally defensible claim to special
expertise *vis-à-vis* the insane....

We need to explain how and why insanity came to be exclusively defined as an
illness, a condition within the sole jurisdiction of the medical profession; to
answer the related question of why the mad-doctors and their reformist mentors
opted for the asylum as the domain within which the insane were to receive their
'treatment'; and to delineate the effects of these choices. Such questions deserve
to be raised and answered in the first instance because the adoption of the
state-run asylum system, the transformation of madness into mental illness and
the subsequent reverberations of these developments represent the most striking
and lasting legacy of the reform movement. Furthermore, it is not at all obvious
on the face of things why these changes took the form that they did. Since the
initial and continuing costs of making this separate provision for the mentally ill
were obviously high, and apparently cheaper means of sustaining them were
already in existence, ... the successful 'capture' of such a group by the medical
profession and the large-scale and costly construction of mental hospitals in
which to incarcerate them must be seen as inherently problematic phenomena.

Even apart from their historical importance, such questions have an obvious
contemporary relevance, not least because, as Paul Rock has put it, 'modes of
social control exerted in the past become part of the moral and definitional
context [of the present]... This propensity to preserve earlier moral reactions
means not only that much contemporary deviance is a fossilized or frozen
residue from the past, but that contemporary control is constrained and oriented
by the past. Each new generation does not rewrite the social contract.'[1] As it
happens, since the mid-1950s we have been moving away from one aspect of the
nineteenth-century legacy in the field of mental health – the primary reliance
on the asylum. But even here a historical context is vital if we are to grasp
what is being abandoned and why. The significance of the nineteenth-century
experience is still more incontestable in those areas – state intervention to
control problem populations and the 'medicalization' of deviance – where the
application of nineteenth-century approaches continues to grow in scope and
importance.

Sociologically speaking, the answers to these questions possess in addition a
potentially much wider significance. For [these] developments ... have obvious
parallels with changes occurring almost contemporaneously in other sectors of
the social control apparatus. Thus the key elements which distinguish deviance
and its control in modern societies from the shapes which such phenomena
assume elsewhere likewise grew to maturity in the period stretching from the
late eighteenth through the nineteenth century. Of major importance in this

respect were: (1) the substantial involvement of the state, and the emergence of a highly rationalized, centrally administered and directed social control apparatus; (2) the treatment of many types of deviance in institutions providing a large measure of segregation from the surrounding community; and (3) the careful differentiation of different sorts of deviance, and the subsequent consignment of each variety to the ministrations of experts – which last development entails, as an important corollary, the emergence of professional and semi-professional 'helping occupations'. From this perspective, the differentiation of the insane, the rise of a state-supported asylum system, and the emergence of the psychiatric profession can be seen to represent no more than a particular, though very important, example of this much more general series of changes in the social organization of deviance.

8 Trevor Jones, Brian MacLean and Jock Young

Attitudes towards Crime in Islington

Any assessment of the public's attitude towards crime implicitly involves a number of fundamental questions. Is crime a problem in your area? How big a problem is it in the context of other neighbourhood problems? Do you worry about crime? Are the streets safe? Do you think crime has increased in your area in the past five years? Furthermore, people's attitudes to, and perceptions of, these basic questions constitute a backdrop and pointer to an evaluation of the service provided by the police in any given area.

People in Islington perceive crime as a big problem, second only to unemployment and lack of youth facilities. They place it ahead of housing, education and transport. Interestingly, a majority of people also see crime-related issues like vandalism and lack of child play facilities as a problem whereas only 25 per cent see race relations as a problem, of which 7.9 per cent think it is a 'big problem'. The latter indicates that most people in Islington have no difficulty in getting on with people of a different ethnicity from their own.

This raises the question of what kind of people perceive crime as a big problem in their area. Our findings indicate women rather than men and younger people rather than older. In fact, in terms of overall satisfaction with the neighbourhood, women were more likely to be dissatisfied than men. Blacks are as likely as whites to view crime as a big problem, in contrast to Asians who see it as less of a problem. Amongst blacks, younger women are more likely than men to perceive crime as a big problem, especially those in the 25 to 44 age group. Given the level of victimization of younger women, in general, and the particular kinds of victimization inflicted upon younger black women, these findings are not surprising.

We also asked people if they worried about crime and found that a majority of people worry about being burgled and almost half worry about being a victim of street robbery.

Nearly half of all women in Islington worry about being raped, sexually molested or pestered. There are good reasons for this, particularly among younger women. Substantial minorities of people also worry about having their home or property damaged and about being attacked by strangers. In short, substantial numbers of Islington residents worry about the possibility of being a victim of crime.

Table 1 Viewing neighbourhood issues as a problem (%)

	Big problem	Bit of a problem	Total % problem
Unemployment	65.0	22.1	87.1
Poor housing	35.7	25.3	61.0
Heavy lorry noise	26.8	18.6	45.4
Crime	36.7	34.0	70.7
Poor schools	15.3	19.8	35.1
Poor public transport	10.5	16.0	26.5
Poor street lighting	11.8	23.0	34.8
Race relations	7.9	17.1	25.0
Vandalism	34.2	34.1	68.3
General unfriendliness	5.5	13.0	18.5
Not enough places for children to play	31.5	27.6	59.1
Not enough things for young people to do	38.2	28.2	66.4

Base: All respondents weighted data.

Table 2 Satisfaction with neighbourhood, by gender (%)

	Men	Women
Low	21.4	27.7
Medium	77.7	70.2
High	0.9	2.1

Base: All respondents weighted data.

Table 3 Viewing crime as a big problem, by age, race and gender (%)

	16–24		25–44		45+	
	Men	Women	Men	Women	Men	Women
White	31.0	37.8	40.6	46.4	38.6	27.8
Blacks	35.7	46.9	25.7	55.6	32.1	36.8
Asian	18.9	37.5	21.7	25.8	25.0	14.3

Base: All respondents weighted data.

Table 4 Worrying 'quite a bit' or 'a lot' (%)

	'Quite a bit'	*'A lot'*	*Total*
Being burgled	29.8	26.6	56.4
Being 'mugged and robbed'	24.5	21.5	46.0
Being raped (women only)	22.3	23.2	45.5
Being sexually molested (women only)	22.6	21.9	44.5
Having your home or property damaged by vandals	26.9	18.7	45.6
Being attacked by strangers	23.2	15.5	38.7
Being insulted or bothered by strangers	16.0	10.2	26.2

Base: All respondents weighted data.

Table 5 Scale scores (by age)

	16–24	*25–44*	*45+*
Fear of crime			
Low	11.2	8.4	11.8
Medium	55.6	62.7	55.5
High	33.2	28.9	32.7
Probability of crime in next year			
Low	10.2	11.5	17.2
Medium	69.0	69.8	68.8
High	20.8	18.7	14.0

Base: All respondents weighted data.

We constructed composite tables, 'Scale B' and 'Scale C', to evaluate fear of crime and perception of the likelihood of victimization in the next year. Although the youngest and oldest age groups have the highest fear of crime, there is an inverse relationship with age in terms of likelihood of victimization.

Table 5 illustrates that although people worry about crime, they also have an informed notion of the likelihood of actually being a victim of crime. This is highlighted by the over-45 age group which, although they have a high fear of crime, also have lower notions of probability of victimization.

We asked three questions designed to find out whether people thought the streets were safe in their area. Towards the beginning of the interview, informants were asked:

'Do you think there are risks for women who go out on their own in this area after dark?

If Yes How likely is it that something might happen to them?

And do you yourself ever feel worried about going out on your own in this area after dark?'

The first two questions are about women, and the relevance of trying to evaluate perceptions of vulnerability at night-time is obvious. It is worth noting

Table 6   Risks in going out after dark (%)

	PSI		ICS	
Risks for women				
Serious	41	Fairly likely	60.1
Slight	30	Not very likely	19.9
None	25	None	14.0
Don't know/not stated	4	Don't know/not stated	6.0
Risks for self				
Yes	47	Yes	50.8
No	51	No	49.2
Don't know/not stated	1	Don't know/not stated eliminated from 'ICS'	–

Base: All respondents weighted data.

Table 7   Risks in going out after dark, by race (% believe in risk)

	PSI			ICS		
	Whites	*West Indian*	*Asian*	*Whites*	*Blacks*	*Asian*
Yes	48	28	52	51.4	46.6	46.4
No	52	72	48	48.6	53.4	53.6

Base: All respondents weighted data.

. . . two important differences between Islington residents and the Policy Studies Institute's Survey of Londoners' (henceforth PSI) findings. Firstly, a higher proportion of Islington residents than Londoners as a whole think there are risks for women and secondly, . . . blacks in Islington are more likely to fear for their own safety on the streets.

One would expect to find a higher perception of risk for women in inner city areas, and this level of perception directly relates to the level of risk. Although direct comparison with the PSI report is problematic, our findings cast doubt on the PSI's assertion that blacks may deny that a serious problem exists for them as a reflection of their being made scapegoats for street crime. In Islington, blacks are as likely to fear for their safety on the streets as Asians, and only modestly less than whites.

Finally, we sought to evaluate whether people thought crime had increased in the past five years, as any indication that a majority of people believed this to be the case would point to something being badly wrong.

Respondents were asked if various criminal offences and other problems in their area had become more common, less common or remained the same in the last five years. Overall, 69.8 per cent said they had become more common, 27.1 per cent said they had remained the same and 3.29 per cent said they were less common.

Specifically, respondents were asked about trends in burglary (residential), street robbery, 'rowdiness by teenagers', 'fights and disturbances in the street',

Table 8 Belief about crime, by offence (% believe increase in past five years)

	More common	*Less common*	*Same*
Robbery/mugging	60.7	11.7	28.2
Burglary	67.6	9.8	22.6
Teenage rowdiness	44.3	18.4	37.3
Fights and disturbances in the street	31.0	25.4	43.6
Vandalism	53.0	16.4	30.6
Sexual assault on women	48.1	20.1	31.8
Women being molested or pestered	47.8	19.6	32.5

Table 9 Belief about crime: BCS and ICS (% believe increase in past five years)

	BCS inner-city areas	*ICS*	*% difference (+ or −)*
Burglary	53	67.6	+14.6
Robbery/mugging	72	60.7	−11.3
Teenage rowdiness	60	44.3	−15.7
Vandalism	28	53.0	+25

vandalism, sexual assaults on women and 'women being molested or pestered'. The items about teenagers and 'fights and disturbances in the street' were included to assess the notion floated by the British Crime Survey (henceforth BCS) that the fears urban residents have about crime could be a product of anti-social behaviour and urban decay which then lead residents to believe there was more going on than there was in reality.

Overall, responses were as shown in table 8. Our findings are at variance with the BCS in that Islington residents believe that burglary and vandalism are more prevalent, and street robbery and teenage rowdiness less prevalent, than indicated by the BCS findings. Islington residents, in comparison, see teenage rowdiness as less of a problem and only 31 per cent of them believe that 'fights and disturbances in the street' are more common. In fact the majority of respondents seem to see these phenomena as something that historically has always been a by-product of inner-city life.

9   John Auld, Nicholas Dorn and Nigel South

Irregular Work, Irregular Pleasures: Heroin in the 1980s

The recent period has witnessed a real and substantial increase in the use of heroin, particularly among young adults and those in their late teens. Rather than being injected, the drug has also become more typically smoked or snorted (although a relatively small proportion of recent new users are injecting). A wide variety of social groups are involved; several street agencies report seeing many more women users than in previous years. . . .

Evidence of the increased use of heroin and other drugs in the UK comes from four principal sources:

1   evidence relating to international trafficking and seizures;
2   criminal and health services statistics of persons apprehended or reported as being involved with heroin;
3   local prevalance studies, ranging in quality from the systematic to the frankly inane;
4   experience of practitioners and self-help groups in the fields of welfare, advice work, unemployment projects, etc.

A consistent picture emerges from these various forms of evidence. While there may be a 'moral panic' over heroin (following an earlier one over solvent sniffing) and while that panic may distort our view of heroin use today, there is no doubt that more people in Britain today have used heroin than ever before. Perhaps the only rough parallel in quantitative terms would be the nineteenth century, when large proportions of the population used the plant extract, opium. Admittedly, they would have been eating it, drinking it as tea or taking it as part of patent medicines rather than smoking or snorting the stronger manufactured derivative of opium, heroin. Nevertheless, what this comparison brings out is the common feature of consumption via mouth or nose, with injected use being the practice of a minority. The changes that have occurred in the dominant mode of administration in more recent times will be considered in some detail presently. Suffice it to say in the present context, however, that many more persons in Britain are familiar with opiate drugs today than has been the case for about a century.

The total international trade in opium (from which heroin is made) has been estimated as amounting to thousands of tons, with profit levels running into hundreds of billions of dollars. . . . [P]art of the explanation for third world cultivation of plant drugs, including opium, should be sought in the pressures of maintaining both personal income and the payment of interest on national debt in circumstances where there is a lack of alternative profitable crops or sources of income. However, we agree with the staff of the Drug Indicators Project when they state that while supply has increased, 'it is not being suggested that supply in itself created demand. There were a number of domestic factors which meant that increased supply would find a ready market.' We [now] examine some of these 'domestic factors' that have provided a market for heroin in Britain and other Western countries. . . .

Throughout the 1970s there developed a growing body of literature which discovered or, more accurately, rediscovered a variety of activities that seemed hidden from the official purview of the formal economy. Such activities are highly diverse. Some take place within the sphere of waged work, others in and around households, local communities and informal exchange networks. Some of the minor perks, fiddles and benefits associated with them are basically legal, others clearly not, while there are a number of other activities which occupy a great area of the law. In the absence of agreement over the matter of precise conceptual definition, we can employ the term 'informal economies' as a means of referring to these activities. Our present concerns focus upon more unambiguously illegal patterns of thieving, dealing and exchange involving a variety of commodities and centred primarily on streets and housing estates and best described, we believe, as the *irregular economy*. We suggest that it is within the context of a degree of involvement in this irregular economy that the bulk of heroin use among young people is currently taking place. The irregular economy provides multiple conduits for the distribution and exchange of drugs, and for a variety of other goods and services: prostitution, the disposal of stolen goods, and so on.

Activity within the irregular economy has as a defining characteristic a temporal sense of irregularity. It takes the form of a bunching together of intensive periods of work (buying, selling, contacting, getting money together, etc.). In between these intensive bursts of activity the business of survival requires one to be always searching for further opportunities, and to be on the look-out for potential dangers. Patterns of irregular and even sometimes 'chaotic' styles of drug use mesh with the irregularity of this economy and the subcultures that it underpins.

This perspective carries implications for the way in which one approaches two issues with which the use of heroin (and, indeed, illegal drugs in general) has traditionally been associated – namely, ill health and crime....

The involvement of drug users in the irregular economy, where stolen goods also circulate, necessarily makes an important contribution to current stereotypes of drug users as being not only sick but also criminal, being pushed into crime in order to support their expensive habits. As Helmer observed of the typical response in the United States, the 'approach to the narcotics problem is the same one today as it has always been; narcotics cause crime'.[1] In London, a senior police officer discussing the rising use of heroin in a BBC news interview (19 June 1984) ventured the opinion that while there were no official figures which proved a link between rising heroin use and crime, none the less a substantial source of income is required to sustain the use of heroin, and he felt quite sure that this income was not coming from the welfare state: the clear implication being that drug users must be stealing in order to get money to supply themselves with drugs.

We would agree that there are links between widespread heroin use today and criminality. However, the nature of these links is mystified in the statement that heroin causes crime. Our argument is very simple. Social security benefits and youth training allowances are at too low a level for satisfaction of basic needs – for housing, clothing, heating and food – let alone buying much in the way of intoxicants. It is partly in order to secure a standard of living better than mere survival that people get involved in aspects of the irregular economy, and it is through their involvement in this partially petty-criminal economy that they may come to buy, exchange, sell and consume heroin. There is a sense, then, in which crime can lead to heroin use: the very opposite of the conventional view. One implication of this might be that a shift in economic policies that reduced the extent to which the irregular economy permeates increasing numbers of inner-city and other areas would reduce petty crime, and with it much heroin use in its presently expanding forms. A direct assault by law enforcement agencies against episodic heroin users, by contrast, would do relatively little to dent the criminal aspects of the irregular economy in which they play only a part.

How one responds to the activities of importers and large-scale suppliers of drugs such as heroin is another question. Organized crime of this kind is by no means new, and has been the subject of lengthy discussion elsewhere, especially with regard to the context of the USA. Here in Britain, at the same time as the street-level irregular economy has significantly expanded, there have been changes in the organization of drug supply at national and regional levels:

> The illicit market has become more organized and has attracted the atten-
> tion of criminal groups who, a few years ago, would not have been willing
> to become involved in drugs. This is particularly true of cannabis and in
> the past two years of heroin.[2]

The large-scale importation and supply of drugs have always been a lucrative source of income – in this respect the illegal market simply reflects that in alcohol, tobacco and pharmaceuticals – and the combination of a ready interna- tional supply of heroin and a ready irregular market in Britain makes large-scale pushing even more attractive to established criminal organizations. What is of note is that even here – as on the lower level of the street and local community – *existing* patterns of large-scale criminal and petty criminal activity are expanding to incorporate drugs. . . .

Modes and meanings of administration

Although sample survey evidence is as lacking on this matter as it is on the issue of the total numbers of young people involved, it has come to be widely accepted that the bulk of heroin use among those whose use began during the last few years takes the form of either smoking or (less commonly) snorting the substance. Rather than being injected, in other words, the drug is heated and the smoke fumes thereby given off are inhaled.

There are a number of reasons for thinking that this particular mode of administration makes an important contribution not only to the intrinsic com- patibility of heroin use with the structural features of the irregular economy, but also to an understanding of why the now widely used description of the rate of increase in the activity among young people as an epidemic might be a particular misnomer. The first and arguably most important one connects with the distinc- tion between the categories of 'sickness' and 'irregularity' referred to earlier. Throughout the 1960s and early 1970s there was a labour market quite favour- able to white males in many parts of Britain, offering opportunities for consider- able freedom of movement between jobs and, significantly, ease of movement out of the labour market and back again. The adoption of the sick role in the manner made possible by being officially labelled and treated as an addict provided an important vehicle for such movements in and out of the labour market, and offered other rewards besides. The role of 'addict' was one which – provided one played one's cards right by both acknowledging the undesirability of one's predicament and at least appearing to accept the kind of technically competent medical treatment then being offered by drug treatment clinics – one might have a good chance of occupying indefinitely. There was, of course, a certain price to pay: specifically, an acceptance of the moral stigma which conventional society tends to bestow upon those whom it views as being un- avoidably or irresponsibly dependent upon its beneficence, and a corresponding obligation to conform with the stereotypically defined role.

For many young people today, however, the distinction between being either 'inside' or 'outside' respectable society and the formal economy has become very blurred. They cannot easily *choose* whether to be 'in' or 'out', the choice already having been made for them. For those effectively excluded from wage employ- ment there is little advantage to be derived in adopting the sick role, since the primary benefit of the sick role is that it allows one to evade temporarily the obligations of waged work. There is a sense, then, in which the market itself has diminished the appeal of sick/addict styles of involvement with heroin, and in doing so has undermined one possible rationalization for injecting drugs. Injection is an unappealing prospect for most people, but one that can be 'made sense of' within the context of an acceptance of oneself as a 'junkie' or addict. Injection is made less acceptable when circumstances weaken the rationale for adopting the sick/addict role.

The practice of smoking heroin, by contrast, has a number of relatively positive aspects. In the most straightforward sense, of course, it is simply easier at a psychological level to relate it to and view it as an unproblematic extension of more conventional pursuits such as the smoking of tobacco or, in the case of some young people, cannabis.

However, it is also necessary to consider certain consequences arising from the contemporary supply situation. The fact that the bulk of heroin currently entering this country is of high quality, low in cost and easily obtainable (at least in many urban areas) has been a recurrent theme in the expressions of alarm being made by the various agencies concerned with trying to deal with the problem. But it ought to be recognized that the widespread availability of cheap, good-quality heroin makes the practice of smoking it a considerably more rational activity than it would have been in former times when the supply situation was not such a favourable one from the consumer's point of view. Only when the drug is relatively plentiful and cheap can the user contemplate letting some of it quite literally go up in smoke.

It should also be pointed out that smoking has certain health advantages in comparison with injection. Firstly, infections, sores and vascular problems sometimes associated with injection of heroin and other substances are not risks run by the smoker. Secondly, smokers may be less likely to overdose. With injection, it is sometimes difficult for the user to calculate precisely how much of the drug to inject in order to achieve the desired effect – a matter of practical inconvenience on many occasions and death by overdose on some. Smoking, by contrast, is a more easily controlled and safer mode of administration.

Summarizing our discussion, we suggest that the easing of heroin supply on an international level, the shift to the new modes of administration (most commonly smoking) that this facilitates and the relatively casual (non-needle/non-addict) and episodic styles of involvement that emerge in the context of a more general involvement in the irregular economy, may reasonably be described as contributing to a quantitative increase in the numbers of heroin users, and to a qualitative shift towards less dangerous patterns of use. Putting it in fewer and plainer words – Britain has acquired rather more of a slightly less bad thing.

10   Michael Clarke

The Nature of Business Crime

The most consequential feature of business crime is the private context in which business crimes are committed. This is true almost as much of organizations in the public sector, such as schools and hospitals, as it is of private-sector business. The differences lie in the service ethic which predominates in the public sector, as against the profit orientation of the private, and in the greater penetration of public-sector organizations by oversight and funding agencies in the state hierarchy – area health authorities, local education authorities, and beyond them the relevant government ministries. Private businesses are subject to the shareholders and non-executive directors in the case of companies with shares held by the public, neither of which group has easy access to the detail of the companies' activities, and are easily deceived, not so much by the refusal of relevant information as by not knowing the pertinent questions to ask. Both companies with public shareholders and those where shares are held privately are subject to audit by external accountants, but, as a number of decisive court cases have shown, auditors are not required as part of their inquiries into whether the company's accounts constitute a true and fair view of the company's affairs, to ensure that they check for possible malpractices; and accountants who ask awkward questions and provoke embarrassing cover-ups may not be engaged for the following year's audit.

The principal points about privacy for present purposes – others will emerge later – are first, that members of business organizations are protected from detection by the veil of privacy. This is formally and legally the case in respect of the limited company form, which is designed to protect commercial confidentiality and not to give information away to competitors. But privacy is also inherent in the relatively complex and specialized work and context of the organization. The minutely organized, bureaucratized division of labour which characterizes modern business renders its activities opaque to outsiders, even outsiders to the section, unit, office or division within a large organization, who measure its success and probity by its inputs and outputs, not by a detailed scrutiny of its working routines. It is thus only too easy for individuals or groups within an organization to shield misconduct from prying eyes and to manipulate outputs so that all appears to be normal.

Secondly, therefore, privacy means that business offenders are legitimately present at the scene. Offences consist of violations of the trust implicit in them as officers of the organization and exploitation of the resources of the organization for personal gain. The scope for such exploitation and the ease with which it can be covered up vary partly because of chance aspects of organizational structure – individuals or groups may happen to find themselves in a position in the organization where it is particularly easy to steal organizational property or funds, where others, located elsewhere, would find this very difficult. More systematically, however, opportunities vary with discretion, autonomy and access to a range of organizational resources, and these of course increase as one ascends the organizational hierarchy. Delivery drivers, for example, may be able physically to divert goods from their vehicles, but will probably need the co-operation of the warehousing and despatch departments to reconcile the necessary paperwork. Similarly, clerks in accounts departments may have no difficulty making use of company telephones, postage and photocopying, but, although dealing with company cheques, receipts and invoices, may find it very hard to embezzle without a collective effort. The accounts manager, by contrast, has less need to communicate such misdeeds to others, and much greater discretion, and probably also has the knowledge of the company and the expertise in accounting necessary to enable him to embezzle company funds and to manage the paperwork to disguise the fact.

This disguise of even serious offences can continue successfully for long periods, and no doubt in some cases, especially where the misconduct ceases undetected, offences are never discovered. The chief executive of the Grays Building Society was discovered in 1978 to have embezzled £2 million over a period of forty years, successfully deceiving the auditors, with whom he enjoyed a good relationship, and his staff, by always making up the books himself, sometimes working late to do so. He was discovered only because the auditors were changed on the retirement of the accountant after twenty-seven years. Similarly, the chief accountant at Pitman's Secretarial College admitted in 1987 to stealing £1.4 million over twenty years, at a rate in later years of £50,000 per annum, mostly in cash fees paid by students. He was discovered only as a result of a company reorganization and special audit, in the course of which he was made redundant.

Unlike conventional crimes, such as burglary and robbery, therefore, in the case of business crime there is not necessarily an immediate complainant. Those whose interests have been damaged may not be aware of it, or, as in the case of shops which write off stock losses through shoplifting, staff theft and accidental damage under the one heading 'stock shrinkage', not fully aware of it. Business crime is certainly not victimless, but the principal objective of the offender is to prevent the victim recognizing the loss. For, in the case of business crime, it is the offence which is difficult to discover because it is hidden by the normality of the organization's functioning and by the legitimacy of the offender's presence in the organization. Of course, some major offences emerge because their extent is so great as to cause the financial breakdown of the organization. Once the offence is uncovered, however, it is usually relatively simple to establish who committed it or at least colluded in it, as a result of checks back on individuals' actions and responsibilities. This is the reverse of the case of conventional crime, where the householder who is burgled is immediately aware of the fact of the loss but finds it extremely difficult to detect the offender precisely because he had no legitimate access to the premises.

A consequence of this is that public order is not violated in business offences as it is in conventional crime. There is normally no violence to persons or property, and the conduct in question takes place in private not public places, between people with a pre-existing and usually continuing relationship, not between strangers. This in part accounts for the much less threatening character of business offences: not only do they not involve violence, but they become possible at all only if citizens enter into a situation where they can be deceived and defrauded. While there is a substantial contemporary debate on the citizen's reasonable expectations, there is also some expectation of caution and self-protective measures against deceit. Trust is necessary between employer and employee, businessman and customer, creditor and debtor, but trust has to be established, not merely taken for granted.

This explains the relatively limited interest of the police in business crime. Its privacy and complexity make it difficult to investigate; the pre-existing relationships between victim and offender make for the likelihood of claim and counterclaim as to who occupies which role; and in many cases the police may take the view that their victims have only themselves to blame for their lack of caution, or have the necessary resources to remedy the situation by civil action. Indeed, in legal terms, the whole field of business crime is beset by ambiguity as to whether offences are to be dealt with by the criminal or the civil route. Disputes between private parties are normally dealt with through civil litigation, and the public authorities are often reluctant to act, even where a criminal offence has clearly been committed, if matters can be settled privately. There is a strong tendency for matters to be dealt with privately, and thus for the question whether the misconduct was criminal never to be formally raised. This is reflected in the disposition of manpower in the police forces: about 5 per cent of detective manpower and 0.5 per cent of overall police personnel nationally, totalling 588 police in the UK, were allocated to the fraud squads in 1987. The police see their primary responsibility as the maintenance of order in the public realm, and the pursuit of conventional crimes which violate it as well as damaging the interests of private citizens. In addition, the police and other public agencies can normally gain access to premises to pursue inquiries only where they have reasonable grounds to suspect that a criminal offence has taken place. Restraints upon the power of public authorities in a liberal democracy act to protect the accessibility of private domains.

As will become clear below, however, this tendency for business crime to be dealt with privately and often non-legally is not a matter for alarm but rather an inevitable outcome of its character. Certainly it is much more effective and flexible in coping with what are in most cases quite ambiguous patterns of conduct. Research, even on embezzlers, the most obviously criminal of business offenders, suggests a pattern not of calculated villainy but of opportunism, financial stress and, at times, an intention to repay embezzled money well before being stimulated to do so by detection. In many other areas the issue is precisely: has an offence been committed, or is it at worst error or misunderstanding, or more often a loss that the victim must accept as legitimate, as 'just business'?

It is evident from the foregoing that the detection and control of business crime are primarily, and at least in the first instance, internal to the organization, and hence private. It is up to those with a direct interest in the business to decide how much effort they devote to ensuring that probity is maintained and wrongdoing is detected and sanctioned, and as to how they define wrongdoing: does it include arriving five minutes late for work, using company phones to call home or giving lifts to friends in company vehicles, for example? When misconduct is detected or suspected, however, the mobilization of resources to deal with it internally is potentially very great. Here the privacy, enclosure and the official allocation of tasks of the business environment act to the advantage of control. The existence of rules and routines, of task responsibilities and specialized competencies, of authority clearly delimited and of extensive record-keeping and accounting makes the tracing of misconduct and its pinning down to individuals possible in a way that is immensely difficult in the case of conventional crimes. Membership of the organization requires the constant generation of evidence of activities in discharging job responsibilities, evidence that has as its counterpart the meagre traces left to scene-of-crime officers in conventional offences, which only in the fictional cases of such as Sherlock Holmes routinely provide anything like a substantial lead to the offender.

This advantage to internal control once suspicion is aroused is further enhanced by the range of sanctions available. Ideally proof and confession, and hence the introduction of effective remedies against repetition, are desirable, but even suspicion that is not cleared can be followed by, for example, the transfer of individuals to other duties, or a simple failure to promote them. Suspicions which are confirmed can be sanctioned not only by dismissal, but by demotion, involving of course recurrent loss of pay, and at worst perhaps by public exposure outside the organization, involving loss of occupational standing. In the case of professionals this may include loss of professional accreditation, but for all employees dismissal for specified misconduct will make re-employment in any position of trust very difficult. All of this is at the discretion of the organization, and its procedures for implementing investigation and imposing sanctions, while subject to the powers of the trade unions and to legislation such as the Employment Protection Acts, usually combine the formal and the informal. The scope for the control of the employee if the organization wishes to exercise that control is hence very great, and the great majority of misconduct in organizations is dealt with in this way, by procedures ranging

from a reprimand from an immediate superior to formal inquiry and arraign-
ment before a special disciplinary panel.

The position of the employee is hence very much weaker than that of the
employer. Where the employer engages in abuses, his staff have to organize
strongly if their interests are affected, and may still find it difficult both to gain
access to information essential to proof of misconduct, and to resist selective or
even collective dismissal. Outside interests such as customers, creditors and the
Inland Revenue may find all the privileges of private enterprise deployed to
frustrate them: information is refused, lies are told, meetings postponed, correspondence unanswered, worthless promises made and managing directors become inaccessible. . . .

The obvious recourse of those suffering from recalcitrant and fraudulent
businessmen is to the public domain of the law, usually by suing for damages or
bankruptcy, or by calling on the Department of Trade to investigate the affairs
of the company. As has already been remarked, the police are by no means
always ready or able to act, and usually do so only if clear evidence of a criminal
offence is presented to them, or where the number of complaints becomes
substantial. The victims, however, are caught in a dilemma. The law is slow,
uncertain and expensive; worse still, at the end of the day its use may well have
the effect of closing down the business, leaving little behind but debts. This may
be in the public interest in not ensnaring any more people as victims, but it does
nothing to secure the interests of existing victims in recovering their money,
whether this consists in repayment of the debt, the provision of goods not
supplied, or supplied but defective, or in continuity of employment. There is
therefore a powerful incentive for the victim to keep matters in the private
realm, and to attempt to negotiate a solution. In practice recourse to the law
and the public agencies is usually indicative of despair and a thirst for vengeance
on the part of the victims. It is hence in the interests of the offender to continue
negotiations for as long as possible by making offers, promises and part-
payments. . . .

A point which has already been alluded to but needs stating more fully is the
ambiguity of business crime, which ranges from calculated and singleminded
fraud to hotly debated misconduct. It includes, as has been remarked, losses
consequent upon incompetence, naïvety and negligence, as well as deliberate
misappropriation; and misappropriation itself may be opportunist or pressured,
as well as sheer, cold theft. The most comprehensive study to date of the most
classically criminal of frauds, the long-term credit fraud, in which the perpetra-
tor builds up his creditworthiness with prompt payments for a time, and then
takes as much credit as he can obtain before disappearing, shows that a substantial proportion were not the unaided efforts of habitual criminals. Some cases, it
is true, involve criminals financing 'front men' to set up businesses with the sole
objective of building up credit and then maximizing the fraud on suppliers.
Many, however, involve businessmen who have fallen on hard times and who,
despairing at last of ever recovering – a corner shop squeezed out of the market
by the arrival of a supermarket, for example – decide that years of honest
trading deserve some substantial reward, and decide to go bankrupt for a large
amount rather than a small one. Sometimes too, professional criminals prey
upon such businesses by offering loans to get them through a difficult period,
and then take over the business and use the proprietor as a 'front man'.

The ambiguities of business crime extend also to the corner-cutting and sharp
practice from which almost no great modern business organization and business
tycoon has been free at some point in their careers. Doubts and complexities
here are legion. If your competitor does not realize the weakness of his position,

is it your job to inform him? Is it illegitimate to obtain contracts by offering lavish entertainment to clients and key personnel? In some circumstances this may fall foul of the Corrupt Practices Acts, in others not. Goods ordered are not available and others are supplied in their stead. How does this affect the contract in respect of quality, performance and price? Are professional services to be charged at their cost plus a reasonable rate per hour, or at whatever the client can be persuaded to pay, and at what stage does this constitute fraudulent misrepresentation?

One has also to recognize the readiness of a very large sector of the public to collude in or connive at some illegal and underhand practices. Who voluntarily insists on paying VAT when they have their car serviced, their plumbing fixed or their windows repaired? Who will refuse the offer of a friend to run off some photocopies on the office machine, or do some calculations on the office computer? Who will resist the offer of the company van to move furniture or other heavy goods, or the offer of a load of 'cheap' tarmac to improve their drive?...

The ambiguity of business crime is hence profound and pervasive, and furthermore there is no prospect of eliminating it.... [D]ebate about how acceptable conduct is to be distinguished from unacceptable must be informed by the practice and practitioners of business itself.

It follows from this that business crimes have an essentially contested character. They are basically political offences, not in the parliamentary sense of the term, but in that they involve the mobilization of power to make the accusation of wrongdoing stick. Where conventional crimes are self-evidently so, business crimes, as has been outlined above, have to be shown to be crimes and not something else. The compilation of evidence and successful denunciation require the mobilization of sufficient powerful interests to overcome the offender, who will naturally secrete or destroy damning evidence, interpret his actions as legitimate (if perhaps mistaken) and counterclaim malevolence on the part of his accusers. Because he is inside the organization and may remain close to the scene of the offence, he has maximum opportunity to resist exposure, and he will of course mobilize the support of friends and colleagues if possible. Above all it is difficult to prove *mens rea* (malign intent) in business offences, even though the evidence of the records may easily show wrongful conduct. It is hard for the surprised burglar to explain forced entry, but the business offender is in the reverse position, and will use it to deny, not that he was the offender, but that the offence was an offence. Even the embezzling employee may deny theft, on the grounds that it was only a loan that he intended to repay. No burglar can credibly make such a claim; the employee's may be doubtful but not necessarily entirely so....

Underlying ... concern with the control of business crime lies a tension fundamental in all societies, but particularly characteristic of modern Western industrialized democracies: between private self-interest pursued through the institutions of business, and the service ethic of the public good, of fairness and distributive justice, developed in Britain by the civil service after the reforms of the latter part of the nineteenth century, and further developed and expanded by the welfare state. The danger of unfettered private enterprise is that it degenerates into greed, ruthlessness and deceit, to the oppression of the interests of those insufficiently cunning, skilled, wealthy or powerful to protect themselves, and so polarizes the haves from the have-nots. The danger of the service ethic and of distributive justice is that if applied to all institutions of society it imposes minimum standards but at an ever-increasing cost, while also stifling initiative with bureaucracy, restrictive practices and heavy taxation. This is not a problem that can ever be resolved. Much of political debate will continue to concern the relative balance of advantage to be given by government policy to each alternative. Whilst the demands for cost-cutting, measured efficiency and the elimination of waste constitute the assault by a business ideology upon the public sector, efforts to ensure higher standards of business conduct through regulation and public debate constitute an attempt to render business more compatible with the ideals of the service ethic.

11   Josie O'Dwyer and Pat Carlen

Surviving in a Women's Prison

Britain has six closed prisons for women: Holloway in London, Styal in Cheshire, Cookham Wood in Kent, a wing of Durham prison, Cornton Vale just outside Stirling in Scotland and Armagh Prison in Northern Ireland.

For England and Wales there is one closed Youth Custody Centre, Bullwood Hall in Essex, and an open Youth Custody Centre, at East Sutton Park. There are three open prisons for women: Drake Hall in Staffordshire, Askham Grange in Yorkshire and East Sutton Park in Kent. The three remand centres which take women and girls are: Low Newton in Durham, Pucklechurch in Bristol and Risley in Cheshire. Scotland has no open prison for women as all penal facilities – remand wing, young prisoners' wing, Youth Custody Centre and prison – are concentrated on one site at Her Majesty's Institution, Cornton Vale. In Northern Ireland a separate part of Armagh Prison is used as the female young offenders' centre. Additionally, women on remand are often held for one night (or more) in police cells and, at various times, certain convicted women prisoners have been temporarily housed in one of the male institutions. Josie O'Dwyer has served sentences (or been remanded) at Pucklechurch, Bullwood Hall, Cookham Wood, Styal, Holloway and Mountjoy Gaol in Ireland. Although she is only twenty-eight she has, since the age of fourteen, spent eight of those twenty-eight years in a variety of penal institutions, including Approved School, Borstal, remand centre, and four closed prisons. And Josie has survived. The purpose of this [discussion], therefore, is to describe exactly how Josie did survive those years and, in telling the story of one prisoner's survival, to describe also the violence, the injustices, the pain, the degradations and the other, different modes of survival (or not) which characterize British women's imprisonment.

On any day of the year around 1,500 women are held captive in British prisons. Many of them will be remand prisoners, only 27 per cent of whom will eventually receive a custodial sentence; over a quarter of the convicted women will be in prison for failing to pay a fine, and over half of them will be there for some minor crime of stealing. Of the remainder, less than 10 per cent of the convicted women will have been found guilty of violent crime and a sizeable number of prisoners in all categories will be those whose biographies embody accounts of all kinds of social, emotional and mental problems often either unrelated or related only tangentially to their criminal activities. A sizeable number of this latter group, too, will have either been brought up in institutions from an early age or will have been taken into either 'care' or the old Approved School system in their early teens. Either way these 'state-raised' children will have learned early on in their careers that the main name of the game in institutions is SURVIVAL.

Josie O'Dwyer is just one of the many women whose penal careers began at the age of fourteen in circumstances which make a mockery of the terms 'care', 'training' and 'in the child's best interest'. Josie's account of her first taste of the penal system is one which is studded with references to feelings of fear and memories of violence. As a consequence of being apprehended by the police for 'breaking and entering' the full force of the penal and judicial machinery engulfed the adolescent Josie in a quick processing through police cell, prison remand wing and Approved School.

> They took me in a police-car, up the motorway to Bristol. I was only little: aged fourteen, four-feet-ten inches in height and just six stone. It seemed a long journey from Exeter to Bristol and I was terrified, absolutely terrified. But I was stroppy with it. I had already spent the night in the police-cell at Exeter and I had been in a cell with a junkie who was really sick. I got myself in the top bunk and sat in the corner clutching a pillow; I actually chewed off the corner of that pillow watching this woman thrashing about. Then in the morning they took me to Pucklechurch. They had told me that it was a remand centre but it looked like a prison. I had thought that it was going to be a kids' home, maybe with bars on the windows so that I couldn't get out, but it wasn't, it was a real prison. They took me to the women's section and the police handed me over to the prison officers. All that I wanted to do was to curl up in a corner with something over my head and stay there, but I had to get undressed. I took my clothes off and put on this dressing-gown and I felt terrified. I've never felt such fear and yet the prison officers were being really nice to me compared with how I've seen them since with other people! They eventually coaxed me out with cigarettes and took me down this long corridor with cell doors on either side. They took me to a cell, locked me up for the night and came along in the morning and said that I was to go and see the Chief. I wouldn't get dressed though. I was still terrified, still had the dressing-gown over my head. Then I looked out of the window and I saw the prisoners exercising in the yard. I couldn't believe my eyes; I really thought that some of them were men! The prison officers kept coming in and encouraging me to go out and exercise – 'Come on, love' etc., but I would not go.

Josie was terrified and, as is often the case when people are afraid, she soon realized that one effective way to counter one's own fear is to inspire fear in others. Women's prisons, no less than men's, are places of violence; places where explicit violence will gain credit for its perpetrators and where a known capacity for violence is the necessary currency for efficient and healthy survival. In prison, moreover, the newcomer does not have to be predisposed to violence in order to engage in violent modes of behaviour – lessons in violence come at her from all sides.

> In the cell next to me there was a Pakistani woman; I think that she was waiting to be deported. They had taken her baby away from her because she had kept trying to kill herself and the baby. She actually wrecked her cell, there was a lot of blood and I was terrified. Then I wrecked my own cell. I put all the windows out and smashed all the furniture. The officers came in and told me to take all my clothes off. Then they put me in this special dress and did something up at the neck so that it could not be taken off. It took me four hours to chew through it. I wouldn't come out of that cell for ten days and then I came out to go to church. After that the prison

officers managed to coax me out for the last hour of Association and I was amazed at everyone wanting to mother me because I was so tiny. They gave me chocolates and they wanted me to sit on their lap. I didn't mind at all, I liked it. Then came the bombshell. I was told that I was being moved to the Approved School.

Within the penal system those who want to survive counter their own fear by inspiring fear in others and meet violence with violence or, better still, the threat of violence. Boredom and loss of freedom, however, call for different survival tactics and in the case of children and young people held in less secure conditions, the most obvious way to regain their freedom and self-respect is to go straight back out, either over the wall or through the gate. Josie was eventually to find that, in fact, the senior Approved School provided a good academic education but when she first arrived there was no way that she intended to stay. She became a 'runner'.

Seventeen times I ran away from that school and seventeen times they took me back. Each time they took me back I spent twenty-four hours in the detention room. I eventually dislocated my knee jumping out of a window but I still tried to run away, on crutches! Next morning they gave me a skirt to put on, but I kept my jeans on and went for the nearest window, with tennis-rackets and anything else that came to hand. The school was in Bath and I used to run back to Truro. I don't know what I was running to really; it was just an instinct. If I could get out, I got out.

But Josie, recognizing that she, like many other runners, had in reality no one and nowhere to run to, eventually settled down to O levels, horse-riding, forced religion (it was a convent school) and more lessons in the seamier side of life.

There were girls who had been through more than me, they had been prostitutes. It was mostly sex they talked about and sex was seen as a crime anyway, because we were in a convent school. Some of those girls went on to remand centres and then to Borstal.

When Josie left the school at sixteen the process of her social isolation and stigmatization as a delinquent had already begun.

I was sixteen when I left. I had never had a letter or a visit all the time that I had been there. I went back to Cornwall and tried for various jobs but they soon found out about my past, what I'd done and where I'd been, and they weren't prepared to forgive and forget. I used to sit for hours and stare into space. None of my friends understood; they all thought that I was mad. After about five months I took myself back up to Bath and it was there that I overdosed – I just didn't know what to do next. Then I actually went breaking and entering with the full intention of getting myself nicked.

I went to Borstal after I had been convicted on a burglary charge. They sent me off to Bullwood Hall along with two others and again, I was terrified. This time there was real reason to be afraid. An air of viciousness pervaded the whole place. The tougher you were the better. If you weren't tough people insulted you and took your cigarettes off you. You had a dog's life. It's the way the prison officers ran it which made it like that. Inmates couldn't really retaliate, but having a go at an officer gave them some kind of credit. They tore up each other's photos and ripped up each other's clothes. I'd been on the Assessment Unit for about five days and it was my first night on the wing when I happened to be going for a bath that I saw one inmate being kicked by about five others. It was not done quickly to get it over with; they were actually thoroughly enjoying it. The message was 'Don't mix-it with us.' Everyone was frightened of everybody else. Anything could start off a fight. Everything or nothing. The officers could have stopped it if they'd wanted to. They could have run the place differently. They stood down on the ground floor and everything that went on that was bad went on either on the landings or in somebody's cell – and in the recess anyhow. Unless you were one of the toughest you were absolutely terrorized. Borstal was amazing. Whereas the grown women in Pucklechurch could take things in their stride, in Borstal the slightest little thing could make someone hit the ceiling and the officers would just go in. There would be no 'Come on, dear, calm down.' None of that. They just went in and grabbed you and took you off down to the punishment block. You got the same treatment whatever you did so you knew that you might as well hit the roof, make a big show out of it and get some credit out of it.

At that stage Josie did not have time to think about the whys and wherefores of the viciousness which permeated Bullwood. She did not realize then that the viciousness was a product of the system itself rather than of the system's victims. She only had time to suss out how best to ensure her own survival.

You weren't allowed to do your sentence quietly. You survived by being the most vicious. But you couldn't just be vicious – you also had to have no fear, to be able to take the punishment and the lock-up. At first I was probably the most frightened. I was terrified. The whole place terrified me. The air was electric, always someone doing something, alarm bells going, a fight going on, screaming, shouting, banging. They used to sing 'A...G...G...R...O...' It was terrible – just bang, bang; bang, bang, bang. You *had* to scream, you had to let go. You just couldn't contain it within yourself. Every single day there was some sort of trouble and people were screaming out of the windows all the time in Bullwood. If one person started banging on the door the whole wing would take it up. I discovered that if I got all wound up, ready to blow, the whole wing would be all simmering, waiting for the action and it gave me credit. But it didn't just come from me, it was there all the time, just waiting for someone to set light to it. You had to have fights with the screws as they dragged you off to punishment because you were considered a sissy if you just walked there. Everyone struggled. They bent your arms so you tried to bite and you spat and kicked. They weren't exactly gentle either. Some of the officers were a little more vicious than the others so you worked out which ones to go for. You worked out who was soft, who was hard and who would hurt you most. So when you saw them coming at you – about eight or nine prison officers and a couple of men in the background – you tried to let the gentler ones get hold of you. To me it was just a game and you had to play the game well or you got hurt. Most of my stuff looked good, but it was all bravado, all for show, to give me more credit, so that I could survive. I never really hurt anyone.

...By the time Josie had finished her Borstal sentence she had completed her apprenticeship in violence and she was ready for bigger things. She knew that her Borstal days were over and, like many of the other Borstal girls, she knew also that the next stop would be prison.

Most of the girls had an idea that they were going on to prison anyway so you thought that whatever crimes you did when you were out, next time you went in you'd have more 'cred.' It was happening to me like that, though I didn't realize it at the time. But now when I go back and think, I think, 'Huh! What a wally!' Because when I came out of Borstal my ambition in life was to be the top dog, the most hardened criminal, the worst, the most vicious. There was no other reason to be alive as far as I was concerned. Anything outside wasn't going to give me a chance anyway, so if I was going to make it anywhere, it had to be in there.

Part 4

Gender and Sexuality

For many years sociology proceeded as if gender divisions – divisions between men and women – were largely irrelevant to social analysis. Today, in substantial part as a result of the impact of feminist thought, such a position is completely untenable. Gender refers to learned sexual identity and therefore in principle concerns men as much as women. Yet since women's experience has until recently been effectively blanked out in sociology, we have to give it particular attention in order to redress the pre-existing bias.

In reading 12, Debbie Taylor provides a concise assessment of some of the differences which tend to separate women's lives generically from those of men, relating her discussion to the contrast between unpaid domestic work – virtually everywhere mainly carried out by women – and paid work outside the home. Many women find themselves engaged in a double workload since in addition to their domestic labour they are engaged in paid work outside the home. Sue Sharpe's discussion (reading 13) further develops these observations. Unpaid domestic work, both authors conclude, has a massively important economic role, but this goes largely unrecognized. Where women's lives are circumscribed by domestic responsibilities, Sharpe argues, their self-esteem may become wholly bound up with the care and services they provide for other members of the family, a phenomenon which has its rewards but may also be both constricting and damaging in its psychological consequences.

Anna Coote's contribution describes the experiences of Lesley Smith, who set out to undertake a job normally regarded as exclusively within the male domain (reading 14). Smith trained to drive large long-distance lorries. She found that mastering the technical skills needed to control the vehicle was a relatively minor problem compared to coping with the antagonism and puzzlement which her adoption of the career of lorry driver aroused in the male fraternity. What happened to Lesley Smith ultimately, we do not know. She was looking forward to getting married and assuming new domestic responsibilities. Did she then find herself in the position referred to above, effectively carrying out two full-time jobs?

Reading 15, by Marc E. Mishkind et al., examines the sexual identity of men. According to the authors, cultivation of a definite 'body image' is an important aspect of men's attempt to reshape masculinity in circumstances in which women – like Lesley Smith – now commonly carry out occupations once regarded as exclusively a male province. If, as Mishkind et al. suggest, many men identify with an image of male bodily power, this is distinctly worrying in respect of the questions discussed by Jane Dowdeswell in reading 16. An emphasis upon male physical prowess might well reinforce the attitudes which lead men to commit rape, a form of crime which, with a small number of possible exceptions, is wholly a male phenomenon. Dowdeswell emphasizes that rapists are not necessarily pathological individuals, but men who are in most respects apparently quite ordinary and 'normal'; and that the majority of rapes happen in familiar circumstances, rather than in dark streets or unfrequented neighbourhoods.

The possibility of rape associates sexuality with danger. The advent of AIDS links sexuality to danger in a different way. All forms of sexual liaison involving certain forms of physical contact now, in principle, constitute a risk to life. No one knows how far the HIV virus, which is at the origin of AIDS, has spread through the British population or that of other countries throughout the world. Nor is there much reliable evidence about how far various categories of people have altered their sexual practices in the light of their knowledge of the risks of contracting the disease. Reading 17 by Stuart Weir and Claire Sanders suggests that while heterosexual people are conscious of the risks that AIDS presents, this awareness does not necessarily lead them to alter their pre-existing sexual behaviour.

12   Debbie Taylor

Women: Work and Domestic Responsibilities

One third of a million women are in labour as you read this – faces contorted, bodies straining in contractions that will have pushed another 300,000 infants into the world by the time today becomes tomorrow.

Some of those women are lying on clean linen under electric lights, the sharpest edge of their pain blunted by the drugs of white-coated doctors. Others – oblivious to the woodsmoke in their nostrils and the whine of mosquitoes in their ears – are riding raw pain, their bodies buffeted from peak to trough of each contraction, soothed by the voices of mothers, aunts, neighbours, kneeling on the earth floor beside them.

Pregnancy and childbirth: the pain, the power and the privilege that define a woman as different from a man. From two cells, to four, to eight; a tiny pink crescent; the buds of arms and legs; fingers, fingernails, eyelashes: only a woman's body can cherish and cradle and create a new human being. It's a miracle only she has the power to perform.

But the power of childbearing is a blessing laced with bitterness, because in every society in the world it is a power that is turned back against her. And, instead of defining just one difference between men and women, women's ability to bear children is used to define their entire lives. It is used to create and justify a role for women that extends their responsibility for caring for children far beyond the nine months of pregnancy. The labour of childbirth is just the beginning. Though the cord that binds mother to child is severed, the role that binds woman to domestic work and child-rearing holds fast throughout her life.

There can be few generalizations that hold as true throughout the world: unpaid domestic work is everywhere seen as woman's work, woman's responsibility. It is important, vital work. Food must be cooked, infants fed, clothes washed and mended, water and firewood collected. And it all takes time. A woman in a Pakistani village, for example, spends around sixty-three hours a week on domestic work alone. Even in the rich world, where water comes from taps and cookers heat at the flick of a switch, a housewife works an average of fifty-six hours a week. And if she has small children that average jumps nearly 40 per cent.

But housework is invisible work. Those long hours – totalling 40 billion each year in France alone – go unvalued, unrecognized, unpaid. Yet their contribution to society is enormous. If the services provided free by a housewife in the US in 1979 had to be purchased with wages at market rates, they would cost $14,500 a year. On this kind of calculation it is estimated that unpaid housework done in the industrialized countries contributes between 25 and 40 per cent of gross national product (GNP).

Domestic work is not, however, the only work women do. There are relatively few women anywhere in the world who can claim to be 'just a housewife'. Even in Europe 35 per cent of married women have a job. And of those remaining women without formal employment nearly half are either retired, in full-time education or looking for work.

But a working woman in Europe can expect little or no help from her husband at home. In Italy 85 per cent of mothers with children and full-time jobs outside the house are married to men who do no domestic work at all. And in Europe as

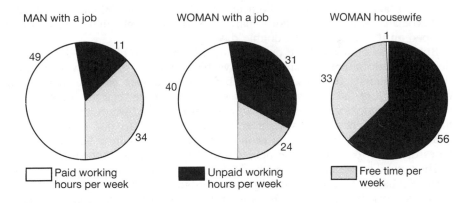

Figure 1 Paid and unpaid work of husbands and wives: data from twelve countries in 1975 – Belgium, Bulgaria, Czechoslovakia, France, Federal Republic of Germany, German Democratic Republic, Hungary, Peru, Poland, United States, USSR, Yugoslavia
Source: Alexander Szalai, reported in Worldwatch Paper 37, May 1980.

a whole, a working woman has, on average, only two-thirds of the free time her husband has.

In the developing world the picture is the same. There is 'man's work' and there is 'woman's work'. And, because many women do additional work outside the home, whereas few men would dream of doing any additional work inside it, 'woman's work' always ends up simply being 'more work'. In a village in Rwanda, for instance, men tend the banana trees and do most of the paid labour outside the home. Women, on the other hand, do virtually all the domestic work, three-quarters of the other agricultural work and half of the work with animals. Taken together, women in this village work over three times as much as men. In Java, too, where men do a more equal share of the agricultural work, a survey in one village found that women still worked over 20 per cent longer than men.

Women do not choose to take on extra work in addition to their domestic responsibilities. They have no option. In most parts of the world a woman's labour – in the fields growing food, packing transistors on a production line, typing a never-diminishing pile of letters – is absolutely vital to her family's survival. In fact it is a rare family indeed which can manage on the proceeds of just one person's labour. Eighty-three per cent of women with four children in France have full-time jobs outside the home too. And they are working because they need the money.

The chief injustice lies less in the extra work women must do outside the home than in the assumption that it is their role – and their role alone – to do all the work inside it. This assumption is a triple injustice. It is unjust because it means that women around the world end up working twice as many hours as men. It is unjust because they are not paid for those hours of work. And – the final insult – it is unjust because domestic work is looked down on as not being 'real' work at all – *because* it is unpaid. The circle is finally closed by men's refusal to take on work that is both unvalued and unpaid. Woman's work it is and woman's work it will stay – part of a vicious circle that keeps women trapped on the treadmill of a double day.

But it may not always have been like this. Many social historians believe that domestic work became unvalued and invisible as a result of the development of the cash economy. It seems likely that before people were paid for their labour or their produce, no one type of work was valued more than any other. Work was simply work: for survival. And in parts of the world where cash and wages have not yet penetrated, women and men still tend to do relatively equal amounts of work. But the cash economy only pays certain people for certain types of work, so setting those people and that work above the rest.

There were no wages for woman's domestic work in her own home. Yet it was work that had to be done. And it is this two-edged imperative – the necessity for domestic work to be done, plus men's refusal to do it – that etches women's domestic role so deeply into the structure of society.

13   Sue Sharpe

'Just Like a Girl': Gender Differences, Home-making and 'Real Work'

Women today have two recognized roles: one at home, and the other increasingly in the workforce. But rather than these being alternatives, the domestic role is assumed to be a natural part of being a woman. Any other activities like having a job are then performed as additional work. In the isolation of every home, women perform never-ending tasks of cleaning, cooking, washing up, washing clothes, and all the repetitive services that maintain the home. Mothers have the more exhausting demands of childcare. This work seems very far away from the grind of production. It is not counted as 'real work' because it is unpaid and done in the privacy of home. Here, women are given the illusory freedom to organize these tasks. It is an implicit part of being wife and mother, although the same things done for other people are counted as employment. The work itself is not light, and mothers may often work eighty or ninety hours a week in their homes. Housework has become easier and less time-consuming through domestic technology, but there are no consumer products to make children less demanding.

This unrecognized work is in effect the service and maintenance of the workers of today and tomorrow. It *is* related to the external world of production, but indirectly. A man is forced to rely on his wife's labour at home in order to be fit and able to earn a wage. With his wage he is expected to provide for a wife and family. Their survival on this money is dependent on a wife's economical shopping, and the provision of her free services. Every day she reproduces labour power, her man's capacity for another working day. Her work produces things, not for exchange, but for immediate consumption. Meals are eaten, floors and clothes are made dirty over and over again. It is because she does not produce for exchange that a woman's labour is deceptively unconnected with the 'real' economic markets. Therefore it is seen as 'unreal', or 'invisible labour', but it is certainly real enough to reduce greatly the cost of maintaining and reproducing workers (and to be, at least at present, cheaper than any other method), and therefore makes an important contribution to the total profits received by capital. Women have accepted this definition of themselves enough to say, 'I don't work. I'm only a housewife.' Their sons and daughters also absorb this perception of women's role and develop their appropriate relationships to production.

Home-making and childcare are obviously real work in every physical sense, but as women's work and as so-called 'unproductive' work they are different because they operate on a social and personal level. The power of labour lies usually in its capacity to be sold and withdrawn at will. If housework is 'real' work, then a woman should be able to withdraw her services. But the crucial difference here is that it is not alienated labour but 'love-labour'. The relationship between man and wife is not that between worker and employer. The emotional ties and responsibilities run very deep: 'love-labour' is capable of sustained production out of all proportion to that of wage-labour. It appears disguised as something that has escaped reduction to sordid economic terms, and yet without it the cost of reproducing and looking after the workers would have to be borne by capitalism itself.

From childhood, women have learned to give themselves freely as a natural extension of character and role. The reward is love and security, which is highly valued by women in a society where love is a human feeling out of place and often distorted in the productive world, and where the development of capitalism has forced women to become dependent on finding a husband for their support. In such a society, what you are worth is more important than what you are, and it is no wonder that women stand aloof from this and express views like that of the fourteen-year-old girl who said: ' . . . when you have a career you just work, and you might have a lot of money but you never have love'.

But what are the consequences for a woman whose whole life is measured in terms of the love she gives and receives from her husband and children? Often her identity gets lost, submerged within her caring. Her success is the reflection of their success, their problems are treated as her problems, their happiness becomes her happiness. At first, her own self may hang suspended, sometimes returning for moments of expression, but when the children come, and life gets filled with immediate demands, this becomes a luxury, drawing further and further back and finally forgotten. Her world is encapsulated within home and family.

A man's relationship to the home is very different. He has an independent role at work where he becomes someone in his own right, whatever his job and however well he does it. For him home is a place to return to, to relax in and be recharged for the next day's work. It is the place where he is by tradition the head, however token this has become. Here he can dominate and satisfy expectations of masculinity denied to most workers in their subordinate position within capitalism. The masculine ideal demands assertiveness, aggression, competitiveness and initiative, and such attributes are valued as necessary for success within capitalism. . . .

Women at home have adopted many strategies to cope with their situation, to refract its real causes and transfer them into some other form. They often develop minor illnesses and nervous complaints. They may become neurotic and obsessional over trivial things, overreacting to small crises. To ease these symptoms, doctors prescribe tranquillizers or sleeping pills, which dull the senses enough to enable them to do the family duties. But the main criterion of women at home's 'normality' is how far they stay within the domestic role. If they reject this in an exaggerated way, doubts may even be cast on their sanity. In traditional social work, a woman may be judged according to her 'femininity' and domesticity, and increased neatness and cleanliness is seen as 'improvement' in her condition. But on the other hand, intense concern with domestic tasks is rational if there seems to be no alternative, and many women draw much of their self-esteem from their indispensability to the family. To deny this seems to remove the whole purpose of their existence.

Very few women today spend all their lives at home, and girls growing up now have lots of ideas about vocations. But this has not necessarily changed women's dependence on home and family as much as may be expected, as the ideology defining their role as wife and mother has lagged behind. Women's primary place is still at home with work running a closer second place than before, but still only acceptable with convincing reasons and adequate provision at home. This has masked the fact that many women, especially working-class women, have been doing two jobs for many years, accepting their 'love-labour' and blaming themselves if they could not cope with the double workload.

14   Anna Coote

Lesley Smith: Lorry Driver

'Have you got a single room for the night?'
  'Yes, indeed, Madam.'
  'Is it all right if I leave my vehicle in your car park?'
  'Certainly, Madam.'
  'It's the one with the 40-foot trailer behind it . . . '
It was Lesley's first long-distance trip. She had to deliver 18 tons of frozen food from a Doncaster cold store to two depots in Scotland. And it was getting late. She had made her first drop in Edinburgh and phoned through to the Glasgow depot to make sure it didn't close down for the night leaving her with a lorry full of carrots and peas. When she arrived in Glasgow it was dark. The depot was on the edge of the Gorbals and she'd heard alarming stories about the area. A small boy asked her for 10p to guard her waggon for the night and she remembered another driver telling her how he'd turned down a similar offer – and found all his wheels gone the next morning.

Most of the transport lodging-houses in that part of town were full, except the ones with three beds to a room. In desperation, she headed out towards Renfrew where she was due to reload the following day, stopped at the big hotel near the airport and asked for a room for the night.

When they'd recovered their composure, the hotel staff were most helpful. Could Madam park her lorry round the back? It would be safer there. The night porter would keep an eye on it. Lesley was grateful – the vehicle was worth around £30,000.

That hotel room cost Lesley's firm £5 more than a regular stop-over, but they didn't complain as it was the first time and it never happened again. Soon she was making regular long-distance trips down to Cornwall via Avonmouth and up to Fort William in the Highlands where the roads got narrower and narrower, calling on all her skills at manoeuvring. Like the other drivers, she got to know the best lodging-houses along her routes, and established her favourite transport cafés where the faces were familiar and she didn't have to keep explaining herself.

It was always the same when she went into a café for the first time. The drivers all fell silent. Then they looked out into the park for a car. When they saw no car, they assumed she was a hitchhiker and asked her where she wanted to go. She would then explain and wait for the usual handful of jokes about women drivers. On the whole, however, the men were a lot friendlier and more courteous once they learnt that she too was a driver. They were careful with their language, and always curious. After a while Lesley wished she could carry a tape-recorded message, so she wouldn't have to answer the same questions again and again: Why did she want to be a lorry driver? How did she start? Where did she learn?

Her dad is a lorry driver, but it was never her intention to follow in his footsteps. She was brought up in a small mining village outside Doncaster, an only child and thoroughly spoilt. Her mother has worked, since well before Lesley's birth, as a nurse in the local hospital.

> My parents gave me everything I wanted. I was crazy about horses, so they saved up and bought me horses of my own. I left school at 15 without taking any exams because I was determined to start working with horses as soon as possible. I was sent to the local riding school to train as an instructor. My dad built me some stables on the land behind our house – we had a four-acre smallholding left to us by a relative. When I was 17, I started working from home, training other people's horses and giving a few free lessons to kids who helped me out in the stables.

It was her friend Hilda who introduced her to lorry driving. An unconventional woman herself, being managing director of a local sand and gravel company, Hilda gave Lesley a rather unusual 21st birthday present: a ten-day training course for the heavy goods vehicle driving test. So Lesley went to the training centre in Rotherham and took the course to please her friend. She learnt to drive Class 1 vehicles, the biggest on the road.

The main practical skill she learnt was how to manoeuvre a large vehicle, reversing and turning a 10-ton lorry which was 12 feet wide, 40 feet long and 14 feet high – in spaces more suited to Minis and Escorts. 'When you turn a corner you don't stay close to the kerb as you do in a car. You're taught to use more of the road you're leaving than the one you're entering, and to stick to your own side of the road once you've made the turning. And you're told never to use the weight and size of your vehicle to get you around – in other words, don't play Big Brother with the little cars, they pay for use of the road too.' She had to learn the relevant sections of the Highway Code, what the law said about juggernauts, and the restrictions on hours of driving. She didn't need any detailed knowledge of motor mechanics, although she was expected to know what was wrong if, for instance, black smoke was pouring from the exhaust. In fact, she knew a lot more than that, as she had often watched her father strip down engines when she was a child.

'It's a hard test. Quite a lot of people fail. I managed to pass first go and then started to look for a job. I can't explain why – I just wanted to go on driving.'

She telephoned or visited one local company after another. 'I'll be truthful with you, love,' said one old Doncaster trucker. 'There's no way I'm going to trust twenty thousand quids' worth of my vehicle in a woman's hands.' At least he was honest. There were others who tried to fob her off by saying they might have some work in a week or two. They never did.

In the end, Lesley's father had to step in. He'd telephone a company, ask if there was a job going and find out all the details. When they said 'come and see us', he'd casually mention the job was not for him but for his daughter. Six weeks later, she was hired by a general haulage company. When the boss first saw her, he felt sure she wouldn't last for more than a fortnight. She certainly didn't look the part – a slim, delicately built young woman with pale blonde hair, dressed in neat pretty clothes. (If she turned up at your front door you might think she was the Avon lady, never the driver of a 32-ton truck.) But looks can deceive, of course, and Lesley stayed in her first job for more than a year. . . .

The driving itself wasn't physically taxing. With power steering and smooth gears, the lorry was no heavier to handle than the average family car. But power steering is a fairly recent innovation. Not long ago drivers really did need a lot of muscle, as Lesley discovered on the one occasion when she had to drive a very old vehicle. 'It was an ancient 32-ton truck. It had no power steering, there seemed to be nothing powered about it at all! I had to drive 17 miles to the Hull docks. When I came to the first roundabout I found I couldn't steer and change gear at the same time. I had to stop in the middle of the road, put it into gear, then lean on the steering wheel with all my weight to ram it round. Nowadays a child could get into a truck and steer with one hand.'

After thirteen months she moved over to Hull to work for a container firm. It was easier than her last job. She picked up the loaded containers at the docks and drove them to various destinations, up to 100 miles away, where they were unloaded so she could return them empty to the docks. The only drawback was that she had to live in digs during the week. Hull was 50 miles away and she couldn't do a day's work and get back to Doncaster each night without breaking the legal limits on driving hours. (The maximum time was ten and a half hours with a half-hour break after five hours; now it's eight hours, under EEC laws.) She was very attached to her home and she missed her boyfriend Robert, a young farmer with whom she'd been going steady since she was 17. So after six months she moved back to her old firm in Doncaster.

It wasn't long before another local company offered her a better job. This was the one which took her to Scotland, delivering frozen food from the Doncaster cold store. It was the main depot for all the farmers in the area, who sent in their produce to be frozen and stored. When the produce was purchased, the farmers employed Lesley's firm to make the deliveries which usually went in 18-ton loads to one or two customers at a time. Lesley was in charge of a larger and newer vehicle with a 40-foot refrigerated trailer which didn't need roping or sheeting. . . .

Though she travels all over the country, she is still based in Doncaster with her parents and manages to get back there most nights of the week. When I last saw her she told me she and Robert were about to get engaged. 'He's been looking at houses, and we want to wait until he's found one before we get married; it may take a while because he wants to buy a small farm. Robert's been on about buying me my own lorry when we're married – just the front without the trailer – so that I could contract to pull grain vehicles and potato carts for the local farmers. There'd be plenty of work. I like the idea – as long as it would leave me time to look after Robert. I'm quite looking forward to being a housewife. Mind you, I'm like my mother. She never gave up her job, she couldn't bear to stay in the house all day.'

15   Marc E. Mishkind et al.

A Man's Body and his Sense of Self

How important is a man's body to his sense of self? How connected to a man's self-worth are his feelings about his body? Studies have revealed consistently a significant correlation between men's body satisfaction and self-esteem. . . . How a man feels about himself is thus tied closely to how he feels about his body. It remains for researchers to examine the relative importance of body image to a man's sense of self when compared with other variables such as career achievement, but the data already available suggest that feelings about body play a significant role in self-esteem.

[A] great number of men acknowledge a gap between their actual and ideal body types, and . . . the greater this gap, the lower their self-esteem. As a result, men feel motivated to close this gap. This often depends upon which parts of the body are the foci of dissatisfaction.

In a large-scale factor-analytic study, Franzio and Shields found three primary dimensions along which men's bodily satisfaction and dissatisfaction occur.[1] The first factor, 'physical attractiveness', includes the face and its constituent features, such as cheekbones, chin, ears and eyes. These features contribute to making a man appear 'handsome' or 'good-looking'. The second factor, dubbed 'upper-body strength', contains muscle groups that men typically want to build up in order to improve their physique: biceps, shoulder width, arms and chest. The third factor, 'physical conditioning', contains items that reflect a man's concern with being physically 'fit' or in 'good shape', such as physical stamina, energy level, physical condition, stomach and weight.

Each of these three dimensions – facial attractiveness, upper-body strength and physical conditioning – suggests specific ways in which men could attempt to narrow the distance between their real and ideal selves. A man who wishes to improve his facial attractiveness may perhaps modify his hairstyle or undertake cosmetic surgery. However, we believe that men pursue this kind of self-improvement less frequently. First, facial appearance is viewed typically as less malleable than one's body: 'good looks' are seen as something with which one is or is not endowed. Second, this dimension seems more closely tied to aesthetic dimensions of attractiveness than functional dimensions, and the latter are more central to masculine physical attractiveness.

A man who desires to increase his muscle size and strength – that is, to embody the muscular mesomorphic ideal – may engage in weight-lifting or use weight-training machines. Physical conditioning is most likely to be achieved through long workouts of running, swimming, aerobic exercising or other activities that build stamina and endurance while decreasing body fat. Given that the physical effects of endurance workouts may be less readily visible than the effects of body-building, we surmise that men who want to be widely recognized for their physical masculinity are more likely to opt for muscle-building as their form of physical exercise. There is evidence that weight-lifting men, compared with those who engage in other athletic activities, are more likely attempting to compensate for a lowered sense of masculinity, but replications with current samples are needed.

A different route to altering one's body shape involves dieting. Although women continue to be the largest consumers of diet books and diet products, men constitute a rapidly increasing market. Light beers and diet sodas are promoted by male athletes in order to establish a masculine association to products with formerly feminine connotations. The 'drinking-man's diet' was an effort to capture a relatively untapped male market, and the businessman's lunch is being replaced now by salad bars and lighter fare. Our clinical experience suggests that men are entering diet programmes in increasing numbers for both appearance and health.

Increased efforts expended on exercise and dieting are reinforced by a societal attitude that everyone can improve himself or herself through sufficient effort. People believe that body size and shape are almost totally under volitional control. In fact, this is largely a myth. Individual differences in body build have a large genetic component. Identical twins, for example, even when reared apart, are significantly more similar in weight than fraternal twins or siblings. Adopted children resemble their biological parents in weight, far more than their adoptive parents. For those men who are genetically disposed to deviate from the muscular mesomorphic ideal, the costs of attempting to achieve this ideal may be considerable.

A man who strives to bridge the self-denial gap will experience a heightened attentiveness to and focus on his body. This may render his standards more perfectionistic (and hence perhaps more out of reach) and enhance his perceptions of his shortcomings. Both his limitations and the gap itself can become increasingly salient. To the extent that he feels that he falls short, he will experience the shame of failure. He also may feel ashamed at being so focused on his body, presumably because this has been associated traditionally with the female sex-role stereotype. . . .

Body-building attempts [to reach an ideal body-type may] carry hazards. Men tend to see an overdeveloped muscular body as the most masculine physique, and many body-builders ingest male hormones and steroids in their efforts to attain this exaggerated hypermesomorphic look. These represent only a minority of body-conscious men, but the health ramifications for them may be significant. . . .

[However, the pursuit of the ideal body has] potentially powerful positive consequences. The more a man experiences himself as closing the self–ideal gap – for example, through exercising – the more positive he will feel toward body and self. Higher frequencies of exercise have been associated with greater body satisfaction, and programmes of physical activity have led to more positive feelings towards one's body. The more a man works towards attaining his body ideal and the closer he perceives himself as approximating it, the greater his sense of self-efficacy.

Some men opt not to involve themselves in the deliberate pursuit of the mesomorphic ideal, which can also have both positive and negative effects. Lack of concern with changing one's physical appearance may protect a man from intense bodily preoccupation and its ramifications, but those who experience dissatisfaction but do not strive to change their physiques are likely to suffer from guilt and self-criticism. A recent Gallup survey reports that many people who refrain from exercising feel that their lives would be better if they were to do so.

The increased cultural attention given to the male body and the increasing demands placed on men to achieve the mesomorphic build push men further along the continuum of bodily concern. Men are likely experiencing more body dissatisfaction, preoccupation with weight and concern with their physical attractiveness and body shape now than they did even two decades ago. Fashion designers currently are broadening the chest and tapering the waist of men's clothing lines in order to fit their male customers. However, research is needed to document these current trends.

At the extreme, such concerns could lead to excessive attention to one's body and to an obsessive preoccupation with body-altering behaviour such as weight-lifting, exercising and dieting. With women, extreme bodily concern, coupled with difficulties in achieving the ideal body type, portends disregulated eating patterns such as bulimia – frequent and compulsive binge eating, sometimes followed by purging. Those subcultures of women that amplify the sociocultural emphasis on appearance and weight (e.g., dancers, models) manifest higher rates of eating disorders. Similarly, we might expect that subgroups of men that place relatively greater emphasis on physical appearance would be at greater risk for excessive weight-control behaviours and even eating disorders.

An illustrative group is the gay male subculture, which places an elevated importance on all aspects of a man's physical self – body build, grooming, dress, handsomeness. We predicted that gay men would be at heightened risk for body dissatisfaction and for eating disorders. In a sample of heterosexual and homosexual college men, gay men expressed greater dissatisfaction with body build, waist, biceps, arms and stomach. Gay men also indicated a greater discrepancy between their actual and ideal body shapes than did 'straight' men and showed higher scores on measures of eating disregulation and food and weight preoccupation. If the increased focus on appearance continues for men in general, such concerns and eating disorders may begin to increase among all men.

We have argued that men are moving further along the continuum of bodily concern. But why do men at this time in history appear to be pursuing the muscular mesomorphic ideal to a greater extent than ever before? Western society currently places an unprecedented emphasis on lifestyle change and self-management as the major health-promoting activities. The burden of illness has shifted from infectious diseases to cardiovascular disorders, automobile accidents and cancers, many of which are considered preventable through behaviour change. Looking healthy is the external manifestation of the desired healthy state, so the body symbolizes the extent of one's self-corrective behaviour. Further, what were once considered exclusively male abilities and domains are decreasingly so. Whereas once a man could be assured of his masculinity by virtue of his occupation, interests or certain personality characteristics, many women now opt for the same roles. Gerzon writes that the five traditional archetypes of masculinity – soldier, frontiersman, expert, breadwinner and lord – are now archaic artefacts, although the images remain.[2] The soldier archetype conveys the image of the strong, muscle-armoured body. The frontiersman and lord are no longer viable roles for anyone, and the expert and breadwinner are no longer exclusively male. Thus men may be grasping for the soldier archetype – that is, building up their bodies – in an exaggerated attempt to incorporate what possible options remain of the male images they have held since youth. One of the only remaining ways men can express and preserve traditional male characteristics may be by literally embodying them.

It is worth considering whether this ubiquitous interest in achieving the maleness-as-soldier ideal is a reflection of the conservative militaristic trends in our society. Is it a coincidence that men are opting for muscle-building at a time of greater US military intervention in foreign governments and increased xenophobic patriotic media events such as *Rambo*, which features an overly-muscled mesomorph who returns to Vietnam to avenge American pride and honour for a war we 'lost'? Perhaps, also, the current ideal of thinness for women represents the flip side of this phenomenon. The thin female body connotes such stereotypically feminine traits as smallness, weakness and fragility, which are the mirror opposite of the strength and power represented by the muscular male body. The current female body ideal may be considered the 'last bastion of femininity'.

We therefore propose a second, 'polarization' hypothesis: the male and female body ideals, which are physically and symbolically opposite extremes, may be a reaction against sexual equality, an expression of a wish to preserve some semblance of traditional male–female differences. Lippa found that what people considered the 'ideal' male and 'ideal' female body shapes were more different from each other than what people believed to be the 'typical' male and female body shapes.[3] Even these typical body shapes were more differentiated than men's and women's actual body shapes.

16   Jane Dowdeswell

The Act of Rape

Contrary to the stereotype image of the stranger who strikes in a dark alleyway or churchyard, you are more likely to be raped by someone you know or have seen before the assault. Strangers are involved in less than half the number of attacks, and it is more likely to be a casual acquaintance, ex-boyfriends, friends, family or neighbours. Rapists can be husbands, lovers, fathers, employers, the boy next door, the delivery man, the man you work with:

> I thought I'd be able to spot a rapist a mile off. But somehow when a man is attractive, well dressed and so pleasant, it doesn't occur to you that he could rape you. It was our office party and I got talking to this bloke who'd been working with us for just a week. He seemed really nice: very friendly. I didn't fancy him or anything, and he was telling me about his wife; they'd been married for two years. Anyhow, it turned out he lived a couple of roads away from me, so he offered me a lift home. I wouldn't just accept a lift from anyone: I'm not stupid, but he seemed so nice. Instead of driving straight home, he took another route as he said he had to call in at a friend's house. He drove to the ring road round the airport, stopped the car, and raped me. I don't remember much of what happened, I was so shocked. It was as though I'd been knocked out with chloroform. I thought of getting out of the car and running, but where to? I've not been to work since, and hardly go out in case I see him. Sometimes I remind myself that it wasn't me that did wrong. But when it's someone who's so pleasant you can't help thinking it was your own fault. (*Sandra, 28, from Slough*)

Rapists can be 'nice' men too: women are not prepared for this and find it difficult to talk about it to anyone when the man concerned is well known and well-liked.

> I'd been babysitting for Dave and Ann since I was fourteen. They both played for the local darts team and had a regular night out each week. He had always been my childhood dream: he used to tease me and joke around with me. They only lived next door and Ann was my mum's best friend. A year ago, Dave came home early one Tuesday without Ann: he said they'd had a row and she'd gone home with a friend. I said I'd go as I was feeling tired, I went to get up and he grabbed me by the hair. I didn't know what he was doing at first, it was as if he was mucking about with me. He pulled me up the stairs: I was so frightened I was making these little sobbing noises, trying to scream. I was on my hands and knees, trying to get away, but he was very strong. He tried to have sex with me, but couldn't do it, he got angry and started swearing at me saying I'd always

led him on, teased him. He said if I ever said anything he'd tell Ann that I'd wanted him to do it, and that everyone would know that I was easy. I see him almost every day: sometimes if I'm in the garden I see him looking out of the window at me. I hate him more than I can say, but everyone else thinks he's wonderful. (*Joanne, 19, from Lewisham*)

It is generally held that being raped by a man you know is less damaging and distressing to the victim, but through talking to women it is clear this is just another myth.

Jenny, a student from Brighton, was raped when she was eighteen by the person she most trusted:

My rapist wasn't the violent stranger most people imagine rapists are. This was my boyfriend. I was doing 'A' levels, intending to study for a degree and aiming for a good career. The last thing I wanted was a baby. I had a physical relationship with him in which I enjoyed him entering my vagina with his hand. He knew this was as intimate as I was prepared to be.

Unfortunately, this made rape very easy for him. He simply swopped his hand for his penis. I did not consent, I did not even realize what was happening. I did sense a change in his movements and was afraid of what this meant, but I was numb. In my confusion I was absolutely silent. He confirmed my fear immediately afterwards by apologising. I can remember thinking 'This is Rape'; he looked like a stranger all of a sudden, but he was looking at me with concern and feeling in his eyes. No, he couldn't be a rapist, but then why did I feel so cold? Subtle seduction or subtle rape? I believe the latter.

Questioning ourselves about whether it is rape reveals our own confusion. Julie from Northampton would agree:

I always used to think that girls and women were raped or attacked by strangers, but I knew the boy who raped me. I was walking home with a friend at night, and on the opposite side of the road we saw a lad we knew: he had been out with one of my friends from school. We called over hello, and he came over. I thought he was drunk because he had a glass in his hand – it was Whit weekend and people were taking their glasses around with them from pub to pub. He held the glass and smashed it against the wall, holding it close to my face, and said, 'Shut up, or you'll get this.' I laughed, as I thought he was joking, but he pushed me into a garden. My friend ran off as she said she was scared, and I was screaming and had cut my hand. He was lying on top of me and I remember trying to get up and seeing my legs under his body so I couldn't move. He held me down half-way between my chest and neck, and pulled my knickers down. I just kept screaming and eventually he ran off. I had marks on my thighs for weeks after, and when I got home my face and legs were streaked with blood – I think he'd cut himself on the glass. I've not told my mum or anyone else about it, as I think a lot of people wouldn't believe me and would think I encouraged him.

Often the rape or assault seems unreal even to you. At first you may find it difficult to see it as 'rape', particularly if the man involved is known to you. In an attempt to survive, mentally, some women tell how they tried to convince themselves it wasn't really happening to them.

Sandra was raped by a man who was given her address by a friend:

She was chatted up by this South African guy we met at a nightclub and because of some instinct or something, she tried to get rid of him, so she gave him a false name and address (mine!). The next day, Sunday, at about 9 a.m. the doorbell rang and this guy was standing there. I recognized him, and he became very angry and said my friend had been playing games with him and he didn't like it. He just pushed his way into the house and threw me down on to the hall floor, then dragged me into the living room. I had slept with a man before the rape, my second boyfriend, and I tried to think that this was what I had done with my boyfriend and tried to blank out the fact that this man was not someone I cared for. I just knew instinctively there was nothing I could do to dissuade him, and in a way I just went off into a sort of a trance. It was like going out of your body, trying to disassociate myself from what was happening to me. I felt like I was in a time warp – while I could keep myself in this cocoon where it was all unreal, I'd be able to survive whatever he did to me!

This 'blocking out' of everything around them is not uncommon says Dr Gillian Mezey from the Institute of Psychiatry, who has spoken to many rape victims in the course of her research. She says:

There is often a narrowing of perception that occurs during attacks when women are not really aware of what is going on around them. One said, 'All I could think about was the blue button, that blue button on the rapist's shirt.' So while he was doing all these dreadful things, all the senses became narrowed down to this one single perception. I found this helps a lot of women get through it. Another woman remembers the area in the small of the back that was being rubbed up and down on concrete and the skin being grazed. She was just concentrating on that so much she couldn't remember anything else.

We are led to believe that rape occurs often in streets and dark alleys but the circumstances can be wide and varied. As examples, here are four very different settings. Read them through and decide which you think was the place and who the victim of a crime:

- 7 a.m.   a fourteen-year-old girl sets out on her paper-round in Sevenoaks. It's her regular route and she sees the same few joggers and workers on their way to the station...
- Noon   a pensioner leaves the busy shopping centre, already crowded with shoppers, calls into Woolworth's and the Post Office to collect her pension...
- 3 p.m.   a nurse on nightshift sleeps in the flat she shares with her friend, also a nurse, who is getting ready to leave for work...
- Midnight   two girls walking home after a night at the local club. They stop at the bus shelter to check on the last buses. A car pulls up – it's the father of one of their friends – and offers them a lift. They are relieved: it was going to be a long walk home.

The frightening answer is that each setting we've described was witness to rape. No better proof, if it is needed, that rape can happen *anywhere*, to *any one* of us at *any time*.

17   Stuart Weir and Claire Sanders

Dangerous Liaisons: AIDS and Unsafe Sex

Luke is 29. He is a commodity broker in the City and earns over £200,000 a year. He is a calm and reflective man and talks very precisely about his life and feelings. Two years ago a long-standing relationship broke down.

I have been a bachelor ever since, travelling quite a bit. I work very long hours, normally until 8.30 p.m. and in my work there is a lot of tension and stress and emotion. Because of the stresses of work, I like my relationships to be as easy as possible. Emotionally, it is very difficult to carry on a strong relationship with a fixed partner because I don't have the time to deal with all the consequences of that. So I have many relationships.

In the first place I was very concerned about contracting HIV. I went out with some girls I knew, who were kind of friends, and eventually I was having sexual relationships without any protection. One day I met a girl who said, 'Do you know if you have AIDS or not?' I said I don't think so. She said, 'How do you know?' and she sent me to a doctor. He tested me and I was all right. He was a specialist in this kind of disease and he explained that the main risk is with homosexuals or prostitutes. I think purely from a statistical point of view this is possibly true, but you just need one unlucky occasion and you can contract AIDS.

But in saying that, I must say that I take some risks. Although it doesn't follow any logic, I am still having sex with girls without protection. It's always with girls I have known for several months, it's very unusual for me to have sex with a person at the first meeting. And I always discuss AIDS and other relationships before I have intercourse, I ask specific questions about those kind of things. You know, 'Do you think you have AIDS, if you don't, how do you know that precisely?' The funny thing is that though I am always very honest and say that I go out with several other girls and have sex with them, and we talk very seriously about safe sex and using condoms, no bullshit – you know, we are going to do this thing seriously – the relationship kind of evolves and when it comes down to it, I have never had a girl ask me to wear a condom. Over the past year I have probably met about twenty different girls, and the girls I go out with are perhaps university graduates, you know, they have very responsible jobs, but none have insisted I wear a condom.

So in effect you have a very serious discussion and then you both act entirely differently?

Well, we have a serious discussion about it and we say that it could be dangerous, you have to be careful. We don't normally talk too specifically about what we have to do. We both realize that the decision is serious, but we don't say, 'OK, we're going to do this, buy a condom.' It's more, 'OK, we have to be careful.' But eventually, having met and talked as a couple, there is no more discussion.

Why do we take such risks? I don't know, it is very difficult for me to explain. Maybe it is in our minds, or at least in mine, and it must be somewhere very remote, that using condoms is not really natural. And also if you really think about it, it is really ridiculous. So you don't want to be bothered with that, it is not pretty, it is not practical, it is not poetic. Of course, it can also save your life – but you are sure the person is OK, after all.

COLEG MENAI
BANGOR, GWYNEDD LL57 2T

So in a sense you are judging each other on some notion of responsibility and respectability?

Well, for example I met a French girl and she said she hadn't had sex for quite a while. Maybe it was true, maybe it was not, for some reason I thought it was. Then I said, 'What about me? I could have AIDS, you know.' And she said, 'No, I know you haven't got AIDS.' I asked why, and she said, 'Well, because you look fairly straight.' I think that people for some reason seem to trust me. But they don't realize that by trusting me they have to trust all the partners I have been with, which is a different thing.

Do any of them ask you if you are bisexual?

No, nobody asks me that.

Or if you take drugs?

No, but I think anyone who knows me would know that I am neither of the two.

But they have only known you for weeks in some cases.

Yes, that is true. There is no doubt that there is some discrepancy in people's lives, perhaps they don't want to see some things. They may be very mature and very adult in their business life, and in taking these big risks there, but they change in their social life, they become immature, and I include myself.

Have you yourself ever decided that you don't quite trust a woman you've met?

Yes, definitely. There are a couple of girls that I didn't trust, I couldn't tell you exactly why. I just decided to stop the relationship. And perhaps in 25 per cent of the cases where I go to bed with a girl, I stop before penetration.

What about anal intercourse, does that come into it at all?

Yes, whenever it gets to anal intercourse I tend to pick the girls that somehow I trust more than the others.

And what about your partners, are they more careful with that?

That's the odd thing. When it gets down to being in bed with somebody, the whole thing is somehow not there for them any more. That kind of thought is outside the bedroom somehow.

Obviously, the women take a greater risk than you, as penetrative sex is much more dangerous for them than for you. Would you behave the same way if you felt you were running an equal risk?

I always thought I was running an equal risk. And when it comes to oral sex, when it is the man using his mouth, that is one of the great risks for the man. It is not that I have oral sex with any girl I go with, but on some occasions I have and in that particular instance I take an equal risk. I have a hard time to really pinpoint why I am taking this risk. If you think about it, it is ridiculous and I have a hard time to find out why you take risks. And I have been telling myself a hundred times never again, you know, this is crazy...

Do you think the risk in any sense actually makes things more exciting?

That is an interesting question, I guess I would say no, because if I thought about it during intercourse it would make me less excited. The idea that I could be contracting HIV is not the kind of thought I like to have when I am in bed with someone.

Is it your impression generally that the risk of infection has not really affected most people's behaviour very much?

In my experience, exactly. I've met girls who talk very straight about it, so you know where you are, and then you go to bed with them and they haven't got a condom. Once you get into a very physical relationship it is all over. That happens so many times. I even had a girlfriend who was a model in New York and her best friend died of AIDS and she is still suffering from that emotionally because he was a very close friend. You would think that she would be more cautious than anybody else and that is the way she talked. I said I don't like condoms, and she said, 'Don't worry, with me there is no way you won't use them, it's crazy not to.' But we met several times, and then began a physical relationship without penetration and eventually a week later we had penetration with no protection and I thought about it only later on.

But didn't you think that she might be dangerous for you?

Oh yes. I only trusted her because she was so assertive and so strict about it that I thought it was impossible she would ever take the risk. Afterwards, I thought I don't know about her any more, I got very nervous and I went and had a check. That was pushing my luck a bit too far. I did realize that somehow I would have to calm down, because if you push your luck too far one day you might get HIV, there is no question about it.

Joan is 35. She is a solicitor who concentrates on legal aid work, mostly in family law. She has been living with a regular partner for seven years and they have bought a flat in south London together.

I have a full sex life with my partner, I mean, we have probably done most things people do together. I am on the pill so he never has to use a condom. We have never discussed the question of safe sex together and I don't think that we ever would. I don't think that we have to.

Do you know that some people say that even people in stable relationships should discuss and practise safe sex, simply because surveys of sexual behaviour suggest that no one can actually trust their partner not to sleep with someone else.

Some people say that, do they? I can't agree with that. You have to trust somebody and surely you've got to trust the person you live with. I trust my partner completely. I am sure that he has never been out with any other woman. I know him very well and I know he thinks the world of me and I know he wouldn't – it sounds awful, but I do know him, I am 100 per cent sure of him.

Is he 100 per cent sure of you?

No. He knows that I had an affair very early on in our relationship. In fact, I knew the man – a colleague – before I moved in with Michael and we have been close friends for years. One night when I'd been with him Michael asked me if I was having an affair and I said, yes, and he was so upset that I broke the thing with Peter off. But we have remained friends since and there have been periods of time, maybe a year has gone past, when we haven't been out and haven't slept together, but then we get back together again. Over the last year or so we were seeing each other, say every two months. Peter has got his own house and he is single. He has had a long-term relationship with a woman which was supposed to be over, but then she found out she was pregnant so she has actually moved in with him now, about a month ago. Since then I haven't seen him.

So Peter was having sex with at least one other person while you were having an affair with him. Did you practise safe sex?

No.

Did you think that you might be running a risk?

No, because the way I think about it – and probably will continue to think about it – is that the people I choose to have a sexual relationship with, who now are very few and far between anyway, are people I have known for years. I know a lot about them, and they are responsible people, they don't sleep around, they have probably only had one partner for the last three or four years and I suppose that that is what makes me feel safe.

How much do you know about Peter's other lover? Do you think she may have had other lovers too?

From what he has told me, yes, I do know about her. I don't think she would have had other partners while she was seeing him – not from the way he talked about her, and what he said. I mean, it is conceivable, but she was so keen on Peter, and wanted to get married, I don't think she's the sort.

You talked about the people you have had affairs with. Has Peter been your only lover over the last few years?

There's only been one other, and that was just a one-off with my partner's best friend a few months ago. It was nothing spectacular and it was a great mistake. It took place in the afternoon and didn't last very long, and that was it. It wasn't 'safe sex', he didn't use a condom. But again, and I'm sorry if this sounds boring, I have known him for about eight years and he's been married for five of those years, and I am sure that he doesn't have other partners, except possibly a one-night stand when he's away, but I doubt that too. I mean, we have been friends for a long time and he is the sort of person who talks about it and I am very easy to talk to about it. I think I would know. So I simply didn't worry about AIDS because I know he is a responsible person.

But he has just done so with you.

Well, he knows that I have only got one partner and that I have been very good for the last so many years. And I know all about his habits with his wife. I can tell you, if I fancied somebody and was going to have perhaps a one-night stand, there is no way I would sleep with that person if I didn't know them. If I had only met them that very day at a conference or something, there is no way I would sleep with them without protection, without using a condom.

Jon is a hospital doctor in Birmingham. He is 45 and has been married for twenty-three years. He and his wife have two teenage children. He has a strong outgoing character and has always had affairs with other women.

I am in a rather complicated situation at the moment. I am going out with three women, but one of them who is married has got very, very keen and now she wants to ditch her marriage. I have been trying to drift away slightly and I haven't seen her for three weeks. I was seeing her once every week and we were speaking on the telephone four or five times a day and she was writing letters and poems.

Then there are one or two other little forays. I met a very attractive doctor, quite small, about 35, at a conference in London recently. We went back to her flat and drank some champagne and she said, 'Would you carry me into the bedroom?' I do still see her when I am in London, but she's rather neurotic. There is another one which is not so complicated in one of the provincial towns which I have to visit quite often. So when I go there that is quite a nice interlude. I would say that none of them are risky from the point of view of HIV infection.

How many women have you slept with in the past five years?

Maybe thirty, yes around thirty. I don't like using condoms, but I do if they ask me to. The doctor insists that I wear a condom, she always does. And the one in the provinces normally says I have to wear one, she thinks of some trumped-up reason, you know, she has got her period or something, but really it is because she is frightened of AIDS. Anyway, I do. But I never use a condom with the married woman that I have been seeing quite a lot. And not many people ask for it and I don't like it, I think condoms really do affect it.

But you don't think your own safety depends on it?

I still am very arrogant, I still think the risks are at the moment extremely small, you would have to be extremely unfortunate. Most of the heterosexual AIDS sufferers have contracted it through drug users or homosexuals. There are very few cases of AIDS being passed on by straight sex. Of course, in three or four years' time the risks will increase. But here at the moment the risk is very, very slight. I'm far more likely to get gonorrhoea or syphilis, or be run over or be killed in a car crash.

But if you get AIDS it doesn't just affect you, it affects all of your partners, your wife, their families and in a way your own children. Do you worry about affecting them?

Well that would be terrible, it would be an awful thing. If you start thinking about it, it would be an absolutely awful thing to have to inflict on a family. But talk to any doctor. Most doctors are basically saying there was a justifiable kind of hysteria a few years ago, but I don't think any of us now believe – apart from a small number – that AIDS is going to be anything like the scourge that people thought before.

Basically, you've got to realize there are two factors here. One, it was in the interests of the government to create a slight panic about it to try and get people to change their sexual habits. Two, some of it was generated by the gay community who didn't want to be scapegoated and wanted the whole thing to be generalized. What developed in the medical world was a small group of doctors who very cynically – this is probably not a very nice thing to say, because a lot of them I know and some of them are very decent and honourable people – but it is in their interest to try and maintain a kind of AIDS culture for their careers.

But at a personal level, if you consider your partner in the provincial town, she has presumably some inkling of your behaviour and she's right to be worried . . .

I don't know that I have been quite so, she knows my track record very well. I think among working people, perhaps among those who don't feel they have so much to lose, that their behaviour hasn't changed as much as middle-class behaviour which hasn't probably changed an awful lot either.

Your married partner, is she too a doctor, and does she know that you have other partners?

Yes, and she knows more than the others about me.

Doesn't it alarm her?

Do you know any straight person with AIDS?

Yes, because we interviewed someone who became infected with HIV without knowing it from one random sexual encounter and she had at least one lover before she found out. Possibly you could meet someone like her who didn't know and then you could have problems.

Was she working-class?

Actually she is a middle-class person. Do you think that you're safe with middle-class people, then?

At the moment, I just think there are an awful lot of things to be frightened of which are far worse.

Part 5

Class and Stratification

All social systems are stratified – that is, material and cultural resources are distributed in an unequal fashion. In modern societies, class is the most significant (although by no means the only) form of social stratification. In spite of, or perhaps because of, its centrality in sociology there is no general agreement over how the concept of class should best be formulated.

Reading 18 compares the two most influential conceptions of class advanced in classical social thought, those of Karl Marx and Max Weber. According to Marx, class is above all linked to control of private property and 'surplus production'. Class relations are not just incidental to modern social orders, but absolutely essential to them, as are mechanisms of class conflict. Weber accepted a good deal of Marx's viewpoint, but argued that economic factors other than ownership or control of property are important in determining class divisions. Class concerns the differential distribution of 'life-chances', and these are affected by economic influences such as the structure of labour markets as well as by who controls property in the means of production.

Reading 19, by Nicholas Abercrombie and Alan Warde, considers one of the most important empirical studies of class divisions in Britain, which is concerned not only with class formation but with social mobility – in other words, levels and rates of movement of individuals between the major class divisions. The Nuffield Mobility Study indicates that, while there is a considerable amount of social mobility in Britain, most such mobility does not reflect the development of an increasingly 'open' society. Upward mobility is primarily a consequence of changes in the class system, deriving from industrial and technological development. Traditionally working-class jobs have been declining in number relative to occupations associated with higher class positions, thereby providing opportunities for generalized upward movement (one should note that the Nuffield Mobility Study dealt only with men, thereby, its critics assert, continuing the 'gender-blind' nature of traditional sociology).

John Scott's contribution (reading 20) is directed at the upper echelons of the class structure. At the core of the upper class is the 'Establishment', a network of people who wield power in a diversity of major institutions. In terms of social mobility, the Establishment is substantially self-recruiting, such social reproduction being achieved primarily through the influence of the public schools and ancient universities. Within the business sector, Scott demonstrates, similar patterns of recruitment are found to those in other elite areas, such as the Church, army or judiciary.

Together with most other analysts of social class, Marx and Weber saw class divisions as closely related to political views and voting patterns. In reading 21, Robert Waller looks at a particular class group, skilled manual and supervisory workers, to investigate their specific role in modern politics. He finds good reason to question whether this class group influences voting outcomes as decisively as is often suggested.

In the concluding selection of this part (reading 22) Hakon Leiulfsrud and Alison Woodward discuss some basic issues of gender and class. Critical of the Nuffield Mobility study as well as of other orthodox approaches to class analysis, they claim that it is mistaken to treat women workers as being in the same class position as their husbands. They develop this argument by means of a discussion of 'cross-class' marriages, in which one partner in a couple is in a different class position from the other. They show that where the female in the marriage is in a higher-class occupation than the male, the woman tends to have correspondingly more power in the home. In such circumstances, women are not merely 'appendages' of their partners in class terms.

18   Anthony Giddens

Marx and Weber on Class

According to Marx's theory, class society is the product of a determinate sequence of historical changes. The most primitive forms of human society are not class systems. In 'tribal' societies – or, in Engels' term, 'primitive communism' – there is only a very low division of labour, and such property as exists is owned in common by the members of the community. The expansion of the division of labour, together with the increased level of wealth which this generates, is accompanied by the growth of private property; this involves the creation of a surplus product which is appropriated by a minority of non-producers who consequently stand in an exploitative relation *vis-à-vis* the majority of producers. Expressed in the terminology of Marx's early writings, alienation from nature, which characterizes the situation of tribal society, yields place to an increasing mastery of the material world, whereby [human beings] both 'humanize [themselves] and develop [their] culture; but the increasing dissolution of . . . alienation . . . is attained only at the price of the formation of exploitative class relationships – at the price of an increase in human self-alienation.

Marx was not always careful to emphasize the differences between capitalism and prior forms of class system which have preceded it in history. While it is the case that all (written) history 'is the history of class struggles',[1] this most definitely does not mean that what constitutes a 'class' is identical in each type of class society (although, of course, every class shares certain formal properties which define it as such), or that the process of the development of class conflict everywhere takes the same course. Marx's rebuke to those of his followers who had assumed the latter is instructive in this respect. Several of the factors which characterized the origins of the capitalist mode of production in Western Europe in the post-medieval period existed previously in Ancient Rome, including the formation of a merchant/manufacturing class and the development of money markets. But because of other elements in the composition of Roman society, including particularly the existence of slavery, the class struggles in Rome took a form which resulted, not in the generation of a 'new and higher form of society', but in the disintegration of the social fabric.[2]

The diverse forms and outcomes of class conflict in history explain the different possibilities generated by the supersession of one type of society by another. When capitalism replaces feudalism, this is because a new class system, based upon manufacture and centred in the towns, has created a sort of enclave within feudal society which eventually comes to predominate over the agrarian-based structure of feudal domination. The result, however, is a new system of class domination, because this sequence of revolutionary change is based upon the partial replacement of one type of property in the means of production (land) by another (capital) – a process which, of course, entails major changes in technique. While capitalism, like feudalism, carries 'the germ of its own destruction' within itself, and while this self-negating tendency is also expressed in the shape of overt class struggles, their underlying character is quite different from those involved in the decline of feudalism. Class conflict in capitalism does not represent the struggle of two competing forms of technique, but stems instead from the incompatibility of an existing productive technique (industrial manufacture) with other aspects of the 'mode of production' – namely, the organization of the capitalist market. The access of a new class to power does not involve the ascendancy of a new form of private property, but instead creates the conditions under which private property is abolished. The proletariat here is the equivalent of Saint-Simon's '*industriels*': because it becomes the 'only class' in society, its hegemony signals the disappearance of all classes.

The problem of Marx's usage of the term 'class' is complicated, given the fact that he does not provide a formal definition of the concept. In approaching this matter, it is valuable to make a distinction between three sets of factors which complicate discussion of the Marxian conception of class – factors which have not been satisfactorily separated in the long-standing controversy over the issue. The first of these refers simply to the question of terminology – the variability in Marx's use of the word 'class' itself. The second concerns the fact that there are two conceptual constructions which may be discerned in Marx's writings as regards the notion of class: *an abstract or 'pure' model of class domination*, which applies to all types of class system; and more concrete descriptions of the specific characteristics of classes in particular societies. The third concerns Marx's analysis of classes in capitalism, the case which overwhelmingly occupied his interests: just as there are in Marx 'pure' models of class, so there are 'pure' and 'concrete' models of the structure of capitalism and the process of capitalist development.

The terminological issue, of course, is the least significant of the three sets of questions here. The fact of the matter is that Marx's terminology is careless. While he normally uses the term 'class' (*Klasse*), he also uses words such as 'stratum' and 'estate' (*Stand*) as if they were interchangeable with it. Moreover, he applies the word 'class' to various groups which, in theoretical terms, are obviously only parts or sectors of 'classes' properly speaking: thus he speaks of intellectuals as the 'ideological classes', of the *Lumpenproletariat* as the 'dangerous class', of bankers and moneylenders as the 'class of parasites', and so on. What matters, however, is how far this terminological looseness conceals conceptual ambiguities or confusions.

The principal elements of Marx's 'abstract model' of class domination are actually not difficult to reconstruct from the generality of his writings. This model is a dichotomous one. In each type of class society, there are two fundamental classes. Property relations constitute the axis of this dichotomous system: a minority of 'non-producers', who control the means of production, are able to use this position of control to extract from the majority of 'producers' the surplus product which is the source of their livelihood. 'Class' is thus defined in terms of the relationship of groupings of individuals to the means of production. This is integrally connected with the division of labour, because a relatively developed division of labour is necessary for the creation of the surplus product without which classes cannot exist. But, as Marx makes clear in his unfinished discussion at the end of the third volume of *Capital*, 'class' is not to be identified with source of income in the division of labour: this would yield an almost endless plurality of classes. Moreover, classes are never, in Marx's sense, income groupings. Modes of consumption, according to Marx, are primarily determined by relations of production. Hence his critique of those varieties of socialism which are directed towards securing some kind of 'distributive justice' in society – which seek, for example, the equalization of incomes: such forms of socialism are based on false premises, because they neglect the essential fact that distribution is ultimately governed by the system of production. This is why it is possible for two individuals to have identical incomes, and even the same occupations, and yet belong to different classes; as might be the case, for example, with two bricklayers, one of whom owns his own business, while the other works as the employee of a large firm.

It is an axiom of Marx's abstract model of classes that economic domination is tied to political domination. Control of the means of production yields political control. Hence the dichotomous division of classes is a division of both property and power: to trace the lines of economic exploitation in a society is to discover the key to the understanding of the relations of super- and subordination which apply within that society. Thus classes express a relation not only between 'exploiters and exploited', but between 'oppressors and oppressed'. Class relations necessarily are inherently unstable: but a dominant class seeks to stabilize its position by advancing (not usually, of course, in a consciously directed fashion) a legitimating ideology, which 'rationalizes' its position of economic and political domination and 'explains' to the subordinate class why it should accept its subordination. This is the connotation of the much quoted assertion that:

> The ideas of the ruling class are in every epoch the ruling ideas: i.e., the class which is the ruling *material* force of society, is at the same time its ruling *intellectual* force. The class which has the means of material production at its disposal, has control at the same time over the means of mental production, so that thereby, generally speaking, the ideas of those who lack the means of mental production are subject to it.[3]

In the abstract model, classes are conceived to be founded upon relations of mutual *dependence* and *conflict*. 'Dependence' here means more than the sheer material dependence which is presupposed by the division of labour between the classes. In Marx's conception, classes in the dichotomous system are placed in a situation of reciprocity such that *neither class can escape from the relationship without thereby losing its identity as a distinct 'class'*. It is this theorem, heavily influenced by the Hegelian dialectic, which binds the theory of classes to the transformation of types of society. Classes, according to Marx, express the fundamental identity of society: when a class succeeds in, for example, elevating itself from a position of subordination to one of domination, it consequently effects an overall reorganization of the social structure. In the dichotomous system, classes are not, of course, 'dependent' upon each other in the sense of being collaborating groups on a level of equality; their reciprocity is an asymmetrical one, since it rests upon the extraction of surplus value by one class from the other. While each class 'needs' the other – given the continued existence of the society in unchanged form – their interests are at the same time mutually exclusive, and form the basis for the potential outbreak of open struggles. Class 'conflict' refers, first of all, to the opposition of interests presupposed by the exploitative relation integral to the dichotomous class relationship: classes are thus 'conflict groups'. This is, however, a point at which Marx's terminology is again variable. Whereas in his normal usage a 'class' represents any grouping which shares the same relationship to the means of production, regardless of whether the individuals involved become conscious of, and act upon, their common interests, he occasionally indicates that such a grouping can be properly called a 'class' only when shared interests do generate communal consciousness and action. But there is not really any significant conceptual ambiguity here. On the contrary, by this verbal emphasis, Marx seeks to stress the fact that class only becomes an important social agency when it assumes a directly political character, when it is a focus for communal action. Only under certain conditions does a class 'in itself' become a class 'for itself'.

Most of the problematic elements in Marx's theory of classes stem from the application of this abstract model to specific, historical forms of society – that is to say, they turn upon the nature of the connections between the 'abstract' and 'concrete' models of class. The first question to consider in this respect is the relationship between the dichotomous class system, presupposed by the abstract model, and the plurality of classes which, as Marx admits, exist in all historical forms of (class) society. Although Marx nowhere provides an explicit discussion of this matter, there is no serious source of difficulty here. Each historical type of society (ancient society, feudalism and capitalism) is structured around a dichotomous division in respect of property relations (represented most simply in each case as a division between patrician and plebeian, lord and vassal, capitalist and wage-labourer). But while this dichotomous division is the main 'axis' of the social structure, this simple class relation is complicated by the existence of three other sorts of grouping, two of which are 'classes' in a straightforward sense, while the third is a marginal case in this respect. These are: (1) 'transitional classes' which are in the process of formation within a society based upon a class system which is becoming 'obsolete': this is the case with the rise of the bourgeoisie and 'free' urban proletariat within feudalism; (2) 'transitional classes' which, on the contrary, represent elements of a superseded set of relations of production that linger on within a new form of society – as is found in the capitalist societies of nineteenth-century Europe, where the 'feudal classes' remain of definite significance within the social structure. Each of the first two examples results from the application of two dichotomous schemes to a single form of historical society. They represent, as it were, the fact that radical social change is not accomplished overnight, but constitutes an extended process of development, such that there is a massive overlap between types of dichotomous class system. (3) The third category includes two principal historical examples: the slaves of the ancient world, and the independent peasantry of the medieval and post-medieval period. These are 'quasi-class groupings', in the sense that they may be said to share certain common economic interests; but each of them, for different reasons, stands on the margin of the dominant set of class relationships within the societies of which they form part. To these three categories, we may add a fourth 'complicating factor' of the abstract dichotomous system: (4) sectors or sub-divisions of classes. Classes are not homogeneous entities as regards the social relations to which they give rise: Marx recognizes various sorts of differentiations within classes.

It should be noted that none of these categories involves sacrificing the abstract conception of the dichotomous class system: but they do make possible the recognition of the existence of 'middle classes', which in some sense intervene between the dominant and the subordinate class. 'Middle classes' are either of a transitional type, or they are segments of the major classes. Thus the bourgeoisie are a 'middle class' in feudalism, prior to their ascent to power; while the petty bourgeoisie, the small property-owners, whose interests are partly divergent from those of large-scale capital, form what Marx sometimes explicitly refers to as the 'middle class' in capitalism. If the terminology is again somewhat confusing, the underlying ideas are clear enough....

For the most significant developments in the theory of classes since Marx, we have to look to those forms of social thought whose authors, while being directly influenced by Marx's ideas, have attempted at the same time to criticize or to reformulate them. This tendency has been strongest, for a combination of historical and intellectual reasons, in German sociology, where a series of attempts have been made to provide a fruitful critique of Marx – beginning with Max Weber ... As in Marx, we find in Weber's writings treatments of 'classes' and 'capitalist development' as abstract conceptions; and these can be partly separated from his specifically historical discussions of the characteristics of particular European societies.

In the two versions of 'Class, status and party' which have been embodied in *Economy and Society*,[4] Weber provides what is missing in Marx: an explicit discussion of the concept of class. There are two principal respects in which this analysis differs from Marx's 'abstract model' of classes. One is that which is familiar from most secondary accounts – the differentiation of 'class' from 'status' and 'party'. The second, however, as will be argued below, is equally important: this is that, although Weber employs for some purposes a dichotomous model which in certain general respects resembles that of Marx, his viewpoint strongly emphasizes a *pluralistic conception of classes*. Thus Weber's distinction between 'ownership classes' (*Besitzklassen*) and 'acquisition classes' (*Erwerbsklassen*) is based upon a fusion of two criteria: 'on the one hand . . . the kind of property that is usable for returns; and, on the other hand . . . the kind of services that can be offered on the market', thus producing a complex typology. The sorts of property which may be used to obtain market returns, although dividing generally into two types – creating ownership (*rentier*) and acquisition (entrepreneurial) classes – are highly variable, and may produce many differential interests within dominant classes:

> Ownership of dwellings; workshops; warehouses; stores; agriculturally usable land in large or small-holdings – a quantitative difference with possibly qualitative consequences; ownership of mines; cattle; men (slaves); disposition over mobile instruments of production, or capital goods of all sorts, especially money or objects that can easily be exchanged for money; disposition over products of one's own labour or of others' labour differing according to their various distances from consumability; disposition over transferable monopolies of any kind – all these distinctions differentiate the class situations of the propertied. . .[5]

But the class situations of the propertyless are also differentiated, in relation both to the types and the degree of 'monopolization' of 'marketable skills' which they possess. Consequently, there are various types of 'middle class' which stand between the 'positively privileged' classes (the propertied) and the 'negatively privileged' classes (those who possess neither property nor marketable skills). While these groupings are all nominally propertyless, those who possess skills which have a definite 'market value' are certainly in a different class situation from those who have nothing to offer but their (unskilled) labour. In acquisition classes – i.e. those associated particularly with the rise of modern capitalism – educational qualifications take on a particular significance in this respect; but the monopolization of trade skills by manual workers is also important.

Weber insists that a clear-cut distinction must be made between class 'in itself' and class 'for itself': 'class', in his terminology, always refers to market interests, which exist independently of whether men are aware of them. Class is thus an 'objective' characteristic influencing the life-chances of men. But only under certain conditions do those sharing a common class situation become conscious of, and act upon, their mutual economic interests. In making this emphasis, Weber undoubtedly intends to separate his position from that adopted by many Marxists, involving what he calls a 'pseudo-scientific operation' whereby the link between class and class consciousness is treated as direct and immediate. Such a consideration evidently also underlies the emphasis which Weber places upon 'status groups' (*Stände*) as contrasted to classes. The contrast between class and status group, however, is not, as often seems to be assumed, merely, nor perhaps even primarily, a distinction between subjective and objective aspects of differentiation. While class is founded upon differentials of economic interest in market relationships, Weber nowhere denies that, under certain given circumstances, a class may be a subjectively aware 'community'. The importance of status groups – which are normally 'communities' in this sense – derives from the fact that they are built upon criteria of grouping other than those stemming from market situation. The contrast between classes and status groups is sometimes portrayed by Weber as one between the objective and the subjective; but it is also one between production and consumption. Whereas class expresses relationships involved in production, status groups express those involved in consumption, in the form of specific 'styles of life'.

Status affiliations may cut across the relationships generated in the market, since membership of a status group usually carries with it various sorts of monopolistic privileges. None the less, classes and status groups tend in many cases to be closely linked, through property: possession of property is both a major determinant of class situation and also provides the basis for following a definite 'style of life'. The point of Weber's analysis is not that class and status constitute two 'dimensions of stratification', but that classes and status communities represent two possible, and competing, modes of group formation in relation to the distribution of power in society. Power is *not*, for Weber, a 'third dimension' in some sense comparable to the first two. He is quite explicit about saying that classes, status groups and parties are all 'phenomena of the distribution of power'.[6] The theorem informing Weber's position here is his insistence that power is not to be assimilated to economic domination – again, of course, a standpoint taken in deliberate contrast to that of Marx. The party, oriented towards the acquisition or maintenance of political leadership, represents, like the class and the status group, a major focus of social organization relevant to the distribution of power in a society. It is, however, only characteristic of the modern rational state.

Weber's abstract discussions of the concepts of class, status group and party, while providing the sort of concise conceptual analysis which is missing in Marx, are nevertheless unfinished expositions, and hardly serve to do more than offer a minimal introduction to the complex problems explored in his historical writings. In these latter writings, Weber details various forms of complicated interconnection between different sorts of class relationships, and between class relationships and status group affiliations. In the history of the European societies, there has been an overall shift in the character of predominant types of class relationship and class conflict. Thus in ancient Rome, class conflicts derived primarily from antagonisms established in the credit market, whereby peasants and artisans came to be in debt-bondage to urban financiers. This tended to cede place, in the middle ages, to class struggles originating in the commodity market and involving battles over the prices of the necessities of life. With the rise of modern capitalism, however, relationships established in the labour market become of central significance. It is evident that for Weber, as for Marx, the advent of capitalism dramatically changes the character of the general connections between classes and society. The emergence of the labour contract as the predominant type of class relationship is tied to the phenomenon of the expansion of economic life, and the formation of a national economy, which is so characteristic of modern capitalism. In most forms of society prior to modern capitalism, even in those in which there is a considerable development of manufacture and commerce, status groups play a more important role in the social structure than classes. By creating various sorts of restriction upon enterprise, or by enforcing the monopolization of market privileges by traditionally established groups, status affiliations have in fact, as is shown in Weber's studies of the Eastern civilizations, directly inhibited the formation of modern capitalist production.

19   Nicholas Abercrombie and Alan Warde
Social Mobility: The Nuffield Study

Social mobility concerns movements between social classes. It is usually estimated by reference to occupational positions. Movement may happen within an
individual's lifetime, called *intragenerational* mobility, as for example the cases
of the promotion of a clerk to a manager or a manual worker obtaining
qualifications permitting access to a profession. Or the movement may occur
between generations, children coming to fill places in a different occupational
class to their parents, which is called *intergenerational* mobility. Examples would
be the child of an engine driver who becomes a solicitor, or the child of a
solicitor who becomes an engine driver. The former would be an example of
upward social mobility, the latter of *downward* social mobility. It is assumed
that occupational classes can be graded in a hierarchy of prestige, and that the
criterion of mobility is to shift across a class boundary. It should be noted that
people also obtain new jobs without crossing a class boundary, moving sideways,
so to speak.

Deciding what are *relevant* class boundaries is bound to be contentious. For
many people, upward mobility used to be associated with a move from blue-
collar to white-collar occupations. However, since many routine white-collar
jobs now pay less well and are less satisfying than skilled manual jobs, that
boundary may well be thought less meaningful. The most authoritative recent
study of mobility in Britain concentrates on movement into and out of the
service class (composed largely of professional and managerial occupations),
on the grounds that for most people upward mobility is achieved by entering
professional and managerial occupations. It is to the findings of this study, the
Nuffield Mobility Study, reported by Goldthorpe, Llewellyn and Payne,[1] that we
will [now] turn. To make sense of the findings of this study, however, it is
necessary to be familiar with the class categories being used.

The definitions of the seven occupational classes used by Goldthorpe et al. are
listed in figure 1. For many purposes, these seven classes are grouped into three
– the service class, the intermediate class and the working class. For Goldthorpe
et al., the 'service class' includes higher and lower professionals and middle
management...; the intermediate class comprises routine white-collar workers,
small proprietors and supervisory workers; the working class is defined as
manual workers without positions of authority.... Importantly, although Goldthorpe et al. study movement between all seven occupational classes, they
consider *only movement into and out of the service class* as socially meaningful
mobility.

Goldthorpe et al. discovered more intergenerational mass social mobility in
Britain since the Second World War than might have been expected. Previous
studies had suggested that classes in Britain were largely self-recruiting. Sons
would usually end up in the same class as their fathers. (Regrettably, almost
all mobility studies, including the Nuffield one, only analyse the movement of
men.) It was believed, on the basis of a survey in 1949, that there was a lot
of short-distance but little long-distance movement, that the elite was highly
self-recruiting and that the blue/white collar boundary was a major barrier.
Goldthorpe et al. paint a different picture.

Consider table 1. This is an 'outflow' table, showing the class *destination* of

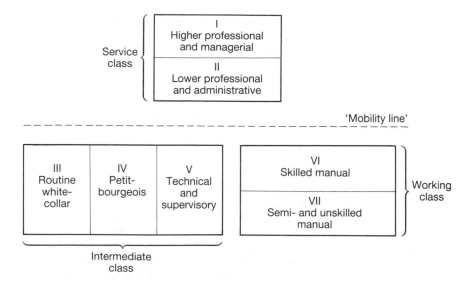

Figure 1   Model of the British class structure (Nuffield Mobility Study), showing 'occupational' class (with roman numerals). Contains the following types of occupation: I   higher-grade professionals; higher-grade administrators and officials; managers in large establishments; large proprietors; II   lower-grade professionals and higher-grade technicians; lower-grade administrators; managers in small establishments; supervisors of non-manual workers; III   routine non-manual workers (largely clerical) in administration and commerce; sales personnel; other rank-and-file employees in services; IV   small proprietors, including farmers and smallholders; self-employed artisans; other 'own account' workers (except professionals); V   lower-grade technicians; supervisors of manual workers; VI   skilled manual wage-workers; VII   all manual wage-workers in industry in semi- and unskilled grades; agricultural workers
Source: J. H. Goldthorpe, C. Llewellyn and C. Payne, *Social Mobility and Class Structure in Modern Britain* (Oxford: Oxford University Press, 1980), pp. 39–41.

sons, which indicates the extent to which opportunities are equal. If classes were perfectly self-recruiting, every son would be in the same class as his father and the diagonal boxes would all register 100. What we observe is, rather, much movement between classes. Consider, for example, the row of fathers in class VII – semi-skilled and unskilled manual workers and agricultural labourers: 6.5 per cent of sons of such fathers were in class I occupations (higher managerial and professional) in 1972; another 7.8 per cent were in the lower professional grade, class II. However, 34.9 per cent of such sons were, like their fathers, in class VII; and a further 23.5 per cent were in the other class of manual workers – class VI, skilled manuals. In effect, then, about six out of ten became blue-collar workers.

It is in some degree a matter of judgement whether you will be impressed by the number of sons who were upwardly mobile, or by the number who remained in class VII. But, whatever your judgement, the table does show different degrees of self-recruitment. Looking at the diagonal boxes you can see that only one in eight of sons of routine white-collar workers (class III) were to be found in that class in 1972. The sons of such workers were, in fact, fairly evenly

Table 1 Intergenerational occupational mobility of men aged 20–64 in England and Wales, 1972, outflow[a] (%, by row)

Father's class when son aged 14 years	Son's class[b] (1972)							Fathers in sample	
	I	II	III	IV	V	VI	VII	No.	%
I	45.2	18.9	11.5	7.7	4.8	5.4	6.5	688	7.3
II	29.1	23.1	11.9	7.0	9.6	106	8.7	554	5.9
III	18.4	15.7	12.8	7.8	12.8	15.6	16.9	694	7.3
IV	12.6	11.4	8.0	24.8	8.7	14.4	20.5	1,329	14.1
V	14.2	13.6	10.1	7.7	15.7	21.2	17.6	1,082	11.5
VI	7.8	8.8	8.3	6.6	12.3	30.4	25.9	2,594	27.5
VII	6.5	7.8	8.2	6.6	12.5	23.5	34.9	2,493	24.6

[a] i.e. class distribution of sons by the class of their father when son was aged 14 (a measure of equality of opportunity).
[b] For definitions of classes see figure 1.
Total number of respondents = 9,434.
Source: J. H. Goldthorpe, C. Llewellyn and C. Payne, *Social Mobility and Class Structure in Modern Britain* (Oxford: Oxford University Press, 1980), p. 48.

distributed across all occupational classes. By contrast, class I fathers were the most likely to pass on their 'class position' to their sons. Nearly one in two class I sons had class I jobs. It is this capacity for privilege to be transmitted intergenerationally that arouses suspicion about the social significance of the, undeniably large, absolute amounts of mobility. Clearly, the class into which a man was born did not *determine* his class destination; lots of men were upwardly mobile in the period 1928–72. But the chances of ending up in class I were weighted heavily in favour of those with fathers there already.

Issues relating to class formation are best illustrated by considering an 'inflow' table, table 2. Based on exactly the same data as the previous table, this shows the *composition of social classes* in 1972, in terms of the class origins of sons. Reading down the columns you can see who has arrived in which classes. Compare class I and class VII. Class I, which comprised about one worker in eight (13.6 per cent) in 1972, had drawn its members from all social classes. Although one in four members also had fathers in class I, the rest came more or less equally from the six other classes in Goldthorpe et al.'s classification. Class I in 1972 was, then, very heterogeneous (i.e. of very mixed origin); 28.3 per cent of class I were sons of manual workers. Class VII, by contrast, was largely composed of sons of manual workers (69.6 per cent). Only 2 per cent of class VII had fathers in class I. Skilled manual workers had similar origins. Thus Goldthorpe et al. propose that Britain now has a 'mature' working class, alike in its origins, and therefore capable of exhibiting considerable solidarity. If they are correct, and being in the same class for two or more generations does increase solidarity, then their study does suggest the existence of a solidaristic working class and considerable fragmentation among the other occupational classes.

Given the very considerable movement between classes, it might be imagined that Britain had become a fairer, more open, society, opportunity becoming less and less dependent on class origins. In an important sense, though, this is a

Table 2 Intergenerational occupational mobility of men aged 20–64 in England and Wales, 1972, inflow[a] (%, by column)

	Son's class[b] (1972)						
	I	*II*	*III*	*IV*	*V*	*VI*	*VII*
Father's class when son aged 14							
I	24.2	12.0	9.1	6.0	3.0	1.9	2.0
II	12.5	11.8	7.6	4.4	4.9	3.0	2.2
III	12.0	10.0	10.2	6.1	8.3	5.4	5.3
IV	13.0	13.9	12.2	36.5	10.6	9.6	12.3
V	12.0	13.5	12.5	9.4	15.6	11.4	8.6
VI	15.7	21.0	24.8	19.2	29.2	39.4	30.3
VII	12.6	17.8	23.6	18.5	28.5	29.4	39.3
Sons in sample							
No.	1,285	1,087	870	887	1,091	2,000	2,214
%	13.6	11.5	9.2	9.4	11.6	21.2	23.5

[a] i.e. class composition, by class of father when son was aged 14 (a measure of class formation).
[b] For definitions of classes see figure 1.
Total number of respondents = 9,434.
Source: Goldthorpe et al., *Social Mobility*, p. 44.

misleading impression. Much of the upward mobility into the service class is merely a consequence of changes in the occupational structure. The number of positions in the service class increased sharply in the period examined by Goldthorpe et al. Men occupied in service-class occupations rose from around 1.2 million in 1931 to 3.5 million in 1971. Compare the proportions of *fathers* in the service class (classes I and II) in Goldthorpe's et al. sample – 13.2 per cent (see table 1) – and the proportion of *sons* – 25.1 per cent (see table 2). What Goldthorpe et al. point out is that the service class increased in size to such an extent that, even if every son of a service-class father had obtained a service-class job, there would still have been more men with origins in other classes in the service class in 1972. This can be seen in table 3, which summarizes information on movement across the boundary of the service class. Boxes A and D are percentages of men intergenerationally stable; box B is the percentage downwardly mobile; box C is the percentage of men upwardly mobile. The upwardly mobile vastly outnumbered the downwardly mobile. Put another way, the service class of the previous generation did not breed fast enough to fill all the new service-class occupations made available in the long boom after the Second World War. A large amount of upward social mobility was inevitable.

   This fact led Goldthorpe et al. to try to separate out *absolute* mobility, of which we have seen there is a great deal, from *relative* mobility, which is a measure of whether class differentials have narrowed. In other words, if there had been no change in the occupational structure, would there still have been an expansion of opportunities for the lower classes? Answering such a question is fraught with difficulty, not least because the occupational structure is always

Table 3 Intergenerational social mobility into and out of the service class, men aged 20–64, in England and Wales, 1972 (%)

	Son's social class (1972)		
	Service (I–II)	Other (III–VII)	All
Father's social class when son aged 14			
Service (I–II)	7.7 A	5.4 B	13.1
Other (III–VII)	17.4 C	69.5 D	86.9
All	25.1	74.9	100.0

Total number of respondents = 9,434.
Source: From tables 1 and 2.

changing. However, it is an important question because it is unlikely that we will see, during the rest of the twentieth century, further 'upgrading' of the occupational structure which would allow the service class to continue to expand. It will, then, matter to what extent exclusive class privileges can be maintained from generation to generation. Goldthorpe et al. suggest that, relatively speaking, the capacity of service-class fathers to transmit privilege did *not* decline between 1928 and 1972. The simplest indication of this is the low rate of downward mobility from, especially, class I. Look at table 1 again: 64.1 per cent of class I sons ended up in the service class; only one in three moved down: and this may be an underestimate given the nature of *intra*generational mobility. It seems, then, that a use of material resources accumulated by fathers in lucrative careers and a capacity to secure high educational qualifications for their children has ensured that sons of the service class are heavily protected against downward mobility.

The importance of the mobility data for understanding class relationships is harder to interpret. Only the working class is intergenerationally stable, being composed predominantly of sons of manual workers, in a ratio of 30.9 per cent with fathers from classes VI–VII to 13.8 per cent with fathers from classes I–V (see table 4). Whether that 30 per cent, or three men in ten, does constitute a 'mature' working class in the political arena remains to be seen. Voting behaviour until 1979 bore this out to some extent. Heath shows that working-class men with working-class fathers and working-class fathers-in-law are more likely than any other category to vote Labour.[2] He, indeed, shows that men with working-class connections at any level of the class hierarchy were more likely to vote Labour than those without. This corresponds to information on the friendship and leisure patterns of the upwardly mobile. Such patterns provide strong evidence that men who are intergenerationally stable, whether in the service class or the working class, mostly have social contact with people of their own class. As might be expected, a man upwardly mobile is more likely to have working-class friends and associates than a man born into the service class. However, there seem to be few problems for the upwardly mobile in becoming assimilated into their new class position. (It used to be thought that such men

Table 4　Intergenerational social mobility into and out of the manual working class, men aged 20–64, in England and Wales, 1972 (%)

	Other (I–V)	Son's class (1972) *Working (VI–VII)*	*All*
Father's social class when son aged 14			
Other (I–II)	34.1	13.8	47.8
Working (VI–VII)	21.2	30.9	52.1
All	55.3	44.7	100.0

Total number of respondents = 9,434.
Source: From tables 1 and 2.

might be isolated or unwelcome, but such problems have probably been overcome through the sheer volume of the upwardly mobile.) The upwardly mobile have sociable relations across classes.

The third, intermediate, class seems to have relatively little identity, either over time or internally. With the exception of sons of men in class IV, the *petite bourgeoisie*, who because they inherit property are relatively likely to continue in the same line of business as their fathers (see table 2), the other intermediate classes spread out across the class structure almost at random. This is, in important part, due to the typical patterns of *intra*generational mobility in the period. Men tend to pass through jobs in the intermediate classes. Hardly any men spend their entire working life in occupational classes III–V. Stewart et al. showed that young men who were routine white-collar workers would, before they reached 35 years of age, either be promoted into managerial occupations or would leave to try other jobs, usually manual ones.[3] The other main group of male, routine white-collar workers were older men, over 50, who had been promoted from the shop floor, often because they were no longer physically capable of manual tasks. These are both instances of changes which can be understood in terms of *careers*. (It is important to bear in mind that many people's social and political behaviour may be oriented to their anticipated future rather than to their current situation.) People may be mobile during their lifetime, *intra*generationally.

Again, Goldthorpe et al. demonstrate a considerable amount of *intra*generational mobility among men. In their survey, they asked for a man's first full-time job and for the job he held after ten years of working life. A very considerable proportion (73 per cent) of those aged 35 and over in the service class in 1972 had had first jobs in other classes. Moreover, there was no evidence that this route into the service class was closing up. (It used to be thought that increased numbers of people getting qualifications in higher education would block channels of upward mobility within firms and organizations.) Another interesting feature of intragenerational mobility is that, while sons of service-class fathers often have first jobs in other social classes, after ten years of working life they have secured service-class posts. Only 27 per cent of service-class sons were direct entrants into service-class occupations, while a further 36 per cent had first jobs elsewhere.

There are two major limitations of existing survey-based studies of social mobility, and the Nuffield study in particular. First, the greatest exclusiveness of social groups is at the very top of the occupational hierarchy, the elite being more highly self-recruiting than any other. Second, the mobility experiences of women are ignored.

The Nuffield Mobility Study examined *mass* mobility. It would be false to imagine that the existence of considerable mobility into the service class meant that *all* top positions were equally accessible. While the son of a manual worker may become a solicitor, he is very unlikely indeed to become a High Court judge.... People at the very top of the hierarchy tend to have impeccable upper-class backgrounds. To take just a single example, of those bank directors listed in *Who's Who* in 1970/1, 45 per cent also had fathers listed in earlier editions of *Who's Who*. This is 300 times greater than chance. It does not leave much space for others to be upwardly mobile into top banking jobs! Of course, sample surveys like the Nuffield one could never pick up sufficient of these kind of people to allow effective analysis. These elites are too small for that. But, at the same time, they are exceptionally powerful, very important persons. No complete understanding of social mobility can afford to ignore this upper class.

The Nuffield study examined only men, as have other studies of mass mobility. It is very doubtful whether the same kind of study could be undertaken if it included women, because women's experience of social mobility is so different from men's. Men move from one occupational class to another fairly infrequently during their lifetime and are unaffected by marriage and divorce. Women's intragenerational experience is likely to be much more varied and hard to capture with orthodox sociological categories. Most women work full time as housewives for part of their life, but that work is not included in occupational classifications. Then, the jobs available to women are more restricted, there being few women in class I, while a great many shift in and out of white-collar and manual work. Women's economic position is much more precarious than that of men, and much less well paid. We have seen that two jobs with the same name may be of a different nature for women; young male clerks tend to be promoted to become managers, women clerks rarely are.

It is equally problematic to analyse women's intergenerational mobility. Should a daughter's occupation be compared with that of her mother, rather than her father, for instance? Should we take account of the occupation of a woman's husband when considering her work experiences, or not? Our present state of knowledge allows us to say very little about women and mobility. That implies, however, that we do not understand a major experience of one half of the British population.

20   John Scott

The Old Boy Network

The Establishment has been defined as 'a body of people, acting, consciously or subconsciously, together, holding no official posts through which they exercise their power but nevertheless exercising a great influence on national policy'.

That is to say that whatever formal power its members may or may not have, the Establishment has a considerable amount of informal power and influence. This influence is based upon its role as a means of opinion formation: it facilitates communication among those who are familiar with one another, share a common social background and meet in numerous formal and informal contexts. . . .

The Establishment is not simply a group of people; it is a group of people allied around certain social institutions. These institutions are the Conservative Party, the Church of England, the public schools and ancient universities, the legal profession and the Guards regiments; and the lifestyle of Establishment members has traditionally been expressed in the 'season' of social activities in London, the gentlemen's clubs and country-house life. The dominant status group can be termed 'an establishment' so as to bring out the 'assumption of the attributes of a state church by certain powerful institutions and people'. In its informal aspect the Establishment is the 'old boy network', the system of social contacts which stem from family and education. Such contacts 'are maintained largely in an informal manner by membership of the London clubs, by the social round of dinners and parties as well as, more formally, in business meetings and at official events'. The contacts which constitute this informal network of social relationships are important in the determination of the life-chances of those who go through the public school and Oxbridge system. Their contacts 'both facilitate their careers and enable them to have more influence in the posts where they eventually land'. . . .

The public schools and the ancient universities are crucial mechanisms for the integration and recruitment of both the Establishment and the wider business class. They maintain a high level of closure in access to positions of privilege, and they ensure the assimilation of those newcomers who have necessarily to be granted entry. Directly through their 'old boys', and indirectly through the influence which they exert on the older grammar schools, they bring about a social and cultural unity among those who possess superior life-chances. In the monopoly sector of the economy; in parliament, government, the military and paramilitary forces, and the civil service; in the Church and the legal profession; and in the various bodies and agencies which bridge the gap between the state and the economy are to be found people with a similar social and cultural background and a similar set of life-chances. Within and between these various occupational milieux, intragenerational and intergenerational mobility is frequent. It is with a description of these milieux and the connections between them that the rest of this section will be concerned.

For most of this century government has been dominated by the Conservative Party; and over that period the Conservative Party has been dominated by the products of the public schools. . . . [T]he proportion of public-school MPs on the Conservative benches dropped immediately after 1950 from 83 per cent to 70 per cent and fluctuated between 75 and 80 per cent after 1955. Within this figure the role of Eton has been particularly great, though the proportion has fallen from 26 per cent to 17 per cent. While the proportion of all boys attending public schools is extremely low, three-quarters of all Conservative MPs in the postwar period were public-school boys. Similarly, over 50 per cent of Conservative MPs attended Oxford or Cambridge colleges: and the proportion of Oxbridge MPs was actually higher in 1974 than in 1945. Almost a half of all Conservative MPs in the postwar period have followed the public school and Oxbridge route. The public-school MPs tend to have the safest seats and to form a core of long-serving Conservative MPs whose numbers are periodically enlarged by the arrival at Westminster of non-public-school, non-Oxbridge men when the party wins sufficient marginal seats to attain power. For this reason those from the public schools are likely to be the more established and influential MPs. Other things being equal, they are more likely to attain ministerial posts. At this level, and especially in the Cabinet, the products of Eton and Harrow have been particularly prominent.

In the period 1901–57 a total of 317 MPs moved on to the House of Lords. Allowing for inheritance of titles and for MPs who died in office, about one-fifth of MPs could expect to end their careers with a peerage. Of these 317 peers, 180 had been backbench MPs and 137 had been ministers. Given the small number of ministers – 89 ministers out of 635 MPs in 1980 – it is clear that the chance of attaining a peerage is greater for those who reach ministerial posts. The normal grade of peerage for a minister or backbencher is a barony, nowadays a life peerage, and backbenchers have also qualified for the lesser titles of baronet and knight. Those who have held senior posts as Leader of the House or Home Secretary, and those who have been Speaker, have traditionally been able to expect a viscountcy; and a Prime Minister has usually been able to claim an earldom. As well as a peerage being a reward at the end of a political career, it can be used in the time-honoured way for building up a bloc of support in the Lords – though the declining power of the Lords makes this less necessary than in the past. More usually a peerage can be a short cut to a parliamentary career, obviating the need for selection and election in a parliamentary constituency. . . .

[Outside government, t]he scions of the privileged classes have monopolized the military profession from the time that it became established as an integral part of the national state. The same is true of the Church and the law, which have provided profitable sources of income for the younger sons of the great families and have acted as essential adjuncts of the state's social control functions of legitimation and discipline. While the declining salience of religion in British life and the increasing bureaucratization of the Church have perhaps restricted the power and influence of the Church of England in modern Britain, it remains the established Church and, as such, retains an important role in state ceremonials. There were, in 1980, 144 Church of England bishops, of whom the twenty-six most senior sit in the House of Lords. The bishops, still appointed by the Prime Minister and the Patronage Secretary, stand at the head of a formal hierarchy in which many important managerial functions have been delegated to the numerous deans, provosts and archdeacons. The legal profession does not have this hierarchical structure, though the judicial bench remains the position of highest status in the profession and the members of the judiciary are themselves formed into a hierarchy of superior and subordinate courts. The number of top judges is similar to the number of Church of England bishops: in 1980 there were 136 people holding the most senior judicial appointments (see table 1). Those judges who are required to sit in the House of Lords to enable it to fill its role as a court of law have, since 1850, been accorded peerages for life. The House of Lords does, of course, include many other former lawyers and judges among its membership, just as it includes former churchmen who have received peerages in their own right.

Both the law and the Church show a high degree of self-recruitment, showing the existence of Church families and lawyer families. Those who fill the senior posts within the professions tend to be recruited from the business class, and especially from its dominant status group. In the years 1900–9 there were 43 per cent of judges whose fathers had been in the legal profession and 18 per cent whose fathers or uncles had been judges. By the period 1960–9 both of these figures had increased: 52 per cent of judges had lawyer fathers and 29 per cent

Table 1   The senior judiciary[a] (1980)

	Number
Law Lords	13
High Court	95
Scottish Court of Session	21
Northern Ireland Supreme Court	7
Total	136

[a] With the Law Lords are counted the Lord High Chancellor, the Master of the Rolls and the Lord Chief Justice of England. The Court of Appeal is counted with the High Court.
Source: Calculated from *Whitaker's Almanack*.

had fathers or uncles who were judges. In terms of their general patterns of recruitment the judiciary of the 1960s and 1970s had four-fifths of its members drawn from the public schools, with 39 per cent of judges in 1963 coming from Eton, Winchester, Harrow and Rugby alone. In the same year 18 per cent of judges were the sons or close relatives of peers. For the period 1947–70 it has been found that a consistent two-thirds of bishops were public-school products, though the proportion of Oxbridge bishops declined slightly from nine-tenths in 1920–39 to four-fifths in 1960–70. Bishops remain a university-based group, but the proportion of university men among the clergy as a whole has decreased. This has led to a greater educational separation of the episcopacy from the parochial clergy. At the same time the tendency for bishops to come from Church families has increased to a current level of over one-half.

Within the business world itself the same patterns of gentlemanly recruitment are to be observed. [It is clear] that business leaders tend to be drawn from the wealthiest levels of society and that the inheritance of wealth plays a crucial role in the perpetuation of business fortunes. Among the business leaders there is a high degree of self-recruitment, and the top positions tend to be monopolized by members of the Establishment. Erickson's widely cited study of intergenerational mobility among steel executives suggests that there may have been a move towards relatively greater openness.[1] Erickson's study shows that the proportion of steel executives whose fathers were major landowners declined towards the end of the nineteenth century and has since remained at a level of between 7 and 10 per cent. The main group of steel executives consisted of those whose fathers had come from a business background, though she shows that the proportion declined from 55 per cent in the period 1905–25 to 34 per cent in 1953. Although the proportion of steel executives drawn from the professions may have increased, the main increase was in those who came from clerical and skilled manual backgrounds. Erickson argues that the decline in the proportion coming from a background of business leadership is mainly due to the failure of sons to take up positions in family firms. During the interwar years, she argues, the heirs of these family businesses found more congenial career lines available to them and so began to abdicate from control in their own firms. Further light is thrown on this by two other discoveries from Erickson's research: the proportion of steel executives from public schools remained constant at about one-third, and the proportion of Oxbridge executives increased from 15 per cent in

Table 2 Social origins of business leaders (1906–1970)

	From propertied and wealthy background (%)					
	1906	*1920*	*1946*	*1952*	*1960*	*1970*
Top 50 industrials	62	61	53	48	50	39
Top 30 financials[a]	78	73	71	68	69	55

[a] In the original source the figure for financial companies in 1952 was incorrectly given as 48. This has been corrected above.

1905–25 to 21 per cent in 1935–47. These figures suggest that a gentlemanly education was important for the second- and third-generation steelmen who remained in the industry and for the financiers who dominated the boards of the steel companies in the interwar years. That is, the entrepreneurial capitalists and finance capitalists continued to follow the public-school and Oxbridge route, though Erickson gives no information on how important this route might be for those internal capitalists who enter business leadership from outside the ranks of the business class.

Erickson's findings are drawn from one particular industry and relate to those who are actively involved in management; they have less relevance to the question of the social background of other participants in business leadership. In particular, the finance capitalists whose interests spread across the monopoly sector as a whole are not covered by the research. Fortunately, a number of recent studies have concentrated their attention on precisely these groups. Whitley has shown that one-half of the directors of the largest industrial companies in 1970 were former public-school boys, with one-sixth coming from Eton alone. Among financial companies it was found that about one-half of the directors of clearing banks and large insurance companies in 1957 came from six major public schools, with one-third from Eton alone. Among clearing-bank directors of 1970 three-quarters were public school products: one in three from Eton and one in ten from Winchester. Between one-half and three-quarters of bank directors had graduated from Oxford or Cambridge. The most recent figures on the social origins of business leaders, presented in table 2, seem to show that the proportion of directors of top companies coming from a background of 'substantial property or wealth' has declined over the period 1906–70 for both industrial and financial companies. An important qualification to be made about these figures, however, is that those whose fathers were in the professions were classified as being of upper-middle-class origins. In view of the monopolization of the higher levels of the older professions by members of the business class, this is an important qualification.... While only 6 or 7 per cent of directors were from such a background in 1906, fully a quarter were in 1970. Indeed, the total of 'upper-class' and 'upper-middle-class' origins over the period shows virtually no decline at all. Clearly, any alteration in the openness of recruitment to positions of business leadership must be far less than the figures in table 2 suggest.

It has been argued that the business class has exercised a high degree of closure over recruitment to a number of privileged occupations, and that members of the establishment have been able to monopolize those positions of

Table 3 Occupational background of Conservative MPs (1945–1974)

Occupation	Numbers of MPs at each election[a]									
	1945	1950	1951	1955	1959	1964	1966	1970	1974a	1974b
Barrister	37	51	55	60	66	58	48	50	50	47
Solicitor	4	10	11	11	12	13	13	13	11	9
Civil service	3	2	2	1	1	0	0	0	1	1
Diplomatic service	8	11	12	14	14	17	14	12	11	8
Military	30	30	31	36	30	20	11	12	4	4
Director	67	100	109	113	122	85	74	94	83	81
Banking and finance	1	4	2	2	3	3	4	7	13	13
Commerce and insurance	7	8	10	14	17	13	9	13	11	9
Farmer, landowner	25	28	32	30	36	36	34	35	28	22
Other	31	53	56	62	64	56	46	94	85	83
Total	213	297	320	343	365	301	253	330	297	277

[a] The two entries for 1974 relate to the two elections of that year.

greatest privilege through the mechanisms of sponsored mobility. The business class, despite the diversity in occupations followed by its members, has been able to achieve a high degree of unity and cohesion because of the amount of circulation that takes place between positions of privilege. Mobility between the various class situations, both intergenerationally and intragenerationally, has been frequent enough to counteract any tendency towards the formation of distinct class fractions. Although there are to be found Church families, army families, political families and business families, there is sufficient circulation to prevent the formation of separate groups. While this is true for the business class as a whole, it is particularly true for the Establishment. Members of the Establishment have been able to perpetuate its position as a group with an extremely high degree of social solidarity. Table 3 shows the occupations of Conservative MPs prior to their election. The fact that many of these occupations are continued concurrently with membership of the House of Commons is a further source of solidarity between the various positions of privilege. It can be seen that the largest groups of Conservative MPs in 1945 were those from the law, the armed forces, business and the land. By 1974 the number of military MPs had fallen away considerably, even after allowing for the inflation of the figures in the immediate postwar period by those who were commissioned for war service. The law, business and industry all held their positions over the thirty-year period, indicating that the social composition of the Conservative Party has altered only very slightly. It is perhaps particularly significant that two-thirds of Conservative MPs in the 1970s held a business directorship at the time they sat in the House.

The solidarity and cohesion of the business class has depended on the extent to which it could maintain its social distinctiveness. Members of the business class have, however, increasingly tended to eschew the language of class division in formulating images of their own social positions. Instead, they have projected a view of themselves as part of an extensive 'middle class'. Such a claim is made realistic by the formal position of business executives and directors at the head of managerial hierarchies, and by the absence of any obvious distinctions between those professional employees who do and those who do not come from a background of wealth and privilege. Unequal life-chances are, in many respects, invisible; and this invisibility lends plausibility to the image of a continuous and hierarchical middle class. The business class, then, has a degree of social anonymity: it no longer sees itself and is no longer seen by others as constituting a distinct social class. Business class and service class appear to merge into a unified middle class. . . . Although it makes sense to speak of a partial normative convergence between business class and service class, there remains a crucial economic and relational differentiation between them – and the survival of the Establishment involves the survival of distinctive normative standards and a distinct lifestyle. Centred on the honours system and its gentlemanly values, this meaning system is a crucial aspect of social legitimation. The hierarchical character of the system of honours, leading from the peerage through the knightage to the 'officers' and 'members' of the Order of the British Empire, overlays the formal hierarchies of authority which permeate modern British society. In this way the norms of the Establishment are an important condition for the plausibility of the image of a hierarchical middle class. The social anonymity of the business class is, paradoxically, enhanced by the survival of the gentlemanly meaning system. The relational differentiation of the business class from the service class is apparent in the myriad contexts of informal interaction, in patterns of intermarriage, and in political and leisure activities. The lifestyle of the Establishment constitutes a paradigm of social behaviour for other members of the business class. Those who are outside the established social circles may follow the precepts of this paradigm because they aspire to the higher social status with which it is associated, or they may simply accept the activities it enjoins as being normal features of a civilized lifestyle. The tendency for members of the business class to live in half-timbered houses in areas commonly referred to as the 'stockbroker belt' or to live in carefully modernized cottages in 'rural' areas, their preference for private education and private health care, and their regular involvement in such sporting activities as golf, racing, shooting and hunting are all reflections of the salience of the Established lifestyle. . . .

[However, despite such differences in lifestyle, it] would be wrong to depict the business class as totally closed to outsiders. The evidence shows that this is not the case. While members of the business class are able to pass on their own privileges to their children, the growth in size of the occupational groups which they have traditionally monopolized has necessitated relatively high rates of recruitment from other sectors of society. As a result, many newcomers are to be found in the fringes of the business class, and together with others who reach high managerial and professional positions they may be able to secure access to the business class for their children. It is difficult to judge the full extent of such openness at the upper levels, since studies of those reaching the peaks of their careers in the 1960s and 1970s are concerned with people who were educated before the Second World War and whose fathers were educated before the First World War. The new entrants to the business class are still likely to have followed the public-school and Oxbridge route and so are likely to be endowed with the appropriate habits of class behaviour, but they are far less likely to owe their positions to the operation of the old boy network. Educational assets and technical expertise are increasingly prominent factors in executive recruitment and in recruitment to the professions. Any changes in rates of upward mobility into the business class may not yet be apparent in the available statistics. The relative decline of the Establishment and the possibility of increased openness mean that the traditional means of representing the interests of the business class within the political system are likely to prove increasingly inadequate.

21   Robert Waller

Social Class and Voting Patterns

Politicians, journalists, academics and pollsters constantly seek to identify a key group of voters who will decide the next election: first-time voters, mortgage holders, shareholders in newly privatized industries. Or they might try to identify key electoral battlegrounds, like the Midlands marginals (presumably because they are seen as holding the balance between a fictional Labour north and Conservative south). The most fashionable key voters now are the C2s – skilled manual and supervisory workers. They are supposed to have put Mrs Thatcher into power.

A theory of this sort is no mere daydream. It has considerable influence in setting the agenda according to which politicians speak and even, occasionally, act. It shapes the allocation of resources before and during election campaigns. Few voices now challenge the idea that the C2s are 'the all-important swing group that will decide the next election'. It's prevalent on television, in the newspapers, and in the inner counsels of the parties. But it is quite wrong.

This is not to say that the C2s are not important, or even necessarily that they aren't the single most influential social class. But they are not all-important. They were not solely, or mainly, responsible for Mrs Thatcher's electoral 'triumphs' . . . and they should not be the focus of political attention and advertising.

Let's look at a few figures. The ITN Harris exit poll at the last election gave the Tories a 7 per cent lead over Labour among the C2s. But has there really been a mass defection of these skilled workers to Labour since then? I have aggregated nine months of Harris *Observer* polls [in 1989] to create a sample . . . large enough to be broken down into social classes. Labour has had a 14.5 per cent lead during this period – a swing of around 13 per cent from Conservative to Labour since 1987. The strongest swing to Labour is indeed among the C2s, at 16.5 per cent. But the DEs – unskilled workers, unemployed people and state beneficiaries – have swung almost as much, by 14.5 per cent. And there are more DEs (30 per cent in the 1989–90 sample) than C2s (28 per cent). All in all, the 16.5 per cent swing within the C2 category represents just over 4.5 per cent of all voters. The 14.5 per cent swing among DEs represents just under 4.5 per cent.

To all intents and purposes, the DE group is equally responsible for the reversal of the Tory lead as the C2s, and indeed the C1s (white-collar workers) are not far behind, accounting for 2.5 per cent of the total 13 per cent swing. Only the ABs, the smallest social group and the most loyal to the Tories, give little cause for worry – here the Labour advance has come predominantly at the expense of the centre parties.

There is little convincing evidence, either, that the C2s played a dominant role in the 'Thatcherite triumphs' of the eighties. While the C2s played a leading part in securing Mrs Thatcher's election victories, they were not alone in responding favourably to her party's image and policies. The C2s swung slightly more to the Tories than other social groups in the eighties, and since 1987 they have swung very slightly more away; but there is no real evidence to suggest that they are a significantly more vital 'swing' group than, say, the DEs – especially bearing in mind that there are slightly more DEs (and certainly there were considerably more at the height of unemployment in the mid-eighties).

All this seems blindingly obvious to me. Who could seriously think that any group comprising less than 30 per cent of the electorate can be all-important? But the popularity and widespread acceptance of the C2 myth is explicable. Journalists like to find a new 'angle', a 'new' revelation, to enliven political debate. Advertising men and women live by targeting; in many branches of consumer marketing, the identification of a narrow group which can be persuaded to part with money can make a career; the doubling of a market from, say, 5 to 10 per cent is more than enough to win fame and fortune. Yet targeting is surely a different matter when the goal is to achieve 40–45 per cent of the vote – the likely minimum necessary to win a general election. C2s cannot do this on their own. Nor can the Midlands. Nor can share-owners.

Resources are limited and must be prioritized. Yet the search for 'the' key group or groups in the electorate is always doomed to fail, and it's about time that was recognized. Each and every vote still counts as one, although sometimes a mixture of illusion and hype may persuade us that that is not so.

22   Hakon Leiulfsrud and Alison Woodward

Women at Class Crossroads: Repudiating Conventional Theories of Family Class

There can be little doubt that within the conjugal family it is still overwhelmingly the husband who has the major commitment to labour market participation, and there are, furthermore, various indications that the pattern of employment of married women is itself conditioned by their husband's class position . . . 'cross-class' families may thus in turn be regarded far more as artefacts of an inappropriate mode of categorisation than as a quantitatively significant feature of present-day society.[1]

The contention that women's participation in the labour force has only marginal implications for the position of families in the class system resurfaced with some vigour recently. [It has been argued] that even when women hold jobs placing them in a different class from their mate, the importance of such cross-class combinations for class analysis is little. Generally, families should be classified as units in class analysis. Given the rising participation of women in the labour force in most highly developed capitalist countries, it was natural that this contention inspired considerable discussion, coming at a time when more than a decade of feminist study had nailed down the autonomous importance of women's work.

The main lines of the revitalized conventionalist approach can be quickly summarized. First, 'it is the family rather than the individual which forms the basic unit of social stratification'.[2] The head of the family (i.e. the partner with the major commitment to the labour market, who is usually male) determines the family's place in the class structure. Secondly, as the family is the unit of class analysis, the argument assumes that the family also *acts as a homogeneous* unit in the class structure. Finally, the analysis presupposes that women are less well anchored in the labour force, implying that 'the pattern of employment of married women is more likely to be class-conditioned than class-determining'.[3]

Contrary to Goldthorpe, as well as to Eriksson, who makes similar arguments using Swedish data,[4] we contend that female workers are *directly* influenced by the class structure in many matters, rather than receiving indirect messages mediated by their husband's position. Women's participation on the labour market has implications for all families, whether class-homogeneous or class-heterogeneous. Further, families with partners in different class positions, cross-class families, are not merely 'an artefact of an appropriate mode of categorisation', but a *significant element within the class structure*.

The existence of cross-class families presents problems, as the conventionalists themselves admit: 'A truly problematic situation would be created only if it could be shown that the extent and nature of female participation in the labour market is now such that . . . in many cases there are in effect two "heads" with, quite often, different class positions.'[5] Such combinations offer potential for embourgeoisement, proletarianization or ambivalence, all depending on the class composition of the family in question. It becomes difficult to talk about 'typical' working-class or middle-class families. While it may be true that life within the family sphere moderates experience from the world of work, this does not obviate our contention that the cross-class experience is significantly different. Attitudes and orientations toward work, gender roles as related to the division of labour in the home and values in child-rearing are affected by these class meetings. The confrontation of different social classes within the family decisively affects everyday life both at home and in areas such as political engagement and class awareness. [Various analyses] indicate that, politically, voting behaviour in the cross-class family is extremely unstable. Likewise, members in cross-class families appear to participate in labour organizations to a greater or lesser extent than their class and gender identities would lead one to expect from theories based on homogeneous families. Such issues are not pre-decided by traditional gender roles, as the conventionalist position might lead one to expect, but rather are to a high degree dependent upon the class composition of the family and which of the spouses is most interchangeable in the world of work.

This [discussion] contends that the conventional position as posed by Goldthorpe is difficult to defend. We illustrate everyday situations which present serious problems for conventional models. Here, we focus specifically on the division of labour at home and access to cultural capital within the familial sphere. Our arguments are based on recent Swedish data as well as an ongoing study of cross-class marriages. . . .

Is it the case that the family rather than the individual provides the basic unit of social stratification? Goldthorpe revives the convention of allowing the 'family head' to determine the placement of a family in a class categorization scheme. What are the consequences of this approach?

It immediately defines as irrelevant one partner's class experiences, rooted in the relations of production and brought into the family. Working-class female workers married to middle-class men are clumped together with non-working homemakers married to middle-class mates. Are these families' positions really comparable or equivalent? Experiences from the world of work may be modified or reformulated through the mirror of the family, but it is still the case that the relations extending from the productive sphere remain directly relevant for the individual, be he or she wage-earner or capitalist. Even within the family, we are not only family members, but also remain members of unions, political parties and other collectivities which may serve as bases for class action. Individuals act within the class structure from a variety of starting platforms. Thus in class analysis, as in all sociology, the unit of analysis should be chosen to illuminate the issue under study.

Using a unitary family in analysis further conceals the fact that 'the family' is not a given. This point is often shuffled over, even by the most conscientious authors. Families shift over time. Ignoring the class position of one or the other partner in classifying a two-partner family leads to obvious anomalies if the conjugal bond is broken. If a working-class woman is married to a middle-class man, then she is classified in a conventional analysis as belonging to the middle class. Does her class position suddenly change after the death of her husband? This problem leads authors such as Stanworth to argue for a strongly individual-based class analysis.[6] The revived conventional approach underestimates the potential of women in families as 'autonomous' actors in class struggle. An argument that women work less than men, whether measured in hours or during a lifetime, conceals the obvious fact that such basic issues as job content, working hours, and domination and subordination on the job affect *all* workers, as individuals.

Yet shifting completely to an individual analysis also presents problems. Most people are members of two-partner families at one time or another, even if that unit changes character over time. That unit is the meeting-place for men and women, filtering relations of gender and power. It can be a meeting-place for like and unlike class experience, with outcomes for questions of class formation rather different than the mere sum of two individual class positions might suggest. The family unit may either moderate or amplify experience gained in the relations of production.

Assuming that the family acts as a homogeneous unit in class analysis obscures the possibility of seeing that families can nurture both tensions and continuities in the same unit. Families with members in different class positions do not necessarily defend common class interests or values. Although literature is rich with samples of this sort of conflict, where Strindberg's *Miss Julie* and Shaw's *Pygmalion* immediately come to mind, sociologists seem to prefer a more 'homogeneous' world.

Previous critics of the neo-conventionalist position have generally focused on the problems of ignoring 'women's work' in class analysis. The next step is the recognition of the consequences of ignoring women's work. The 'family unit' approach is unable to deal with autonomous and contrasting class experiences within the same family. It is not only the case that women increasingly bring the experience of class into the family through their own wage-earning activity, but further, that the structure of the labour market for men and women makes it a virtual necessity that cross-class constellations appear. . . .

The most extreme cross-class constellation pits a working-class partner against one from a contradictory or employer-class location. The first explicit study of this phenomenon, the recent work by McRae, only focuses on the problems presented by the *non-traditional* cross-class relationship, where a working-class man, very broadly defined, is married to a non-working-class wife.[7] The *traditional* cross-class combination, which forms the majority of all cross-class pairings, mates a non-working-class male with a working-class wife. We maintain that *both* traditional and non-traditional partnerships foster contradictions simply swept under the rug by conventional analysis.

Such families present a potential for both embourgeoisement and proletarianization. Each polarity exerts a pull, but neither can be taken to its ultimate extension. Contradictions may thus appear in many spheres of family life. Below we focus on the traditional gender-based division of labour in the home, but cross-class couples also reveal new patterns of political engagement, child-rearing, socializing and so on.

Discussion is based on the experiences of thirty Stockholm cross-class families. Only one partner was working-class, using a very strict definition. In

Table 1   Swedish National Class Study, division of labour in two-partner
households by class: women's share of shopping, cleaning, dishwashing, laundry
and food preparation compared to spouse in households with varying class
composition

| | Housework done by wife % | | | | |
	0–25	26–50	51–75	75+	No.
Household class, composition (F–M)[a]					
Worker–worker	2	11	33	54	97
Non-worker–non-worker (employees)	1.5	12	45.5	43	67
Worker–non-worker (employees)	4	11	39	46	72
Non-worker–working-class	0	9.5	57	33.5	21
Total percentages	2.5	11	39.5	47	257

[a] Employer constellations are excluded given their small number in this sample,
22 spread over three constellations.

contrast to McRae, the working-class partner was almost as often male as
female. Fourteen males and sixteen females comprised the working-class side of
the partnerships. The other partner occupied one of the 'contradictory positions'. The sample was theoretically selected to illustrate patterns of interaction
between sex and class proceeding in both traditional and non-traditional directions. It does not depict the general distribution of cross-class families in the
population, but rather illuminates some key contradictions.

One such contradiction is based on the relationship between gender and class.
Cross-class couples have the potential either to reinforce established gender role
patterns or undermine them. This depends on the specific constellation of
gender and class. The most common class mix of working-class woman married
to a non-working-class spouse frequently follows more 'traditional' sex role
patterns. When the positions are reversed, we begin to see patterns of radical
change in gender role behaviour.

Many of the examples in this study illustrate that in today's two-parent
families female labour-market participation upsets the traditional division of
labour in the home. Results from the 1980 Swedish national study [see table 1]
support observations made in the qualitative study about the division of such
tasks as shopping, cleaning, washing clothes and cooking.

Non-working-class women married to workers are less often entrapped in
'traditional' division of household tasks. Thirty-three per cent of these women
did more than 75 per cent of these tasks. At the other extreme, working-class
women in homogeneous relationships show the most 'traditional' behaviour,
with 53.5 per cent doing more than 75 per cent of such household tasks.
Cross-class situations in Sweden seem to have much greater potential for up-
setting the 'traditional' scheme of things than is suggested in McRae's British
material.

Our material substantiates Engels' early perception that when women are
more intensively engaged in the world of work than their partners the delegation
of domestic labour is no longer self-evidently based on gender. Many examples
of changing gender roles in the family can be clarified by examining the partners'
situations at work.

The working hypothesis here is that, in questions concerning gender roles and
family patterns, position on the labour market highly influences behaviour at

Table 2 Stockholm Family Study, responsibility for staying home with sick children by individual class position (working class–non-working class)

Male job	Female job	Number of husbands who stay home various percentages of the time		
		50% or more	*49% or less*	*Hardly ever*
Worker	Non-worker	9	5	0
Non-worker	Worker	4	3	0

home. Our study indicates an erosion of dominant class and gender roles in certain family constellations. Decisions about who stays at home with a sick child and who deals with a difficult school administrator turn out not to be eternal givens, but rather to be related to the interaction of gender and class position within the family.

Despite changes in employment patterns, it is still the case that women have prime responsibility for childcare. They stay at home with sick children, even though husbands can also be economically compensated. However, in cross-class families it is often the partner with the working-class job who stays at home, regardless of sex. Table 2 illustrates that in most cases working-class men stay at home with sick children at least as often as their non-working-class wives.

In those cases where the working-class partner did not stay at home, there tended to be extenuating circumstances. Job content made it hard for some working-class respondents to take unexpected leave. For others, the wage system penalized the working-class partner more than the spouse. An important factor which helps explain some of the variation is the difference that private versus public sector employment makes. Many public-sector jobs can be seen as an extension of the social state.The rules for childcare leave are made by the state. To maintain legitimacy, at least with public-sector employees, it must honour its own rules. Thus, labour-market regulations are virtually always respected in this sector, regardless of job content. A department director may, theoretically, stay home with a sick child without fearing reprisal. Many highly placed male Swedish public officials have made public relations capital by demonstrating their private contribution to the battle for gender equality on the home front. Thus, of the non-working-class men who stayed at home half the time or more in table 2, all were in public-sector employment! Of male working-class partners who stayed at home less often than their wives, on the other hand, most were privately employed. A small employer explained that for his workers:

> It just isn't done, if you work in a little firm like mine, then it just isn't done, to take off . . . the guy wouldn't be welcome back . . . if you take a whole month, well, you might as well see that you are through for good . . . It's really hard, and probably hardest in the private sector, it's tougher there in a way.

His wife, a municipal office worker, cut in, 'I usually say it's a good thing I work for the state. If I didn't, we could never make our family life go 'round!'

Despite male peer pressure against staying at home for family reasons, the male working-class respondents in our sample took leave freely. In part, the willingness to take childcare leave despite gender prejudices can be explained by looking at the differences between the conditions of working- and non-working-class labour. Working-class respondents felt they were *interchangeable*, that their job could easily be done by someone else. A fireman who usually stayed with his sick children while his managerial wife tackled her duties synthesizes the interchangeability argument:

> Since we have such a large group, there is always someone who can cover for me if I am home. Besides, parent insurance covers staying with sick children, so for me there are no problems in staying home. If there should happen not to be enough staff, well, that's a problem for the fire chief and the politicians, not for me.

This problem can be contrasted with the ideology fostered in the private sector. Both men and women are encouraged to consider themselves unique and irreplaceable. This individualistic orientation is usually at the cost of a fair division of labour at home. A semi-autonomous male office worker related that while his working-class wife increasingly demanded he stay home when their daughter was ill,

> there is naturally a built-in conflict situation here. I have double loyalties, on the one hand in the type of job I have, I have an imposed loyalty. I am, after all, alone on my job, at least within my department. There is no one else that can just hop in on the spur of the moment. On her job, there is a totally different overlap.

Thus, for a non-working-class spouse to stay with a sick child was exceptional. Women with non-working-class jobs had a position to defend, both economically and socially. Therefore, their husbands stayed home. A printer, discussing this situation with his teacher wife, mused:

> I think I have been at home more than you have when they're sick. That's out of consideration for your pupils. One or two days with a substitute, and then it's hard. I have an easier time . . . since we have a bigger group that does the work. So if one of us is gone, well, it's not the whole world, you know. Naturally, somebody has to do my job too, but it doesn't have the same effect, really.

Although there are some social penalties for men who stay at home for child-care, the working-class men in our sample who took leave at childbirth did it confidently, as this transport worker married to a nursing supervisor reports:

> The guys at work thought it was bizarre (his taking leave when his second son was born) but I said they sure shouldn't worry about it more than the foreman did. I said to them that they couldn't do anything about it, because it was my legal right, and that's the way it went . . . and yeah, the first time, O.K. it was really fun . . . but it was a full-time job here, since there were two kids.

The males who broke traditional gender role patterns saw primarily advantages. As one painter pointed out, getting away from a job full of paint fumes and tedium, even to stay with a sick child, was very attractive. His teacher wife related: 'The few times the kids have been sick, Ralf has been glad to stay home; and I think it's good that I can go to work . . . I know that most women have a problem the opposite way, that *he* never wants to stay home, but here, it's just the opposite.' Her husband feels little pressure from his workmates. They also stay at home with sick offspring. However, 'there's more trouble from employers. They don't seem to understand that the wife also has a job, they just

Table 3 Stockholm Family Study, economic decisions in cross-class families: who pays the bills, and who wins most in economic arguments?

	Bills paid most often by whom?			Who wins most often in economic arguments?		
	M	F	Both	M	F	Both
Male worker–non-working-class wife (N = 14)	2	8	4	0	1	13
Male non-worker–working-class wife (N = 16)	9	3	4	6	0	10

think she should stay home. But then *her* employer goes crazy...'. Ralf tends to ignore the pressure from his employer, while his non-working-class wife is full of consideration for the problems of capital, saying, 'I think we should divide up who stays home a little. It feels embarrassing otherwise. I love to go to work, but I think we ought to divide up (the obligation when children are sick) a little more for the sake of his firm, so that's what we usually do.' Yet this woman, and others in non-working-class jobs, often had work obligations which were less easily fulfilled by a substitute, and thus, when possible, availed themselves of their husband's comparative 'freedom'. These women were pursuing what can be termed a 'professionally adapted' family life, while the working-class men and the majority of working-class women can be said to represent a 'family adapted mode of working life'. The tightrope between home and work can be strung at many angles.

Despite dramatic changes in labour market participation for women, many established gender role patterns do tend to persist. For example, men still handle major financial planning for the family. Again, however, this division of labour may reflect family class composition rather than revealing a gender given. We found a number of examples among our cross-class families where non-working-class women broke established patterns of financial decision-making [see table 3]. In several cases, women owned the family dwelling, paid the family taxes or controlled long-range economic planning. Some of these women reported that in economic conflicts they dominated and won. In such feuds they held the better cards, not necessarily on the basis of their higher income but because of their class-related competence in analysis and negotiation.

Some suggest that the amount of money brought in by respective partners influences who decides about financial matters in the family. For instance, Stamp in her pilot study of primarily middle-class professional couples with unemployed male partners saw a shift in financial power to the bread-winning woman in the family.[8] On closer examination, however, the issue of control over household finances is more complicated. While Pahl also suggests that money confers power, and fails to take full account of the class dimension, she helpfully contributes a model for breaking down financial tasks in the home, noting that:

> It is important to make a distinction between control, management and budgeting ... Control is mainly exercised at the point where money enters the household ... While management is partly concerned with the way in which money is allocated between expenditure categories, budgeting is primarily concerned with spending within expenditure categories.[9]

Many studies show that working-class women budget and sometimes also manage, but they also often demonstrate that ultimate *control* rests with the male. We suggest that, irrespective of income contributions and sex, the issue of control will tend to fall with the non-working-class partner.

A factory repairman described himself in our interview as taking each day as it came. He pointed with pride as well as bemusement at his wife's middle-class penchant for planning everything from purchases to vacations long in advance. Likewise Erik, a train mechanic, allowed that money was the centre of many family arguments, but that in the end it was probably for the best that his nursery school director wife controlled the purse strings:

> I always want to have five or six irons in the fire. It's usually me who comes home with ideas for new purchases, like a new tape deck . . . there we are very different. Maria, she's very restrictive when it comes to finances. I'm much more for daring and redistributing. I say 'let's take that money which we were going to use next month and fill in the hole when next month rolls around.'

When it comes to family economy, it was often the case that the non-working-class partner brought a resource to the family which helped effectively manage the outside world. . . .

This discussion of Swedish evidence may suggest that it is a little early to close discussion on the question of the unit of analysis in class research. While the effects of women's work on class issues may be difficult to discern in the homogeneous family unit, the heterogeneous partnership draws the confrontation into the light. The conventionalists, who have used data from the early seventies to decide that women's economic participation is transitory, appear ill-advised. Things are changing, even in Great Britain.

We allow that Sweden appears a polar case, but suggest that statistics in many Western economies show similar tendencies. What has happened in Sweden is that family and labour legislation have closely followed political demands for gender equality. Thus Swedish women entered the labour force at a faster rate than British women after the war and, when working part-time, work longer weeks than in Great Britain. Importantly, the situation even for part-time working women is much more favourable in Sweden than in Britain. Almost all working women are covered by social insurance for sick leave and by relevant employment security legislation.

The expansion of the welfare state has worked in two ways to institutionalize and secure women's workforce participation. First, the greatest proportion of new jobs for women has occurred in the public sector, where 61 per cent of the women in a 1980 nationwide survey were employed. Second, the welfare state provides a new situation for families with children. Paid leave at childbirth for both parents, compensation for staying at home with sick children and expanding municipal day care ease some everyday problems. Thus, the largest portion of increased participation in the labour force among women came from mothers of children under school age. In 1970, 48.5 per cent of all such mothers were employed, while in 1985 the figure was 81.5 per cent. Only 48 per cent of British mothers of children under ten were employed in 1980.

Further anchoring Swedish women in the workforce are a number of structural changes, which are sometimes held in common with other countries in the West. Taxation systems, job security legislation and rising costs for families in general all favour a trend towards two-income families. Concretely, it is virtually impossible for a couple with children to remain above the poverty line on only one income.

Although women in the 1940s and 1950s may have left work out of consideration for their families, today, the opposite is the case. Women enter the labour market for the sake of their families. They may have a shorter work career than men, due to late entrance, but once in interruptions are few and short.

The change has been rapid and dramatic, but there are few signs that the clock will turn backwards to that brief period in the past when stratification theorists could calmly build models leaving women out. Social policy and public opinion support full employment for all; twenty-five of our thirty female respondents could not imagine staying home full-time for any longer period, even if able to afford it. In Scandinavia, this working-class woman's opinion is typical:

> It's good for your self-conception to get out. I think that every adult person should support themselves to the degree they can, if you don't have 5 or 6 kids, because then you have to be at home. As it is today, I would want to work, to have self-confidence, to have a life of one's own, and to meet other people. I think I am a better mother if I work than if I stay at home the whole day.

The conventionalists invite critics to show that 'it is increasingly hard to say whether the husband or wife could be better regarded as the household head' and that in the rare cases where there are two 'heads', they would often occupy different class positions. We meet this challenge by demonstrating both that this situation exists in an ever-increasing proportion of families, and further that this has important consequences for any consideration of class in the family.

The sexual segmentation of the labour market, coupled with increasing female labour-market participation, makes the appearance of cross-class families a virtual inevitability. We argue that when partners have diametrically opposed class experiences this has significant effects on life within the family and the relations of the family to the outside world. In such families, there are different divisions of labour and attitudes about children, politics and the world from those found in class-homogeneous families.

Ignoring a pattern which appears in a significant proportion of families when discussing social class inevitably distorts our picture of reality and ability to make accurate predictions. Life would be simpler if one could classify all families as units based on the major breadwinner's class position, but the most elegant solution is not necessarily the correct one. Neither men nor women in class-mixed marriages behave exactly as their counterparts in homogeneous partnerships. Using the 'conventional' approach to analyse the family in class society forces us to ignore the important consequences these new class constellations show. Searching for a better approach is worth the effort!

Part 6

Politics and the State

Modern societies are nation states – that is to say, they have clearly marked territorial boundaries and a centralized governmental apparatus, and are associated with the fostering of national sentiments. The various readings in this part all deal with distinctive features of modern nation states.

Jean Blondel (reading 23) investigates the nature of political parties. Parties did not exist in traditional states, which were ruled by monarchs, emperors, kings and the members of aristocratic groups. In virtually all modern states, however, political parties of some kind exist, although some states are 'one-party' states. Parties, Blondel suggests, represent conflict groups, including class groups, and their specific character is influenced by how far they need to seek mass electoral support.

We often think of a further distinctive feature of the modern nation state – the importance of ideals of democratic participation – as intrinsically linked to existence of political parties, which allow individuals to represent their interests in the political arena. As the discussions by Gøsta Esping-Andersen and David Held (readings 24 and 25) make clear, conceptions of democracy range more widely than this.

'Social democracy' is one main form a democratic order can assume. The term refers to a political order in which working-class groupings or their representative organizations have a major role in determining political processes. Social democracy only becomes a dominant political form, Esping-Andersen argues, when it comes to approximate to democracy in the wide sense: that is, when 'class politics' is subordinated to the overall interests of the political community as a whole. David Held's analysis extends this observation into a generalized interpretation of the conditions of democratic participation. Ideals of democracy, he asserts, are connected to the 'principle of autonomy': the establishing of circumstances in which human beings can most effectively develop their capabilities and are able both to understand their best interests and act upon them.

Until quite recently, in common with the other societies of Eastern Europe, the Soviet Union was a one-party state. The Communist Party dominated most aspects of both political and economic life in the country.

The initiation of *perestroika* (reform) in the USSR was initially directed towards reconstructing the economic system, but seems likely to eventuate also in the emergence of a multi-party political order. In reading 26, David Lane discusses the emergence of social, economic and political reform in the Soviet Union, analysing its origins and its possible outcomes. As I write in 1991, the Soviet Union has effectively ceased to exist. In its place, there stands a loosely grouped confederation of states. Wherever the changes now under way lead, it is clear that nationalist impulses will play a major part in determining the sequence of events.

In the final contribution to this part, Ernest Gellner (reading 27) addresses the issue of the nature of nationalism and its relation to the modern state. Nationalism, he proposes, is essentially a theory of political legitimacy, by means of which ethnic boundaries are made subordinate to the overall political integration of the state. Sentiments of nationalism, and the boundaries of nation states, he stresses, do not necessarily coincide; hence the impact of nationalist beliefs can foster the disintegration as well as the cohesion of states.

23   Jean Blondel

What are Political Parties for?

Parties are groups – but how does one distinguish them from other groups which seem close to parties? A national liberation movement in a colonial territory may not be called a party, but is it very different from a political party? What about organizations like the Campaign for Nuclear Disarmament in Britain in the 1950s or anti-war movements in the United States in the 1960s? There is a distinction between pressure groups, such as trade unions or employers' organizations, and political parties. There are other intermediate groups whose aims are openly political, and the boundary between parties and such groups is not very precise.

To approach these questions realistically, it is better to eschew a theoretical definition or description of goals and concentrate more practically on the existence of parties. Political parties emerge under different conditions and with different viewpoints. Behind the facade lie conflicting desires, which may explain some of the difficulties faced by political parties.

Parties exist in some countries and not in others. Given certain conditions parties are more likely to exist; these conditions are of three types.

[First, p]arties are more likely to exist where many members of the society *perceive* the existence of social conflict and perceive these conflicts to be large and long-standing. There is no need for parties if everyone agrees about everything. This is why, typically, parties do not emerge in traditional societies. The elders of tribes are expected to take the decisions which need to be taken. Social conduct and order are their province by right. There are few new problems; past experience is the best guide. Within tribes, at least, social conflicts are either few or non-existent.

For parties to develop there must be broad social conflict. Parties organize large sections of society for major battles; if conflicts involve only a few individuals, parties will not be formed. For parties to emerge conflicts must run deeply into the fabric of society and sharply divide its members. Parties might emerge, for example, if there are conflicts *between* tribes or *between* ethnic groups within the same country, as in Nigeria, Ghana and many other African countries. Deep conflicts between religious groups or between social classes may produce the same effect. When this occurs, members of the society are not simply confronted with isolated clashes over one issue; on the contrary, individual conflicts can become absorbed into one major social conflict. In Northern Ireland, for instance, conflicts over housing and job discrimination are sucked into a broad religious conflict. Similarly, in many Western democracies, numerous conflicts become branded as part of a class conflict between workers and the 'bourgeoisie'.

Perception of the conflict is more important than actual conditions; antagonisms become acute only when they are perceived as such by members of the society. This is true of all major types of social conflict. In two countries where income and status as between rich and poor are objectively similar, perception of class conflict may be very different. It may be very weak in one of them, very strong in the other. Broadly speaking, despite large income differences on both sides of the Atlantic, perception of class conflict is much greater in Europe than it is in North America. Thus it is hardly surprising that parties in Europe are based on class conflict while this is not so marked in the United States and

Canada. Indeed, there are gradations in the perception of social conflict as there are gradations in objective differences. Only in traditional societies is conflict hardly perceived at all; in modern societies, variations in the intensity of social conflict can be very wide. There is some perception of class conflict in the United States, where to some extent parties are based on class. Conversely, in Europe class conflict is dominant, but not overwhelming; parties are not exclusively based on class, they may also be based on religion. But religious conflicts also vary in intensity: the religious composition of Glasgow and Belfast is almost the same, for example, yet religious conflict is strikingly higher in Belfast than it is in Glasgow.

Since social conflict is based on the perception of this conflict, it can be engineered. The development of class consciousness is an endeavour to engineer social conflict where it has not been perceived. Marxists often say that class consciousness must be increased. They mean that efforts have to be made to increase the perception of objective conflicts, because the basis for a class party will be more assured when class conflict is perceived to be high. But Marxists are not the only ones wishing to increase the perception of conflict. The Nazis encouraged conflict with the Jews. In many countries, especially third world countries, conflict with 'foreign elements' is deliberately fostered. More generally, single-party systems are often set up with a view to increasing some conflict: social conflict may thus be perceived intensely even when there is one party only. . .

Parties are unlikely to emerge if there is little or no perceived conflict. But, even if conflict is relatively high, parties will only arise if politicians need popular support and if traditional social hierarchies are weak. In a traditional society, the absence of social conflict accounts in part for the absence of parties; but, even if there are conflicts, for instance *between* tribes, the existence of a well-defined tribal structure which is accepted by members of the various tribes makes a party organization superfluous. Those in government can rely on these hierarchies to implement their decisions. Feuds only occur between the leaders of tribes, or between aristocrats. In an absolute monarchy, politics is therefore limited to the factions of courtiers, and so long as no political leader wishes to appeal to the people, parties will not be created.

A party is thus more than a faction or a conspiracy, although it may originate from one. It results from the desire or the need to obtain or strengthen support among the population. It entails trying to attract, if not the 'common man', at least many helpers and followers. A party is to a faction or conspiracy what the army is to a band.

All parties face problems of organization and leadership which differ from, and are more complex than, those of a faction. Members of a faction know each other, face-to-face. Decisions are taken among friends although some members of the group may be more influential than others. In a party, there are followers as well as leaders; followers may merely execute leaders' decisions. Only some members are directly involved in party activities; others, the majority, are less active. Leaders do not know more than a small fraction of these followers and communication between leaders and followers becomes difficult and complex. Questions of organization therefore cannot be avoided in a political party. Indeed, they tend often to be one of the major aspects of the life of political parties.

The extent to which a party needs popular support varies: the complexity of party organization varies accordingly. Some parties have little popular support; in some, the leader commands – or wants to command – the allegiance of millions. What begins as a faction – for instance, near or around the palace

– may slowly become a party with outside support. A party is created when supporters of a faction acquire followers. Parties emerged in this way in Britain in the seventeenth and eighteenth centuries; they developed, in a similar way, in Western Europe in the eighteenth and nineteenth centuries.

Traditional societies do not need parties, as we saw, because existing tribal or feudal links are sufficient for day-to-day government. A party is only formed when some individuals want to change the social structure, achieve more power for themselves or the group to which they belong, or develop the country economically or socially. The response to these efforts may be slow, however; people may not understand or agree with party goals. The party may not take roots in the community. This happened in Europe in the past and currently happens in the third world. Parties may be set up to achieve popular involvement, but traditional bonds – tribal, for instance – may scarcely be touched. The new parties are artificial, and easily disbanded or abolished by a *coup d'etat*.

We need to account for the link between the formation of a party and expectation of political victory. Why do many believe that, by setting up a party, they are more likely to achieve their political goals? The reason lies in the fact that it is usually *assumed* or *believed*, not just by political leaders but by most of us, that 'unity is strength'. We feel that good results will be achieved if we unite with like-minded people.

This belief is general. Many organizations exist because men believe it is worthwhile to unite with others. Yet it is worth remembering that this is only an assumption for which little real 'proof' can be given. Indeed, there is evidence for and against the assumption. For example, members of trade unions believe that workers should be 'organized' because they will obtain better living conditions as a result. The causal link is not proved. It is true that workers have obtained better living conditions in the last hundred years *at the same time* as trade unions developed; but there is no appreciable difference between the workers' standards of living in those industrial countries where they are well organized and those where they are not. From the examination of policies and achievements it is even more difficult to prove that the conditions of the poor are better in those countries where they are politically united than in those where they are not.

Most of us believe that 'size is strength'. Most men and women who are concerned with social and political action feel that, in order to win, they must enlist the support of large numbers. This belief is rarely questioned. We are told that support attracts more support and brings victory nearer. Parties often use their current support as bait for prospective followers. We are thus told, for instance, that we will find hundreds or thousands of friends and comrades if we join a party.

Although the belief in the necessity of large numbers is very common, it is not universal. Indeed, all of us are probably inconsistent in this respect. For instance, some men profess to believe in the value of 'active minorities' rather than in large groups. Many small groups – factions, conspiracies – have attempted to take power and some have succeeded. The supporters of this view place greater stress on the dynamism and dedication of a few than on the role of large numbers. They point to the limited achievements of trade unions and established political parties and state that 'real' revolutions are only made by a few men.

Moreover, even if we believe that 'size is strength', we are also often prepared to be somewhat inconsistent and not to consider ourselves defeated when we fail to muster large numbers of supporters. In the West the principle of majority rule is applauded and institutionalized. But, even in the West, this principle is often thwarted, one way or another, by the action of minorities. Outside the West, the principle of majority rule plays a less significant part; it is often not legally entrenched. Everywhere in the world minorities are very powerful, in political parties and in other associations, and use dubious tactics to undermine majority groups. It seems as if, the more one feels unable to muster a majority, the more one uses conspiratorial tactics to achieve one's aims. Thus, we are coming close to recognizing that only those who can rally support of large segments of the population really adhere to the principle that 'size is strength'; the minority live by different principles.

Indeed, political parties exist precisely because of this inconsistency. The need for both large support and smaller groups is at the origin of political parties. Parties exist only where there is conflict; but conflict means disunity. Parties thrive both on the disunity of the society and on a popular desire to rally to a common cause. . . .

At first sight, the function of parties seems straightforward: they exist to propose and implement policies. But what policies? The British Labour Party may exist to improve the conditions of the common man in Britain, but what are the conditions which need improvement? And who exactly is the common man or the 'working man'? And what does 'improvement' mean?

These are questions which we usually brush aside because no one really knows the answers. If we talk about improvement, we must have some goal, some ideal, some general principles. This may be equality for all, or a hierarchy of classes and groups, or a combination of various goals. But one thing is certain: an understanding of human nature must precede any improvements. It is no good saying that some situations are scandalous and obviously need redress. First, if they are so obvious, why were they not redressed before? Is it only because our forefathers were wicked or stupid? And second, do we know really what our goals are? Can we say that any party really knows what its goals are?

But this is not all. Policies are based on a principle – be it conservative, socialist or liberal. It is difficult to see the link between these principles and specific policies. If a party states that pensions should be increased because older citizens should not be allowed to live in poverty, we see a relationship between principles and policies. But the link is imprecise because we do not know *by what amount* pensions should be increased. It is also imprecise because we do not know whether pensions, rather than sickness benefits for instance, should be increased. A party may propose social improvement as a general principle, but this proposal does not help in deciding on pension increases or choosing between pensions and sickness benefits.

There is another question: should party supporters decide on policies or should policies be 'sold' to supporters? Which do we think should come first, the policies or the supporters? In practice, most parties follow both strategies at one and the same time; they are influenced by supporters and adopt some policies as a result, while they also adopt policies and 'sell' them afterwards. This messy practical approach does not answer the question: who should decide policy?

These three problems – general principles, links between principles and policies, the relationship between policies and support – are not easily solved. They are rarely solved except in a pragmatic, muddled way. As parties need support, they 'bend' their principles, they 'bend' even more their policies and postpone their goals. Popular support is seen as indispensable and the first priority; policies based on principle recede into the background.

Parties are often tempted to go further and see organization as an end in itself. Lukewarm or passive followers must be encouraged to be more active. Party organization becomes separated from principles and policies: 'If only our branches and sections would increase, if only our members could be more active at branch meetings, we would be closer to victory.' In almost all parties, party organization is as important as the search for policies and the analysis of ideology.

In a subtle fashion, all parties are thus infected by the curse of oversimplification. For the most dedicated party activists, the 'goodness' of the party cause seems obvious. If the party's goals are obviously good, popular support should automatically be forthcoming. If it is not forthcoming, this can only be because people cannot see what the party wants to do. Why should anyone not see the bright sunshine? Because the curtains are drawn. Thus lack of support is not seen as a lack of policies or goals, but as a lack of good public relations. Party activists rarely ask themselves why people do not automatically support the party. They have to avoid the issue; they can answer only in terms of 'enemies' or of lack of understanding, lack of awareness, lack of 'consciousness'.

Oversimplification creeps in, and it does so in two ways. It creeps in because party activists always have a ready-made answer to the problem of lack of support: people are not aware, opponents beguile the masses; if only people could see, if only we could lift the curtain, there would be no problem. And oversimplification also affects the party programme. The message must be simple; by saying that 'if only such and such were done, a solution would be found', party workers hope to find more support. Parties tend to oversimplify every problem, idea or difficulty. They oversimplify ideologies because they believe that people will understand matters better this way, and they oversimplify solutions by not showing problems of priorities, or constraints. To win the contest, parties always underestimate the case of their opponents and overestimate their own programme.

This, in turn, has two consequences. First, it reinforces the importance of organization. Ideas, principles, programmes and policies are less important than the need to put the idea across. Principles become subservient to the need to communicate them; they are gradually simplified into simpler messages. And, second, party activists and leaders become infected by the message which they try to put across. They, too, come to believe that matters are simple, that principles are clearly defined, that priorities are self-evident and that time is unimportant.

24   Gøsta Esping-Andersen

Social Democracy in Theory and Practice

Social democracy is, and has always been, the most successful expression of working-class politics in capitalist democracies. In northern Europe it has enjoyed virtually a monopoly over workers' votes, and it has been dominant almost everywhere else. Where, as in Italy or France, communism has held sway, the trend is nevertheless towards a 'social democratization' of working-class politics. Thus it is puzzling that we have no adequate theory of such a historically powerful force.

Although social democracy may be a pervasive political force, its fate has come to diverge quite sharply from nation to nation. Where once it was unshakable, it is apparently losing ground; where once it was peripheral, it is coming to the fore. It is particularly fascinating to observe that three such historically similar social democracies as the Scandinavian countries are now moving in different directions. Yet, we have no adequate theory to explain the conditions under which social democracy will succeed or fail. . . .

Few writers pause to ask what social democracy is. Party labels alone hardly clarify matters. There exist some self-declared social democratic parties, the Italian version, for example, that few would consider genuine. . . . Some even believe that America's Democratic Party is social democratic in nature. Nor is membership in the Socialist International a satisfactory criterion, even if admission is reserved for those parties formally dedicated to parliamentarism and in some way programmatically committed to socialism. . . .

[One] method of defining inclusion is to compare party organization. One of the most important historical distinctions between communist and social democratic parties has to do with their principles of party membership, internal authority and relations between central executive officers and the rank and file. Duverger counterposes the social democratic party to the loose electoral aggregation typical of the bourgeois party, on one hand, and the centralist and disciplined apparatus of the communist party, on the other.[1] Where the one rarely builds a strong organization with strict membership criteria, the other is typified by exclusiveness of membership, by a 'ghetto character' that fosters the creation of an entire world separate from society at large, and by democratic centralism, recurrent purges and calls for discipline. But, to Duverger's credit, he refuses to make a categorical distinction between communist and social democratic parties; rather, they are viewed as being on a continuum shared by all modern mass parties.

Many social democratic parties were originally 'ghetto' parties. Until the First World War, all three Scandinavian social democratic parties followed the model of the later communist parties, building a separate socialist world by means of athletic associations, boy scout movements, educational institutions, organized leisure activities and so forth. In respect of centralized authority and strict control over party militants and local cells, a hard-and-fast distinction between communist and social democratic parties is difficult to make. As Michels has shown, the social democratic party was hardly an open and democratic organization.[2] There is little doubt, too, that the traditional vanguard party model is decaying. Duverger notes that even the comparatively rigid French Communist party (PCF) could not maintain control of its local cells. By the 1970s, the PCF [was] only residually a 'democratic centralist' vanguard party.

The relationship between party and trade union has had tremendous historical significance. Before the First World War, socialist parties usually viewed the trade union movement as a political instrument and hence refused to grant union autonomy. Frequently the parties insisted on collective trade union membership in the party and loyal subordination to party strategy. While the political subjugation of trade unionism was retained in most Third International communist movements, it was abandoned by most social democratic parties. According to Sturmthal, trade union autonomy was crucial in moving social democratic leaders to put aside ideological orthodoxy in order to face the crisis of world depression and further the survival of democracy and the labour movement itself.[3] The emancipation of trade unionism occurred under very different conditions from country to country. In Britain, it was the Trades Union Congress (TUC) that provided the main impetus for the Labour Party's formation in 1906. In Sweden and Denmark, the unions were originally under social democratic party control, but divorce came soon after the turn of the century. Even if the Mannheim Resolution of 1906 granted the German unions independent status, the process had not quite been completed before the Nazi seizure of power – at least not to the degree that the ADGB could influence party policy. . . .

Organizational characteristics, then, are certainly necessary in any definition of social democracy, but they are not sufficient. They tell us very little about the relation of the party to social structure, to the state or to historical change. Przworski has provided a definition of social democracy that has the great advantage of being grounded in the parties' strategic choices rather [than] in their professions of ideology.[4] The question is how working-class parties historically have resolved three crucial issues: whether to participate in the political institutions of capitalist society; whether to seek support outside the working classes; and whether to pursue reformist or revolutionary policy. I agree with Przworski on the first two dimensions, but disagree on the third.

According to Przworski's definition, social democracy differs from communism in that the former adheres to, rather than opposes, parliamentary democracy. Social democrats, contrary to their Marxist forebears or their Leninist opponents, insist that it is both possible and imperative to struggle for socialism within parliamentary institutions. The decision to commit the proletarian cause to parliamentary procedure did not everywhere evolve with ease. In Britain and Denmark there was hardly ever any contemplation of anti-parliamentary strategies. In Germany, the social democrats eventually became the main bastion in defence of 'bourgeois democracy', but the party was never quite united on the question. At one extreme were the Lassalleans. For decades, however, the party vacillated between a variety of positions, ranging from acceptance (or cautious distrust) to the almost purely strategic-instrumental view that democracy might be exploited for socialist mobilization. In Norway, the social democrats joined the Comintern during the early 1920s, but even after their departure, the leadership generally opposed the parliamentary strategy.

An important source of ambivalence was concern that the bourgeoisie would not abide by parliamentary rules if the social democrats should finally muster the strength to vote socialism into existence. This was certainly true in the case of the Swedes – at least until the parliamentary crisis of 1918 had been fully resolved – as well as among the Austrians and Germans. If complete and unconditional surrender to the rules of electoral competition and parliamentary majoritarianism is one hallmark of social democracy, the opportunity to surrender varied dramatically before the Second World War. In Scandinavia, where socialists allied with peasants and farmers in the struggle for political democracy, trust in parliamentarism came relatively easily. Bourgeois resistance there was generally modest, and even under limited suffrage the socialists had managed to gain representation and affect policy at both the local and the national level.

The second definitional element concerns the party's strategy for class mobilization. Until 1918, socialist parties typically adhered to the view that the socialist transformation was a strictly proletarian affair. Social democratic parties, until 1918, saw themselves as class parties. To abandon a strict class image, however, does not necessarily mean that a political party becomes class-diffuse.

The issue was partly one of theoretical analysis, partly one of strategic choice. Theoretically, Marxist revisionism – led by Eduard Bernstein – reassessed several fundamental Marxian propositions concerning the evolution of class structure.[5] In opposition to the polarization-cum-immiseration thesis underpinning the justification of the class-oppositional strategy, Bernstein argued that class polarization was countered by the rise of the new middle classes. For a party already committed to parliamentarism, this naturally provoked a reexamination of how the requisite electoral majority would materialize.

Revisionism did not necessarily prescribe broader class alliances, but it did offer a theoretical rationale for their eventuality. The decisive impetus came from strategic choices in the realm of practical politics. The Scandinavian experience of fighting for democracy in unison with liberal farmers opened up new vistas. Liberals learned that the socialists were not necessarily a threat; socialists discovered that significant strides could be made through class collaboration. It seemed logical that additional reforms were possible through *ad hoc* alliances. Furthermore, while national power still seemed only a remote possibility, socialists occasionally gained influence in local government. Their experience with 'sewer socialism' showed that political collaboration with other 'progressive elements' on local issues could bear fruit. And, whether or not they had studied Bernstein, socialist leaders themselves began to realize that a strictly proletarian majority was depressingly slow to materialize. Pressed from below to deliver immediate material improvements, socialist leaders were obviously weary of Kautsky's 1904 Amsterdam Socialist International congress resolution prohibiting collaboration with bourgeois parties. As Schumpeter and Przworski have put it, the main problem was how to build a majority on the basis of ideological purity alone.[6] If the class party image were abandoned, the party would risk losing its left-wing clientele; by remaining pure, it risked having to wait forever for the socialist opportunity.

Social democracy, then, distinguished itself by the decision to subordinate class purity to the logic of majority politics. The organization moved from 'working-class party' to 'people's party'; its platform addressed the 'national interest' rather than the 'proletarian cause'. In the words of the late Swedish socialist leader Per Albin Hansson, social democracy strived to erect a 'people's home'. It is worth noting, however, that the difference between socialist and communist parties does not have to do so much with the actual class composition of the party's constituency as with the conditions under which allied classes are admitted. Whereas the vanguard party admits only recruits who are willing to adhere to its manifesto, the social democratic party is prepared to realign its programme in response to current requirements for alliance formation. For communist parties, programme dictates parliamentary power; for social democratic parties, parliament dictates programme....

The first two components of Przworski's definition emphasize, respectively, social democracy's relation to the state and to the class structure. The third element focuses on the party's posture concerning social transformation. According to Przworski, social democracy is characterized by a willingness to 'seek improvements, reforms, within the confines of capitalism [as opposed to dedicating] all efforts and energies to its complete transformation'.[7] Social democracy is without a doubt reformist, but to say this is to miss the point. To differentiate 'revolutionary' from 'reformist' in this manner assumes that we have a way of knowing when a given policy has long-range revolutionary consequences. In some instances, we probably do. Almost certainly, old-age homes will have no revolutionary consequences for the social structure. But in all too many cases, we have no accepted criteria for deciding which actions will merely reflect the status quo and which will accelerate historical transformation.

25 David Held

What Should Democracy Mean Today?

There are several reasons why the critical assessment of existing models of democracy and the pursuit of alternative positions is important. First, we cannot escape an involvement in politics, although many people seek to do so. Whether one explicitly acknowledges adherence to a political perspective or not, our activities presuppose a particular framework of state and society which does direct us. The actions of the apathetic do not escape politics; they merely leave things as they are. Secondly, if we are to engage with problems of democracy, we need to reflect on why for so many people the fact that something is a recognizably 'political' statement is almost enough to bring it instantly into disrepute. Politics is frequently associated today with self-seeking behaviour, hypocrisy and 'public relations' activity geared to selling policy packages. The problem with this view is that, while it is quite understandable, the difficulties of the modern world will not be solved by surrendering politics, but only by the development and transformation of 'politics' in ways that will enable us more effectively to shape and organize human life. We do not have the option of 'no politics'.

Thirdly, scepticism and cynicism about politics are not necessarily inevitable facts of political life. By establishing the credibility and viability of alternative models of 'governing institutions', showing how these can be connected to systematic difficulties that occur and recur in the social and political world, a chance is established that mistrust of politics can be overcome. A political imagination for alternative arrangements is essential if the tarnished image of politics is to be eradicated. Fourthly, we cannot be satisfied with existing models of democratic politics. [T]here are good grounds for not simply accepting any one model, whether classical or contemporary, as it stands. There is something to be learnt from a variety of traditions of political thought, and a propensity simply to juxtapose one position with another, or to play off one against another, is not fruitful.

In what follows, one strategy for advancing beyond the current debate between perspectives is elaborated. It is important to stress that the position set out below does not claim to represent a tightly knit, definitive series of ideas; rather, it amounts to a number of suggestions for further examination. It is an attempt to offer a plausible response to the question: what should democracy mean today? But clearly the response will need a considerably more detailed defence than can be offered here, if it is to be found ultimately compelling. The approach I describe involves an attempt to reconceptualize a key notion common to a number of strands of political thought and to show how aspects of these perspectives could, indeed should, be integrated in an alternative position. I shall begin by looking briefly again at aspects of new right and new left thought.

The new right thinkers have in general tied the goals of liberty and equality to individualist political, economic and ethical doctrines. The individual is, in essence, sacrosanct, and is free and equal only to the extent that he or she can pursue and attempt to realize self-chosen ends and personal interests. Equal justice can be sustained between individuals if, above all, individuals' entitlement to certain rights or liberties is respected and all citizens are treated equally before the law. In this account, the modern state should provide the necessary conditions to enable citizens to pursue their own interests; it should uphold the rule of law in order to protect and nurture individuals' liberty, a state of affairs in which no one is entitled to impose their vision of the 'good life' upon others. This has been, of course, a central tenet of liberalism since Locke: the state exists to safeguard the rights and liberties of citizens who are ultimately the best judge of their own interests; the state is the burden individuals have to bear to secure their own ends; and the state must be restricted in scope and restrained in practice to ensure the maximum possible freedom of every citizen. Liberalism has been and is preoccupied with the creation and defence of a world in which 'free and equal' individuals can flourish with minimum political impediment.

By contrast, new left thinkers have defended the desirability of certain social or collective means and goals. For them, to take equality and liberty seriously is to challenge the view that these values can be realized by individuals left, in practice, to their own devices in a 'free market' economy and a minimal state. Equality, liberty and justice – recognized by them as 'great universal ideals' – cannot be achieved in a world dominated by private ownership of property and the capitalist economy. These ideals, according to them, can be realized only through struggles to ensure that society, as well as the state, is democratized, i.e. subject to procedures that ensure maximum accountability. Only the latter can ultimately guarantee the reduction of all forms of coercive power so that human beings can develop as 'free and equal'. While new left thinkers differ in many respects from traditional Marxist writers, they share a concern to uncover the conditions whereby the 'free development of each' is compatible with the 'free development of all'. This is a fundamental common goal.

The views of the new right and new left are, of course, radically different. The key elements of their theories are fundamentally at odds. It is therefore somewhat paradoxical to note that they share a vision of reducing arbitrary power and regulatory capacity to its lowest possible extent. Both the new right and the new left fear the extension of networks of intrusive power into society, 'choking', to borrow a phrase from Marx, 'all its pores'. They both have ways of criticizing the bureaucratic, inequitable and often repressive character of much state action. In addition, they are both concerned with the political, social and economic conditions for the development of people's capacities, desires and interests. Put in this general and very abstract manner, there appears to be a convergence of emphasis on ascertaining the circumstances under which people can develop as 'free and equal'.

To put the point another way, the aspiration of these traditions to a world characterized by free and equal relations among mature adults reflects a concern to ensure the:

1 creation of the best circumstances for all humans to develop their nature and express their diverse qualities (involving an assumption of respect for individuals' diverse capacities, their ability to learn and enhance their potentialities);
2 protection from the arbitrary use of political authority and coercive power (involving an assumption of respect for privacy in all matters which are not the basis of potential and demonstrable 'harm' to others);
3 involvement of citizens in the determination of the conditions of their association (involving an assumption of respect for the authentic and reasoned nature of individuals' judgements);
4 expansion of economic opportunity to maximize the availability of resources (involving an assumption that when individuals are free from the burdens of unmet physical need they are best able to realize their ends).

There is, in other words, a set of general aspirations that 'legal' and 'participatory' theorists have in common. Moreover, these aspirations have been shared by thinkers as diverse as J. S. Mill and Marx, and by most of those eighteenth- and nineteenth-century theorists who have sought to clarify the relation between the 'sovereign state' and 'sovereign people'.

The concept of 'autonomy' or 'independence' links together these aspirations and helps explain why they have been shared so widely. 'Autonomy' connotes the capacity of human beings to reason self-consciously, to be self-reflective and to be self-determining. It involves the ability to deliberate, judge, choose and act upon different possible courses of action in private as well as public life. Clearly, the idea of an 'autonomous' person could not develop while political rights, obligations and duties were closely tied, as they were in the mediaeval world-view, to property rights and religious tradition. But with the changes that wrought a fundamental transformation of mediaeval notions, there emerged a new preoccupation in European political thought with the nature and limits of political authority, law, rights and duty.

Liberalism advanced the challenging view that individuals were 'free and equal', capable of determining and justifying their own actions, capable of entering into self-chosen obligations. The development of autonomous spheres of action, in social, political and economic affairs, became a (if not *the*) central mark of what it was to enjoy freedom and equality. While liberals failed frequently to explore the actual circumstances in which individuals lived – how people were integrally connected to one another through complex networks of relations and institutions – they none the less generated the strong belief that a defensible political order must be one in which people are able to develop their nature and interests free from the arbitrary use of political authority and coercive power. And although many liberals stopped far short of proclaiming that for individuals to be 'free and equal' they must themselves be sovereign, their work was preoccupied with, and affirmed the overwhelming importance of, uncovering the conditions under which individuals can determine and regulate the stucture of their own association – a preoccupation they shared with figures such as Rousseau and Marx, although both the latter dissented, of course, from liberal interpretations of this central issue.

The aspirations that make up a concern with autonomy can be recast in the form of a general principle – what I call the 'principle of autonomy'. The principle can be stated as follows:

> Individuals should be free and equal in the determination of the conditions of their own lives; that is, they should enjoy equal rights (and, accordingly, equal obligations) in the specification of the framework which generates and limits the opportunities available to them, so long as they do not deploy this framework to negate the rights of others.

... What is the status of the principle of autonomy? The principle of autonomy ought to be regarded as an essential premiss of liberalism and Marxism, and of their various contemporary offshoots. It ought to be considered one of their central elements, a basic and inescapable aspect of their rationale. All these traditions have given, and continue to give, priority to the development of 'autonomy' or 'independence'. But to state this – and to try to articulate its meaning in a fundamental but highly abstract principle – is not yet, it must be stressed, to say very much. For the full meaning of a principle cannot be specified independently of the conditions of its enactment. Liberalism and Marxism may give priority to 'autonomy', but they differ radically over how to secure it and, hence, over how to interpret it.

The specification of a principle's 'conditions of enactment' is a vital matter; for if a theory of the most desirable form of democracy is to be at all plausible, it must be concerned with both theoretical and practical issues, with philosophical as well as organizational and institutional questions. Without this double focus, an arbitrary choice of principles, and seemingly endless abstract debates about them, are encouraged....

A starting point for reflection is provided by table 1, which sums up (albeit in rather stark form) some of the central positions of liberalism and Marxism.

Table 1 Justified prescriptions of liberalism and Marxism

Liberalism	*Marxism*
1 Hostility to and scepticism about state power, and emphasis on the importance of a diversity of power centres	1 Hostility to and scepticism about concentration of economic power in private ownership of the means of production
2 Separation of state from civil society as an essential prerequisite of a democratic order	2 Restructuring of civil society, i.e. transformation of capitalist relations of production, as a prerequisite of a flourishing democracy
3 The desirable form of the state is an impersonal (legally circumscribed) structure of power	3 The 'impersonality' or 'neutrality' of the state can only be achieved when its autonomy is no longer compromised by capitalism
4 Centrality of constitutionalism to guarantee formal equality (before the law) and formal freedom (from arbitrary treatment) in the form of civil and political liberties or rights essential to representative democracy: above all, those of free speech, expression, association, belief and (for liberal democrats) one-person-one-vote and party pluralism	4 The transformation of the rigid social and technical division of labour is essential if people are to develop their capacities and involve themselves fully in the democratic regulation of political as well as economic and social life
5 Protected space enshrined in law for individual autonomy and initiative	5 The equally legitimate claims of all citizens to autonomy are the foundation of any freedom that is worth the name
6 Importance of markets as mechanisms for co-ordinating diverse activities of producers and consumers	6 Unless there is public planning of investment, production will remain geared to profit, not to need in general

There are good grounds for taking seriously some of the central arguments and, thus, some of the central prescriptions of *both* liberalism and Marxism. The principle of autonomy can only be conceived adequately if we adopt this (somewhat eclectic) approach. It is important to appreciate, above all, the complementarity of liberalism's scepticism about political power and Marxism's scepticism about economic power. To focus exclusively on the former or the latter is to negate the possibility of realizing the principle of autonomy.

Liberalism's thrust to create a sovereign democratic state, a diversity of power centres and a world marked by openness, controversy and plurality is radically compromised by the reality of the so-called 'free market', the structure and imperatives of the system of private capital accumulation. If liberalism's central failure is to see markets as 'powerless' mechanisms of co-ordination and, thus, to neglect – as neo-pluralists, among others, point out – the distorting nature of economic power in relation to democracy, Marxism's central failure is the reduction of political power to economic power and, thus, to neglect – as participatory democrats, among others, point out – the dangers of centralized political power and the problems of political accountability. Marxism's embodiment in East European societies [was] marked by the growth of the centralized bureaucratic state; its claim to represent the forces of progressive politics [was] tarnished by socialism's relation in practice, in the East and also in the West, with bureaucracy, surveillance, hierarchy and state control. Accordingly, liberalism's account of the nature of markets and economic power must be rejected while Marxism's account of the nature of democracy must be severely questioned.

It is important to take note, furthermore, of some of the limitations shared by liberalism and Marxism. Generally, these two political traditions have failed to explore the impediments to full participation in democratic life other than those imposed, however important these may be, by state and economic power. The roots of the difficulty lie in narrow conceptions of 'the political'. In the liberal tradition the political is equated with the world of government or governments alone. Where this equation is made and where politics is regarded as a sphere apart from economy or culture, that is, as governmental activity and institutions, a vast domain of politics is excluded from view: above all, the spheres of productive and reproductive relations. The Marxist conception of politics raises related matters. Although the Marxist critique of liberalism is of great significance, its value is ultimately limited because of the direct connection it postulates (even within the framework of the 'relative autonomy' of the state) between the political and the economic. By reducing political to economic and class power, and by championing 'the end of politics', Marxism itself tends to marginalize or exclude certain types of issue from politics. This is true of all those issues which cannot, in the last analysis, be reduced to class-related matters – the development of power in organizations, for instance.

The narrow conception of 'the political' in both liberalism and Marxism has meant that key conditions for the realization of the principle of autonomy have been eclipsed from view: conditions concerning, for example, the necessary limits on private possession of the means of production, if democratic outcomes are not to be skewed systematically to the advantage of the economically powerful (insufficiently examined by liberalism); and the necessary changes in the organization of the household and child-rearing, among other things, if women are to enjoy 'free and equal' conditions (insufficiently examined by both liberalism and Marxism). (This is not to say, of course, that no liberal or Marxist has been concerned with these things; this would clearly be untrue. Rather, it is to argue that their perspectives or frameworks of analysis cannot adequately encompass them.) In order to grasp the diverse conditions necessary for the adequate institutionalization of the principle of autonomy, we require a broader conception of 'the political' than is found in either of these traditions.

In my view, politics is about power; that is, it is about the *capacity* of social agents, agencies and institutions to maintain or transform their environment, social or physical. It is about the resources that underpin this capacity and about the forces that shape and influence its exercise. Accordingly, politics is a phenomenon found in and between all groups, institutions (formal and informal) and societies, cutting across public and private life. It is expressed in all the activities of co-operation, negotiation and struggle over the use and distribution of resources. It is involved in all the relations, institutions and structures which are implicated in the activities of production and reproduction in the life of societies. Politics creates and conditions all aspects of our lives and it is at the core of the development of problems in society and the collective modes of their resolution. While politics, thus understood, raises a number of complicated issues – above all, about whether a concept of the private is compatible with it (a matter returned to later) – it usefully highlights the nature of politics as a universal dimension of human life, unrelated to any specific 'site' or set of institutions.

If politics is conceived in this way, then the specification of the conditions of enactment of the principle of autonomy amounts to the specification of the conditions for the participation of citizens in decisions about issues which are important to them (i.e. us). Thus, it is necessary to strive towards a state of affairs in which political life – democratically organized – is, in principle, a central part of all people's lives. Can this state of affairs be specified more precisely? How can 'the state' and 'civil society' be combined to promote the principle of autonomy?

If the force of the above argument is accepted then, for the principle of autonomy to be realized, it would require the creation of a system of collective decision-making which allowed extensive involvement of citizens in public affairs. A powerful case can be made, as it has been by Dahl, that for such a system to be fully democratic it would have to meet the following criteria:

1. Equal votes: The rule for determining outcomes ... must take into account, and take equally into account, the expressed preferences of each citizen as to the outcome; that is, votes must be allocated equally among citizens.
2. Effective participation: Throughout the process of making ... collective decisions, each citizen must have an adequate and equal opportunity for expressing a preference as to the final outcome.
3. Enlightened understanding: In order to express preferences accurately, each citizen must have adequate and equal opportunities ... for discovering and validating his or her preferences on the matter to be decided.
4. Final control of the agenda by the demos: The demos must have the exclusive opportunity to make decisions that determine what matters are and are not to be decided by processes that satisfy the first three criteria.
5. Inclusiveness: The demos must include all adult members except transients and persons proved to be mentally defective.[1]

These criteria will be examined here in order to delineate the general conditions of democratic decision-making.

If the right to 'equal votes' is not established, then there will be no mechanism that can take equally into account, and provide a decision procedure to resolve differences among, the views and preferences of citizens (even though the latter may decide not to deploy a decision-making system based on voting in all circumstances). If citizens are unable to enjoy the conditions for 'effective participation' and 'enlightened understanding', then it is unlikely that the marginalization of large categories of citizens in the democratic process will ever be overcome, nor that the vicious circles of limited or non-participation will be broken. If the 'final control' of the 'political agenda' is out of the hands of citizens, then 'rule by the people' will exist largely in name only, and Schumpeter's technocratic vision is more likely to be the order of the day.[2] If the *demos* does not include all adults (with the exception of those temporarily visiting political 'units', whether these be nation states or smaller-scale associations, and those who 'beyond a shadow of doubt' are legitimately disqualified from partici-pation due to mental incapacity and/or severe records of crime), then it will clearly fail to create the conditions for 'equal involvement'. For individuals to be 'free and equal' the above criteria would have to be met. It is hard to see how persons could be politically equal if any of the criteria were violated and how, as Dahl put it, 'any process that failed to satisfy one or more of the criteria could be regarded as fully democratic'.[3] . . .

Advocates of liberal democracy have tended to be concerned, above all else, with the proper principles and procedures of democratic government. By focus-ing on 'government', they have attracted attention away from a thorough ex-amination of the relation between: formal rights and actual rights; commitments to treat citizens as free and equal and practices which do neither sufficiently; conceptions of the state as, in principle, an independent authority and involve-ments of the state in the reproduction of the inequalities of everyday life; notions of political parties as appropriate structures for bridging the gap be-tween state and society and the array of power centres which such parties and their leaders cannot reach; conceptions of politics as governmental affairs and systems of power which negate this concept. None of the models of liberal democracy is able to specify adequately the conditions for the possibility of political participation by all citizens, on the one hand, and the set of governing institutions capable of regulating the forces which actually shape everyday life, on the other. The conditions of democratic participation, the form of democratic control, the scope of democratic decision-making – all these matters are insuf-ficiently questioned in the liberal democratic tradition. The problems are, in sum, twofold: the structure of civil society (including private ownership of productive property, vast sexual and racial inequalities) – misunderstood or endorsed by liberal democratic models – does not create conditions for equal votes, effective participation, proper political understanding and equal control of the political agenda, while the structure of the liberal democratic state (including large, frequently unaccountable bureaucratic apparatuses, institution-al dependence on the process of capital accumulation, political representatives preoccupied with their own re-election) does not create an organizational force which can adequately regulate 'civil' power centres.

The implications of these points are profound: for democracy to flourish today it has to be reconceived as a double-sided phenomenon: concerned, on the one hand, with the *re*-form of state power and, on the other hand, with the restruc-turing of civil society. The principle of autonomy can only be enacted by recognizing the indispensability of a process of 'double democratization': the interdependent transformation of both state and civil society. Such a process must be premised by the acceptance of both the principle that the division between state and civil society must be a central feature of democratic life and the notion that the power to make decisions must be free of the inequalities and constraints imposed by the private appropriation of capital. But, of course, to recognize the importance of both these positions is to recognize the necessity of recasting substantially their traditional connotations. . . .

To analyse democracy as a 'double-sided' process is more than simply an attempt to clarify the framework that would empower citizens in different spheres of life. The limits and forms of state action and civil society are becoming a crucial theme in certain contemporary European discussions of alternative democratic policies, a debate which can be usefully illustrated by new initiatives in the areas of investment, trade unions and the reorganization of social welfare provision. These policy examples, it must be stressed, are import-ant not because they can be 'imported' and straightforwardly adopted by any particular country, but because they explicitly recognize the requirement to confront both the undesirable elements of state regulation and the systems of power in civil society which currently distort democratic life.

Since 1975, for instance, extensive discussions have occurred in Sweden about the ways in which a gradual extension of social ownership of productive property can be achieved. From these discussions emerged the Meidner Plan. Its details are complex, but the thrust of its programme is to create the means for increasing the level of socially controlled investment. This would be done by formulating an egalitarian, planned wages policy (promoting a direct attack on poverty and low pay) while using increased taxes on profits to create investment funds on a local and regional basis which are citizen-controlled. This proposal seeks to avoid the problem whereby wage restraint leads traditionally to an increased rate of private profit without increasing investment, let alone greater social control over productive resources. In the long run, it also aims to break with the conventional view that state economic planning plus the nationalization of industry advances citizen autonomy. It is this idea which is important; the proposal itself, of course, needs much further examination.

Considerations like the Meidner Plan have radical implications for trade unions, some of which have been explored since 1978 by the French Democratic Labour Confederation. The CFDT has attempted to create a new 'non-sectarian social solidarity' against employer and state power. This means meeting concerns not only about immediate working conditions, but also about the divisions in, and the fragmentation of, the working class, by agitating for the recognition of the needs of workers with low wages, precarious jobs and no trade union representation. The CFDT's priorities have been increases in the minimum wage, remuneration for the lowest wage groups, an overall reduction of the working week, flexible working hours and greater self-management. The CFDT is concerned to stimulate the independent formulation of broad social demands upon the state. While recognizing the importance of the state in pushing through reforms for all workers (unionized or not), the CFDT strategy is, significantly, opposed to corporatist strategies and reliance upon state power. It proposes a strategy for enhancing the powers of the least powerful in civil society, not for increasing trade union power for its own sake, ordered and managed by the state.

The final example of new democratic policy strategies concerns Scandinavian proposals to 'lease back' institutions of social policy to the community. These proposals are a response to the evident increase in concern with bureaucratic and hierarchical state institutions such as planning authorities, schools and housing agencies. At the same time, such proposals attempt to counter directly the new right strategy of privatization, returning to the private sector control of state services and resources. These proposals suggest that state institutions of social policy can be transformed into more responsive, effective and democratic units if control of them is reclaimed or leased back to the people who use and service them. Although they would remain publicly funded, the policies of such organizations would be guided neither by capitalist markets nor by state direction, but by criteria of social need generated by producers' and consumers' decisions. As a consequence, the state would guarantee the resources and facilities for childcare, health clinics and schools, while leaving the government of these organizations to local constituencies.

Policy examples like the ones above do not necessarily lead to more egalitarian patterns of social life. They would require vigorous political support, including legal protection and state funding, if the conditions for their survival and expansion are to be established. In short, without a secure and independent civil society, the principle of autonomy cannot be realized. But without a democratic state, committed to providing tough redistributive measures, among other things, the democratization of civil society is unlikely to succeed.

26 David Lane

Soviet Politics under *Perestroika*

The Soviet Union under Gorbachev has undergone radical changes that make many of the characteristics of earlier periods obsolete. The changes ushered in by Gorbachev (like the short-lived ones of Dubček in Czechoslovakia, twenty years earlier) cast in doubt the validity of the antinomy between capitalism and communism and the associated competing organizing principles of planning and market, private and public, individual and collective. A look at the political, economic and ideological developments between the leadership of Khrushchev and that of Gorbachev will provide a foundation for understanding the changing nature of the goals of Soviet communism. Two major watersheds in recent Soviet history may be distinguished: Khrushchev's Programme of the CPSU (Communist Party of the Soviet Union) and its revised version brought out under Gorbachev. For important dates in recent Soviet history see [table] 1.

The Programme of the CPSU adopted at the Twenty-second Party Congress on 18 October 1961 reflected the optimism and confidence of the political leadership under Khrushchev. The Programme asserted that the world socialist system would triumph given the cumulative 'crisis of world capitalism'. It was proclaimed that within twenty years the Soviet economy would catch up with the standard of living of the United States. This goal would be ensured by the advantages of state ownership, central planning and Communist Party leadership based on Leninist principles. The 1961 Programme marked, in its own words, the beginning of a period of 'full-scale communist construction'.

Almost a quarter of a century later, on 25 February 1986, Gorbachev presided over another version of the Party Programme at the Twenty-seventh Party Congress. This time the tone was more cautious. In his introductory remarks, after praising previous Soviet achievements, he said, 'The leadership considers its duty to tell the Party and the people honestly and frankly about the deficiencies in our political and practical activities and the unfavourable tendencies in the economy and the social and moral sphere.' The claims of the revised Party Programme of 1986 are more modest. There are no references to the attainment of communism. If a fundamentalist regards Khrushchev as wanting to dig a grave for capitalism, Gorbachev may be said to be doing the same for the traditional Soviet concept of communism. Ideologically, the Party's revised Programme makes no reference to the attainment of communism, to the expansion of collective forms of welfare outside the price system, nor does it refer to the withering away of the state.

The problems of socialist construction have now become the centre of the Party's attention. As Gorbachev emphasized in January 1987 at a plenum of the Communist Party, 'No accomplishment, even the most impressive ones, must obscure either contradictions in the development of society or our mistakes or failings.' Furthermore, Gorbachev's speech at the Twenty-seventh Party Congress was in many ways a more fundamental critique of the deficiencies of Soviet society than was Khrushchev's secret speech in which the cult of personality of

Table 1 Some important dates in recent Soviet history

1953	Death of Stalin
1956	Twentieth Congress of the Communist Party of the Soviet Union (CPSU): Khrushchev exposes Stalin's excesses
1961	New programme of the CPSU adopted at the Twenty-second Party Congress
1964	Brezhnev and Kosygin come to power
1982	Andropov comes to power
1984	Chernenko comes to power
1985	Gorbachev comes to power
1986	Twenty-seventh Congress of the CPSU; programme of the CPSU revised
1988	Nineteenth Conference of the Communist Party of the Soviet Union
1989	USSR Congress of People's Deputies elected
1990	Party plenum relinquishes monopoly of power by CPSU

Stalin was denounced. Khrushchev offered few structural criticisms of Soviet society whereas Gorbachev provided a critique of the state system and its methods of bureaucratic control, and he outlined inadequacies in the nature of the economic and political systems.

In a speech before the Twenty-seventh Party Congress, Gorbachev defined in Marxist phraseology four major contradictions within the system: a contradiction between the way work is organized and carried out, and what is needed to operate a modern economy; a contradiction between the form of ownership under socialism and the way that management and control are performed; a contradiction between the commodities that are produced and the money that is available to distribute them to consumers; and a contradiction between the centralization of the economy and the need to give economic units independence to organize things efficiently. As Gorbachev put it, there is a 'lack of correspondence between productive forces and productive relations, between socialist property and the economic forces of its implementation, in the relations between goods and money and in the combination of centralization and independence of economic organizations' (February 1986).

Among the many objective reasons for this change of emphasis, Khrushchev's economic aims did not materialize. Over a long period, the expectations generated in the 1960s were not fulfilled. Considering the goals of the Party Programme of 1961 against achievements reached in 1980, real conditions fell considerably short of anticipations. National income was 36 per cent less than the long-term plan, gross agricultural production was 56 per cent short, electric power was 57 per cent down, and grain production fell 39 per cent below the estimate. The quality and regularity of food delivered to the urban areas was inadequate. This does not mean that there were no improvements: compared to the 1960 levels, the actual level of national income had risen 320 per cent, gross agricultural production had risen 65 per cent, electric power 470 per cent, and grain production 141 per cent. Standards had improved, but they had not improved enough to meet the high expectations engendered by the political leadership of Khrushchev.

This process of underfulfilment of plans continued in the early 1980s. Economic indicators comparing objectives and achievements of the eleventh Five Year Plan (1981–5) were underfulfilled, particularly in agriculture (plan 13 per cent, actual 6 per cent) and industrial productivity (plan 23 per cent, actual 17 per cent). Nevertheless, by the mid-1980s conditions had improved and it cannot be doubted that standards had been rising. In industry as a whole the work week has shortened from 47.8 hours in 1955 to 40.5 in 1985, and the average number of holidays rose from 18.5 in 1958 to 22 in 1983. The index of consumption (a measure of the standard of living) had risen from 100 in 1970 to 176 in 1981 (and remained the same in 1982); it rose to 189 in 1984 and 196 in 1985. Even according to estimates made by the Central Intelligence Agency of the United States, the USSR had an annual rise in gross national product of from 2 per cent to 2.5 per cent in the early 1980s. A later revised CIA figure put the latter figure at 1.9 per cent. Of Western European states, according to the Organization for Economic Co-operation and Development (OECD), this record was matched only by Ireland in the 1980–5 period; the Federal Republic of Germany had an average rate increase of 1.3 per cent and Britain 1.2 per cent.

While Brezhnev was consoled by the steady though slow rate of progress, Gorbachev and many others were not. Moreover, the Soviet Union has experienced a long-term decline in its rate of economic growth. Official figures show a reduction in growth rates; the average increase in produced national income was 8.9 per cent for 1966–70; 6.3 per cent for 1971–5; 4.7 per cent for 1976–80; and 4.0 per cent for 1981–3. Economic growth in the 1980s was further negatively influenced by the decline in the growth of the working population, its shift to the non-Slavic east, and by an increase of the economically dependent population, for example, those in old age. The defence burden was immense. It is confidently estimated in the West that Soviet defence spending was some 15 per cent of its gross national product compared to only 7 per cent of that of the United States. (In 1989 Gorbachev conceded that defence accounted for 15.6 per cent of the total budget.)

The Soviet Union's problems, furthermore, had not been confined to internal economic ones. On the international front the Soviet Union's military position became much stronger *vis-à-vis* the United States during the period after Khrushchev, but under Brezhnev the policy of peaceful coexistence and *détente* was in crisis. The Soviet Union since the end of the Second World War had steadily lost its hegemony over the world communist movement. It had conceded ideological leadership: some of the sacred assumptions of Marxism–Leninism, central planning and collectivism, were shrouded in doubt. Those assumptions have been cast aside by movements ranging from Eurocommunism to economic reform programmes in China and Hungary. And the Soviet mould of socialism had been openly challenged by diverse forces such as the Czechoslovak Reform Movement and the Solidarity movement in Poland.

The current international economic and political system is of a qualitatively different type [from] the system in which the Soviet command economy developed under Stalin. The Soviet model of growth has appealed to relatively underdeveloped countries. The centralization of political and economic control facilitated the allocation of resources necessary to create an industrial society. The technological hardware of the advanced countries was relatively easily transferred and adopted by the underdeveloped ones. Full employment and a relatively equal society in terms of consumption was a major appeal to observers in the West and the growth rates of the economy compared well during times of depression.

Since the end of the Second World War, the world economy has changed fundamentally. The advent of high technology, the rise of the service industries in the West, the dependency on scientific advance for the achievement of state defence and economic growth has put a greater store on internal innovation and dynamism. The world economy has seen the rise of new economies in south-east Asia as well as technological progress in the advanced Western societies. The

Soviet model has failed in this international competition. The technological gap, particularly in the evolving weaponry of the United States, has been a cause for concern in the USSR. Rising Japanese economic power has brought it into contention with the USSR as the world's second largest producer of economic wealth.

Advanced technology itself has brought the image of the advanced capitalist countries into the USSR. Communication is international in scope and contact with the West has 'contaminated' the Soviet public. The population has developed a consumer mentality and a yearning for Western artefacts.

This, then, was the political and economic legacy inherited by Gorbachev. It was one of frustration on the part of the political leadership and the Soviet people as a whole. While the USSR remained a major world power claiming a quantitative gross national product second only to that of the United States, the country had experienced a cumulative decline: political, economic and ideological.

Gorbachev's answer to the malaise facing the Soviet Union is a policy of *uskorenie*, meaning acceleration or rapid growth. It is a general strategy involving 'a new quality of growth: the all-round intensification of production on the basis of scientific and technical progress, a structural reshaping of the economy and efficient forms of managing and stimulating labour'.

The means to achieve such acceleration mark a radical break from previous thinking and practice. '*Perestroika*' is the term used to describe the process of change. It may be translated as restructuring, or radical reform, or even revolutionary transition. *Perestroika* is significant because it is a comprehensive and theoretically based policy of change. Reforms, it may be argued, were undertaken under Khrushchev, Kosygin and Brezhnev, but they tended to be piecemeal rather than systemic; these leaders assumed that the underlying political and economic structures devised under Stalin were essentially sound and needed improvement to correct distortions in their administration rather than radical reform. The process of *perestroika* must be considered a different phenomenon. The present reforms are comprehensive in scope, politically radical, have been executed with positive skill and enjoy, at least as principles, widespread support. Underlying the process of *perestroika* is a major theoretical reappraisal and critique of social relations in the USSR that will provide the basis for the working-out of a comprehensive reform programme.

Soviet thinking has undergone a revision in its focus on the various forms of incompatibilities, tensions and conflicts generated in society. In Soviet phraseology, there has been a redefinition of the nature of 'contradictions' under socialism. 'Contradictions' is a concept that describes any incompatibility, tension or conflict between people, groups or institutions. In Marxist theory, antagonistic contradictions involve irreconcilable conflicts of interests: under capitalism, for instance, that between the proletariat and the bourgeoisie. Such contradictions are resolved, not by compromise or accommodation of mutually opposed positions, but by a change of state. The antagonistic interests under capitalism are abolished through a movement, by a revolution, that ushers in socialism. In contrast to capitalism, however, contradictions under socialism may be resolved peacefully, with mutual goodwill, through common understanding and good leadership. To distinguish these contradictions from those under capitalism, they are termed 'non-antagonistic'.

Under Stalin and during the period from Khrushchev to Chernenko, the leadership held that under Soviet socialism the 'fundamental interests' of state and society coincided. The social order was one of social harmony and conformity. The conflicts that arose were incompatibilities rooted in the non-antagonistic contradictions between the 'survivals of capitalism' and the emergent social formation of socialism. Incompatibilities had their source in backwardness – the idiocy of traditional peasant life, the superstition of religion – or were the direct negative influence of the capitalist West (through malevolent propaganda and sabotage). Leaders held that with the maturation of the Soviet economy and with the growing strength of socialist states in the world political order, such antagonisms would sharply decrease, though the Soviet state would have to continue until capitalism had been finally buried.

The need for state power is a contradiction under socialism, for Marxists conceive of the state as an expression of a ruling class. Under socialism the need for a state is justified by the necessity of maintaining vigilance against an external class enemy in the shape of the hostile capitalist states. As Khrushchev envisaged it, in the future the internal role of the state would 'wither away'.

Internal policy operated through compromise designed to promote and solidify internal social harmony. Under Brezhnev, a 'social contract' between leaders, government and people developed. The political leadership provided a framework of stability and peace. The government apparatus was secure under the traditional forms of central planning. The working class enjoyed full employment, an undemanding work environment and a steady but slow amelioration of pay and conditions. There was a liberalization of conditions for the intelligentsia: within restricted circles discussion was not curbed. (Many of the policies adopted by Gorbachev were worked out by reform-minded intellectuals under Brezhnev.) When reforms were suggested, they were experimented with but when problems or resistance arose, reforms were quietly dropped. These are the roots of what is now called the 'period of stagnation'.

The cumulative economic, political and international decline of the Soviet Union under Brezhnev led to a reassessment of the assumptions on which policy was based. This thinking is epitomized in the 'Novosibirsk document' attributed to a leading Soviet sociologist, T. Zaslavskaya, and circulated in the USSR in 1983. Contradictions under socialism were indeed non-antagonistic – they did not have the explosive character of class conflict under capitalism – but they were less benign than the incumbent leadership assumed, for two reasons. First, they originated not just in the 'left-overs' of capitalism but in the structure of Soviet socialist society itself, which generated group and class interests. Second, such interests gave rise to contradictions, conflicts and antagonisms between groups.

Zaslavskaya contended that the antagonisms between groups are at the heart of the malaise of Soviet society and they account for the deceleration of growth and the lack of dynamism. Furthermore, the political leadership under Brezhnev was a source of contradiction in that it perpetuated bureaucratic forms that acted as a brake on the development of productive forces. Production relations (the system of economic management and political control) were in conflict with the potentialities of the productive forces. This conflict, in turn, led to 'stagnation' – the retardation of economic development, corruption, a decline of socialist morality, public apathy and alienation.

The recognition that contradictions are built into socialism gave rise to the conception of a society with policy preferences linked to individuals and the positions they occupy and the privileges they enjoy. 'Interests', then, are at the centre of contemporary Soviet political analysis. At the February 1988 plenum of the Central Committee, Soviet society was defined in terms of a 'plurality' of opposing 'interests and views'. According to this reassessment, various vested interests and groups at the heart of the political system have prevented development; they are a brake or a fetter on the development of productive forces. They were legitimated by the cult of personality under Brezhnev and administered by the apparatus of government and Party. To break out of the vicious circle of complacency, decline and stagnation, the mechanisms that perpetuate them have to be replaced and those individuals and vested interests who benefit must be removed....

Perestroika (restructuring or radical reform) is a set of tactics aimed at resolving contradictions. Rather than a set of policies, *perestroika* is an attitude or approach to politics and society. Its major components, illustrated in figure 1, are explained below to give the reader an overview, and in later chapters we shall take up its component parts in more detail.

Perestroika involves four mobilizing strategies:

● individual (and group) self-interest (including *khozraschet*);
● public criticism (*glasnost*);
● democracy (*demokratiya, demokratizatsiya, plyuralizm*);
● law and control.

Self-interest is a mobilizing principle. The underlying assumption of *perestroika* is that if self-interest is allowed to take its course, higher levels of economic and political efficiency are achieved. While self-interest and economic accounting had been espoused even under Stalin, their role now is much more important than in the past. *Khozraschet* involves economic accountability and independence (literally, it means autonomous profit-and-loss accounting). It may apply to individuals (they should be given initiative and rewarded for what they do), institutions (enterprises should be given greater independence over production and rewarded or penalized for their efforts), even regions of the country are encouraged to manage their own affairs. The important shift in the organizing principles of Soviet society involves changing from an administered model – in which the public interest is determined centrally by the authorities – to a system wherein individuals and groups are allowed to express their own interests.

Glasnost means public criticism and access to information. It legitimates the articulation of individual group interests and the answerability of decision-makers to criticism; and thus involves greater individual and group autonomy. The mass media, rather than being merely a conduit for the transmission of government policy, ha[ve] the responsibility to articulate a spontaneously expressed range of views. Thus *glasnost* entails a pluralism (*plyuralizm*) of points of view rather than the previously centralized and controlled media.

Demokratiya (democracy) and *demokratizatsiya* (democratization) involve a transformation in participation in decision-making. The process of transition to 'democracy' is 'democratization'. The objective is to place more authority with the rank-and-file citizen or member of a collectivity or group. A thorough restructuring of the apparatus of the state will devolve power to the government apparatus (the Soviets) and place a limitation on the centralized role of the Party. *Demokratiya* seeks to involve the masses in a more positive way in public affairs and in so doing to restrict the power of the political leadership. A *plyuralizm* of interests is to be encouraged. Hence democratization is an important mechanism to combat traditional interests that maintain the status quo but it is also a necessary condition to ensure the acceleration of economic development, *uskorenie*.

The principles of discipline and control originated with Andropov (the short-lived leader of the USSR who preceded Gorbachev). Their objective was to strengthen commitment and obedience to socialist laws, while opposing corruption and administrative privilege. In the early days of *perestroika* Andropov's principles led to administrative measures against malingerers and an alcoholism

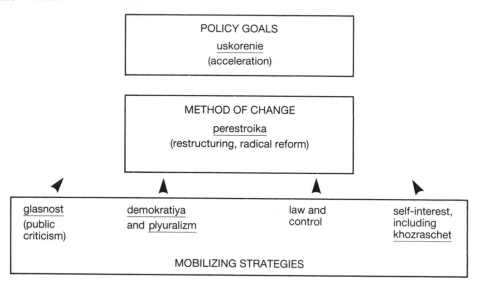

Figure 1   Gorbachev's reform strategy

campaign. With the advent of *perestroika* the notion of law and control means that the Soviet Union is moving toward a legally constituted state. Prescribed laws intended to guarantee civil rights to the population are to define the legal operation of the state. As Gorbachev put it at the Nineteenth Party [Congress] in June 1988, 'The process of the consistent democratization of Soviet society should complete the creation of a socialist state governed by the rule of law.' A major shift in the relationship between the individual and society should provide citizens with rights, although they will also be constrained by law. Laws are shaped by the Party: the state will make and enforce laws and define the context in which individuals and groups enjoy rights (see figure 1).

At first sight, there appears to be an odd combination of traditional concepts (law and control) and a more open market-orientated approach with concern for democracy, pluralism and public criticism. There are two explanations for this paradox. First, the significance of stressing law and order and the drive against corruption is an attempt to strengthen the integrity of Soviet society. The aim is to provide a framework of morality, discipline and rules enforced by law, which is an attempt to move to a legal–rational type of society. If market relations and private trade are to develop, it is necessary to have effective legal control.

Secondly, democracy is in essence a form of control from below. The objective of the reform leadership is to appeal over the heads of the bureaucracy and middle management to the rank and file: using lower levels in the power structure as levers of change is the strategy for overcoming inertia and maladministration. The arrows in figure 1 illustrate that policy goals are achieved from below, rather than from the top down. A policy involving a shift of power away from the centrally controlled bureaucracy to lower levels gives people a greater chance to participate. It legitimates the articulation of group and individual interests. The introduction of competitive elections will put pressure on incumbents of political position to become more responsive to the demands of the people they represent.

The boundaries of democracy, *glasnost* and financial autonomy have not yet been fully worked out. In my view, the leadership adopted this strategy as a device to precipitate change, to involve the public in new policies, and to weaken forces opposed to the new incumbent political elite under Gorbachev. This has led to greater participation, a more open exchange of information and *'plyuralizm'* (that is, a limited form of group autonomy). But when the invocation of these principles appears to threaten the existing order, limits are established in the name of control and socialist legality.

Perestroika is an orientation and approach to the politics of radical reform. It is a comprehensive mode of action and policy. The strategy has undergone changes through time. First, it involves a psychological campaign to alert the public to the need for change, to raise levels of consciousness, to overcome inertia and moral turpitude. Various anti-alcoholism, anti-corruption, anti-malingering campaigns were started, and claims were made to institute socialist 'justice'.

Second, a vigorous personnel (or cadres) policy was instituted that sought to install 'from the top and from below' people in authority who supported the new policy.

Third, a new style in leadership was initiated. This has been more direct, honest and open, and has involved public participation and debate. It has led to direct open communication with the West, and in practice to a more American presidential style for Mr Gorbachev (and the cultivation of a First Lady role for Mrs Gorbachev).

Fourth, a comprehensive set of interrelated reforms has been introduced. These have ranged over the industrial enterprise, health, electoral and mass media practice, the rule of law, individual and group rights, education, the organization of the economy, and government and foreign affairs.

Fifth, the fundamental object of socialism has become the policy of the development of socialism in the USSR; any remaining concern with a struggle against capitalism has been dropped. As Gorbachev put it in February 1987: 'Our desire to make our own country better will hurt no one, with the world only gaining from this.' Social development takes priority over class interests.

Sixth, *perestroika* involves a view of the interdependence of the capitalist and socialist systems. They cannot develop separately or even in parallel. The two systems interact within one framework. For progress on both sides, co-operation and mutual trust [are] essential. This has involved a major change in foreign policy. There has been a genuine movement towards disarmament and a reduction in international tension. The Soviet government has also allowed the socialist states of Eastern Europe to move to more pluralistic governments.

Finally, the general principle that underpins these changes has been to allow the articulation of interests by individuals and groups and resolving them through political exchange. A pluralistic and interest-driven social and political system has been added to the existing centralized forms of political control. This has created its own form of tension. This principle involves relying on markets in politics (more competition through elections) and in economics (prices are intended to reflect supply and demand). Unlike Khrushchev's reforms, which were institutional and personal in character, *perestroika* entails an impetus 'from below', which represents a change in the direction of power, which had been directed from the top down. . . .

To what extent will the changes under Gorbachev lead to a fundamental readjustment in the nature of Soviet society? Is the initially grudging acceptance and later admiration of Gorbachev in the West an indication of a profound convergence with capitalism? Are the proposals operational within the context of Soviet society? Would their implementation lead to social collapse?

All societies hold some tenets as sacred: in the West the underlying values of individualism, the market (in economics and politics), rights and private property underpin the political system. What are the sacred components of Soviet society? In a February 1988 speech to the Central Committee Plenum, Gorbachev emphasized that the USSR is 'not departing by one step from socialism, from Marxism–Leninism'. For Gorbachev, the essence of socialism lies

> in establishing the power of the working people and giving priority to the good of the individual, the working class and all the people. Ultimately socialism's task is to put an end to the social alienation of the individual which is characteristic of the exploitative society, alienation from power, from the means of production, from the results of his labour and from spiritual assets.

In an economic sense, the foundations of socialism lie not only in state ownership, but also in other forms of co-operative and individual economic activity. Under *perestroika* central planning has to take place in the context of economic incentives for growth and has to overcome individual alienation. The centrally directed and authoritarian political system, argue the reformers, is no longer appropriate for the kind of social structure that has developed in the USSR in the past twenty years. By making the political system more open and responsive, Gorbachev hopes that alienation (in the sense of disenchantment with conditions and processes) will be overcome. Enhanced forms of participation, moreover, are also the means by which *uskorenie* can be achieved: the forthcoming higher quality of political input will lead not only to a more legitimate political system but also to more efficient decision making.

The economy's performance is a crucial pivot on which the new regime's strategy turns. The market under socialism will play an important role in increasing levels of efficiency. The traditional form of planning was supply-based – planners decided what and how much should be produced and the prices at which commodities should be sold. Demand by consumers did not have any direct effects on the kinds or prices of goods produced. The reforms seek to give the forces of demand greater salience. The incentive of making money is a motivating principle for workers and, in the sense of income generation and self-financing, for managers and the directors of institutions (such as research institutes). Reformers are also seeking the means to use money, rather than planned quantitative indicators, as a measure of performance. For instance, some have suggested that educational institutions should be financed from fees received from employers of graduating students: this would be a direct measure of the value of an educational institution's contribution.

There are, however, significant limits on the development of private property and on the market as a determinant of economic activity. The direction of investment, for example, will be largely determined by the central planners, rather than through decisions of a stock exchange or joint stock companies and banks. (There are no plans for the institution of a proper stock exchange.)

Democratization is a key feature of the form that socialism will take under *perestroika*. Such democratization involves a growth in the autonomous activity of civil society: the encouragement of group interests that may flourish without state involvement or surveillance. The notion of 'socialist pluralism', coined originally in Czechoslovakia during the days of the Prague Spring under Alexander Dubček, is considered a component characteristic of socialism. The extent of such pluralism and the operation of 'independent groups' within this system are legitimate only within the context of a reformed Marxist–Leninist state. As Party Secretary and Politburo member V. A. Medvedev has put it: 'Socialism must create a political system which takes account of . . . the multitude of interests and aspirations of all social groups and communities of people. What is meant, of course, are healthy, economically and morally substantiated interests which do not run counter to our system.'

The most important condition here is that the interests of the working class (as Gorbachev stated in the earlier quotation) will continue to be defended by the political leadership of the Communist Party. Here, then, we may pinpoint a contradiction in the strategy of *perestroika* between Party hegemony and the freedom to form associations in civil society.

27 Ernest Gellner

Nations and Nationalism

Nationalism is primarily a political principle, which holds that the political and the national unit should be congruent.

Nationalism as a sentiment, or as a movement, can best be defined in terms of this principle. Nationalist *sentiment* is the feeling of anger aroused by the violation of the principle, or the feeling of satisfaction aroused by its fulfilment. A nationalist *movement* is one actuated by a sentiment of this kind.

There is a variety of ways in which the nationalist principle can be violated. The political boundary of a given state can fail to include all the members of the appropriate nation; or it can include them all but also include some foreigners; or it can fail in both these ways at once, not incorporating all the nationals and yet also including some non-nationals. Or again, a nation may live, unmixed with foreigners, in a multiplicity of states, so that no single state can claim to be *the* national one.

But there is one particular form of the violation of the nationalist principle to which nationalist sentiment is quite particularly sensitive: if the rulers of the political unit belong to a nation other than that of the majority of the ruled, this, for nationalists, constitutes a quite outstandingly intolerable breach of political propriety. This can occur either through the incorporation of the national territory in a larger empire, or by the local domination of an alien group.

In brief, nationalism is a theory of political legitimacy, which requires that ethnic boundaries should not cut across political ones, and, in particular, that ethnic boundaries within a given state – a contingency already formally excluded by the principle in its general formulation – should not separate the power-holders from the rest.

The nationalist principle can be asserted in an ethical, 'universalistic' spirit. There could be, and on occasion there have been, nationalists-in-the-abstract, unbiased in favour of any special nationality of their own, and generously preaching the doctrine for all nations alike: let all nations have their own political roofs, and let all of them also refrain from including non-nationals under it. There is no formal contradiction in asserting such non-egoistic nationalism. As a doctrine it can be supported by some good arguments, such as the desirability of preserving cultural diversity, of a pluralistic international political system and of the diminution of internal strains within states.

In fact, however, nationalism has often not been so sweetly reasonable, nor so rationally symmetrical. It may be that, as Immanuel Kant believed, partiality, the tendency to make exceptions on one's own behalf or one's own case, is *the* central human weakness from which all others flow; and that it infects national sentiment as it does all else, engendering what the Italians under Mussolini called the *sacro egoismo* of nationalism. It may also be that the political effectiveness of national sentiment would be much impaired if nationalists had as fine a sensibility to the wrongs committed by their nation as they have to those committed against it.

But over and above these considerations there are others, tied to the specific nature of the world we happen to live in, which militate against any impartial, general, sweetly reasonable nationalism. To put it in the simplest possible terms: there is a very large number of potential nations on earth. Our planet also contains room for a certain number of independent or autonomous political units. On any reasonable calculation, the former number (of potential nations) is probably much, *much* larger than that of possible viable states. If this argument or calculation is correct, not all nationalisms can be satisfied, at any rate at the same time. The satisfaction of some spells the frustration of others. This argument is further and immeasurably strengthened by the fact that very many of the potential nations of this world live, or until recently have lived, not in compact territorial units but intermixed with each other in complex patterns. It follows that a territorial political unit can only become ethnically homogeneous, in such cases, if it either kills, or expels, or assimilates all non-nationals. Their unwillingness to suffer such fates may make the peaceful implementation of the nationalist principle difficult.

These definitions must, of course, like most definitions, be applied with common sense. The nationalist principle, as defined, is not violated by the presence of *small* numbers of resident foreigners, or even by the presence of the occasional foreigner in, say, a national ruling family. Just how many resident foreigners or foreign members of the ruling class there must be before the principle is effectively violated cannot be stated with precision. There is no sacred percentage figure, below which the foreigner can be benignly tolerated, and above which he becomes offensive and his safety and life are at peril. No doubt the figure will vary with circumstances. The impossibility of providing a generally applicable and precise figure, however, does not undermine the usefulness of the definition.

Our definition of nationalism was parasitic on two as yet undefined terms: state and nation.

Discussion of the state may begin with Max Weber's celebrated definition of it as that agency within society which possesses the monopoly of legitimate violence. The idea behind this is simple and seductive: in well-ordered societies, such as most of us live in or aspire to live in, private or sectional violence is illegitimate. Conflict as such is not illegitimate, but it cannot rightfully be resolved by private or sectional violence. Violence may be applied only by the central political authority, and those to whom it delegates this right. Among the various sanctions of the maintenance of order, the ultimate one – force – may be applied only by one special, clearly identified and well centralized disciplined agency within society. That agency or group of agencies *is* the state.

The idea enshrined in this definition corresponds fairly well with the moral intuitions of many, probably most, members of modern societies. Nevertheless, it is not entirely satisfactory. There are 'states' – or, at any rate, institutions which we would normally be inclined to call by that name – which do not monopolize legitimate violence within the territory which they more or less effectively control. A feudal state does not necessarily object to private wars between its fief-holders, provided they also fulfil their obligations to their overlord; or again, a state counting tribal populations among its subjects does not necessarily object to the institution of the feud, as long as those who indulge in it refrain from endangering neutrals on the public highway or in the market. The Iraqi state, under British tutelage after the First World War, tolerated tribal raids, provided the raiders dutifully reported at the nearest police station before and after the expedition, leaving an orderly bureaucratic record of slain and booty. In brief, there are states which lack either the will or the means to enforce their monopoly of legitimate violence, and which nonetheless remain, in many respects, recognizable 'states'.

Weber's underlying principle does, however, seem valid *now*, however strangely ethnocentric it may be as a general definition, with its tacit assumption of the well-centralized Western state. The state constitutes one highly distinctive and important elaboration of the social division of labour. Where there is no division of labour, one cannot even begin to speak of the state. But not any or every specialism makes a state: the state is the specialization and concentration of order maintenance. The 'state' is that institution or set of institutions speci-fically concerned with the enforcement of order (whatever else they may also be concerned with). The state exists where specialized order-enforcing agencies, such as police forces and courts, have separated out from the rest of social life. They *are* the state.

Not all societies are state-endowed. It immediately follows that the problem of nationalism does not arise for stateless societies. If there is no state, one obviously cannot ask whether or not its boundaries are congruent with the limits of nations. If there are no rulers, there being no state, one cannot ask whether they are of the same nation as the ruled. When neither state nor rulers exist, one cannot resent their failure to conform to the requirements of the principle of nationalism. One may perhaps deplore statelessness, but that is another matter. Nationalists have generally fulminated against the distribution of political power and the nature of political boundaries, but they have seldom if ever had occasion to deplore the absence of power and of boundaries altogether. The circum-stances in which nationalism has generally arisen have not normally been those in which the state itself, as such, was lacking, or when its reality was in any serious doubt. The state was only too conspicuously present. It was its bound-aries and/or the distribution of power, and possibly of other advantages, within it which were resented.

This in itself is highly significant. Not only is our definition of nationalism parasitic on a prior and assumed definition of the state: it also seems to be the case that nationalism emerges only in milieux in which the existence of the state is already very much taken for granted. The existence of politically centralized units, and of a moral–political climate in which such centralized units are taken for granted and are treated as normative, is a necessary though by no means a sufficient condition of nationalism.

By way of anticipation, some general historical observations should be made about the state. Mankind has passed through three fundamental stages in its history: the pre-agrarian, the agrarian and the industrial. Hunting and gathering bands were and are too small to allow the kind of political division of labour which constitutes the state; and so, for them, the question of the state, of a stable specialized order-enforcing institution, does not really arise. By contrast, most, but by no means all, agrarian societies have been state-endowed. Some of these states have been strong and some weak, some have been despotic and others law-abiding. They differ a very great deal in their form. The agrarian phase of human history is the period during which, so to speak, the very existence of the state is an option. Moreover, the form of the state is highly variable. During the hunting–gathering stage, the option was not available.

By contrast, in the post-agrarian, industrial age there is, once again, no option; but now the *presence*, not the absence of the state is inescapable. Paraphrasing Hegel, once none had the state, then some had it, and finally all have it. The form it takes, of course, still remains variable. There are some traditions of social thought – anarchism, Marxism – which hold that even, or especially, in an industrial order the state is dispensable, at least under favourable conditions or under conditions due to be realized in the fullness of time. There are obvious and powerful reasons for doubting this: industrial societies are enormously large, and depend for the standard of living to which they have become accustomed (or to which they ardently wish to become accustomed) on an unbelievably intricate general division of labour and co-operation. Some of this co-operation might under favourable conditions be spontaneous and need no central sanctions. The idea that all of it could perpetually work in this way, that it could exist without any enforcement and control, puts an intolerable strain on one's credulity.

So the problem of nationalism does not arise when there is no state. It does not follow that the problem of nationalism arises for each and every state. On the contrary, it arises only for *some* states. It remains to be seen which ones do face this problem.

The definition of the nation presents difficulties graver than those attendant on the definition of the state. Although modern man tends to take the centralized state (and, more specifically, the centralized national state) for granted, nevertheless he is capable, with relatively little effort, of seeing its contingency, and of imagining a social situation in which the state is absent. He is quite adept at visualizing the 'state of nature'. An anthropologist can explain to him that the tribe is not necessarily a state writ small, and that forms of tribal organization exist which can be described as stateless. By contrast, the idea of a man without a nation seems to impose a far greater strain on the modern imagination....

A man must have a nationality as he must have a nose and two ears; a deficiency in any of these particulars is not inconceivable and does from time to time occur, but only as a result of some disaster, and it is itself a disaster of a kind. All this seems obvious, though, alas, it is not true. But that it should have come to *seem* so very obviously true is indeed an aspect, or perhaps the very core, of the problem of nationalism. Having a nation is not an inherent attribute of humanity, but it has now come to appear as such.

In fact, nations, like states, are a contingency, and not a universal necessity. Neither nations nor states exist at all times and in all circumstances. Moreover, nations and states are not the *same* contingency. Nationalism holds that they were destined for each other; that either without the other is incomplete, and constitutes a tragedy. But before they could become intended for each other, each of them had to emerge, and their emergence was independent and contingent. The state has certainly emerged without the help of the nation. Some nations have certainly emerged without the blessings of their own state. It is more debatable whether the normative idea of the nation, in its modern sense, did not presuppose the prior existence of the state.

What then is this contingent, but in our age seemingly universal and normative, idea of the nation? Discussion of two very makeshift, temporary definitions will help to pinpoint this elusive concept.

1   Two men are of the same nation if and only if they share the same culture, where culture in turn means a system of ideas and signs and associations and ways of behaving and communicating.

2   Two men are of the same nation if and only if they *recognize* each other as belonging to the same nation. In other words, *nations maketh man*; nations are

the artefacts of men's convictions and loyalties and solidarities. A mere category of persons (say, occupants of a given territory, or speakers of a given language, for example) becomes a nation if and when the members of the category firmly recognize certain mutual rights and duties to each other in virtue of their shared membership of it. It is their recognition of each other as fellows of this kind which turns them into a nation, and not the other shared attributes, whatever they might be, which separate that category from non-members.

Part 7

Organizations and Bureaucracy

Large-scale organizations are a pervasive phenomenon in the modern world. Modern organizations, as Max Weber pointed out, tend to be bureaucratic in nature: they are structured in terms of formal rules, a hierarchy of offices, and regularized duties which 'officials' are called upon to perform. In reading 28, Henry Jacoby considers how far bureaucracy generates administrative effectiveness and whether or not bureaucratic systems are compatible with democratic involvement. Bureaucratic systems often develop nominally to serve the interests of underprivileged groups – such as trade unions – yet bureaucratic organization tends to centralize power and administrative responsibility at the top.

Organizations always involve a formal designation of tasks, but in all organizational settings other factors are also influential, including informal social relations, expressive actions, humour and laughter. Gary Alan Fine (reading 29) shows that having fun is not necessarily incompatible with bureaucratic procedures and may indeed on occasion be the means of carrying them out in an efficient fashion. Studying the work environment of a restaurant, he tries to show that playful activity, a constant part of the life of the organization, reinforces work solidarity and satisfaction in various specific ways.

A restaurant is not, in Lewis Coser's terms (reading 30) a 'greedy' organization: those who work in a restaurant typically only spend certain parts of the day and week there. Some organizations, however – greedy institutions – claim exceptional loyalty and commitment on the part of their members. Since greedy organizations tend to pressurize individuals to weaken ties to all other groups, they can cause major strains and conflicts for their members. An example would be the tensions between the obligations members of the armed forces have towards the military, as contrasted with those they have towards their families, discussed in the concluding reading (Mady Wechsler Segal, 'The Military and the Family', reading 32 in part 8).

28 Henry Jacoby

The Bureaucratization of the World

Bureaucracy is not an unambiguous term. Although it generally refers to a group of people concerned with organization and management, its usage is often limited to government officials. The term has also acquired a derogatory meaning which points to such shortcomings in the performance of administration as slowness and cumbersomeness.

There are many variants among bureaucracies, especially state bureaucracies. They can conduct themselves rationally or arbitrarily. Their performance can be efficient and precise, or protracted and inefficient. A bureaucracy may be characterized by honesty or corruption. Its political orientation and social origin, as well as its status in society, can vary greatly. It may function collectively, even if its hierarchical structure permits only a very uneven distribution of authority, to the point where it may be non-existent among the lower echelons. Bureaucracy can serve as the mere tool of authority and still be significant enough to influence those in control.

Differences exist not only between the upper and lower levels within bureaucracies, but also between specialists and administrators.

The bureaucratic *concept*, however, refers to a system of social interaction which forms in all varieties of bureaucracies and bureaucratic organizations. Franz Neumann has provided a detailed analysis: 'Bureaucratization, correctly understood, is a process operating in both public and private spheres, in the state as well as in society. It means that human relations lose their directness and become mediated relations in which third parties, public or private functionaries seated more or less securely in power, authoritatively prescribe the behavior of man.'[1] This has become a comprehensive process in modern society. Neumann points out that a gigantic organizational network surrounds almost every aspect of human life, even including culture. Sports and the arts are also administered by professional bureaus, and special departments in the mass-media system figure out how much light and how much classical music, how many lectures and how much news are to be presented to the public.

The *real problem* posed by the bureaucratic process is its relationship to democratic values. However, the public pays much more attention to the way in which the bureaucracy functions than to its actual influence. Perhaps it is precisely this fact which shows to what extent the process has succeeded. The negative factors in the bureaucratic system are seen in the way it conducts its business, which has been described as 'the disease of bureaucracy'. The fundamental difficulty does not stem from its 'superfluous', but from its 'indispensable' aspects. Bureaucracy holds disintegrated society together. The nature and history of the bureaucratic system have to be studied so we can understand the interpersonal relationships which it forms. After all, the administrative bureaucracy itself complains about its 'superfluous' aspects and the 'disease of bureaucracy' and wants to rationalize its organization.

Whether the 'disease' is curable, whether it is part of the system, whether indispensable bureaucracy must always include superfluous administration, are by no means unimportant questions to which varied answers can be given. 'Parkinson's Law' shows how the bureaucratic balloon is permanently inflated, how it wastes funds and promotes the selection of mediocrities. There is no lack of examples. However, there is also evidence that modern offices function more efficiently than they did in the past; electronic machinery has replaced red tape, and the efficiency of many skilled administrative officials is noticeable. It has been shown that bureaucratic business management is not a uniform phenomenon, but is subject to many influences. Government and industrial bureaucracies, and those of the unions and political parties, react differently and reveal variants in their conduct which have provided the topics of innumerable individual investigations. What is apparently evident in intrabureaucratic relationships, and in relationships between administrators and those they administer, is considerable 'dysfunction'. 'Dysfunction' is inherent in bureaucracy, but it is only one of the many difficulties connected with it, and not even the essential one.

The problem presented by bureaucratization in social interaction is only seen clearly when the former is considered in the light of its irrevocability:

> Bureaucratic organization is a first-class sociological work of art which has been fashioned over many centuries. It is an illusion to maintain that it could be suppressed and replaced by 'self-government.' The contrary is proved by 'communal bureaucracy'... [and] the bureaucracy of political parties in all countries possessing a parliamentary and democratic system. It is the indispensable machinery of an official administration which orients itself toward formal law. Its systematic structure, the way in which it turns all that is personal into something functional, is a necessary attendant symptom of the inevitable process by which it becomes a large-scale enterprise.[2]

From an historical as well as objective point of view, the expansion of government activity and the centralization of its social responsibilities and actions must be considered particularly problematical since they concern society as a whole. These special problems were already touched upon by Wilhelm von Humboldt in 1792:

> It has been from time to time disputed by publicists whether the State should provide only for the security, or for the whole physical and moral well-being of the nation. Concern for the freedom of private life has in general led to the former proposition; while the idea that the State can give something more than mere security, and that the injurious limitation of liberty, although a possible, is not an essential, consequence of such a policy, has influenced the latter theory. And this belief has undoubtedly prevailed, not only in political theory, but in actual practice. This is shown in most of the systems of political jurisprudence, in the more recent philosophical codes, and in the history of constitutions generally. Agriculture, handicrafts, industry of all kinds, business, the arts and learning itself, all receive life and direction from the State.[3]

The conclusion reached in the last sentence is particularly surprising when one considers to what extent the state has increased its functions since then. However, in view of the new areas which fall to the responsibility of government, the problem as described by von Humboldt must be dealt with on quite a different level. The basis for extensive changes in the social structure is being established in the area of industry in particular, where the 'new industrial state' must constantly submit to new regulations. Schumpeter has already pointed out that capitalist economics invariably tend towards a socialist model. But he could not conceive of a socialist organization except as an all-embracing bureaucratic apparatus. Schumpeter was not unaware of the problems presented by a comprehensive bureaucracy, nor of the 'diseases' which accompany administrative activity. Yet he maintained of the latter: 'The elimination of the profit and loss motive that is often exclusively stressed is not the essential point. Moreover, responsibility in the sense of having to pay for one's mistakes with one's own money is passing anyhow...and the kind of responsibility that exists in the large-scale corporation could no doubt be reproduced in a socialist society.' Schumpeter also recommended the expansion of bureaucratic activity:

It is not enough that the bureaucracy should be efficient in current administration and competent to give advice. It must also be strong enough to guide and, if need be, to instruct the politicians who head the ministries. In order to be able to do this it must be in a position to evolve principles of its own and sufficiently independent to assert them. It must be a power in its own right. This amounts to saying that in fact though not in form appointment, tenure and promotion must depend largely – within civil service rules that politicians hesitate to violate – on its own corporate opinion in spite of all the clamor that is sure to arise whenever politicians or the public find themselves crossed by it as they frequently must.[4]

The danger envisaged by Schumpeter is not the limitation of political activities by bureaucracy but the way in which politicians might jeopardize a true understanding of administrative relationships. Inefficient political interference could endanger the results of long-term administrative labour. The official who identifies with his particular task might be forced into defending himself against political showmanship. The administration is often better able to recognize and to represent society's needs in the face of the egoistic interests of pressure groups and the indifference of all those who do not consider themselves concerned.

It is not possible to deal with the heart of the problem until this reality has been acknowledged. As Schumpeter phrases it, 'recognition of the inevitability of comprehensive bureaucratization does not solve the problems that arise out of it.'[5] The accumulation of power is promoted by the fact that a growing number of functions have become centralized. There is no guarantee that this power is administered in the interests of one and all. But this is only part of the difficulty. The conflict between reality and democratic values cannot be seen in its entirety until one takes into account the reaction of those who are administered to the continuous accumulation of central power and responsibility – an accumulation which renders them impotent and undermines their responsibility.

29   Gary Alan Fine

Letting off Steam? Redefining a Restaurant's Work Environment

In much sociocultural analysis the concept of play has been posed in opposition to that of work. Play is conceived as being that which work is not. Perhaps the critical distinction in the definitions is that, whereas work is seen as motivated by external rewards (often in the form of monetary payment), play is defined as activity that is intrinsically motivated. Work is seen as being explicitly goal- or task-directed, whereas play is emergent and hence has no necessary direction.

Further, work is often depicted as forced, whereas play is considered purely voluntary. I argue that it is unnecessary to establish this rigid dichotomy between these two categories of human activity.

The world of work is also a world of play and expressive behaviour. As a long series of ethnographies of work environments have shown, there are few, if any, occupations that can be characterized by continuous grimness. In most occupational settings – factories, coal-mines, hospitals or bakeries – the opportunities for play are abundant. Fun is part of the successful completion of tasks and is necessary for the creation and maintenance of a sense of satisfaction. The now classic time-and-motion studies that suggested that a work organization should be based on efficiency of motion do not, in fact, produce maximal efficiency *in human terms*. The social demands of workers take precedence over considerations of logic.

Most writers on organization theory now dismiss time–motion studies, at least in their classic form, in part because they don't allow for the display of expressive behaviour; in its place they have postulated a view that expressive behaviour is necessary to 'let off steam'. This view suggests that play in itself doesn't directly accomplish the doing of tasks; rather, its role is to permit work by providing a safety valve or outlet for energy that otherwise would negatively affect production. This is essentially a hydraulic model of behaviour, which suggests the successful worker will be the worker who lacks hostility towards what he is doing (since hostility is drained by the play).

An alternative approach I shall emphasize is that the work culture may directly contribute to productivity by supporting values that, in turn, support the conditions of work. The first approach sees play as essentially opposed to work, while the second sees work and play as expressing the same value system and as promoting the adjustment of the worker to his or her environment. Work and play are mutually reinforcing. Although joking or other play time formally represents time away from work, in practice it contributes to increased satisfaction and productivity by changing the definition of the work environment from an institution of coercive control to an arena in which the workers have some measure of control over the conditions of their own employment.

In this essay I focus my discussion of the world of work on one particular industry – restaurants (sometimes known generically as 'the hospitality industry'). I have conducted intensive ethnographic observation and in-depth interviews in the kitchens and with the staffs of three restaurants in the Twin Cities metropolitan area. The first, La Pomme de Terre, is an *haute cuisine* French restaurant, by all accounts one of the best and most creative restaurants in the Upper Midwest. The second restaurant, The Owl's Nest, a multi-year Holiday Award winner, is a continental-style restaurant, best known for its fresh fish. Its primary clientele are wealthy businessmen. The third restaurant is Stan's Steakhouse. Stan's is family-owned and operated. It is particularly well known in its part of the Twin Cities, an area that is not acclaimed for the quality of its restaurants. Stan's has received metropolitan awards for the quality of its beef.

In terms of organizational structure these three restaurants are quite similar. In all three the owner and/or his children manage the restaurant and are on the premises virtually very day. Each restaurant has a head chef, two or three other cooks working every evening and a crew of waiters (in the case of La Pomme de Terre), waitresses (Stan's) or both (The Owl's Nest). All can be classified as small restaurants in terms of the size of their staff, although they differ in their customer turnover. On an average Saturday night Stan's serves 500 customers, The Owl's Nest 150, and La Pomme de Terre 75.

Every occupation must deal with particular problems that derive from the specific conditions of work, and each develops its own solutions. For cooks, one of the major strains they must face is working under intense pressure for a relatively short part of the day, and having relatively little pressure for the rest of the time. Typically the period 6.30 until 8.30 in the evening will be hectic in the kitchen, and the rest of the time from 3.00 until 11.00 will be much more leisurely. This provides the opportunity for cooks to prepare for their 'real work', and time for them to relax after the pressure. This temporal organization of the work day structures the location of play for the workers. Up until the rush, work is leisurely, mostly consisting of preparing everything for the busy period so that work can proceed smoothly and efficiently. Unless there is a large party coming in that night, or a huge number of reservations, or a shortage of cooks, the cooks know they can complete their tasks with time to spare, and so can joke with each other, take breaks, or talk about personal matters while they work. During the rush the focus is much more task-oriented; cooks rarely take breaks or leave the kitchen, and most talk is oriented to the work at hand. By the time the rush has ended (either with all the customers seated or with few more reservations on the books), joking can resume. It is particularly in this period after the rush that joking and playing will occur and cooks will take lengthy breaks. Clean-up need not end at a particular time, so cooks don't feel they are on a schedule after the rush.

I suggest that play in the kitchen reinforces kitchen work in four ways. First, kitchen play fits into the work day in such a way as to diminish the likelihood of boredom. Second, play, like work, builds collective co-operation. Third, the existence of expressive behaviour at work serves to maintain the worker's allegiance to the workplace and prevents turnover. Fourth, one may play at work, and add 'joy' to one's occupational requirements.

Play in the workplace doesn't just happen; rather, it is socially situated. Much play occurs when there is a lull in work. Most cooks agree that they prefer busy nights to slow nights, because slow nights are boring. The hardest part of cooking for many cooks is just standing around doing nothing, waiting for something to happen. It is at this time that cooks will trade jokes or will play pranks on each other. For example, on slow evenings at Stan's, when one of the cooks takes a break and leaves the kitchen, the other cooks will quickly put up a large number of old tickets so it will appear to the returning cook that they were suddenly flooded with orders. At such times, too, cooks play catch with items of food or spike each other's soda with Tabasco sauce. Cooks try a wide variety of entertaining devices to maintain their interest throughout the evening. At busy times such playful activity is not necessary, because the work provides a sufficient challenge for the cook.

From this perspective work and play have a reciprocal relationship, but not a contradictory relationship. Play doesn't let off steam from work, but provides for a continuation of interest.

Play is also found after a long period of intensive work, and here play is used to contrast with the strain that occurred over the evening. The play provides a counterpoint to the hectic activity of work by slowing down the activity – as in jocular discussions about one's female friends, recreational drug or alcohol use, or entertainment preferences. Play can be seen here as a way of providing an alternative to the demanding requirements of cooking.

Several things should be apparent in this discussion of the social and temporal locus of play. First, not all play is identical. Play takes different forms and consequently has different positions in kitchen work. Some play fills slots in which cooks need to be motivated. Other play fills slots in which cooks need to regain their cognitive and affective equilibrium after a long period of rushed activity. However, play always is fitted into one's schedule; that is, play is responsive to the requirements of the work situation. In all three of the work sites examined, work took priority over play, and play did not interfere with work but supported it.

Any efficient work organization relies on the co-operation of its members. Workers are expected to aid each other in the completion of their duties. In each restaurant cooks were willing to help co-workers in the performance of their work roles, and it was common for one cook to ask another to help him do something when that other cook was not busy on a project. In some cases cooks asked their colleagues to take over for them when they wanted a break. In all three restaurants cooks defined themselves as members of a team. However, to think of oneself as a member of a team one must not only have similar work tasks or a similar physical location, but one must also recognize a sense of community.

It is in the construction of a sense of community that play at work is important. In many occupations rituals of initiation occur. In some cases this is a formal initiation, although perhaps more often (as is true in these restaurants) the initiation simply consists of establishing the recognition that one's fellow cook is 'a good guy', can 'take a joke', and can be trusted.[1] In the early days on the job cooks send new workers on mock errands. One cook commented: 'Sometimes when we have a new busboy we tell him to go down and get a can of prunes and we don't have any prunes at all. [Prunes don't come in cans.] We had a busboy and a bartender down there for half an hour looking for them.' It is even better if one can convince a new worker to look for something ridiculous like a left-handed knife or a can of steam. The social importance of these tricks emerges in the reaction of the novice. If he shows that he is a good sport about it, he is accepted. This play serves as a signal that all are willing to give up something of their 'self-image' for the enjoyment of their fellow workers: they have given part of themselves to the organization. They, therefore, can be trusted.

This initiation to the group also ties them to the *goals* of the group. One now can hardly refuse the request of a co-worker. If the workers were alienated strangers, any request for aid could be met by a refusal – it is not the job of the other person to help. But if informal friendly relations have been established, the aid flows naturally through the social network. Thus the co-operation that is cemented in the playful activities of the cooks can be duplicated in their task-orientation to the benefit of organizational efficiency.

Every organization needs the members of its workforce to be loyal to it and to its goals. When the work is not intrinsically interesting and the pay is not high, there exists the potential for alienation from one's employer with detrimental effects on productivity and quality. How can organizations help to increase the likelihood of organizational loyalty? In the last decade, students of organization have discovered the motivating power of corporate culture. Much of the discussion of corporate culture has focused on the imposition of this culture 'from the top down'. In this article I wish to discuss the creation of corporate culture (or 'expressive culture') from 'across'.

I have previously suggested that every small group develops a small-group culture – what I term an 'idioculture'. This is 'a system of knowledge, beliefs, behaviours, and customs shared by members of an interacting group to which members can refer and employ as the basis of further interaction'.[2] This cultural creation was found in each of the restaurants examined. Each restaurant had customs and traditions of its own – after-hours activities, nicknames, rituals or simply ways of doing things that were functionally irrelevant to the task at hand. This culture ties the workers into the organization. In the words of Robert Freed Bales: 'Most small groups develop a subculture that is protective for their members, and is allergic, in some respects, to the culture as a whole ... They [the members] draw a boundary around themselves and resist intrusion.'[3]

These symbols of the idioculture serve as badges of belonging, and even though some forms of expressive behaviour may take time away from the formal requirements of the job, the consequences are sufficient to produce benefits for the organization. One of the important conditions of work is how a person feels about his fellow employees, and expressive culture not only ties one to the organization, but also connects one to one's co-workers. Rarely is cooking a high-paid occupation and the work is often boring and routine, particularly for short-order cooks who do not have much opportunity for creative cookery; yet cooks report that they remain on the job primarily because of their affection for their co-workers. They find the work environment to be pleasant, primarily because of their interpersonal relations and the expressive behaviours that go along with them. The relatively low rate of turnover helps employers' profit, because they do not have to advertise for, or train, new workers, and so the existence of an expressive culture among the workers directly contributes to corporate efficiency.

At two of the restaurants, cooks would occasionally sing together as they prepared the meals. Perhaps this off-key vocalizing was distracting, but it also lightened the mood in the kitchen, and had attendant psychological benefits for the performers. The tradition at two of the restaurants for the staff to form sports teams (outside of work) also contributed to the *esprit de corps* that small organizations need in order to survive. It is my contention that expressive behaviour is not only a means of letting off steam (in a psychological hydraulic model), but that it very directly contributes to the doing of work in the kitchen; hence, playing is not subsidiary to the process of working.

Mihalyi Csikszentmihalyi speaks of the phenomenon of 'flow' that he finds in several intense leisure-time activities.[4] In a state of flow the actor immerses himself fully in the activity without a sense of self-consciousness. One is totally engaged in the action. Such a concept of flow applies most directly to what we call our 'peak experiences' – those components of ourselves that could be considered self-actualizing.

Such a state of flow is not normally considered part of the work experience. However, there were some occasions in restaurant kitchens when something very much like flow seemed to characterize the cooks' activities. This was especially evident in the busiest periods in the restaurants. On those occasions when things go smoothly, cooks may transcend their work roles, feeling that a sense of joy or a 'high' characterizes their actions. As one cook commented, 'I just love the activity ... I concentrate totally, so I don't know how I feel ... It's like another sense takes over.' Mundane experiences are transformed into something resembling joy. The cooks are working very hard and are in constant motion, but while this is occurring they are not conscious of their mounting exhaustion. When everything goes well, the cooks are totally immersed in the requirements of their roles without being aware of them. The restaurant operates like a well-oiled machine. As one cook commented when I asked what constitutes a 'good' day:

> When everyone's working together and you have an awful lot to do. Your time is spent real constructively. You organize it so that everything gets done and everything works smoothly like that. When the restaurant opens, you're ready. You're set up and everyone feels good and everything's done and the restaurant is busy.... That doesn't happen often.

As this cook implies, the joy or flow in one's work is a rather fragile phenomenon. Many things can break the mood. A dish that burns, a customer who sends his food back to the kitchen, or a mistake such as switching around orders can change a 'good' night to one that is disappointing. Yet, there are times in the experience of most cooks during which everything works right, and they feel happy in doing something that would otherwise be tiresome. Of course, after the 'rush' is over, cooks typically find themselves exhausted, and it is at this point that the more overt aspects of play manifest themselves.

This sense of 'joy' or 'flow' in one's work clearly contributes to the smooth working of the kitchen and, as a result, to the efficient operation of the restaurant. Once again we see that expressive activity need not be seen in contradiction to the doing of work requirements but as part of them.

30   Lewis A. Coser

Greedy Institutions

Organized groups are always faced with the problem of how best to harness human energies to their purposes. They must concern themselves with mechanisms which ensure that people will be sufficiently motivated to be loyal even in the face of competing appeals from other sources within the wider social structure.

Such competition for loyalty and commitment is a perennial problem because these are scarce resources. Not only do human beings possess only finite libidinal energies for cathecting social objects, but their resources of time are similarly limited. As a consequence, various groups having a claim on individuals' energies and time compete with one another in the effort to draw as much as they can, within normative limits, from the available pool of resources. The struggle over their allocation is as much a root fact of social life as is the competition among users of scarce resources in economic affairs.

In relatively undifferentiated societies, the claimants on the loyalties of individuals are few, but even there conflict among them over the members' allegiance is the rule rather than the exception....

In the modern world, to use Georg Simmel's terminology, the individual lives at the intersection of many social circles. 'He is determined sociologically in the sense that the groups "intersect" in his person by virtue of his affiliation with them.'[1] Modern man is typically enmeshed in a web of group affiliations and hence subject to the pushes and pulls of many claimants to his commitment.

Lest this description give the impression of a perennial tug of war between all in which the individual, whose energies are claimed from all directions, could hardly survive, it must be added that this multiplicity of claims is patterned and channelled through normative regulations and preferences. Thus, in modern society, for example, the amount of time that an individual legitimately owes to his employer is normatively and even legally established; this makes it possible for him to have time for his family or other non-occupational associations. Similarly, democratic societies limit the areas in which the claims of the state upon the citizen are considered legitimate. In non-totalitarian societies, a distinction is made between the private sphere, in which the state cannot intrude, and a public sphere, in which it can claim the loyalty of the citizen. Thus, a wife cannot be made to testify against her husband, due to the assumption that loyalty to her spouse is to be given preference over her loyalty to the state and its judicial system. Just as in the economic sphere competition between individuals and groups is subject to normative and legal limitation, so in this respect also no society could exist without normative restrictions on the competition for the loyalty of individuals.

Modern non-totalitarian societies typically come to terms with such competing demands on individuals through a structural arrangement by which these individuals, far from being fully immersed in a particular subsystem, are in fact segmentally engaged in a variety of social circles, none of which should demand exclusive loyalty. People are expected to play many roles on many stages, thus parcelling out their available energies so that they can play many games. Their multi-faceted involvements with a plurality of role partners, though possibly often resulting in role conflicts, are not likely to present insoluble dilemmas as long as none of the claimants to the individual's commitments makes totalistic claims; as long, in other words, as all of them are content with controlling only a segment – large though it may be – of the personality. To put the matter a little differently, the segmental structure of a society is viable to the extent that concomitant patterns of normative priorities assign the claims for loyalty in such a way that little choice has to be made by the individuals concerned.

As the modern world slowly emerged from the middle ages, norms gradually evolved for people's adjustment to the complexity of modern life styles. As a rule, in the urban and industrial world (except for totalitarian countries), each person belongs to a variety of groups and circles all of which claim allegiance while none makes exclusive demands on commitments.

When the child emerges from the protective circle of the family, he slowly learns to participate in the world of the school and the peer group. Such participation may at times conflict with obligations to the family but it usually does not, since normally neither group will require exclusive loyalty. As the life career of the mature person begins to take shape during and especially after the groping of adolescence, he becomes involved in a variety of circles that correspond to his various status positions in the world at large. He is a father, an employee, a trade unionist and a church member, and he learns to navigate, as it were, among the various obligations that these different roles impose and require. The demands of competing claims to allegiance are handled in such a way that they can be reconciled with each other, and this is feasible because modern social institutions tend to make only limited demands on the person. The multiple obligations of modern men, though they may in concrete fact lead to conflicts among various status positions, are nevertheless of such a nature that they can be composed by the person, even though often at the price of significant compromise and painful adjustment. During the process of social differentiation, tensions and conflicts develop precisely where a new normative pattern for differential allocation of time and energy has not yet been established. When compulsory public education was established, for example, farmers protested that they had a right to the full-time labour of their children. Today, there is no choice in the matter of whether children should leave the home for school in the morning.

Yet the modern world, just like the world of tradition, also continues to spawn organizations and groups which, in contradistinction to the prevailing principle, make total claims on their members and which attempt to encompass within their circle the whole personality. These might be called *greedy institutions*, in so far as they seek exclusive and undivided loyalty and they attempt to reduce the claims of competing roles and status positions on those they wish to encompass within their boundaries. Their demands on the person are omnivorous.

Such organizations may, for example, as does the Catholic Church, require celibacy of their priests, so as effectively to minimize the divisive pull of family obligations. They may, as in the case of utopian communities, attempt to counteract tendencies towards 'singularization' or 'particularization' by disapproving of dyadic attachments which have the potential of withdrawing energy and affect from the community. They may, as in monastic and utopian communities, erect strong boundaries between insiders and outsiders so as to hold the insider in close bonds to the community to which he owes total loyalty. They may, as in the case of the family, require that the wife be always available to cater to all its needs.

Examples of such totalistic claims abound in history. They range from the demands of charismatic leaders of new religious communities – as in St Luke's account of Jesus' appeal: 'If any man come to me, and hate not his father, and mother, and wife, and children, and brethren, and sisters, yea, and his own life also, he cannot be my disciple' – to the well-known claims for allegiance of totalitarian ideologies in the modern age, as in the recent Chinese pronouncements about the importance of the thought of Chairman Mao in even the most private and apolitical spheres of daily life.

Greedy institutions need to be distinguished from what Erving Goffman has called 'total institutions'. Goffman uses this term to characterize institutions whose encompassing character is symbolized 'by the barrier to social intercourse with the outside and to departure that is often built right into the physical plant, such as locked doors, high walls, barbed wire, cliffs, water, forests, or moors'.[2] Among the several types of such institutions Goffman lists homes for the aged and the infirm, mental hospitals, gaols, concentration camps, army barracks and boarding schools. He argues further that it is a basic social arrangement in modern society that individuals tend to 'sleep, play, and work in different places with different co-participants, under different authorities, and without an overall rational plan', while 'the central feature of total institutions can be described as a breakdown of the barriers ordinarily separating these three spheres of life'.[3]

There are evident overlaps between 'total' and 'greedy' institutions, yet these terms denote basically different social phenomena. Goffman focuses on physical arrangements separating the 'inmate' from the outside world, while I shall show that greedy institutions, though they may in some cases utilize the device of physical isolation, tend to rely mainly on non-physical mechanisms to separate the insider from the outsider and to erect symbolic boundaries between them. The celibate servants of the Church, or the Court Jew serving a German prince with his whole person, are not physically separated from the rest of the population with which they are, on the contrary, engaged in continuous social intercourse. They are nevertheless socially distant from the ordinary run of citizens because of the nature of their statuses and prerogatives.

Nor are greedy institutions typically marked by external coercion. On the contrary, they tend to rely on voluntary compliance and to evolve means of activating loyalty and commitment. The monk or the Bolshevik, the Jesuit or the sectarian have·chosen a way of life in which they engage themselves totally even though they may be subject to rigid social controls, and most women accept the mandate of completely committing themselves to their families. Greedy institutions aim at maximizing assent to their styles of life by appearing highly desirable to the participants.

Greedy institutions are characterized by the fact that they exercise pressures on component individuals to weaken their ties, or not to form any ties, with other institutions or persons that might make claims that conflict with their own demands. Merton's work on role-sets helps us to understand the manner in which this is being accomplished.[4] He deals with the structural circumstance that each social status an individual occupies involves not a single role, but an array of role relationships. For example, the status of schoolteacher involves him or her not only with students but with a whole distinct role-set, of colleagues, principal, superintendent and students' parents. Similarly, people occupy not just one status, but a complex of distinct status positions. For example, they are at the same time placed in the stratification system, the marital order, the division of labour, the religious order. Expectations emanating from different role partners or from various status partners may be incompatible or conflicting. The consequences of this could be highly dysfunctional. However, there are mechanisms available that make it possible for the status occupant to articulate his role or status by assigning priorities to certain behaviours at given times.

One such mechanism consists of the fact that a status-occupant's behaviour is not observable by all his role partners or status partners at the same time. His periodic insulation from their observability, and, as a corollary, the fact that he does not interact with all of them at the same time, reduces the burden of their contradictory expectations.

In greedy institutions, conflicts arising from contradictory expectations are being effectively minimized because outside role partners have, so to speak, been surgically removed or because their number has been sharply limited. These institutions concentrate the commitment of all of their members, or of selected members, in one overall status and its associated central role relationships. Being insulated from competing relationships, and from competing anchors for their social identity, these selected status occupants find their identity anchored in the symbolic universe of the restricted role-set of the greedy institution....

[There exist] structural conditions that favour the recruitment and use of servants of rule who are totally beholden to the ruler because they lack roots in the society at large. Cases in point are heads of non-familistic organizations who attempt to destroy all family and sexual, as well as local, attachments of their devoted servants so as to monopolize their energies and interests. The phenomenon of *political eunuchism* in various oriental empires is grounded in mechanisms by which total allegiance to the ruler could be assured through the eunuch's effective exclusion from kinship and sexual involvement.

Even if they are permitted sexual involvements and family attachments, persons who are socially uprooted can serve powerful or power-hungry rulers in essentially similar ways. As aliens who are distant from the population at large and hence unable to build enduring ties to it, they can serve as ideal servants to rulers who wish to minimize their dependence on other power centres, be they nobles, estates, guilds or bureaucratic bodies. Court Jews in seventeenth- and eighteenth-century Germany, and converted Christians at the court and in the armed forces of the Ottoman Empire, are two types from among many.

The use of aliens as instruments of rule has been extremely widespread in history. The Greeks were used by the Romans as administrators and counsellors; Peter the Great reformed the Russian empire with the help of foreign experts; the British used Tikhs and Gurkhas as choice military troops in India; Jews served in the courts of Babylon and later in Spanish Christian courts; and alien mercenaries or tax-collectors served as the mainstay of rule in a great variety of historical constellations. A vivid description of the uses of ethnically German officials in the Hungarian portion of the Hapsburg empire bears quoting at some length, since it vividly exemplifies the general uses of aliens as servants of the powers to be.

> These district officials, who were combed out of the German and Bohemian crown land offices and spread over the Empire, were loyal, honest, tyrannical, and in their small way efficient. They would be sent down to some little backward village in Hungary to teach an almost illiterate staff the rudiments of official paper work. They struggled to keep their tax collecting and recruiting from falling in arrears. They labored in the midst of hostility, suspicion, and incompetence, for the displaced aristocrats whose functions they had usurped despised them as parvenus, and the population detested them as foreign meddlers. Often they were ignorant of the language of the district to which they were sent. The minister of interior kept a firm hand on them, prescribing their clothes, and even the cut of their beards. The type was not peculiar to the Hapsburg Monarchy; it was the type of servant to which the modern state inevitably resorted whenever it could not entrust local government to the free action of the residents of a district. Wherever, as in Schleswig where Danes ruled Germans, or in Hungary where Germans ruled Magyars, a language barrier intervened between the official and the populace, the hard mechanical character of the system was seen at its worst.[5]

Such uses of aliens need not be limited to political administration of nations by their rulers. In the novel (and movie) *The Godfather*, the trusted adviser of Don Vito Corleone (the Godfather) is an Irish foundling who is completely isolated and without a future in the Mafia because he is not a Sicilian, and is similarly estranged from respectable American society because of his close association with the underworld.

Though not specifically dealing with aliens as servants of rule, Max Weber nevertheless highlighted the sociological reasons for the frequent recourse of rulers to their services when he wrote:

> The recruitment of officials from among the propertyless strata increases the power of the ruler. Only officials who belong to a socially influential stratum which the monarch believes to have to take into account as support of his person . . . can permanently and completely paralyze the substance of his will.[6]

The propertyless are more pliable instruments than those who own property or are otherwise men of substance. It follows that men who are complete aliens in the lands they serve are even more unlikely to challenge the powers of the ruler and are hence even more suitable instruments for him. When Alessandro de Medici and his successor Cosimo I transformed Renaissance Florence from a patrician republic into a dukedom, they successfully bypassed and controlled the previously powerful patrician families which they had defeated but not eliminated by staffing a whole new set of political and administrative offices predominantly with foreigners.

Generally, rulers are especially likely to want to rely on foreigners when there exist rival forces in competing centres of power. Official mistresses at the court of France in the age of Louis XIV and Louis XV were at times used by their master as instruments of rule in situations in which they feared the emergence of rival centres of power. Such mistresses were used for political rule only if they came from lower social strata. In this way, the danger of their gaining independent power for their kinsmen and thus to rival the power of the King was minimized. The mistresses could become an instrument of rule only to the extent that they were 'alien' to the dominant social strata of the kingdom.

Part 8

Military Power and War

In spite of the obvious influence of military power and war upon patterns of social development, it is only in fairly recent years that sociologists have attempted to come to terms with them. War (defined as the actual engagement of the military in armed confrontations) is an intermittent activity. Military organizations, on the other hand – the armed forces – form more or less permanent parts of modern institutions. Wars have dramatically changed the course of modern history. The impact of the military, however, is not confined to periods of warfare and we have to assess military power as a basic aspect of the distribution of power in modern social systems.

In the first selection in this part (reading 31), Mary Kaldor argues that, when real wars are not being fought, the military conduct 'imaginary wars' with perceived enemies. An 'imaginary war' is a combat fought out in the minds of military strategists rather than in reality. Imaginary wars, nevertheless, help fuel programmes of military development and spending. The cold war, between the United States and its allies on the one side and the Soviet Union and the countries of Eastern Europe on the other, was a specific form of imaginary war. Elaborating upon this theme, Kaldor is able to question orthodox accounts of the origins of the cold war period.

In reading 32, Segal considers some important aspects of the military as an organization. The military, she points out, is a 'greedy institution', in the sense discussed in part 7. Joining, or being conscripted into, the military means entering an organization within which one risks injury or death and which places a comprehensive set of demands upon the individual. These demands are not limited to the soldier alone but extend to his or her family. In her discussion, Segal analyses the impact of membership of the armed forces upon the family, indicating the strains to which family life can be subjected by greedy institutions.

War has traditionally been a male activity. Women have always been directly involved in war, but mostly 'from the sidelines', as the mothers, daughters or lovers of the men who fight on the battlefield. Increasing gender equality may actively alter the character of military institutions, since such institutions seem plainly to be bastions of 'male values' of dominance and physical force. On the other hand, the outcome may be simply that women increasingly become combat soldiers on a direct par with men, while wars go on much the same as before. In the selection from Jean Elshtain's book *Women and War* (reading 33), the author discusses some instances in which women have directly participated in combat situations.

31   Mary Kaldor

The Debate about the Origins of the Cold War

Most studies of the cold war, in the general sense, are historical and they have been undertaken largely in the United States. They focus on the origins of the cold war in the 1940s, and on the preoccupations, motivations and inclinations of the key political figures of the period. They tend to presuppose a fundamental conflict between East and West and they seem mainly concerned to assign responsibility to one side or the other. Basically, they seem to be interested in the question of who started the cold war.

My concern is somewhat different.... [M]y primary interest is to discover why the fundamental elements of the East–West conflict – the military confrontation, the hostile rhetoric, the games of diplomacy and espionage – persisted for so long, why the structures and institutions established during the cold war period were reproduced, why it was so difficult to introduce policies which departed significantly from those of the cold war period. The starting-point is less important than the question of why it continued.

During the Second World War, rather different political models for the postwar period were envisaged. Roosevelt and the New Dealers espoused an idealist vision of the world expressed in the Atlantic Charter in which global collective security arrangements and international economic liberalism would respect the self-determination of peoples. The European resistance movements hoped for a united socialist Europe which would banish for ever European nationalism and imperial ambitions. And Churchill and Stalin, in their different ways, dreamed of a relative harmony between competing spheres of influence – the American, the Russian and the British empires. None of these aims or anticipations were entirely fulfilled, although the international political system came close to the spheres of influence concept both immediately before the onset of the cold war and during the *détente* period. How was it, therefore, that Truman and Stalin chanced on a formula in the late 1940s that was to dominate international politics, to a greater or lesser degree, up to the present day? ...

The orthodox story largely deals with the early 1940s and Stalin's occupation of Eastern Europe. The orthodox view holds that once the Red Army was installed in these territories there was nothing much the West could do except to halt further expansion. The containment policy, the Marshall Plan, the creation of NATO, it is implied, all follow from Stalin's actions during this earlier period. The orthodox historians emphasize the nature of the Stalinist system and Stalin's basic insecurity and concern with establishing a defensive perimeter, although, of course, defensive obsessions may become expansionary. Less sophisticated variants of the argument that were current at the height of the cold war period in the early 1950s tended to equate all totalitarian systems, and assume that Stalin had a master plan just like Hitler. Some of the orthodox historians also argue that it was Anglo-American tolerance in that early period, and also the failure to open a second front earlier, that allowed Stalin to get away with his sphere of influence in Eastern Europe. Litvinov told Edgar Snow in an interview in 1945: 'Why did you Americans wait until now to begin opposing us in the Balkans and Eastern Europe? ... You should have done this three years ago. Now it's too late and your complaints only arouse suspicion here.'[1]

The revisionist historians tell a different story. They concentrate on the period immediately after the Second World War. They assume that, at that point, some kind of agreement was possible on Germany and on troop withdrawals from Central Europe. However, a series of American actions prevented such an agreement and sealed the division of Europe. These actions included the Marshall Plan, the Truman doctrine of 1947, the West German currency reform and later (after the Berlin blockade) the introduction of the Basic Law which established a West German state, the formation of NATO and the subsequent military build-up. The refusal to provide economic assistance to Eastern Europe, the trade embargoes, the atmosphere of hostility, forced Stalin to tighten his grip on Eastern Europe and adopt an equally hostile posture.

The revisionist historians explain American behaviour in terms of the inner dynamic of American society. William Appleman Williams was the first revisionist historian to relate the cold war to the frontier thesis: the notion that American political cohesion and stability had stemmed from the continuous possibility of westward expansion. When the Pacific Ocean had been reached, the United States economy had to expand overseas and this gave rise to the 'open door' policy of the 1890s. National economic rivalries in the 1930s, especially the creation of the sterling bloc in 1931, resulted in a new version of the open door: the New Dealer's conception of an international liberal economy which was incorporated into the Atlantic Charter and in conditions attached to lend–lease and subsequent American loans. This conception was, however, thwarted by the socialist ideas and policies in Europe in the last years of the war. The next best thing was to push the socialist countries out of the states system so that an international liberal economy could be realized in the rest of the world. The Marshall Plan and high levels of military spending both served to expand American markets.

The post-revisionists cover both the early and late 1940s and assign some degree of responsibility to both sides. They deplore the excessive militarization of the cold war but they see no alternative to the balance of power system and the coexistence of spheres of influence. John Lewis Gaddis elaborates this position in his essay 'The Long Peace' and concludes that historians in the future might look back on 'our era, not as "the Cold War" at all, but rather, like those ages of Metternich and Bismarck, as a rare and fondly remembered "Long Peace"'.[2] And Daniel Yergin ends his fascinating and detailed account of the diplomatic and bureaucratic complexities of the period with a plea for *détente*, in the sense of an uneasy but somewhat less dangerous coexistence, within the framework of the balance of power.[3]

The post-revisionists tend to see a sharp break between Roosevelt and Truman, what Yergin calls the Yalta and Riga axioms. Roosevelt was pursuing at that time a policy of co-operation with Stalin, which involved mutual respect for spheres of influence. Truman broke with that policy and adopted an openly confrontational approach. The post-revisionists seem to imply that the period of the cold war, the period of confrontation, could have been avoided, and that a continuation of Roosevelt's policies would have led to a more or less permanent *détente*.

The post-revisionists consider themselves close to the later views of George Kennan. Kennan, it will be remembered, is generally credited with the doctrine of containment, both as a result of his famous 'long telegram' to Truman in 1946 when he was based in Moscow and the anonymously authored 'X' article which appeared in the journal *Foreign Affairs* in 1947. Kennan has subsequently made it clear that he never meant containment to be interpreted as a military response to the Soviet threat. Indeed, he saw the Soviet threat as political and not military. He supported the Marshall Plan and Truman doctrine (although not the universalist language in which the doctrine was presented) because he believed that economic aid to Western Europe and military aid to Greece and Turkey were ways of combating the internal communist threat. But he was doubtful about the West German currency reform and opposed the formation of NATO because he believed that these would preclude any possibility of agreement about overcoming the division of Europe in the future.

My own view, coming from a European perspective, is that both the orthodox and the revisionist versions are partly right. The orthodox historians were probably right in arguing that once the Soviet Union had occupied Eastern Europe, there was nothing much the West could do to prevent communist takeovers within those countries. Even though bourgeois parties participated in coalition governments up to the winter of 1947–8, the communists from an early date took charge of the ministries of the interior and controlled the police apparatus. They also became, presumably on instructions from Moscow, the most dynamic agents in the process of reconstruction. For a variety of reasons, having to do with the sense of insecurity and paranoia built into the Stalinist system, it was likely that, sooner or later, the Soviet Union would impose more direct forms of control.

On the other hand, there was no obvious reason why the West should have reacted to the occupation of Eastern Europe through such devices as the Truman doctrine or the formation of NATO. The explanation given by the revisionists for the American policy of confrontation is much more convincing. Moreover, the failure to offer economic aid to Eastern Europe on purely humanitarian grounds (without political strings) and the subsequent trade embargoes undoubtedly hastened the process of Stalinization and left less room for possible autonomous development. This was certainly a widespread view in Europe at the time and is illustrated by a Polish joke circulating in the spring of 1947: 'What is it that is red and eats grass?' Answer: 'Us, next year.' Subsequently, the formation of NATO, the military build-up and all the paraphernalia of the early postwar years undoubtedly fed Stalin's megalomania and provided a perfect legitimation for Soviet behaviour in Eastern Europe.

Paradoxically, this view is closer to both the orthodox and revisionist historians than to the post-revisionists. The post-revisionists tend to play down both the logic of the Soviet role in Eastern Europe and the internal dynamic of American policy, even though they ascribe some responsibility to both sides. They would not agree with this assessment, I hasten to add. On the contrary, Gaddis concludes his book on containment with the following reflection:

> George Kennan made the point, in both the Long Telegram and the 'X' article that Soviet foreign policy was the product of internal influence not susceptible to persuasion, manipulation, or even comprehension from outside. Without pushing the point too far, the same might be said of American foreign policy during the thirty years that separated Kennan's appointment as Director of the Policy Planning Staff from Kissinger's retirement as Secretary of State. To a remarkable degree, containment has been a product, not so much of what the Russians have done, or what has happened elsewhere in the world, but of internal forces operating within the United States.[4]

But the whole tenor of Gaddis's argument is that internal pressures somehow thwarted a rational international policy, that they represented a distortion of a policy that was fundamentally directed towards an external reality. This becomes clear in the chapter of his book on *détente* where he notes what he sees as an inconsistency between the behaviour of Nixon and Kissinger towards communist states and their behaviour towards social movements. He seems bemused by the fact that Nixon and Kissinger could tolerate China and the Soviet Union but could not tolerate 'independent Marxism'. They could not allow a victory for Hanoi and hence invaded Cambodia and prolonged the Vietnam war for four years. They could not tolerate the Allende government in Chile, nor the Eurocommunists in Western Europe.

Kennan, in fact, expresses a similar bewilderment:

> The greatest mystery of my own role in Washington in those years, as I see it today, was why so much attention was paid in certain instances, as in the case of the telegram of February 1946 from Moscow, and the X-article, to what I had to say and so little in others. The only answer could be that Washington's reactions were deeply subjective, influenced more by domestic political moods and institutional position.[5]

The puzzle is resolved if we interpret the East–West conflict in a different light. The post-revisionists see the East–West conflict as a traditional great-power conflict of interest, in which irrational behaviour is sometimes induced by domestic pressures. The orthodox historians see American behaviour as a rational response, a great-power response, to Soviet behaviour which stems from the internal nature of the Soviet Union. The revisionists, on the other hand, by and large see Soviet behaviour as a more or less rational response to American behaviour which has to be explained in terms of the inner nature of the American system. The different positions can be expressed schematically, [as in figure 1].

If we were to interpret the East–West conflict in a way that could be fitted into the fourth box, as an *imaginary* conflict which conceals parallel but largely separate internal conflicts, then the paradox of Nixon and Kissinger's behaviour is explained. On this interpretation, cold war and *détente*, conflict and co-operation, are different ways of managing internal conflicts. Kissinger and Nixon *needed détente* precisely in order to manage domestic, that is intra-West, conflicts at less cost.

These different stories about the origins of the cold war stem from different world-views. Inherited language and theory combined with political predispositions define the contours of what is considered appropriate to investigate. Both the orthodox and post-revisionist historians are realists. They see the world largely through a politico-military lens. The orthodox historians are perhaps more idealist. They put more emphasis on democracy and see the totalitarian nature of the Soviet system as an obstacle to global democracy. The post-revisionists are willing to take economic factors into account in so far as they explain divergences from a rational realistic approach, but they do sometimes seem nervous of any argument that might appear to smack of socioeconomic determinism, and this sometimes results in unrealism.

The revisionists, on the other hand, emerge from a Marxian tradition; they see the world through a socioeconomic lens. This is perhaps why their analyses do not seem able to take into account the nature of the Soviet system.

These mindsets inherited from the past imply a certain blindness about aspects of the postwar period. Certain events, phenomena or developments were ignored or bypassed by all these schools of thought. The orthodox and post-revisionist historians often seem unaware of the deep-rooted internal conflicts within the West and in the third world. Kennan himself is remarkably distant and even dismissive about the third world. The revisionist historians, on the other hand, often appear to be apologizing for what happened in Eastern Europe, with the exception of a few Trotskyist accounts. Indeed, on the whole,

Soviet Union reacting to:

		External conflict	Internal conflict
US reacting to:	External conflict	Post-revisionists	Orthodox
	Internal conflict	Revisionists	

Figure 1

reading this literature one is struck by an extraordinary callousness towards the fate of the East European peoples. The orthodox historians and polemicists weep crocodile tears for the peoples of Eastern Europe. They loudly proclaim the injustices of Stalinism. And yet it was Western governments who halted Western credits and imposed trade embargoes in 1947. The East European countries were much poorer than the West European countries and their war devastation was proportionately greater. What is more, it has been calculated that the Soviet Union extracted from these countries – in the form of war reparations, profits from joint stock companies and unfair pricing procedures – an amount which totalled around $14 billion, approximately the same as was spent on Marshall Aid. The post-revisionists, on the other hand, consider that the fate of Eastern Europe is secondary to the concern with great-power stability.

Part of the explanation is the cold war itself. Any well-meaning liberal or socialist who tried to tell the truth about Eastern Europe found himself or herself in the same dilemma as George Kennan in 1945. Kennan, who had lived mostly abroad for many years, expressed in his long telegram a genuine outrage about Stalinism. But that genuine outrage merely fed domestic anti-communism in the United States, and domestic anti-communism is a phenomenon distinct from serious criticism of the Soviet Union. For a long time, the Western situation has been such that any critical statement about Eastern Europe and the Soviet Union was used as a justification or legitimation for the structures of the imaginary war. And yet, such is the ingenuity of the cold war formula, that the failure to be critical, to tell the truth about the East, discredited and marginalized the left.

A similar, perhaps worse, situation pertained in the East, where the threat from imperialism explained repression within. Anyone brave enough to challenge the Western threat hypothesis used to risk the charge of being an agent of imperialism. At the same time, criticism of the West was a kind of collusion with oppression.

The alternative was myopia, assisted by the division of Europe itself. The reduction in trade, the restrictions on travel and so on gave rise to real ignorance about events on the other side of the East–West divide. The actual behaviour of the socialist states did not, in fact, impinge in tangible ways on Western society (and vice versa). The 'other side' became a blank sheet on which to sketch the mirror image of one's own preoccupations. Views about what was happening, on the other hand, tended to be a reflection of domestic political positions rather than descriptions of what was actually happening. And these views inevitably influenced the thinking of historians.

In a sense the imaginary war was, and is even today, so effective because it drew on deeply rooted modes of thought. Realism, Marxism and idealism grew out of the separation of the economic and the political and the civil and the military which accompanied the rise of capitalism and the states system. They provided the language in which different political positions were expressed. While all three modes of thought, but especially Marxism and idealism, had something to offer an analysis of the postwar system, all missed certain novel aspects of the postwar system which required a new language to be understood. Or, [to] put it another way, all three modes of thought gave rise to stories about the cold war that, in effect, upheld the cold war. They both gave rise to good–bad stories which reflected and indeed served to maintain domestic differences. Even though this was far from what was intended, by the revisionists at least, the stories were used to conceal alternative interpretations which might have helped to undermine the cold war.

32   Mady Wechsler Segal

The Military and the Family

The military is unusual in the pattern of demands it makes on service members and their families. Although each specific organizational requirement can be found in other occupations, the military is almost unique in the constellation of requirements. (Perhaps the only other occupation that exerts a similar set of pressures is the foreign service.) Some demands vary in frequency and intensity among and within the services, but over the course of a military career, a family can expect to experience all the specific demands. Characteristics of the lifestyle include risk of injury or death of the service member, geographic mobility, periodic separation of the service member from the rest of the family and residence in foreign countries. Normative pressures are also directly exerted on family members regarding their roles in the military community.

The risk that military personnel will be wounded or killed in the course of their duties is an obvious aspect of the institution's demands. The legitimacy for the institution to place its members at such physical risk is perhaps the greediest aspect of all. Although this risk is, of course, greatest in wartime, even peacetime military training manoeuvres entail risk of injury, and military personnel can be sent at any moment to areas of armed conflict. The effects on military families of the potential for injury and death in both peacetime and wartime are studied relatively seldom. Therefore, we know less about them than about the effects of other military demands on families. The potential for casualty has been studied as a source of stress during certain kinds of separations. Studies of military families conducted during and after the Second World War emphasized the impact of wartime separation. Similarly, recent research has focused on the families of American prisoners of war and those missing in action in Vietnam. There is much less research on the grieving process in families of servicemen who were killed.

The US armed forces periodically transfer personnel to new locations, for new tours of duty as well as for specific types of training. Both frequency of mobility and length of duty tours vary among the services as a function or organizational policy. Results of the 1978–9 DOD Survey of Officers and Enlisted Personnel show that, across all services, '[twenty-nine] percent of surveyed enlisted personnel have been at their present location less than one year, 36 percent between one and two years, and 21 percent between two and three years. Among officers, 33 percent have been at their present location less than one year, 33 percent between one and two years, and 22 percent between two and three years.' Thus, 86 per cent of enlisted personnel and 88 per cent of officers had moved at least once in the three years preceding the survey.

Families of military personnel move less often than the service members themselves, but relocation is still frequent, especially for officers' families. For all personnel, regardless of length of service, the number reporting at least three family moves was 43 per cent for enlisted personnel and 69 per cent for officers; for those with seven to ten years of service, the corresponding figures are 41 per cent and 59 per cent, respectively. For enlisted personnel who had been in the military for more than fourteen years, 9 per cent reported that their spouse and/or children had moved more than nine times; the corresponding figure for officers is 31 per cent.

Although many service members and their spouses view the opportunity to travel as a benefit of military service, geographic mobility is also seen as a hardship that disrupts family life and necessitates adjustments under the best of circumstances. The most obvious component of geographical mobility is the requirement to move frequently. Less obvious and less often discussed in the literature on military families is the first move, which perhaps calls for the greatest adjustment. Whether a service member is already married when entering the military or marries later, the spouse's first residence during military service is usually away from home. This has special implications for young enlisted families because they are likely to be away from their families of origin and long-term friends for the first time. In contrast, junior officers are older and have gone to college, often away from home. Similarly, officers' spouses are more likely than enlisted spouses to have gone to college, though they too (like enlisted spouses) may be away from their extended families for the first time. All, however, are geographically separated from their usual interpersonal networks and sources of social support. If they manage to become integrated into new supportive networks, these relationships are severed when they are required to move to a new location, an experience that is repeated with each additional move.

Besides the social disruption of moving are the other adjustments to a new location. The place is unfamiliar and one must learn one's way around. For families with limited resources and/or small children, this can be especially stressful. Junior enlisted families often must make do without a car or access to public transportation. The physical environment and climate may also be quite different from what the family members are accustomed to. Whatever the type (including size) of the community, some military families will be used to another type. For example, people from rural areas often find large military installations intimidating; they are unaccustomed to living close to neighbours. The regional dialect may also be unfamiliar to them, straining communication with others and possibly making them feel like outsiders.

Moving affects families differently, depending on where they are in the life-cycle. Those early in their military careers (especially enlisted personnel) have the least control over when and where they move. They also have the fewest military institutional supports, such as family housing on post. For children in school, moving disrupts their education; the lack of standardized curricula among states can cause gaps or repetition in what they are taught. Moving can be particularly stressful for teenagers. Adolescence involves a search for personal identity, which usually requires integration into a peer group; moving not only disrupts relationships with peers, but also hampers participation in extra-curricular activities, which may be an important component of the teenager's self-concept.

Moving is especially harmful to spouses' employment possibilities and career continuity. Unemployment rates are substantially higher for military than civilian wives. Family income is lower in military families than in civilian families, due largely to lack of employment opportunities for wives. For officers' wives, who are more likely to be oriented to a career rather than just to employment, geographic mobility interferes with normal career progression. Even if they can find work in their field, they lose seniority when they move. Thus, employment problems create economic hardships for the family and problems of personal identity and worth for the wives.

While the military provides subsidies for moving expenses when a service member is transferred to a new location, these are often inadequate, forcing the family to pay some of the expenses. For both officer and enlisted families, the frequent moves leave them less likely than civilian families to own their own home, which is not only a cultural goal in American society, but also is often a family's major financial asset.

Military demands often necessitate that service members be away from their families. The extent and nature of these requirements vary among and within the services. In peacetime, the most common types of assignments that result in family separations include military schooling, field training, sea duty and un-accompanied tours. On some assignments, the family is allowed to accompany the service member but for various reasons chooses not to. The length of peacetime separations generally varies from a few days to a year; wartime separations can be much longer and indefinite. Certain military units (e.g., submariners and the 82nd Airborne Division) experience frequent or prolonged separations.

Hill reports that 75 per cent of families of career military personnel 'have experienced one or more prolonged periods of father absence'.[1] At the time of the 1978–9 DOD survey, 15 per cent of all married enlisted personnel and 5 per cent of officers reported that they were not accompanied by their families. Among the services, separation rates were lowest in the air force (8 per cent of enlisted, 4 per cent of officers) and highest in the Marine Corps (23 per cent of enlisted, 10 per cent of officers).

These proportions of unaccompanied personnel do not include separations caused by temporary duty and field training. Thus, at any one time, the proportions of service members who are away from their families are much higher. Results of the 1978–9 DOD survey show that, of those with spouses and/or children, 55 per cent of enlisted personnel and 63 per cent of officers had been separated from their families for some time during the year preceding the survey, including 25 per cent of enlisted personnel and 29 per cent of officers who had spent at least five months away from their families.

Some effects of separations on families depend on the type of separation, and others are common to most, if not all. Separations always require adjustments by service members and their spouses and children. Because little attention has been given to service members either in research or in the provision of services, we know less about their reactions to separations than about those of their wives. The most common problems experienced by the latter are loneliness, problems with children, physical illness and loss of their usual social role in the community. The wife is thrust into the role of sole parent. Research on military children with psychological problems has often identified the absence of the father as a contributing factor. Even when families cope well with separation, they still view it as a stressful experience requiring adjustment.

The strains of separation may be especially difficult at certain stages of family life. Newly married couples, who have had less time to solidify their relationships, are vulnerable to the disruption of separation. Men who are away during their wives' pregnancies and/or childbirths miss an important family event. Service members separated from their young children miss periods of rapid growth and change in their children. Similarly, they sometimes are absent for special events in their children's lives (e.g., a child's first step, first word, first ride on a bicycle, birthday; an adolescent's participation in competitive athletic events, graduation from high school). Family separation during children's adolescence may also interfere with parent–child relationships and, therefore, with the adolescents' psychological development. In general, such absences can cause distress for the service family; sometimes family members harbour long-term feelings of resentment and abandonment. . . .

Although the demands on military service members impact indirectly on family life, the military also exercises more direct constraints on families through normative pressures on the behaviour of spouses and children. Family members informally carry the rank of the service member, and behavioural prescriptions vary accordingly. In the traditional institutional military, wives of service personnel 'are expected to initiate and take part in a panoply of social functions and volunteer activities'.[2] Wives of officers and senior non-commissioned officers are integrated into a military social network with clearly defined role obligations and benefits determined by their husbands' ranks and positions.

Wives are socialized through various mechanisms. Traditional expectations are clearly spelled out in handbooks, such as Nancy Shea's *The Army Wife*, which cover military customs, rank courtesy, entertaining, etiquette, calling cards and so on. Wives are informed that their husbands owe their primary loyalty to the military, not the family: 'Early in your new role as an Army wife you must understand that your husband's "duty" will come first – before you, before your children, before his parents, and before his personal desires and ambitions.' Additionally, various social obligations are specified: 'It is every wife's duty not only to join, but to take an active interest in the wives' club on the post where her husband is stationed.'[3] Although some of these prescriptions do not now carry the normative force they have had traditionally, most are still communicated and enforced through informal interpersonal processes.

Family members learn that their behaviour is under scrutiny and that the degree to which it conforms to normative prescriptions can affect the service member's career advancement. Social pressures are especially exerted on officer's wives and, to a lesser extent, on senior NCO wives. For enlisted wives and for military children, there are fewer prescriptive obligations; rather, pressures on them are more proscriptive in nature. Enlisted wives are generally not required to engage in military community activities; they are expected, however, to refrain from 'troublesome' behaviour. Violations of such norms by enlisted wives or by children that come to the attention of military authorities result in pressure on service members to control their families. Such pressures are most likely for families who live on military installations because they are more subject to military control and attention than are those who live off post.

Although military wives may experience normative constraints as pressures, wives also benefit when they are incorporated into the military system. With their roles institutionalized, wives have defined social identities and are more readily integrated into supportive social networks. Such integrative social mechanisms are likely to make important contributions to personal well-being, especially during stressful times such as routine family separations, relocation and combat deployment.

33 Jean Bethke Elshtain

Women and War

We know women can be brave but doubt they can be ruthless. We know those made of sterner stuff will defend themselves and their children in the final redoubt, the home/land itself, but doubt women will march out to a nation's defence. We know women have been in uniform, but think of auxiliary services, support, non-combat duties. We can accept female spies, for that is a sexualized and manipulative activity given our Mata Hari-dominated image of it. We think rarely of women who have actually fought, who have signed up by disguising themselves as men or volunteering their services to resistance and guerrilla movements; and these, too, get slotted as exceptions that prove *the* rule.

The woman fighter is, for us, an identity *in extremis*, not an expectation. Joan of Arc proves this truism through her challenge to it, as her uniqueness as myth and legend in Western history shows. Joan gripped my childhood imagination, but as much for her brave martyrdom as for her warrioring. I suspect it was and has been so for many who have cherished her story in the nearly six centuries since her death. She didn't enter sainthood until this century. Her martyrdom figured centrally. So did her virginity. She may have donned male garb, but she was a *pure* woman whose violence, or leadership of violence, was sanctified officially once others granted her voices the epistemological privilege she gave them . . .

Should the few [female fighters] become not merely many but more – and yet more? Join the ranks of male combatants? In France in the Second World War, '*in the tradition of Joan of Arc*, women led partisan units into battle . . . During the liberation of Paris women fought in the streets with men'.[1] Some 'regulars', members of the armed services, recalling events forty years later, remain vexed by restrictions on what they could and could not do – for example, women pilots for Britain's Air Transport Auxiliary – as others detail wartime camaraderie and equality with men. 'I was considered a comrade, just the same as them,' reports one French Resistance fighter. But she adds that this was true only in the Resistance: the professional army never accepted a woman as equal.

Women have described their wartime activities as personally *liberating* despite pervasive fears and almost paralysing anxieties. None regrets her choice to fight or to be in the thick of the fighting. They would, to the woman, do it all over again. But they hope no one else will have to in the future. All report gaining respect, in the words of a Soviet woman fighter, for 'men – soldiers – born not out of idolatry from afar, but out of sharing this with them, exposed to their weaknesses, seeing how they coped, and showed more human sides . . . They cried, they were frightened, they were upset about killing.' So were the women. But they did what they had made their duty.[2]

Today the United States Marines are training women for combat despite the no-combat rule because women 'can be assigned to support units that might unexpectedly come under attack and since there is always a danger of terrorist activities'. Because women Marines are not assigned to units that are likely to be direct combat units, they are not instructed in 'bayonets, offensive combat formations, offensive techniques of fire', and a few other skills. Women comprise about 5 per cent of the active-duty strength of the Marine Corps.

More interesting than almost-Marines or future conflict is the little-known or remembered story of Soviet women in combat in the Second World War. Soviet women formed the only regular female combat forces during the war, serving as snipers, machine-gunners, artillery women, and tank women. Their peak strength 'was reached at the end of 1943, at which time it was estimated at 800,000 to 1,000,000 or 8 per cent of the total number of military personnel'.[3]

Soviet women formed three women's air regiments and participated in minesweeping actions. Nadya Popova, a Soviet bomber pilot, has recounted her wartime experience in the language of pure war, the classic language of force Clausewitz would recognize and endorse: 'They were destroying us and we were destroying them . . . That is the logic of war . . . I killed many men, but I stayed alive. I was bombing the enemy . . . War requires the ability to kill, among other skills. But I don't think you should equate killing with cruelty. I think the risks we took and the sacrifices we made for each other made us kinder rather than cruel.' Despite this unusual – given the numbers of women involved and the tasks to which they were assigned – experience with women as wartime combatants in regular forces, the Soviets have returned to the standard model, with women designated as non-combatants and vastly outnumbered by the men, fewer than 10,000 by estimate. Just as the Greek term for *courage* is elided to the word for *man*, in Russian *bravery* is by definition masculine. Pointing this out, Shelley Saywell has noted that all the woman fighters she interviewed said that women 'do not belong in combat', and that they took up arms only because Russia faced certain destruction.[4]

Part 9

Race and Ethnicity

Ethnic divisions – divisions between groups based upon differences of culture and/or physical appearance – are frequently linked to profound social tensions and conflicts. There are few multi-cultural societies that have no history of antagonism between the members of their constituent ethnic communities. Lines of opposition and prejudice frequently centre upon 'racial' differences between whites and non-whites. In reading 34, Frances Aboud discusses the development of ethnic awareness in childhood, concentrating upon 'racial' differentiations. She finds that ethnic awareness develops at an early age, although the differentiations that are drawn are complex and shift quite rapidly.

The prejudices which whites have entertained towards blacks have to be understood in a broad historical context. In substantial part their origins are bound up with Western expansionism and colonialism. In reading 35, Paul Gilroy emphasizes that the cultural development of black groups in Britain similarly has to be seen against an international backdrop. Black cultural styles in the United Kingdom form part of a 'diaspora' – a network of cultural connections and oppositions spanning many countries. Blacks in Britain are linked by many ties to blacks elsewhere: something which is also the case, however, Gilroy argues, for whites within British culture.

In reading 36, Ellis Cashmore analyses aspects of discrimination against blacks in British society today. In spite of the barriers which they face, some blacks are successful in business activities. Paradoxically, once they have got to the top, they might find themselves perpetuating forms of discrimination from which they themselves have suffered. A black who becomes a company director is faced with a dilemma. Appointing other blacks as top managers can place business efficiency under pressure, precisely because of the prejudice and discrimination which they are likely to confront in the white population with whom they deal. Appointing whites in recognition of this fact, on the other hand, means consolidating the very barriers which make it difficult for blacks to achieve economic success in the first place.

34   **Frances Aboud**

The Development of Ethnic Awareness and Identification

Applying an ethnic label correctly or identifying which person goes with a given ethnic label is usually measured by showing pictures or dolls from different ethnic groups and asking the child to point to, for example, the white, the black and the Native Indian person. A significant proportion of children make correct identifications at 4 and 5 years of age and this proportion increases with age. By 6 and 7 years the children reach close to 100 per cent accuracy especially when identifying whites and blacks. Two studies found that 3-year-olds were very inaccurate in that less than 25 per cent of them correctly pointed to the white and black when given those labels.[1] However, 4- and 5-year-olds reached close to 75 per cent accuracy or better in both white and black samples. Most of these studies also indicate a significant improvement with age, suggesting that 3 to 5 are the critical years for acquiring this form of label awareness. By improvement, I mean that a larger proportion of children made accurate identifications. Older white and black children of 6, 7 and 8 years usually reached a level of 90 per cent to 100 per cent accuracy.

According to Fox and Jordan, it is also between the ages of 5 and 7 years that white and Chinese Americans acquire the ability to identify Chinese people.[2] However, the identification of Hispanics or Mexican Americans seems to be more difficult for both white and Hispanic children. They improved in accuracy between 4 and 9 years of age and reached asymptote around 9 or 10 years. Similarly, the identification of Native Indians by both white and Indian children was fairly good by 6 years of age but continued to improve during the next 3 years. Presumably the children were using features such as skin colour and hair type for whites and blacks and so found Hispanics, Indians and whites less distinctive in these features than whites and blacks.

The child's awareness of ethnic groupings also takes the form of perceiving certain similarities between members of the same group and perceiving certain differences between members of different groups. Vaughan gave children sets of three pictures of people and asked them which two were similar and different from the third. By 6 years of age the children had reached a level of 68 per cent accuracy and this improved to 83 per cent by 11 years.[3] Similarly, Katz et al. asked children to rate the degree of similarity between pairs of people. At 8 years of age, white and black children rated same-ethnic pairs as more similar than different-ethnic pairs.[4] That is, two whites were perceived as very similar and two blacks were perceived as very similar despite their different facial features or different shades of skin colour. Black children rated two whites as slightly more similar than two blacks. However, a white and a black were always perceived as very different. An interesting result from the Katz et al. study was that in later years, perceptions of dissimilarity were not always based on race but were sometimes based on individual features such as emotional expression. In other words, the children had acquired perceptions of racial similarity and difference by 8 years, had continued to use these perceptions for the following three years, and then abandoned them at 11 or 12 years in favour of perceptions of individual features. Thus, we must keep in mind the fact that racial awareness is often overused when it is first acquired, but that it may lose its salience later on when other types of awareness become more useful.

Another method was used by Aboud and Mitchell to examine how children perceive similarities and differences among different ethnic members.[5] The Native Indian children in this study were first asked to place photographs of men from four different ethnic groups on a similarity board to indicate how similar the men were to themselves. Then a peer from each ethnic group was placed (one at a time) at the end of the board. The children were asked to repeat the rating procedure, this time to indicate how similar the men were to each ethnic peer. The children, who ranged from 6 to 10 years of age, accurately perceived the same-ethnic man as most similar to the peer and the three different-ethnic men as equally dissimilar. On a second task, they were asked whom each ethnic peer would most want as an uncle or brother. It was expected that these kinship selections would closely parallel the similarity ratings as indeed they did.

When white children of the same age were given the same task they made a number of interesting errors. Younger children often made egocentric errors in that they assigned the uncle they wanted, a white uncle, to another ethnic peer. Both younger and older children also made mismatch errors in that they assigned an incorrect non-white uncle to the peer. These mismatches were especially frequent when the peer came from a disliked ethnic group, or when the peer, whether from their own or a disliked group, spoke his non-English native language (e.g., the Asian child spoke Chinese, the Hispanic Spanish and the white French). Perceptions of ethnic similarity or kinship received interference both from the child's own strong preferences and from his or her strong dislikes. It seemed that the older children were able to control their own strong preferences but not their dislikes. The errors for the disliked group were probably due to a lack of knowledge or attention to details. Johnson et al. also found that children possessed least knowledge about national groups that they disliked.[6] This lack of knowledge or attention to detail has manifested itself in several different ways. For example, in the Aboud and Mitchell study, many children chose the wrong, but not their ingroup, ethnic uncle. In the Middleton et al. study, it was reported that British children from 7 to 11 years were egocentric in suggesting that a disliked outgroup peer would prefer a British person.[7] The opposite was found by Genesee et al., where more ingroup preference or ethnocentrism was attributed to disliked nationalities.[8] The egocentric judgements of British children support Piaget's observations of Swiss children, but not the reports of North American children. Perhaps egocentrism persists longer when one is assigning preferences to national groups with whom one has little contact rather than ethnic groups living in one's community.

Vaughan found that children were able to categorize by race and to give appropriate labels to people only after they were relatively accurate at perceiving similarities.[9] He claimed that categorizing and labelling required certain cognitive skills, such as classification, that matured later than perceptual skills. For example, Vaughan asked children to sort white and Maori dolls by race. At 5 and 6 years of age, only 60 per cent of the children could do this correctly. However, by 7 years of age 85 per cent of the children were accurate, and 100 per cent were at 8 years. Similarly, when Vaughan showed them a doll and asked 'What sort of doll is this?' not until 7 years of age did a significant proportion of the children give the correct racial label: 85 per cent at 7 years of age and 100 per cent at 8 years.

Other researchers have used the sorting task but they have used it to measure the salience of race over other cues such as sex and age rather than as a measure of awareness of categories. Madge and Davey presented children with pictures of people who varied in race, sex and age.[10] The children sorted these pictures into two boxes of people who 'belong together'. Almost half the children sorted the people according to race; this was true for white, black and Asian children who ranged from 6 to 10 years of age. Sorting by race increased with age for the white children only. Given Vaughan's data, we cannot be sure whether the younger children sorted by sex or age because they were unable to sort by race or because sex and age were more salient to them. However, the older children were presumably capable of sorting by any one of the categories but chose race because it was the most salient. We might expect, then, that sorting by race or ethnicity increases from 4 to 7 years as children develop a cognitive awareness of racial categories. Whether it increases or decreases thereafter depends on the other categories available. Relative to sex and age, race remained salient for Davey's children. However, relative to personality or individual features, race became less salient for the white children in Katz et al.'s study.

A more mature form of ethnic awareness involves understanding that race and ethnicity are tied to something deeper than clothing and other superficial features. Adults think of a person's ethnicity as being derived from his or her family background. However, young children are not aware of this deeper meaning of ethnicity; they are fooled by superficial features. For example, not until the age of 9 or 10 do black children seem to be aware that a person remains black even though she puts on white makeup or a blond wig, or even though she may want to be white. This deeper awareness manifests itself in many ways. One of these is constancy or the constant identification of a person's ethnicity despite transformations in superficial features. Aboud examined constancy by showing children a photograph of an Italian Canadian who was labelled as such.[11] Then a sequence of four photos was shown of the Italian Canadian boy donning Native Indian clothing over the top of his ordinary clothes. In the final photo, the boy's appearance had changed except for his face. The children were asked to identify the boy in the final photo. Constancy was said to be present if the child said that he was Italian and not Indian (label), that he was more similar to photos of other Italian children than to photos of Indians (perceived similarity), and that he should be put into the pile of other Italians (categorization). Constancy increased from 5 to 9 years of age but was not really present until 8 years. Most children younger than 8 years thought the boy was Indian.

Furthermore, when asked if the boys in the first and last photos were the same person or two different persons, half the 6-year-olds said they were two different persons. Over 90 per cent of the 7-year-olds knew they were the same boy, but not until a year later did they attain ethnic constancy. Children of 8 years and older were certain that the boy was Italian and not Indian. Consistent with our previous discussion, the two cognitive identifications of labelling and categorization were more difficult than the perceived similarity identification. At 8 years they not only identified the boy as Italian but also inferred that he would prefer an Italian over an Indian playmate. However, although the 8- and 9-year-olds understood that ethnicity was deeper than clothing, they were not able to articulate the reason for this. When asked what makes a person Italian or Indian, only a few mentioned country of birth or family but most did not know.

Another manifestation of children's maturing awareness of ethnicity is that they understand the cause of skin colour. Clark et al. tested the notion that with age children dispense with their early view that skin colour is caused supernaturally or through arbitrary association (e.g. being American or being bad) and begin to understand that it is transmitted via a physical mechanism from parents to children.[12] Children were asked, 'How is it that this person is white . . . this one black?' Their answers were coded in terms of seven levels of understanding the cause of skin colour. Children became aware that there were physical origins of a person's skin colour after the age of 7, though they did not make the link to parents till some time later. Understanding the physical basis of skin colour was acquired after they had mastered conservation. This awareness developed around the same time as identity constancy, measured here as the understanding that kinship remains constant despite a change in age and family size. It is clear, then, that ethnic constancy and a mature understanding of skin colour are later developments and require a fairly mature level of cognitive development. Clark et al. also found that this level of awareness was necessary for the decline in white children's prejudice towards blacks.

35   Paul Gilroy

'There Ain't No Black in the Union Jack'

As black styles, musics, dress, dance, fashion and languages became a determining force shaping the style, music, dress, fashion and language of urban Britain as a whole, blacks have been structured into the mechanisms of this society in a number of different ways. Not all of them are reducible to the disabling effects of racial subordination. This is part of the explanation of how [black] youth cultures became repositories of anti-racist feeling. Blacks born, nurtured and schooled in this country are, in significant measure, British even as their presence redefines the meaning of the term. The language and structures of racial politics, locked as they are into a circular journey between immigration as problem and repatriation as solution, prevent this from being seen. Yet recognizing it and grasping its significance is essential to the development of anti-racism in general and in particular for understanding the social movements for racial equality that helped to create the space in which 'youth culture' could form. The contingent and partial belonging to Britain which blacks enjoy, their ambiguous assimilation, must be examined in detail for it is closely associated with specific forms of exclusion. If we are to comprehend the cultural dynamics of 'race' we must be able to identify its limits. This, in turn, necessitates consideration of how blacks define and represent themselves in a complex combination of resistances and negotiations, which does far more than provide a direct answer to the brutal forms in which racial subordination is imposed.

Black expressive cultures affirm while they protest. The assimilation of blacks is not a process of acculturation but of cultural syncretism. Accordingly, their self-definitions and cultural expressions draw on a plurality of black histories and politics. In the context of modern Britain this has produced a diaspora[1] dimension to black life. Here, non-European traditional elements, mediated by the histories of Afro-America and the Caribbean, have contributed to the formation of new and distinct black cultures amidst the decadent peculiarities of the Welsh, Irish, Scots and English. These non-European elements must be noted and their distinctive resonance must be accounted for. Some derive from the immediate history of empire and colonization in Africa, the Caribbean and the Indian subcontinent from where postwar settlers brought both the methods and the memories of their battles for citizenship, justice and independence. Others create material for the processes of cultural syncretism from extended and still-evolving relationships between the black populations of the overdeveloped world and their siblings in racial subordination elsewhere.

The effects of these ties and the penetration of black forms into the dominant culture mean that it is impossible to theorize black culture in Britain without developing a new perspective on British culture *as a whole*. This must be able to see behind contemporary manifestations into the cultural struggles which characterized the imperial and colonial period. An intricate web of cultural and political connections binds blacks here to blacks elsewhere. At the same time, they are linked into the social relations of this country. Both dimensions have to be examined and the contradictions and continuities which exist between them must be brought out. Analysis must, for example, be able to suggest why Afrika Bambaataa and Jah Shaka, leading representatives of hip-hop and reggae culture respectively, find it appropriate to take the names of African chiefs distinguished in anti-colonial struggle, or why young black people in places as different as Hayes and Harlem choose to style themselves the Zulu nation. Similarly, we must comprehend the cultural and political relationships which have led to Joseph Charles and Rufus Radebe being sentenced to six years' imprisonment in South Africa for singing banned songs written by the Birmingham reggae band Steel Pulse – the same band which performed to London's RAR carnival in 1978.

The social movements which have sprung up in different parts of the world as evidence of African dispersal, imperialism and colonialism have done more than appeal to blacks everywhere in a language which could invite their universal identification. They have communicated directly to blacks and their supporters all over the world asking for concrete help and solidarity in the creation of organizational forms adequate to the pursuit of emancipation, justice and citizenship, internationally as well as within national frameworks. The nineteenth-century English abolitionists who purchased the freedom of Frederick Douglass, the distinguished black activist and writer, were responding to an appeal of this type. The eighteenth-century settlement of Sierra Leone by blacks from England and their white associates and the formation of free black communities in Liberia remain an important testimony to the potency of such requests. The back-to-Africa movements in America, the Caribbean and now Europe, Negritude and the birth of the New Negro in the Harlem Renaissance during the 1920s all provide further illustrations of a multi-faceted desire to overcome the sclerotic confines of the nation state as a precondition of the liberation of blacks everywhere.

Technological developments in the field of communication have, in recent years, encouraged this desire and made it more powerful by fostering a global perspective from the memories of slavery and indenture which are the property of the African diaspora. The soul singers of Afro-America have been able to send 'a letter to their friends' in Africa and elsewhere. The international export of new world black cultures first to whites and then to 'third world' markets in South America and Africa itself has had effects unforeseen by those for whom selling it is nothing other than a means to greater profit. Those cultures, in the form of cultural commodities – books and records – have carried inside them oppositional ideas, ideologies, theologies and philosophies. As black artists have addressed an international audience and blues, gospel, soul and reggae have been consumed in circumstances far removed from those in which they were originally created, new definitions of 'race' have been born. A new structure of cultural exchange has been built up across the imperial networks which once played host to the triangular trade of sugar, slaves and capital. Instead of three nodal points there are now four – the Caribbean, the US, Europe and Africa. The cultural and political expressions of new world blacks have been transferred not just to Europe and Africa but between various parts of the new world itself. By these means Rastafari culture has been carried to locations as diverse as Poland and Polynesia, and hip-hop from Stockholm to Southall.

Analysis of the political dimensions to the expressive culture of black communities in Britain must reckon with their position within international networks. It should begin where fragmented diaspora histories of racial subjectivity combine in unforeseen ways with the edifice of British society and create a complex relationship which has evolved through various stages linked in different ways to the pattern of capitalist development itself.

The modern world-system responsible for the expansion of Europe and consequent dispersal of black slave labourers throughout Europe and the new world was from its inception an international operation. Several scholars have pointed to its uneasy fit into forms of analysis premised on the separation of its economic and cultural subsystems into discrete national units coterminous with nation states.[2] The social structures and processes erected over the productive and distributive relations of this system centred on slavery and plantation society and were reproduced in a variety of different forms across the Americas, generating political antagonisms which were both international and transnational in character. Their contemporary residues, rendered more difficult to perceive by the recent migration of slave descendants into the centres of metropolitan civilization, also exhibit the tendency to transcend a narrowly national focus. Analysis of black politics must, therefore, if it is to be adequate, move beyond the field of inquiry designated by concepts which deny the possibility of common themes, motives and practices within diaspora history. This is where categories formed in the intersection of 'race' and the nation state are themselves exhausted. To put it another way, national units are not the most appropriate basis for studying this history, for the African diaspora's consciousness of itself has been defined in and against constricting national boundaries.

As the international slave system unfolded, so did its antithesis in the form of transnational movements for self-emancipation organized by slaves, ex-slaves and their abolitionist allies. This is not the place to provide a full account of these movements or even of the special place within them occupied by ideas about Africa. However, that continent has been accepted by many, though not all, who inhabit and reproduce the black syncretisms of the overdeveloped world as a homeland even if they do not aspire to a physical return there. Ties of affect and affiliation have been strengthened by knowledge of anti-colonial struggles which have sharpened contemporary understanding of 'race'. These feelings, of being descended from or belonging to Africa and of longing for its liberation from imperialist rule, can be linked loosely by the term 'pan-Africanism'.[3] The term is inadequate as anything other than the most preliminary description, particularly as it can suggest mystical unity outside the process of history or even a common culture or ethnicity which will assert itself regardless of determinate political and economic circumstances. The sense of interconnectedness felt by blacks to which it refers has in some recent manifestations become partially detached from any primary affiliation to Africa and from the aspiration to a homogeneous African culture. Young blacks in Britain, for example, stimulated to riotous protest by the sight of black 'South Africans' stoning apartheid police and moved by scenes of brutality transmitted from that country by satellite, may not feel that shared Africanness is at the root of the empathy they experience. It may be that a common experience of powerlessness somehow transcending history and experienced in *racial* categories; in the antagonism between white and black rather than European and African, is enough to secure affinity between these divergent patterns of subordination. As Ralph Ellison pointed out long ago: 'Since most so-called Negro-cultures outside Africa are necessarily amalgams, it would seem more profitable to stress the term 'culture' and leave the term 'Negro' out of the discussion. It is not culture which binds the people who are of partially African origin now scattered throughout the world but an identity of passions.'[4]

... [These struggles] have, since the very first day that slaves set out across the Atlantic, involved radical passions rooted in distinctly African history, philosophy and religious practice. Passions which have, at strategic moments, challenged the political and moral authority of the capitalist world-system in which the diaspora was created. The ideologies and beliefs of new world blacks exhibit characteristically African conceptions of the relationship between art and life, the sacred and the secular, the spiritual and the material. Traces of these African formulations remain, albeit in displaced and mediated forms, even in the folk philosophies, religion and vernacular arts of black Britain.

36   Ellis Cashmore

Black Entrepreneurs: No More Room at the Top

'I don't believe it's possible to run a successful business unless the *majority* of your senior management is white,' says Ishaq Kassim, managing director of a West Midlands food company. His company turns over about £60.5 million per year and employs about 150 people.

> We have a number of hygiene managers who have to deal with officials from the Department of Health. One of the white managers is quite slack in his standards, but he gets on well with the inspectors when they come to visit our premises. He'll sit down with them and have a drink and we never have a moment of trouble. But with the other manager, this time an Asian guy, who is better and maintains much higher standards, we keep getting hassle from the inspectors. It happens so often that there is only one conclusion. So it makes sense from our point of view to keep a white manager at the front of things.

The efforts of Britain's black bourgeoisie to open up opportunities for other blacks are being undermined by a form of racism that has made them unwilling, though not unwitting, accomplices. This is the unseen discrimination actively practised by other blacks who have moved into positions of economic power, yet find themselves hamstrung, not by people, but by abstract factors with their source in market forces. The result adds new twists to the already perverse logic of racism.

Let us imagine how one facet of it might work. You are a black director of a company that employs 200 people, ten of whom are senior managers. These are charged with the responsibility of negotiating with government bureaucrats. It becomes clear to you that the negotiations are made painfully difficult for your black managers, yet seem to run smoothly for your white managers. Do you: (1) appoint only whites to senior management positions? (2) appoint on merit and risk further complications which may threaten your business? (3) complain to the relevant bureaucracies?

Ishaq Kassim's option, disheartening as it may be, is based on pragmatism. 'I know the problem exactly, but, in a way, it's the same one facing all ethnic businesses that reach a certain level of growth. First and foremost we are in business. We have a sense of responsibility. But we have to keep the business going as efficiently as possible.'

The view is typical of many members of Britain's new black bourgeoisie, a group of Asians and, to a lesser extent, Afro-Caribbeans, who have in recent years made the transition from paid employment or self-employment to the ownership of medium and sometimes large businesses. In building a management structure, they have found that resisting pressures to discriminate against other members of ethnic minorities defies business sense.

Roland Laing, the Caribbean owner of a Surrey nursing home, was prepared to do exactly this.

> I appointed a black male as a matron. It never occurred to me for a second that it might affect the business. It was only brought to my notice at a later stage. But no such thought had entered my mind. In fact *he* suggested that we weren't filling rooms so quickly because of him. If I had suspected that his appointment could have caused the problem, I wouldn't have made it.

In business, the stern Mammon of market forces usually dictates, and finer moral ideals are often sacrificed. 'The alternative is to go under. Then where do you go? Out of business and with no chance of creating any more work opportunities at all for blacks. You have to grin and bear it.' This Afro-Caribbean woman, Fay Warr, owns a specialist recruitment agency in London and screens customers before she sends them along to client companies as job candidates. Her agency keeps a file of clients who have specifically ruled out ethnic-minority candidates. Do they know that she is black herself when they issue their instructions? 'I don't make a point of telling them, if that's what you mean.' Do they change policy when they find out? 'No.' Do they change agencies? 'No, we're too good.'

The hard-nosed approach means that many suitably qualified and proficient job-seekers do not get access to positions in some leading companies. Trite solutions are easy: tell the companies concerned to get lost and threaten to squeal to the Commission for Racial Equality (CRE). This would be a course of action in a perfect world. Business is not so perfect, and many firms are not so strong that they can snub big customers and escape unscathed. The costs of taking a moral stand can be punishing.

Markets are frequently fine-tuned to the requirements of whites, and trying to change them can prove disastrous. Running a London model agency in which half the female models were black was cumbersome to one Afro-Caribbean entrepreneur, trying at that stage to establish himself in a market dominated not only by white agencies but by white models. His decision to rationalize took on an unwholesome racial character when he removed all but two of his black models. Yet the sleeker business drew rewards: the remaining black models' diaries soon filled up, as did those of the rest of the models on his books.

Within a couple of productive years, agent Derek Leigh not only established his business, but diversified into new areas, one of which was publishing. 'I used to get many black girls coming to me and saying, "Can you get me work?" I couldn't get them any.' His attempted solution was to publish his own fashion magazine, using only black models. 'If I could stimulate interest in black models in this country, then I thought it might well lead to more work for them.'

The area of business most susceptible to changing markets is, of course, sales. Not surprisingly, black people have been consciously excluded from sales teams for reasons not so different from those wheeled into play during the 1950s. 'The public doesn't like dealing with black people,' was once a standard rationalization for unequal opportunities, with a little too much truth in it to be totally dismissed.

Twelve years ago, when a then-aspiring insurance company director in Birmingham began to assemble a sales team around him, he was aware that selling policies was an awful struggle for a black person. Chris Martin's awareness came from several years' slog door to door. Much more successful were his sales from what the trade terms 'cold calling': telephoning potential clients and reeling off the sales spiel. But his own venture could not rely on cold calls, so he deliberately hired white sales personnel. Over the years, as his confidence grew, he incorporated more Asians and Afro-Caribbeans into his teams. It was a gradual programme, a microcosm of how many Western societies proceed. His sales force is now divided equally between whites, Asians and Afro-Caribbeans.

Black business owners have one more problem. They have been a much-maligned group at least since 1957, when E Franklin Frazier's book, *Black Bourgeoisie*, set the tone. It was critical of the upwardly mobile blacks' attempts to mimic whites. It also disdained the way in which they cut themselves off from the working-class majority of blacks, on whose lives the black bourgeoisie made no material impact.

Britain's new ethnic elite shows more encouraging signs. Here is a fast-growing class of entrepreneurs, some well established by the turn of the 1980s, others breaking new ground over the past few years in areas traditionally dominated by whites (industrial manufacture, publishing, training, hotels). Feathering one's own nest is obviously a priority of any entrepreneur. But those from ethnic-minority backgrounds see other functions in their remit. A great many wish to become catalysts, facilitating change through personal inspiration or job creation. They do not wish their success to be isolated, leaving the ethnic population to lurch from one fortuitous break to another. Their hope is to plant seeds that reflower seasonally, rather than a freak Thatcherite bloom that might die as suddenly as it was born.

The inspirational role of Asian and Afro-Caribbean entrepreneurs is beyond doubt. Among Asians, the presence of a prospering business class has been a virtually direct stimulus to all manner of endeavour. The waves started by the growing number of young, female, Afro-Caribbean entrepreneurs will be felt by many in years to come. They are inscribing a new template for women from all ethnic backgrounds, and Afro-Caribbeans of both genders.

But their success as inspirators seems unlikely to be matched in job creation. Equal opportunities are upon us. Countless employers augment their job advertisements with statements and many even go through the ritual of ethnic monitoring. If the ethnic composition of a workforce accurately reflects that of the surrounding environment, then everyone is satisfied the policy is working.

Ethnic-minority-owned businesses rarely announce their equal opportunities policies. They see little need. Recruitment is no longer the problem; *advancement* is. Black people are getting in, but not going up. And, while black business owners might like to expose the sham of equal opportunities, they are being pressured into making a Mephistophelean pact with the market. The alternative is to challenge the inequity at every turn and probably go broke in the process. There is nothing new or startling about black people hitting an invisible ceiling once in industry or commerce. It is very commonplace for companies to mystify their promotion arrangements, so that injustice and unfairness [are] covered up. I was recently approached by a large national retail store company to design its equal opportunities (EO) training. The company insisted it had 'no problems' and operated an EO policy; it required specialized training for its 120 store managers. Its ethnic record-keeping did not extend far enough up the hierarchy to include these managers, so that when I asked how many came from ethnic minorities, the personnel director, his deputy and the director of training were at a loss. 'Would I be right in assuming fewer than five?' I enquired, to be answered with three solemn nods. No prizes for guessing the real answer. The company's policy is approved by the CRE.

It is a measure of the persistence of racism that even ethnic employers have not found a resolution to the riddle of how to boost their ethnic colleagues into senior management positions without jeopardizing their enterprise. Racism-by-proxy arrives like an old friend of the family, then surreptitiously wreaks damage. For all the optimism generated by the new black bourgeoisie's glittering success, there remains a forbidding pessimism about its ability to transform particular triumphs into something more resonant for all black people.

Part 10

Intimacy, Marriage and the Family

Among the changes now affecting modern societies few are more profound than those acting to transform the nature of personal life. Over the
past several decades, in virtually all the industrialized countries, divorce
rates have risen sharply, while the proportion of people in the 'orthodox'
family (biological father and mother living with their children in the same
household) has declined very substantially. The family is not disintegrating
and marriage remains a massively popular institution; yet there is a great
deal of experimentation in personal life, and no one can be sure where
patterns of family development will lead in the future.

The first selection in this part, by Lawrence Stone (reading 37) gives
an historical perspective upon marriage and divorce in England. Divorce
has long been possible (although in most periods difficult to obtain) for
aristocratic groups. Procedures for breaking up marriage, although not
formally recognized as divorce, were available to the poor. But for the
mass of the population sandwiched in between, marriage tended to be
an indissoluble union.

Reading 38, by Gwynn Davis and Mervyn Murch, considers the causes
of marriage breakdown in current times. The authors identify several
factors which might underlie high rates of divorce. Possible influences
include a reduction in the stigma associated with divorce; the movement
from marriage as an economic division of labour towards a personal
relationship valued for the intimacy it provides; and the increasing emancipation of women. As the authors point out, the majority of divorce
petitions are now lodged by women rather than men – a reversal of major
proportions, when considered in historical terms.

In spite of growing gender equality, the income of men is on average
much higher than that of women. What impact does this differential have
upon control of finances and patterns of spending within marriage? Jan
Pahl (reading 39) studied the issue by interviewing more than a hundred married couples from varying class backgrounds. She found that the
higher the income group, the more likely the husband is to control the

family finances. Where finances are pooled, women tend to be more responsible for domestic expenses, while husbands are more likely to determine major financial decisions.

The family is often associated in people's minds with a cosy environment of warm domesticity. While the image may frequently be an appropriate one, the family is often the site of violence. Most such violence, although not all, is directed by men against women. As Elizabeth Stanko (reading 40) points out, only a tiny proportion of wife-battering ever comes to the notice of the authorities. The phenomenon is extremely widespread; yet many women, for a mixture of practical and psychological reasons, find that escaping from a violent marriage or relationship is difficult.

The family has always been the main setting of human reproduction. For most of human history, reproduction was a 'natural' process; today, however, it is more and more influenced by modern science and technology. As Michelle Stanworth points out (reading 41), several different types of reproductive technology can be distinguished; all have important implications for the family and marriage, as well as for gender relations more broadly. Modern forms of contraception represent one type of reproductive technology; other types include those concerned with labour and childbirth, those to do with the modification of the foetus and, most controversial of all in terms of their possible implications, those bound up with overcoming infertility.

37   **Lawrence Stone**

Divorce and Separation in Eighteenth-century England

For most people in England marriage was an indissoluble union, breakable only by death; this point was emphasized by Defoe in 1727, and by that acidulous spinster Miss Weeton in a sarcastic poem in 1808 about a discontented husband:

> 'Come soon, O Death, and Alice take.'
> He loudly groan'd and cry'd;
> Death came – but made a sad mistake,
> For Richard 'twas that died.

Unlike the other Protestant churches, the Anglican Church, largely because of historical accident at its inception, failed to provide for remarriage by the innocent party in cases of separation for extreme cruelty or adultery. This question remained in some doubt throughout Elizabeth's reign, but was finally clarified by number 107 of the canons of 1604, which forbade the remarriage of 'divorced' persons. To the aristocracy this created an intolerable situation, since it meant that a nobleman whose wife committed adultery before producing a son was precluded from marrying again and begetting a legal male heir to carry on the line and inherit the property. It was to circumvent this difficulty that in the late seventeenth century, as the concept of marriage as a sacrament ebbed with the waning of religious enthusiasm, divorce by private Act of Parliament became a possible avenue of escape for wealthy noblemen and others who found themselves in this predicament. But this was a very expensive procedure, and it was almost entirely confined, especially before 1760, to those who had very large properties at stake to be handed on to a male heir by a second marriage. Between 1670 and 1799, there were only 131 such Acts, virtually all instituted by husbands, and only seventeen passed before 1750.

At the other end of the social scale, among the propertyless, there were also alternatives to death as a means of finally dissolving an unsatisfactory marriage. In a society without a national police force, it was all too easy simply to run away and never be heard of again. This must have been a not infrequent occurrence among the poor, to judge by the fact that deserted wives comprised over 8 per cent of all the women aged between 31 and 40 listed in the 1570 census of the indigent poor of the city of Norwich. The tragic victims of this solution to marital discord or economic stress were the wives and children, who were left destitute and inevitably became charges on the community. In 1762, for example, the parish officials of East Hoathly recaptured one William Burrage, who had run away five years before. He had left behind him a wife and six small children, the support of whom over these years was estimated to have cost the parish about £50 in all, partly because the deserted wife had gone mad from grief. The villagers were divided about what to do with Burrage: the moralists wanted to clap him in the House of Correction as a punishment, but the pragmatists wanted to pardon him so that he could earn a living and take his family off the parish poor rates. The second alternative was bigamy, which seems to have been both easy and common. In the eighteenth century, more or less permanent desertion was also regarded as morally dissolving the marriage. Thus when in the 1790s the husband of Francis Place's sister was transported for life for a robbery, she soon remarried an old suitor, apparently without any qualms or objections on the grounds that she already had a husband who was presumably still alive. In 1807 a Somerset rector agreed to put up the banns for a second marriage of a woman whose husband had gone off as a soldier to the East Indies seven years before and had not been heard of since. But the man unexpectedly turned up and reclaimed his wife, only to desert her again when he found her consorting with her second husband. He was said soon after to have remarried, despite the existence of this first wife.

A third alternative for the poor in the eighteenth century was the unofficial folk custom of divorce by mutual consent by 'wife-sale'. As described in 1727, the husband 'puts a halter about her neck and thereby leads her to the next market place, and there puts her up to auction to be sold to the best bidder, as if she were a brood mare or a milch-cow. A purchaser is generally provided beforehand on these occasions.' This procedure was based closely on that of the sale of cattle. It took place frequently in a cattle-market like Smithfield and was accompanied by the use of a symbolic halter, by which the wife was led to market by the seller, and led away again by the buyer. The transaction some-times even included the payment of a fee to the clerk of the market. In the popular mind, this elaborate ritual freed the husband of all future responsibility for his wife, and allowed both parties to marry again. Very often, perhaps normally, the bargain was pre-arranged with the full consent of the wife, both purchaser and price being agreed upon beforehand. The latter varied widely, from a few pence to a few guineas. Sometimes the husband actually paid to have his wife taken off his hands. In 1796 a Sheffield steel-burner sold his wife for sixpence to a fellmonger and then gave the purchaser half a guinea to take her out of town to Manchester on the next coach. At other times, the price was higher, for example in 1797 when a London butcher sold his wife for three guineas and a crown to a hog-driver. A little higher up the social scale there is even some evidence of the use of written contracts: one has survived from 1768 which was made between a clothworker and a gentleman (for six guineas), being duly signed and witnessed like an ordinary deed of sale. In this case, the transaction took place without the wife's knowledge or consent, but neither here nor in any other case is the object of sale recorded as having raised any objection. She presumably calculated that any purchaser was likely to treat her better than a husband who was prepared to sell her publicly for a modest sum in order to get rid of her.

It appears that this procedure was almost exclusively confined to the lower classes, and was centred mostly in the big towns and the west of England. It had a medieval origin, but evidence for it becomes far more frequent in the late eighteenth century, then dies away in the nineteenth, the last recorded case being in 1887. Whether this means that the practice was on the increase in the late eighteenth century is doubtful. It seems more likely that the newspapers were picking up more of these cases and reporting them since they were increas-ingly regarded as scandalous to bourgeois morality. By the 1790s, reports usually ended with some hostile comment about 'such depraved conduct in the lower order of people'. To the labouring classes, however, this ritualized procedure was clearly regarded as a perfectly legitimate form of full divorce, to be followed by remarriage, despite its illegality in both secular and ecclesiastical courts, and despite increasing condemnation in the public press. Indeed, the courts made intermittent and half-hearted attempts to stop it, Lord Mansfield treating it as a criminal offence, a conspiracy to commit adultery.

One may conclude, therefore, that in the late seventeenth and eighteenth centuries, full divorce and remarriage was possible by law for the very rich and by folk custom for the very poor, but impossible for the great majority in the middle who could not afford the cost of the one or the social stigma and remote risks of prosecution of the other.

38   Gwynn Davis and Mervyn Murch

Why Do Marriages Break Down?

In this [discussion] we pose the deceptively simple question: why do marriages break down? There is a tendency *either* to provide answers in terms which are broadly sociological (such as 'the emancipation of women') *or* to offer psychological explanations based on the individual personalities of husband and wife, or on the interaction between them. Both these ways of describing the causes of marriage breakdown may have validity, but there is an inevitable distortion if they are considered separately. We shall try, wherever possible, to relate the private trouble to the public issue.

One set of explanations has to do with the gradual reduction in the social pressures to remain married. There is certainly less of a social stigma attached to divorce, and even, some would argue, a process of social imitation. Clearly the view of marriage as a religious sacrament, entered into for life, is no longer as potent or as widespread as it once was. It is also suggested that the development of urban living, leading to uprooting and greater social isolation, has both contributed to the stresses within marriage and made it easier to leave. There is, indeed, some evidence that marital breakdown and divorce are more prevalent in urban, especially metropolitan, than in rural areas.[1]

Secondly, it can plausibly be argued that there has been a change in our explanations of what marriage ought to provide. This can be summarized as a move from 'institutional' to 'companionate' marriage. If the essence of marriage is seen as a personal relationship, and if it is no longer necessary to preserve the bond for *economic* reasons, fulfilment may legitimately be sought in a second union. It has been suggested that it was much easier to fulfil the demands of institutional marriage, these being largely economic, or entailing the provision of basic domestic services, than it is to meet the expectations of companionate marriage (intimacy, sexual gratification, shared friends and interests). As Rheinstein puts it, 'In all these more subtle aspects of marriage we need more, we expect more, and we are more easily disappointed.'[2] Peter and Brigitte Berger are likewise of the view that

> the high divorce rates indicate the opposite of what conventional wisdom holds: people divorce in such numbers *not* because they are turned off marriage, but rather because their expectations of marriage are so high that they will not settle for unsatisfactory approximations. In other words, divorce is mainly a backhanded compliment to the ideal of modern marriage, as well as a testimony to its difficulties.[3]

Thirdly, we might point (as many others have done) to 'the emancipation of women'. There are a number of key areas where it is possible for a growing proportion of women to have the same opportunities and to behave in the same way as do men – in education, in employment and in marriage. These steps towards equality have been accompanied by the granting of increased legal rights, in marriage as in other spheres. Even more important, women now enjoy greater financial independence of their husbands. Three obvious examples which bear directly on the incidence of divorce are, firstly, the provision of state-financed legal advice and representation, enabling women to petition for divorce in large numbers; secondly, the availability of Supplementary Benefit, allowing women to leave their husbands without fear that they (or their children) will starve; and thirdly, a pool of local authority accommodation, generally awarded on the basis that children (and their carers) should have priority.

All this only matters to the extent that women *want* to abandon their marriages. Jessie Bernard has suggested that

> we do our socialising of girls so well . . . that many wives, perhaps most, not only feel that they are fulfilled by marriage but even hotly resent anyone who raises questions about their marital happiness. They have been so completely shaped for their dependency and passivity that the very threat of changes that would force them to greater independence frightens them. They have successfully come to terms with the condition of their lives. They do not know any other. They do not know that other patterns of living might yield greater satisfactions, or want to know. Their cage can be open. They will stay put.[4]

The most fundamental aspect of 'emancipation' may be that a growing proportion of women appear to be dissatisfied with marriage as they experience it. Bernard has referred to 'his' and 'her' marriage in order to suggest the idea that there are two marriages in every marital union and that these do not always coincide. Furthermore, in Bernard's view, 'his' marriage is better than 'hers'. Our own research evidence lends support to the by now familiar idea that marriage means something rather different to men than it does to women. 'The emancipation of women' has therefore had an impact on divorce rates in two ways: firstly, in provoking more women to question the terms of the bargain which they appear to have struck, and secondly, in giving them freedom to leave.

The relative number of men and women who initiate divorce proceedings has fluctuated dramatically throughout this century. Prior to 1914, more decrees were granted on the petition of husbands than of wives. The proportion of husband petitioners increased after the war, reaching over 76 per cent in 1920, the highest this century. In 1923, wives were, for the first time, enabled to petition for divorce on the same footing as their husbands. In the following year, over 50 per cent of divorces were, for the first time, granted to wives. The Second World War again saw a substantial increase in the proportion of decrees granted on petition of the husband (64 per cent in 1946), but since 1949 more women than men have petitioned for divorce. Indeed, the proportion of female petitioners has risen steadily since 1960, reaching 74 per cent in 1982. This has coincided with the seemingly inexorable rise in the overall number of divorce petitions.

Financial assistance to litigants of limited means who wished to divorce was first introduced in 1950 and has been uprated a number of times since then, with the most generous increase in real terms coming in 1960. It has therefore been suggested that the thirty-year trend towards an increased proportion of female petitioners is due to the way in which the Legal Aid fund operates, with both parties being separately assessed so that it pays them (quite literally) to ensure that the poorer of the two (in terms of current assets and income) does the petitioning. But while the way in which the Legal Aid fund operates is bound to have an influence, we found that the high proportion of women petitioners does

Table 1   Who took the decision to divorce? (Conciliation in Divorce survey)

	View of wives		View of husbands	
	No.	*%*	*No.*	*%*
Wife's decision	104	72	77	61
Husband's decision	25	17	36	28
Joint decision	14	10	14	11
Not recorded	1	1	–	–
Total	144	–	127	–

indeed reflect the woman's role as the key decision-maker, determining if and when the marriage should end.

We asked all those interviewed in the course of the Conciliation in Divorce study[5] whether it was they or their former spouse who had taken the decision to divorce. The results, broken down by sex, are given in table 1....

Can we assume from this that men are, in general, more committed to sustaining the marital relationship? Not necessarily. It was clear from a few cases which we studied that while the husband had not wanted a divorce, he had not wanted much of a marriage either – and it was this which had prompted his wife to issue proceedings. As one husband recalled:

> Well, I was going out with somebody, but she didn't know anything about it – you know, sort of once, twice a week. I don't think that would have broken my marriage up. I was quite happy, until she started hearing rumours about it, like. She questioned me about it and I denied it all. But she got up one Monday morning and started ranting and raving again and then she just up and went.

This was not the only man whom we interviewed who confessed to having had a somewhat 'laid back' approach to his marriage. This was the husband's account in a different case: 'I didn't really want a divorce. I was happy going on as I was. I mean, I wasn't a good husband. The fact is I was always out, always drinking, but I mean she never went without. It wasn't a wonderful marriage. I'd have carried on.'

It also appeared in a few instances that the wife's filing of the divorce petition was a kind of desperate last throw, hoping against hope that it would make her husband realize the enormity of what he was doing. Perhaps because we were interviewing members of the divorced population, we gained the impression that, as a strategy for achieving reconciliation, this was not to be recommended. This was one woman's account:

> I never really took the decision. I never actually sat down and thought about it. It just happened. When I first went ahead and filed for a divorce I thought it might pull him to his senses. Everybody kept saying, like friends would say, 'Ah, this'll make him think', but it didn't make him think. It just didn't affect him at all.

But these cases were the minority. In general, we found that not only were women the initiators of divorce, they were correspondingly less likely to regret

Table 2   Would you have preferred to have stayed married? (by sex)

	Women		Men	
	No.	%	No.	%
Yes	41	28	65	51
No	99	69	52	41
Uncertain	1	1	6	5
Other. e.g. reconciled, spouse died	3	2	4	3
Total	144	–	127	–

the ending of the marital relationship. We asked everyone whom we interviewed in Bristol in the course of the Conciliation in Divorce study whether they would have preferred to have remained married. The breakdown of replies is given in table 2. The figures certainly suggest that it is women who, by and large, resolve to end the marriage tie. This has also been found to be the pattern in Australia, where it is reported that divorced husbands are much more likely to regret the ending of the marital relationship than are their wives. This may in turn have implications for second marriages, since we found that even among the thirty-eight men in our Conciliation in Divorce sample who had remarried, 37 per cent said that they wished they had remained married to their former partner (21 per cent of remarried women said the same thing). Apart from throwing a new light on the alleged high failure rate amongst second marriages, these findings reinforce the general impression of male regret.

These responses lead one to wonder whether there might not be another section of the married population, perhaps just as large, who soldier on rather unhappily together. Certainly our interviews suggest that in many of these cases the impulse to divorce had existed for some years prior to the eventual decision to separate. Our evidence is consistent with the arguments advanced by Brigitte and Peter Berger, who describe marriage as the creation of a world in which the individual may achieve power and intelligibility, enabling him or her to become 'a somebody'.[6] As these authors note, this is not an aspiration that one gives up easily; or, as one of the women whom we interviewed remarked, 'Who would willingly subject themselves to this indignity and heartbreak?'

Very few of the people whom we interviewed had taken a *sudden* decision to end their marriage. For example, one couple had separated three times altogether: on the first occasion they had two children; when they finally divorced they had four – one extra, it appeared, for each reconciliation. Women, especially, were inclined to suggest that the cause of the problems lay far back in the marriage, perhaps unacknowledged for years.

> As the years go by . . . I suppose if you look into every nook and cranny, it starts off with one thing, which leads into another, which goes on to something else, and then you go and do something – and that's the end. And it's only that actual end bit that anybody wants to know about – 'Oh, she went off with somebody else' and that's it. Nobody asks 'why?' That's what amused me – they are all too busy making up their own stories. This all sort of started a few years after [child] was born and I was pregnant and my husband made me have an abortion. That's where it all began. If it

hadn't happened, if he hadn't kept on nagging and nagging until I had the blasted abortion, it would never have come to this. In the end, you felt you didn't want him to touch you. You'd had enough, sort of thing.

One of the strongest messages to emerge from these interviews is that people will put up with an extraordinary amount – years of unhappiness – in order to try to keep their marriage and family together. If divorce is 'too easy'... this can only be in relation to crossing the legal boundary; one could never accuse the couples in our sample of having taken the decision lightly. One woman, for example, had been married for nineteen years to a very violent man – a heavy drinker – who used to terrify her. She had tried to divorce him fifteen years previously, but, in the face of cross-examination from her husband's barrister, had fled the courtroom in tears – to return to her husband for what she regarded as another fifteen wasted years.

The final decision to leave was often prompted by this sense of waste – of time wasted in the past and of being unable to bear such waste in the future.

I really didn't want it [divorce]. My mother had been divorced and I thought when I eventually got married, I didn't want that to happen to me. I tried very, very hard for it not to happen. I had left a couple of times and gone back, just because I thought I should stay and I should try as much as I possibly could – especially having a child. I was so unhappy by then, I would drink a bottle of wine during the day just to make life more bearable, you know. I suddenly decided, well look, if I don't leave now, I will sacrifice the rest of my life just to live with someone I feel sorry for. I didn't want to hurt him, but I didn't want to stay with him and perform the duties of a wife. It wasn't a thing to take lightly – it meant a lot to me to get a divorce.

This was the view of one husband in a different case.

The biggest thing was the waste of time, the years we were married. Getting married at twenty and divorced at thirty, you've lost ten years. We were a long time in ignorance. It took us a lot of time to wake up. Once we had taken stock of ourselves and realized what we were doing to each other, then it didn't take very long at all [to be divorced]. We spent a lot of time destroying each other until we realized what we were doing: that sort of creeps up on you gently, like old age.

Many of the people we spoke to were at pains to point out that they took the responsibilities of marriage very seriously. As another husband explained, 'I'm the only person in my family that has ever been divorced. My mother and father have been married for donkey's years. My grandparents are still alive and they are still married. I'm the only one of five children that has ever been divorced – and I've been divorced twice. I feel it's not a family tradition.' Others were keen to distance themselves from any suggestion of radicalism in personal relations; they were certainly not critical of marriage as an institution. As one woman put it to us, 'If you haven't got it right, then it's best to do something. But to me, marriage and a family is everything. I'm not a burn-your-bra type – I don't want to go it alone. I like to think there's someone around.'

There was also, even among some of those who had clearly been the instigators of their divorce, a sense of profound regret that they had felt bound to take such a step. The wife in a different case, asked why she left, replied:

That's difficult. I loved him and the security is very important – especially when you have children. I'd have preferred none of it to happen. I'm a very loving person and I try to see the good in everyone. I loved my husband with all my heart, but the drink won. It's a thing you can't fight. There'll always be that little something between us. You can't love like that twice. We had the best from each other. It only comes once. I haven't found anyone else to love like him.

39   Jan Pahl

Household Spending, Personal Spending and the Control of Money in Marriage

The aim of this article is to examine the extent to which money is shared within marriage and to consider the implications of this for patterns of spending. The article draws on my own study of the control and allocation of money within marriage.[1] Two sets of quotations from the interviews carried out in the course of the study may serve to set the scene: in both cases it is the husband who is speaking.

> My wife is totally dependent on me. We are basically traditional: she has a set amount of housekeeping money and I pay the bills as they come in. I wouldn't want a joint account: I like to feel I'm in control of the family scene and I feel more in control this way.

> Marriage is a joint partnership: the money is there for both of us. I wouldn't want to keep our incomes separate. I earn more than my wife and it equalises incomes putting them in a joint account. My wife controls the money and decides how much she needs to spend on housekeeping.

These quotations raise complicated issues about the transfer of resources within households and about responsibility for spending. Where one partner is the main earner and the other the main spender, what social and economic processes shape the transfer of resources from earner to spender? We know that household spending patterns reflect household income levels: do they also reflect the control and allocation of money *within* the household? The working hypothesis which underpins the article is summarized in figure 1.

[I examine] these issues in the light of data drawn from a study of the control and allocation of money within the household. The study focused on households containing two adults, who were married in all but one case, and at least one dependent child. The words 'household', 'family' and 'couple' may be used interchangeably in the pages which follow. However, it is important to remember that both households and families can take many different forms. The extent to which money is shared within other social groups offers a rich field for further research.

The main aim of the study was to gain a better knowledge of patterns of allocation of money within households and to investigate the significance of different allocative systems for individual members of households. Husband and wife were interviewed first together and then separately, and interviews were completed with 102 couples. The small number of respondents means that it would be rash to claim that they were representative of a wider population of families; it is likely that unhappy marriages and couples with money problems were underrepresented. However, in many respects the study couples had characteristics which one would have hoped to see in a representative sample.

Figure 1   Earning, sharing, spending

There are many different criteria which might be used to create a classification of household financial arrangements. However, for the purpose of this analysis it seemed important to focus on the extent to which income was pooled and on the control of the pool, if there was one. The existence of joint and separate bank accounts offered a relatively objective way in which to assess the jointness or otherwise of a couple's financial arrangements. Having a joint bank account suggested some degree of pooling, so couples with a joint account were divided from those without.

Next the couples were sorted according to the wife's answer to the question 'Who really controls the money that comes into this house?' The possible answers to this question were 'wife', 'husband', and 'both'. However, where 'both' were said to control finances, the analysis showed that husbands were likely to be responsible for paying major bills, checking the bank statement and financial arrangements which most closely resembled those where husbands controlled finances. In the analysis which follows 'both' and 'husband' have been combined in order to reduce the number of categories. Support for the choice of the wife's answer came from the interviewers, who at the end of the joint interview noted discreetly which partner had been the most authoritative in talking about money. A very significant correlation existed between the husband appearing authoritative in the joint interview and his being described by his wife in her separate interview as controlling the money: conversely, wives who appeared authoritative were likely to control the money.

Sorting in this way the 102 couples in the sample produced four categories. The first category contained couples where there was a joint bank account and where the wife described herself as controlling the money. There were twenty-seven of these and they were described as 'wife-controlled pooling'. Among these couples it was usually the wife who paid the bills for rates, fuel, telephone, insurance and mortgage or rent. In the majority of cases, neither partner had a separate bank account and all finances were handled from the joint account.

The second category was described as 'husband-controlled pooling'. This contained couples where there was a joint bank account, but where the wife considered either that the husband controlled the finances or that they were jointly controlled. There were thirty-nine couples in this category. Among this group husbands were typically responsible for the bills for rates, fuel, telephone and insurance and for paying the mortgage or rent.

Lack of a joint account implied one of two things. Either the couple were paid in cash and were too poor ever to need a bank, or one or both partners rejected the idea of a joint account. The third category contained couples where there was no joint account and where the wife considered that control was in the husband's hands. There were twenty-two couples in this category, which was described as 'husband-controlled'. Typically the husband had his own personal bank account and he was responsible for all the main bills.

Finally, there was a small group where there was no joint bank account and the wife considered that she controlled the finances. This category contained fourteen couples and was described as 'wife-controlled'. These couples typically had no bank accounts at all and operated in cash, with the wife controlling and managing the finances and taking responsibility for the major bills.

Wife control of finances was particularly common in low-income, working-class households where neither partner had any qualifications. Wife control was associated with the payment of wages in cash and with the absence of any bank accounts. Typically the wife also managed the money, paying for food and for rent, fuel, insurance and so on, while the husband had a set sum for his personal spending money. Thus in many respects wife control was synonymous with wife management.

Husband control was associated with relatively high income levels.... Most of these couples kept their money separate. When the wife was earning her wages typically went into the housekeeping purse, while the husband was responsible for larger bills. Husband control was characteristic of couples where the husband was the main or sole earner, and there was a tendency for it to be associated with marital unhappiness for both partners.

There were interesting differences between wife-controlled pooling and husband-controlled pooling. Wife-controlled pooling was associated with medium income levels, while husband-controlled pooling was more typical of higher income levels. Wife-controlled pooling was associated with the employment of both partners; when only the husband was in employment he was likely to control the pool. Table 1 shows that the more the wife contributed to the household income the more likely it was that she would control household finances; this effect was particularly marked among pooling couples. Where wives' earnings were 30 per cent or more of their husbands' earnings, wives were twice as likely as husbands to control the pool; where wives had no earnings, husbands were three times more likely than wives to control the pool. When neither partner was employed there was a tendency for wives to control finances; however, the term 'wife control' of finances seems a misleading way to describe what was essentially a struggle to make ends meet in very poor households.

The effect of social class was particularly marked among pooling couples, especially where husband and wife were of different classes. Social class was defined according to the Registrar General's classification. Where the husband was classified as middle-class and the wife as working-class, the husband always controlled the pool, or joint account. Where the wife was middle-class and the husband working-class, she controlled the pool in all but one instance. The same pattern occurred for qualifications. If one partner had more qualifications than the other he or she was likely to control finances: where both partners had gained some qualifications after leaving school there was a tendency for the husband to control finances.

To sum up this section, then, where a wife controls finances she will usually also be responsible for money management; where a husband controls finances he will usually delegate parts of money management to his wife. Thus where a wife controls finances she will usually be responsible for paying the main bills and for making sure that ends meet, as well as for buying food and day-to-day necessities. Where a husband controls finances he will typically delegate to his wife the responsibility for housekeeping expenses, sometimes giving her a

Table 1   Control of finances by wife's earnings as a proportion of husband's earnings

	Wife's earnings		
	Over 30% of husband's earnings	Under 30% of husband's earnings	Wife had no earnings
Wife control	6	–	8
Wife-controlled pooling	12	8	7
Husband-controlled pooling	5	14	20
Husband control	5	5	12
Total	28	27	47

housekeeping allowance for this purpose. Marriages where the wife controls the money and the husband manages it are rare. There were no examples of this pattern in the study sample, nor were there examples of the small number of marriages where the husband both controls and manages the money. Evidence from other studies suggests that in these circumstances there is likely to be extreme inequality between husband and wife and deprivation on the part of the wife and children.[2]

What is the relationship between the control of money within the household and patterns of spending by individual household members? Patterns of spending were investigated in the joint interview, when each couple was asked who was responsible for spending on each item in a long list. They were asked 'who actually buys each item or pays each bill?' Patterns of spending were differentiated by gender. Wives were likely to pay for food, clothing for themselves and their children, presents and school expenses such as dinner money. Husbands were likely to be responsible for paying for their own clothing, the car, repairs and decorating, meals taken away from home and alcohol. Joint responsibilities, paid for by either partner or by both together, included consumer durables, donations to charity and Christmas expenses. This pattern is similar to that found by Todd and Jones: the main difference between the two studies lies in the increase in goods purchased by 'either or both', a change which reflects the spread of joint bank accounts.[3]

Responsibility for spending varied significantly according to the control of finances within the household, but only for some items of expenditure. In general the person who controlled finances, whether or not there was a joint account, was also responsible for the major bills. This applied in the case of the bills for mortgage or rent, rates, fuel, phone and insurance. However, the pattern for consumer goods was rather different: where there was a joint account, whether it was controlled by husband or wife, it was likely that they would both be responsible for buying the washing machine, refrigerator or other household item. However, where there was no joint account, husbands were likely to be responsible for spending on consumer goods....

In this study the question of spending on leisure was approached in various different ways. In the joint interview each individual was asked to identity a source of money for personal things 'like cigarettes, tights, a drink out with friends, a present for your spouse'. In the separate interviews each was asked about their personal spending money, the sums involved and the items it had to cover; each was asked what leisure activities he or she pursued and how much was spent on each activity. Each was then asked to describe their partner's leisure pursuits and to estimate how much he or she spent on them.

What determined the amount of money which each person felt they could spend on leisure and personal needs? [The] part of the household budgeting system [from which] each person drew her or his personal spending money [appears to be an important factor]. Husbands were more likely than wives to take their personal spending money from their earnings, while wives were likely to use housekeeping money for their personal needs, especially if they were not earning. The source of personal spending money varied according to how the couple organized their finances. Where there was a joint account and money management was shared, both partners tended to get their own spending money from the pool. When money was managed independently both partners took their personal spending money from their earnings. Where there was an allowance system the husband's personal spending money tended to come from his earnings, while the wife's money came from the housekeeping money, a situation which was particularly likely to make a woman feel that she had no right to spend on herself.

[S]pending on leisure varied depending on the control of money within the household. In the sample as a whole husbands were likely to spend more than their wives, but this was especially so when there was no joint account. Husbands were particularly likely to spend more on leisure than wives in those households where wives controlled finances, that is, in households with the lowest incomes. A rather unexpected result was found, however, when wife-controlled pooling couples were compared with husband-controlled pooling couples. It was among the latter category that wives who spent more on leisure than their husbands were most commonly found. Of the seventeen women who spent more on leisure than their husbands, ten were found in those households where the husband controlled finances and there was a joint account. Perhaps these were the households where a larger-than-average income was combined with an ideology of financial sharing?

40   Elizabeth A. Stanko

Wife Battering: All in the Family

More than anything else, the experiences of women battered by husbands, boyfriends or lovers expose the underside of the ideal family or the happy couple. To hear battered women recount these experiences is to hear stories of abuse which are often characterized as 'normal' interaction of intimate couples. Blinded by patriarchal notions about the privacy of family matters, deafened by the rhetoric which maintains these notions, society once again focuses blame on individual women who, because of their assumed weakness, 'choose' battering relationships. Masochistic women, they are called. Battered women live within their own state of siege; they know, to the core of their being, the weight of the contradictory demands of their roles as women....

Physical intrusion within intimate relationships reflects a pattern similar to sexual intimidation and violence: women are overwhelmingly the recipients of 'domestic violence'. So too, women are blamed for their powerlessness, and labelled as passive, submissive, even desirous of their own harm. Hence dominant stereotypes of women provide the common-sense information to divide women in two categories, those who are nurturers and caregivers, and those who are nagging, selfish and in violation of women's expected role. And men's behaviour? Too often, it is seen as 'typical'.

While the stereotype of the blameworthy battered wife remains steadfast, researchers have found that wife beating is perhaps the most underreported crime. One estimate suggests that only one out of 270 incidents of wife abuse is ever reported to the authorities.[1] When incidents do come to police attention, they compose a significant proportion of assault complaints. Rebecca and Russell Dobash's analysis of 3,020 reported cases of violence in two Scottish cities, for instance, found assault against wives to be the second largest category of assault that comes to police attention.[2] Researchers who examine violent incidents outside police involvement find even higher incidence of wife abuse. Diana Russell's recent random survey on women's experiences of sexual assault revealed that 21 per cent of women who had ever been married reported physical violence by a husband at some time in their lives.[3] Murray Straus, Richard Gelles and Suzanne Steinmetz, in a random survey of 2,143 households in the US, found evidence of 'domestic violence' in 28 per cent of households.[4] It is important to note here, however, that domestic violence and wife battering are different concepts. In one – domestic violence – the researcher assumes that all violence is experienced by men and women alike and that the damage administered by a wife is equivalent to that administered by a husband. In fact, the Straus et al. survey found that the incidence of husband battering exceeded that for wife battering. As Russell points out in her critique of these findings, Straus et al. 'fail to distinguish between offensive and defensive violence', ignoring strength differences, variation in fighting skills and the sustained injuries of women and men.[5] The term 'wife abuse', then, stresses the social position of women *vis-à-vis* men. The context of women's position is what needs to be explained, not 'exchange' of physical abuse. Furthermore, wives who fight back might be more severely injured. Women who are beaten either try to defend themselves or remain physically passive: there is no set pattern. What remains a 'social fact', as the Dobashes emphasize, is that violence between adults in the family is directed at women.

Common among women's experiences of physical assault are reports of sexual assault. Approximately 10 per cent of Russell's respondents who had ever been married reported being raped and beaten by their husbands. So, too, Irene Hanson Frieze's research reveals widespread sexual abuse among the battered women in her US study; one of every three women she interviewed had been battered. Of the battered women, one-third of her respondents had been raped, two-thirds felt they had been pressured into having sex with their husbands and 40 per cent felt sex was unpleasant because it was forced. Clearly men's sexual intimidation and violence toward women goes hand in hand with physical intimidation and violence.[6]

Behaviour referred to as wife battering – the violent action on the part of husband against wife – includes forms of pushing, kicking, slapping, throwing objects, burning, dragging, stabbing or shooting. Assaults over time may have cumulative physical effects; severe bruising and all around bodily soreness accompany emotional distress. For example, in answering 'What kind of injuries were inflicted on you?' asked by a member of the Select Committee on Violence in Marriage, UK, one woman replied:

> I have had ten stitches, three stitches, five stitches, seven stitches, where he has cut me. I have had a knife stuck through my stomach; I have had a

poker put through my face; I have no teeth where he knocked them all out; I have been burnt with red hot pokers; I have had red hot coals slung all over me; I have been sprayed with petrol and stood there while he has flicked lighted matches at me. But I had to stay there because I could not get out. He has told me to get out. Yet if I had stood up I know what would have happened to me. I would have gotten knocked down again.

Pat Calen, in her research on Scottish women in prison, came upon many women's accounts of violent attacks at the hands of men.[7] These attacks included severe beatings, with a range of bodily injuries from the loss of an eye and a tooth to physical mutilation: a carved swastika on one woman's forehead. Women's discussions about their lives eventually focused on the common occurrence of male violence, which some women attributed to 'Scottishness'. (Some American, English and Welsh women subjected to violence might also attribute it to that which arises from a particular cultural context. The similarities across cultures, however, reinforce the commonness of male violence in both British and American societies.) The 'cult of aggressive and assertive masculinity' is attributed to a Scottish working-class ethos; women's experiences of male violence elsewhere show how this cult crosses class boundaries. Equally important, the cult of aggressive and assertive masculinity is taken by some women to be typical male behaviour.

Ultimately, women's injuries reflect the effects of aggressive masculinity. In the Dobash study, nearly 80 per cent of the battered women reported going to a doctor at least once during their marriage for injuries resulting from attacks by their husbands; nearly 40 per cent stated they sought medical attention on five separate occasions. Dobash and Dobash conclude:

> Untreated injuries and vicious attacks often result in permanent disfigurement such as loss of hair, improperly healed bones, and severe scars from cuts, burns, and abrasions.... The women we interviewed... suffered serious woundings, innumerable bloodied noses, fractured teeth and bones, concussions, miscarriages and severe internal injuries that often resulted in permanent scars, disfigurement and sometimes persistent poor health.[8]

The medical profession too participates in perpetuating wife battering by ignoring women's complaints of physical injury as symptomatic of a pattern of battering. So do those who feel that the sanctity of marriage is, above all, more important than a woman's physical safety.

> By late afternoon I still hadn't come up with a specific plan of action. All I knew was that I would have to get away from Florida. Just before dinner my mother said she wanted to talk to me.
> 'Chuck has been calling all day,' she said. 'I've talked to him a few times now and all I know for sure is that he really loves you.'
> 'Mother, you don't know what you're talking about.'
> 'Oh, you never think that I know what I'm talking about,' she said. 'I've been married a good long time, longer than you've been alive, and after all this time I guess I know a thing or two about husbands and wives. You don't want to forget that he's your husband and you're his wife. No matter what little difficulties you've been having, you should be able to work them out.'
> 'Little difficulties? *Little* difficulties!'
> 'Chuck has told me everything,' my mother said. 'He told me enough so that I know this is just a lovers' quarrel.'

All day I had been thinking about how I could tell my parents what was going on in my life. I felt that I should break it to them gently. Well, all those plans just flew out the window. I laid the situation flat-out, using the bluntest words I knew.

'Mom, Chuck has beaten me bloody,' I began. 'He has held a gun to my head and made me do awful things. He has forced me to have sex with women and other men. And now he is talking about making me have sex with animals. He has made me pose for dirty pictures and he is turning me into a prostitute. He is always threatening to kill me. He has even threatened to kill you and Daddy.'

'But, Linda, he's your *husband*.'[9]

That women are to blame – the strongly entrenched male point of view often held by many doctors, police, neighbours, parents and so forth – is difficult for battered women to confront. Many women still envision a life of domestic tranquillity. Yet the economic and emotional ties wrap tightly around women's uncertainty about the domestic tranquillity when violence arises. All too often, battered women's responses, similarly to incestually assaulted or raped women's responses, end up in self-blame.... Battering may be interpreted by the woman as an indication, not of her husband's problem but as her failure as a wife. Mortified, ashamed, humiliated, a woman may then remain silent about her abuse to others, fearing most of all that she is ultimately to blame.

I don't know. I kept thinking he was changing, you know, change for the better.... He's bound to change. Then I used to think it's my blame and I used to lie awake at night wondering if it is my blame – You know, I used to blame myself all the time.[10]

I was concerned, I didn't do anything to deserve it. I mean, I never went out. I never went out of the house, you know. I never looked at anybody.[11]

The feeling of helplessness due to the fact that it was my fault that I got battered, which I think is common that a woman is blamed because she provoked him. Certainly my husband immediately blamed me. 'If you had done so and so; if you hadn't done so and so.' And the fact that he did almost kill me and threatened if I said anything to the police he *would* kill me and the destruction of confidence or any way out. I had no money, I had kids. I couldn't for years see my way out of this situation, in myself I didn't have any sense of it. If I left, he'd follow me. He'd take my kids away. He threatened to do that. I believed all that. Getting the strength came with my finally deciding that I was dying, and that if I was going to die, I was going to die fighting, which meant I had to leave. I could not die this way any longer in this relationship and if he came after me, damn it, I was going to give him what he was trying to give me. It was a giving up of his power over me and my acknowledgement of his power over me [that] gave me power to move. It was a long time before I was able to – ten years – get over really being afraid of that man. I'm just now getting to a point to where I am not afraid of him, and move forward into my life. My life has always been attached to this kind of powerlessness. If I do this, what's he going to do. It's a reaction instead of an action. It's always a reaction instead of moving with the confidence of no matter what he does I can somehow manage, maybe get killed in the process. I don't think that anymore but I did for a long time. And I talk to other women who have had other experiences like that who have the same kind of hopelessness and in many instances, without resources, without the ability to make a living, find a house, to solve all these terrible problems, these real problems, practical problems. Where they are as bad as this, it is better than that [the battering situation], better than going into an absolute abyss of nothing.[12]

For a period of time – days, months, years – many battered women are caught within the web of violence, unable to predict when more violence will occur or to understand why violence is occurring in the first place. During this period, many report symptoms of stress, such as lack of sleep, weight loss or gain, ulcers, nervousness, irritability, and [for] some even thoughts of suicide. Moreover, depression slows down a battered woman's ability to escape the battering, an act that, by its very nature, is an assertive one. Phyllis Chesler describes women's depression as a 'continual state of mourning for what they [women] never had – or had too briefly – and for what they can't have in the present, be it Prince Charming or direct worldly power.'[13] Battered women have neither Prince Charming nor worldly power: they see themselves as failures, as their husbands treat them. 'When women feel excluded from direct participation in society [and many women, regardless of social position, do], they see themselves as subject to a consensus or judgment made and reinforced by the men on whose protection and support they depend and by whose names they are known.'[14]

Keeping the relationship together, despite the violence, is also important for practical reasons – financial support, shelter, even access to the ability to earn a living many times rest with the husband/boyfriend. Getting out is almost as bad as staying in the relationship. Women often feel inadequate to cope with self-sufficiency; the lack of self-confidence often acts as a trap to keep women within a violent home.

Women stay within battering situations because of the real conditions of their lives within a male-dominated world. Men's power is not an individual, but a collective one. Women's lives are bounded by it. The threat of male violence outside the home, as women currently within violent relationships told Russell, is an acutely intimidating reality of women who endure violence within their own homes. Keeping women in relationships with men, says Adrienne Rich, is a primary 'means of assuring [the] male right of physical, economical, and emotional access.'[15] Having women react instead of act, as the woman stated above, is a response pattern fostered by women's dependence upon men.

Many women do leave violent husbands/boyfriends. In doing so, many women leave, return, leave again, return again and leave never to return. The process could take years, or it could happen immediately after the first beating.

> I went to my parents and of course, he came – I left him because of his hitting and kicking me – and I went home to them, but he came there and I had to go. I went back really to keep the peace because my parents weren't able to cope with it.[16]

> [I returned to my husband] because I was sure there was something in me that could make the marriage work. I was quite positive about that.[17]

Reasons for returning are similar to those for staying: hope that the husband will change or, because he has apologized, hope that he will never strike again; concern for the children; worry over financial difficulties; resignation to the 'inevitability' of violence; fear for the safety of others; fear of being outside the home; fear of losing the status of 'wife'; just plain fear – these are but a few of the motivating forces affecting women's decisions to leave or stay.

41 Michelle Stanworth

Reproductive Technologies and the Deconstruction of Motherhood

Technologies designed to intervene in the process of human reproduction fall, roughly speaking, into four groups. The first and most familiar group includes those concerned with fertility control – with preventing conception, frustrating implantation of an embryo or terminating pregnancy. According to the General Household Survey, in Britain three women out of four aged between 18 and 44 use some form of contraception; just over 140,000 residents of England and Wales underwent an abortion in 1985. Many of the technologies of fertility control – diaphragms, intra-uterine devices, sterilization, abortion, even the newly visible condom – have been known in some form for centuries. Hormone-suppressing contraceptive drugs are one of the few genuine innovations in contraceptive technology this century. Since by the late 1970s the market for the pill in many Western countries was saturated, pharmaceutical companies now devote much of their research efforts to finding new ways of administering contraceptives that would open up expanding markets in the third world.

A second group of reproductive technologies is concerned with the 'management' of labour and childbirth. In the course of the past 150 years in Europe and America, childbirth changed from a home-based activity, undertaken primarily with the assistance of female healers and friends, to an activity defined as the province of medical professionals. The extent of the shift is illustrated by the rising proportion of British babies born in hospital – from 15 per cent in 1927 to 99 per cent in 1985. In its wake, a range of technologies for monitoring and controlling the progress of labour and delivery – instruments to assist delivery, caesarian sections, ways of inducing labour, episiotomies, techniques for measuring foetal heart rate and movement – have been applied on an increasingly routine basis; the caesarian section rate in the United States, for example, rose from 4.5 per cent in 1965 to 19 per cent in 1982. In many Western countries, the potential for effective intervention in the management of labour and childbirth is approaching saturation point, not only because of the high proportion of birthing women who are already subject to these techniques, but also because of objections to 'high-tech' deliveries from women themselves.

A current focus in terms of the development of reproductive technologies is upon extending obstetric services backwards into the antenatal period, through the use of more elaborate technologies and screening procedures for monitoring foetal development in the early stages of pregnancy; at least one-third of all pregnant women in the United States now experiences ultrasound. The focus is also upon perfecting new techniques for neonatal care; and upon research that might eventually enable the modification of inborn 'defects' through human genetic engineering. In short, the third and one of the growth areas in reproductive technology is concerned with improving the health and the genetic characteristics of foetuses and of newborns – with the search for, as some have said, 'the perfect child'.

The fourth and perhaps most controversial group are the conceptive technologies, directed to the promotion of pregnancy through techniques for overcoming or bypassing infertility. Estimates for Britain suggest that 50,000 new cases of infertility present for treatment each year and the number of people requiring treatment at any one time may be as high as two million. Yet for much of this century, the treatment of infertility has been relatively static; apart from the clinical introduction of artificial insemination in the 1930s and the 'fertility drugs' of the 1960s, no new technologies were introduced until in vitro fertilization burst upon the scene in the late 1970s as a 'miracle cure'. Most research in the area of infertility is now devoted to the refinement of in vitro fertilization and to the development of new applications – through combination with, for example, egg donation, embryo donation, low-temperature storage of gametes and embryos or surrogacy – rather than to alternative approaches to infertility. The conceptive technologies, often treated as if they were synonymous with 'high-tech' medicine, in fact are immensely varied; they range from surrogacy or artificial insemination – both of which can be and are practised in ways that require no medical intervention at all – to in vitro fertilization, which involves very sophisticated medical, surgical and laboratory procedures.

As the history of reproductive technologies is gradually being written, we have come to know more about the range of groups or institutions that have an interest in their development. Women themselves, as consumers of services concerned with reproductive care have, to be sure, 'demanded' techniques that would help them to control their fertility, their pregnancies, their experience of birth and the health of their children. Yet it is clear that there is no simple cause-and-effect relationship between the 'demands' made by women and the 'supply' of reproductive technologies. For one thing, the 'demands' of those who can afford to pay are likely to be catered for far more assiduously than the 'demands' of those with smaller resources; and the greater the proportion of total health costs that is met by individuals, the more powerfully such inequalities are likely to assert themselves. For another, part of the 'demand' for reproductive technologies comes from state-subsidized programmes, and the objectives of the state in providing resources for the introduction of some technologies and withholding funding from others are not likely to reflect women's wishes in any straightforward way. The state responds to women's demands in the area of reproductive care selectively, in terms of its own priorities with respect to population policy, health expenditure and political payoff. So, for example, in the context of rigorous insistence on reduction of public expenditure over the past decade, in vitro fertilization programmes have received virtually no public funding in Britain, while the Department of Health and Social Security viewed benignly – in hopes of saving money on the care of handicapped children – the possibility of mass programmes of antenatal screening.

There are other reasons too, why the demands of women for technologies to aid in reproductive care are insufficient to explain the technologies currently on offer. What we 'demand' (that is, what we are willing to tolerate) as consumers depends on the options available to us. Undoubtedly, the demand among heterosexual women who wished to avoid pregnancy for a 100 per cent reliable contraceptive technique that carried no risks to health or quality of life would be overwhelming; but in real life, women have to divide their 'demands' more or less grudgingly between a range of less-than-satisfactory options. Even our notions of what 'satisfactory' would be are shaped partly by our knowledge of existing or potential alternatives. If we come to believe that home births are dangerous (whether or not that belief is objectively 'true') we are unlikely to be able to articulate clearly our dissatisfactions with hospital confinements.

Many of the groups most directly responsible for developing and promoting reproductive technologies have an agenda in which women's 'demands' play only a small part. For obstetricians and gynaecologists, specific types of reproductive technologies may carry advantages quite separate from their impact on mothers and infants. Reproductive technologies often enhance the status of medical professionals and increase the funds they can command, by underpinning claims to specialized knowledge and by providing the basis for an extension of service. Such technologies may, in addition, help a profession in its attempts to dominate other competitors for control of an area of work; the application of new forms of technology has been one way that obstetricians have succeeded in reducing midwives to a subordinate status in the field of maternity services. Perhaps most significantly, new technologies help to establish that gynaecologists and obstetricians 'know more' about pregnancy and about women's bodies than women do themselves. When the majority of the profession is male, it is perhaps not surprising that medical practitioners have been attracted to techniques that enable them to brush aside a woman's own felt experience of menstruation, pregnancy and birth.

Medical practitioners are themselves dependent upon the research and development activities of pharmaceutical and medical supply companies, and many of these corporations have a vast financial interest in the manufacture and promotion of technologies concerned with reproductive care. The buoyant market for infertility treatment has attracted considerable private finance for research and development, but even this is probably outstripped by investment in the realm of genetic engineering. Feminists have raised troubling questions about the accountability and public scrutiny of reproductive technologies, the development of which is motored by private investment.[1]

Precisely because of the different and sometimes conflicting interests at stake in the application of reproductive technologies, women have not been content to leave the evaluation of the impact of technology to 'the experts', who are often the very people involved in their promotion. Instead, they have highlighted the ambivalent effects of reproductive technologies on the lives of women. Women in Western Europe and North America today, compared with their foremothers, have fewer pregnancies, bear fewer babies against their wishes, are less likely to die in childbirth and less often experience the death of their babies. This is no small matter – and it is due, in some part, to technologies for intervening in human reproduction. But the view that reproductive technologies have given women control over motherhood – and thereby over their own lives – simply will not do.

First, this view takes insufficient account of the impact of changing social definitions of motherhood. While women today spend less time in pregnancy and breast-feeding than in the recent past, the care of children has come to be defined in a far more rigorous way; mothering involves responsibility not only for the physical and emotional care of children, but for detailed attention to their psychological, social and intellectual development. Motherhood is seen, more than in the past, as a full-time occupation. Mothers may be expected now to lavish as much 'care' on two children as they might previously have provided for six. In short, the reproductive technologies address themselves to only a small part of the experience of motherhood.

Secondly, reproductive decisions continue to be constrained by the shortcomings of existing means of fertility control. For example, the pill and the intra-uterine contraceptive device – heralded in the 1960s as instruments of women's liberation – appear now to carry worrying health risks and a range of distressing side-effects. Some contraceptive techniques, including some of the most reliable for preventing pregnancy, appear also to increase the risk of infertility, creating a Catch 22 situation for women who wish to control the timing of childbearing. The failure to develop safer and more acceptable means of birth control is not simply a technical problem; in part, it reflects the low priority given to women's health and a tendency to disregard symptoms and issues that women themselves think are important.

Thirdly, the way that access to means of fertility control is managed indicates how women's options regarding childbearing are linked to their location in the social structure. In Britain, the recent Gillick case represented an attempt to restrict through the courts the access of younger women to contraceptive information and supplies. Controversial contraceptives such as the injectable long-acting Depo-Provera, though considered unsuitable for the majority of women in Britain, have been used extensively on their Asian and black compatriots. Although the 1967 Abortion Act entitles British women to legal abortion on medical and social grounds, access to safe abortion in many parts of the country – as in the United States – depends on ability to pay; the bulk of legal abortions in Britain today are performed outside the National Health Service. Infertility, and especially the infections that lead to tubal closure, are particular problems for black women and women on low incomes in Britain and the United States, but these are precisely the women who have least access to new conceptive technologies like in vitro fertilization.

Fourthly, the technical possibility of fertility control coexists with a powerful ideology of motherhood – the belief that motherhood is the natural, desired and ultimate goal of all 'normal' women, and that women who deny their 'maternal instincts' are selfish, peculiar or disturbed. At a conference in Oxford in 1987, Patrick Steptoe, the obstetrician who is credited with 'creating' the first test-tube baby, declared: 'It is a fact that there is a biological drive to reproduce. Women who deny this drive, or in whom it is frustrated, show disturbances in other ways.' Research suggests that many members of the medical profession share this view.

While many women wish to have children, the views of medical personnel are not simply a reflection of that fact. The idea of maternal instinct is sometimes used to override women's expressed wishes with regard to childbearing – discouraging young married women from sterilization or abortion, for example, while denying single women the chance to have a child. In other words, a belief in maternal instinct coexists with obstacles to autonomous motherhood – obstacles, that is, to motherhood for women who are not in a stable relationship to a man. According to ideologies of motherhood, all women *want* children; but single women, lesbian women (and disabled women) are often expected to forgo mothering 'in the interest of the child'.

Finally, technologies for 'managing' pregnancy and childbirth are often embedded in a medical frame of reference that defines pregnant women as 'patients', pregnancy as an illness and successful childbearing in terms that de-emphasize the social and emotional dimensions. In some respects, reproductive technologies have made childbearing safer for women and their infants, but they have also brought new dangers in their wake. Apart from medical risks and benefits, as the process of pregnancy and childbirth has come under the control of medical professionals, the majority of whom are men, many women are left with a sense of being mere onlookers in the important process of giving birth.

Thus, medical and scientific advances in the sphere of reproduction – so often hailed as the liberators of twentieth-century women – have, in fact, been a double-edged sword. On the one hand, they have offered women a greater technical possibility to decide if, when and under what conditions to have children; on the other, the domination of so much reproductive technology by the medical profession and by the state has enabled others to have an even greater capacity to exert control over women's lives. Moreover, the 'technical possibility' of choosing an oral contraceptive or in vitro fertilization is only a small aspect of reproductive freedom. For some women, motherhood remains their only chance of creativity, while economic and social circumstances compel others to relinquish motherhood altogether.

Against the stark backcloth of the history of technologies for controlling fertility, pregnancy and birth, how are we to analyse the emergent technologies concerned with promoting conception and with eliminating 'defects' in the unborn? One powerful theoretical approach sees in these new techniques a means for men to wrest 'not only control of reproduction, but reproduction itself' from women.[2] Following O'Brien,[3] it is suggested that men's alienation from reproduction – men's sense of disconnection from their seed during the process of conception, pregnancy and birth – has underpinned through the ages a relentless male desire to master nature, and to construct social institutions and cultural patterns that will not only subdue the waywardness of women but also give men an illusion of procreative continuity and power. New reproductive technologies are the vehicle that will turn men's illusions of reproductive power into a reality. By manipulating eggs and embryos, scientists will determine the sort of children who are born – will make themselves the fathers of humankind. By removing eggs and embryos from some women and implanting them in others, medical practitioners will gain unprecedented control over motherhood itself. Motherhood as a unified biological process will be effectively deconstructed: in place of 'mother', there will be ovarian mothers who supply eggs, uterine mothers who give birth to children and, presumably, social mothers who raise them. Through the eventual development of artificial wombs, the capacity will arise to make biological motherhood redundant. Whether or not women are eliminated, or merely reduced to the level of 'reproductive prostitutes',[4] the object and the effect of the emergent technologies is to deconstruct motherhood and to destroy the claim to reproduction that is the foundation of women's identity.

The problem with this analysis is not that it is too radical, as some have claimed; rather, in seeking to protect women from the dangers of new technologies, it gives too much away. There is a tendency to echo the very views of scientific and medical practice of women and of motherhood, which feminists have been seeking to transform. This analysis entails, in the first instance, an inflated view of science and medicine, the mirror image of that which scientists and medical practitioners often try themselves to promote. By emphasizing the continuities between technologies currently in clinical use, and those that exist merely in the fantasies of scientific commentators; by insisting that the practices involved in animal husbandry or in animal experimentation can unproblematically be transferred to human beings; by ignoring the ways in which women have resisted abuses of medical power and techniques they found unacceptable: by arguing this way, science and medicine have been portrayed as realms of boundless possibility, in the face of which mere human beings have no choices other than total rejection or capitulation. Any understanding of the constraints within which science and medicine operate, and of the way these can be shaped for the greater protection of women and men, is effectively erased.

Also integral to this approach is a view of women that comes uncomfortably close to that espoused by some members of the medical professions. Infertile women are too easily 'blinded by science'; they are manipulated into 'full and total support of any technique which will produce those desired children';[5] the choices they make and even their motivations to choose are controlled by men. In the case of doctors, it is the 'maternal instinct' that allows women's own assessments of what they want from their bodies or their pregnancies to be overlooked; in this analysis, it is patriarchal and pronatal conditioning that makes infertile women (and, by implication, all women) incapable of rationally grounded and authentic choice. I argued above that the ideology of motherhood attempts to press women in the direction of childbearing, and that in this sense women's motivations are socially shaped. But 'shaped' is not the same as 'determined'; and a rejection of childbearing (for infertile women or fertile) is not necessarily a more authentic choice. The very existence of a range of sanctions and rewards designed to entice women into marriage and motherhood indicates, not that conformity is guaranteed, but that avoidance of motherhood (and autonomous motherhood) are genuine options, which efforts are made to contain.

Finally, this approach tends to suggest that anything 'less' than a natural process, from conception through to birth, represents the degradation of motherhood itself. The motherhood that men are attempting to usurp becomes a motherhood that is biologically defined, and to which all women are assumed to have the same relationship. While it is the case that the lives of all women are shaped by their biological selves, and by their assumed or actual capacity to bear children, our bodies do not impose upon us a common experience of reproduction; on the contrary, our bodies stand as powerful reminders of the differentiating effects of age, health, disability, strength and fertility history. There is, moreover, little reason to assume that the biological potential to give birth has an identical meaning for women, regardless of their social circumstances or their wishes with regard to childbearing. How can the experience of women who have chosen to remain childfree be fitted into a framework that sees the continuous biological process that culminates in birth as the core of our identity as women? How can we make sense from this perspective of women (such as those interviewed by Luker,[6] who value children and childbearing highly, but who experience pregnancy itself as merely an unpleasant reality *en route* to raising children? How can we explain the fact that fewer working-class women in Britain attend antenatal clinics, demand natural childbirth or breast-feed their infants? Luker's analysis suggests the possibility that while for many middle-class women pregnancy may be a scarce resource – time out from a hectic professional life to enjoy the sensations of being a woman – for a greater proportion of working-class women pregnancy may be more a taken-for-granted prelude to social motherhood, not an experience to be cherished in itself. Far too many women have experienced the type of reproductive care that is insensitive to their own wishes and desires; but shared reaction against unsatisfactory medical treatment should not be allowed to mask differences in women's own sense of what authentic motherhood might be. Women may legitimately, as Rayna Rapp said, 'want other things from reproductive technology than merely to get it off our backs'.[7]

Feminist critics of technologies have always and rightly insisted that technologies derive their meaning from the social and political context in which they emerge. But where the context that is invoked in connection with reproductive technologies is the universal victimization of women, then it is easy to underestimate the significance of political struggles concerning the future of reproduction which are currently being waged. Reproductive technologies are controversial – not only amongst feminists, but among a wider public – because they crystallize issues at the heart of contemporary controversies over sexuality, parenthood, reproduction and the family; a concern for self-determination for women must engage, above all, with these struggles.

Part 11

Education and Media

Mass education is a phenomenon of the relatively recent past, dating in most industrial countries only from the late nineteenth century. In pre-modern societies, the majority of the population was non-literate. Mastery of formal educational skills was confined to a very small stratum. Education became generalized partly through the efforts of liberal reformers, who wished to extend the benefits of education to the working class, and partly because it became generally recognized that the functioning of a complex society depends upon a populace having at least minimal educational qualifications.

The intrinsic value and social importance of education are not always evident to those obligated to attend schools – more specifically, children from underprivileged backgrounds, who often see the authority system of the school as oppressive rather than liberating. Paul Willis's study (reading 42) describes the outlook of a group of working-class boys ('the lads') in a school in Birmingham. The lads feel alienated from the dominant culture of the school and seek every opportunity to challenge or contest it. They have developed an informal culture of their own, the main tenets of which diverge radically from the orthodoxy of the school. The lads seek every opportunity, Willis points out, to frustrate the formal objective of the school, which is to make pupils 'work'.

The selection from Ivan Reid (reading 43), based as it is upon a quantitative survey, contrasts methodologically with Willis's study, but provides material upon much the same issue: the relation between social class and education. The early educational reformers believed that universal schooling would provide a means of social advancement for individuals from lower-class backgrounds. The evidence from work such as Reid's, however, suggests that education serves to consolidate existing class inequalities more often than to undercut them. Even where IQ is held constant, the educational attainments of children from working-class backgrounds are significantly lower than those from more affluent homes.

Children from minority group backgrounds also commonly face a clash of values when attending school. Parents and children may wish to keep alive cultural values and practices which the school system, in combination with the wider social environment, tends to dissolve. Reading 44, by Saeeda Cahanum, discusses an instance in which the members of an Asian community in the north of England took an active approach to the question of education and cultural development. The Bradford Moslem Girls' School was established as a means of providing Asian girls with an educational setting which would stress the religious and cultural values of Islamic life. Although the context of the school is a 'protected' one, both the teachers and pupils experience problems in following a set of subcultural practices in a society whose overall values are very different.

Formal education is clearly only one way in which information is acquired in the modern world. The rise of mass education has occurred more or less simultaneously with the development of mass media – large-circulation newspapers, magazines, radio and television – and indeed, the two developments have tended to converge. Many phenomena which form 'common knowledge' in modern societies are transmitted via the media rather than by the formal mechanism of the school. How far people's attitudes and outlooks are influenced by the various media is a controversial issue in contemporary sociology. Reading 45, by Tamar Liebes and Elihu Katz, analyses the popularity and possible impact of the television programme *Dallas*. *Dallas* reaches a truly global audience. Yet how the programme is interpreted varies considerably between different countries and subcultures within countries. Liebes and Katz argue that the educational and ethnic backgrounds of viewers filter which aspects of the programmes they pick out and focus upon.

John B. Thompson (reading 46) similarly emphasizes that the reception of the 'messages' conveyed through the mass media is an actively organized one. Audiences respond to media messages selectively and in a critical fashion. The term 'mass' in mass media, Thompson points out, is somewhat misleading: media audiences may be very large, but they are also highly differentiated.

42   Paul E. Willis

Dossing, Blagging and Wagging: Countercultural Groups in the School Environment

On a night we go out on
the street
Troubling other people.
I suppose we're anti-social,
But we enjoy it.

The older generation
They don't like our hair,
Or the clothes we wear
They seem to love running
us down,
I don't know what I would
do if I didn't have the gang.

(Extract from a poem by Derek written in an English class)

...Counterschool culture is the zone of the informal. It is where the incursive demands of the formal are denied – even if the price is the expression of opposition in style, micro-interactions and non-public discourses. In working-class culture generally opposition is frequently marked by a withdrawal into the informal and expressed in its characteristic modes just beyond the reach of 'the rule'.

Even though there are no public rules, physical structures, recognized hierarchies or institutionalized sanctions in the counterschool culture, it cannot run on air. It must have its own material base, its own infrastructure. This is, of course, the social group. The informal group is the basic unit of this culture, the fundamental and elemental source of its resistance. It locates and makes possible all other elements of the culture, and its presence decisively distinguishes 'the lads' from the 'ear'oles'.

The importance of the group is very clear to members of the counterschool culture.

[In a group discussion]
Will: [...] we see each other every day, don't we, at school [...]
Joey: That's it, we've developed certain ways of talking, certain ways of acting, and we developed disregards for Pakis, Jamaicans and all different... for all the scrubs and the fucking ear'oles and all that [...] We're getting to know it now, like we're getting to know all the cracks, like, how to get out of lessons and things, and we know where to have a crafty smoke. You can come over here to the youth wing and do summat, and er'm ... all your friends are here, you know, it's sort of what's there, what's always going to be there for the next year, like, and you know you have to come to school today, if you're feeling bad, your mate'll soon cheer yer up like, 'cos you couldn't go without ten minutes in this school, without having a laff at something or other.
PW: Are your mates a really big important thing at school now?
–   Yeah.

\-   Yeah.
\-   Yeah.
Joey: They're about the best thing actually.

The essence of being 'one of the lads' lies within the group. It is impossible to form a distinctive culture by yourself. You cannot generate fun, atmosphere and a social identity by yourself. Joining the counterschool culture means joining a group, and enjoying it means being with the group:

[In a group discussion on being 'one of the lads']
Joey: [...] when you'm dossing on your own, it's no good, but when you'm dossing with your mates, then you're all together, you're having a laff and it's a doss.
Bill: If you don't do what the others do, you feel out.
Fred: You feel out, yeah, yeah. They sort of, you feel, like, thinking the others are...
Will: In the second years...
Spanksy: I can imagine... you know, when I have a day off school, when you come back the next day, and something happened like in the day you've been off, you feel, 'Why did I have that day off', you know, 'I could have been enjoying myself'. You know what I mean? You come back and they're saying, 'Oorh, you should have been here yesterday', you know.
Will: [...] like in the first and second years, you can say er'm... you're a bit of an ear'ole right. Then you want to try what it's like to be er'm... say, one of the boys like, you want to have a taste of that, not an ear'ole, and so you like the taste of that.

Though informal, such groups nevertheless have rules of a kind which can be described – though they are characteristically framed in contrast to what 'rules' are normally taken to mean.

PW: [...] Are there any rules between you lot?
Pete: We just break the other rules.
Fuzz: We ain't got no rules between us though, have we?
[...]
Pete: Changed 'em round.
Will: We ain't got rules but we do things between us, but we do things that y'know, like er...say, I wouldn't knock off anybody's missus or Joey's missus, and they wouldn't do it to me, y'know what I mean? Things like that or, er... yer give 'im a fag, you expect one back, like, or summat like that.
Fred: T'ain't rules, it's just an understanding really.
Will: That's it, yes.
PW: [...] What would these understandings be?
Will: Er... I think, not to... meself, I think there ain't many of us that play up the first or second years, it really is that, but y'know, say if Fred had cum to me and sez, 'er... I just got two bob off that second year over there', I'd think, 'What a cunt', you know.
[...]
Fred: We're as thick as thieves, that's what they say, stick together.

There is a universal taboo among informal groups on the yielding of incriminating information about others to those with formal power. Informing contravenes the essence of the informal group's nature: the maintenance of oppositional meanings against the penetration of 'the rule'. The Hammertown lads call it 'grassing'. Staff call it telling the truth. 'Truth' is the formal complement of 'grassing'. It is only by getting someone to 'grass' – forcing them to break the solemnest taboo – that the primacy of the formal organization can be maintained. No wonder, then, that a whole school can be shaken with paroxysms over a major incident and the purge which follows it. It is an atavistic struggle about authority and the legitimacy of authority. The school has to win, and someone, finally, has to 'grass': this is one of the ways in which the school itself is reproduced and the faith of the 'ear'oles' restored. But whoever has done the 'grassing' becomes special, weak and marked. There is a massive retrospective and ongoing reappraisal among 'the lads' of the fatal flaw in his personality which had always been immanent but not fully disclosed till now:

[In a group discussion of the infamous 'fire extinguisher incident' in which 'the lads' took a hydrant out of school and let it off in the local park]

PW: It's been the biggest incident of the year as it's turned out, hasn't it?

Joey: It's been blown up into something fucking terrific. It was just like that [snapping his fingers], a gob in the ocean as far as I'm concerned when we did it, just like smoking round the corner, or going down the shop for some crisps.

PW: What happened [...]?

– Webby [on the fringes of the counterschool culture] grassed.

Joey: Simmondsy had me on me own and he said, 'One of the group owned up and tried to put all the blame on Fuzz'. But he'd only had Webby in there.

Spanksy: We was smoking out here.

Spike: He's like that, you'd got a fag, hadn't you [to Fuzz].

Spanksy: And Webby asks for a drag, so he give Webby the fag. Rogers [a teacher] walked through the door, and he went like that [demonstrating] and he says, 'It ain't mine sir, I'm just holding it for Fuzz'.

Will: Down the park before, [...] this loose thing, me and Eddie pulled it off, didn't we, me and Eddie, and the parky was coming round like, he was running round, wor'he, so me and Eddie we went round the other side, and just sat there, like you know, two monkeys. And Webby was standing there, and the parky come up to him and says, 'Come on, get out. Get out of this park. You'm banned'. And he says, he walks past us, me and Eddie, and he says, 'I know you warn't there, you was sitting here'. And Webby went, 'It warn't me, it was...', and he was just about to say summat, warn't he?

Eddie: That's it, and I said, 'Shhh', and he just about remembered not to grass us.

Membership of the informal group sensitizes the individual to the unseen informal dimension of life in general. Whole hinterlands open up of what lies behind the official definition of things. A kind of double capacity develops to register public descriptions and objectives on the one hand, and to look behind them, consider their implications, and work out what will actually happen, on the other. This interpretative ability is felt very often as a kind of maturation, a feeling of becoming 'worldliwise', of knowing 'how things really work when it comes to it'. It supplies the real 'insider' knowledge which actually helps you get through the day.

PW: Do you think you've learnt anything at school, has it changed or moulded your values?

Joey: I don't think school does fucking anything to you [...] It never has had much effect on anybody I don't think [after] you've learnt the basics. I mean school, it's fucking four hours a day. But it ain't the teachers who mould you, it's the fucking kids you meet. You'm only with the teachers 30 per cent of the time in school, the other fucking two-thirds are just talking, fucking pickin' an argument, messing about.

The group also supplies those contacts which allow the individual to build up alternative maps of social reality, it gives the bits and pieces of information for the individual to work out himself what makes things tick. It is basically only through the group that other groups are met, and through them successions of other groups. School groups coalesce and further link up with neighbourhood groups, forming a network for the passing-on of distinctive kinds of knowledge and perspectives that progressively place school at a tangent to the overall experience of being a working-class teenager in an industrial city. It is the infrastructure of the informal group which makes at all possible a distinctive kind of *class* contact, or class culture, as distinct from the dominant one.

Counterschool culture already has a developed form of unofficial bartering and exchange based on 'nicking', 'fiddles', and 'the foreigner' – a pattern which, of course, emerges much more fully in the adult working-class world:

Fuzz: If, say, somebody was to say something like, 'I'm looking, I want a cassette on the cheap like'. Right, talk about it, one of us hears about a cassette on the cheap, y'know, kind of do the deal for 'em and then say, 'Ah, I'll get you the cassette'.

Cultural values and interpretations circulate 'illicitly' and informally just as do commodities.

Opposition to the school is principally manifested in the struggle to win symbolic and physical space from the institution and its rules and to defeat its main perceived purpose: to make you 'work'. Both the winning and the prize – a form of self-direction – profoundly develop informal cultural meanings and practices. By the time a counterschool culture is fully developed its members have become adept at managing the formal system, and limiting its demands to the absolute minimum. Exploiting the complexity of modern regimes of mixed ability groupings, blocked timetabling and multiple RSLA options, in many cases this minimum is simply the act of registration.

[In a group discussion on the school curriculum]

Joey: [...] of a Monday afternoon, we'd have nothing right? Nothing hardly relating to school work, Tuesday afternoon we have swimming and they stick you in a classroom for the rest of the afternoon, Wednesday afternoon you have games and there's only Thursday and Friday afternoon that you work, if you call that work. The last lesson Friday afternoon we used to go and doss, half of us wagged out o' lessons and the other half go into the classroom, sit down and just go to sleep [...]

Spanksy: [...] Skive this lesson, go up on the bank, have a smoke, and the next lesson go to a teacher who, you know, 'll call the register [...]

Bill: It's easy to go home as well, like him [Eddie]...last Wednesday afternoon, he got his mark and went home [...]

Eddie: I ain't supposed to be in school this afternoon, I'm supposed to be at college [on a link course where students spend one day a week at college for vocational instruction]

PW: What's the last time you've done some writing?

Will: When we done some writing?

Fuzz: Oh are, last time was in careers, 'cos I writ 'yes' on a piece of paper, that broke me heart.

PW: Why did it break your heart?

Fuzz: I mean to write, 'cos I was going to try and go through the term without writing anything. 'Cos since we've cum back, I ain't dun nothing [it was half way through term].

Truancy is only a very imprecise – even meaningless – measure of rejection of school. This is not only because of the practice of stopping in school for registration before 'wagging off' (developed to a fine art among 'the lads'), but also because it only measures one aspect of what we might more accurately describe as informal student mobility. Some of 'the lads' develop the ability of moving about the school at their own will to a remarkable degree. They construct virtually their own day from what is offered by the school. Truancy is only one relatively unimportant and crude variant of this principle of self-direction which ranges across vast chunks of the syllabus and covers many diverse activities: being free out of class, being in class and doing no work, being in the wrong class, roaming the corridors looking for excitement, being asleep in private. The core skill which articulates these possibilities is being able to get out of any given class: the preservation of personal mobility.

[In a group discussion]

PW: But doesn't anybody worry about your not being in their class?

Fuzz: I get a note off the cooks saying I'm helping them [...]

John: You just go up to him [a teacher] and say, 'Can I go and do a job'. He'll say, 'Certainly, by all means', 'cos they want to get rid of you like.

Fuzz: Specially when I ask 'em.

Pete: You know the holes in the corridor, I didn't want to go to games, he told me to fetch his keys, so I dropped them down the hole in the corridor, and had to go and get a torch and find them.

For the successful, there can be an embarrassment of riches. It can become difficult to choose between self-organized routes through the day.

Will: [...] what we been doing, playing cards in this room 'cos we can lock the door.

PW: Which room's this now?

Will: Resources centre, where we're making the frames [a new stage for the deputy head], s'posed to be.

PW: Oh! You're still making the frames!

Will: We should have had it finished, we just lie there on top of the frame, playing cards, or trying to get to sleep [...] Well, it gets a bit boring, I'd rather go and sit in the classroom, you know.

PW: What sort of lessons would you think of going into?

Will: Uh, science, I think, 'cos you can have a laff in there sometimes.

This self-direction and thwarting of formal organizational aims is also an assault on official notions of time. The most arduous task of the deputy head is the construction of the timetables. In large schools, with several options open to the fifth year, everything has to be fitted in with the greatest of care. The first weeks of term are spent in continuous revision, as junior members of staff complain, and particular combinations are shown to be unworkable. Time, like money, is valuable and not to be squandered. Everything has to be ordered into a kind of massive critical path of the school's purpose. Subjects become measured blocks of time in careful relation to each other. Quite as much as the school buildings the institution over time *is* the syllabus. The complex charts on the deputy's wall show how it works. In theory it is possible to check where every individual is at every moment of the day. But for 'the lads' this never seems to work. If one wishes to contact them, it is much more important to know and understand their own rhythms and patterns of movement. These rhythms reject the obvious purposes of the timetable and their implicit notions of time. The common complaint about 'the lads' from staff and the 'ear'oles' is that they 'waste valuable time'. Time for 'the lads' is not something you carefully husband and thoughtfully spend on the achievement of desired objectives in the future. For 'the lads' time is something they want to claim for themselves now as an aspect of their immediate identity and self-direction. Time is used for the preservation of a state – being with 'the lads' – not for the achievement of a goal – qualifications.

Of course there is a sense of urgency sometimes, and individuals can see the end of term approaching and the need to get a job. But as far as their culture is concerned time is importantly simply the state of being free from institutional time. Its own time all passes as essentially the same thing, in the same units. It is not planned, and is not counted in loss, or expected exchange.

43   Ivan Reid

Social Class and Education

Interest in the relationship between class and education is . . . not only sociological. It has its roots in the whole philosophical and political question of equality (or rather the legitimate criteria for inequality) in education. . . .

While the concept of social class is very complex, for our present purpose we can accept the way it is operationalized in empirical research: 'a grouping of people into categories on the basis of occupation'.[1] Class is used in educational research in two main and distinct ways – as an individual characteristic and to characterize a geographical or other area. [Here we will consider] the first and most common approach, the relationship between parental class and child's achievement.

The main weight of research and concern has been with social class and terminal educational qualifications (O and A level GCE/further and higher education). It is possible, however, to trace class differences in participation and performance throughout the educational system. In the early 1970s access to preschool education was clearly related to class. At the extremes, twice the percentage of children of 'professional' fathers went to nursery school than those with unskilled manual fathers (14 per cent compared with 7 per cent) and nearly three times the percentage attended day nurseries or playgroups (18 per cent compared with 7 per cent). Following a government White Paper in 1972,[2] there was some expansion of provision which, together with a drop in the number of children in the relevant age group and a spread of part-time places, brought the class differences in respect of the chance of preschool education much closer. Whether, and how, such experience affects subsequent performance at school is not clearly indicated by research. What can be shown, however, is that by the age of seven, the differences in performance of the social classes in infant or first schools in the essentials of reading and arithmetic are marked. Table 1 contains figures based on the test scores of some 15,000 children, showing that those from social class V were six times more likely to be poor readers than those in class I (see top row of table). The study reveals even greater differences in respect of children who are 'non-readers', class V being fifteen times more likely than class

Table 1   Reading and arithmetic attainment test scores of 7-year-old children by social class of father (%)

	I	II	III (nm)	III (m)	IV	V	All[a]
				Social class			
Grouped Southgate reading-test scores							
0–20	8	15	14	30	37	48	29
21–8	37	39	43	41	38	34	39
29–30	54	47	43	29	25	17	32
Grouped problem arithmetic-test scores							
0–3	12	19	19	30	34	41	29
4–6	38	39	43	42	42	37	41
7–10	50	42	38	28	24	22	31

[a] Of whole sample, including those without father or social class information.
Source: I. Reid, *Social Class Differences in Britain*, 2nd edn (Oxford: Blackwell, 1981).

I to be in that category. The table also shows similar differences for mathematics. Note, too, the clear divide between the middle (I, II, IIInm) and the working classes (IIIm, IV, V) and how class I stands out as being better in terms of performance than the other middle classes while social class V performs correspondingly worse than the other working classes.

These early class differences increase with further schooling. Commenting later on the same children, Fogelman and Goldstein wrote:

> For a given 7-year score the children whose fathers were in non-manual occupations are, at the age of 11, about 1.0 years ahead of social classes III manual and IV, who in turn are about 0.4 years ahead of social class V. This, of course, is additional to the pre-existing differences at the age of 7, which were respectively 0.9 years and 0.7 years. Thus the overall differences at 11 have increased to 1.9 years and 1.11 years respectively.[3]

Very similar results were found for arithmetic. Douglas, in a similar longitudinal study using a battery of standardized tests including intelligence, reading and school attainment, showed that between the ages of 7 and 11 middle-class children's scores increased, whereas working-class children's scores declined, so that the difference between them increased.[4] Both these longitudinal studies found that the divergence of attainment test scores between the social classes observed at ages 7 and 11 continued through secondary school. So the overall picture is one of a widening gap between children from different social classes, which is greatest at ages 15 and 16. Fogelman et al. comment that their figures imply that at 16 years only about 15 per cent of children in social class V could be expected to score above the mean of non-manual children.[5] These findings are perhaps surprising. It could be held that schools ought to operate so that at least initial differences are not heightened while it might be argued that their purpose should be to equalize differences by improving the performance of weaker pupils.

The most crucial stage of schooling is clearly the leaving examinations. Burnhill provides a dramatic view of the relationship between social class and secondary school examination achievement among Scottish school-leavers.[6]

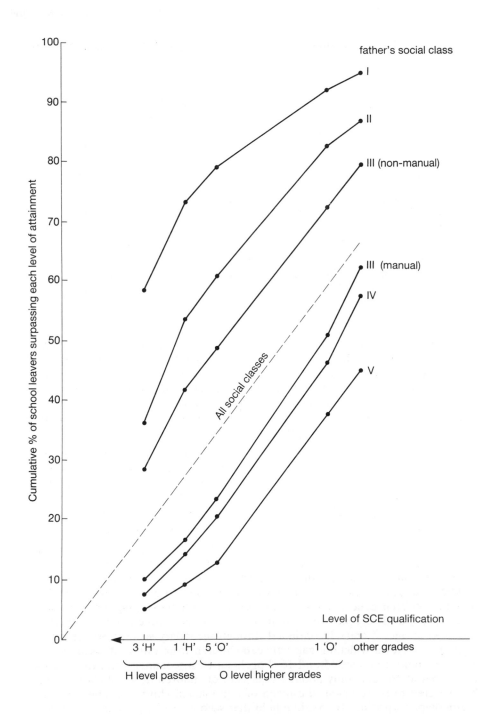

Figure 1 School examination performance of leavers from Scottish schools, 1975/6, by social class of father (cumulative percentages)
Source: P. Burnhill, 'The Relationship between Examination Performance and Social Class', *CES Collaborative Research Newsletter*, 8 (1981), fig. 1, p. 178.

Table 2 Highest educational qualification attained by persons, aged 25–49, by sex and social class of father, Great Britain 1981/2 (%)

	I	II	III	IV	V	VI	All
			Father's social class				
Males							
Degree or equivalent	40	20	22	6	5	4	10
Higher education below degree	17	15	13	10	7	8	11
GCE A level or equivalent	13	12	12	9	8	6	10
GCE O level/CSE higher grades or equivalent	16	20	17	15	11	8	15
GCE/CSE other grades/ commercial/apprenticeship	2	6	8	13	12	12	11
Foreign/other	5	6	5	4	3	2	4
None	7	22	22	44	55	60	40
Females							
Degree or equivalent	23	8	9	2	1	1	4
Higher education below degree	27	15	15	7	5	4	9
GCE A level or equivalent	9	8	6	3	3	1	4
GCE O level/CSE higher grades or equivalent	22	25	22	17	13	8	17
GCE/CSE other grades/ commercial/apprenticeship	6	11	14	12	11	9	12
Foreign/other	6	6	4	3	3	3	4
None	7	27	30	57	64	75	50
Social class of sample	3	17	10	44	19	7	100

Source: *General Household Survey 1982* (London: OPCS/HMSO, 1984), table 7.5(a).

[Figure 1] shows that at each level of achievement the percentage passing declines across the social classes from I to V, and this can be compared with the overall percentage (the hatched line) which neatly divides the non-manual from the manual classes. As can be seen, at the extremes 95 per cent of children from class I left school with at least some qualification and 58 per cent had three or more higher SCE passes, compared to only 45 per cent and 4 per cent respectively of those children from social class V. A more general view of the relationship is provided by the *General Household Survey 1982*.[7] Table 2 shows, by sex, the highest educational achievements of a large sample of adults related to the social class of their fathers. The expected pattern – the 'higher' the class the larger the proportion with qualifications – is sustained together with very clear indications of differences between the sexes. Some 40 per cent of males with fathers in social class I had degrees compared to 23 per cent of females, while only 7 per cent of both sexes had no qualifications. Of those with fathers in class VI, 60 per cent of males and 75 per cent of females had no qualifications, while only 4 per cent and 1 per cent respectively had a degree....

[The question of intelligence is] clearly important when viewing the terminal education achievements of the social classes.... Consequently, although the

Table 3   Academic achievement by pupils[a] at LEA grammar schools, by grouped IQ scores at age 11 and social class of father, England and Wales[b] (%)

| | | Social class | |
IQ score	Achievement	Non-manual	Manual
130+	Degree course	37	18
	At least 2 GCE A levels	43	30
	At least 5 GCE O levels	73	75
115–129	Degree course	17	8
	At least 2 GCE A levels	23	14
	At least 5 GCE O levels	56	45
100–114	Degree course	6	2
	At least 2 GCE A levels	9	6
	At least 5 GCE O levels	37	22

[a] Born in 1940/1.
[b] Figures for degree course are for Great Britain.
Source: *Higher Education (The Robbins Report)*, Cmnd 2154 (London: HMSO, 1963), table 5, appendix 1, part 2.

data in table 3 are dated, they are particularly valuable for our purpose since they hold constant the type of school attended and the measured IQ ranges of the children studied. The table shows that, other than for children of the highest IQ range (130 or more) at the O-level stage, differences in achievement existed between middle- and working-class children in distinct favour of the former. In the middle IQ range (115–29) a quarter as many more middle-class children gained five or more O levels than did the working-class, two-thirds as many more gained two A levels and more than twice the number entered degree-level courses. Note, however, that these are not measures of pure achievement. They also involve staying on at school and using educational qualifications to enter higher education rather than employment. Hence part of the difference in A-level success between the classes was due to differences in entry to sixth forms. Even at the highest IQ range the percentage of those who actually gained two A levels and subsequently went on to degree courses was 86 per cent for the middle and 60 per cent for the working class. Very similar results were obtained in a study some six years later, which held constant the type of school and the grade of 11+ secondary school selection examination.[8] Here, although the overall achievements at O level were higher, the social class differences remained. They are again revealed in the cohort from the study mentioned [in note 4]. The follow-up study, in which ability measured at age 15 was held constant but not the type of school attended, revealed that the percentage of the top-ability group (16 per cent) who had gained five or more O levels (including at least three from English language, mathematics, science and a foreign language) varied from 77 per cent for upper-middle-class children across the classes to 37 per cent for lower-working-class children.[9] These findings are broadly supported by Rutter et al. who, having controlled for verbal reasoning, found parental occupation to be related to the examination performance of children in

Table 4 Percentage distribution of full-time university entrants, United Kingdom, 1984, and further education students, Great Britain, 1977, by social class[a]

| | Class | | | | | | | |
	I	II	III (nm)	III (m)	IV	V	Middle	Working
University	22	48	10	12	6	1	80	19
Advanced further education	13	37	19	20	9	2	69	31
18-year-olds[b]	5	20	10	40	18	7	35	65

[a] The UCCA social class classification is based on occupational information provided by candidates and does not always include employment status.
[b] Based on 10–14-year-olds in 1971 Census.
Source: *UCCA: Twenty-second Report 1983–4* (Cheltenham: UCCA, 1985), p. 7; J. H. Farrant, 'Trends in Admissions', table 2.18, in O. Fulton, *Access to Higher Education* (Surrey: SRHE, 1981); Household Composition Tables (10% sample), *Census 1971, England and Wales* (London: OPCS/HMSO, 1975), table 46.

their sample of London schools.[10] The relationship was particularly strong among children in the middle band of ability and slightly less so for those in the higher-ability band.

Post-school education presents the starkest picture of the relationship between social class and education. The most comprehensive research was that of the Robbins Report,[11] which surveyed about one in every 200 people born in 1940/1. In terms of full-time degree-level courses the survey revealed that while a third of class I entered such courses, only 1 per cent of classes IV and V did so. In other words, a person from social class I was 33 times more likely to end up on an undergraduate course than someone from classes IV and V. At the other extreme, only 7 per cent of social class I failed to gain any educational qualification compared with 65 per cent (nearly two in every three) of classes IV and V. An interesting aspect of this research was that it also looked at the relationship between *mother's* social class (occupation before marriage) and children's educational achievement, with very similar results to those of father and child. The study did not, however, consider mothers and fathers together.

The evidence is brought more up to date in table 4, which shows the social class profile of university and advanced further education students. The bottom line of the table gives the overall distribution of the population by social class for comparison (though see footnote). There is a clear overrepresentation of the middle classes – who are only 35 per cent of the population, but 80 per cent of university undergraduates – and underrepresentation of working classes – 65 per cent of the population, only 19 per cent of undergraduates. The figures for advanced further education (which includes public sector undergraduates) are only slightly less pronounced at 69 and 31 per cent for middle and working class respectively. Class differences are stark at the extremes: 22 per cent of university undergraduates came from class I, 1 per cent from class V, despite the latter being larger in the population (7 per cent compared to 5 per cent).

44   Saeeda Cahanum

Finishing School: Asian Girls in the British Educational System

I hail a taxi to go to spend the day at Bradford Muslim Girls' School. The Asian taxi driver smiles and turns his gaze away from my face. This is a mark of respect on his part and a change from the normal flirtatious attitude of Asian drivers to a Westernized Asian woman with uncovered hair. He commends me on my choice of school and hopes that I will make a good student.

More than thirty girls attend this private school which is in an old stone building in the city centre. Parents pay for their daughters to receive a strong grounding in Islam in a place that sustains the religious and cultural values of Muslim home life. The school also acts as daytime custodian to ensure that the girls do not have the opportunity to stray from orthodoxy.

The school's existence owes much to the row in 1983 when an article by Bradford headmaster Ray Honeyford entitled 'Multiracial Influences' appeared in the right-wing *Salisbury Review*. Asian parents complained that Bradford Education Authority's multi-racial policy had failed to accommodate the religious beliefs of Muslim students. Some suggested separate schooling for girls and the Bradford Muslim Girls' School was born.

After assembly, the girls disperse to rooms named after the Prophet's wives and daughters to begin their studies. The classrooms are spartan, small and decorated with posters showing details of prayer, pilgrimage and the life of the Prophet. The school costs £100,000 a year to run – but only £28,000 is raised in fees. Private donations and school merchandizing help cover some of the costs but the school is run on a deficit. It employs seven part-time teachers and a headmistress, Nighat Mirza. Last year pupils were able to take GCSEs in Urdu, Childcare and Religious Studies. This year, French and English have been added. Next year maths and science are promised.

'Sacrifices have to be made,' says Mrs Mirza. 'I'm not sad that the girls in previous years left with no qualifications, but proud that they have the satisfaction of knowing that they did something for someone else.'

Mrs Mirza began her career after marriage and motherhood. She denies that by teaching the girls to be good wives and mothers she is placating Muslim men. 'By teaching the girls about Islam we are giving them tools with which to challenge and fight for their rights. Empowering women doesn't frighten men but creates a more stable society,' she says. 'Islam teaches us that men and women are equal but different.' Girls are also taught to understand the restrictions on their lives and that Islam is a preparation for the life hereafter.

Molly Somerville, a charismatic white woman, dressed in a *shalwaar-kameez* and wearing earrings shaped like the continent of Africa, teaches French and the Christian element of religious studies. The only presence of Islam in the French lesson is the press cuttings of the three French Muslim Alchaboun sisters involved in the campaign to allow them to wear the *hijab* (veil) to school. In the afternoon the same classroom doubles as a room for religious studies. Today the girls are learning about leprosy. They are told to look it up in the Bible and the Koran and compare the two. The girls then discuss modern-day equivalents of outcasts. Suggestions made include people with AIDS, the homeless and people with disabilities.

During the lunch hour I am surrounded by girls in their maroon uniform.

What do they like about the school? 'We get to learn all about our religion and can pray when we like. There is no racism here. No one laughs at the way we dress, because we are all the same,' they say.

Few dispute the fact that they could get the same religious education by going to an ordinary state school during the day and attending a supplementary school run by the mosque in the evenings. They agree that they would not be getting an education unless it was compulsory. They say they are educating themselves because 'they might need it one day'. 'If I am lucky I might get married to a man who will let me use my education and get a good job,' says one 15-year-old. A 16-year-old can't decide whether she wants to be a doctor or a lawyer, but says it will depend on what her parents allow her to do. This strikes a familiar chord with all of them. 'I want to be a hairdresser,' says another. Does she think she'll realize her ambition? 'No, because my parents won't let me.'

One tiny 14-year-old with freckles has hopes of being a journalist. I take to her immediately. She doesn't think her dream will come true because 'Asian parents don't allow their daughters to go into such professions.' A moment of silent confusion follows when I point out that they're talking to such a woman.

Mrs Mirza says she wants her 10-year-old daughter to get the best education possible. So will she send her to the school? 'Yes, but only if things improve.' Her daughter, she claims, doesn't need to come to the school to get the good grounding in Islam, because, says Mrs Mirza, 'I can provide that at home for her.'

The dilemma for the Muslim community is that having an educated daughter has a particular value, if only for the prestige in the marriage market. The conflict arises when education leads to independent thought among women and so a desire for independence. In response, parents opt for separate schooling as a means of social control. The girls, too, believe in education but end up aborting their own aspirations when faced with massive pressures.

At Belle Vue Girls' School, a Bradford comprehensive where most of the girls are Muslim, there are similar conflicts. Yet none of the girls wishes to go to a segregated school.

They see themselves as the 'lucky ones' for they have been brought up to see education as a privilege, not a right. They are unsure of the future. 'We all have our own plans, but we don't actually know what will happen,' says one lively 17-year-old about to sit her A levels. Girls who lack qualifications discover that the only alternative is marriage. These girls see marriage as the end of their individual identity and describe it as a form of death. One 18-year-old is getting involved in as many activities as possible before she gets married this summer. 'My in-laws are sexist and won't let me do anything once I'm married.' Yet she doesn't see herself as being oppressed. 'My parents' choice is my choice. My freedom is in my mind.'

Community pressure plays an overwhelming role in their lives, and 'mistakes' by other women in the community cause more restrictions. 'Asian parents don't understand the concept of individuality, we're always judged by someone else's standards, never our own,' says Farrah, a 17-year-old Muslim and former heavy metal fan who found her identity at 13 when she became a practising Muslim. Dressed in a *hijab*, she says Islam has taught her her rights, that she no longer lets people take advantage of her and that religion is the dominant force in her life. 'It answers all my questions, makes sense and is perfectly logical.' Muslim women, she adds, are oppressed not because of religion but through a lack of religious education. 'Women have to be educated to use religion as a tool and not leave the interpretation up to men.'

For Asian women teachers, social pressures impose particular restrictions and difficulties. The younger generation of women teachers in particular work hard to challenge their students' cultural and religious upbringing and to use their own experience as a model and guide.

Saira had been teaching in a Bradford state school for one year when a colleague reprimanded her for challenging an Asian girl who said arranged marriages work because there are hardly any divorces. The white teacher accused Saira of 'arrogance' and told her to stop confusing the girl and learn to be more 'objective' about cultural concerns. 'As a black teacher in this school...' began Saira. 'You're not a black teacher, you're *a* teacher,' came the response.

This incident, says Saira, highlights the complexities and contradictions of her position. 'As a professional I'm expected to detach myself from the concerns of Asian pupils. However, as an informed insider who has experienced the intolerable pressures the community brings to bear on girls, I feel I have a duty to encourage pupils to hope for more from life.'

Some girls assume that because Saira is young, drives a car, wears Western clothes and teaches a subject other than Urdu her experiences are completely different to theirs. To them she's distant and totally 'free'. 'This is just one step away from seeing me as an Uncle Tom, a mere token,' says Saira.

Asian parents also have different expectations of an Asian teacher. On the one hand, they welcome the fact that Saira is Asian, but they also expect her to police their daughters on behalf of the community. 'Tell me straight away if you see her hanging around with boys after school, won't you?' they say.

Saira's ambivalent relationship with her pupils is paralleled by a story told by Asha, a 24-year-old teacher in a Leeds state school. A stone was recently thrown at her in the classroom in what she describes as a display of 'tabloid fundamentalism'.

'I have an extremely good relationship with my 14-year-olds. They love a teacher who relates to them in both language and experience. On this particular day, a new Asian girl had joined the class and I suppose the others were trying to impress her by seeing what they could do to rile me,' says Asha. 'I turned to the blackboard and felt this stone whiz past my head and hit the board.' Asha's calm response resulted in the culprit coming forward to confess the full story. The girls had had a meeting during break and collected nine stones each, the size of pebbles, and decided that if 'Miss' gave a negative response to the question 'Are you fasting?' then they would discharge their missiles at her. All but one lost their nerve.

Asha and another teacher tried to make sense of the episode and there is talk of bringing parents in to discuss it and reiterate the school's philosophy of tolerance. She now thinks that all the girls have an ambivalent attitude towards her. 'Part of them finds me and all I stand for enticing, yet another part of them finds me threatening. It was this conflict and in-bred conditioning that made them respond to me in what I regard as a fundamentalist way.'

The Rushdie episode has put Muslim girls' schools back on the agenda and the gains made in state schools since 1984 are under threat. Although the Bradford Muslim Girls' School was set up in 1984 it did not represent the feelings of the majority of Asians. Polls taken by the Commission for Racial Equality in 1984 found little support for separate schooling in Bradford. This put paid to plans by the Muslim Parents' Association to buy four state girls' schools and transform them into separate Muslim girls' schools. At that time, the Bradford Council for Mosques also opposed the demand for separate schooling, opting instead for a compromise with Bradford council in which they accepted concessions in dress and food. In public, the Bradford Council for Mosques said the proposal had not been thought out properly.

Other Asian organizations said the idea smacked of 'educational apartheid'. Privately, it was rumoured that the Council for Mosques decided tactically that the time was not right to pursue the campaign because of the atmosphere created by the Honeyford affair.

The Rushdie affair has reinforced the Bradford Muslims' siege mentality and with this has come talk of separate schools. A culture besieged in this way throws up its own notions of what a 'good Muslim woman' should be. Religion then becomes a substitute for a kind of cultural conformity. In practice, Islam comes to represent what is allowed rather than what is possible. For women the idea of *Izzat*, or chastity and honour, has become the means of social control, and separate schools the perfect institutions for exercising that control. And as Saira and Asha have learnt through their own experiences as Asian teachers, intellectual freedom is meaningless unless it goes hand in hand with social freedom. The girls of the Bradford Muslim Girls' School have yet to learn the lesson but if – and when – they do, they too will go on the offensive in their fight for self-determination.

45   Tamar Liebes and Elihu Katz

Dallas and Genesis: Some Questions of Education and Popular Culture

Despite the universal popularity of American films and television, and the allegations of cultural imperialism that accompany their diffusion, almost no-body has bothered to find out how they are decoded or indeed whether they are understood at all. Our subjects are persons of some secondary schooling drawn from four ethnic communities in Israel – Arabs, newly arrived Russian Jews, Moroccan Jews and kibbutz members – and non-ethnic Americans in Los Angeles. Groups of six persons – three couples, all friends, meeting in the home of one of them – are asked to discuss an episode of *Dallas* immediately after seeing it on the air. We have begun to conduct a parallel study in Japan – one of the few countries in which *Dallas* failed – but have only preliminary results so far. . . .

Before we summarize these findings, we wish to dismiss the widely-held view that the success of programmes like *Dallas* can be explained in terms of their simplemindedness or in terms of their rich visual appearance. The fact is that the programme is not simple at all – one must learn the complex relationships among the large number of characters, and one must learn how to make a coherent story out of the 'staccato' series of scenes and subplots that are presented to the viewer without benefit of narration. Moreover, the pretty pictures are by no means sufficient to an understanding of the narrative. One cannot decode the story without its words, and in Israel, for example, these words appear in subtitles in two languages, Hebrew and Arabic.

We think, rather, that the secret of *Dallas* is in the ways in which it offers viewers at different levels and in different cultures something they can understand from within themselves.

We are not referring here to the superficial problem of understanding; in fact, we find that all of the groups we studied have an elementary understanding of the story as a drama of human relationships (whether this is true of the whole world, we cannot yet say, but we assume that it is). What we do wish to do here is to distinguish, first of all, among different types of understanding. Then we wish to show that these types of understanding are related to different types of involvement. Finally, we will argue that programmes like *Dallas* invite these multiple levels of understanding and involvement, offering a wide variety of different projects and games to different types of viewers.

It is often remarked that *Dallas* provokes conversation. An essay on *Dallas* in Algeria, for example, argues that the programme replaced the conversation following grandmothers' storytelling around the fireside.[1] Our study documents this phenomenon extensively. A kibbutz member says that the secretariat of the kibbutz is occupied with talk of *Dallas* on the day after the programme. A new immigrant from Russia says that *Dallas* is compulsory viewing for anybody who wants to be part of Israeli society!

What we want to say is that to view *Dallas* overseas – perhaps even in America – is to view a *programme* and not – as certain critics think – to view moving wallpaper. It is, in fact, more than viewing a programme, it is becoming engaged with a narrative psychologically, socially and aesthetically, depending on the background of the viewer. Programmes like *Dallas* appear to be able to activate very different kinds of viewers.

To analyse these different types of understanding and involvements, we distinguish, first, between the referential and the metalinguistic. In answer to our question, 'Why all the fuss about babies?' some viewers refer to real life and explain that families, especially rich ones, need heirs. Others, using a metalinguistic frame, say that babies are good material for conflict, and the narrative of soap opera needs conflict to keep going. Within the referential, we distinguish between real and ludic keyings. The one makes serious equations between the story and life, the other treats the programme more playfully, subjunctively and interactively – turning the group discussion into a kind of psychodrama. Making a further distinction within the referential, some viewers key the programme normatively, judging messages and characters moralistically; others treat the programme as observers and withhold value judgements. The moralizing statements tend to be couched in the language of 'we': 'Their women are immoral; our Arab women would not behave that way.' Less moralizing statements come either in the language of 'they' – for those who generalize from the programme to the universals of life – and in the language of 'I' and 'You' for those who treat programme and life more playfully.

Applying these distinctions to viewers of different education and different ethnicity reveals how understanding and involvement may vary among groups. While all groups make many more referential than metalinguistic statements, the better-educated viewers use the metalinguistic frame much more. Better-educated viewers decode the programme at two levels – referential and metalinguistic – thus involving themselves not only in the narrative but in its construction.

Patterns of involvement vary by ethnicity as well. The more traditional groups – Moroccan Jews and Arabs – do not stray far from the referential. Even the well-educated among them make comparatively few metalinguistic statements. They accept the programme as real, and deal seriously with its relationship to their own lives. The Arabs in particular discuss the programme moralistically, and in terms of 'them' and 'us'. This pattern of relating to the programme is at once involving and defensive: the programme is discussed referentially and seriously, but, at the same time, it is rejected as a message for 'us'. Even if this rejection serves as a buffer against the influence of the programme, it nevertheless reflects a high level of engagement.

The American and kibbutz groups show an altogether different pattern of involvement. The rate of their metalinguistic statements is high, and their use of the referential is often in the ludic mode. Some of their dialogue reminds one of fantasy games.

Like the Americans and kibbutzniks, the Russians also have a high proportion of metalinguistic statements – the highest proportion, in fact. They are critical not only of the aesthetics of the story (comparing it unfavourably to Tolstoy and other literary sagas) but about the message, which they regard as an ideological manipulation. Beware, say the Russians, of the false message of the programme. They tell us that the rich are unhappy because that's what they want us to think!

Note the difference between these forms of criticism and those of the traditional groups. The Arabs, as we have said, criticize the seeming real-life behaviour of the characters as immoral but believe the surface message of the narrative that the rich are unhappy. This decoding is precisely what the Russian criticism warns against.

Curiously, however, when the Russians use the referential frame, they seem to set aside their ideological suspicions and treat the programme, as the Arabs and Moroccans do, as if it were a documentary. Going even further than the traditional groups – who accept the programme as the truth about Americans but reject the programme as a portrayal of themselves – the Russians seem to be saying that entire classes of people – women, businessmen and so on – behave as their *Dallas* counterparts do. The seriousness of their sweeping universal generalizations from the programme to life are altogether different from the ludic keyings of the Americans and kibbutzniks.

Thus we see at least three different patterns of involvement in these decodings. The more traditional viewers remain in the realm of the real (and the serious), and mobilize values to defend themselves against the programme. The more Western groups – the Americans and the kibbutzniks – are relatively more aware of, and involved in, the construction of the programme, and deal with its reality more playfully. The Russians are also metalinguistic – most of all, in fact – but they show more awareness of the message of the programme than of its structure. This concern seems to go together with the seriousness with which the Russians enter the referential just as the more constructionist concerns of the other Western groups go hand in hand with their more playful keyings of the referential.

It is evident that each pattern of involvement includes a mechanism of defence. The Arabs, accepting the programme's reality, reject the values of the characters. The Russians reject the values of the producers. The Americans and kibbutzniks reject the idea that the values – either of characters or producers – are to be taken seriously.

We cannot answer the question whether these forms of distancing – any one or all – reduce the extent of viewer vulnerability. While it may appear, at first glance, that ludic keyings and metalinguistic framings are more resistant to influence, we are by no means certain that this is so. The ludic may be seductive in the sense that fantasy and subjectivity invite one to be carried away. Similarly, constructionst concerns distract attention from the ideological message. Even ideological decodings are vulnerable to influence in the sense that the decoders believe that their oppositional reading is the truth!

Whatever the answer to this question, the fact that the progamme invites very different – educationally and ethnically – kinds of viewers to become involved in their several ways is the concern of this [discussion]. We turn, therefore, to the next question: namely, what it is about a programme like *Dallas* – or perhaps, what is it about the soap opera genre to which it is related – that makes this kind of multi-dimensional participation possible?

In attempting to answer this question, we are led by the viewers to two dimensions of the *Dallas* genre: the semantic dimension, which draws so heavily on primordial themes of human relations, and the syntactic dimension of seriality, which regularly combines and recombines this set of basic relational elements to tell endless variations of the same story. In other words, we are suggesting that these two dimensions of the genre constitute invitations to the viewer to invest his or her emotions, empathy, and expertise as a card-carrying member of a kinship group and to invest his or her imagination and puzzle-solving predilections in the game of how they are going to do it this week.

We cannot claim to be discovering more than our colleagues have, and cannot prove that we were first. In fact, the idea of the universal appeal of soap opera as a drama of kinship in which we are all connoisseurs has been stated by others, both in general[2] and with respect to programmes like *Dallas*.[3] And the idea of seriality as a form of aesthetic pleasure has also been stated, most recently by Umberto Eco.[4] What we can say is that our point of departure does not proceed from content analysis of the text to some imagined reader supposedly constructed by the text, but inductively, from real readers – and the variations in their readings – to those aspects of the text that invite different levels of decoding and different forms of involvement. Thus we can show that Eco's two readers – the 'naive' and the 'smart', which ostensibly correspond to semantic and syntactic decodings – may, in reality, be the same person. To show that these two model readers can coexist in the same minds and hearts is one of the advantages of our method.

Primordiality: Dallas is a primordial tale echoing the most fundamental mythologies . . . [T]he mythic reverberations figure in many of the group discussions. For example, Ayad, in one of the Arab groups (group 40), tells the *Dallas* story as follows:

> It's about a rich family who have a large inheritance. They have oil, and two sons. The older son is a cheat. He wanted to grab control of all the wealth of his father and mother. The younger one tried to share in the property but the older one schemed and plotted to get the money. And the two brothers quarreled.

Notice how this quote omits the name of the characters in favour of their primordial roles, and how familiar it all sounds to teller and listener.

A more sophisticated version of this same kind of telling is Eitan's in one of kibbutz groups (group 80): 'He was the elder son, and it's as if he was constantly trying to prove his worth to his parents. There was another (a third) brother whom the mother loved, and baby Bobby was loved by the father.'

A Japanese viewer also recognizes the primordial quality of these relationships but makes clear that these are better forgotten: 'It certainly reminds us of the Japanese before the war. Elements such as inheritance, relationship between bride and mother-in-law and powerful eldest son – these are points we want to forget.'

There are different levels of sophistication, different theories that are invoked in telling, attributing motivation and interpreting, and a different selection of issues that are focused upon. But sophisticated or not, mythic or not, we all are connoisseurs of these human relations and the psychology, sociology and politics that define them. In other words, all viewers – each at his own level of sophistication and embedded in his own culture – will find familiar the narrative of the embroilments of kinship, and can become involved in how these characters are organizing their lives by comparison with all of the other kinship texts we know – our own, our neighbours', and our forefathers'. It is likely that these kinship stories become so engrossing that the rest of social and political reality is shut out and not missed. This clearly has a political consequence.

Seriality: Our involvement in these characters and their stories not only reflects their enactment of human texts that are familiar to us but reflects no less our week-to-week familarity with them. We are connoisseurs not just of the situation but of these very people. The familiarity that results from these weekly visits leads, for one thing, to what is known as parasocial interaction, whereby people talk back to the characters approvingly or disapprovingly, wishing them well or ill, urging them on, warning them of danger, worrying about the shame they will bring upon themselves. Indeed, seriality at the referential level often puts the viewer in a position where he knows more about a character than the character knows about himself, thus increasing the viewer's sense of control over the goings-on. . . .

The open-minded nature of the family serial, of course, distinguishes it from some of the formulaic constraints of the series in which each story is self-contained and has to be resolved within fifty minutes. The serial allows for greater character development, more ambiguity and more complexity. In a word, soap opera *is* more like reality, and it is no wonder that the stories enter into the realm of gossip. Moreover, the incomplete nature of each episode that leaves us hanging on a cliff is reminiscent of the Zeigarnik effect, which posits that interrupted tasks are better remembered than completed ones. This is yet a further dimension to help explain the active nature of reader involvement in serial narratives, as literary theorists have already noted.[5]

Seriality as an invitation to viewer involvement operates not just at the referential level but also at the metalinguistic level. At this level, viewers can name the genre and compare it to others: they can define its attributes and dramatic conventions, such as its division into subplots woven around characters and the staccato succession of two- and three-person dialogues. While the Americans compare the dynamics of *Dallas* to those of other television dramas, the Russians use the classic novel, much to the detriment of *Dallas*. From our study, it is clear that television viewers are much better critics than they are usually given credit for. They become quite involved in these analyses and comparisons, which are often emotionally loaded. Indeed, some viewers show considerable sophistication about the constraints that operate on producers. Thus certain kinds of viewers can identify the elements out of which the story is constructed and the characters created. In other words, viewers in the meta-linguistic frame can do what they do not do in the referential frame, namely, to put the pieces together – to combine and recombine them – as the writers do, while managing, nevertheless, to switch back and forth from referential to the metalinguistic.

The key to viewer involvement at this level is in the realization that the story is like a contest in which the outcomes can repeatedly change or like a game in which the pieces can be put together in different ways. For long periods of time, the pieces are the characters as given – in number, gender, personality and kinship roles. These characters can be rotated through an elementary series of changing problems and relationships that are necessary to keep the story going. Viewers who relate to the programme at this level become interested in how the characters will next confront a problem or each other. Consider Deanne (American group 9), who says, 'Now it seems that Katherine has got her eye on

Bobbie, and in this one episode there is just a little bit of hint she will have her way.' Continuing her thought, Jill says, 'This will snap Pam out of her depression fast enough.' And Deanna adds, 'Or put her into a worse one.'

Another viewer, Greg (American group 3) sees a seesaw domination and subordination at work. He says it's like a wrestling match.

> The bad guys keep squashing the good guys using all the dirty tricks and then every once in a while some good guys will resort to the bad guy's tricks and, you know, stomp on the bad guys for a while, and all the crowd will go yeah yeah yeah and then the next week the bad guys are on top again squashing the good guys.

Greg's involvement is in his intellectual perception of the programme as contest, and not in the emotions of soap opera. In the longer run, the character of the characters also changes, and viewers get the idea that the true building blocks, or pieces, of the puzzle may not be the characters as given once and for all but structural attributes that are redivided among the characters. Thus the good and the bad guys may not only struggle for domination but actually exchange roles.

46   John B. Thompson

Mass Communication, Symbolic Goods and Media Products

The advent of mass communication, and especially the rise of mass circulation newspapers in the nineteenth century and the emergence of broadcasting in the twentieth, has had a profound impact on the modes of experience and patterns of interaction characteristic of modern societies. For most people today, the knowledge we have of events which take place beyond our immediate social milieu is a knowledge largely derived from our reception of mass-mediated symbolic forms. The knowledge we have of political leaders and their policies, for instance, is a knowledge derived largely from newspapers, radio and television, and the ways in which we participate in the institutionalized system of political power are deeply affected by the knowledge so derived. Similarly, our experience of events which take place in contexts that are spatially and temporally remote, from strikes and demonstrations to massacres and wars, is an experience largely mediated by the institutions of mass communication; indeed, our experience of these events as 'political', as constitutive of the domain of experience which is regarded as politics, is partly the outcome of a series of institutionalized practices which endow them with the status of news. The role of the media is so fundamental in this regard that it would be partial at best to portray the nature and conduct of politics at a national and international level without reference to the processes of mass communication.

In this [discussion] I want to begin to explore some of the ways in which the advent of mass communication has transformed the modes of experience and patterns of interaction characteristic of modern societies....

Let me begin by analysing some of the general characteristics of what is commonly called 'mass communication'. It has often been pointed out that, while 'mass communication' is a convenient label for referring to a broad range of media institutions and products, the term is misleading in certain respects. It is worth dwelling for a moment on some of the respects in which this term can lead astray. The expression 'mass' derives from the fact that the messages transmitted by the media industries are generally available to relatively large audiences. This is certainly the case in some sectors of the media industries and at some stages in their development, such as the mass circulation newspaper industry and the major television networks. However, during other periods in the development of the media industries (e.g. the early newspaper industry) and in some sectors of the media industries today (e.g. some book and magazine publishers), the audiences were and remain relatively small and specialized. Hence the term 'mass' should not be construed in narrowly quantitative terms; the important point about mass communication is not that a given number or proportion of individuals receive the products, but rather that the products are available in principle to a plurality of recipients. Moreover, the term 'mass' is misleading in so far as it suggests that the audiences are like inert, undifferentiated heaps. This suggestion obscures the fact that the messages transmitted by the media industries are received by specific individuals situated in particular social–historical contexts. These individuals attend to media messages with varying degrees of concentration, actively interpret and make sense of these messages and relate them to other aspects of their lives. Rather than viewing these individuals as part of an inert and undifferentiated mass, we should leave open the possibility that the reception of media messages is an active, inherently critical and socially differentiated process.

If the term 'mass' may be misleading in this context, the term 'communication' may also be, since the kinds of communication generally involved in mass communication are quite different from those involved in ordinary conversation. I shall examine some of these differences in the course of the following discussion. Here I shall call attention to one important difference: namely, that mass communication generally involves a one-way flow of messages from the transmitter to the receiver. Unlike the dialogical situation of a conversation, in which a listener is also a potential respondent, mass communication institutes a fundamental *break* between the producer and receiver, in such a way that recipients have relatively little capacity to contribute to the course and content of the communicative process. Hence it may be more appropriate to speak of the 'transmission' or 'diffusion' of messages rather than of 'communication' as such. Yet even in the circumstances of mass communication, recipients do have some capacity to contribute, in so far as recipients are also consumers who may sometimes choose between various media products and whose views are sometimes solicited or taken into account by the organizations concerned with producing and diffusing these products. Moreover, it is possible that new technological developments – such as those associated with fibre optic cables – will increase the interactive capacity of the medium of television and give viewers greater control over the transmission process, although the extent to which this will become a practical reality remains to be seen.

In the light of these preliminary qualifications, I want to offer a broad conceptualization of mass communication and to highlight some of its key characteristics. We may broadly conceive of mass communication as *the institutionalized production and generalized diffusion of symbolic goods via the transmission and storage of information communication*. By conceiving of mass communication in terms of the production and diffusion of symbolic goods, I wish to stress the importance of viewing mass communication in relation to the institutions concerned with the commodification of symbolic forms. What we now describe as mass communication is a range of phenomena and processes that emerged historically through the development of institutions seeking to exploit new opportunities for the fixation and reproduction of symbolic forms.

I . . . want to analyse mass communication in a more theoretical way by focusing on the following four characteristics: the institutionalized production and diffusion of symbolic goods; the instituted break between production and reception; the extension of availability in time and space; and the public circulation of symbolic forms. . . .

The first characteristic of mass communication is *the institutionalized production and diffusion of symbolic goods*. Mass communication presupposes the development of institutions – that is, relatively stable clusters of social relations and accumulated resources – concerned with the large-scale production and generalized diffusion of symbolic goods. These activities are 'large-scale' in the sense that they involve the production and diffusion of multiple copies or the provision of materials to numerous recipients. This is rendered possible by the fixation of symbolic forms in technical media and by the reproducibility of the forms. *Fixation* may involve processes of encoding whereby symbolic forms are translated into information which can be stored in a particular medium or material substratum; the symbolic forms may be transmitted as information and then decoded for the purposes of reception or consumption. The symbolic forms diffused by mass communication are inherently *reproducible* in the sense that multiple copies may be produced or made available to numerous recipients. The reproduction of forms is generally controlled as strictly as possible by the institutions of mass communication, since it is one of the principal means by which symbolic forms are subjected to economic valorization. Forms are reproduced in order to be exchanged on a market or through a regulated type of economic transaction. Hence they are *commodified* and treated as objects to be sold, as services to be paid for or as media which can facilitate the sale of other objects or services. In the first instance, therefore, mass communication should be understood as part of a range of institutions concerned, in varying ways, with the fixation, reproduction and commodification of symbolic forms.

A second characteristic of mass communication is that *it institutes a fundamental break between the production and reception of symbolic goods*. These goods are produced for recipients who are generally not physically present at the place of production and transmission or diffusion; they are, literally, *mediated* by the technical media in which they are fixed and transmitted. This characteristic is not, of course, unique to mass communication: the fixation and transmission of symbolic forms on papyrus or stone also involved a break between production and reception. But with the rise of mass communication, the range of producers and receivers affected by this process has greatly expanded. Moreover, as I noted earlier, the mediation of symbolic forms via mass communication generally involves a one-way flow of messages from the producer to the recipient, such that the capacity of the recipient to influence or intervene in the processes of production and transmission or diffusion is strictly limited. One consequence of this condition is that the processes of production and transmission or diffusion are characterized by a distinctive form of *indeterminacy*. Symbolic forms are produced for audiences and transmitted or diffused in order to reach these audiences, but these processes generally take place in the absence of a direct and continuous monitoring of the audiences' responses. In contrast to face-to-face interaction, where the interlocutors can question one another and observe one another's responses, in mass communication the personnel involved in the production and transmission or diffusion are generally deprived of immediate feedback from the recipients. Since the economic valorization of mass-mediated symbolic forms may depend crucially on the nature and extent of reception, the personnel involved typically employ a variety of strategies to cope with this indeterminacy. They draw upon past experience and use it as a guide to likely future outcomes; they use well-tried formulas which have a predictable audience appeal; or they try to obtain information about recipients through market research or through the routine monitoring of audience size and response. These and other techniques are institutionalized mechanisms which enable personnel to reduce the indeterminacy stemming from the break between production and reception, and to do so in a way which concurs with the overall aims of the institutions concerned.

A third characteristic of mass communication is that *it extends the availability of symbolic forms in time and in space*. Again, this characteristic is not unique to mass communication: all forms of cultural transmission involve some degree of space–time distanciation. But the media of mass communication generally involve a relatively high degree of distanciation in both space and time; and, with the development of telecommunications, space–time distanciation is severed from the physical transportation of symbolic forms. The transmission of symbolic forms via telecommunications – for example, via a network of terrestrial and satellite relays – enables the institutions of mass communication to achieve a high degree of spatial distanciation in a minimal amount of time. Moreover, since the symbolic forms are generally fixed in a relatively durable medium, such as paper, photographic film or electromagnetic tape, they also have extended availability in time and can be preserved for subsequent use. The space–time distanciation involved in mass communication is also affected by the conditions under which symbolic forms are received and consumed. By virtue of the instituted break between production and reception, the nature and extent of distanciation may depend on the social practices and technical conditions of reception. For example, the extension of availability of a book in time and space may depend as much on the ways in which the book is received – whether it is recommended or ignored, incorporated into curricula or actively suppressed, and so on – as it depends on the channels of diffusion and the nature of the technical medium itself. Similarly, the extension of availability of a television programme or film may depend on whether potential recipients have the technical means to receive the programme, whether the scheduling concurs with the social organization of their everyday lives, and so on.

A fourth characteristic of mass communication is that *it involves the public circulation of symbolic forms*. The products of mass communication are produced in principle for a plurality of recipients. In this respect, mass communication differs from forms of communication – such as telephone conversations, teleconferencing or private video recordings of various kinds – which employ the same technical media of fixation and transmission but which are orientated towards a single or highly restricted range of recipients. This basic difference between established forms of mass communication and other forms of electronically mediated interaction may be called into question by the increasing deployment of new communication technologies, but this is a development which has yet to be fully realized. As the institutions of mass communication have developed hitherto, their products circulate within a 'public domain', in the sense that they are available in principle to anyone who has the technical means, abilities and resources to acquire them. While the nature and scope of this public domain may be unlimited in principle, it is always limited in practice by the social–historical conditions of production, transmission and reception. The institutions of mass communication often aim to reach as large an audience as possible, since the size of the audience may directly affect the economic valorization of the products concerned. Today the audiences for some films and television programmes may amount to hundreds of millions of viewers worldwide; a single Christmas Day television broadcast can command more than 30 million viewers in Britain alone. The nature and scope of the audiences for the products of mass communication vary enormously from one medium to another, and from one product to another within the same medium. The ways in which these products are appropriated by the recipients – whether, for example, they are appropriated by a collective gathering in a cinema or by a private viewing in the home – also vary considerably, depending on the medium, the product, the channels of diffusion and the social and technical conditions of reception. One consequence of the intrinsically public character of media products is that the development of mass communication has been accompanied by attempts to exercise control, on the part of state authorities and other regulatory bodies, over the institutions of mass communication. The very capacity of these institutions to make symbolic forms available to a potentially vast audience is a source of concern for authorities which seek to maintain order and regulate social life within the territories under their jurisdiction.

Part 12

Religion and Society

The classical social thinkers, such as Marx, Weber and Durkheim, all believed that with the progressive development of modern societies, religion (at least in its traditional sense as the belief in supernatural beings) would disappear. This has not happened: religious beliefs and ideals seem not only to have remained strong, but in certain contexts to have undergone a significant revival and further elaboration.

Yet everyone agrees that the role of religion in modern societies is substantially different from its role in pre-modern times, and that in some respects the hold of religion over people's day-to-day lives has weakened. It remains widely debated how far such a process of weakening, or secularization, has occurred, and what its implications are for other social institutions. In the first two selections in this part (readings 47 and 48), Thomas Luckmann and Jeffrey Hadden consider different aspects of the question of secularization. Luckmann argues that, in modern societies, personal identity is essentially formed through individual experience, rather than structured in terms of public or group critieria. To a much larger degree than in traditional cultures, the individual is left free to choose her or his mode of life, friends, marriage partners and so forth. The position of religion in modern societies has to be understood in relation to such individualization: religious belief increasingly becomes a matter of individual decision and represents a search for self-fulfilment.

Hadden provides a balanced assessment of the various arguments involved in the secularization debate. He points out that the major difficulty with the thesis of progressive socialization is that there is little accurate historical evidence about patterns of belief and religious practice in the past. If we cannot be sure how strong religious beliefs used to be, and whether or not individuals regularly took part in religious practices, we cannot easily assess how far profound changes have taken place.

Hadden concludes that secularization has almost certainly occurred in certain spheres, and in respect of particular aspects of religious organization and practice; but he argues that other aspects of religion remain of basic importance. Religion and political movements, he points out, have become closely intertwined. An example is provided by Emmanuel Sivan (reading 49) in his discussion of Islamic fundamentalism. This religious orientation, Sivan makes clear, has to be understood in some part as a reaction against the impact of Western culture upon other parts of the world.

47   **Thomas Luckmann**

Religion and Personal Identity in Modern Society

The history of Western civilization is marked by the continuous expansion of institutional specialization of religion.... In the heterogeneous, geographically and socially mobile urban milieu of the Hellenistic world, the sacred cosmos that had become part of that world lost its original, relatively simple relationship to more or less self-contained societies. The partly 'disembodied' sacred cosmos was drawn into syncretistic developments which could be accommodated – although with some difficulty – within the framework of the dominant and institutionally non-specialized religion of the Roman Empire – traditionally rooted in the political and kinship structure of ancient Rome. The eschatological texture of Christian beliefs of the early period and its influence upon the Christian conception of the extent of legitimate political control made such accommodation extremely difficult in the case of Christianity. While submitting to the 'properly' defined authority of political institutions, Christianity resisted their traditional *religious* claims. The outcome of the ensuing struggle affected both the character of political institutions in the subsequent history of Europe *and* the direction that was taken by the further development of the incipient church-structure of Christianity. The autonomy of the state was defined in 'secular' terms – despite some vestiges of earlier conceptions that survived in the Holy Roman Empire through the feudal period. The autonomy of the Church gained a specifically religious significance – despite the 'secular' entanglements of religious institutions. The definitions of religious and political jurisdictions were the basis for the variety of arrangements and conflicts between Church and state that characterize the subsequent history of Europe.

The Church, having remained victorious in a situation of 'pluralistic' competition and having adapted herself to the requirements of institutional survival *vis-à-vis* the state, became the visible, specialized institutional basis for *one* well-articulated and obligatory sacred cosmos. Identity between Church and religion, and congruence between the 'official' model of religion and the prevalent individual systems of 'ultimate' significance, was taken for granted in ecclesiastic ideology. For some time it was also approximated – although not fully accomplished – in fact. The factors that cause a growing incongruence between the 'official' model and individual religiosity and disrupt the identity of church and religion are incipiently present in this social form of religion. Until the late Middle Ages these 'seeds of secularization' were here placed in infertile soil. The circumstances which generally retard the growth of incongruence between the 'official' model and individual religiosity prevailed. With the waning of the feudal order, however, the situation began to change. The structural basis for the approximate identity of Church and religion was dissolving. The change in the social order transformed the everyday lives and the effective priorities of ever wider strata of the population. The growing discrepancies between the socially prevalent effective priorities and the 'official' model undermined the latter and bestowed upon it an increasingly rhetorical status for certain groups in the population – thus permitting, beginning with the Renaissance, the articulation of 'secularist' countermodels. In spite of the adjustments of the 'official' model of religion during the Reformation and Counter-Reformation, the discrepancies between the 'official' model and the socially prevalent effective priorities were not successfully overcome. Church–state relations during the period of absolute monarchies; the political and social context of the 'religious wars'; the proliferation of sects; the development of scientific thought and its effect on philosophical and – eventually – popular conceptions of life and the universe; the French Revolution and its repercussions in 'traditionalist' and 'liberal' movements in Catholicism and Protestantism; the social consequences of the industrial revolution and the emergence of a working class; and the rise of ideologically oriented political parties, biblical criticism and its effects on theology, to mention only a few major factors affecting the Christian churches, attest to the danger of oversimplification. Summarizing a complex process it may be said, none-the-less, that the long-range consequences of institutional specialization of religion as part of an overall process of social change resulted, paradoxically, in the loss of what institutional specialization originally accomplished in the 'pluralistic' religious context of the Hellenistic world and the Roman Empire: monopoly in the definition of an obligatory sacred cosmos.

Political and theological rearguard actions could retard but did not succeed in preventing eventual legal recognition of a *fait accompli*. 'Secular' ideas were competing successfully with the churches in determining the individual systems of 'ultimate' significance, especially among those members of the population whose lives and effective priorities had been most radically transformed by 'objective' social changes and who were increasingly willing to abandon the traditional 'official' model – even as a system of rhetoric. The wealth, power and administrative perfection of the churches notwithstanding, religion was defined as a private matter. This meant, in practice, that the church could no longer rely on the state to enforce its jurisdictional claims. The church [has become] an institution among other institutions....

In comparison to traditional social orders, the primary public institutions no longer significantly contribute to the formation of individual consciousness and personality, despite the massive performance control exerted by their functionally rational 'mechanisms'. Personal identity becomes, essentially, a private phenomenon. This is, perhaps, the most revolutionary trait of modern society. Institutional segmentation left wide areas in the life of the individual unstructured and the overarching biographical context of significance undetermined. From the interstices of the social structure that resulted from institutional segmentation emerged what may be called a 'private sphere'. The 'liberation' of individual consciousness from the social structure and the 'freedom' in the 'private sphere' provide the basis for the somewhat illusory sense of autonomy which characterizes the typical person in modern society....

The sense of autonomy which characterizes the typical individual in modern industrial societies is closely linked to a pervasive consumer orientation. Outside the areas that remain under direct performance control by the primary institutions, the subjective preferences of the individual, only minimally structured by definite norms, determine his conduct. To an immeasurably higher degree than in a traditional social order, the individual is left to his own devices in choosing goods and services, friends, marriage partners, neighbours, hobbies and, as we shall show presently, even 'ultimate' meanings in a relatively autonomous fashion. In a manner of speaking, he is free to construct his own personal identity. The consumer orientation, in short, is not limited to economic products but characterizes the relation of the individual to the entire culture. The latter is no longer an obligatory stucture of interpretive and evaluative schemes with a distinct hierarchy of significance. It is, rather, a rich, heterogeneous assortment of possibilities which, in principle, are accessible to any individual consumer. It goes without saying that the consumer preferences still remain a function of the consumer's social biography.

The consumer orientation also pervades the relation of the 'autonomous' individual to the sacred cosmos. One highly important consequence of institutional segmentation, in general, and institutional specialization of religion, in particular, is that the specifically religious representations, as congealed in the 'official' models of the churches, cease to be the only and obligatory themes in the sacred universe. From the socially determined systems of effective priorities new themes of 'ultimate' significance emerge and, to the extent that they are socially articulated, compete for acceptance in the sacred cosmos. The thematic unity of the traditional sacred cosmos breaks apart. This development reflects the dissolution of *one* hierarchy of significance in the world view. Based on the complex institutional structure and social stratification of industial societies, different 'versions' of the world-view emerge. The individual, originally socialized into one of the 'versions', may continue to be 'loyal' to it, to a certain extent, in later life. Yet, with the pervasiveness of the consumer orientation and the sense of autonomy, the individual is more likely to confront the culture and the sacred cosmos as a 'buyer'. Once religion is defined as a 'private affair' the individual may choose from the assortment of 'ultimate' meanings as he sees fit – guided only by the preferences that are determined by his social biography.

An important consequence of this situation is that the individual constructs not only his personal identity but also his individual system of 'ultimate' significance. It is true that for such constructions a variety of models is socially available – but none is 'official' in the strict sense of the term. None is routinely internalized *au sérieux*. Instead, a certain level of subjective reflection and choice determines the formation of individual religiosity. Furthermore, themes of 'ultimate' significance emerge primarily out of the 'private sphere' and are, on the whole, not yet fully articulated in the culture. The individual systems of 'ultimate' significance tend to be, therefore, both syncretistic and vague, in comparison with an 'official' model internalized *au sérieux*.

It should be noted that the traditional, specifically religious representations still form part of the heterogeneous sacred cosmos in modern society. They are, indeed, the only part of the sacred cosmos that is commonly recognized as religious. The other elements are usually described as 'pseudo-religious' or are not perceived as part of the sacred cosmos, despite the fact that they may be dominant themes in the prevalent individual systems of 'ultimate' significance. The specifically religious representations, furthermore, still form something not unlike a model, a model that bears some resemblance to traditional 'official' models of religion. It should be remembered, however, that once the *traditional* sacred cosmos came to reside exclusively in a specialized institution, the jurisdiction of this institution and, indirectly, of the sacred cosmos, was increasingly restricted to the 'private sphere'. This, in turn, tended to neutralize – although, perhaps, not completely – the privileged status of the traditional 'official' model in relation to other themes of 'ultimate' significance that addressed themselves to the 'inner man'. The 'autonomous' individual today confronts the traditional specifically religious model more or less as a consumer, too. In other words, that model is one of the possible choices of the individual. But even for those who continue to be socialized into the traditional model, specifically religious representations tend to have a predominantly rhetorical status. Various studies have shown that church-oriented religiosity typically contains only a shallow 'doctrinal' layer consisting of 'religious opinions' which do not stand in a coherent relation to one another.

The conflict between the claims of the traditional model and the socially determined circumstances of everyday life rarely, if ever, becomes acute – precisely because it is generally taken for granted that these claims are rhetorical.

They find no support from other institutions and fail to recieve 'objective' reaffirmation in the daily lives of the individuals. The subjective neutralization of these claims, on the other hand, makes it possible for the former 'official' model to survive as rhetoric. In the typical case, a conscious rejection of traditional forms of religion, merely because they are not congruent with the effective priorities of everyday life, becomes unnecessary. The neutralization of the claims does, however, contribute to further dissolution of the coherence of the model and reinforces the restriction of specifically religious representations to the 'private sphere'.

The social location of the churches in the contemporary industrial societies decisively influences the selection of those social types who continue to be socialized into the traditional 'official' model and determines the manner in which the model is likely to be internalized. [T]he more 'modern' the constellation of factors determining the socialization of the individual, the less likely is the routine internalization of the model and, if internalization still occurs, the less likely will it be *au sérieux*. But even in the case of church-oriented individuals it is likely that effective priorities of everyday life, the subjective system of 'ultimate' significance and the rhetoric of the traditional 'official' model are incongruent – for reasons...already indicated. An additional reason is the sociability and prestige-substitution function which church religion may continue to perform in the lives of certain types of persons even after the specifically religious function is neutralized.

In view of this situation it is useful to regard church religiosity in two different perspectives. First, we may view church religiosity as a survival of a traditional social form of religion (that is, institutional specialization) on the periphery of modern industrial societies. Second, we may view church religiosity as one of the many manifestations of an emerging, institutionally non-specialized social form of religion, the difference being that it still occupies a special place among the other manifestations because of its historical connections to the traditional Christian 'official' model. Many phenomena of contemporary church religion make better sense if placed in the second, rather than the first, perspective....

The social form of religion emerging in modern industrial societies is characterized by the direct accessibility of an assortment of religious representations to potential consumers. The sacred cosmos is mediated neither through a specialized domain of religious institutions nor through other primary public institutions. It is the direct accessibility of the sacred cosmos, more precisely, of an assortment of religious themes, which makes religion today essentially a phenomenon of the 'private sphere'. The emerging social form of religion thus differs significantly from older social forms of religion which were characterized by the diffusion of the sacred cosmos either through the institutional structure of society or through institutional specialization of religion.

The statement that the sacred cosmos is directly accessible to potential consumers needs to be explicated. It implies that the sacred cosmos is not mediated by primary public institutions and that, correspondingly, no obligatory model of religion is available. It does not imply, of course, that religious themes are not socially mediated in some form. Religious themes originate in experiences in the 'private sphere'. They rest primarily on emotions and sentiments and are sufficiently unstable to make articulation difficult. They are highly 'subjective'; that is, they are not defined in an obligatory fashion by primary institutions. They can be – and are – taken up, however, by what may be called secondary institutions which expressly cater to the 'private' needs of 'autonomous' consumers. These institutions attempt to articulate the themes arising in the 'private sphere' and retransmit the packaged results to potential consumers. Syndicated advice columns, 'inspirational' literature ranging from tracts on positive thinking to *Playboy* magazine, *Reader's Digest* versions of popular psychology, the lyrics of popular hits, and so forth, articulate what are, in effect, elements of models of 'ultimate' significance. The models are, of course, non-obligatory and must compete on what is, basically, an open market. The manufacture, the packaging and the sale of models of 'ultimate' significance are, therefore, determined by consumer preference, and the manufacturer must remain sensitive to the needs and requirements of 'autonomous' individuals and their existence in the 'private sphere'.

The appearance of secondary institutions supplying the market for 'ultimate' significance does not mean that the sacred cosmos – after a period of institutional specialization – is once again diffused through the social structure. The decisive difference is that the primary public institutions do not maintain the sacred cosmos; they merely regulate the legal and economic frame within which occurs the competition on the 'ultimate' significance market. Furthermore, diffusion of the sacred cosmos through the social structure characterizes societies in which the 'private sphere', in the strict sense of the term, does not exist and in which the distinction between primary and secondary institutions is meaningless.

The continuous dependence of the secondary institutions on consumer preference and, thus, on the 'private sphere' makes it very unlikely that the social objectivation of themes originating in the 'private sphere' and catering to it will eventually lead to the articulation of a consistent and closed sacred cosmos and the specialization, once again, of religious institutions. This is one of the several reasons that justify the assumption that we are not merely describing an interregnum between the extinction of one 'official' model and the appearance of a new one, but, rather, that we are observing the emergence of a new social form of religion characterized neither by diffusion of the sacred cosmos through the social structure nor by institutional specialization of religion.

The fact that the sacred cosmos rests primarily on the 'private sphere' and the secondary institutions catering to the latter, combined with the thematic heterogeneity of the sacred cosmos, has important consequences for the nature of individual religiosity in modern society. In the absence of an 'official' model the individual may select from a variety of themes of 'ultimate' significance. The selection is based on consumer preference, which is determined by the social biography of the individual, and similar social biographies will result in similar choices. Given the assortment of religious representations available to potential consumers and given the absence of an 'official' model it is possible, in principle, that the 'autonomous' individual will not only select certain themes but will construct with them a well-articulated private *system* of 'ultimate' significance. To the extent that some themes in the assortment of 'ultimate' meanings are coalesced into something like a coherent model (such as 'positive Christianity' and psychoanalysis), some individuals may internalize such models *en bloc*. Unless we postulate a high degree of reflection and conscious deliberation, however, it is more likely that individuals will legitimate the situation-bound (primarily emotional and affective) priorities arising in their 'private spheres' by deriving, *ad hoc*, more or less appropriate rhetorical elements from the sacred cosmos. The assumption seems justified, therefore, that the *prevalent* individual systems of 'ultimate' significance will consist of a loose and rather unstable hierarchy of 'opinions' legitimating the affectively determined priorities of 'private' life.

Individual religiosity in modern society receives no massive support and confirmation from the primary public institutions. Overarching subjective structures of meaning are almost completely detached from the functionally rational norms

of these institutions. In the absence of external support, subjectively constructed and eclectic systems of 'ultimate' significance will have a somewhat
precarious reality for the individual. Also, they will be less stable – or rigid –
than the more homogeneous patterns of individual religiosity that characterize
societies in which 'everybody' internalizes an 'official' model and in which the
internalized model is socially reinforced throughout an individual's biography.
In sum, while the systems of 'ultimate' significance in modern society are
characterized by considerable variability in content, they are structurally similar.
They are *relatively* flexible as well as unstable.

48   Jeffrey K. Hadden

Challenging Secularization Theory

[An] assessment of the status of secularization theory reveals four important
challenges. First, a critique of secularization theory itself uncovers a hodgepodge
of loosely employed ideas rather than a systematic theory. Second, existing data
simply do not support the theory. Third, the effervescence of new religious
movements in the very locations where secularization appears to cut deeply into
established institutional religion suggests that religion may really be ubiquitous
in human cultures. Fourth, the number of countries in which religion is significantly entangled in reform, rebellion and revolution is ever-expanding. This
reality challenges the assumptions of secularization theory that would relegate
religion to the private realm.

Critique of the theory

C. Wright Mills once translated Talcott Parsons' 555-page tome, *The Social
System*, into four short paragraphs.[1] Here's a translation of secularization theory
in three short sentences:

> Once the world was filled with the sacred – in thought, practice and
> institutional form. After the Reformation and the Renaissance, the forces
> of modernization swept across the globe and secularization, a corollary
> historical process, loosened the dominance of the sacred. In due course,
> the sacred shall disappear altogether except, possibly, in the private realm.

Secularization, thus understood, is properly described as a general orienting
concept that causally links the decline of religion with the process of modernization. That is, it is more appropriately described as a proposition than as a
theory.

Beyond its use as a general orienting proposition, secularization has been used
in many ways ranging from the 'decline' or 'loss' of religion, to the 'differentiation' of the religious from the secular, to an Enlightenment myth 'which views
science as the bringer of light relative to which religion and other dark things
will vanish away'.[2]

Two decades ago David Martin argued for the abandonment of the concept.[3]
Later, Larry Schiner reviewed the uses of the term secularization and found six
discrete meanings.[4] Noting that several of these meanings were infused with
polemical and ideological overtones, Schiner, too, thought abandonment was a
reasonable way of dealing with the problem.

Encased within this general orienting proposition are the elements of a theory. Many scholars have highlighted one or more of these elements, but for all that has been written about secularization, probably only Martin, who decided not to abandon the concept, has written a treatise that would qualify as a theory.[5]

More recently, Karel Dobbelaere has achieved a remarkably thorough and systematic review of secularization literature which reveals the absence of a general theory.[6] Dobbelaere's review differentiates three distinct levels of use: (1) societal, (2) organizational and (3) individual. A Belgian, Dobbelaere sees the evidence of secularization all around him and is reluctant to challenge the utility of the theory. Rather, he concludes that we need to be more conscious of the fact that different theorists, working with different paradigms, mean different things. 'All classifications of secularization theories,' he writes, 'should also take into account the sociological paradigms used by the builders of these theories.'[7]

Dobbelaere's analysis is extremely useful. More clearly than anyone else, he has illuminated the sad fact that in the lexicon of sociological inquiry, 'secularization means whatever I say it means'. But Dobbelaere's solution to the problem seems ill-advised. He seems prepared to give the idea of secularization a life of its own, free to yoke or splinter in as many directions as there are crafters with moulds and chisels. I think the sounder conclusion to be reached from his work is the same that Martin and Schiner reached two decades ago.

To summarize, the idea of secularization is presumed to be a theory, but literature reviews support this assumption only in a very loose sense. This, however, does not diminish its importance. It is believed to be a theory and is treated as such. The fact that the theory has not been systematically stated or empirically tested is of little consequence. It has dominated our assumptions about religion and guided the types of research questions scholars have asked. Its imagery is powerful, and it is unlikely that it will disappear from our vocabulary or thought processes. But developments in the social scientific study of religion have begun to erode its credibility.

I turn next to the empirical evidence we have about secularization in support of this prediction.

Examining the data

Charles Glock not only warned us about the limited utility of data on religion, he further counselled that 'It is extremely doubtful that accurate statistics can be produced through manipulating the unreliable ones.'[8] A decade later, N. J. Demerath III thoroughly documented the point that Glock had only asserted.[9] In a 95-page contribution to Eleanor Sheldon and Wilbert Moore's *Indicators of Social Change*, Demerath meticulously examined indicators of church membership, religious belief, organization and ecumenical activity.

Some types of data are more reliable than others, Demerath concluded, but for every argument that can be made in defence of a data set, there exists a rebuttal. The result of Demerath's extensive evaluation and critique of many data sources leaves us with a single plea: 'If there is a single recommendation that emerges from this review,' Demerath pleads, 'it is that *the Census should include questions concerning religion in its regular enumerations*.' 'Indeed,' Demerath continues, 'this recommendation is so urgent ... that it deserves a postscript of its own.'[10]

In the face of such a passionate admonition, one must be cautious in trying to build a case either for or against secularization with existing data. But if we must not throw caution to the winds, neither are we compelled to silence, or forbidden from examining and interpreting the data.

To me, the data, with all their recognized faults, speak clearly. And their most important message is that *the data cannot confirm the historical process predicted by secularization theory*. One must also add the caution that neither can the data disconfirm the process. But when one examines the large corpus of literature that provides some longitudinal perspective, I don't see how one can fail to conclude that religion stubbornly resists the prophecies of its early demise. If that simple proposition is entertained, then we open the door for alternative ways of thinking about religion in the modern world.

Marking 1935 as the beginning of scientific polling, the Gallup Organization's annual *Religion in America* report for 1985 highlights a half-century assessment of religion. In the introductory essay, George Gallup, Jr, concludes: '. . . perhaps the most appropriate word to use to describe the religious character of the nation as a whole over the last half century is *"stability"*. Basic religious beliefs, and even religious practice, today differ relatively little from the levels recorded 50 years ago.' [11]

Unfortunately, early polling included only sporadic questions about religion, and when they were included, the wording was frequently changed just enough to leave one wary about comparability. Most of the items for which Gallup now provides trend data were not available in the early years of polling. But when one picks one's way through the poll data, plus other types of data that permit some inferences, Gallup's conclusion of stability seems to me a prudent assessment.

Still, within the general context of stability, there are some important changes. I shall briefly identify *six significant deviations from the theme of stability*.

1   The most reliable indicators we have confirm the existence of a *religious revival in the post-Second World War era*. We can't precisely pinpoint the beginning, but it seems to have lost steam by the end of the 1950s.

2   During most of the second half of this century, the 'mainline' or *liberal church traditions* have struggled and mostly *lost membership and influence*.

3   During this same time period, *conservative religious traditions*, evangelicals and fundamentalists, have *experienced sustained growth*. Growth continues within these groups, although there is some evidence of a slowing of the process.

4   *The Second Vatican Council dramatically affected the beliefs and behaviour of Roman Catholics in America*. Attendance at mass and confession fell dramatically. Catholics became much less likely to report that religion was 'very important' in their lives. But these indicators of decline now seem to have levelled off and stabilized.

5   While Catholics now seem positioned to fight among themselves over the essentials of belief, meaning and purpose of the Church, and the authority of their leaders, the *authority of the Roman Catholic leadership is now greater than at any point in American history*.

6   Primarily as a result of immigration from Central America and the Caribbean, *Catholics have increased their proportion of the American population* from roughly 20 per cent in 1947 to almost 30 per cent in 1985, *and their proportion* of the total population *can be expected to continue to grow*.

Each of these patterns of change either has had or will have important implications for the future of religion in America. Nested within these trends and countertrends are social forces that portend changes which could alter the face of religion during the next fifty years. But the indicators of stability also provide clues to the future. I shall identify five among many possible indicators of stability.

1   The overwhelming proportion of Americans report that they *believe in God*, and that proportion has fluctuated very little over the forty years for which we have data. The proportion professing belief in God has never dipped below 94 per cent and has moved as high as 99 per cent during the revival period of the 1950s [according to the Gallup poll].

2   Church *membership* statistics have fluctuated only a little over the past forty years. Self-reported membership surveys consistently run a little higher than statistics reported by religious organizations. By Gallup survey estimates, church membership was 73 per cent in 1937 and 68 per cent in 1984. A high of 76 per cent was reached in 1947 and the low was 67 per cent in 1982.

3   *Church attendance* has fluctuated in some religious sectors, but the overall picture of church attendance is amazingly stable. Essentially the same proportion reported attending church in 1984 as was the case in 1939. After the revival of the 1950s, reported church attendance dropped back to the range of 40 per cent and has remained at that level since 1972.

4   Some differences in *personal devotion* can be noted, but the bigger picture is again one of stability. In 1985 almost as many people reported that they prayed (87 per cent) as in 1948 (90 per cent). Whereas fewer people reported frequent prayer (twice a day or more), the proportion who read the Bible at least daily was half again as great in 1984 as in 1942. And religious knowledge grew significantly between 1954 and 1982: this during a period when most types of cognitive skills seemed to be declining.

5   Contributions to charitable or voluntary organizations are higher in the United States than any other country in the world. And there is but scant evidence that either proportional or per capita giving to religion has declined. In 1955, 50 per cent of all charitable contributions were given to religious organizations. That proportion slipped to 44 per cent in 1975, but has since climbed back to 46.5 per cent. On a per capita basis, *in constant dollars, Americans gave almost 20 per cent more to religious organizations in 1982 than they did in 1962.*

During the period for which we have data, some dramatic shifts in people's perceptions about religion have occurred. For example, the proportion believing that the influence of religion was increasing in society peaked at 69 per cent in 1957 and then plunged to only 14 per cent in 1970. Since that date, the figure has risen steadily to 48 per cent in 1985. Also, people are less likely to report today that religion is 'very important' than in the revival period of the 1950s. But after a significant plunge following the revival period, these figures now have stabilized, even risen slightly.

Other short-term trends may be interpreted as supportive of the secularization hypothesis. Space permitting, I could comment on each. In the absence of that opportunity, I would offer two general conclusions. First, there is abundant evidence to support the conclusion that *what* people believe and *how* they practise religion is a dynamic, ever-changing process. For example, over the past twenty years we have experienced a significant decline in the proportion of Americans who believe that the Bible is the actual word of God and is to be taken literally, word for word. But, as we have seen, rejecting biblical literalism does not mean that people cease to believe. Similarly, weekly attendance at mass has fallen dramatically for Roman Catholics in the quarter of a century since the Second Vatican Council. But this is not *prima facie* evidence that people are ceasing to be Catholic or that they are 'less religious' because they don't go to mass every week.

Second, it is clear that some indicators are affected by the broader cultural milieu. Demerath noted this possibility in his essay on religious statistics: 'There may be a self-fulfilling prophecy crescendoing as the phrase "religious revival" is trumpeted from steeple to steeple. The tendency to conform artificially to this newly religious image in a poll response may be a factor in documenting the image itself.'[12] It should be equally obvious that downside trends may be triggered by media-pronounced prophecies of religious demise. The Gallup question on the perception of the importance of religion seems to support the self-fulfilling prophecy generalization.

Claims about trends in religions are not likely to be sustained and reinforced for long in the face of contrary evidence, but we can hypothesize that any trend is likely to get some self-fulfilling action from mass public perceptions. But the general conclusion this suggests is that we can expect indicators of religious behaviour to continue to fluctuate.

To summarize this all too brief assessment of trends in religious behaviour, I would say that the balance of data supports the proposition that religion is changing within a context of broad stability. There is a general absence of indicators which would support the long-term secularization hypothesis. Religion is dead in the minds, hearts and feet of large sectors of American society. But just as certainly, religion is alive for other broad sectors. There is no evidence to support a decisive shift either towards or away from religion.

New religious movements

A third factor which has served to challenge the secularization thesis has been the emergence of new religious movements. The countercultural movement of the late 1960s involved a wholesale rejection of our materialistic world and its concomitant secularized ethos. The search for a 'new consciousness' took many bizarre turns, but there was a profound religious quality to the search for new meaning.

This happened on the heels of a radically different perception of what was happening in America. In the early 1960s, a small group of theologians proclaimed the 'death of God', and their proclamation captured substantial national media attention. Arguing that man is by anthropological nature a religious animal, Harvey Wheeler concluded that 'a death-of-God era is also a god-building era'.[13] And certainly the late 1960s and early 1970s were an era of frantic 'god-building.'

The growth of new religions was stimulated in part by Lyndon Johnson's repeal of the Oriental Exclusion Acts in 1965. The disoriented but searching counterculture became a missions field for gurus of Eastern religions. Their seeds multiplied, as did the seeds of many new sectarian visions of the Christian faith and the indigenously manufactured religions and quasi-religions.

[By the mid-1980s] many of the more prominent new religions [had] collapsed. Most of the others [were] struggling. At the moment it does not seem likely that any of the new religions of the 1960s and 1970s will experience the kind of sustained growth that has characterized the Mormons, the most successful of several surviving new religious movements of the nineteenth century.

In the final analysis, the significance of the new religious movements of the 1960s may be not so much their contributions to religious pluralism in America as the fact that their presence stimulated a tremendous volume of scholarly inquiry. And the result of those inquiries has been an enrichment of our understanding of the process of sect and cult formation and dissolution.

Many scholars have contributed to this literature. The single most important development to emerge out of these studies has been the comparative study of new religions over time and across cultures. . . .

I offer here four important generalizations that are emerging from the research on new religious movements:

1   Historical investigations have led us to understand much more clearly that sectarian fissures (splintering from established traditions) and cults (newly created or imported) have been forming for the whole of human history.
2   Furthermore, the parallelisms in the patterns and process of sect and cult formation appear to be highly similar over a very long period of time.
3   'Religious schisms are inevitable.'[14] In a free market-place, new religious organizations will spring abundantly from established traditions. Even under conditions of an established state Church and the suppression of unsanctioned religions, new groups spring forth.
4   Cults (new inventions or exports from another culture) flourish where traditional established religions are weakest.

The last proposition is less well documented with cross-cultural evidence. Nevertheless, the comparative ecological research of Stark and Bainbridge for the US during the nineteenth and twentieth centuries, with more limited data for Canada and several European nations, provides some provocative conclusions. 'Secularization, even in the scientific age,' they argue, 'is a self-limiting process.'[15]

Referring to the West Coast region as the 'unchurched belt' in America, Stark and Bainbridge demonstrate that this pattern has persisted for a century. Cults, thus, do not automatically 'fill the void' in areas that have experienced a high degree of secularization. But cult activity is greatest in those areas with the lowest levels of 'established' religious activity. With but a slight twist on Egyptian mythology, the phoenix may be consumed by the fires of secularization, but it is sure to rise again from its own ashes.

The study of new religious movements introduces a certain irony to the view that our heritage from the founding generations provides ample evidence that religion will eventually fade from our collective consciousness. Durkheim, perhaps more than any other founding scholar, took us into the abyss which follows discovery that society itself is the object of collective worship. How can we believe once we have discovered we are the creators of the gods?

In the context of scepticism, if not open antagonism toward religion, perhaps we sociologists have parted from our guide before the journey was finished, presuming we had learned all there was to learn. 'There is something eternal in religion,' concluded Durkheim, 'which is destined to survive all the particular symbols in which religious thought has successively enveloped itself.'[16]

Religion and political authority in global perspective

One way that secularization theorists have accounted for the persistence of religion in the midst of the secular is with the notion of *privatization*. Within Kuhn's conception of 'normal science', this concept may be viewed as a 'mopping-up' operation; the filling in of details and accounting for anomalies.[17]

According to this reformulation, religion becomes a personal matter in the modern world, anchored in individual consciousness, rather than a cosmic force. Religion may be capable of maintaining its traditional function as a mechanism of social control, at least in some sectors of human societies. But certainly religion is not to be taken seriously as an earth-moving force.

This assignment of religion to the private sphere is rather like having your cake and eating it too. One can hold steadfastly to the Enlightenment image of the demise of religion and still account for its embarrassing persistence. It is not necessary to establish a timetable for the disappearance of religion. In due course it will happen. And in the meantime, its only significant effects are in the private sphere.

The anomalies have been ignored for a long time. Notwithstanding the omnipresence of religious leadership during the civil rights movement of the 1960s, we tended not to think of this as a religious movement. The periodic outbursts of violence in Northern Ireland have something to do with historical conflict between Protestants and Catholics. The present conflict involves only a small minority of fanatics. We got over our differences earlier this century, and surely they will too.

Jews have been fighting Arabs since the establishment of the state of Israel, but that's a struggle over turf. After all, the Zionist leaders of Israel were highly secularized. What do their quarrels with their neighbours have to do with religion? Mohandas Gandhi was a religious leader, of sorts, but the nation he led in revolt against colonialism was hardly a modern secular state. And besides, with Hindus and Muslims and Sikhs all fighting one another, it didn't make much sense. And if one thought about it at all, it was much easier to see India's ongoing unrest grounded in the great ethnic diversity of the Asian subcontinent. One thing is for certain, the Europeans know how to have a good brouhaha without bringing religion in. Remember the Second World War?

Examples of such myopic analysis could go on and on. Because of our assumptions about secularization, we have systematically engaged in a massive wholesale dismissal of the religious factor when considering sociopolitical events in the modern world.

In 1979 and 1980, the United States encountered two nearly simultaneous developments which radically altered our consciousness about religion. In 1979, fanatical Muslims overthrew the Shah of Iran, a man and government believed to symbolize the modernization of the Middle East. That same year, Jerry Falwell heeded the call of secular right-wing leaders and formed the Moral Majority. In 1980 a small band of Ayatollah Khomeini's followers held hostage more than 400 Americans from the diplomatic and military corps. And Falwell held captive the attention of the mass media with claims that his organization registered millions of conservative voters.

Since these developments at the turn of the decade, our consciousness has been bombarded almost continuously with evidence of religious entanglement in the political. Even as I write, we are learning daily new details regarding the central role of the Roman Catholic Church in the overthrow of the corrupt regimes of Ferdinand Marcos in the Philippines and Jean-Claude Duvalier in Haiti. Pope John Paul II is a tormented man trying to curb ecclesiastical involvement in the praxis of liberation theology in Nicaragua and Brazil while tacitly encouraging political engagement in Poland and the Philippines.

The remarkable Kairos Document signed by more than 150 South African clergymen confesses prior timidity even as it charts a bold course of engagement in the political crisis of that nation. Like Martin Luther King, Jr, Nobel Peace

Prize winner Bishop Desmond Tutu is but a symbol of courageous religious leadership.

Not all of the religion and politics stories of the 1980s involve courageous voices speaking out for peace and justice. And in many tension spots, distinguishing the heroes from the villains is very much an ideological issue. In Lebanon, Egypt, Iran and Iraq, we mostly agree that the Muslim extremists are villains. But when the same Islamic zealotry is unleashed against Soviet invaders in Afghanistan, we see them as heroes and seek to minimize the similarities with their Middle East brothers. Turning to Central America, if you are a 'liberal', you're likely to admire the courage of the priest brothers Ernesto and Fernando Cardenal. If you are a 'conservative', they are traitors to their Church and dupes of the Sandanista regime.

In many tension-ridden areas there is the tendency to reduce religious conflict to 'just ethnic hostilities', and there are no heroes at all. Sikhs assassinating Hindu leaders, Hindus doing battle with Muslims, Buddhists oppressing Tamils and Tamils striking back with guerilla warfare tactics are all part of a complex mosaic of ethnic conflict.

Such simplistic explaining by labelling reduces our need to come to grips with one of the most important developments of the second half of the twentieth century. But the extensiveness of political entanglement around the globe is simply too great to be ignored. Each episode cries out for explanation, not as an isolated event, but as part of a global phenomenon. The present data base for comparative analysis consists mostly of case studies. We do not yet have a very good conceptual model, much less a theory, to account for the tumultuous entanglement of religion in politics all around the globe. The one thing that is clear is that the classical imagery of secularization theory is not very helpful.

49   Emmanuel Sivan

Radical Islam

Islamic revival – while activist and militant – is essentially defensive; a sort of holding operation against modernity. And though it has no doubt a sharp political edge, it is primarily a cultural phenomenon. Its very strength proceeds from this alliance of political and cultural protest.

The refrain of all fundamentalist litanies is 'Islam is isolated from life.' This is nowhere more evident, in their eyes, than in the mass media. Television comes in for most of the blame because it brings the modernist message in the most effective, audio-visual form into the very bastion of Islam – family and home. But the same holds true for radio and for tape cassettes, be they specially produced or recordings of radio programmes. The electronic media carry out a 'destructive campaign' that overwhelms the efforts of religious militants by 'broadcasting indecent and vulgar songs, belly-dancing, melodramas on women kidnapped in order to serve in the palaces of rulers, and similar trash'.[1] Pop music, Arab style, comes in for more criticism than explicitly sexual plays (or films), perhaps because of its popularity. According to a field study quoted by *al-Da'wa*, preference for variety programmes was expressed by 60 per cent of Egyptian viewers and listeners (as against 54 per cent for Koran reading). They are all the more dangerous for being indigenous and at the same time impregnated with 'the Western poison'. A content analysis of the lyrics propagated by popular singers like Umm Kulthum, Muhammad 'Abd al-Wahhab and 'Abd al-Halim Hafiz comes up with 'terms and ideas diametrically opposed to Arab and Islamic concepts, encouraging loose morality and immediate satisfaction, placing love and life and its pleasures over everything else, totally oblivious of religious belief, and of punishment and reward in the Hereafter'.

Sociological surveys revealed indeed that love songs take up to 37.8 per cent of Egyptian broadcasting time compared with 9 per cent for religious programmes.[2] Worship of TV, film and singing stars – generated by the media itself – only tends to make things worse, as it creates idols that subsume the superficial character of this popular culture, lionized for achievements based on image and not on substance. Popular mourning over the death of 'Abd al-Halim Hafiz, given an aura of respectability by the participation of prominent intellectuals and pundits, made one commentator scoff: 'All the martyrs of Sinai and Golan . . . did not get the same amount of solicitude from the media. . . . To hear their eulogies, one could think that insipidity is heroism, vulgarity is an uplifting experience, and singing is tantamount to glorious struggle. The populace learned that their problems, grief, and suffering are of no significance, compared with the death of that entertainer.' TV 'personalities' build up a trivialized hero-worship around themselves, enabling them to spread consumerism all the more efficiently by incorporating commercial publicity into their talk shows. Even worse is professional sports, which brings the idolatry of pagan-inspired body worship to a peak.

Not that the sexually explicit products of popular culture are made light of; it is only that as Islamic criticism of modernity became more sophisticated, it learned that the indirect approach is sometimes more dangerous, precisely for being implicit. But articles on the permissive morality of TV dramas and films (let alone underground pornographic films, whether imported or produced locally) are legion. Here Egypt is no doubt the most prolific centre of production in the Arab world, although Lebanese writers find much to complain of about Beirut. This is less true of pulp novels and popular magazines – whether of the implicitly or explicitly sexual variety – but their availability to the public, even in the proximity of mosques, is often lamented. Buttressed by other forms of popular culture such as beauty contests, the result is inevitable: 'the weakening of family bonds battered by the unleashing of carnal appetites'. 'Rare are the films and plays in which one cannot watch at least one of the following: seminude dancing, wine cups filled, easy-to-learn tricks to woo young females, criticism of the conservative older generation for blocking marriage between lovers, description of the beloved merely in terms of sex appeal, justification of the adultery of a young woman given in marriage to an old man or that of an older woman married to one she does not love.'

Other forms of 'recreation' – that hated term which signifies, for the fundamentalists, an attempt to divert the mind from the moral values – have their share in this [discussion]. Foremost is the nightclub industry, which prospered as a result of the growing tourism from puritanical oil states (encouraged by the demise of Beirut). This is a case where moral protest is linked with an economic one: criticism of an unbridled 'open-door policy' bent on maximization of foreign-currency income by every means. The 'commerce in the human body', bordering on, or even incorporating, high-class prostitution, is rendered all the more obnoxious to the True Believers, as alcoholic beverages can be sold in the same tourist precincts. This 'cancerous growth' is bound to spread to the indigenous society as well as through those natives who are associated with the tourist trade or with foreigners.

Religion does figure in the Syrian and Egyptian mass media, but significantly enough, it is a religion made of externals, of gestures shorn of values: prayer, fast, pilgrimage. This is particularly evident in the context and manner of their presentation. The call for the daily prayer comes over television and radio in the middle of entertainment programmes (whether belly-dancing or a love scene) with no introductory and concluding presentation designed to separate the holy from the profane. Koran readings are not only much shorter than they used to be, but are also not reverently separated from the preceding (and following) pop songs; they are often recorded 'live' in mosques, making them part of show business, complete with the non-aesthetic cries and wailings of ignorant men in attendance. During the month of Ramadan, while more attention is given to religious programmes, their impact is neutralized by quiz and prize shows that foster 'material obsessions', and by belly-dancing and erotic films. Small wonder that the few, supposedly serious, religious talk shows deal with technicalities of devotional acts and seldom with the application of Islam in daily life....

A much more systematic introduction of modern culture is detected in Syrian and Egyptian education. Concerning school curricula, the radicals voice the all-too-expected complaint that the teaching of science, though not openly critical of religion, is subverting Islam quite efficiently, precisely by being oblivious to it. Science offers an alternative explanatory model, supposedly value-free and objective; it does not even deign to try to reconcile this model (as, they claim, could be done) with Islam. The implication is, of course, that by transfer through training, the same approach will be applied to other spheres. In like vein, the radicals attack the teaching of philosophy for giving too much place to Western thinkers and above all for having Islamic philosophy represented by rationalistic, Greek-style medieval philosophers such as the Mu'tazila school, Avicenna and Averroes, branded as deviationists in their own times. This is deemed a victory for Orientalism and its disciples, who had tried to trace back a sort of proto-modernist strand in Islam. Traditional philosophy of the Ash'ari and Ghazzali variety is barely taught.

Somewhat less expected is the critique of Arab language and literature studies. Arabic is, after all, the sacred language of Islam, heavily permeated with its terminology, history and culture. Yet the language in question is the classical literary one. Schools and universities do not do enough to promote it, with the result that most university graduates cannot speak it properly and prefer the colloquial or the 'middle language' (*wusta*), an amalgam of colloquial dialects, modern vocabulary and syntax, and a debased classical (*fusha*) backdrop. Quite often, it is reported, dissertation defence – even in departments of Arabic – is held in the colloquial (*'amiyya*) medium for lack of ability to converse formally in *fusha*. The schools, of course, did not unleash this danger, for the mass media tend toward a growing use of the *'amiyya* and *wusta*, as do political leaders in assemblies. It is not unusual for an imam in his Friday sermon to resort to the colloquial whenever at a loss for *fusha* terms and structures. Modern literature – increasingly taught in the schools – is moving in the same direction, towards a language not far from that of journalism. This so-called contemporary (*mu'asira*) language is rapidly losing historical – that is, Islamic – connotations.

As for the content of literary studies, it is quite in tune with ambient popular culture. Not only are junior high-school students taught an ode to Umm Kulthum, 'making singing appear as a sublime value', but modern poetry anthologies include works in praise of physical culture 'where struggle is equated with playing football and happiness with healthy bodies'. Other poems praise the beauty of nature in the pagan manner of pop songs, with no mention of any values other than self-gratification. Prose is skewed by a heavy dose of political speeches of the president-of-the-day, part of the ritual of state worship. No attempt is made to produce separate texts for boys and girls to foster the values that suit each sex (courage and endurance, family orientation and chastity, and so on); schools thus enhance the growing promiscuity typical of mass culture. (The education system, it is lamented, is almost completely integrated at the elementary and university levels, and is becoming increasingly so at junior and senior high school levels.) Religious texts tend to be relegated to 'religious culture' classes, and at the university level there are even cases where Syrian and Egyptian students of Arabic are no longer required to take courses in Koran and Sunna.

Teaching 'religious culture' cannot help matters. Treating it as a separate topic legitimizes the separation between religion and daily life, which is much more bothersome for the Muslim radicals than the more formal separation between religion and state, a danger they do not consider imminent. Moreover, religious culture is a 'parasitic teaching matter': its time allocation is small; its prestige low because it is not judged by schools to be a criterion of scholarly aptitude; the calibre of teachers is low (mostly Arab-language teachers who treat it in an offhand manner); the curriculum is dull, designed to have students memorize a few sacred texts and learn some acts of devotion rather than inculcate values. The 'religious vacuum' so many youth suffer from – and which was the most popular topic in a youth essay contest organized recently by the Egyptian Muslim Brethren – is certainly not being filled by what is judged a perfunctory endeavour. Not that it would have been an easy task, for as one teacher remarked to an investigative reporter:

> What if I teach that taking interest is forbidden by the Shari'a when our whole economic structure, consecrated by law, is based on it? What if I teach Koranic verses on the virtues of modest dress when my students see décolleté and miniskirts in public places? And what about teaching Islamic doctrine that the rich are morally and legally bound to help the poor when inequity in income distribution is steadily growing?[3]

Part 13

Work and Industry

One of the unique features of modern societies consists in the fact that the majority of the population is propertyless. In order to achieve livelihood, people must sell their labour power on the market, or be funded by others who do so. In all prior types of social order, the economy was fundamentally localized. Even in the most developed traditional states, 90 per cent or more of the population lived in rural areas and worked in agricultural production. With the emergence of modern economies, however, most people no longer directly produce their own food, but participate in a complex division of labour in which their own occupation is only one among a multitude of other jobs which are carried out. Labour markets – markets on which individuals offer their labour power – as Claus Offe (reading 50) explains, differ from markets upon which other types of goods or services ('commodities') are bought and sold. From these differences, as Offe demonstrates, stem major variations in the power of employers as compared to that of employees.

As various of the readings in part 4 ('Gender and Sexuality') pointed out, 'work' cannot be identified solely with a job in the labour market. The labour market is at the core of modern production systems, but is bolstered by other forms of labour which are either unpaid, such as the domestic work of housewives, or which is funded in various 'irregular' ways. The 'formal economy' of the labour market, as J. I. Gershuny and R. E. Pahl (reading 51) show, exists alongside a complex series of informal economic arrangements. The informal economy, they argue, should be thought of as involving three main components: the household economy, the 'underground' or 'hidden' economy and the 'communal' economy. In each of these three segments, goods and services are created, modified and exchanged without passing through orthodox economic institutions. For instance, a neighbour might help repair a part of another person's house in exchange for produce which the first individual has grown in his or her market garden. As the authors indicate, the informal economy is not only fundamental to modern industrial production, but tends to grow in a way paralleled with the formal economic system.

Modern industrial production was pioneered in the West, but today, of course, has spread widely throughout the world. Among non-Western countries, Japan in particular has emerged as an extremely strong producer and exporter, able to compete in a more than effective way with Western firms. Japanese styles of management differ in certain important ways from those characteristic of most Western countries. In recent years, some Japanese corporations have begun to initiate joint ventures with Western companies, others to set up their own production facilities in Europe and the United States. Reading 52, by Jeremy Seabrook, looks at a joint endeavour established by the Japanese firm Mitsubishi and the American car-maker Chrysler in Illinois. The study indicates that the US employees adapt fairly quickly to the Japanese type of administrative system. A feature of that system, in this particular plant at least, is a very high level of technological sophistication and automation.

Levels of open conflict in Japanese organizations appear to be low, although union–management clashes of one kind or another are by no means absent. In Western industrial settings, by contrast, open struggle in some economic sectors is more or less chronic. The contribution by Paul Routledge (reading 53) discusses a particular example of industrial conflict which occurred at Times Newspapers Ltd. The newspaper industry in the UK has periodically been the site of large-scale industrial confrontation. In particular, technological changes affecting printing have led newspaper proprietors to alter the conditions of employment to which printers are subject; the printing unions, for their part, have sought to resist or limit what they see as the unfortunate consequences of such developments for the members they represent.

The next two selections in this part move to an international level. The internationalizing of production is a primary feature of globalizing processes. Schoenberger's article (reading 54) analyses the interaction between internationalization and the decline of 'Fordism'. Fordism refers to mass production for standardized markets, initiated by Henry Ford in the era of early assembly-line car production. Partly as a result of technological changes, and partly as a result of intensifying international competition, the author argues, Fordism is now being replaced by more flexible production systems. Flexible production differs from pre-established mass-production technology in so far as machines are now programmed by computer to be able to produce in small batches according to specific customer demands.

Some analysts argue that, rather than simply being replaced by flexible production, mass-production methods are in part being shifted to countries outside the developed nations, where labour power is cheaper and workers are less prone to produce organized union resistance to strict managerial control of production. Women workers make up a large proportion of the labour force in many such settings, a phenomenon discussed by Ruth Pearson in reading 55. The international corporations, she claims, have discovered that women's productivity tends to be higher than men's under similar conditions, while the wages paid to women are not generally as high as those which male workers receive.

David Lyon (reading 56) analyses the possible implications of a further set of technological changes now affecting industrial production: the widespread use of information technology. Many have claimed that modern economies no longer depend so centrally, as they once did, upon the production of manufactured goods; in place of manufacture, the production of information becomes a core resource. Lyon submits to critical scrutiny the idea that we are moving from an industrial order towards an 'information society'. As he says, it is impossible to resist the conclusion that information technology has already changed our lives significantly and is likely to alter them further in the future. Yet, as Lyon shows, upon examination the idea of the information society turns out to be a complicated one, and there is good reason to be cautious about some of the wilder claims which have been made about its potential consequences, good and bad.

50   Claus Offe

The Political Economy of the Labour Market

In capitalist societies the labour market is the main institutional solution to a dual allocative problem that must be solved in all societies: on the one hand, the production system must be supplied with the labour inputs it requires; on the other, labour power must be provided with monetary (income) and social (status) means of subsistence. The labour market solves both of these allocative problems simultaneously, while in non- or pre-capitalist societies we find predominantly institutional forms in which the type and level of the means of subsistence provided to individuals depend on factors other than the individual's contributions to social production. The important point is that the labour market organizes production and distribution as an exchange relationship of wages and labour inputs, and that here, as in all other markets, suppliers and buyers of 'labour' stand opposed. A further similarity is that in all markets the relationship of competition is given: supplier and buyer compete with other suppliers and buyers against whom they must assert themselves if, respectively, their offer is to be successful or their demands are to be satisfied. This relationship of competition therefore also necessitates the pursuit of specific rational strategies of supply and demand. On the supply side, these strategies involve specifying, as fairly as possible, the type, quantity, location and timing of the labour inputs offered, as well as adjusting the price demanded (wages) to the willingness of the demand side to pay. Conversely, for the actors on the demand side, the aim is to reduce the specificity of their demands for the type and quantity of labour needed or, if necessary, to raise the price offered (wages) in such a way that the demand of the individual employer can be satisfied from the available supply (e.g. 'wage-drift' as an internal competitive strategy of individual purchasers of labour). An important adaptive strategy for both sides of the market is for them to free themselves from their respective dependencies upon the other side by putting themselves in the position of finding substitute sources for the satisfaction of this need. The labour market – like every other market – requires both sides to engage in continuous and complementary strategic adaptations. This forced adaptation arising from market relations is often viewed as a powerful source of the social processes of rationalization which are especially reflected in continuous productivity increases.

The arsenal of strategic options associated with the dynamic and the results of market processes is, however, not exhausted by the individual strategies of particular suppliers and purchasers of labour. A further important strategic option for both sides consists in reducing the intensity of the relations of competition on one's own side of the market relative to the intensity of competition on the 'other' side. This occurs primarily through forming coalitions and engaging in other types of collective action. For example, workers come to a mutual understanding by forming a coalition to establish maximum limits for the supply of services or minimum limits for price/wage demands; by not violating these limits, they avoid either continuously outbidding each other with respect to the level of labour offered, or continually underbidding each other with respect to the level of wages demanded. The same effect is sought by hindering access to the market of those potential suppliers who would be prepared or even compelled to violate one limit or the other. Internal solidarity and external (possibly violent) discrimination are thus rational strategies for attaining market advantages on the supply side. The same holds true for the demand side: the purchasers of labour can form an alliance to moderate their internal relations of competition and/or negatively sanction 'more attractive' buyers (e.g. through their exclusion from employer associations). The common principle of these strategies, in short, is the lessening of the intensity of competition in one's own 'camp' relative to the level of competition in the other.

In addition to the techniques of solidarization (coalition formation) and discrimination (exclusion), the same strategically advantageous effect can also be achieved when the intensity of competition in the other camp is successfully heightened, assuming a constant intensity in one's own camp. The purchasers in a market can succeed in doing this when, for example, they are in a position relatively to increase the numbers of suppliers entering the market, or to ensure that attempts undertaken on the supply side to create coalitions or discrimination fail. Analogous possibilities for influencing the intensity of competition are also available in principle to the supply side, which can draw upon a rich and complex repertoire of strategies, both individual and collective, solidarizing and discriminating.

But the various markets – for raw materials, goods, captial and labour – differ fundamentally according to the criterion of whether, and to what extent, buyers and sellers can actually utilize this 'in principle' symmetrical catalogue of rational market strategies. Should one or other side of the market find itself in a position of having exhausted its reservoir of strategic options to a greater extent than the other side, an asymmetrical power relationship would be evident in the market process itself. Of interest to us here with regard to the relationship between the supply and demand sides are the peculiarities of the labour market which make it possible to speak of a differential in the availability of the diverse rational market strategies, and consequently of a power differential in favour of the demand side and to the disadvantage of the supply side.

The peculiarly disadvantaged market and strategic position of the 'commodity' labour power consists in 'the employee always ending up in a position unfavourable to him when concluding a labour contract under free competition'.[1] The first reason for this alleged 'peculiar position' or 'fictive' character of the 'commodity' labour power,[2] is that while it is indeed treated as a commodity in markets, it does not reach these markets in the way most other commodities do. The quantity and quality, place and time of supply of other commodities depend on the expectations of the respective sellers of these commodities concerning their marketability. The entry of 'real' commodities into markets is regulated, or at least codetermined, by the criterion of their expected saleability. This is not the case with the 'commodity' labour power. Even in purely quantitative terms, the rising 'supply' of labour power is determined by non-strategic demographic processes and the institutional rules of human reproductive activity. It is also determined by socioeconomic processes which 'set free' labour power from the conditions under which it could maintain itself *other* than through sale in the market. To the degree that labour power is prevented from turning to modes of subsistence outside the labour market (e.g. through utilizing private agricultural land), the labour supply pressing into the market becomes quantitatively inelastic: 'Above all other factors that can otherwise still influence elasticity stands the massive question of physical existence, the question of whether it is possible to remain above water by other means, and for this the distribution of property is certainly of fundamental importance.'[3] An initially important peculiarity of labour power, therefore, is that while it is indeed treated as a commodity in the market, it enters this market for reasons other than those of other commodities. One could thus speak of a structural handicap of labour power in the market, for the supply side has no way of controlling its own volume of supply in a market-strategic manner.

A second handicap of the supply side of the labour market is that labour power, continuously dependent on the supply of the means of subsistence which can only be acquired through its 'sale', is not (or only within very narrow limits) in a position to 'wait' for favourable opportunities. This difficulty is related to the temporal parameters of supply. The inability to 'wait' before selling results from the typical situation whereby labour power does not control the (natural or manufactured) means of production which would allow it to either live on the sale of *products* manufactured from these means of production, or to use these (agricultural) products themselves as a means of subsistence. An essential aspect of the capitalist process of industrialization consisted precisely in destroying these conditions of economic independence (i.e. the self-sufficiency of agricultural and household production), as well as the preconditions of strategically 'waiting' for favourable demand conditions. To the degree that these preconditions are destroyed, the supply of labour power that does not meet with demand is in itself totally 'worthless'. As a result, it is structurally compelled extensively to relinquish its own strategic options, to submit to any presently given conditions of demand, and to accept the going wage it is offered. Labour power also cannot afford to sell its labour for a longer period of time 'for less than its value', that is, at a minimal level of subsistence, even when its long-term market opportunities would be increased by such a self-subsidy. It is dependent upon the *continuous* flow of *adequate* means of subsistence.

For the supply side of the labour market, the existence of its own numbers is a given and strategically invariable quantity; it can additionally be influenced by the demand side, namely, through the strategic utilization of the technological change that sets labour power free and thus expands the potential supply. A quantitative policy related to the supply side becomes possible, historically as well as systematically, only when an authority *external* to the market appears in the form of state social- and labour-protection policies. On the one hand, these policies guarantee the right to coalition formation; on the other hand, they hinder portions of the available labour supply from entering the market (e.g. the prohibition of child labour, the setting of maximum working hours, the standardization of the working day). But at the same time they make available *non-market* means of subsistence (e.g. retirement insurance) to the labour power 'excluded' from the supply side, such that this labour power is no longer forced to offer itself on the market. This means that the strategic options that are otherwise available to the suppliers of other commodities must, in the case of the 'commodity' labour power, be facilitated and guaranteed from the outset through political regulation. Only through the presence of a politically organized unemployment insurance scheme are the suppliers of labour power (at least partially) able to strategically 'wait', instead of directly and immediately accepting each demand, that is, every wage offered.

A third peculiarity of labour power and its limited strategic options is that its own need for subsistence means is largely constant within the framework of a materially and culturally defined 'minimum standard of living'. At any rate, its need is essentially more rigid than the reciprocal need of employers. If wages procure the means of subsistence of workers and if, inversely, the allocation of labour is a means for producing goods and services, an asymmetry between these two relations becomes evident: through the use of technological change, production can very well be maintained even with a fall in labour input per unit of output, while reproduction of labour power *cannot* be maintained with a fall of income per household. An asymmetry between the two sides of the market is based on the fact that (at least on average, and in the long term) the buyers of labour can more easily make themselves independent of supply than is the case with the suppliers of labour with respect to the demand side. The purchasers of labour can increase the efficiency of production, but the suppliers cannot increase the efficiency of their reproduction; the latter have only the option of cutting their standard of living as soon as possibilities for 'economizing' on their incomes (e.g. by walking to distant discount stores) have been exhausted.

A fourth handicap lies in the *qualitative* potential for adaptation on the supply side of the labour market. No doubt, both individual suppliers and purchasers of labour are qualitatively 'determined'. Concrete labourers can be combined only with certain functions in the production process (because of their special occupational training and experience, for instance), just as certain concrete machines require specifically skilled operators. What is decisive, however, is the greater degree of qualitative 'liquidity' of capital in comparison with labour. Every unit of capital, whether over the short or long term, passes through a phase of 'liquidity' – a phase of liquefaction into money. At the end of a phase of the capital cycle, the owners of capital are free to decide whether or not they wish to purchase other means of production suitable for combining with labour power (with less or other qualifications) for the next phase in that cycle. Herein lies a qualitative opportunity for mobility that has virtually no equivalent on the side of labour power (where one would have to think of unlimited possibilities of retraining as an equivalent). In fact, and quite unlike capital, the concrete labour capacity that suppliers of labour have to offer does not pass through a phase of 'liquidity', in which it could rid itself of all qualitative determination and, so to speak, start a new life; strictly speaking, capital does not 'age', but rather moves in a circular pattern of constant renewal. Suppliers of labour power, by contrast, can vary the quality of their offer only within very narrow limits, and again only because of such forms of external (political) support as education and retraining.

The only variable through which the supplier of labour power can possibly improve its strategic position in the market is that of the spatial dimension. Accordingly, the historically most important adaptive responses by labour *without* public assistance have taken place in the spatial dimension, through such movements as emigration, urbanization and commuting. But it is obvious that even in spatial processes of adaptation, which represent the sole dimension in which the supply side of the labour market can employ autonomous strategies against the demand side, labour is forced to make sacrifices. These become evident in the destruction of local family and social relations, but also in specific risks of impoverishment or marginalization, as in the urban development not only of third world countries, but also in the USA and, increasingly, Europe.

The relative strategic rigidity of the supply side of the labour market, which is evident in the dimensions of the quantity, quality and timing of supply, and which distinguishes this particular market for labour power from all other markets, is paid for above all through relative losses of income. Because the individual seller of labour power – or workers organized as a whole – cannot, for the structural reasons already discussed, employ market strategies, they must compensate for these strategic handicaps through a drop in the rate of pay demanded for labour. Exploitation results from the asymmetrical strategic capacity of supply and demand – even more so in the case of labour power than in the standard market constellation of agricultural production, where farmers can of course strategically vary the type, but not, as a rule, the timing and quantity of their products. Producers are, therefore, often forced to sell their usually 'perishable' products at a price far below their production costs. The example of agricultural production is also instructive, since in both cases only voluntary forms of collective action (trade unions or co-operatives) or public guarantees (guaranteed producers' prices or labour-protection and social policies) make it possible to equalize at least partially the power differentials between the supply and demand sides of these markets.

51   J. I. Gershuny and R. E. Pahl

Implications and Future of the Informal Economy

People have always fiddled, had perks, worked on the side, and helped a neighbour with 'cheap goods'. This is the way the workers have always survived and, at another level and in a different style, the rich have got richer. (Those in the middle may have missed out.) Attempts by the state to organize, tax and control, have shifted various activities from the formal economy or the domestic economy into the informal economy. Yesterday's 'enterprise' becomes part of today's hidden economy. But the political parties huff and puff about the importance of getting people into employment rather than helping people to do their own work.

Obsession with what can be easily counted leads to false ideas about the British disease and our national performance. The political agenda ignores, or misunderstands, the main economic tendencies in our society. This would not matter much if the 'formal' and 'informal' modes of production maintained a constant interrelationship over time. If the informal economy grew at the same rate as the formal economy, then the significance of GNP as an indicator of change would be unaffected by the fact that it only measures formal activity. And if the amount of work done in the two economies rose or fell in parallel, then statistics of formal employment levels would indicate the overall availability of work.

But our thesis is that, on the contrary, the two economies develop at different rates. A consequence of social and technological development is the transfer of particular spheres of production between them.

We must first deal with some definitional problems. We are using the term *informal economy* to cover the following three areas, of which the first two are the most important for our argument:

1   *Household economy*: production, not for money, by members of a household and predominantly for members of that household, of goods or services for which approximate substitutes might otherwise be purchased for money.
2   *Underground, hidden or black economy*: production, wholly or partly for money or barter, which should be declared to some official taxation or regulatory authority, but which is wholly or partly concealed.
3   *Communal economy*: production, not for money or barter, by an individual or group, of a commodity that might otherwise be purchasable, and of which the producers are not principal consumers.

Like any economic definitions, these have fuzzy edges. Where, for example, do we place those small businesses which rely heavily on family workers, and are less than absolutely scrupulous in their VAT returns? But the definitions will stand up for our present purpose – which is to demonstrate that there are good reasons for expecting the informal economy to grow at the expense of the formal.

In most of the developed world, the massive increase in material production over the last 150 or 200 years has been associated with technological developments and with an increasing scale in organization. Now this process is showing clear signs of breaking down. With new technology, production can be cheaper, more efficient and often more convenient when it is carried out on a small scale. Work can be done in the household or in the hidden economy which once was done only in the formal economy.

The man who finds that it pays him to take a week off work to paint the house, or rebuild the engine in his car, will probably do a better job than if he went to a firm in the formal sector. With sewing machines, power drills and food mixers, we can (if we have the skills) get smart clothes, fine carpentry and gourmet food by working in our own time with our own tools. Technology has created this new freedom.

Technology is not the only driving force. Legal changes also push production from the formal into the informal economy. VAT means that money payments in cash become illegal and unrecorded. Steep rates of personal taxation, obligations to pay high national insurance contributions, and employment protection legislation: all these encourage both casual work 'for cash' and do-it-yourself. Changes in relative prices increase DIY, too. Technical innovation has pushed down the price of goods. But rising wages rates have pushed up the price of services. And the satisfactions of informal work – relative autonomy, self-direction and self-pacing – also encourage its growth.

Seen in this perspective, development is not a one-way progress – from reliance on primary production, through manufacturing production, to a society whose major efforts are devoted to the production of services. Nor is there a simple transition from a society in which economic relationships are based on custom to a modern society in which an increasing proportion of social relationships are cash-based – i.e. converted from generalized to specific exchange. The pattern is less tidy. [Figure 1] shows that, instead of a steady one-way flow of economic activity – whereby things move, over time, from the household to the industrial production system – there is a whole series of little transformations of production (perhaps taking place simultaneously) between the formal economy, the household economy and the underground economy. The direction of flow is determined by the social and technical conditions for the production of particular commodities at particular times. As [figure 1] shows, this involves six possible flows among three types of economy.

Here are some examples. The washing of clothes and linen, which moved from the wash-house at home into the laundry, and then back into the home with the technological help of a washing machine, illustrates the two-way flow between households and the formal economy (1 and 2 in the [figure]). The current prevalence of household construction work paid for in cash may indicate a shift from formal to underground, or 'black' production (3 in the [figure]). And if unemployment levels rise, the cost of black work will drop and some jobs, now DIY, will move across (6).

There is much discussion about the 'de-skilling' of the workforce in the formal economy. But there may be a re-skilling in the informal one. Some people who in the past might have called in a plumber or a carpenter are now more ready to try to do the job themselves. 'How-to' books democratize skills in the informal economy. Hiring a cook or a chauffeur has always been a minority pastime. The same is now coming to apply to carpenters and glaziers.

Though we argue for a wide range of different sorts of flow between three

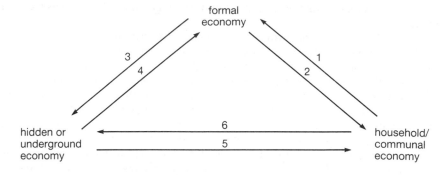

Figure 1   The three economies

types of economy, we wouldn't deny that over the last couple of centuries, the aggregate effect has been an overall shift from household/communal production to formal industrial production. But it may be that the most significant transformation in the future will be from the formal economy to the underground and household economies.

We are both engaged in research work, attempting to explore the implications of this hypothesis. One of us (Gershuny) is analysing published and unpublished data to assess more precisely the growth of informal economic activity. For example, the official Family Expenditure Survey shows that, rather than buying formal transport, household and entertainment services, the British have increasingly bought *goods* like cars and TV sets – which are used in the informal household production of services.

Another source is the national sample of people's activity patterns, carried out by the BBC Audience Research Department. Reanalysis of the diaries which respondents kept over a number of weeks in 1961 and 1974–5 shows that time spent working for money declined; time devoted to the informal production of services increased.

The other author (Pahl) is exploring the detailed social and economic transactions within and between families in one community. He is trying to document a new kind of rationality, which allocates time and energy between the three economic spheres according to a very subtle calculus. There is employment for which one gets money, and perhaps social satisfaction; and there is work with one's own tools in one's own time, for which one gets much satisfaction and perhaps some money as well.

Work and sociability can get more intertwined in the informal economy than in the formal one. A woman calls on her sister and looks after her child while she has her hair done; she returns with some commodity got through her sister's employment. A man who goes to the pub for a drink and a chat gets suggestions for people who will help him build his house extension.

The whole of everyday life is suffused with contacts, exchanges and reciprocities. Yet the standard economic model is of a market-place in which you sell your labour for money, and this in turn pays for the goods and services you need. Certainly, that is one option. But, for many people, it is not very satisfactory or rewarding. Any government which assumes that everyone is longing to sell their labour to an employer ought to get closer to the people.

But what will it be like to live in a world dominated more by the household and hidden economies, and less by the formal economy? Let us construct some alternatives. Two grim ones, and a pleasant one.

The first kind of future goes like this. If current trends continue, the 'self-service' sector of the economy will continue to grow at the expense of the formal sector. The demand for commodities from the formal sector will be concentrated in the manufacturing sector, which is also the sector with high growth in manpower productivity. This productivity is dependent on shedding labour, which in turn may produce faster growth in the underground economy.

The non-manufacturing and less productive part of the formal economy will be forced to pay minimal wages and to use part-time labour – probably women, and children still at school or the retired. They will expect to augment their wages through tips and fiddles.

This will produce a dual labour market: (a) a high-technology sector, aiming at an international market and obliged to be as efficient and productive as possible, and probably paying relatively high wages; paired with (b) a low-wage sector, largely relying on female and part-time workers.

Below this dual labour market, the informal economy will flourish uncontrolled, and perhaps uncontrollable. This would be a world of *mafiosi*, of big bosses and little crooks. The working class will become divided within itself. The new labour aristocracy of the high-technology growth industries in the manufacturing sector will get high wages and be able to afford an expensive, even ostentatious lifestyle. Those less fortunate, in the low-wage sector, may sink yet further.

Women obliged to work part-time, a shifting workforce of young people or immigrants, and a fluctuating and unstable pattern of employment – all these help to provide the ingredients of a nasty, increasingly inegalitarian world.

The second glimpse into the gloomier side of the crystal ball is perhaps not so much an alternative to the first – rather, a consequence of it. On this view, the state, fearful of the unstable situation in the first scenario, increases its power of surveillance and control. It attempts to enforce taxation and employment legislation by increasing the penalties for non-compliance, and by bolstering the police force and other law-enforcing agencies. It keeps up employment in the formal sector by spending the increased tax yield on more public services, and developing a larger bureaucracy. This creates more resentment among the mass of the population. The social satisfactions of the informal economy could not be re-created in the formal economy. People would feel much like those caught in the 'socialism' of Poland or Czechoslovakia.

Both these forecasts are extremely disagreeable and unpleasant prospects. What is the third and better route? This would be based on the state's recognizing certain realities in our new economic life, encouraging the most desirable features, and mitigating the less desirable. Governments are now uncomfortably caught. On the one hand, they feel they should try to maintain, or increase, the present number of jobs. On the other hand, the efficient industrial production which is necessary to compete in international markets means reducing employment. The dilemma can only be resolved by a deeper understanding of the socially good aspects of the informal economy, and then by encouraging them.

The formal economy can provide efficient material production, but the informal economy can provide services which, since they are not widely traded, need *not* be efficient in their use of labour. So the state could adopt a 'facilitative' role. It would support community-based services in such fields as care for old people, children and the chronically sick. It would modify the laws relating to very small companies in order to relieve them of administrative and tax burdens. It would change social security benefits, in order to reduce the high tax rates on low-wage earners, and to protect anyone working exclusively in the small-scale informal sector. Above all, the state would *encourage* people to participate simultaneously in both the formal and the informal sectors. There would be job-sharing schemes in the formal economy; and education and training schemes to develop the skills needed for the informal economy.

Clearly, some aspects of the way the informal economy is developing are unpalatable. Some people are expelled or excluded from the formal economy. Their participation in the informal economy is not voluntary. They do not gain any intangible, personal benefits from informal production. They are vulnerable to exploitation by those with access to jobs (and therefore cash) from the formal economy. The growth of the informal economy is no grounds for complacency about formal unemployment.

But positive government action could extend the range of genuine options open to people. Action should be taken to reduce the discriminatory impact of unemployment, and to promote shorter working hours. This would improve things. It is the only kind of strategy that will cope with rising levels of unemployment in the formal economy.

The problem that still faces us is lack of knowledge. We do not thoroughly understand the social processes that underlie the flows between the formal and informal economies. We need new concepts as well as more detailed ethnography. The scale of adjustment in intellectual frameworks is enormous. The only reason we have for thinking that this adjustment will take place is that it is necessary. If we are to cope with a world in which jobs are lost inside the formal economy, we must come to understand the nature of work outside it.

52   Jeremy Seabrook

House of the Rising Sun: The Nature and Impact of Japanese Corporations

This joint venture between Mitsubishi and Chrysler looks incongruous set in the rich black earth of McLean County in central Illinois. The plant is one of the most highly automated and robotized in the world. Ninety per cent of welding is done robotically, releasing the associates (there are no workers) from dangerous and tedious operations. Almost half a billion dollars' worth of investment has gone into the 636-acre site. This has produced just under 3,000 jobs.

There is a stamping shop, body shop, plastic moulding shop, paint shop and final assembly area; the conveyor lines are 8 miles in length. A 1.5-mile track allows for the test-driving of every vehicle. The low white building is surrounded by a wire mesh fence and rows of barbed wire. It looks like something between a military installation and a hospital.

Although this is an equal venture, few people in the plant can be unaware that Mitsubishi accounts for almost 10 per cent of the gross national product of Japan. One in ten of the Diamond Star Mitsubishi (DSM) workforce will be trained in Japan for a period up to thirty-seven weeks. There are about fifty Japanese employees at present, and 100–150 technical assistants on short-term visits to help production under way. The plant opened in the autumn of 1988.

The Japanese say they have been surprised by the dedication of the Bloomington workforce. It is no accident that the site chosen is the middle west, where the work ethic remains strong. The office hours of DSM are 7.30 a.m. until 4.12 p.m. When the first 300 jobs were advertised, there were more than 30,000 applicants. You don't have to travel far in Bloomington before you meet disappointed aspirants. Those accepted are the object of envy and admiration, forming, as they do, a new aristocracy of workers in a community whose egalitarianism is only apparent.

All applicants are screened by the Illinois Department of Social Security for information about their work record and basic skills. The next step is a battery of State-administered general aptitude tests before further screening at the DSM Assessment Center. A physical examination and routine drug test are also mandatory.

It goes against the grain for many people in the middle west to acknowledge the industrial superiority of the Japanese. There is some overt xenophobia, and an understandable reserve on the part of those who were on the death marches of the Second World War. Others insist that it is now time for Japan to share the burden of defending the free world.

There is also much criticism of the Japanese for having unfairly protected their industries. But perhaps the most common response would be familiar to us in Britian. It clearly echoes the proprietorial tolerance with which Britain once regarded the US, seeing in it an extension of an energy and vigour which originated in Britain. In the US, the reasoning goes like this: 'We are the true initiators and innovators, the Japanese take over our inventions, improve upon them, perfect them.' In this way, the Americans feel that they remain the orginal source of all that is most vital in the world, even though they get less of the credit for it, and little of the profit.

It turns out that Japanese management can be seen as simply a matter of common sense. 'Kaizen', or continuous improvement, is at the heart of the Mitsubishi philosophy, and who could quarrel with that? As an employee of DSM, your advice and suggestions are sought for the enhancement of safety and efficiency. All suggestions are considered; if they are not implemented, you are given an explanation. It is easy to buy into such a system, so different from traditional manufacturing plants, where suggestions boxes grew dusty with disuse.

The training manual applies to all 3,000 associates. There is a common programme of work discipline. All wear the grey and maroon DSM uniform, which removes the last traces of any 'them and us' attitude. All are part of the Diamond Star family. The United Auto-Workers' Union of American was recognized by the Company in 1988; although it is hoped that the need for it will wither away.

The team concept pervades the plant. There are teams of ten to fifteen people, who all work together under a team-leader. Each team has twenty to thirty job responsibilities. People are trained in all of these, and work rotated on a two-hourly basis, so that the working day remains varied. It also means that there is flexibility: if an employee is absent, someone else can cover. It is the antithesis of the monotony of the assembly line, where people have always been given one simple, repetitive function. Naturally, the strong sense of belonging means there are many collective social activities. On the Friday I was there, I was told, 'tomorrow some people are going to the ball-game in Peoria, there is a golf outing to Chicago, some women are shopping in Chicago, and there is a trip to the home of Abraham Lincoln in Springfield'.

Among the associates are former bank-tellers, farmers, housewives, day-care workers, students. The level of educational attainment is relatively high. There is sophisticated equipment to operate and no quality inspection is carried out until the vehicle is completed. The teams themselves are responsible for quality, which is superb.

Donald Schoene is Executive Vice-President, Finance, and Treasurer. Before joining Diamond Star, he spent more than twenty-five years with Chrysler, and was Controller for Chrysler UK. He says: 'Our eastern friends are very good at learning our western trades. They know how to modify and enhance our technology. This places us in the role of teachers, and the knowledge we impart is then transferred back, improved, to the USA.'

While the robots take care of the work that is monotonous and dangerous, the associates become responsible only for what is most creative. There are three key words in Japanese: 'Muri' means unreasonable; 'Mura' means uneven; 'Muda' means unnecessary. The approach is to remove all these from the workplace experience. This gains their loyalty.

> In the past, the typical US plant would try to control waste by making the worker responsible for it; the workers became estranged from the company's ideals by having to do tasks that were not enhancing. The Japanese believe in consensual decision-making. This is also more efficient: our plant is two-thirds the size of the average US car plant. We have two million square feet, producing 240,000 cars a year, one thousand a day. The flow of work is so well planned that it can be carried out in a smaller space. It is a process-driven product and plant.

... When Diamond Star settled on Bloomington, they were anxious not to arrive in the middle west like a whirlwind. They wanted to stay on a par with the community, not offer sky-high wage rates that would disrupt the local economy. Everything has been discreet and without ostentation. The wage rates are comparable to those in the area, lower than in traditional assembly plants. The associates are paid $9.95 an hour, and skilled maintenance people $11.74. DSM didn't want to strip other industries of their employees. Even so, there have been complaints in Peoria and Springfield that some heavy industrial works have lost people to DSM. The Japanese believe in 'wa', harmony among people at all levels, and have sought to insert themselves as unobtrusively as possible in Bloomington-Normal.

In spite of its compactness, the workplace is so big that it is difficult to see from one end of the building to the other. A subdued white light pervades the space, from where the great rolls of metal arrive in the press shop to the finished product. In the press shop, the panels are delivered to a computer-controlled storage area; they are stored robotically, and distributed to the body shop by automatic guided vehicles. Front and rear bumper fascias are moulded in the plastic shop. In the body shop, panels and undercarriage are welded together. There are more than 250 robots, and 90 per cent of the operations are automated. The conditions in the paint shop are said to be 'hospital clean'.

More than seventy robots seal the welded seams of the car body. The doors are then removed and the 'operating hardware' is installed; instrument panel, heater, air conditioner are also set in place automatically. There is a 'just in time' inventory management practice, which means that local suppliers can be alerted automatically when a new consignment of seats or tyres or some other component is due. This saves storage space.

The whole process moves forward at considerable speed: one vehicle is produced for every twenty-three work hours. There is something disturbing about the robots: they are installed like some vast giant human body. They emerge from their place of rest in the form of skeletal arms, fingers, claws, eyes, an exposed musculature deftly lifting and placing with the greatest precision. Each movement goes forward at a precisely calculated pace, and is preceded by an electronic warning tune that sounds like 'Mary Had a Little Lamb', so that the employees can be clear of the arena of operation. When this is completed, the people move in to add their touch – so much lighter than the machines. The vehicles emerge in such a way that those who must work beneath them can work at eye level.

The guided vehicles taking the parts to the body shop emit a euphonic robotized warning as they go, following predetermined, computerized tracks along the floor. Although it all seems smooth and effortless, enormous force is used. The robotic welding process with its cascade of blue sparks is noisy and dazzling, the thud of the metal each time the whole ensemble moves forward demands ear-plugs, hard hats and goggles. There is little space for the employees to communicate beyond co-ordinating their specific function. Some of the operations are spectacularly graceful – the double or triple-jointed flexibility of metal arms that lift the windshield with suction-pads and dexterously place it in the aperture of the car.

Yet the subordination of the people to the process remains: the dwarfing, indeed, the inferiorizing of human beings who must wait until the warning music comes, and then, with precision, accomplish their task, and then withdraw, so that the whole lot can proceed to the next work station.

There are two eight-hour shifts at present, with a 42-minute meal break (this because time is measured in tenths of one hour). The shifts begin at 7 a.m. and 3 p.m. and are preceded by 90 seconds of stretching exercises. Thirty-five per cent of the employees are women. Most are young. There has been only one serious accident so far – one associate thought a robot was in a training mode, i.e. was still being taught the operation it had to perform, when it was already in the production mode.

That production can take place with such scant human intervention is both exalting and appalling: exalting because it makes the possibilities seem endless; appalling because so little of the labour saved is of any benefit to all the underoccupied and unemployed in the world. The finished products, the Eclipse and the Laser, stand on plinths in the reception area, a place of bare functional metal and marble, with only photographs of the Illinois countryside on the walls as ornament.

The embodiment of such power and strength in these robots is disturbing, because it represents the successful neutralization of the working class, and celebrates the triumph of international capital which has, contrary to some predictions, proved itself to be the gravedigger of labour. This is perhaps the meaning of that dispersal of disembodied energies and powers in these tame machines. The flesh and blood has been liberated into the benign functions required by the service economy of Bloomington-Normal.

No wonder the associates of DSM must have intelligence, communicative ability and psychosocial skills. As well as doing their job, they are custodians of the funerary monument of a defunct working class.

53   Paul Routledge

Lock-out at Times Newspapers Ltd

Times Newspapers Ltd incorporates five publications, namely *The Times*, its three *Supplements* (*Educational, Higher Education* and *Literary*) and *The Sunday Times*, and is among the most famous and prestigious newspaper groups in the world. It operates from Fleet Street, a small concentrated jungle with

its own traditions and customs, particularly regarding its trade union organization. The unions figuring large in this case are: SOGAT – the Society of
Graphical and Allied Trades, representing publishing room workers, van
drivers and circulation representatives; NGA – the National Graphical Association, representing skilled print workers, including compositors, machine managers and readers; NUJ – the self-explanatory National Union of Journalists;
and NATSOPA – the National Society of Operative Printers, Graphical and
Media Personnel, representing semi-skilled grades and clerical and administrative staff. In all, fifty-six chapels existed at the start of the dispute.

It is now generally recognized that the 'big bang' theory of industrial relations
did not work when it was tried at Times Newspapers Ltd (TNL) in the long,
costly and often bitter lock-out of 1978–9. TNL management insisted after the
11.5-month suspension of its five titles that it had achieved 70 per cent of its
objectives. Little more than a year later, when *The Times*, its three supplements
and *The Sunday Times* were put up for sale, it was admitted that industrial
disruption had not ceased 'and it has not been possible to operate the new
technology on even the most limited basis'.

In the calmer operating climate of today, and with the benefit of the more
accurate science of hindsight, it is possible to determine why events did not
unfold as management had foreseen and perhaps to draw some general conclusions about the nature of trade union power in the national newspaper industry.

To begin more or less at the beginning, the background to the dispute was
clearly laid out in a letter to print union general secretaries sent by M. J. 'Duke'
Hussey, managing director and chief executive of Times Newspapers, on 26
April 1978. He complained of 'crippling disputes' which had cost 7.7 million
copies of the paper because of unofficial industrial action over a period of just
three months – 20 per cent of total output. Losses due to this action amounted
to £1,750,000, equal to the total profit in 1977, which was easily the best year in
the company's history.

Hussey told the unions: 'It is not an exaggeration that almost the total
working hours of our Board and senior managers are now occupied with trying
to prevent disputes, solving disputes and repairing the damage they cause.
Virtually no effort is going in to improving the turnover and profitability of the
company.' No board of directors – and no responsible trade union official –
could stand aside from a crisis of this nature, he argued.

TNL accordingly proposed 'urgent discussions' on four basic company demands: (1) absolute continuity of production; all arbitrary restrictions to be
lifted; no unofficial action to prevent publication; (2) negotiation of a new,
fast-acting and effective disputes procedure; (3) negotiation of a general wage
restructuring based on new technology and computer-based electronic printing
systems; (4) a timetable insisting on completion of these negotiations by 30
November. If this deadline was not met, publication of the titles would be
suspended unilaterally by the company, and staff who had not accepted these
terms would be dismissed.

There was another underlying factor, rarely articulated but playing a key role
in managerial attitudes: restoration of 'the right to manage'. Hussey let the cat
out of the bag in a television interview, saying that Fleet Street had 'allowed
situations to develop which it should never have done . . . the right to manage is
one of the issues at stake, it is a Fleet Street problem'. As Martin points out,
'management became more committed to new technology as a means of achieving a once-for-all transformation in the company's industrial relations, with an
assertion of management's authority'.[1]

As Martin further observes, 'Times management was asking for the moon,' and it was not available.[2] The company had chosen to fight on too many fronts. In the first place, the steady shift of power from the centre to the workplace that had been such a feature of trade union development in the 1960s had given further 'clout' to the print union chapels, which were already in a strong position because of the pre-entry closed shop universally operating in the industry. Even if they had wished to, the print union full-time officials could not give *absolute guarantees* of continuity of production.

Secondly, by requiring full use of computerized typesetting – including direct input to the computer by journalists – the company was demanding that the NGA, the most powerful, disciplined and wealthy print union, give up its traditional monopoly of the keyboard. The NGA had watched its counterparts in the USA and West Germany fight, and lose, this battle, with catastrophic consequences in terms of de-skilling and job losses. Joe Wade, general secretary of the NGA, said in an eve-of-conflict message to his members that the rest of Fleet Street, provincial managements and general printing firms were 'waiting like vultures to see the union break its back' at *The Times*; 'So there is no going back. There can be no surrender. We fight for our union. We fight until we have won.'

And thirdly, the company made the cardinal error of assuming that *Times* journalists would behave with their customary moderation and meekly accept the conditions for continuing employment. They did not. On the last day of publication, they voted 142 to 92 to be dismissed along with the printers. It was a passionate debate within the chapel of the National Union of Journalists, fuelled partly by a sense of professional outrage at the management taking the paper off the streets for an indefinite period, and partly by a sense that here was an opportunity to close the earnings gap with *The Sunday Times* and win greater concessions for operating new technology.

After recovering from the initial shock of this decision, TNL moved swiftly to prevent the break-up of its editorial team. The NUJ negotiated an interim agreement under which journalists 'would not be asked to do work that had not been voluntarily relinquished by another union'. That proviso, which remains in force at the present time, took them out of the firing line but it also had a considerable psychological impact on the company's bargaining position.

Few substantive negotiations had taken place elsewhere by the time the deadline was reached. Only four of the fifty-six bargaining units had signed deals, covering circulation representatives, maintenance engineers, the *Sunday Times* NUJ and a handful of building workers. It had taken several months to get all the print union general secretaries into one room, and they then complained that there was insufficient time to conclude agreements before 30 November. The NGA simply refused to discuss surrendering its control over typesetting, while personal rivalries and chaotic lines of communication in SOGAT and NATSOPA between chapel, branch, region and national leadership sharply diminished the prospects of peace talks.

William Rees-Mogg, editor of *The Times* and a director of TNL, who supported the lock-out policy, was to complain later:

> Negotiation is a process which offers at every stage the opportunity to say 'No', regardless of the policy of the Government, regardless of the policy of the trade union movement, regardless of the wishes of the members and regardless of the interests of the members.
>
> Our position at *The Times* is like that of a man at the end of a windswept pier in some cold and out of season seaside resort – perhaps Scarborough in late November. We are confronted with a set of seven

rusty and ancient fruit machines. To reach agreements we have to line up three strawberries in each of the fruit machines at the same time.

Somehow, heaven knows how – we have managed to line up three of the strawberries on two of the machines, and we have a couple of strawberries in the third. Of the others, some reject the coin that is put in – however large – while one has a lemon and another has a raspberry rusted permanently in place on the centre of the dial.

His exasperated comments were colourful but misplaced. The company was asking for too much and usually asking the wrong people – the union general secretaries, rather than the chapels – to deliver it. This policy continued through an abortive two-week postponement of the deadline to 14 December, during which the then Employment Secretary of the Labour government, Albert Booth, attempted to bring the warring parties together. The delaying move cost the company £1 million but yielded no settlement, and the first 580 employees who were on two-week notice periods were sacked as the new year came in. Dismissals thereafter continued at the rate of about 100 a week as individual notices expired, and the repetitive experience of people leaving (sometimes accompanied by emotional scenes) inevitably prompted rising resentment on the shop floor. Members of NATSOPA and the NGA voted not to reopen talks with management until all the dismissed employees had been reinstated. An All-Union Liaison Committee bringing together rank and file leaders of the various chapels was formed, supplying a platform for lay officials and further extending the role of the in-house union leaders.

The dispute ran into its fourth month with Albert Booth once again seeking to act as peacemaker. He called on both sides on 8 March and persuaded the company to re-engage those already dismissed and retain those still on TNL books until 17 April, a planned date for republication of the titles. The Booth initiative was essentially to win time for realistic negotiations, this time bringing in the chapel leaders. But these talks, too, foundered on the rock of NGA intransigence. The craft printers would agree to a 'back end' system which retained their monopoly of the keyboard. But they would not go to arbitration on the possibility of moving to a 'front end' system giving journalists and tele-ad clerks access to the computer. Les Dixon, president of the NGA, insisted: 'It's a matter of principle and you can't arbitrate on a matter of principle.'

As breakdown came at the Easter weekend, the notices of the 620 NGA men expired and they were dismissed. The union then declared an official dispute, and began paying £40 a week benefit to its members, a sum topped up by the same amount raised in a Fleet Street levy. Later in the dispute, the NGA allowed its members to take work elsewhere, and on several occasions the full authority of its leaders was required to hold its TNL membership together. NATSOPA also found its members work elsewhere in Fleet Street, even where this meant (as it did at the *Daily Mirror*) displacing temporary staff. The union's undeclared but actual role as a labour exchange for the industry was never more tested, and other national newspaper proprietors found themselves paying the wages of ex-*Times* employees to whose dismissal they were giving moral support through the Newspaper Publishers' Association, the employers' body for the industry. Like other national newspapers, TNL has for long acquiesced in the system of virtual 'subcontracting' by which the trade unions supply labour and allocate tasks in the production areas.

The temptation to produce some form of newspaper in the run-up to the 1979 general election is thought to have been a major factor in the company's decision, announced on 20 April, to print and publish a European edition of *The*

Times, to circulate exclusively abroad. Journalists were allowed to follow their own conscience in deciding whether to work for it, and after many months of inactivity many did contribute.

The reaction of the print unions was predictably wrathful. It was not long before the 'secret' location – Frankfurt in West Germany – was known. The NGA sent over a national officer to establish contact with the German printing union, IG Druck und Papier, so that the plant could be picketed. Only one edition of the 'Eurotimes' was printed, on the presses of the right-wing Turkish language newspaper *Tercumen*, close to Frankfurt airport. Pickets had stuffed a petrol-soaked rag into an air vent connected to machine room compressors, and police advised that they could not guarantee safe production of the paper. Amid charges from Rees-Mogg that 'violent and criminal elements' had halted the venture, the NUJ chapel changed its mind and decided that publication of the 'Eurotimes' was an obstacle to a negotiated solution of the dispute. No further editions were printed.

Two more idle months passed before the real breakthrough came in late June over dinner between the NGA leaders and Lord Thomson of Fleet, son of the Canadian entrepreneur who bought *The Times* from Lord Astor in 1966, adding it to his large portfolio of media investments which already included *The Sunday Times*. TNL had been a subsidiary of the Thomson organization since 1967, and as such was part of a massive conglomerate with substantial and profitable North Sea oil interests. *The Times* had consistently turned in a loss, though TNL had in good years made a profit. The large profits of the Thomson organization from oil, travel, publishing and provincial newspapers contributed to a widely held (though eventually erroneous) assumption that even though he did not share his father's attachment to *The Times*, the new Lord Thomson would not quit ownership of the titles. Conversely, it was also held in some quarters that the oil revenues were being used to break the power of the print unions.

Whatever his motives, Lord Thomson finally agreed to drop the company's insistence on single key-stroking, i.e. to allow the NGA to keep its monopoly of the keyboard. With this obstacle out of the way, negotiations began in earnest.

'Duke' Hussey, flanked by his top managers, attended a meeting of the All-Union Liaison Committee and told the chapel leaders: 'You will find us very flexible. We are newspaper makers, not executioners.' The company conceded that it had missed the signs of change in the balance of power within the unions; that power, it argued, should now be used constructively. Whether TNL had in mind what followed is unlikely; it took four more months to construct a return-to-work formula, which was the subject of in-fighting between the chapels as each working group scented victory and sought to wring the maximum possible gains from the company. Pay negotiations in the machine room were particularly abrasive, with the NGA machine managers accusing the NATSOPA machine assistants of endangering the peace process by disturbing hallowed differentials.

Within NATSOPA, there was a revolt among the white-collar chapels led by the wily and charismatic Barry Fitzpatrick who objected to what had been signed on their behalf. A clutch of operating agreements for new technology had to be renegotiated, with the chapels once again stamping their authority on the bargaining process. Fitzpatrick had emerged as a key figure in the dispute, leading the rank and file Liaison Committee. He is now a full-time national officer of SOGAT 82, into which NATSOPA disappeared through merger. His main rival in NATSOPA–TNL politics, Reg Brady, leader of the *Sunday Times* machine assistants, left the shop floor by another traditional Fleet Street route: to become an industrial relations executive under the new Murdoch regime.

The negotiations went through a series of broken deadlines, frequently lasting most of the night and pushing the negotiators on both sides 'beyond the limits of physical endurance'. Agreement was reached on the morning of the last day of the 'final, final' ultimatum period; Lord Thomson told waiting newsmen the suspension had been worth it if it secured the long-term future of the papers.

Before the champagne poured by a toastmaster at the front door had disappeared down the print workers' throats, it was clear that the lock-out had achieved nothing of the kind. The NGA had accepted a back-end system of computerized typesetting, which would cut composing room manning levels by 40 per cent; but this had been on offer before the shutdown. Fewer men were to be employed in the machine room, though how many were notional shifts was anybody's guess; this issue also went to an ineffective ACAS investigation. A new disputes procedure had been signed, but it had scarcely been put to the test before the company was back in dispute, this time with the NUJ after refusing to honour an arbitration award. The suspension cost TNL £39 million, and the NGA still had control over the new technology.

The strategy might have worked in the United States, but it did not work in Britain because of the unusually tightly knit nature of the industry, concentrated in a few square miles rather than dispersed in large cities. The print unions' 'labour exchange' had prevented any real privation, and the power of the chapels survived largely intact. In the view of one veteran print union leader, the shutdown 'made no contribution at all to improving relations in Fleet Street'.

However, it did tear away any remaining sentimentality within the Thomson organization parent company towards its difficult dependant. The week-long NUJ strike of autumn 1980 is credited with being the final straw for Lord Thomson, but there were already signs that the firm had decided that *The Times* was a prestigious luxury which would have to be ditched for the sake of the group as a whole. Under Thomson, Times Newspapers had practically become ungovernable, as his lordship said when the titles were put up for sale on the 23 October 1980. His continued support for the papers was 'conditional on the overall cooperation of the newspapers' employees, and I have sadly concluded that this cooperation will not be forthcoming under our ownership'.[3]

It had been a costly love affair with 'the old lady of Printing House Square'. From the formation of Times Newspapers in 1967, more than £70 million was advanced from Thomson sources for investment, working capital and losses incurred. The pretax loss in the year after suspension was £15 million, and TNL had to borrow £22 million from Thomson British Holdings to keep the papers afloat until their eventual sale to the Australian media magnate Rupert Murdoch.

54   E. Schoenberger

From Fordism to Flexible Accumulation: Technology, Competition and the Internationalization of Production

In the midst of crisis, one is naturally inclined to grasp at any and all apparent solutions. A particularly acute example is provided by the response of beleaguered manufacturing firms in the US and other advanced countries to their present predicament. Alone or in combination with other solutions, this response has included rationalization of existing capacity, a wave of mergers and acquisitions, plant shutdowns, the shifting of production to low-cost areas overseas, the adoption of new manufacturing technologies and new ways of organizing production, the restructuring of supplier and subcontracting relationships, and all manner of formal and informal co-operative and joint ventures on a national and international scale. This bewildering proliferation of strategies in the face of intensifying international competition, declining profits and stagnating markets in many core countries defies easy analysis. We appear to be in the midst of a transition from one form of social and economic organization to another and it is quite likely that a period of extensive and often disruptive experimentation and restructuring is inherent to this process.

One of the principal arenas of experimentation concerns the introduction of new, so-called flexible automation technologies in production. It is, as yet, far from clear that they will live up to expectations and it is certainly premature to predict that they will successfully resolve problems of industrial competitiveness and economic growth. Despite this uncertainty, however, it is important to develop an analytical framework for understanding why the move to flexible technologies is occurring, how they are likely to be used, and what this implies for employment, the use of labour and the spatial allocation of production.

The answer to the first of these questions may appear obvious – new technologies are being adopted because the system based on the old ones is breaking down. But we need to know more specifically what it is about the old system that is breaking down in order to understand to what precise problems the new flexible technologies are responding. This lays the groundwork for analysing how the new systems need to be used in order effectively to restore the competitiveness and profitability of firms seeking a way out of the Fordist dilemma.

The Fordist regime of accumulation, which was fully elaborated in the decades after the Second World War, encompasses both a characteristic technology and organization of production, and the nature of and mechanisms underlying consumption at a societal scale. In essence, Fordism is to be understood as an historically specific 'articulation between process of production and mode of consumption'.[1]

The labour process under Fordism is structured around the semi-automatic assembly line – the familiar standardized mass production operation based on costly fixed-purpose machinery. This has given rise to huge productivity gains with accumulation driven primarily by the extraction of relative surplus value.

This very productivity itself, however, poses a problem to the system. Mass production must have as its counterpart mass consumption in order to absorb the fabulous output of the production system. The possibility for mass consumption arises from a transformation of the conditions of the working class, especially through the institutionalization of the capital–labour relation in collective bargaining. Relative labour peace is traded for wage increases in line with productivity growth. This is, in a sense, the real originality of Fordism, although it was significantly reinforced by the rise of the welfare state to broaden the basis of mass consumption to important segments of the population who were not employed in those sectors organized along Fordist lines or who were not employed at all. Similarly, the adoption of Keynesian macroeconomic policies helped to insulate the system against cyclical fluctuations in demand. The whole is set within the context of particular institutional and social structures and norms of conduct that constitute the mode of regulation. The essence, however, is this dual and interrelated movement along axes both of production and of consumption.

The eventual breakdown of the regime of accumulation can be attributed to several factors. Aglietta stresses in particular the technical and social limits to Fordism that have resulted in a declining rate of productivity growth and a declining rate of exploitation.[2] One of the problems that Fordism helped to resolve was increasing the amount of the working day that was actually spent working. This is partly a question of disciplining the labour force, where possible by regulating the intensity and continuity of the work process via the machinery itself. The problem, however, is also associated with decreasing the amount of necessary downtime associated with start-up and switching between tasks, transfer of materials, retooling, etc; that is, reducing the 'porosity' of the working day.

Eventually, however, the increasingly refined technical division of labour within the production process generates an increase in what Aglietta refers to as 'balance delay time' or the mismatch among cycle times of the various segments of the production process. Production as a whole is, in a sense, regulated by the slowest segment of the work process, which means that some operations – and the workers tied to them – may be made temporarily redundant while the rest of the process catches up.

Along with the technical problems generated by Fordism, the intensification of the labour process is argued to have hit mental, physical and social limits. The pace of the semi-automatic equipment cannot exceed the ability of humans to process information and to respond to events. Moreover, the increasingly intolerable pace of the production process leads to a more generalized worker backlash.

These limits are seen to account for the slowdown in productivity growth and the slowdown in the decline of real social wage costs evident since the late 1960s, thus laying the foundation for a crisis of the system. Another element of the crisis, however, rests on the intensification of international competition consequent on the very spread of Fordism geographically.

The exacerbation of international competition and the spread of what Lipietz refers to as 'global Fordism' has not, of course, gone unremarked in the literature.[3] Nevertheless, there are several aspects to this question that merit elaboration.

It should be noted that Fordism as a regime of accumulation is, in principle, internal to a given national social formation. Aglietta, of course, was writing about the United States, which was the first country fully to implement Fordism as a production system. By virtue of its enormous lead in productivity, the US remained relatively immune for several decades to foreign competition despite extremely high wage rates (by world standards).

However, as Aglietta notes in a later article, 'each epoch-defining mode of capitalist regulation involves the emergence of a hegemonic centre, followed by an uneven spread of that mode's principles which undermines the original hegemony'.[4] In other words, the international spread of the production system poses serious problems of competitiveness to the very area in which it has been most fully elaborated. The high wages (and high levels of state expenditure) that are needed to sustain and stabilize the mass consumption base underlie this vulnerability and bear the brunt of the inevitable restructuring. This eventuality was already foreseen by Gramsci, who observed:

> In reality, American high wage industry is still exploiting a monopoly granted to it by the fact that it has the initiative with the new methods. Monopoly wages correspond to monopoly profits. But the monopoly will necessarily be first limited and then destroyed by the further diffusion of the new methods both within the United States and abroad (compare the

Japanese phenomenon of low-priced goods), and high wages will disappear along with enormous profits.[5]

In this view, then, the Fordist regime of accumulation can be maintained relatively intact so long as it is confined to one (or a few) core countries. The inevitable diffusion of the production techniques associated with Fordism, however, spells the end of this protected dominance and the system is thrown into disarray.

Lipietz approaches the issue from a somewhat different angle. He emphasizes the technical and social failure of Fordism in the core (manifested in declining productivity and profit rates) as a crucial element underlying the spread of Fordist production methods to the periphery, chiefly via direct investment by multinational firms in search of low-cost labour. Global Fordism, in this light, is a strategy to ward off the impending crisis, although by its very nature it ends up exacerbating it in precisely the way that Aglietta and Gramsci suggest. Thus, in the peripheral countries, the combination of Fordist techniques and the extraordinarily low level of wages and worker organization allows the extraction of both absolute and relative surplus value to proceed apace. However, if the problem of the extraction of surplus value is thereby ameliorated, the integrity of the system is still not assured. For the process of realizing the surplus value produced entails intensified international competition in the formerly insulated domestic markets of the US and other core countries.

Without necessarily disputing these analyses, I believe that two additional factors – concerning the timing and the form of internationalization – need to be considered. In the first instance, it can be argued that Fordism was an international system virtually from the beginning in the sense that foreign markets and foreign outlets for surplus capital were always necessary even after the system was more or less consolidated in the US. Significantly, the huge postwar growth of US manufacturing investment overseas was directed primarily to other advanced industrial nations and to this day nearly three-fourths of the total foreign manufacturing investment remains in these areas. This is particularly significant to the extent that direct investments expand foreign market shares beyond the level that could be achieved by exports alone.

In short, it appears that even the vast and insulated domestic market could never by itself suffice to absorb the output that the system was capable of producing. Looked at in another way, the domestic economy could not absorb the surplus that was being accumulated at such an extraordinary rate. Part of this capital, then, was channelled into investments abroad. Thus, although it is true that the US economy is very little dependent on *exports*, it does not follow from this that the development of Fordism in the US was essentially self-contained or autonomous.

This does not diminish the importance of the role played by domestic consumption in the major loci of Fordism in North America and Europe if taken as a whole. If the US was first, it was soon followed and in some respects surpassed by changes in these other areas of the core. Productivity-linked wage rises, the expansion of state collective consumption and welfare expenditures and the regulation of labour markets all contributed to the necessary extension of consumption to absorb the output of the production system and to generate outlets for the continual reinvestment of the surplus produced. In this sense, one may be justified in speaking of the *internalization* of the regime of accumulation as the system was maintained largely on the strength of the powers of consumption and the scope for investment in the core countries themselves.

Under these circumstances, the eventual advent of Fordism as a production system in Europe did not throw the system as a whole into crisis because it was rapidly articulated with the expansion and deepening of the mass consumption base. Indeed, given the magnitude and the pattern of postwar international investment, it seems likely that the stability of the system depended precisely on the rapid geographical expansion (beyond the borders of the US) of what constituted the Fordist core.

Crucially, this has not been the case for the subsequent extension of Fordist production techniques to other areas of the globe, at least to the same degree. To a considerable extent, the newly industrializing countries and even Japan (although less so now than in previous decades) have developed a highly *externalized* Fordist system in the sense that Fordist production techniques have been adopted while the expansion of domestic mass consumption has lagged far behind. This has allowed these countries to keep wage costs extremely low while relying on foreign markets to absorb a large share of their output. It is this change in the way that Fordism has spread geographically that helps to explain the timing of the crisis.

In brief, geographical expansion played an important role in sustaining the accumulation process under Fordism by, in effect, staving off a general crisis of overaccumulation. Although there is little reason to suppose that this could have continued indefinitely, the way in which Fordism expanded beyond the North Atlantic core almost certainly influenced the timing of the present crisis and shaped its character. In the struggle over who will bear the brunt of this crisis, firms in the traditional core countries have proved to be particularly vulnerable, the more so as they have been prevented from altering the foundations of competition by the rigidities built into the Fordist system. . . .

The key distinction between flexible technologies and traditional mass production techniques is that what the machine actually *does* is programmed in via computer software rather than built into the machinery at the outset. This means that a given machine can be used in the manufacture of a range of product types and configurations; hence its flexibility in contrast to fixed-purpose dedicated machinery. Significantly, the existence of machines that can perform several functions, or variations of a given function according to product configuration, allows shorter runs and a mix of product types on the line without sacrificing economies of scale. Economies of scope can be exploited across a range of product types, while aggregate production volumes can remain quite high in principle.

Although the use of these technologies in production is arguably still in its infancy, in theory they offer the promise of substantial cost savings. Quite possibly, they will prove to be capital-saving in the long run as they can be reprogrammed (rather than replaced) to cope with product changes. Moreover, for a given amount of output, the demand for labour and, significantly, physical plant space is likely to be much reduced. In this they go some way to resolving one of the Fordist competitive dilemmas – intensified price competition.

Nevertheless, it should not be thought that the implementation of this technological shift is unproblematic for the firm. First, the equipment itself is still quite imperfect. Beyond the ordinary 'bugs' that need to be worked out in practice, serious technological problems remain to be resolved (for example, in the areas of machine sensing, manipulating large weights within close tolerances, etc.). By the same token, combining individual pieces of flexible equipment into flexible *systems* is proving more difficult than anticipated. Second, the capital outlays required in the transition are quite large and pose a severe burden to firms coming off an extended period of poor profits and growing debt.

A third obstacle to a smooth transition is the need for extensive redesign of products that will adapt them to the requirements of the new automation techniques. This means, in particular, the simplification and standardization of components and intermediate goods.

Last, the flexibility of the technology also appears to benefit from a much greater flexibility in the use of labour in production. This arises from several factors. In the first instance, the fact that much or all of what the machine does is controlled by the program means that the worker has less to do in relation to any single piece of equipment. If what the worker does is better described as supervising rather than operating the machine, with direct intervention largely limited to instances of malfunction, then the desirability of assigning him or her to several machines in order to reduce the total amount of production labour in use is clear. Moreover, where flexible *systems* of interrelated machines are achievable, the need to group them together (connected by automated transfer processes) increases the ability of an individual worker to monitor several machines. However, this type of flexibility runs directly counter to the traditions of industrial unionism (in the US, at least) where rigid task demarcations have been viewed as a means of enhancing the security of workers. This factor underlies increasingly intense corporate interest in renegotiating work rules to allow for flexible job assignments – a process that has met with some success.

There remain, however, great risks and uncertainties in the sphere of capital–labour relations. It is undeniable that labour has been severely chastened by the experience of the last ten to fifteen years of rationalization, plant closings and layoffs. This helps to account for the evident willingness (however reluctant) of unions to participate in the restructuring of work relationships. However, in some respects, an interlinked flexible system of machines is more fragile than a situation where individual free-standing machines are producing for stock. Any failure within the linked group of machines renders the whole group idle. In this sense, the supervisory function of the worker is strategically important, even if it does not entail any effective re-skilling. This suggests that firms will need to cultivate the co-operation and active participation of those workers who remain on the production line. Needless to say, this effective empowerment of the worker, however limited, is in sharp contrast to Fordist and Taylorist practices and may undermine to some degree the principle of tight managerial control over the labour process.

Given the costs and problems of adjustment involved, it must be anticipated that the uptake of the new technologies will be quite gradual and uneven. Moreover, whatever these flexible technologies may offer in theory, there is no guarantee that they will be used in a particular way in practice simply by virtue of their inherent qualities. The hardware itself can be used in quite traditional Fordist ways without a costly and in many respects risky reorganization of production, encompassing the technical, social and spatial divisions of labour. This would still help to resolve the problem of meeting increased price competition as suggested above. Crucially, however, it would leave the firm less well equipped to deal with the second competitive dilemma centring on the need to respond flexibly to an increasingly fragmented and rapidly changing market.

The advent of flexible technologies, then, is particularly relevant to resolving the difficulty, characteristic of Fordism, of quickly altering product configuration or product mix. If the latter can be changed through reprogramming rather than re-equipping, then the ability of the firm to react to changes in market demand and the behaviour of increasingly numerous competitors is greatly enhanced. At the extreme, this can be one of the selling-points of the product – that it can be tailored to some extent to the needs of the individual consumer.

More precisely, the reorientation of competitive strategies in an era of flexible accumulation is likely to hinge on greater specialization and differentiation of products with a heightened rate of change in product design and product mix. The reorganization of production, in its various dimensions, must be made consistent with the implementation of flexible competitive strategies. In other words, if one accepts that the adoption of a new technological system in production is carried out at least in part to serve the needs of a new competitive orientation, then one needs to ask how this competitive strategy will influence the way these technologies are used in practice.

The essence of flexible competition is flexible and rapid response to changes in the market, whether these result from the behaviour of competitors or from demand shifts. This means that at any given time there must be greater flexibility in the mix and configuration of the products that are actually manufactured than was true under Fordism. It also means that product lines and configurations must be able to evolve rather rapidly.

One result is that the operational connections among various functions of the firm – including marketing, product design, product engineering, prototype development and testing, manufacturing engineering and manufacturing itself – stand to be significantly tightened with a far greater degree of simultaneity and feedback among these various tasks. In this scenario, time takes on tremendous importance.

First, the firm has to reduce dramatically the product-development cycle time from initial design to scaled-up production, a process which, under Fordism, could stretch over months or even years. Again, this underscores the rather paradoxical importance of standardizing components and, perhaps even more significantly, standardizing the design process itself in order to alter rapidly and smoothly the configuration of final output. This process could conceivably engender renewed labour–management tensions as heretofore privileged white-collar workers (designers, engineers, programmers, etc.) find themselves subject to increasing time pressures while the craft content of their work is eroded.

Second, turnaround time through the whole sales and manufacturing cycle must be significantly tightened. Manufacturing must be able to adjust quickly to changes in final output demand, even for consumer products. In addition, for products that enter into the production processes of other 'flexible' firms, the premium placed on rapid turnaround from order to delivery is very high. . . .

At present, 'flexibility' is rapidly becoming a kind of buzzword with all sorts of unspoken suggestions of renewed competitive 'spirit', leanness and suppleness. This optimism has even extended to the analysis of working conditions in flexible production systems with what amounts very nearly to a vision of the resurgence of the autonomous craftsperson freed from the deadening specificity of traditional Fordist assembly-line work.

55   Ruth Pearson

Female Workers in the Third World

Nimble-fingered young women working in serried ranks in a south-east Asian electronics factory is by now a widespread image. More than that, it is *the* image of women industrial workers in the third world. Virtually all of the analysis of women's work in the industrial sector in the third world is based on the experience of export platform factories. From a number of often first-hand research and other reports about women working in a variety of sectors, regions and countries in the third world an ideal and universal picture has emerged which has tended to coalesce the third world into a single undifferentiated country where women factory workers are young, industrious, naïve and passive. And it seems likely that the same kind of generalizations are being translated to the analysis of women working in the new-technology industries of the industrialized world.

This simplistic analysis captures some aspects of the emergence of a specific demand for female labour for assembly operations in factories mainly owned by foreign capital and producing for the world market as part of what has been termed the new international division of labour. However, this framework of analysis, which refers to the trend during the 1960s and 1970s for foreign companies to relocate production to low-wage countries, belies the complexity of the wider process of capitalist restructuring at a global level. The analysis assumes the existence of an ubiquitous pool of 'suitable' female labour – a kind of global reserve army activated directly, and without contradictions, by international capital seeking low-paid workers with high productivity.

Partly responsible for this undifferentiated image of third world women workers is the way in which the analysis of the new international division of labour has ignored the complexities and contradictions of producing the desired social relations of production involved in creating a new sector of waged labour. The analysis focuses primarily on the international mobility of capital which facilitates rational location decisions on the basis of comparative costs. Labour is cheap in Mexico but cheaper still in Sri Lanka and even cheaper in Malawi. Which location was chosen depended, of course, on a number of other considerations, including the scope of incentives provided by third world governments eager to attact foreign investment in the industrial sector, for such investment offers foreign exchange earnings and industrial employment opportunities and at least the promise of escape from the third world's traditional place in the international division of labour. Indeed, the competition to attract international investment of this kind is so intense that many third world countries have established special locations – free trade zones (FTZs) or export processing zones (EPZs) – which provide international capital with relevant industrial infrastructure and services and effectively cede large areas of sovereignty over foreign companies operating within these areas in terms of trade and employment regulations. By 1984 there were some eighty such zones with another forty planned or in the process of establishment.

It is clear, therefore, that location decisions are not just a matter of seeking the lowest-cost environment; in addition the state, in the guise of the host government, has to intervene to deliver such environments to international capital in a variety of ways. They have to guarantee political and economic security, which could be provided by a strong military regime or could be delivered by enacting legislation about the control or absence of labour unions, as well as provide the industrial inputs necessary to make the environment feasible for an internationally controlled and organized operation. This means providing telecommunications, air freight services, power and water supplies and basic infrastructural and internal transportation investments. The governments representing the multinational companies' home state have also been required to intervene to provide a feasible environment for this mode of international accumulation. The United States, for example, made special provision in its tariff schedule to allow US components assembled abroad to be allowed back into the United States free of import tax on the value of those components.

What has not been addressed is the availability or construction of cheap labour. It has not been acknowledged that either capital or the state might need to intervene to deliver the suitable labour required; it has been assumed that this was axiomatic on the existence of high levels of unemployment or underemployment in the third world locations. Given that it has been female labour which was targeted to provide labour power for third world export factories it was assumed that the absence of industrial employment for women in the immediate economic history of the country meant that there would be no problem in making this labour available in the quantities and qualities required.

The analysis of women's employment by multinationals involved in manufacturing for export in the third world has established that women constitute an overwhelming proportion of the 'operator' (i.e. unskilled and manual worker) level of employment and that such employment constitutes up to 90 per cent of total employment generated by such investments. It is also clear that women are employed in both traditional and 'new-technology' industries in spite of the unequivocal existence of unemployed male labour in the third world. The reason why women's labour is the preferred 'cheap' labour in a situation of surplus labour of both sexes is complex. First, women's wages are generally lower than those paid to male workers in comparable occupations, though this is not always the case. But also it has been demonstrated that women's productivity under the production conditions determined by specific production processes is higher than men working under the same conditions.[1]

From this analysis of how and why women are the preferred labour force, a stereotypical picture of the average or ideal third world woman factory worker has emerged, comprising four essential components:

1   that she is young – recruited from an age cohort ranging from 15 to 25, concentrated in the 18–21 age group;
2   that she is single and childless;
3   that she is 'unskilled' in the sense of having no recognized qualifications or training;
4   that she has no previous experience of formal wage employment in the industrial sector – 'virgins in terms of industrial employment that need not be retrained or untrained', to quote one not untypical researcher writing about women's employment in the Mexican border industries.[2]

In fact, when we come to examine in detail different case studies of women factory workers in different areas and regions of the third world it becomes clear that there exists considerable variation in the characteristics of the workers recruited. For what the management of multinational companies consciously, if not explicitly, operated was indeed a strategy of providing for themselves a labour force which would incur minimum costs in terms of wages, fringe benefits, management control, discipline and militancy. And these are not necessarily supplied by recruiting a single age cohort from the vicinity of these factories and setting them to work in a standard context.

The most deeply held aspect of the stereotype of women workers in third world factories is that they are young women; the age range varies in different accounts, but it is generally within the range 15–25, bunching in the 18–21 age group. However, research has indicated that there is in fact a considerable variation in the age range. In some countries women as young as 12 are employed; in other countries (e.g. Barbados) the labour force in the electronics factories are considerably older, starting in the late twenties and going throughout the thirties age group.

This last example is interesting because it relates to another aspect of the stereotype, that women factory workers in the third world are *single*. It is clear why this should form part of the employers' construction of their ideal labour force: single women, with few alternative industrial job opportunities, can deliver the highest level of compliance and loyalty to the firm. They are deemed not to have domestic and economic responsibilities to their own conjugal households and children – a kind of international teenager ready to exchange their hours of industrial activity for the monetary rewards and concomitant independence this brings. However, what single really means in the context of this analysis is *childless*, and in different social contexts the two characteristics do not necessarily go together.

In Barbados, where the age of first childbirth is earlier and age at marriage later, and the provision of maternity leave and payments more historically integrated into the island's labour practice, older women are recruited who have passed through their intensive phase of childbearing.

In locations where there is a large supply of women applicants for jobs in export processing factories, the criterion of childlessness can be used as part of a complex recruitment mechanism for selecting 'ideal' applicants. In Mexico, where there is an excessive supply of female labour and a range of export factories in different sectors, and where for social, economic and cultural reasons there is a high rate of illegitimate births, electronics factories include pregnancy tests as well as declarations of childlessness as a routine measure. In Malaysia, where recruitment takes place within a less homogeneous and different social and cultural context, different strategies have been adopted. Among the social classes from whom electronics workers are recruited, there is a strong prejudice against married women working in factories, and a much more cohesive family structure, so recruitment of single high-school graduates will provide motivated childless women. But where the prejudice against factory work extends to daughters because of its implications in undermining forms of control of fathers and brothers over young women, capital may have to alter its strategy in order to 'release' the required labour power. One multinational company operating in Malaysia pursues a policy of reinforcing traditional forms of patriarchal power. Instead of undermining the father's authority over the daughter by encouraging modern, Western independent behaviour, it pursues a policy of reinforcement: 'The company has installed prayer rooms in the factory itself, does not have modern uniforms and lets the girls wear their traditional attire, and enforces a strict and rigid discipline in the workplace.'[3] In another case the firm has allowed traditional leaders on to the production line to talk to the women and check the modesty of the company uniform. Young women recruited from rural areas may be provided with supervised hostel accommodation and in some cases the wage is paid to the male kin rather than directly to the women workers.

What these variations in the composition of the labour force and in the employment conditions demonstrate is that women's potential labour power, as a commodity available for exploitation by capital, has to be negotiated for with forms of patriarchal control and with her childbearing and reproductive role; and at the same time these can be used to control the composition and characteristics of those employed. In addition, it must be recognized that different production processes and industrial branches require different kinds of labour power which may be supplied by different subsectors of the female labour force. For example, Fernandez-Kelly has documented wide variations [between] the characteristics [of] women recruited into the electronics and garments sectors on the Mexican border – demonstrating that workers in the garments plants are less educated, older (median age 26 years compared to 20 years in electronics plants), more likely to have held waged employment before (70 per cent compared to 40

per cent) and have a greater number of children.[4] This is related to the 'enfee-
bled position of "older" women in the labour market and the inability of the
garment sector to attract workers who are seen to be ideal (i.e. young single
childless women) because of the higher instability and temporality of employment as well as the extremely inadequate working conditions.'[5] In addition to this
it can be argued that workers employed making garments whose design, size,
material, etc. change frequently are required to bring a specific kind of experience and skill to the job, suggesting that older women with previous experience
are a preferable workforce in this sector.

> The reduction of workers to the notion of 'cheap labour' may fail to
> identify variations which have theoretical and practical significance. Varia-
> tions derive from the different competitive and technological conditions
> of different manufacturing branches which will determine the nature of
> labour recruitment strategies and the form that control over workers takes
> in each industry.[6]

Moreover, the firms do not face an undifferentiated supply of homogeneous
cheap female labour and can utilize differences within the potential female
labour force to structure their recruitment strategy according to their own
perceived requirements....

A further aspect of working conditions refers to one of the characteristics
of the multinational company's target female labour force frequently cited by
commentators, that of docility. Many commentators, often quoting management
and industrial promotion agencies in the third world, have pointed to the
docility of women operators in the face of boring, tedious and repetitive work.
The explanations for why women should be so accepting of these conditions
varies from the fact that women are naturally submissive [and] that domestic
work suffers from the same disadvantages, to cultural factors concerning the
pattern of behaviour of women in a given society. The rigid sexual hierarchy of
production in the factories contributes to the promotion of such a response from
the women workers as all authority and responsibility is firmly in the hands of
male technical, managerial and supervisory personnel. So too are the elaborate
management strategies aimed at emphasizing the 'femininity' and accepted feminine characteristics of women workers. Management sensibly does not rely
entirely on nature to ensure an unresistant labour force, though it does take
advantage of the various historical reasons why women are less likely to respond
to unionization, where legally permitted.

One final point about the variations in conditions of employment in the third
world must be made. Much of the literature assumes a single type of production
situation and relations of production; that is, of young women recruited from
the school-leaver cohorts with no industrial experience, working in manufacturing plants organized along conventional factory lines. In reality, as we have
seen, there is a range of production relations which vary according to the
historically determined situation of women in any given situation. While the
majority of third world women industrial workers are employed as 'free' wage
labour, this is not always the case. In Turkey, women weaving carpets for export
in village-based workshops do not receive any payment from the subcontractor,
who instead pays according to a piece-rate scale to the male head of the
household. In Haiti women employed in American-owned firms making toys
and soft goods frequently take work off the plant to their homes to complete; in
Puerto Rico a large proportion of the production of garments for the export
market takes place in illegal 'underground' domestic workshops whose output is
then marketed by the multinational retail groups in the United States.

What this analysis demonstrates is that the female labour recruited for third world market factories is not available in a prepackaged form. While it is clear that women workers offer capital labour power which can be low-paid and highly productive, both the state and capital need to intervene to release this labour power in the particular form required by concrete production conditions. Nor can it be assumed that this labour is available in unlimited quantities from a given age cohort anywhere in the world; the characteristics of the female labour force – in terms of age, education, marital status, class and ethnic origin – and how their work process is organized will depend as much on the historically determined availability of female labour and the interaction of gender and class systems as on the demand for cheap labour from foreign capital.

56 David Lyon

Information Technology and the 'Information Society'

The 'information society' expresses the idea of a novel phase in the historical development of the advanced societies. Not just a 'postindustrial' society, but the advent of new social patterns is predicted, consequent upon a 'second industrial revolution' based above all on microelectronic technologies. A growing proportion of people, it is claimed, is involved in an unprecedented variety of information-related jobs. Scientific and technical workers gather and produce information, managers and supervisors process it, teachers and communications workers distribute it. From domestic life to international relations, and from leisure activities to industrial relations, no sphere of social activity is left untouched by this 'informatizing' process.

Notions such as Alvin Toffler's 'third wave' – virtually synonymous with 'information society' – have entered popular imagination. A television film has been made of the *Third Wave*, and in the UK, the 'Third Wave' is the slogan for a British Telecom advertising campaign. The 'information society' is increasingly used as a handy catch-all for focusing discussions of 'the future' as we approach the third millennium. Government policy also draws upon this concept, particularly with regard to education. The British are assured, for instance, that 'Our educational system will be a major, perhaps the dominant factor in ensuring the economic prosperity of the UK in a world-wide information society.'[1]

However, certain questions are too frequently left unanswered or treated only to oblique or opaque responses. What are the connections between new technology and society? To what extent and under what circumstances does technological potential become social destiny? Is it warranted to see an epochal social transformation in the kinds of economic and social restructuring currently taking place? And whether or not we are witnessing the emergence of a 'new kind of society', are its advocates correct to assume, as they often tend to, that the social effects of information technology are generally benign? . . .

All manner of vested interests are involved in [information technology (IT)], but the concept of the information society is all too often used in ways that obscure their role. Sometimes those interests are intertwined in ways that have yet to be carefully explored. The coincidence that defence funding supports so much research in IT *and* that the world of IT frequently excludes women deserves just such exploration. Technology in general is undoubtedly associated with maleness, socially and culturally; IT no less so.

Secondly, the information society concept papers over not only the cracks but also opposing movements in society. Underlying contradictions are even less likely to be exposed than inequalities and conflicts on the surface. Opposing movements may be seen, for instance, in the IT context, along the fault-line of information as public good versus saleable commodity. The real threats of current IT development to public service broadcasting and to public libraries are manifestations of deeper dynamics of opposition.

Thirdly, the coming of the information society is viewed (by its popular proponents at least) as an entirely natural occurrence. It is the obvious way forward. The future lies with IT. The new technologies must be 'wholeheartedly embraced', declare the captains of industry. This is why educational systems have to be reoriented, the market unshackled and high-technology research and trading deals engineered. It is also why Luddism has to be stamped out.

This particular ideological aspect – information society as a natural and logical social advance – is further buttressed by the typically Western belief in progress via unlimited economic accumulation. What Shallis calls 'silicon idolatry' resonates with this still-strong belief. As Bob Goudzwaard observes, if indeed this faith is a driving force within economic and technological expansion then two things follow. One, the 'overdevelopment' of both spheres comes as no surprise, and two, it is 'accompanied by an expectation of happiness that relativises anything that might raise objections against them'.[2] . . .

Anyone worried about the encroaching tyranny of technocratic power embodied in IT should not ignore countervailing movements also present in contemporary societies. True, the information society idea is strong and popular, but there are many for whom it is remote and unreal, and yet others who regard it with suspicion and hostility. For them, the critique of ideology may itself appear as a less than central task; more urgent is actual resistance to the adoption of new technology. Examining forms of resistance – particularly the 'Luddism' scathingly referred to above – is one thing, however; joining the quest for alternatives is another. I shall argue that both strategies are required if the information society as depicted here is not to become a self-fulfilling prophecy.

The intrusion of IT into numerous areas of life – only this week I discovered that my plastic card could buy a train ticket at the local station and that my office is soon due to be connected with a central IBM computer – has revived interest in Luddism as a mode of opposing technology. While some use it as an epithet to be directed at all 'anti-progressives' who quite irrationally wish to 'put the clock back' by refusing to adapt to new technology, others – both conservative and radical – willingly accept the label as correctly portraying their stance. 'If Luddite means the preservation of all that is good from the past and the rejection of things that destroy good', says Michael Shallis, 'then I would welcome the term.' . . .

What form should be taken by 'alternative visions' to the 'information society' idea? At least two criteria should be satisfied. One, the normative basis of the alternative(s) must be made clear. Two, the different levels on which intervention might take place, and modes whereby policies may be implemented, must be indicated. This involves offering practical examples of altered practice and of the potential for choice in technological innovation.

Technocratic thought, especially that embodied in today's computer logic, tends to minimize or exclude debate about ethics. Discussion of 'alternatives' brings this into the foreground. Unfortunately, as Hans Jonas observes, an ethic suited to the global and long-term aspects of today's technology is largely lacking.[3] The ethics of the personal is far better developed. That said, once it is recognized that the 'information society' gives the false impression that we are entering an *entirely* novel social situation, then certain long-trodden ethical paths become pertinent.

A further problem here is the relative lack of contexts within which such moral debate may take place. Professions, for instance, have always provided such opportunities (even though they have sometimes been self-interestedly abused). Medicine, involving 'technologies of the body' has traditionally been hedged by moral qualification, dating back to the Hippocratic Oath. Today's computer professionals evidence a very low level of membership or interest in any comparable organizations.

It may be that IT raises new moral problems. The ease with which data can be permanently and untraceably erased may be one, the way in which privacy is invaded by computers, another. But among the most pressing issues is that of the status of information itself. This raises old questions about the proper relation between data, information, knowledge and a fourth category, which has a low profile today, wisdom. But IT gives their ethical consideration a new urgency, and also connects them with another cluster of problems to do with property: information as a commodity. 'Information' is produced for sale in the market-place. But what should rightly be defended as 'public information', as a 'resource'? What should be the limits to commodification?

The second criterion is that of realism about strategies. It is all very well for 'processed' (read 'alienated') San Francisco office-workers to parade the streets wearing cardboard visual display terminals over their heads, but such demonstrations do not exhaust the possibilities of strategic action relating to IT. The kind of realism required is that which connects possibilities for alternative action with actual conditions in a given social context. Despite the apparent cohesiveness of the 'information society' vision, it is unlikely that alternatives to it will be similarly homogeneous.

Although it may be possible theoretically to show how modern societies are increasingly divided between classes of people with and without control over and access to information, in real life their struggles are on numerous and often unconnected fronts. The labour process and industrial relations offer some obvious examples of appropriate strategies. New Technology Agreements, for whatever reason they are introduced, may be used to monitor and control the process of adapting to new technologies. Demonstrations of automation and robotics whose introduction does not de-skill or displace labour are vital here.

Other strategies run through a spectrum including formal political activity within existing parties, involvement in the political process by social movements, attempts to influence communications or educational policy and local grass-roots action. Legislative change, such as data protection, clearly requires activity of the former sort. But concern for IT alternatives may also be expressed in conjunction with other movements. In Britain, the 'Microsyster' organization attempts to redress the gender imbalance within IT, while 'Microelectronics for Peace' encourages the fostering of alternatives to military developments, mainly within the big IT transnationals. Similar organizations, such as the American 'Computer Professionals for Social Responsibility' exist elsewhere.

Part 14

The Globalizing of Social Life

Globalization has already been referred to at various earlier stages in the book. It represents one of the most important processes now transforming social life, both in the industrialized societies and in other parts of the world. As mentioned in the introduction, modern civilization has been expansionist since its early origins; the 'first world' has developed in close conjunction with the transformation of non-Western cultures and regions in a 'less developed' 'third world'. Peter Worsley's contribution (reading 57) charts some of the relatively early contacts which Westerners made with previously 'unexplored' areas elsewhere. As he says, in a striking phrase, 'until our time, human society has never existed': in other words, living in the twentieth century, we are the first generation of human beings who are in some sense in contact with all parts of a known world. In previous ages, no one had any knowledge of the world as a whole, and only a few more literate groups possessed an awareness of regions away from their own community or society.

Reading 58, by Ankie Hoogvelt, continues a theme introduced in part 13: the internationalizing of economic life in the current period. Virtually all third world countries are now to a greater or lesser degree dependent for whatever prosperity they can achieve upon producing for world markets. In some such nations, considerable success with indigenous industrialization has been achieved, while others are almost wholly dependent upon imports for manufactured goods and services they cannot produce for themselves. Hoogvelt echoes the observation made in the introduction that the notion of the 'third world' has become an increasingly difficult one to apply. In the 'newly industrializing' countries, such as Taiwan, South Korea or Singapore, industrialization has reached levels more or less compatible with the 'first world' nations.

Yet those third world countries which have very low levels of industrialization remain extremely poor and in many of them large proportions of the population are undernourished or even starving. According to Jon Bennett (reading 59) there is no need for anyone in the world to go hungry, since more food is actually produced globally than would be required to feed existing populations adequately. In his discussion he contests a number of myths that have developed around the question of global food production and distribution. The problems which prevent the securing of an adequate food supply for the world's population, in his view, are either political or are the result of the selfish pursuit of narrow economic interests on the part of the richer nations.

In reading 60, Thomas L. McPhail considers the possibility that, now colonialism in its traditional sense has disappeared, a new form of 'electronic colonialism' has taken its place. Most forms of mass media and electronic communication are controlled by government agencies or corporations located within the developed countries. Electronic colonialism, he suggests, may be in some ways more insidious than economic colonialism of the pre-existing sort. Media products tend not just to alter economic conditions of life but to influence attitudes, desires and styles of life.

57   Peter Worsley

The Creation of the World

Until our day, human society has never existed. Societies, yes; cultures and empires which extended over large areas and influenced millions of people. Nor could it be otherwise before the growth of civilization. We could expect no worldwide human community in a Palaeolithic Europe only inhabited by a few thousand men. 'In modern terms,' the archaeologist tells us, 'the total output of energy in savage Europe at any one time probably never exceeded that of a single four-engined bomber.'[1]

But even when the great civilizations developed, they set their boundaries somewhere. Whatever their claims to universal dominion – and the Chinese empire had no foreign affairs department, since it *was* civilization, and all else barbarism – they recognized the existence of life beyond the *limes*, but only barbarian life. The line where civilization ended was patrolled by armed men, guarded by Roman and Chinese walls. As to what lay beyond, they were not too interested.

This mutual ignorance was tragi-comic. It could be fatal. Surajah Dowlah, Nawob of Bengal, whom Clive defeated at Plassey, believed that there were only 10,000 people in all Europe. The Chinese too, thought that Europe was short of population.

In 1793, Ch'ien Lung, Emperor of China, addressed a barbarian potentate, George III of England, in response to the mission of Earl Macartney, sent by George to Peking:

> You, O King, live beyond the confines of many seas, nevertheless, impelled by your humble desire to partake of the benefits of our civilization, you have dispatched a mission respectfully bearing your memorial. . . . To show your devotion, you have also sent offerings of your country's produce.
>
> I have perused your memorial: the earnest terms in which it is couched reveal a respectful humility on your part, which is highly praiseworthy. . . .
>
> As to your entreaty to send one of your nationals to be accredited to my Celestial Court and to be in control of your country's trade with China, this request is contrary to all usage of my dynasty and cannot possibly be entertained. . . . It may be suggested that he might imitate the Europeans permanently resident in Peking and adopt the dress and customs of China, but it has never been our dynasty's wish to force people to do things unseemly and inconvenient. . . .
>
> Swaying the wide world, I have but one aim in view, namely to maintain a perfect governance and to fulfil the duties of the State. . . . As your Ambassador can see for himself, we possess all things. I set no value on objects strange and ingenious, and have no use for your country's manufactures. . . .
>
> You, O King, from afar have yearned after the blessings of our civilization. . . . I have already taken note of your respectful spirit of submission. . . .
>
> [Regarding trade] . . . Our Celestial Empire possesses all things in prolific abundance and lacks no product within its borders. There is therefore no need to import the manufactures of outside barbarians in exchange for our own produce. But as the tea, silk, and porcelain which the Celestial

Empire produces, are absolute necessities to European nations and to yourselves, we have permitted, as a signal mark of favour, that foreign *hongs* should be established at Canton, so that your wants might be supplied, and your country thus participate in our benificence.

Regarding your nation's worship of the Lord of Heaven [Christianity] ... Ever since the beginning of history, sage Emperors and wise rulers have bestowed on China a moral system and inculcated a code, which from time immemorial has been religiously observed by the myriads of my subjects. There has been no hankering after heterodox doctrines.... The distinction between Chinese and barbarians is most strict, and your Ambassador's request that barbarians shall be given full liberty to disseminate their religion is utterly unreasonable.

It may be, O King, that the above proposals have been wantonly made by your Ambassador on his own responsibility, or peradventure you yourself are ignorant of our dynastic regulations and had no intention of transgressing them when you expressed these wild ideas and hopes....

Do you, O King, display even more energetic loyalty in future and endeavour to deserve for ever Our gracious affection....'[2]

Despite the high tone and universalistic pretensions of the Chinese emperor, his society was ill-equipped to withstand the incursions of commercial Europe. But for a society that believed that 'as there is one sun in the heavens, so there can be but one great supreme power on earth', it was hard to realize that the sordid opium-dealing foreign devils represented a far greater power than China. Even as late as the Opium War:

> ... the belief that foreigners, and particularly the English, would die of constipation if deprived of rhubarb was widely held ... in China. It had its origin, I think, in the practice, so widely spread in early nineteenth-century Europe, of a great purge every spring, rhubarb-root being often an ingredient in the purgatives used. The seasonal purge was thought to be particularly necessary in the case of children, who without it would be sure to develop worms. However ... later, [the Chinese official responsible for eliminating the opium trade] modified his views about rhubarb, and said that only tea could be considered an absolute necessity.[3]

The gulf between cultures was too great to be easily bridged, too great at times even for mutual comprehension.... When [the Europeans] encountered these civilizations, they asked ...: How could such magnificent civilizations have remained unknown to us? In the thirteenth century, when Marco Polo arrived at the city of Hang-chow, then in decline, he found that it was '... an hundred miles in circuit ... [with] ... ten principal squares or market-places, besides innumerable shops along the streets. Each side of these squares is half a mile in length.... The streets are all paved with stones and bricks.... The whole city must have contained one million six hundred thousand families.'[4] At this time, life in Europe was insecure, communications primitive, and civilization at a low ebb. Even three centuries later, when European civilization had advanced considerably, non-Europe could still astound the European conquerors of Mexico:

> When we saw so many cities and villages built both in the water and on dry land, and this straight, level causeway, we couldn't restrain our admiration. It was like the enchantments told about in the books of Amadis, because of the high towers, *cués* [temples], and other buildings, all of masonry, which rose from the water. Some of our soldiers asked if what we saw was not a dream....

Then when we entered Iztapalapa, the appearance of the palaces in which they quartered us! They were vast, and well made of cut stone, cedar, and other fragrant woods, with spacious rooms and patios that were wonderful to see, shaded with cotton awnings.

After we had seen all this, we went to the orchard and garden, and walked about. I never tired of looking at the variety of trees and noting the scent each of them had. The walks were lined with flowers, rosebushes of the country, and fruit trees. . . .

Today, all that was there then is in the ground, lost, with nothing left at all. . . .[5]

A generation after the conquest there was 'nothing left at all': so thoroughly were the high civilizations destroyed or eroded away that they often became completely forgotten, disbelieved in by whites. Yet the descendants of the conquered remembered. . . .

When Cortes and his companions burned their vessels on the shores of Mexico, the high drama of their action was consistent with the engorged imaginations of men who were not only out for loot, but who also saw themselves as crusading champions of Christianity and as heroes of medieval epic and romance, encountering 'the enchantments told about in the books of Amadis'. A Spain which had been reconquered from the infidel, and which was shortly to be rendered totally uninhabitable for knights by Cervantes, could no longer satisfy the imagination of potential conquistadors. These questing spirits therefore turned abroad, looking for new worlds to conquer. They lusted after the gold of El Dorado, to be sure, but also after the eternal life at the Fountain of Youth. The reality they found – the high civilizations of Mexico and Peru – only confirmed the realism of their wild dreams. But chivalry – and Christian charity – quickly withered as a few hundred men, like ruthless machines, fought for an empire of gold and slaves against hundreds of thousands.

It was Bernal Díaz, the rough foot-soldier whom we saw standing open-mouthed in the Mexican capital of Tenochtitlan (where modern Mexico City stands), Díaz and his comrades, who made Europe's first decisive irruption into the world. They established a fateful relationship of superiority and inferiority which was to sustain the white man in his drive to ultimate world-conquest, and was to lead to the creation of the world as a single social system. However impressed the Spaniards might be at the botanical and zoological gardens of Tenochtitlan, Aztec society did crumble before them. Their sense of superiority is therefore understandable. In Peru, Pizarro, again, conquered an empire of sixteen million people with only 300 men and fifty horses. Despite their great size and their advanced organization, however remarkable their elaborate cultures, the empires of the New World could not withstand the Spanish attack. In Mexico, Cortes had the assistance of hundreds of thousands of Tlaxcalan allies: he was able to exploit internal rivalries also. And he was profoundly aided by the religious belief that the Spaniards were returning gods, a myth which particularly affected the irresolute Emperor Moctezuma. But neither of these factors account for Pizarro's triumph in Peru – except in so far as the Supreme Inca, Atahualpa, had barely assumed the reins of power, following a civil war. Pizarro did, of course, have the example of Cortes to inspire and guide him, too.

Clearly, superior equipment was crucial in the Spanish victory: these hairy white monsters, covered in metal, and mounted on their huge 'deer', struck terror into the hearts of peasant foot-soldiers, bravely though they fought the horsemen and their fears. Bernal Díaz, being a practical fighting man, gives full recognition to the importance of the instruments of war in the Spanish victories:

the horse, armour, crossbows, cannons, dogs, and 'engines' of war. But it was not their iron weapons, nor their iron exteriors, that gave the gold of the New World to men like Cortes and Pizarro. It was also their organization, their discipline, their confidence, and the force of their motivating drives, that gave them crucial advantages. The 'ethic' of the Conquistador was crucial; it helped foster an iron spirit to match their iron fighting equipment: ruthlessness and determination carried the day.

Once Cortes had burned his boats; once Pizarro's men had crossed the line he drew in the Peruvian earth, there was no turning back. Death or victory was the simple choice, and in such circumstances men give no quarter. The Spaniards also had divine support. Cortes' men had been sickened at sacrifices of human beings performed in their honour: the mass sacrifices of the Aztecs horrified them. But at Cholula in Mexico, and at Caxamarca in Peru, the Spaniards themselves did not hesitate to use premeditated, treacherous, large-scale massacre of unsuspecting crowds as a terroristic instrument of policy – and the Church blessed their actions.

Over two centuries later, the superiority of the white man's military discipline and organization was to be demonstrated again, at Plassey, when the fall of another great empire gave Britain the key to a subcontinent. Clive's victory over Surajah Dowlah at Plassey was not due to overwhelming technological superiority – for the Nawob's armies were as well equipped as his – but primarily to British discipline, training and drill.

Clive's victory at Plassey, unlike the Spanish conquest of America, was the victory of a country which was developing into the major capitalist industrial power. Because of this, the impact of the British conquest of India, however destructive of the indigenous economy, and however exploitative, nevertheless ultimately set Indian society on the path to modernization.

A repressive and authoritarian Spain, politically and culturally dominated by the backward provinces of Old Castile and Aragon, had been unable to utilize the gold of the Indies for the 'take-off' to modern capitalist industrialization. The wealth of the New World, instead, was used to bolster up an archaic society. Militarism and xenophobia petrified the social order; an inquisitorial Christianity sanctified it, at home and abroad. Christianity abroad, it is true, produced such noble defenders of the Indian as the great Dominican, Bartolomé de Las Casas. But the Saint of the Indies lost. A Portuguese bishop was to sit on his stone seat at Loanda in West Africa 'blessing the slaves as they entered the holds of the slavers, "and through his apostolic blessing guaranteeing them the inexpressible bliss of a future life with which the short period of earthly tribulation could not be compared"'.[6]

The tradition established on Española (the island divided today between Haiti and the Dominican Republic) – where the Indian population was reduced from some two or three hundred thousand in 1492 to two villages by 1570 – proved irresistible. Violence and terror became an entrenched disposition. War became an art, and colonial war could even inspire art:

> ...all the Kings, who Géntoo [Hindu] gods adore,
> and dare our yoke reject shall rue the wrath
> of hard and hardy Arms, with steel and lowe,
> till low to Gama or to Death they bow....
>
> Lo! he returns and bursts what dares oppose,
> thro' bullet, lance-plump, steel, fire, strongest hold;
> breaks with his brand the squadded host of foes,
> the serried Moor, the Géntoo manifold....[7]

Other European countries, more favourably placed, and notably England, were able to benefit from Spanish and Portuguese pioneering experience, and from their own expanding adventures in 'primitive accumulation'. They refrained no less from stark exploitation: after Plassey, Clive alone picked up £2,300,000 plus an annual income of £270,000 per year.

But unlike Spain, this wealth was not used to perpetuate 'booty capitalism' or traditional mercantilism, or merely to construct a bureaucratic colonial plantation system. It was used to establish a new international division of labour, converting the conquered lands into a resource for a dynamic and expanding industrial capitalism. Out of the prosperity of the 'triangular trade' of the Great Circuit: slaves from Africa to America; minerals and foodstuffs from America to Europe; cheap manufactured goods from Europe and America to Africa: came the prosperity of Liverpool, Manchester, Bristol, and a significant contribution to the mounting of Britain's industrial revolution. Thereafter Europe's edge over the rest of the world became marked. The terms of trade became reversed, as the high civilizations of the East went under one by one, their industry destroyed to make way for the products of Manchester, Lyons, Amsterdam and Brussels, their natural resources transported to feed the factories of Europe.

Objectively, of course, the world had always been one, long before worldwide social relations were established, long before the Spaniards seized America or the British India. Even the most primitive hunters and collectors had never been entirely isolated. Culture was passed along from one society to another, changed and added to, or lost, in the process – by war, intermarriage, conversion, discussion. But the contact was a contact of beads on a thread, though – to use an Irishism – without any thread. Sheer contiguity was the main facilitating mechanism. Small or large, where societies remained politically independent of their neighbours, and were not incorporated into more advanced civilizations, their contacts with the outside were intermittent, accidental or seasonal. Men might acquire a new type of canoe, a new religious cult, a new overlord, from next door – out there – but they never knew what lay beyond, never penetrated 'out there'. The world looked like [the diagram in figure 1] to the Nuer in the twentieth century. Beyond the range of hills, across the other side of the river, they never ventured. That was the territory of enemies, penetrated only for the purposes of trade, war, and marriage – people one needed principally as victims or friends, suppliers or consumers, but who remained essentially separate and marginal to one's own society, and therefore potentially hostile...

[Despite the Europeans' assumption of their own 'natural' superiority,] the civilizations of non-Europe were quite as advanced and cultured, as cruel and as bigoted, as anything Europe could show. As late as 1824, the Ashanti were strong enough to defeat Sir Charles McCarthy's army, and use his skull to adorn the drums of the Asantahene. In 1879, the Zulu could decisively defeat a British army at Isandlhwana, and offer strong resistance to another nomadic pastoral society, that of the Boers, who, as we are reminded, differed in their cultural equipment from the Zulu only in three decisive respects: they possessed the Bible, the wheel and the gun. Even on the eve of the twentieth century, an Ethiopian army could defeat Italy, at Adowa, and as late as 1921, 7,000 Spanish soldiers were wiped out by Abd-el-Krim's smaller army in Morocco.

But these were the death-struggles of doomed cultures. Resistance there might be, but Europe inexorably strengthened her grip. The last sovereign independent Indian state, the Punjab, was conquered and annexed in 1848–9; the last attempt to recreate the old order in the Indian subcontinent came ten years later with the 'Mutiny'. Soon afterwards, the whole process was to be speeded up.

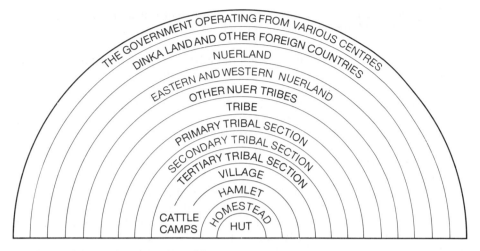

Figure 1   Nuer view of the world
Source: Evans-Pritchard, 'Nuer socio-spatial Categories', in *The Nuer*, p. 114.

The really crucial phase, which ended in the triumphant division of the entire globe between a handful of European powers, came after 1885. The European achievement in this period, therefore, was not merely a repetition of older patterns of 'imperialism'; it marked the dawn of a new era in human history, characterized by an imperialism of a new type, the response to distinctively new economic and financial pressures in Europe itself. It was to result in the unification of the globe as a single social system. . . .

[This] new 'world' was no egalitarian 'family of nations': it was essentially asymmetrical. At the one pole stood industrialized Europe; at the other, the disinherited. Paradoxically, the world had been divided in the process of its unification, divided into spheres of influence, and divided into rich and poor.

58   Ankie Hoogvelt

The New International Division of Labour

We can assess the record of industrialization in the third world on the basis of four criteria:

1   the degree of *structural* transformation of the national economies in terms of the relative contribution of *manufacturing output to GDP*;
2   the degree of structural transformation in terms of the relative absorption of *labour in the manufacturing sector*, for there is little point in having a rapidly advancing manufacturing sector if few people participate in this sector, and, as so often happens, the majority are marginalized from the productive process;
3   the changing *composition of exports*, for this is a measure of a potentially more equal economic relationship with the world market in general, and the advanced industrial countries in particular;
4   the *qualitative pattern of the industrialization process*, because this will tell us something about the extent to which industrialization will take root as a

self-propelling indigenous force, or to what extent it is a mere by-product of industrial development going on elsewhere.

In respect of *structural* transformation there is little doubt that the third world – when viewed as a whole – has made significant advances over the past thirty years. Whereas in 1950, the share of manufactures in the combined GDP of developing countries was no more than 12 per cent, in 1980 it was 20 per cent.

However, this structural transformation has been very uneven between the third world economies, and raises serious questions regarding the continued relevance of the term 'third world' as an adequate descriptive category. At one end of the spectrum there are some forty-eight countries containing about one-quarter of the third world population where industrialization has hardly begun, and is still below or at the 12 per cent mark. At the other extreme we find the eight newly industrializing countries [NICs] of the third world, where the contribution of the manufacturing sector to GDP ranges between 25 [and] 35 per cent, entirely comparable to that of the 'old' industrialized countries. As a matter of fact, the old industrial countries have over the past twenty years experienced 'deindustrialization', an average decline in manufacturing output relative to GDP of 5 per cent since 1960 and an even greater decline of labour employed in industry.

The unevenness of industrial progress between third world countries was succinctly put in the UNCTAD (United Nations Conference on Trade and Development) annual trade report of 1982: 'Fewer than 10 newly industrialized developing countries accounted in 1980 for nearly 30 per cent of developing countries' GDP and nearly half of their manufacturing output, even though their share of the population of the underdeveloped world was no more than 10 per cent.'[1] The big gap between the two groups is largely filled with the near 50 per cent of the developing countries' population who live in India, Pakistan and China. And although industrialization is taking place in these countries as measured by relative and absolute size of the manufacturing sector, as well as composition of exports, the impact of this process of industrialization on the distribution of employment as between agriculture and industry remains insignificant.

Unfortunately, when we examine the *labour absorption rate*, there are no data series available in respect of international comparisons of persons employed in manufacturing industry. What we do have (from the World Bank) is a measure relating to the number of people employed in industry (which includes besides manufacturing also construction and mining). It is interesting that, while for the old industrial countries the percentage share of industrial employment in total employment matches the contribution of industry to GDP (the weighted average for the industrial market economies group being 36 per cent for the industry to GDP ratio and 38 per cent for the industrial employment to total employment ratio), for the newly industrializing countries there is a gap of 11 per cent, with only 28 per cent of people employed in industry as against a weighted average of 39 per cent industrial output in GDP. This gap is even bigger for the World Bank's middle-income group, suggesting for all but the three notorious 'labour exporting' economies, (Singapore, Taiwan and Hong Kong) a pattern of industrialization unable to absorb labour, because of the capital-intensive nature of the industrialization process.

The tell-tale signs of a new international division of labour relate to the *economic exchange* between the old industrial centres and the third world: while for the third world as a group the participation rate in world industrial *production* has remained quite static over a long period, as we have seen, its share in world manufacturing *exports* has grown from practically zero in the colonial period to 6 per cent in 1960 and an estimated 11 per cent in 1979. In fact in this latter period, exports of manufactures from the third world as a group grew faster than either world manufacturing output, or world manufacturing exports. Excluding oil, the composition of merchandise exports from all developing countries as a group changed from one where in 1955 only 20 per cent of the value was contributed by manufactures as against 40 per cent in 1975.

But here too, the distribution in export performance has been so uneven between third world countries as to make a nonsense of the practice of speaking of the developing countries as a group. In 1980, the total value of all the world market economies' manufacturing exports came to just over one trillion dollars. Of this total the old industrialized countries contributed 87.4 per cent, and all the 'developing' world 12.6 per cent. But of this 12.6 per cent, the eight third world NICs took 7.3 per cent while the four southern European NICs took 2.7 per cent, leaving a pitiful 2.6 per cent for the rest of the third world – including India.

Finally in this empirical assessment of the international economic order, a word about the pattern of industrialization, both in the third world in general and in the newly industrializing countries in particular.

A great deal has been written about the dependent nature of the process of industrialization embarked upon by most developing countries soon after their liberation from formal colonial rule. In the 1950s, the eloquent appraisal by various UN specialists, like Raoul Prebisch, put paid to the ideologically conceived wisdom of the theory of comparative advantage, upon which the old international division of labour had rested.[2] They exposed the inherently unequal nature of the exchange between, on the one hand, poor countries trading unprocessed primary commodities, and on the other rich countries trading manufactures. A strategy based on import-substitutive industrialization was – for a time – seen as the only path to development. In brief, this was a development strategy based on the *home* production of hitherto *imported* finished manufactures. Within a decade, however, the strategy of import substitution was itself widely criticized by both conventional and radical economists. While conventional economists debated the many domestic inefficiencies and costs associated with high levels of protection, the radical economists focused on the policy's propensity to generate new forms of external dependency and the associated widening international and domestic inequalities which together distorted the industrialization process. As countries lacking in technological and industrial infrastructure tried to increase their domestic production of finished manufactures, so they had to encourage foreign companies to set up the production facilities for them. The result was a pattern of industrialization subject to foreign ownership and control, frequently slotted into the multinational companies' global strategies of process and product specialization as well as marketing, dependent on foreign inputs of intermediate goods and know-how for which non-market prices had to be paid (so-called 'technological rents'), a return flow of profits (dividends, royalties) which over time exceeded the original value of the capital brought in, and, last but not least, a choice of production technology compatible with the advanced countries' organic composition of capital (i.e. very capital-intensive) but unable to offer much employment for the masses of the population. And so, while – on paper and in national accounting terms – economic progress was being made, domestic inequalities widened and increasing sections of the poor were excluded from the development process. In 1964, the Brazilian President summed it up with the legendary words, 'Brazil is developing but the people are not'. Some radical writers saw the entire thrust of the ideology of developmentalism and modernization with its centre-piece of industrialization as nicely timed and construed to fit the changing needs of the leading branches and countries of world capitalism for new market outlets for producer goods.

After a more or less promising initial start in the majority of the smaller developing countries, the widening social inequalities and the resulting narrowing of the domestic market put a brake on the policy of import substitution. The need to contain popular discontent following this failure led in many countries – especially in Latin America – to the rise of military and bureaucratic authoritarian regimes.

By contrast, the apparent industrial success of the newly industrializing countries was due mainly to two kinds of conditions, each facilitating a further physical expansion of industrial activity.

1   There were a number of countries which had a sufficiently large potential domestic market to stimulate new forms of co-operation with transnational capital, which deepened the industrial structure and which took the import-substitutive strategy one step further into the basic goods sector. Brazil, Mexico, Argentina, India, South Africa and Turkey are examples of this strategy. The consolidation of bureaucratic authoritarian regimes, however, occurred here too because the new dependency created by foreign penetration and control over the industrial producer goods sector increasingly had to rely on the state as direct agent and ally in production. The counterpart of this process was the expulsion of sections of the national bourgeoisie as well as the working class from the productive process. This second stage of import substitution tended to suffer from the same externally induced distortions as the first stage; after a while it too ran up against the same bottleneck of a restricted domestic market. At this historical juncture, which was reached in the larger Latin American economies in the late sixties and early seventies, there were real political options available, as Latin American *dependista* writers Cardoso and Faletto have pointed out.[3] The choice was between, on the one hand, a widening of the domestic market through some degree of social reform and a reorganization of production relations coupled with substantive democratization, or – on the other hand – a redirection of the industrialization process towards exports coupled with a tightening of the grip of the autocratic political machine. For a number of reasons – the new integration of world industrial production on a global scale by transnational capital, and the need to earn foreign exchange imposed by debt-peonage as well as the rigidity of the internal class structure – the 'successful' NICs all opted for the export-orientation strategy. In this way, instead of seizing the opportunity to consolidate their by now relatively well-advanced industrial production structure by integrating it within the wider domestic economy and society, many became instead 'sub-imperialist states', 'relay stations' or 'staging-posts' for transnational capital, penetrating with their industrial products the markets of other less developed countries. And so we find German Volkswagen kits made in Brazil and sold for assembly to Nigeria.

2   Export-oriented industrialization was adopted right from the start – in the early 1960s – by a small group of south-east Asian economies (Singapore, Hong Kong, Taiwan, the Philippines and Malaysia). Skipping the import-substitution phase, the strategy involved attracting foreign 'branch plant' investments by transnational enterprises. Productive activity in these branch plants consists of very specific, labour-intensive, usually assembly-type operations, which are

wholly dependent on imported intermediate goods, equipment and raw materials, and whose output is entirely destined for re-export. The success of this
latter group of countries in attracting such 'split-site' production is due almost
entirely to the availability of a cheap and relatively docile labour force and the
presence of autocratic governments willing to suppress it, as well as willing
to offer favourable tax and other legislation to foreign investors, in especially
designated areas called *free-trade*, or export-processing, zones. A free-trade
zone is like a country within a country, fenced off by barbed wire or concrete
walls from the rest of the territory and guarded in some cases by a 'zone police'.
A survey for the Asian Productivity Organization (APO) defines the free-trade
zone as 'an enclave in terms of customs – territorial aspects and possibly other
aspects such as total or partial exemption from laws and decrees of the country
concerned'.[4]

By 1980 there were fifty-three free-trade zones in developing countries (out of
a total of some eighty the world over) employing just under one million people.
Because production in these zones is part of the multinational corporations'
global product and distribution flows, they are largely irrelevant to the establishment of an integrated industrial complex in these countries, for there are few if
any linkages with the host economy. There are two further reasons why this type
of labour-export oriented industrialization is highly suspect. For one thing,
competition between developing countries for such investments is at present so
intense as to nullify any social advances that have been made in host government bargaining with transnational capital over so-called 'performance requirements' (i.e. local value-added criteria, training of local personnel, ownership
patterns and so on). The cheapness and the degree of oppression of labour are
being used in an ever more ruthless struggle to attract foreign investment.
Second, as a result of cut-throat competition now taking place amongst the
leading branches of world capitalist industry (notably in the electronics and
computer sectors), the competitive advantage of labour-exporting less developed
countries is being eroded because of automation. Some key industries have
already returned to the developed countries, including garment and textile
industries, where computerization has eliminated many of the labour-intensive
tasks, once the competitive preserve of cheap labour economies. A major
impetus for such 'relocation back north' will be the neo-protectionist measures
now gradually and stealthily being reintroduced in all OECD countries and
which effectively place import restrictions on imports from the developing
world.

59 Jon Bennett

Hunger and the Politics of World Food Supply

To understand fully the systems that conspire to produce persistent hunger in
the world today, we must first dispense with some commonly held assumptions
about its causes. It is all too easy to regard the problem as unfortunate, but
inevitable, and perhaps even God-sent. In Ethiopia in 1984, these sentiments
were echoed even among famine victims themselves, many of whom rationalized
their predicament with reference to 'punishment' for past sins.

The first myth: quantity of food

There is plenty of food in the world. In fact, each year the world produces huge surpluses of unused food. The arithmetic is as simple as it is condemning. The food *currently* produced each year is more than enough to feed the projected 6 billion people anticipated by the year 2000. Harvests have been increasing recently at a rate of 2.6 per cent yearly – well ahead of the 2 per cent population growth rate.

Since we evidently have more than enough to feed the world the problem must be one of *access*. Here again, most people of the rich North are favoured. For example, North Americans, representing only 6 per cent of the world's population, by 1978 consumed 35 per cent of the world's resources (including food) – the same as the entire developing world.

The second myth: overpopulation

It is true that current population densities and growth rates are unique in history. As the industrial revolution began, world population also began to expand rapidly. By 1800, we had reached the first billion; by 1930, the figure was 2 billion; by 1975, it was 4 billion; and, by 1987, almost 5 billion. Until very recently, the *rate* of population growth had also been on the increase, reaching almost 2 per cent by the mid–1960s. That growth rate is now declining slowly, yet still there will be 6 billion people on earth by the year 2000. With a few notable exceptions, higher growth rates occur in poorer countries of the South, whereas the slowest-growing nations are all in northern Europe.

Most experts agree that uncontrolled population growth rate and density are worrying factors in the developing world. But are they, in fact, major causes of hunger and poverty? Western Europe has an average population density of about 98 people per square kilometre (with Holland having more than 1,000 per sq km); Africa as a whole has an average of only eighteen people per sq km. Yet the Europeans are among the best-fed people in the world and Africa suffers the highest levels of malnutrition. So there seems to be little relationship between hunger and availability of land. African countries may suffer great shortages of food, but it isn't because of a lack of land. Less than one-third of the potential arable land of this vast continent is being cultivated at present. The fact is that richer countries of the North have enough *money* to support their populations, whereas most countries of the South do not.

World hunger doesn't keep the population down; it actually keeps it up. Africa has the world's fastest population growth rate; yet this is itself an indication of prevailing poverty. Individual families will remain large as long as they lack the economic *security* we take for granted in the North. In rural areas, children are needed as workers to assure the survival of their families and to support parents in their old age. And, since nearly one in five children born in developing countries dies before the age of five, fertility rates remain high as a safeguard.

There is a degree of 'cultural lag' in certain countries, where recent prosperity may belie the argument for more children. The Kenyan middle classes, for instance, continue to have large families; the men cannot 'hold their head high' until they have many sons. Likewise, in India, having many children is perceived as the realization of the marriage vow; for many it has little to do with their economic well-being. Where change has been most rapid, women themselves have fought to regain control of their lives and bodies. Contraception – a complex, sensitive issue when it infringes on cultural or religious mores – is not always the answer. Ultimately more significant will be the slowly changing status of women, from childbearer to breadwinner. Obviously, women should have access to safe contraception, but only they – not foreign family planners – should make the choice.

In the meantime, certain governments continue to experiment with birth-control methods, education and, even, sanctions. Sadly, in countries like China, there is evidence of increasing infanticide where the state's demand for one-child families conflicts with traditional preference given to male offspring. We are witnessing, in the latter half of the twentieth century, a desperate struggle between the imperative for population control and the financial and cultural backlash of millions for whom children represent continuity and security. The fundamental problem, however, must not be understated: high birth rates are primarily related to economic uncertainty. In nearly every country where mal-nutrition has been reduced and child death rates have decreased, birth rates have also dropped dramatically.

The third myth: the weather

For many of us, world hunger became an issue for the first time when famine, in Africa or elsewhere, was causing major upheaval. It is understandable, then, that we tend to associate starvation with natural causes – droughts, floods or earthquakes – that are beyond the control of humankind. True, it was the lack of rain in Ethiopia that ultimately pushed so many highland peasants into a state of destitution; and it was a cyclone in the Bay of Bengal that killed thousands in Bangladesh in 1985.

But, in both cases, it was the *selection* of victims that was the most revealing. No one in the US starves when drought hits the mid-west plains, for the country has mountains of stored grain. Why, then, were no emergency food stocks available for Ethiopians? And why were the poorest Bangladeshis so desparate for land that they risked the dangerous move on to the new islands that appear every year in the Bay of Bengal?

In the Sahel, desertification is the most compelling reason for the drift of thousands from their traditional grazing land. Drought is a natural phenomenon, but its effects could have been minimized with careful planning, equitable distribution of land and appropriate technology. Short-term commercial and political priorities have merely worsened the plight of those living in Africa's semi-arid regions. Likewise, the world's ecosystem is being dangerously tampered with in Brazil where the rain forests are being cut down at an alarming rate. Behind each natural disaster lies a multitude of human errors that cause only the poorest people to suffer the full impact of nature. They are vulnerable to even slight changes in weather patterns, for they already live on the edge of subsistence. In high-income countries the number of people killed per disaster is less than 10 per cent of those killed in low-income countries.

The fourth myth: the miracle of science

We are all familiar with the ways in which transnational companies sell the 'scientific miracle' of fertilizers, pesticides and new high-yield seeds. The scientist's laboratory is no longer contained within the confines of a university, it is now at the forefront of international competition to produce more food on less land. Population pressure and the uncertainties of the weather might have made the quest for higher productivity an incontestably beneficial project in certain countries. But in today's world technology is simply another commodity, bought and sold by those with financial power. If science is to contribute to alleviating world hunger, it must go hand in hand with social and political change.

One scientific response touted as a solution to world hunger – the Green Revolution – certainly fulfilled the promise of producing high-yield varieties of wheat and rice in certain countries of the South. Mexico provided the site for the basic research, and successful programmes were first initiated there and in the Indian subcontinent. In 1970, Norman Borlaug received the Nobel Peace Prize for breeding the first high-yield wheat varieties. The 'revolution' was born.

The Green Revolution did produce more food and enrich some farmers, but as a solution to global hunger it was an expensive failure. In most places it has widened the gulf between rich and poor and has been a cause of social upheavals in peasant cultures. In fact, not only has it failed to improve the lot of the poor, but it has also caused widespread ecological problems. . . .

The ecological hazards of high-technology farming are only now slowly being recognized. Although the Green Revolution research institutes (like CIMMYT in Mexico or IRRI in the Philippines) are making a special effort to breed pest- and disease-resistant varieties of grain, the increasing use of herbicides, pesticides and chemical fertilizers has led to the contamination of both soil and water in many countries where these artificial products are used widely. One of the biggest problems has been the increasing immunity of insects and the fact that the natural balance of nature has been upset to such an extent that new products now have to be invented to compensate for the destruction caused by older products.

Growing more food does not, in itself, end hunger. At one level, diseases of poverty – such as dysentery and diarrhoea – contribute as much to malnutrition as actual lack of food. At another, people starve in countries where millions are spent in storing surplus food. A scientific solution to world hunger cannot, in the real world, be conducted in perfect 'laboratory' conditions. Unless it is accompanied by fair distribution to the poor farmer, equal access to land and the *means* of food production, and a careful assessment of environmental factors, it is doomed to failure. Assuming that the poor are poor because they lack certain things, some governments and aid agencies tend to focus on material redistribution – they bring in what they see as a local requirement. But material incentives invariably fall into the hands of the powerful; what the poor lack more than anything is the power to secure what they really need.

Dispensing with the major myths of hunger is an important step towards uncovering the real causes of the 'scandal' of hunger. . . . The extent of world hunger is gradually receiving more attention in the world's media, and the involvement of ordinary people in the campaign for change is greater than ever before. It is a mark, however, of the fundamental weakness of this campaign that politicians of every persuasion can accommodate the 'famine movement' and sometimes even use it to their political advantage. World leaders are fully aware of the system of social injustice they have created, yet continue to fall very short of significantly changing it; for invested in the system is political and, more important, economic power. . . .

Throughout the 1950s and 1960s, the UN and other national and international aid agencies directed most of their work towards increasing food production, reducing the population growth rate, and promoting the idea of a 'trickle-down' effect of economic growth – that is, that if a nation's *overall* wealth were to increase, poor people within that society would eventually benefit. But the facts have not borne this out. Brazil, now one of the richest nations in the world, has 50 million people living in extreme poverty, 40 million of whom are malnourished. Likewise, enormous disparities in wealth exist in other 'successful' countries of Latin America, Africa and Asia.

What went wrong? The UN World Food Conference in 1974 adopted views that began to show a more politically conscious perspective:

> The situation of the peoples affected by hunger and malnutrition arises from their historical circumstances, including social inequalities – including in many cases alien and colonial domination – foreign occupation, racial discrimination, apartheid and neocolonialism in all its forms, which continue to be among the greatest obstacles to the full emancipation and progress of the developing countries and all the peoples involved.

Such statements have been echoed time and again by other international organizations, such as the European Economic Community (EEC), the Food and Agriculture Organisation (FAO) and the UN Development Programme (UNDP). Yet the analysis of the problem is rarely matched by action. This can hardly come as a surprise; economic or political change on the part of *donor* countries is usually adroitly side-stepped. There are, nevertheless, important differences between the current and previous states of establishment opinion. ... Extreme poverty in the South is now seen as a real *threat* to the survival of the world economic system, rather than something to be dealt with by occasional humanitarian gestures. It is this sense of crisis, of impending economic recession and upheaval *in the North*, that is behind reforms currently being urged upon world leaders.

In Northern countries themselves, unemployment is on the rise. The poor who do not have access to adequate food are a relatively small but growing minority (8–10 per cent in the US). The slow decline of manufacturing industries has condemned many previously rich industrial centres to a 'third world' status, dependent upon increasing levels of state aid.

60   Thomas L. McPhail

Electronic Colonialism and the World Information Order

Over the course of history there have been but a few major trends in empire-building. The first era was characterized by military conquests; these occurred during the Greco-Roman period. The second era involved militant Christianity; the Crusades of the Middle Ages are typical of this expansion movement. The third era commenced with significant mechanical inventions in the seventeenth century and came to a rather abrupt end toward the middle of the twentieth century. It was essentially mercantile colonialism fuelled by the industrial revolution and a desire for empire-building both to import raw materials and to find export markets for finished products. Asia, Africa, the Caribbean and the Americas became objects of conquest by the then European powers. France, Great Britain, Spain, Portugal and Nordic nations systematically set about extending their commercial and political influence. These expanding empires of

Europe sought raw materials and other goods unavailable at home and, in return, sent colonial administrators, immigrants, finished products – and a language, educational system, religion, philosophy, culture, laws and lifestyle that frequently did not suit the invaded country. Yet this caused little concern for the conquerers. During the latter part of this third era, industrialized nations sought to extend their influence through transnational corporations that supplemented and extended more traditional means of control. But the common denominator was a desire for trade links (involving raw materials, cheap labour, expanding markets and so on) that carried with them many commercial imperatives and governmental practices that suited the larger and more powerful industrialized nations rather than their foreign colonies or customers.

The First and Second World Wars not only brought an end to major military expansion movements but also placed the industrialized nations of the West in command of international organizations along with vital trade routes and practices. During the 1950s the business and economic climate allowed transnational corporations to increase and solidify domestic and foreign markets based upon the production of mass produced goods, from cereals to computers. Basically, the industrialized revolution took its logical course. But two major changes occurred during the late 1950s and early 1960s that set the stage for the fourth and current era of empire expansion.

The two major changes are the rise of nationalism, centred mainly in the third world, and the shift to a service-based economy in the West that relies substantially on telecommunication systems, where traditional geographical borders or technological barriers to international communications are being rendered obsolete. The postindustrial society, with information-related services being the cornerstone, has significant implications for industrial and non-industrial nations alike. Military and mercantile colonialism of the past may be replaced by electronic colonialism in the future. A nation state may now be able to go from the stone age to the information age without passing through the intervening steps of industrialization.

Electronic colonialism is the dependency relationship established by the importation of communication hardware, foreign-produced software, along with engineers, technicians and related information protocols, that vicariously establish a set of foreign norms, values and expectations which, in varying degrees, may alter the domestic cultures and socialization processes. Comic books to statellites, computers to lasers, along with more traditional fare such as radio programmes, theatre, movies, wire services and television shows demonstrate the wide range of information activities that make up the broad configuration of what is possible to send and thus to receive – and there lies the rub.

Essentially how much of the foreign and imported material rubs off on the receiver is the critical issue. The displacement, rejection, altering or forgetting of domestic and native customs materials is a major concern for the third world. Electronic colonialism of the twentieth century is just as dreaded as mercantile colonialism of the eighteenth and nineteenth centuries.

Mercantile colonialism sought cheap labour; it was the labourer's hands, feet or body that were required for mining, picking, shovelling, stacking and so on, of raw goods or finished products. Not so with electronic colonialism. Electronic colonialism seeks the mind; it is aimed at influencing attitudes, desires, beliefs, lifestyles, consumer opinions or purchasing patterns of those who consume – by either eyes, ears or both – the imported media fare. Whether it is *Sesame Street* or *Dallas*, there is a great deal of vicarious learning about Western society and ways. It leads to a certain mental set. From spaghetti westerns to soap operas shown around the world, they deliver with them the trappings of an alternative lifestyle, culture, economy or political message that goes far beyond the momentary images flickering on a screen. Electronic colonialism is aimed at examining the mental images, and the long-term consequences of exposure to imported software of all types.

The recent rise of nationalism in many third world countries has resulted in a parallel concern for political, economic and cultural control over their own destinies. Leaving aside the political aspects, it is with the cultural issues that students of journalism and telecommunication find theoretical and research interest. For example, two of the largest international issues that concern the third world and the West, and frequently find them on opposing sides, are the performance of the major wire services and the use of direct broadcast satellites (DBS). The flow, accuracy, emphasis and content of the major Western wire services in reporting third world items have come under considerable criticism and scrutiny, particularly at UNESCO.

The other fear deals with a future broadcasting technology – DBS. It represents to date the ultimate mind- and culture-invading mechanism that is being developed by Canada, Japan, the United States and the Soviet Union alike. In the field of international communications, DBS is to the future what Gutenberg was to the past. DBS may go far beyond the technical and economic aspects of message transmission to create another set of diverse issues that are cultural, political and sociological in nature.

Part 15

Cities in the Modern World

There were few large cities even in the most advanced of pre-modern societies. In traditional China two or three cities numbered as many as half a million inhabitants, but this was very uncommon elsewhere. Medieval Europe boasted no cities which even remotely approached this level of population. With the advent of modern industrial production, however, large numbers of people moved off the land and into newly expanding urban areas; at the same time, substantial processes of population growth were initiated. In the industrialized countries today, more than 90 per cent of the population typically live in urban areas and large cities are commonplace. Some urban conurbations – unbroken built-up areas consisting of several cities in close conjunction – number as many as 40 or 50 million people: an example is that which stretches almost uninterruptedly from Boston through New York to Washington on the north-eastern seaboard of the United States.

In the current century, the trend towards increasing urbanization has become worldwide in scope. Some of the largest cities, in fact, are now to be found in third world countries. In many areas of these cities, dense populations live in conditions of poverty almost unimaginable to people from more prosperous societies of the world. In reading 61 Michael Pacione analyses urbanization in different parts of the world and gives projections of likely future trends. According to him, by the year 2025 over 60 per cent of the world as a whole will have become urbanized.

Reading 62 by John R. Logan and Harvey L. Molotch discusses some of the mechanisms of urban growth in a Western context, concentrating particularly upon American cities. The modern city, they argue, can be seen as a 'growth machine': a series of mechanisms for promoting investment, attracting industry and other installations as a means of enhancing the power of local elites. Fortunes have been made, and continue to be made today, through the boosting of the attractions of local urban areas by those with material stakes in their economic advancement. Public and private prosperity are here highly intertwined.

Processes of urban growth interrelate with modes of neighbourhood decay, and each today is directly influenced by the international division of labour. In reading 63, Edward W. Soja discusses the interrelation of economic development and decline in the Los Angeles urban area. Some neighbourhoods in the Los Angeles region suffered from 'deindustrialization' during the 1970s and 1980s, thereby accelerating forms of urban decay. On the other hand, new industrial development has also been successfully implanted in the Los Angeles basin, leading to accelerated rates of economic growth. The result, in combination with large-scale immigration into Los Angeles, is an extraordinary mixture of urban affluence and decrepitude.

61   Michael Pacione

Major Trends in World Urbanization

The problems of cities and the efforts directed towards their alleviation command global attention because of the increasing proportion of the world's population being affected by such issues. Urbanization and its consequences are worldwide phenomena and the increasing size and scale of urban settlements is a characteristic of the contemporary era. Four out of every ten of the world's population now live in an urban setting and the expectation is that by the year AD 2000 half of the world's inhabitants will be urban dwellers.

In North America 54 per cent of the population was urban in 1925, while fifty years later this proportion had increased to 77 per cent (table 1). Even more dramatic increases in urbanization have been experienced in the USSR, where the urban population rose from 18 per cent in 1925 to 61 per cent in 1975, and in Latin America, where the corresponding figures were 25 per cent and 60 per cent. The rate of world urbanization in general has shown no slackening since 1800 and in all regions the trend is towards increased urbanization and city growth.

The pronounced rate of growth in the world's total urban population is clearly shown in table 2. While the growth rate between 1925 and 1950 was 73 per cent, this figure more than doubled over the next twenty-five years. In some areas the growth of urban population was even more spectacular. In Oceania the number of city dwellers trebled over the half century from 1925 to 1975; in the USSR and East Asia it grew fivefold; in South Asia sixfold; and in Latin America and Africa nearly eightfold. United Nations estimates for the next fifty years call for most of these trends to continue. The distribution of the world's population is also changing. Whereas in 1925 two-fifths was in Europe, by 1975 this proportion had fallen by half. Meanwhile, east and south Asia, which together had about one-quarter of the urban population in 1925, had increased their joint share to 38 per cent by 1975. A continuation of present trends would mean that these two areas together will contain about one-half of the world's urban population by 2025. By the same date the urban populations of both Africa and Latin America will also exceed those of Europe. These trends in urbanization and city growth are reflected in the distribution and different growth rates of metropolitan areas (table 3) and 'million cities' (table 4). In both cases, while the number and relative importance of such cities remain greatest in the developed realm, the fastest rates of growth are occurring in the developing world. Greater Mexico City is already nearing 18 millions and is of almost megalopolitan proportions in itself. Several others are only slightly less vast. Bogota quadrupled in population between 1950 and 1970, while Bombay and Singapore doubled. The reality of these soaring rates of growth and the effect on social and economic conditions is of immediate concern, since the impact of urbanization will press most heavily upon those societies which at present are most deficient in the economic, technological and managerial resources required to maintain and improve a complex urban environment.

The major trends in world urbanization and city growth seem clear, but there are difficulties in predicting future levels of urban population; this is illustrated by the classic S-shaped urbanization curve (figure 1). Different countries reach different points on the curve at different times. Britain was the first country to

Table 1 Percentage of total population in urban localities in the world and eight major areas, 1925–2025

Major area	1925	1950	1975	2000	2025
World total	21	28	39	50	63
Northern America	54	64	77	86	93
Europe	48	55	67	79	88
USSR	18	39	61	76	87
East Asia	10	15	30	46	63
Latin America	25	41	60	74	85
Africa	8	13	24	37	54
South Asia	9	15	23	35	51
Oceania	54	65	71	77	87

Table 2 Urban population in the world and eight major areas, 1925–2025 (millions)

Major area	1925	1950	1975	2000	2025
World total	405	701	1548	3191	5713
Northern America	68	106	181	256	308
Europe	162	215	318	425	510
USSR	30	71	154	245	318
East Asia	58	99	299	638	1044
Latin America	25	67	196	464	819
Africa	12	28	96	312	803
South Asia	45	108	288	825	1873
Oceania	5	8	15	26	38

Table 3 Number of metropolitan areas and average annual growth rate, by world region

World region	Number of metropolitan areas	Average annual growth rate of metropolitan areas (%)	Proportion of regional population in metropolitan areas (%)
World	1387	2.4	–
North America	169	2.4	51.0
Europe	308	1.5	27.0
USSR	220	2.3	27.0
Latin America	125	3.8	30.0
Africa	59	4.5	13.5
East Asia	481	{ 3.4	14.0
South Asia		2.6 }	
Oceania	12	2.4	50.0

Table 4   Million cities, 1950–1985

Region	Number of cities			Million-city population as % of total population		
	1950	*1970*	*1985*	*1950*	*1970*	*1985*
World total	75	162	273	7	12	16
More developed realm	51	83	126	15	20	27
Less developed realm	24	79	147	3	8	13
Europe	28	36	45	15	19	22
North America	14	27	39	23	32	38
USSR	2	10	28	4	9	17
Oceania	2	2	4	24	27	37
East Asia	13	36	54	5	11	17
South Asia	8	27	53	2	6	10
Latin America	6	16	31	9	19	28
Africa	2	8	19	2	5	9

Source: United Nations Population Division (1972).

experience large-scale urbanization, and England and Wales reached the upper portion of the curve shortly after 1900, whereas the USA did not reach the same point until approximately 1950. The initial stage of the urbanization process is characterized by a 'traditional' economic structure. The emphasis is on the agrarian sector of the economy, characteristically accompanied by a dispersed population with a relatively small proportion resident in cities. During the acceleration stage there is a pronounced redistribution of the population, such that from less than 25 per cent the urban component rises to around 70 per cent of the total. This is a phase of concentration of people and economic activity, during which the secondary and tertiary sectors of the economy assume increased importance. As the urbanization curve approaches 100 per cent, it will tend to flatten, as has occurred in England and Wales since 1900. In this terminal stage the urban population is typically in excess of 70 per cent, with the remainder being rural farm and non-farm inhabitants.

Speculation on the future form of the urbanization curve must include the possible flattening of the upper portion at a lower level, or even a reversal of the curve, as has occurred in some parts of the developed world. In the developing world most states are moving into the middle section of the curve, although a distinct minority are still in the initial stage of urbanization. For the foreseeable future the cities in developing countries will continue to grow even if national policy biases favouring urbanization are eliminated and rigorous decentralization measures are deployed. Modern industrial and service activities benefit from the economies of agglomeration and, to the extent that industrialization and structural change are a necessary adjunct of economic development, the impetus for urban growth is well-nigh inexorable.

Study of the magnitude of the urbanization process should not be confused with an analysis of its underlying dynamics. The urbanization process denotes a complex interplay of social, economic, political, technological, geographical and cultural factors. Acknowledgement of the utility of the urbanization curve as a normative model does not carry with it acceptance of the similar-path or con-

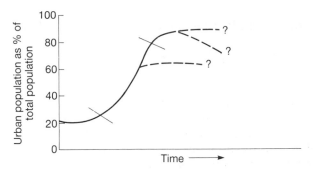

Figure 1 The urbanization curve

vergence theory of development. We must disavow the view that urbanization is a universal process, a consequence of modernization that involves the same sequence of events in different countries and that produces progressive convergence of forms. Neither can we accept the view that there may be several culturally specific processes but that they are producing convergent results because of underlying technological imperatives of modernization and industrialization. Not only are we dealing with several fundamentally different processes that have arisen out of differences in culture and time, but these processes are producing different results in different world regions, transcending any superficial similarities.

Urbanization in the third world exhibits a number of key contrasts with the earlier process in the developed world:

1 It is taking place in countries with the lowest levels of economic development, rather than the highest, as was the case when accelerated urbanization began in Western Europe and North America.
2 It involves countries in which people have the lowest levels of life expectancy at birth, the poorest nutritional levels, the lowest energy-consumption levels and the lowest levels of education.
3 It involves greater numbers of people than it did in the developed world.
4 Migration is greater in volume and more rapid.
5 Industrialization lags far behind the rate of urbanization, so that most of the migrants find at best marginal employment in cities.
6 The environment in cities of the third world is usually more healthy than in their rural hinterlands, in contrast to the industrial cities of the West. Urban fertility is greater in third world cities and net reproduction rates are higher than they ever were in most of the industrial countries.
7 Massive slum areas of spontaneous or transitional settlements characterize most large cities of the developing world.
8 Rising expectations mean that pressures for rapid social change are greater than they were in the West.
9 Political circumstances conducive to revolutionary takeovers of government are present as a result of the recent colonial or neo-colonial status of most of the third world nations.
10 Most of the developing countries have inherited an intentionally centralized administration, with the result that government involvement in urban development is more likely in these countries today than it was in the nineteenth-century West.

62   John R. Logan and Harvey L. Molotch

The City as a Growth Machine

Traditional urban research has had little relevance to the day-to-day activities of the place-based elites whose priorities affect patterns of land use, public budgets and urban social life. It has not even been apparent from much of the scholarship of urban social science that place is a market commodity that can produce wealth and power for its owners, and that this might explain why certain people take a keen interest in the ordering of urban life.

Research on local elites has been preoccupied with the question 'Who governs?' (or 'Who rules?'). Are the politically active citizens of a city split into diverse and competing interest groups, or are they members of a co-ordinated oligarchy? Empirical evidence of visible cleavage, such as disputes on a public issue, has been accepted as evidence of pluralistic competition. Signs of cohesion, such as common membership in voluntary and policy groups, have been used to support the alternative view.

We believe that the question of who governs or rules has to be asked in conjunction with the equally central question 'For what?' With rare exceptions, one issue consistently generates consensus among local elite groups and separates them from people who use the city principally as a place to live and work: the issue of growth. For those who count, the city is a growth machine, one that can increase aggregate rents and trap related wealth for those in the right position to benefit. . . .

The role of the growth machine as a driving force in US urban development has long been a factor in US history, and is nowhere more clearly documented than in the histories of eighteenth- and nineteenth-century American cities. Indeed, although historians have chronicled many types of mass opposition to capitalist organization (for example, labour unions and the Wobblie movement), there is precious little evidence of resistance to the dynamics of value-free city building characteristic of the American past. In looking back we thus have not only the benefit of hindsight but also the advantage of dealing with a time in which 'the interfusing of public and private prosperity' was proudly proclaimed by town boosters and their contemporary chroniclers. The creators of towns and the builders of cities strained to use all the resources at their disposal, including crude political clout, to make great fortunes out of place. The 'lively competitive spirit' of the western regions was, in Boorstin's view, more 'a competition among communities' than among individuals. Sometimes, the 'communities' were merely subdivided parcels with town names on them, what Wade has called 'paper villages', on whose behalf governmental actions could none the less be taken. The competition among them was primarily among growth elites.

These communities competed to attract federal land offices, colleges and academies, or installations such as arsenals and prisons as a means of stimulating development. These projects were, for many places, 'the only factor that permitted them to outdistance less favoured rivals with equivalent natural or geographic endowments'. The other important arena of competition was also dependent on government decision-making and funding: the development of a transportation infrastructure that would give a locality better access to raw materials and markets. First came the myriad efforts to attract state and federal funds to link towns to waterways through canals. Then came efforts to subsidize and direct the paths of railroads. Town leaders used their governmental authority to determine routes and subsidies, motivated by their private interest in rents.

The people who engaged in this city building have often been celebrated for their inspired vision and 'absolute faith'. One historian characterizes them as 'ambitious, flamboyant, and imaginative'. But more important than their personalities, these urban founders were in the business of manipulating place for its exchange values. Their occupations most often were real estate or banking. Even those who initially practised law, medicine or pharmacy were rentiers in the making....

This tendency to use land and government activity to make money was not invented in nineteenth-century America, nor did it end then. The development of the American mid-west was only one particularly noticed (and celebrated) moment in the total process. One of the more fascinating instances, farther to the west and later in history, was the rapid development of Los Angeles, an anomaly to many because it had none of the 'natural' features that are thought to support urban growth: no centrality, no harbour, no transportation cross-roads, not even a water supply. Indeed, the rise of Los Angeles as the pre-eminent city of the west, eclipsing its rivals San Diego and San Francisco, can only be explained as a remarkable victory of human cunning over the so-called limits of nature. Much of the development of western cities hinged on access to a railroad; the termination of the first continental railroad at San Francisco, therefore, secured that city's early lead over other western towns....

The jockeying for canals, railroads and arsenals of the previous century has given way in this one to more complex and subtle efforts to manipulate space and redistribute rents. The fusing of public duty and private gain has become much less acceptable (both in public opinion and in the criminal courts); the replacing of frontiers by complex cities has given important roles to mass media, urban professionals and skilled political entrepreneurs. The growth machine is less personalized, with fewer local heroes, and has become instead a multi-faceted matrix of important social institutions pressing along complementary lines.

With a transportation and communication grid already in place, modern cities typically seek growth in basic economic functions, particularly job-intensive ones. Economic growth sets in motion the migration of labour and a demand for ancillary production services, housing, retailing, and wholesaling ('multiplier effects'). Contemporary places differ in the type of economic base they strive to build (for example, manufacturing, research and development, information processing or tourism). But any one of the rainbows leads to the same pot of gold: more intense land use and thus higher rent collections, with associated professional fees and locally based profits.

Cities are in a position to affect the 'factors of production' that are widely believed to channel the capital investments that drive local growth. They can, for example, lower access costs of raw materials and markets through the creation of shipping ports and airfields (either by using local subsidies or by facilitating state and federal support). Localities can decrease corporate overhead costs through sympathetic policies on pollution abatement, employee health standards and taxes. Labour costs can be indirectly lowered by pushing welfare recipients into low-paying jobs and through the use of police to constrain union organizing. Moral laws can be changed: for example, drinking alcohol can be legalized (as in Ann Arbor, Michigan and Evanston, Illinois) or gambling can be promoted (as in Atlantic City, New Jersey) to build tourism and convention business. Increased utility costs caused by new development can be borne, as they usually are, by the public at large rather than by those

responsible for the 'excess' demand they generate. Federally financed programmes can be harnessed to provide cheap water supplies; state agencies can
be manipulated to subsidize insurance rates; local political units can forgive
business property taxes. Government installations of various sorts (universities,
military bases) can be used to leverage additional development by guaranteeing
the presence of skilled labour, retailing customers or proximate markets for
subcontractors. For some analytical purposes, it doesn't even matter that a
number of these factors have little bearing on corporate locational decisions
(some certainly do; others are debated); just the *possibility* that they might
matter invigorates local growth activism and dominates policy agendas....

Any issue of a major business magazine is replete with advertisements from
localities of all types (including whole countries) striving to portray themselves
in a manner attractive to business. Consider these claims culled from one issue
of *Business Week* (12 February 1979):

New York City is open for business. No other city in America offers more
financial incentives to expand or relocate....

The state of Louisiana advertises:

Nature made it perfect. We made it profitable.

On another page we find the claim that 'Northern Ireland works' and has a
workforce with 'positive attitudes toward company loyalty, productivity and
labour relations.' Georgia asserts, 'Government should strive to improve business conditions, not hinder them.' Atlanta headlines that as 'A City Without
Limits' it 'has ways of getting people like you out of town' and then details
its transportation advantages to business. Some places describe attributes that
would enhance the lifestyle of executives and professional employees (not a
dimension of Fantus rankings); thus a number of cities push an image of artistic
refinement. No advertisements in this issue (or in any other, we suspect) show
city workers living in nice homes or influencing their working conditions.

While a good opera or ballet company may subtly enhance the growth potential of some cities, other cultural ingredients are crucial for a good business
climate. There should be no violent class or ethnic conflict. Rubin reports that
racial confrontation over school busing was sometimes seen as a threat to urban
economic development. Racial violence in South Africa is finally leading to the
disinvestment that reformers could not bring about through moral suasion. In
the good business climate, the workforce should be sufficiently quiescent and
healthy to be productive; this was the rationale originally behind many programmes in workplace relations and public health. Labour must, in other words,
be 'reproduced', but only under conditions that least interfere with local growth
trajectories.

Perhaps most important of all, local publics should favour growth and support
the ideology of value-free development. This public attitude reassures investors
that the concrete enticements of a locality will be upheld by future politicians.
The challenge is to connect civic pride to the growth goal, tying the presumed
economic and social benefits of growth in general to growth in the local area.
Probably only partly aware of this, elites generate and sustain the place patriot-
ism of the masses. According to Boorstin, the competition among cities 'helped
create the booster spirit' as much as the booster spirit helped create the cities. In
the nineteenth-century cities, the great rivalries over canal and railway installations were the political spectacles of the day, with attention devoted to their
public, not private, benefits. With the drama of the new railway technology,
ordinary people were swept into the competition among places, rooting for their

own town to become the new 'crossroads' or at least a way station. 'The debates over transportation,' writes Scheiber, 'heightened urban community conscious-ness and sharpened local pride in many western towns'. . . .

One case can illustrate the link between growth goals and cultural institutions. In the Los Angeles area, St Patrick's Day parades are held at four different locales, because the city's Irish leaders can't agree on the venue for a joint celebration. The source of the difficulty (and much acrimony) is that these parades march down the main business streets in each locale, thereby making them a symbol of the life of the city. Business groups associated with each of the strips want to claim the parade as exclusively their own, leading to charges by still a fifth parade organization that the other groups are only out to 'make money'. The countercharge, vehemently denied, was that the leader of the challenging business street was not even Irish. Thus even an ethnic celebration can receive its special form from the machinations of growth interests and the competitions among them.

The growth machine avidly supports whatever cultural institutions can play a role in building locality. Always ready to oppose cultural and political develop-ments contrary to their interests (for example, black nationalism and communal cults), rentiers and their associates encourage activities that will connect feelings of community to the goal of local growth. The overall ideological thrust is to de-emphasize the connection between growth and exchange values and to rein-force the link between growth goals and better lives for the majority. We do not mean to suggest that the only source of civic pride is the desire to collect rents; certainly the cultural pride of tribal groups predates growth machines. Neverthe-less, the growth machine coalition mobilizes these cultural motivations, legit-imizes them and channels them into activities that are consistent with growth goals.

63 Edward W. Soja

Economic Restructuring and the Internationalization of the Los Angeles Region

The [Los Angeles area] consists of a conglomeration of cities and built-up areas which almost fills a 60-mile-radius circle around its nominal urban nucleus (the civic centre for the City of Los Angeles) and extends over all or part of five counties (Los Angeles, Orange, Riverside, San Bernardino and Ventura). The total population within this area is now nearly 12.5 million and its gross regional product would rank it fourteenth among all the countries in the world (just behind India and The Netherlands and just ahead of Australia and Mexico in GNP). Contrary to many popular images of the region, it is a major industrial metropolis which, since the 1930s, has been the premier growth pole of indus-trial capitalism. Over the past half-century, employment in manufacturing has grown by over 1.1 million as the region not only rode the crest of the war economy and the postwar boom, but also maintained its industrial expansion through the crisis-led economic restructuring of the past two decades.

This apparent continuity of urban and industrial expansion, however, masks the significant changes which have been taking place during this period in the overall fabric of urban social and spatial relations: in the location of industry and the geographical distribution of jobs, in the organization of the labour process and the composition of the workforce, in the incidence and intensity of working-class organization and community struggles, in the scale and structure of external contacts and exchange. The inherited urban mosaic has almost been transformed into a kaleidoscope of changing forms and functions, juxtaposing and interconnecting what may initially appear to be opposing tendencies and contradictory trends.

'Frostbelt' and 'Sunbelt' regional attributes come together in the Los Angeles area, intermeshing to produce a complete mix of selective industrial decline and rapid industrial expansion. The result is a markedly different industrial geography from that which had developed by 1960. Earlier rounds of industrial growth had concentrated production and employment primarily within a broad zone stretching southwards from the city centre of Los Angeles to the twin ports of San Pedro and Long Beach, with important outliers in the San Fernando and San Gabriel valleys and the so-called 'Inland Empire' of San Bernardino County. Within this extensive urban industrial landscape, whole municipalities such as Vernon and the bluntly named City of Industry and City of Commerce became almost entirely devoted to manufacturing and related services, leaving little room for a resident population: almost 50,000 people worked in Vernon, for example, but fewer than 100 lived there. Other cities such as Southgate (next door to Watts and almost midway between downtown Los Angeles and the ports) mixed heavy industrial production with some of the most attractive working-class neighbourhoods in the country. These were almost entirely white neighbourhoods, it should be added, for running through this industrial zone was one of the most rigidly defined racial divides in any American city.

Today, these areas have become the Detroit of the Los Angeles region, with numerous plant closures, high unemployment, economically devastated neighbourhoods, extensive outmigration, and de-skilling and wage-reducing occupational shifts from industry to service jobs. What had once been the second largest automobile assembly industry in the country has been reduced to a single plant in Van Nuys, itself currently threatened with closure. A tyre manufacturing industry second only to Akron has entirely disappeared, along with most of the southern California steel industry. In the four years from 1978 to 1982, at least 75,000 jobs were lost due to plant closures and indefinite layoffs, affecting primarily a segment of the labour market which was highly unionized and contained an unusually large proportion of well-paid minority and female blue-collar workers. . . .

This selective deindustrialization and job loss has had a major effect on the overall strength of organized labour. During the 1970s, unionization rates in Los Angeles County dropped from over 30 per cent to about 23 per cent. In Orange County, the drop was even more pronounced and, in manufacturing, which was experiencing an extraordinary expansion of employment, unionization rates plummeted from 26.4 to 10.5 per cent. This represented an absolute decline of over one-quarter of the union membership in 1971. Declining union membership in turn helped to strengthen management efforts to rescind many of the contractual gains achieved by organized labour in the two decades following the Second World War.

The deindustrialization and deunionization of Los Angeles has reflected national and global trends generated in response to the economic and political crises which shattered the postwar boom and the Keynesian 'productivity deal' that was so much part of the expansionary period. As occurred during similar periods of crisis and restructuring in the past, technological innovation, corporate-managerial strategies and state policies became more directly and explicitly focused on two increasingly vital and closely related objectives: the restoration of expanding profits and the establishment of more effective control over the labour force. Under the rationale of 'rationalization', a renewed celebration of the 'creative destruction' supposed to underlie capitalist development, the economic landscape which became consolidated during the postwar years began to be selectively destroyed and equally selectively reconstructed.

This comprehensive attempt to discipline labour (along with less efficient capitals and major segments of the central and local state) has been the essential core of the contemporary restructuring process, a means through which 'new room' for accelerated accumulation is being opened up: through reduced labour costs, the breakdown of the most powerful working-class organizations, increasing centralization and concentration of capital, intensified capital mobility to establish a constant threat of closure and relocation, induced technological innovation to cut costs and create improved instruments for labour control and efficiency, growing subsidization of large corporations by the state and local government, all wrapped up in ideological programmes to justify sacrifice and austerity by some for the greater national good.

From this more general perspective, the deindustrialization of Los Angeles has not simply been the local expression of an innocent process of modernization and postindustrial evolution, or merely a minor sidelight to an otherwise booming urban region. It has been a critical fulcrum around which the other aspects of social and spatial restructuring revolve. It forms, for example, the necessary introduction and backdrop to the expansive reindustrialization which has been taking place since the 1960s.

The reindustrialization of Los Angeles has been impressive. From 1970 to 1980, when the entire country experienced a net increase of less than a million manufacturing jobs, the Los Angeles region expanded by over 225,000. This net addition was more than that of the next two leading urban growth regions (San Francisco and Houston) combined and contrasted sharply with the combined net loss of 650,000 jobs in New York, Chicago, Philadelphia and Detroit. Most of this employment growth was concentrated in two very different segments of the industrial economy: the first a cluster of technologically advanced sectors based on electronics, aerospace and massive defence contracting, the second a booming garment industry. Employment growth in these and functionally related sectors enabled Los Angeles to maintain its position as a pre-eminent centre of industrial production despite both selective deindustrialization and an extensive switch to the tertiary labour market.

The combined employment growth in the seven sectors specializing in high-technology production (aircraft and parts, guided missiles and space vehicles, office and computing machines, radio and TV equipment, communications equipment, electronic components and accessories, measuring and controlling devices) was over 110,000 in the 1970s. This represented an expansion of over 50 per cent and a net addition greater than the total increment of manufacturing jobs in Houston over the same period. If one compares this job growth with the total employment in the same seven sectors in Santa Clara County for 1979 (about 147,000), it can be claimed that during the 1970s the Los Angeles region *added* a high-technology labour force almost the equivalent of the entire Silicon Valley. More recent data show that by 1985 Los Angeles County alone employed over 250,000 people in the Bureau of Labor Statistics 'Group 3' category, another widely used definition of high-technology industry. The equivalent figure for Santa Clara County was 160,000.

The Los Angeles region is today reputed to contain the highest concentration of mathematicians, scientists, engineers, skilled technicians and high-security-cleared production workers in the country. It has also been a leading recipient of prime defence contracts since the 1940s. Indeed, what ties together the seven

SIC sectors referred to earlier more than anything else has been their shared dependency upon technology arising out of Department of Defense and NASA research and the stimulus of military contracts. Much of the continued growth of high-technology industries into the 1980s can be attributed to the demand stimulation arising from the Reagan administration's Keynesian policy of military expansion....

Both the deindustrialization and reindustrialization of Los Angeles are to some extent continuations of trends which began before the mid-1960s. Their acceleration, however, and their linkage to other changes, have resulted in a major transformation of the sectoral structure of the regional economy and the composition and segmentation of the regional labour market. Over the past twenty years, the Los Angeles labour market has become increasingly polarized as its middle segment of skilled and unionized blue-collar workers dwindles in size, a small number of its expelled workers trickle up to an expanded white-collar technocracy and many more percolate down into a relatively lower-skilled and lower-wage reservoir of production and service workers, swollen by massive inmigration.

To consider only this three-part division, however, is not enough, for the new segmentation and recomposition of the labour market is much more finely grained and complex. Embedded in it is not only the juxtaposition of a Houston and a Detroit but also many of the characteristics of the Boston region, where a deep and prolonged process of labour disciplining, plant closures and capital flight produced the conditions for an economic recovery based in large part on rapidly expanding high-technology and service sectors. This occupational recycling of the labour market reinforces the polarization of wages and skills, while simultaneously increasing the number and variety of employment specializations at the top and bottom bulges of the labour market. Cutting across these occupational shifts and sectoral restructuring is a further segmentation based on race, ethnicity, immigration status and gender. The end-result in Los Angeles is a regional labour market more occupationally differentiated and socially fragmented than ever before in its history....

As has already been noted several times, the restructuring of the Los Angeles urban region has been closely associated with an increasing internationalization of the local economy. Feeding off one another have been first a massive inmigration of almost two million people from third world countries over the past twenty years; and second, an expansive internationalization of capital manifested in the emergence of Los Angeles as a World City, a production and control centre for global banking, finance, trade and industry. This increasing internationalization of both labour and capital has been central to downtown redevelopment, from the new corporate towers to the thriving garment industry, and extends its influence into virtually every aspect of the changing urban structure....

The magnitude and diversity of inmigration to Los Angeles since 1960 is comparable only to the New York-bound wave of migrants at the turn of the last century. A resurgence of migration from Mexico, both legal and illegal, has added at least a million residents to the existing population and the region has also become the primary overseas locus for a score of other countries as well. At least 200,000 Koreans have settled in Los Angeles since 1970 and have become a major influence in retail trade and the garment industry, with Korean family labour proving highly competitive with even the worst sweatshops. Filipinos, Thais, Vietnamese, Iranians, Guatemalans, Colombians and Cubans have arrived in very large numbers and several Pacific Island populations have grown almost as numerous as in their home areas. In what may be the record for inmigration from a single country, it has recently been estimated that the Salvadorean population of Los Angeles has grown by over 300,000 since 1980. Today the 'Anglo' population of the City and County of Los Angeles has probably dropped to well below 50 per cent.

Foreign capital as well as labour has been migrating into Los Angeles at an unusual rate, buying land, building office complexes, investing in industry, hotels, retail shops, restaurants and entertainment facilities. A growing proportion of the prime downtown properties – possibly more than a third – are currently owned by foreign corporations or by partnerships with foreign companies, led by Canada and Japan; and foreign capital is said to have helped finance over 90 per cent of recent multi-storey building construction. Japanese capital has directed the redevelopment of Little Tokyo and a rapidly growing inflow of Chinese capital, especially from Hong Kong, is likely to induce a similar transformation of Chinatown in the very near future. Several high-income residential districts are considered to be owned (if not occupied) primarily by Saudis and Iranians and, although it remains almost totally unexamined, it would not be surprising to find that the inflow of capital from Mexico outweighs the export from waged workers and American corporations. Perhaps only in New York City has there been such a massive urban 'shopping spree' by international capital in so short a time and from so many different sources.

The internationalization of the Los Angeles economy has been produced not only by the inflow of labour and capital, but also by the expanding global reach of domestic economic interests. Large multinational firms headquartered in Los Angeles, or with major local branch offices, have been an important factor in downtown development, and in the complex processes of industrial and spatial restructuring. One reflection of this internationalization of the local economy has been the growth of the Los Angeles port complex to the second largest in the country in dollar volume of overseas trade. Another has been the expansion of international banking and finance to a level surpassed again only by New York. And related to these concentrations has been the establishment in Los Angeles of an apparatus of capital management and control also second only to the so-called 'Capital of Capital' within the United States.

Part 16

Population, Health and Sickness

Modern societies have a different 'demographic profile' from traditional systems. In the pre-modern world, a high proportion of infants died at birth or shortly thereafter and chronic sickness was the lot of much of the adult population. The selection from Roy Porter and Dorothy Porter (reading 64) provides graphic evidence of the level to which illness and the prospect of an early death haunted the lives of individuals in eighteenth-century England. Infectious diseases were rampant and the ordinary individual endured a range of chronic complaints which many of us in modern social conditions would find difficult to tolerate.

Some of the great breakthroughs in the improvement of health care were made in the area of preventive medicine, particularly as a result of improvements in methods of hygiene. Other changes, however, have depended more upon the emergence of organized systems of health care. While such systems exist in all the industrialized countries, there are many variations in terms of how they are structured. In reading 65 Ross Hume Hall compares two contrasting systems of health care, those of the United Kingdom and the United States.

In Britain health care is provided through the National Health Service, funded through public resources. In the US, there is no government-sponsored system of health care directly comparable to the National Health Service. Medical care is provided by means of private insurance, or through government-supported programmes designed to help those who cannot afford to take out adequate health cover for themselves. How far either system is more effective than the other in generating adequate health care is a matter of some contention. Hall points out that the American system provides greater freedom of choice for the more affluent segments of the population, but appears considerably more expensive to run than the National Health Service. On the other hand, it is generally believed that the NHS provides greater medical support for poorer groups than the American system is able to deliver.

The improvements in sanitation and hygiene mentioned above stand behind the world's population explosion. When these innovations in protective health care were first made in the Western countries they were followed by an increase in population. However, heightened population levels began to tail off at a later period. Most Western nations are today experiencing only a very slight population increase, and in some populations rates are less than zero: that is to say, the overall level of population is declining. In non-Western countries, the introduction of modern methods of health care took place in cultural conditions in which there were few incentives for people to reduce their numbers of offspring. Consequently, in many of these countries, population levels have climbed steeply. In reading 66 Betsy Hartmann argues that large-scale population increase is not the same as 'overpopulation'. According to Hartmann, the world's population explosion is now coming under control. The key is economic security. No country which has a high infant mortality rate – that is, where a high proportion of children die at birth or soon afterwards – has managed to bring down its birth rate. For it is only when people can be sure that children will survive that they start to take steps substantially to reduce family size.

64   Roy Porter and Dorothy Porter

Sickness and Health in Pre-modern England

In the eighteenth century in particular, deadly fevers – contemporaries called them 'spotted', 'miliary', 'hectic', 'malignant', etc. – struck down hundreds of thousands, young and old alike, while the so-called 'new' diseases gained ground – some crippling, such as rickets; some fatal, such as tuberculosis. Today's minor nuisance, like 'flu, was yesterday's killer. 'The Hooping Cough is yet with us,' wrote George Crabbe in 1829, '& many children die of it.' And all this against a background of endemic maladies, such as malaria and infantile diarrhoea, and a Pandora's box of other infections (dysentery, scarlatina, measles, etc.) that commonly proved fatal, above all to infants, to say nothing of a hundred and one other pains, eruptions, swellings, ulcers, scrofula, and wasting conditions, not least the agonizing stone and the proverbial gout, which threatened livings and livelihoods, and all too often life itself.

Resistance to infection was evidently weak. This is hardly surprising. Precipitate demographic rise under the Tudors, followed by climatic reverses and economic crises under the Stuarts, had swollen the ranks of the malnourished poor. New and virulent strains of disease possibly emerged. England's good communications network and high job and geographical mobility – it was a land of 'movers' rather than 'stayers' – proved favourable to disease spread: the market society meant free trade in maladies. Few settlements were far enough off the beaten track to escape epidemic visitations travelling along the trade routes (out-of-the-way places could, however, have impressively high life expectancies). And yet the regionality of what was still largely a rural society also meant that disease spread erratically and patchily, with the consequence that there was always a large reservoir of susceptibles, not yet immune, especially among the young, ready sacrificial victims to smallpox or scarlet fever.

Above all, pre-modern medicine had few effective weapons against the infections from which people died like flies. Once smallpox, enteric fever or pneumonia struck, doctors fought a losing battle. In the generation after 1720, the population of England and Wales actually *declined*, primarily because of the ravages of epidemic disease.

Our understanding of the biology of man in history has vastly improved. As yet, however, little attention has been paid to what this ceaseless Darwinian war between disease and populations meant to the individual, considering disease neither as a black block on a histogram nor just as a trope about the human condition betwixt womb and tomb, but as experienced torment and terror. Every soul lived in the shadow of death; indeed, being in the land of the living was itself the survivor's privilege, for so many of one's peers – one's brothers and sisters – had already fallen by the wayside, having died at birth, in infancy or childhood. Life's fine thread was ever precarious, and every statistic hides a personal tragedy. The historical record abounds with sad tales of those who ate a hearty breakfast in the pink of health, only to be dead of apoplexy or convulsions, plague or, later, cholera, before the week was out. Elizabeth Iremonger told her friend Miss Heber the sad tale of her nephew's wife, Eleanor Iremonger, whose delivery of a boy was followed a week later by a 'fever that baffled all art and, on the ninth morning, she sunk finally to this World!'

'Many dyed sudden deaths lately,' lamented the late Stuart Nonconformist minister, Oliver Heywood, ever alert to the workings of Providence:

1, Nathan Crosly buryed Octob 25 1674, 2, Timothy Wadsworth, dyed Octob 23 suddenly in his chair without sickness, 3, Edw Brooks wife dyed under the cow as she was milking, 4, a woman at great Horton wel, had a tooth drawn, cryed oh my head laid her hand on, dyed immediately, 5, one Richard Hodgsons wife at Bradford on munday Nov. 2, dyed on tuesday the day after, &c.[1]

Over a century later, the Somerset parson, William Holland, marked the bitter fate of a father buried on the day his child was christened. Amid the bumper harvest of the Great Reaper recorded in the *Gentleman's Magazine* obituary columns, many expired when apparently in the prime of health – cut off by mad-dog bites, by sudden strokes or through travelling accidents ('I shall begin to think from my frequent overturns', quipped Elizabeth Montagu, 'a bonesetter a necessary part of my equipage for country visiting'). Accidents are not unique to modern technology and urbanism. A Norwich newspaper noted in 1790 how:

On Thursday last (March) a fine boy, about five years of age, fell thro' the seat of the necessary belonging to Mr. Mapes, in the Hay-market, the reservoir to which is not less than 40 feet deep; in this shocking situation he remained from a quarter past ten till three o'clock in the afternoon, before he was discovered by his cries. A person immediately went down to his relief, and when he had raised him halfway up, the bucket in which the child was, striking against a timber that had not been perceived, he was again precipitated to the bottom head forward.[2]

This child survived; so did others, for instance James Clegg, the Derbyshire minister-cum-doctor, who reported 'a very merciful deliverance when mounting [his] mare'. Many, however, fared worse, such as Thomas Day, leading light of the Lunar Society, who died after being thrown from a half-broken-in horse. Visitations came out of the blue, and some deaths were particularly cruel. A Mrs Fitzgerald went to the theatre, and laughed so much she laughed herself to death. Or take the exemplary exit of the Revd Mr M'Kill, pastor of Bankend in Scotland, so 'remarkable' that it 'made an impression upon the minds of his parishioners':

He mounted the pulpit in good health, lectured as usual, and it being the last sabbath of the year, chose for his text these words. 'we spend our years as a tale that is told'. He was representing, in a very pathetic manner, the fleeting nature of human life, and of all earthly things, when, on a sudden, he dropped down in the pulpit and expired instantly.

'He looks much better than you would imagine,' Lady Jane Coke assured a friend about her husband's convalescence on 26 February 1750: 'sleeps well, and I think I may assure you that he is better to-day than he has been for some time, so that I hope the worst is over.' She tempted fate: before sunset, he was dead.

Disease was matched by other dangers, even oncoming thunderstorms. 'William Church', writes the pious Isabella Tindal, 'was speaking to my son John at the time, and saying "The Lord cometh in his chariot, in the clouds to gather his people to himself"... he was struck by the lightning... and fell down dead.' Falls, drownings, fires, firearm explosions, mishaps with tools, knives and poisons, and traffic accidents were perpetual hazards, not least because without ambulance and casualty services, trauma or blood loss readily proved fatal before effectual medical aid was forthcoming. William III, of course, died after his horse stumbled on a mole-hill (Jacobites toasted the little gentleman in velvet), and the third Cambridge Professor of History met his end tumbling off his horse while drunk. The Revd Ralph Josselin recorded scores of such mishaps, or as he saw them, 'Providences':

> I heard that Major Cletheroe, September 21, coming homewards at Redgewell his Horse, stumbled and fell downe upon him and brake his bowells, he was taken up and spake but he dyed about 4 or 5 hours later, Lord in how many dangerous falls and stumbles hast thou preserved mee....[3]

Most ironically of all, William Stout, the Lancaster Quaker who distrusted doctors and championed self-care, received his first blow in years – a broken leg – when he was run down by the local surgeon's horse.

Some mortifications of the flesh had their black comedy: 'Up, and to the office,' wrote Pepys, '(having a mighty pain in my forefinger of my left hand, from a strain that it received last night in struggling avec la femme que je mentioned yesterday).'[4] Yet serious injuries and often death followed from apparent trifles. Erasmus Darwin's son, Charles, a promising medical student, died of septicaemia following a trivial dissecting-room cut. Unable to take life's pains, multitudes of English people took their lives instead. More philosophical minds reflected on their chances. 'The present is a fleeting moment,' mused Gibbon, just turned fifty,

> the past is no more; and our prospect of futurity is dark and doubtful. This day may *possibly* be my last: but the laws of probability, so true in general, so fallacious in particular, still allow me about fifteen years; and I shall soon enter into the period, which, as the most agreeable of his long life, was selected by the judgement and experience of the sage Fontenelle.

He never did; probability, or, perhaps, Providence, was unkind, and the historian of the Roman Empire declined and fell shortly afterwards through postoperative sepsis following surgery on a hydrocele as big as a football.

Yet Gibbon was lucky: all six of his siblings died in infancy. Samuel Pepys was one of eleven children born to his parents. Only one brother and a sister survived into adulthood. A single measles epidemic massacred nine members of Cotton Mather's fifteen-strong household in early eighteenth-century colonial Boston. Half a century later, Dr Johnson's friend, Hester Thrale, produced twelve children: seven of them did not reach their teens. Out of William Godwin's twelve brothers and sisters, only half survived to adult life. His contemporary, William Holland, had four children die within a fortnight of scarlet fever. Francis Place's résumé of the brief lives of his own children conveys the appalling arbitrariness of existence:

1.   Ann – born 1792. Died aged 2 years of the small pox
2.   Elizabeth – April 1794. Died in Chile – Mrs Adams
3.   Annie – 27 Jan 1796 – ... Mrs Miers
4.   Francis – 22 June 1798
5.   Jane – died an infant
6.   Henry – d .... d [dates of birth and death unknown]
7   Mary – 6 Jany. 1804
8.   Frederick Wm. – 14 Oct 1805
9.   Jane – 29 Oct 1807
10. Alfred – died an infant
11. John – 1 Jany 1811

12. Thomas – 4 Augst. 1812. Died at Calcutta 16 Sept 1847. Widow and 5 children
13. Caroline – 29 July 1814. Died 1830
14. William } Twins 6 Feb. 1817 { died – 1829
    Henry   }   { died an infant

The radical tailor himself outlived almost all his offspring.

Thus English people during the 'long eighteenth century' were overshadowed by the facts and fears of sickness and by death itself. He had only three complaints, Byron bantered to his friend, Henry Drury, in 1811:

> viz. a Gonorrhea, a Tertian fever, & the Hemorrhoides, all of which I literally had at once, though [the surgeon] assured me the morbid action of only one of these distempers could act at a time, which was a great comfort, though they relieved one another as regularly as Sentinels.[5]

When John Locke's father wrote to him in 1659, assuring him of his 'health and quiet', the son – then training to be a doctor – responded that this was 'a blessing this tumbling world is very spareing of'. For sickness was all too often the unwelcome, omnipresent guest, and households doubled as hospitals. A letter from Lady Caroline Fox to her sister, the Countess of Kildare, sending for medicines, reads like a dispatch from the front:

> ... as yet there is no amendment in my dearest child [Stephen]; he will be better for some hours almost a whole day sometimes then be as bad as ever again. I wonder I keep my spirits so well as I do, but my trust in Providence is great. My poor Charles was restored to me when there were no hopes left, and I will hope for the same blessing again with regard to my dear Ste. Louisa is perhaps set out by this time; seeing her will be a pleasure to me, but I fear she will find a melancholy house ... Poor William has had a little fever, but was well again when I heard of him. ...

'Every body is ill,' exclaimed Keats to his brother in 1820. This was neither a metaphysical paradox nor a piece of poetic licence, but merely an update on his friends and family.

Not surprisingly, therefore, health was on everybody's mind and filled their conversations. Sickness challenges the stomach (the two are not unconnected) for pride of place in Parson Woodforde's diaries. 'I was very nervous today. My Cow a great deal better this morning,' he chronicled on 17 January 1796. The next day:

> Poor Mr Bodham much altered for the worse. It is thought that he cannot long survive, fallen away amazingly, takes but very, very little notice of anything. Laudanum and Bark his chief Medicine. Dr. Lubbock & Dr. Donne from Norwich have both been there lately, and they say that he is out of the reach of any Medicine, he might live some little time, but is beyond recovery.

Some things improved. The day after, his cow-doctor visited her and pronounced 'her to be ... out of all danger'.

Thus, in the world we have lost, sickness was a constant menace. 'One's very body', suggested Tobias Smollett – himself, of course, a doctor as well as a novelist – should be seen as a 'hospital'. Just as prudence dictated that every man should be his own lawyer, so every man should be his own physician, for he, if anyone, was expert in his own 'case' (contemporary idiom for both 'body' and 'corpse'). So it is hardly surprising that the everyday lives of ordinary people in earlier centuries reverberate with their own ailments, and those of their kith and kin.

65   Ross Hume Hall

Health-care Systems and the Medical–Industrial Complex

What drives the health-care system of industrialized countries? Is it the medical doctors, the government health bureaucracies, people's desire for good health? They all do in a sense, but the main engine that propels the health-care system is high medical technology and the industries that develop and sell the technology. The drug industry, of course, is very much part of this high-technology sector and, as we noted previously, it has become a force in the lives of consumers, the majority of whom consume its products daily. But medical technology also includes medical equipment, diagnostic services, hospitals; and medical care revolves around this technology. Medical care, in fact, could be said to be application of this technology to consumers, who in their ready acceptance of it have come to equate their health with machines, drugs and laboratory tests. This almost total reliance for health care on high medical technology is paradoxical, because in spite of its power to manipulate human biology, this technology fails to deliver on much of its promise of health. It is indeed a tribute to the almost universal acceptance of the technology that its failures are all but ignored....

High medical technology by itself is neutral. It is not the technology *per se* that makes health policy good or bad: it is the institutions that use it. So this [discussion] is not to be taken as a critique of high medical technology, but a critique of its use and misuse.

The one institution that gives high medical technology its life and direction lacks a formal name but is often referred to as the *medical–industrial complex*, a group of industries that develops and markets drugs, medical equipment and supplies and provides a variety of health services. It is closely bound up with the medical profession – absolutely essential for the industry – because only physicians can legally apply medical technology and services to patients. In other words, the industry can only market its products and services through medical doctors. The companies make their money selling their goods and services, the physicians make their money applying the technology; hence the tightness of the complex.

The medical–industrial complex is no small industry. It employs some 10 million people in the United States and comparable numbers in other countries. It operates just as effectively in countries like Britain and Sweden with government-run health-care systems, because these systems are equally dependent on the technologies and services of the medical–industrial complex. It is in the United States, however, that the complex perhaps receives most attention and that public argument over its role in health care is most abrasive. But it is hard to detect in that argument any interest in a place for a preventive health strategy. Rather, public argument revolves around the efficiency of the complex – does it cost too much for the health care it delivers?...

Health policy in the industrialized nations for the past several decades has concentrated almost exclusively on making high medical technology accessible to everyone.

To explore this point further, we will look at two government health programmes: Medicare in the United States and the National Health Service in
Britain.

First Medicare. The United States lacks a single, universal health programme
comparable to the government health services of Sweden and Britain. There is a
mosaic of programmes in the American health sector, but the thrust of all of
them is the same – access to high-tech medical care. The method of paying for
that access, however, varies, with a mixture of private and government payment. And surprisingly, although the United States is thought of as the ultimate
in free-market medicine, the federal government finances 40 per cent of the
country's medical bills. Medicare is the centrepiece of these programmes, providing medical cover to 33 million Americans who are disabled or 65 years of
age and older. As the following anecdote suggests, this cover is not without its
glitches.

In October 1987, Helen Bennett, 72, of Massapequa, New York, was diagnosed as having a tumour in her chest. Her long-time doctor, Arthur Berken,
wanted to put her in hospital for chemotherapy, but Mrs Bennett, living alone,
did not want to leave her dog, so she asked if she could have the course of
treatments in Berken's office. He agreed, and over the next three weeks, Mrs
Bennett spent two hours a day, four times a week, receiving the anti-cancer
drugs Adriamycin and Dacarbazine.

But the system of Medicare disbursement has become highly bureaucratic and
expensive to administer, and moreover, it tries to direct treatment without
regard to cost or benefit to patient. Thus, although Mrs Bennett's treatment
proceeded to the satisfaction of both patient and doctor, the trouble began when
Dr Berken tried to bill the Medicare plan. According to the *New York Times*,
which reported the situation, Berken received an anonymous computer printout
saying that his treatment 'was not reasonable and necessary'. How could Medicare make a value judgement without any knowledge of what's going on?
Berken asked. He explained that chemotherapy is generally given in hospital,
but Mrs Bennett being an outpatient could go home every day, a cheaper
arrangement than spending three weeks in hospital. He tried phoning the Medicare office but received more unsigned printouts rejecting the claim. Exasperated, Berken contacted his Congressman, Robert Mrazek, and solicited his help
in finding 'one human being to explain to me their logic'.

Mrazek, who presumably would rather be dealing with national affairs, was so
overloaded with similar Medicare complaints from his constituents – 240 in the
past year – that he hired a full-time assistant to help sort out the problems. In
the case of Helen Bennett, it was several months before Berken, Mrazek's
assistant and a *New York Times* reporter managed to track down the 'one
human being' they were after: Gloria McCarthy, of a private insurance company
contracted by the government to handle Medicare claims, Empire Bluecross–
Blue Shield. McCarthy, head of the company's Medicare outpatient programme,
said that Empire Bluecross was reconsidering its outpatient chemotherapy policy
and that most such claims would now be paid. But until Berken, and apparently
other doctors, complained, the Medicare insurance company tried to force
patients into the more expensive hospitals by withholding payment for outpatient care.

To understand why Dr Berken had difficulty in recovering his outpatient fee is
to understand one reason for the ballooning cost of Medicare. When the Medicare bill was signed into law by President Johnson in 1965, it was thought the cost
to the government would be modest. In 1967 the programme cost only $3.4
billion, but by 1987, that cost had risen to $158 billion and was still rising.

Joseph Califano predicts that this one government programme alone will cost American taxpayers $600 billion by the year 2000.

As long ago as 1936, the federal government wanted to attach a health-care plan to social security legislation, but opposition from organized medicine, namely the American Medical Association (AMA), so cowed Congressmen that the idea of health benefits for the elderly was dropped. The AMA's lobbying against such legislation continued, and when the idea of a Medicare programme was resurrected in the 1960s, Congressmen realized that the programme would not work without the doctors' co-operation. Congress made substantial concessions to both doctors and hospitals in order to get the legislation passed, concessions that are at the root of Medicare's problems today.

AMA's main opposition to Medicare, which it called socialized medicine, was that it did not want any party coming between doctor and patient. The doctors wanted no interference in how they practised medicine or billed patients. But by the mid-1960s doctors were accustomed to private insurance plans that paid a fee to the doctor or hospital for each patient and for each service rendered. The major insurance carriers in this area were Blue Cross for doctors' bills and Blue Shield for hospital bills, and both carriers were structured to serve the interests of doctors and hospitals. The government, in passing the Medicare legislation, agreed that it would simply foot the bill and that administration of Medicare would be handled through the private insurance carriers. Doctors like Berken simply bill the regional insurance company administering Medicare.

Paul Starr, a Harvard sociologist who has studied the evolution of the American health-care system, noted that in this act, 'the federal government surrendered direct control of the programme and its costs.' In fact, it not only surrendered control over costs, it surrendered control over the introduction and use of high-tech medicine, one reason why in the United States evaluation of new medical technology is virtually non-existent. The medical–industrial complex can develop a piece of equipment or a new procedure and introduce it into wide use – paid for by Medicare or other insurance programmes – unhampered by awkward questions about whether or not it benefits people's health. . . .

Is the dominance of health care by the medical–industrial complex a phenomenon only of the freewheeling open market of the United States or is it more widespread? Let us look at the British National Health Service, a system of universal health care tightly run by the government. . . .

The National Health Service is also structured in [terms of] a two-tier system of doctors. Thirty-five per cent of British doctors practise as independent contractors, called general practitioners (GPs), that is, they are prepared to look after all members of the family. They are the equivalent of family doctors in the United States. General practitioners work in a private office or a community clinic, and each signs up a panel of patients which he or she contracts to look after. Patients select a doctor within their area, establishing a doctor–patient bond – a bond that, ironically, many United States physicians practising in corporate-run clinics have lost. Doctors are paid a capitation fee, a sum for each patient on the panel, regardless of the number of times the patient sees the doctor. A GP has on average 2,200 individuals on his panel, and in the course of a year sees 600 of them with coughs and colds, 325 with skin disorders including dandruff, 100 with chronic rheumatism, 50 with high blood pressure, 8 with heart attacks, 5 with appendicitis and 5 with strokes.[1]

The tier of GPs acts as a primary screen for the National Health Service. GPs treat patients with minor complaints or, if they judge the complaints to be more serious, they refer patients to specialists, called consultants. Consultants occupy the second tier, the top position of privilege and power in the Service. Consultants are attached to a hospital and are relatively few in number. Only about 20 per cent of registered doctors in Britain are consultants, compared with 85 per cent of doctors in the United States who practise a speciality. The National Health Service pays each consultant a salary, and in addition, consultants are allowed a percentage of time to engage in private practice on a fee-for-service basis. Consultants control their own professional standards and have a major voice in the organization and the standard of medical care delivered in their hospitals. Because of their prestige and status, they influence strongly the way the British public and government think about human health.

The work of the consultants revolves around the expensive high-tech medical care delivered by hospitals. In fact, the whole National Health Service revolves around the hospitals and about 65 per cent of the country's doctors (including the consultants) work in hospitals. This is the style of medicine determined by the machines and drugs of the medical–industrial complex. There are differences in degree between British hospitals and American ones, but the high-tech styles are identical. British hospitals tend to have fewer pieces of expensive equipment and because the number of consultant positions in each hospital is controlled, they have, for example, only half as many surgeons per capita as the United States. British doctors are less inclined to subject their patients to major operations and other high-tech procedures. A heart bypass operation, for instance, is performed about one quarter as often as in the United States, and there seems to be no difference in outcome of patients with heart conditions. In fact, according to Roger Hollingsworth, a sociology professor at the University of Wisconsin, who has compared the medical systems of Britain and the United States, there is no real difference in the level of care.

British doctors may use high technology to a lesser degree, but this does not suggest less faith in the technology. They are just as strong proponents of new and improved technology as their American counterparts. They use expensive high technology less because the equipment is not so readily available. But less expensive technology, such as drugs, they prescribe as freely or even more freely than doctors in the United States.

Although both US and British doctors tend to be paternalistic towards their patients – 'doctor knows best' – British doctors carry paternalism to a far greater extent. The plus side, at least from the point of view of cost containment, is that the British doctor is better able to persuade a patient not to undergo treatments for which there is no benefit. They are able to say, 'look, this is all we can do for your cancer or for your chronic arthritis' – and the patient accepts the decision. Contrast this attitude with that in the United States where treatment ends only with the patient's last breath. A British doctor who worked in an American hospital was astounded at the amount of treatment given patients: 'Rarely does an American doctor state that there is no surgery that would help, no drug that is advantageous, and no further investigation is required. There seems to be an irresistible urge always to do something, even though in many cases the doctor concerned must realize that there is no possibility of benefit.'

The more authoritarian relationship between British doctor and patient has its disadvantages. Arrogance and a faith in the infallibility of their own judgement mean that there is little likelihood of doctors questioning their own belief system of health and disease and even less of admitting that there are alternative ways of preserving health. You can see this arrogance expressed in the fate of one experiment in alternative medical care.

This experiment, set up in the London suburb of Peckham in the 1930s by two medical doctors, Scott Williamson and Innes Pearse, created a total health plan for some 2,000 families. The plan, with its own large social centre, encouraged fitness, social conviviality and good health practices. Williamson, Pearse and their medical staff got to know their families very well, giving them the kind of health maintenance that avoided illness. The plan enjoyed great success for about ten years before it was scrapped in 1948 by the newly introduced National Health Service. There were to be no funds for this type of programme.

A dogged group of British doctors and associates, some of whom once worked in the Peckham programme, have tried to rekindle a similar programme since 1948, but the idea of a wellness programme has been consistently rebuffed both by the British medical societies and by the government health bureaucracy. The belief that prevailed in 1948, that such programmes are unnecessary for health maintenance, prevails still.

The National Health Service was founded on the egalitarian principle that although most people do not mind seeing someone else drive a Rolls-Royce, everyone is entitled to a heart bypass operation. Aneurin Bevan, the minister in the British Labour government responsible for introducing the National Health Service in 1948, firmly believed that when the less advantaged citizens – those then unable to afford health care – had access to doctors and drugs, their diseases would vanish. He predicted that the need for medical facilities would decline. What he did not anticipate was the capacity of the modern health-care system to generate new demand based, in large part, on the patient's desire for access to heart transplants and CT scans. Bevan also made the mistake of equating access to doctors and their technology with access to health.

Bevan did not then, nor does the British government now, see human health in its whole relation to society and the natural environment in the way that Williamson and Pearse did. The government is satisfied to limit its focus on health to gritty debates over hospital budgets and the way the National Health Service is run. A comprehensive legislative approach to human health is just as absent as it is in the United States.

But now, forty years after the introduction of the National Health Service, slogan and fiscal reality clash: costs and demands for expensive medical technology keep pushing on the government's limits. Its response was to restrict hospital services, forcing . . . hospital managers to ration the services they offer. But now the government has gone further. It announced plans in 1989 to revolutionize the National Health Service, bringing it closer to the American free-market health-care system. 'For the first time since the NHS was founded in 1948, doctors will be encouraged to see patients as revenue sources and expense centres,' said Gordon Best, director of the King's Fund College, an organization that trains health managers.[2]

So it seems the revolution in health care has more to do with management and costs than with health; the obvious intent is to continue universal access to high-tech medical care, but to make it more revenue-effective.

66   Betsy Hartmann

Rethinking the World Population Problem

An art historian turns to me at a party: 'You're writing a book on population control? My field is aesthetics, and I feel that overpopulation is destroying the beauty of great cities like Paris. Ugly immigrants' housing is springing up all over the place.'

The babysitter turns off the TV. 'I've been thinking about it,' he says. 'If they don't force people to be sterilized in India, how are they going to cope with the population explosion?'

An accounting professor explains how pharmaceutical companies could develop cures for many of the basic diseases that afflict poor people, but don't because the people who need them are too poor to pay. 'Maybe it's not such a bad thing,' he adds. 'After all, if more poor people survive, it will only exacerbate the population problem.'

An economist, known for his radical views on the United States economy, surprises me by saying that many third world countries have no choice but to initiate harsh population control measures. 'Their economic survival is at stake,' he asserts.

I grow to expect such responses from people, no matter how well-meaning or well educated they are. They are repeating a message they have read in the newspaper, heard in the classroom, and seen on television so many times that it has become conventional wisdom. It first captured the popular imagination in 1968, when Stanford University biologist Paul Ehrlich published his famous book *The Population Bomb*. He warned that mankind was breeding itself into oblivion and endorsed stringent population control measures, including compulsion if necessary. Probably most readers have the same impression: that the population bomb is exploding out of control. It is the starting-point of most discussions about population – and, unfortunately, the end-point as well.

The myth of overpopulation is one of the most pervasive myths in Western society, so deeply ingrained in the culture that it profoundly shapes the culture's world-view. The myth is compelling because of its simplicity. More people equal fewer resources and more hunger, poverty and political instability. This equation helps explain away the troubling human suffering in that 'other' world beyond the neat borders of affluence. By procreating, the poor create their own poverty. We are absolved of responsibility and freed from complexity.

But the population issue is complex. To put it into proper perspective requires exploring many realms of human experience and addressing difficult philosophical and ethical questions. It entails making connections between fields of thought that have become disconnected as the result of narrow academic specialization. It demands the sharpening of critical faculties and clearing the mind of received orthodoxies. And above all, it involves transcending the alienation embodied in the very terms 'population bomb' and 'population explosion'. Such metaphors suggest destructive technological processes outside human control. The population issue is about people, about individuals. More than we may realize, it concerns ourselves. . . .

On the surface, fears of a population explosion are borne out by basic demographic statistics. In the twentieth century the world has experienced an unprecedented increase in population. In 1900 global population was 1.7 billion, in 1950 it reached 2.5 billion, and today nearly 5 billion people inhabit the earth. Three-quarters of them live in the third world. The United Nations predicts that world population will reach 6 billion by the end of the century and will eventually stabilize at about 10.5 billion by the year 2110, though such long-term demographic projections are notoriously imprecise.

Initially, this rapid increase in population was due to some very positive factors: advances in medicine, public health measures and better nutrition meant that more people lived longer. In most industrialized countries, the decline in mortality rates was eventually offset by declines in birth rates, so that population growth began to stabilize in what is called the 'demographic transition'. Many countries have now reached the 'replacement level' of fertility and in some the population is actually declining.

Today birth rates are also falling in most areas of the third world, with the exception of sub-Saharan Africa. In fact, the *rate* of world population growth has been slowing since the mid-1960s, and this decline is likely to accelerate in the years ahead. While world population is still growing in absolute terms, the 'explosion' is gradually fizzling out.

Nevertheless, there is still considerable discrepancy between birth rates in the industrialized world and birth rates in the third world. Conventional wisdom has it that third world people continue to have so many children because they are ignorant and irrational – they exercise no control over their sexuality, 'breeding like rabbits'. This 'superiority complex' of many Westerners is one of the main obstacles in the way of meaningful discussion of the population problem. It assumes that everyone lives in the same basic social environment and faces the same set of reproductive choices. Nothing is further from the truth.

In many third world societies, having a large family is an eminently rational strategy of survival. Children's labour is a vital part of the family economy in many peasant communities of Asia, Africa and Latin America. Children help in the fields, tend animals, fetch water and wood and care for their younger brothers and sisters, freeing their parents for other tasks. Quite early in life, children's labour makes them an asset rather than a drain on family income. In Bangladesh, for example, boys produce more than they consume by the age of 10–13 and by the age of 15 their total production has exceeded their cumulative lifetime consumption. Girls likewise perform a number of valuable economic tasks, which include helping their mothers with cooking and the postharvest processing of crops.

In urban settings, children often earn income as servants, messenger boys, etc., or else stay home to care for younger children while their parents work. Among the Yoruba community in Nigeria, demographer John Caldwell found that even urban professional families benefit from many children through 'sibling assistance chains'. As one child completes education and takes a job, he helps younger brothers and sisters move up the educational and employment ladder, and the connections and the influence of the family spread.

Recently some analysts have claimed that the value of children's labour is declining in many third world countries, especially among the rural poor. As the landholdings of the poorest get even smaller, they no longer need as many children to work the land. At the same time, falling wages mean that the landless cannot afford to raise many children to the age at which they would become productive. For these reasons, the desired family size may fall.

However, this argument ignores the other crucial reason for having children: security. In most third world societies, the vast majority of the population has no access to insurance schemes, pension plans or government social security. It is children who care for their parents in their old age – without them one's future is endangered. The help of grown children can also be crucial in surviving the periodic crises – illness, drought, floods, food shortages, land disputes, political upheavals – which, unfortunately, punctuate village life in most parts of the world.

By contrast, parents in industrialized countries and their affluent counterparts among third world urban elites have much less need to rely on children for either labour or old-age security. The economics of family size change as income goes up, until children become a financial burden instead of an asset. When children are in school, for example, they no longer serve as a source of labour. Instead parents must pay for their education, as well as for their other needs, which cost more in a high-consumption society than in a third world village. Today in the United States the cost of raising one child to the age of eighteen ranges close to $100,000, not including the cost of a college education.

At the same time, in industrialized societies personal savings, pension plans and government programmes replace children as the basic forms of social security. These social changes, arising from higher incomes, fundamentally alter the value of children, making it far more rational from an economic standpoint to limit family size.

Son preference is another important motive for having large families. The subordination of women means that economically and socially daughters are not valued as highly as sons in many cultures. Not only does daughters' domestic work have less prestige, but daughters typically provide fewer years of productive labour to their parents, because in many third world countries, they marry and leave home to live with their in-laws shortly after puberty.

Son preference, combined with high infant and child mortality rates, means that parents must have many children just to ensure that one or two sons survive. A computer simulation found that in the 1960s an Indian couple had to bear an average of 6.3 children to be confident of having one son who would survive to adulthood. In the African Sahel, the delicate ecological zone on the southern edge of the Sahara desert, the figure is even higher – the birth of ten children is needed to provide a 95 per cent chance of one son surviving to the age of 38.

High infant and child mortality rates are in fact one of the most important causes of high birth rates. Each year in the third world more than 10 million children die before reaching their first birthday. The average infant mortality rate is more than 90 deaths per 1,000 live births, compared to 20 in the industrialized countries. The situation is especially severe in Africa, where sixteen countries have infant mortality rates in excess of 150 per 1,000.

High infant mortality means that parents cannot be sure their children will survive to contribute to the family economy and to take care of them in their old age. The poor are thus caught in a death trap: they have to keep producing children in order that some will survive.

For many parents, the death of a child is a profound reminder of the basic insecurity of life, leading to the desire for more surviving children than they might have wanted otherwise. A study in an Egyptian village found that a mother who has lost at least one child will have more births and desire more surviving children than women in the same community who have lost no children. In the Philippines, too, total fertility is lower among couples who have not experienced the death of a child.

At first glance, it might appear that reductions in infant mortality would actually *increase* the rate of population growth, since there would be more surviving children to grow up into fertile adults. The third world population surge of the 1950s and 1960s came about through such a reduction in mortality rates without a corresponding reduction in birth rates. Experience has shown, however, that once mortality rates fall to around 15 per 1,000 people per year, the average for the third world today, each further decline in the mortality rate is generally accompanied by an even greater decline in the birth rate, as people adjust their fertility to improved survival possibilities. This has led UNICEF director James Grant to conclude: 'Paradoxically, therefore, a "survival revolution" which halved the infant and child mortality rate of the developing world and prevented the deaths of six or seven million infants each year by the end of the century would also be likely to prevent between 12 and 20 million births each year.'[1]

... Two basic sets of rights are at issue. First is the right of everyone on the earth today, not just in the future, to enjoy a decent standard of living through access to food, shelter, health care, education, employment and social security. Despite present high rates of population growth, most – if not all – societies have the means to guarantee this right to all their people, if wealth and power were shared more equitably. A fairer distribution of resources between the industrialized world and the third world is just as necessary.

Once people's physical survival is ensured and children are no longer their only source of security, history shows that population growth rates fall voluntarily. Higher living standards across the board were the motor force behind the demographic transition in the industrialized world. Similarly, those third world countries, whether capitalist, socialist or mixed-economy, which have made broad-based development a priority have also experienced significant reductions in population growth, often at relatively low levels of per capita income. These include Cuba, Sri Lanka, Korea, Taiwan and China. Meanwhile, a country like India, where the benefits of substantial economic growth have flowed disproportionately to a small elite, still has high rates of population growth despite the massive amount of resources the government has devoted to population control.

The right to a decent standard of living is necessary but not sufficient. The other critical right is the fundamental right of women to control their own reproduction. The expansion of reproductive choice, not population control, should be the goal of family planning programmes and contraceptive research.

What exactly is reproductive choice? Narrowly conceived, it means offering women a broad range of birth-control methods, including legal abortion, from which they can freely choose. But the choice is really less in the specific product than in the ongoing relationship between the provider and the recipient of family planning services. Good screening, counselling, follow-up and genuine informed consent depend on respect for the needs and the experience of the individual woman (or man). She must be the ultimate arbiter in the decision of whether or not to use contraception and which method to choose. Her womb belongs to her.

The question of reproductive choice ultimately goes far beyond the bounds of family planning programmes, involving women's role in the family and in society at large. Control over reproduction is predicated on women having greater control over their economic and social lives and sharing power equally with men.

While reducing poverty reduces birth rates, so does reducing patriarchy. The sheer physical burden of many pregnancies in close succession means that women who are free to control their reproduction seldom opt for having all the children it is biologically possible for them to have. And when women have access to education and meaningful employment, they tend to want fewer children for the obvious reason that they have other options.

To say that guaranteeing these two basic sets of rights will help to reduce population growth is not to say that these rights should be pursued for this purpose. On the contrary, once social reforms, women's projects, and family planning programmes are organized for the explicit goal of reducing population growth, they are subverted and ultimately fail. The individual no longer matters in the grand Malthusian scheme of things, which is by its very nature hostile to social change. Instead, these basic rights are worthy of pursuit in and of themselves; they have far more relevance to the general improvement of human welfare than reducing population growth alone ever will.

Part 17

Revolutions and Social Movements

Revolutions, revolutionary movements and social movements more generally have been key influences shaping the development of modern societies. The American Revolution of 1776 and the French Revolution of 1789 are generally accepted as being the two prime happenings which set the stage for subsequent revolutionary endeavours. In the twentieth century, however, most revolutions have been influenced by Marxism, including those that have affected the largest number of people, the Russian and Chinese Revolutions. However, the revolutionary changes that occurred in Eastern Europe in 1989 were inspired by ideals closer to the American and French Revolutions than to those of Marxism – whose influence, indeed, they have specifically combated.

It is not easy to define what should count as a revolution, as reading 67 by Michael S. Kimmel indicates. Revolutions are usually considered to involve the activities of a mass movement which succeeds in overthrowing an established government by force. However, it is not easy to separate revolution, defined in this way, from a *coup d'état*, which also involves a forcible seizure of power. The 1989 revolutions in Eastern Europe mostly did not involve the use of force, nor was there in any of these instances an organized revolutionary movement. None the less, in terms of the definition which Kimmel arrives at – that revolutions are 'attempts by subordinate groups to transform the social foundations of political power', the 1989 transformations in Eastern Europe would be instances of genuinely revolutionary activity.

The second selection in this part, reading 68 by Johan Galtung, examines a social movement which is not revolutionary in terms of the above definition, but which certainly has radical objectives. The ideals of the Green movement, Galtung points out, cross-cut orthodox political mechanisms. Most Western countries now have 'Green parties' but their aims and objectives can hardly be confined to the normal limits of the political arena. In general terms, the 'Green movement' actually consists of a diverse, and to some extent internally heterogeneous, collection of parties, groups and associations. None the less, there are clear similarities in the aims and ambitions of different sectors of the Green movement. In this reading Galtung offers an overall portrayal of some of these common characteristics, noting how far-reaching are the social changes they imply.

The final item in this part provides a direct discussion of the recent changes in Eastern Europe (reading 69). Deirdre Boden acknowledges that these events in some ways resembled other patterns of revolutionary change, but she insists that they also had new and unusual characteristics. The course of their development, she proposes, has to be understood in terms of the influence of the mass media. (The reader might at this point like to refer back to Part 11, in which general aspects of modern mass communications are discussed.)

Boden points out that the changes of 1989 were more intensively analysed and reported in the media than any comparable set of events hitherto. In the age of satellite communications, images from one context are rapidly transmitted to another, setting up broad waves of mutual influence. We meet yet again here the theme of globalization: according to Boden, the changes of 1989 were triggered and shaped by mediated interactions. The global reporting of events provided models for challenges to pre-existing political orders that would otherwise have seemed unrealizable.

67   Michael S. Kimmel

What is a Revolution?

There's a well-known story about King Louis XVI in France. As the king observed the protests in the streets of Paris in 1789, he turned to his friend, the duc de La Rochefoucauld-Liancourt, and exclaimed, 'My God! It's a revolt!' 'No, Sire,' La Rochefoucauld is said to have replied. 'That is a revolution.'

La Rochefoucauld's reply is justly celebrated because it revealed how the king was unable to perceive what was occurring beneath his window, but it also suggests several questions – questions that lie at the heart of social science thinking about revolution. How could La Rochefoucauld know the difference between a revolt and a revolution? What are the distinguishing features of each? If we were standing at the window with the king and his duc, would we have known enough to agree with the duc?

The central questions in the study of revolution have plagued social scientists, philosophers and even kings, for centuries. What are revolutions? Why do they occur? Why do some succeed and others fail? Are revolutions necessarily violent upheavals, or can there be non-violent revolutions? Why do people rebel? What motivates them to risk their lives for such a cause?

Revolutions are of central importance for social scientists not only because they are extreme cases of collective action, but also because revolutions provide a lens through which to view the everyday organization of any society. '[T]he understanding of revolution is an indispensable condition for the fuller knowledge and understanding of society'.[1] Revolutions are also important for us to understand not as social scientists but as citizens: we live in a world in which over half of the inhabitants of the planet live in a country that has undergone a revolution in this century. Our age is a revolutionary age, and in order to be responsible citizens, it is imperative that we begin to understand this phenomenon. Revolutions are events which deeply affect our lives. In fact, 'excepting war, religion, and romantic love, nothing in ordinary human experience has so inflamed the imagination of men, encouraged so many romantic illusions, or broken so completely with the ordinary routine of existence, as has been true of revolution'.[2]

What is more, revolutions make a moral claim on our sensibilities. Revolutions demand that we take sides, that we commit ourselves to a political position. It is difficult to remain neutral during a revolution. At the more international level, revolutionaries often make large claims about what they will accomplish if they are successful in an effort to enlist support from those of us in advanced industrial countries. The support of the major industrial powers, or at least the withdrawal of support for the established regime, has historically been central to the success of revolutions in the twentieth century. So revolutionaries will make moral and political demands of us, even if we do not live in a revolutionary society ourselves. . . .

Revolutions are a central phenomenon to all theories of society, and have proven a popular subject to study. As the editorial foreword to an issue of *Comparative Studies in Society and History* put it in 1980, '[o]utbursts of violence attract social scientists the way volcanic eruptions draw geologists, as specific events inviting measurement that promise to reveal subterranean forces which may in turn reflect still more basic structures'. As a result of this popularity, and the different theoretical postures which social scientists assume, there seem to be as many theories of revolution as there are theorists. . . .

The first question [we must ask] about revolution concerns what we mean by the term. Definitions abound, and there is little consensus about what a revolution is, let alone why it may occur. Let's start with a definition drawn from a non-social-scientific source: the *Oxford English Dictionary* defines revolution as 'A complete overthrow of the established government in any country or state by those who were previously subject to it; a forcible substitution of a new ruler or form of government.' This definition implies that revolutions take place on the political level, involving governments and rulers, and that they must be 'complete' and successful in order to count as revolutions. It also equates the imposition of a new ruler with a revolutionary transformation of society.

Aristotle understood revolutions to be qualitatively different from these simple changes in political leadership, although he agreed that success was a criterion of the term. In *Politics*, Aristotle wrote that there were 'two sorts of changes in government; the one affecting the constitution, where men seek to change from an existing form into something other, the other not affecting the constitution when, without disturbing the form of government, whether oligarchy or monarchy, they try to get the administration into their own hands'.

These two definitions resonate with many of those offered by social scientists. Most definitions, for example, imply that in order to be labelled a revolution, the uprising must be successful. Baecheler defines revolution as a 'protest movement that manages to seize power',[3] and Neumann expands the definition to include a 'sweeping, fundamental change in political organization, social structure, economic property control and the predominant myth of a social order [thereby] indicating a major break in the continuity of development'.[4] Trimberger calls revolution 'an extralegal takeover of the central state apparatus which destroys the economic and political power of the dominant social group of the old regime', which again implies success in the definition.[5]

The last definition also implies the use of violence in a revolution, and many social scientists have placed violence in the centre of their analysis. Thus Friedrich defines revolution as 'the sudden and violent overthrow of an established political order',[6] and Huntington calls it 'a rapid fundamental and violent domestic change in the dominant values and myths of a society, in its political institutions, social structure, leadership, government activity, and policies'.[7] Skocpol offers perhaps the most comprehensive and succinct structural definition: 'Social revolutions are rapid, basic transformations of a society's state and class structure; they are accompanied and in part carried through by class-based revolts from below.'[8] One writer attempts to modify this requirement of violence by arguing that revolution refers to events 'in which physical force (or the convincing threat of it) has actually been used successfully to overthrow a government or regime'.[9]

But is success a *requirement* for a revolution to be called by that name? Such a definition would mean that revolutions that fail be called something else, thus restricting the number of empirical cases to about twenty. This would be unfortunate, because revolutions that fail can provide as many clues to the causes and the process of revolutions as those that succeed.

To posit success of the revolution as a definitional criterion also leads to a serious teleological problem, in which the theorist interprets the origins by their outcomes. During a potential revolution, an 'urban mob' or a mass of 'traditional peasants' may attempt to seize power, and they may think they are making a revolution. Why would social scientists only permit a successful attempt to be labelled a revolution? Are not all such efforts revolutions – some that succeed and some that fail? Does the content of the revolutionary effort change after the fact if the rebels are unsuccessful?...

One useful suggestion might be to hold to a distinction between revolutionary situations and revolutionary outcomes. We can of course imagine situations in which a revolution takes place, but the outcome does not yield the type of society envisioned by the revolution, or in which the forces of the old regime are victorious, either by their own strength or by soliciting aid from abroad. But these are revolutions also, and they are far more numerous than the successful transformations. To include them in the definition, and to draw contrasts between them and the successful revolutions, will, I believe, prove instructive to students of the phenomenon.

... I offer a fairly fluid and simple definition ... *Revolutions are attempts by subordinate groups to transform the social foundations of political power.* Such efforts require confrontation with power-holders, and must stand a reasonable chance of success to differentiate a revolution from other acts of rebellion, such as a social movement or terrorist act. Such a definition is sufficiently broad to include successful and unsuccessful revolutions, to embrace a large number of sequences over various amounts of time, and yet it is specific enough to allow us to distinguish between revolutions and other forms of social change, such as *coups d'état* and rebellions. Although a revolutionary event must stand a reasonable chance of successfully carrying out a programme of social transformation, success is not inevitable. Social movements and seemingly isolated acts of rebellion may trigger wider movements and become revolutions themselves.

68 Johan Galtung

The Green Movement: A Socio-historical Exploration

The Green movement is puzzling people today, particularly when it takes the form of a Green party, and most particularly in connection with the German party, by far the most important one, *Die Grünen*. They are said to be unpredictable and unable/unwilling to make any compromises with any other actors on the party political scene; consequently they are not really in politics, they are only political. For a party launched in 1981, to break through the 5 per cent barrier (they made 5.6 per cent) already in the elections of March 1983 and then move on to 7, 8 and 9 per cent in subsequent elections, is already an achievement and leads to three obvious hypotheses about the future: the Greens will continue their comet-like career; they will find their natural level as a party below 10 per cent but possibly still above 5 per cent; they will dwindle down to zero again which is where they belong.

The following is an effort to explore the phenomenon, particularly directed at ... readers very used to conceiving of politics in terms of blue and red; market forces, protected by conservative parties, and *étatiste* forces with planning and redistribution protected by socialist parties; both of them found in democratic and dictatorial versions. The Greens are obviously different, neither blue nor red, neither dictatorial nor democratic in the parliamentarian sense of [those words]. In spite of participating in parliamentary elections, mass action, direct democracy, local autonomy, self-reliance and so on are obviously closer to their heart.

Hence, what do they stand for, where do they come from, and who are they? This paper does not claim to have conclusive or any novel answers to these

Table 1 A survey of Green policies

Mainstream characteristics	Green policies, movements
Economic basis	
1 Exploitation of *external proletariat*	Co-operative enterprises, movements; labour buyer/seller difference abolished, customers directly involved
2 Exploitation of *external sector* relations; liberation movements	Co-existence with the third world; only equitable exchange
3 Exploitation of *nature*	Ecological balance person–nature; building diversity, symbiosis; complete or partial vegetarianism
4 Exploitation of *self*	More labour- and creativity-intensity; decreasing productivity in some fields; alternative technologies
Military basis	
1 Dependency on *foreign trade*	Self-reliance; self-sufficiency in food, health, energy and defence
2 Dependency on *formal sector*, BCI-complex	Local self-reliance, decreasing urbanization, intermediate technology
3 *Offensive* defence policies, very destructive defence technology	Defensive defence policies with less destructive technology, also non-military non-violent defence
4 *Alignment with superpowers*	Non-alignment, even neutralism; de-coupling from superpowers
Structural basis	
1 *Bureaucracy*, state (plan) strong and centralized	Recentralization of local level; building federations of local units
2 *Corporation*, capital (market) strong and centralized	Building informal, green economy: • production for self-consumption • production for non-monetary exchange • production for local cycles
3 *Intelligentsia*, research strong and centralized	High level non-formal education, building own forms of understanding
4 MAMU factor; BCI peopled by middle-aged males with university education (and dominant race/ethnic group)	Feminist movements, justice/equality and for new culture and structure; movements of the young and the old; movements for racial/ethnic equality
Bourgeois way of life	
1 *Non-manual work*, eliminating heavy, dirty, dangerous work	Keeping the gains when healthy, mixing manual and non-manual
2 *Material comfort*, dampening fluctuations of nature	Keeping the gains when healthy, living closer to nature
3 *Privatism*, withdrawal into family and peer groups	Communal life in bigger units, collective production/consumption
4 *Security*, the probability that this will last	Keeping security when healthy, making lifestyle less predictable
Chemical/circus way of life	
1 Alcohol, tranquillisers, drugs	*Moderation*, experiments with non-addictive, life-enhancing things
2 Tobacco, sugar, salt, tea/coffee	*Moderation*, enhancing the body's capacity for joy, e.g. through sex
3 Chemically treated food, *panem*, natural fibres removed	Bio-organic cultivation, health food, balanced food, *moderation*
4 *Circenses*, TV, sport, spectatorism	Generating own entertainment, *moderate* exercise, particularly as manual work, walking, bicycling

questions, but they are certainly worth exploring: the Greens have probably come here to stay, and to expand. Hence, three analytical approaches: *ideological, historical* and *sociological*; not necessarily compatible, not necessarily contradictory, but well suited to shed some light on the phenomenon.

[Table 1 sets out] 'a survey of Green policies', divided into twenty points, organized in packages with four points each. The mainstream characteristics in first world societies are then confronted with their counterpoints, Green policies and movements. The list is self-explanatory; suffice it here only to add some remarks about how the list came into being.

The point of departure is a simple model of mainstream society with an economic basis, a military basis and a structural basis. The latter is particularly important, for this is where the pillars of the Western social formation are found: the state with its bureaucracy and its plans, capital with its corporations and its markets, and the intelligentsia with its research, serving both of them. In addition to that there is a peculiar selection of people for these institutions: middle-aged males with university education from the dominant racial/ethnic group being preponderant almost everywhere. It is this structure, then, and composed in that particular manner, that organizes the economic and military basis of society. And all of this is done, manifestly, in order to achieve what is here called the 'bourgeois way of life', with its four characteristics, and the somewhat empty 'chemical way of life', with booze, with *panem et circenses*, in ways known to everybody in the first world.

Let me now formulate two assumptions about the Green movement: (1) The Green movement is an umbrella movement for a number of partial movements, each one of them attacking one or more elements on this list; and (2) the Green movement differs from many other social movements in denying that basic social problems can be solved attacking one single factor; a much more holistic approach is needed.

Thus, the Green movement is a federation of constituent movements and aims at an alternative society roughly characterized by the right-hand column in the survey of the policies. Many such lists can be made. This is one of them, not necessarily better or worse than most others; probably somewhat more comprehensive. To be a 'Green', one does not have to subscribe to all of these ideas; one probably has to agree with more than just one of them, however. There is a correlation in the ideological universe and not only because ideas happen to be held by the same people. There is some kind of internal consistency. For one's inner eye is conjured up the vision of a decentralized society, probably some kind of federation, with strongly autonomous units using the local bases in a self-reliant manner, trying not to become dependent on the outside, including for military purposes. Inside this social formation an alternative way of life is supposed to come into being, more or less as described here.

69 Deirdre Boden

Reinventing the Global Village: Communication and the Revolutions of 1989

The revolutions of 1989 in Eastern Europe have been among the most intensively recorded and extensively observed collective moments in human history. At

the heart of the discussion that follows is a concern with the role of communication, in the broadest sense, in the making of revolution. Clearly, there are vast
differences between the social events I am characterizing as 'the revolutions of
1989', in terms simultaneously of their concrete historical origins, their immediate conditions and their local political ideologies, as well as the vast differences
of language, tradition and culture, to say nothing of the actual outcomes of
which we have only a glimmer of insight at this point. For all their important
differences, the revolutions of 1989 have shared a common variable: they have
been significantly affected by the globalization of information technology and
have, in their turn, interactively shaped those media.

I am thus interested, quite specifically, in the role of the mass media and
telecommunications in the tumultuous social change to which we have all been
witness these past months, indeed, primarily through those same media. The
revolutions of 1989 are like no others in human history in certain highly sugges-
tive ways. The past ten years have seen a radical break with past history;
it is one which, I believe, has gone largely unnoticed not only by academics but
by the very social actors engaged in these activities. Not only did no academic or
government specialist predict any of the revolutions of 1989, none of the revolutionaries themselves would have predicted their relative achievements at any
specific point during those same world-changing activities. Indeed, an interesting
motif of 1989 has been the recurrent astonishment of expert and subject alike.
One reason, I believe, for this remarkable underestimation of the direction, rate
and ultimate totality of social transformation in that year was a lack of appreciation of the now global, instantaneous, simultaneous and total effect of the
telecommunications media as a primary agent of social change.[1]

In the classic sociological literature on the subject, revolutions are generally
described as involving fundamental changes in ideology and values, as well as
in social structures and relations of power.[2] More recently, from a structural
perspective, social revolutions have been defined by Skocpol as 'rapid, basic
transformations of a society's state and class structure . . . accompanied and in
part carried through by class-based revolts from below'.[3] These massive transformations necessarily, according to Skocpol, involve mutually reinforcing
changes in both the political and social realms, that is at the level of both the
state and its citizens. In the revolutionary rhetoric of Marxism and a variety of
related conflict theories, rapid social change depends, on the one hand, on
contradictions in the objective structural conditions of a given society and, on
the other, on the ability of a particular class or coalitions of classes to mobilize
their common interests. Many theories are thus structural in their causes and
explanations of revolution, while some are 'actor-oriented'[4] and an emerging
few are both.[5] In these and other writings in revolution, sociologists and their
founding fathers have had a distinct tendency to characterize such upheavals as
occurring from within, from economic conditions, internal class conflict, relative
and perceived deprivation within a social system and so forth. They are, by and
large, endogenous models of social change.[6]

The revolutions of 1989 are nothing of the kind, in at least one irreversible
and unavoidable way. They are global in their inspiration and in their consequences, as well as in their immediacy and intensity. That is to say that they are, to
some considerable degree, exogenously triggered as well as being endogenously
driven. . . .

In a most cursory way, I shall now trace the essential sequencing of events
in Central and Eastern Europe in the autumn of 1989. It is the sequence and
sequential timing of these tumultuous moments that I want to examine, in
relation to what I take to be a multi-media environment of these chained events.
The world is not only wired in some diffuse and general sense. The unfolding

properties of human action, in their finest detail, are temporally, serially and, especially, sequentially interconnected in such a way as to significantly change the consequences. In today's wired world, people do indeed make history, and in new ways. This single, seamless world in which we all live is interactive – continuously, simultaneously and reflexively. While speculative, my assumption is that there was, in effect, a chain reaction triggered by the media images of China in April, May and even June, and of the triumph of Solidarity in the June elections. That 'reaction' was the altogether human one of hope, at first faint, finally filling hearts from Berlin to Baku; in the short span of six months, from June to December 1989, the face of Europe was to light up with it. And, every night, Europeans and others tuned in to that ever-brightening world, as images of human action bounced across satellites and fed along telephone lines into once-dim living-rooms and lives. At the same time, shortwave radio services of the BBC World Service, Radio France, Radio Free Europe, and Voice of America also stepped up transmission and, in some cases, wattage and the number of broadcast hours in Eastern European languages.[7] The medium had not so much become the message as the many messages, across many media, had merged to become a seemingly unstoppable single signal of hope.

The hearts and minds of the peoples of Central and Eastern Europe are just that: European. Their cultures belong to the West, to Roman Christianity, to the traditions and values of Old Europe. Indeed, many of the peoples and languages of the region we conveniently call 'Western' Europe have their roots in the depths of what we now call 'Eastern' Europe. For a Hungarian, a Czech or a Pole, 'the word "Europe" does not represent a phenomenon of geography but a spiritual notion synonymous with the West';[8] if not part of the West, Kundera argues, they are driven from their destiny. Thus, the lure of the West in recent revolutions cannot be seen as a simplistic craving for consumer culture or for essentially 'foreign' ideals. If we are to treat the notion of 'hearts and minds' seriously, we need to engage ideology with emotion, trust with risk, hope with despair. Here we are on tricky ground to be sure, both theoretically and empirically, but it is my suggestion that the dynamism and intensity of the revolutions of 1989 find little explanation in conventional notions of structural conditions or constraints. If, too, we are to be genuine in our theoretical interest in the 'return of the actor', in 'action and its environments', and, most generally, in the nature of human agency, we must examine what people actually do at the intersections of history. Here, this pervasive problematic is presented as the meeting of people and information. The hearts and minds of the people of Eastern Europe have been lit up by the kinetic effects of global communications and local conditions.

In important ways, of course, the immediate events in Eastern Europe in late 1989 were shaped initially by Solidarity's revolution in the shipyards of Gdansk in 1980–1, which led to the military government of General Jaruzelski and culminated in the suppression of Solidarity in late 1981. Although crushed, Solidarity caught the attention of the world during those dark months, and Lech Walesa was to become a major figure in the years that followed. While some have argued for primarily structural explanations for the Polish revolution at that time, it is equally clear that the reflexive articulation by individual Poles of their emerging independence critically shaped Polish discourse in the years to follow, as well as Polish–Soviet relations, especially with Gorbachev's arrival on the Soviet scene in 1985. Scholars have also argued that these early events in Poland were greeted with considerable hostility in East Germany and Czechoslovakia. By 1988 and 1989, it was nevertheless against the backdrop of Solidarity's successful struggle and extended international image that the unfolding of events across Eastern Europe took place.

330 Revolutions and Social Movements

It may be useful to consider some of the everyday underpinnings of this largely unpredicted shift in national identifications. Note, as an almost simplistic geographic starting-point, that the key countries of Central Europe all share borders with West European countries that now have a considerable mix of radio and television facilities, with enhanced transmission capacities, cable linkages and other penetrating technology. East Germans, for example, have long and longingly viewed the lives of their compatriots, not merely in Berlin but all along their borders with West Germany. In recent years, cable TV services have linked all of East Germany to the images from West German television, and thus with Eurovision and full-scale international satellite connections. Hungary shares television borders with Austria, Yugoslavia with Austria and Italy, Bulgaria with Turkey and Greece, Estonia with Finland, and so on. In addition, Radio Free Europe is located in Munich and staffed by expatriates of each of the East European countries who, in recent years, have mostly travelled freely in their former homelands. Their sophisticated knowledge, combined with the considerable cosmopolitan skills of the BBC, Radio France, Voice of America and other similar services, also contributed to the high-tech saturation of information in the critical weeks of 1989. Indeed, these routine windows on the West were to take on special significance in the tense moments of October and, especially, November. In addition, video recorders have become an important aspect of Soviet bloc life. In Poland and elsewhere in Eastern Europe, a major vehicle for the dissemination of ideas and images has been videotapes and VCRs, and Poland soon earned the name of the 'VCR proletariat'. Videos provided a means for developing a kind of 'magnitizdat' of information and alternative ideology. Rock music and jazz have also played an important role, from Budapest to the depths of the Russian continent.

Throughout the summer of 1989, first in Poland with Solidarity's election success, then in Hungary with demonstrations to commemorate the 1956 uprising and in East Germany with early waves of emigration to the West, a series of relatively sporadic changes began to occur.... The key telecommunication connections were television, radio, telephone, print media and – profoundly, I suspect – the complex and highly collaborative exchange of information, news, rumour and deep-seated fear in face-to-face settings. It was, in fact, a time when the long privately held fears, opinions and hopes of the peoples of Eastern Europe moved from personal and intimate settings into the public domain – from backstage to centre stage – in city squares and on world television....

Were we to rerun the events of 1989 in slow motion and with the retrospective clarity of hindsight, the connections between the execution scenes in Bucharest, the crowds on the top of the Berlin Wall and the vision of the Goddess of Democracy in Tiananmen Square might seem obvious. But are they? We know, for example, that the leaders of East Germany and Romania, to name but two, certainly considered the 'Chinese solution' when confronted with the growing physical presence and psychic pressures of their peoples; yet they did not use it. Why not? Certainly part of the reason is that, in Eastern Europe, that sort of solution would depend on the support of the Soviet Union; indeed, in the past, it had been Russian tanks that had imposed just such 'solutions' on the peoples of Hungary, Czechoslovakia and Poland, to name but three prominent examples. But the Soviet relationship with its Eastern bloc satellites has changed in recent years and, even in the early days of Hungary's border relaxation and the demonstrations in Prague, the role of the Russian Bear was more removed and less menacing than it had been for forty years.

Similarly, if we look for a 'cause' of the revolutions of 1989, it can hardly be located simply in political ideology and economic structure, since the countries involved – despite their journalistic label of 'communist bloc' – are far from monolithic. Nor are their relationships with the Soviet Union identical, though it may be fair to say that the most notable common connection may be the person of Mikhail Gorbachev. The latter has certainly loomed large if rather benignly above the heads of the masses of demonstrators – as a central symbol in Eastern Europe, and as a physical presence in Beijing and East Berlin at the height of the demonstrations. But, apart from subscribing to a 'great man' theory of social change, neither Gorbachev's programmes nor his presence can have 'caused' the sort of contagion of ideas and actions that we have seen. Although the causes of these revolutions may elude us for many years to come, the conditions of these extraordinary events clearly involve one element which has been the central focus of attention in this essay: worldwide communication. As noted earlier, any assessment of the conditions of these multiple revolutionary events, or occurrence of a 'revolutionary situation', must surely include careful attention to the interlaced role of information and communication in 1989. In this world of intense and intensive mass communication and social change, 'everyone must change'.[9] . . .

It is not my purpose to suggest that the media *caused* the revolutions. The political and economic crises in both China and Eastern Europe have been years in the making. The countries of Central and Eastern Europe especially, although treated *en bloc*, are far from identical in their relative economic crises, political sophistication, degree of dependence on the Soviet Union and even level of religious solidarity. Each of these factors, and more, play crucial roles in both the emergence and the eventual resolution of these historically located events. And these are 'events', in the fullest sense suggested by Foucault, in that they appear to be not only singular occurrences but instead represent 'the reversal of a relationship of forces, the usurpation of power, the appropriation of a vocabulary . . ., the entry of the masked "other" '.[10] Today, there are union leaders and playwrights as presidents and premiers in Eastern Europe, and a population larger than Western Europe or North America attempting to appropriate the vocabulary of democracy and of capitalism. There are also, in Romania and Bulgaria for instance, considerable signs of resistance to the proposed shift of power. The outcomes of these watershed events will be complex and far from automatic. Indeed, there is a very real danger of anarchy and a return to highly autocratic structures and political solutions, as well as a well-grounded concern for losing the benefits of socialism in the harsh reality of capitalism.

I have been concerned simply to highlight what I take to be a largely invisible yet new and significant aspect of these spontaneous events: the globalization of communication. A central feature of recent global social change has been the instantaneous, simultaneous and essentially non-linear explosion of images, information and, ultimately, ideology. Historically, revolutions have a number of identifying features including the mobilization of new resources in loyalty, political power, terror and, in modern times, education. We can now add a new and, I believe, prospectively powerful dimension to the revolutionary situation: communication. No society, as noted above, can now operate in the sort of secrecy that was possible barely ten years ago. At the time of writing, the unfolding events in the Baltic republics are but a small sample of the shape of things to come. The role of mass media is, as we have seen, largely unanticipated and unintended, so much so that the functional notion of 'role' is largely misplaced. It would also be a mistake to think of mass media as either monolithic or hegemonic. The media's considerable influence is, moreover, so intertwined with other telecommunication innovations as to be compounded by them. The making of the news has been accelerated to such a degree that careful empirical studies will be needed to disentangle the technological from the social.

Part 18

Sociological Research Methods

Sociology is a very variegated subject and a diversity of research methods are commonly used in the course of social investigation. There is no single method of research which commends itself for all types of study: some methods are more appropriate to the analysis of specific problems than are others. Sociologists do not always agree when one approach rather than another should be employed. For instance, some researchers tend to favour methods which generate rich case materials, while others have a preference for gathering data which can be easily quantified.

One of the most widely used methods for collecting information of a richly detailed kind is fieldwork, also commonly known as participant observation. Two contributions (readings 70 and 71) discuss this approach. Robert A. Georges and Michael O. Jones provide a general interpretation of the nature of fieldwork. Fieldwork research, they stress, cannot be carried on in the way in which a natural scientist might conduct an experiment in a laboratory. The researcher must interact with, and gain the confidence of, those whose activities form the concern of the investigation. Fieldworkers face many problems, including the possibility that their research endeavours might have a strong impact upon their own personal attitudes and identity (a phenomenon which, however, some authors argue is actively desirable: the situation should be one of mutual communication). Anna Pollert's study (reading 71) furnishes a concrete example of a fieldwork project. Her description of her experiences as a participant observer in a tobacco factory yields a graphic yet humorous account of the attitudes and outlook of those working within it.

The survey method is used as widely as fieldwork in social research. Surveys are usually carried out by means of questionnaires, either administered directly by the researcher, or sent by post to the individuals concerned. Other variations include telephone or tape-recorded interviews oriented towards a fixed range of questions. In reading 72, Catherine Marsh gives a general description of the survey method and also points out that it is widely used in other disciplines besides sociology.

Joanna Mack and Stewart Lansley (reading 73) employed the survey method in their investigation of poverty in the United Kingdom. Surveys of the poor formed the basis of the celebrated work by Charles Booth, who in the late nineteenth century first brought to public consciousness the level and extent of poverty in London. Mack and Lansley say that their own study reveals an important point about conceptions of poverty today: that most people now interpret poverty not in terms of the minimal material requirements for subsistence, but in terms of a minimal standard of living which everyone living in the country should rightfully expect to achieve.

The final selection in this part (reading 74) discusses conversation analysis, a type of research investigation which recently has become important in sociology. Conversation analysis concentrates on the study of everyday talk. It not only forms a distinctive research orientation but is also linked to a specific general research programme, that of 'ethnomethodology'. Ethnomethodology is essentially the study of the lay or 'folk' methods which ordinary people use in employing language to make themselves understood and to be understood by others. 'Methodology' here, therefore, has a double sense: it refers to the practices of the research observer, but that observer is in turn studying the methodologies of ordinary day-to-day life.

70   Robert A. Georges and Michael O. Jones

The Human Element in Fieldwork

Two facts about the nature of fieldwork are seldom recognized, acknowledged or discussed. First, as individuals move from the planning to the implementation stages of their field research, they discover that they must engage continuously in a process of clarifying for others and for themselves just who they are, what it is they want to find out and why they wish to obtain the information they seek from the individuals they choose as subjects. Second, as fieldworkers interact with their selected subjects, they are confronted with the necessity of being willing and able to compromise. Unlike laboratory scientists, who can control the phenomena that are the focal points of their investigations by controlling the environments and conditions under which these phenomena are examined, individuals whose research plans call for them to study other human beings while interacting with them in non-laboratory settings must surrender a certain amount of the independence and control they enjoy while they are generating their fieldwork projects. For to gain the co-operation of those from whom they need to learn if they are to succeed in their endeavours, fieldworkers must explain, again and again, their identities and intentions in meaningful and acceptable ways. In seeking assistance, fieldworkers implicitly request permission to assume, and indicate their willingness to accept, a subordinate, dependent status *vis-à-vis* those they have chosen to study.

That fieldworkers must become largely dependent upon their research subjects is one of the ironies of fieldwork, creating a source of tension as fieldwork projects are implemented. The irony stems from the fact that while it is fieldworkers who elect to study others rather than others who choose to be studied by fieldworkers, it is the subjects who are knowledgeable, and the fieldworkers who are ignorant, about the phenomena or behaviours that fieldworkers decide to study. For their project plans to succeed, therefore, fieldworkers must be willing to learn and subjects to teach; and the pupil is necessarily subordinate to the teacher. Tensions arise because fieldworkers' conceptions of themselves as subordinate to their subjects conflict with their images of themselves as investigators to whom research subjects are subordinate. Dealing with this conflict creates an ambivalence with which both fieldworkers and subjects must cope. This coping requires clarifying identities and intentions for, and compromising with, both others and self.

Feelings of ambivalence that require fieldworkers to clarify identities and intentions and to compromise arise not only from the conflict between images of self as both independent and dependent, or dominant and subordinate, in their relations with their chosen subjects, but also from differences between themselves and their subjects that fieldworkers conceive to be significant. The differentiation may be based on any one of some combination of such factors as sex, age, race, nationality, native language, religious background, occupation, social or economic status, living environment, relative degree of technological know-how or overall lifestyle. The greater the significance of differences that fieldworkers conceive to exist between themselves and their chosen subjects, the greater the amount of conflict and ambivalence that is apt to arise, and the greater the number of clarifications and compromises that is likely to occur....

Because they plan fieldwork projects and commit themselves to carrying them out, fieldworkers understandably feel that they have the right to become privy to the kinds of information they set out to obtain; yet they are also aware that their selected subjects are under no obligation to provide that information. Similarly, individuals may determine in advance that the successful implementation of their fieldwork projects is dependent upon their filming, photographing, tape-recording, sketching or making written records of the phenomena or behaviours they have singled out for study; yet they know that those they have chosen to study are not obliged to permit such activities. Individuals may also decide that to accomplish the objectives set forth in their research plans, they must interact on a day-to-day basis and for an extended period of time with their chosen subjects; yet they are also cognizant of the fact that subjects are not required to welcome, accept, accommodate or co-operate with them. Fieldworkers tend to assume as well that subjects have a responsibility to keep interview appoint-ments, provide honest and full answers to questions and submit willingly to any tests or experiments that are part of research designs; yet they also know that their subjects' principal time commitments are not to the fieldworker, but rather to those whose relationships with them are permanent instead of temporary, and that subjects need not tell or do anything unless they choose to tell or do it, regardless of its importance to the fieldworker's aims. In fieldwork involving people studying people at first hand, in sum, rights and responsibilities cannot be legislated by the fieldworker, but must instead be negotiated by fieldworkers and subjects. The negotiating is continuous and requires repeated clarification and compromise.

71   Anna Pollert

Girls, Wives, Factory Lives:
An Example of Fieldwork Research

When I began my study of Churchmans, a tobacco factory in Bristol, I was met with astonishment from management; what could I possibly want to know about 'factory girls'? Was I, then, a 'troublemaker'?

On the shop floor I was met with a mixture of suspicion and curiosity. I was not an employee and had to explain that I felt many people had no idea what factory life was like and I wanted to listen, learn and write about it. Slowly, I became a familiar figure, with notebook and cassette-recorder in hand, and suspicion turned to amusement, even sympathy: 'Go on, my love'; 'I think it's a good thing: people ought to know how people live – not just think about themselves.'

Churchmans was a declining part of Imperial Tobacco, producing pipe and loose tobaccos. Rationalization and insecurity were accepted parts of life, like the din of machinery, the sweet sickly smell of *rag* (the loose, shredded tobacco) and the unyielding pace of work. And indeed the factory is now shut.

It was a small factory. Most of the 140 women worked in the weighing and packing departments, the labour-intensive areas. The largest of these, the machine weighing room, was filled with long weighing machines with conveyor belts to the labellers and baggers.

Each machine contained six scales, each with a little light which went on to register the correct weight of tobacco. Machine weighing needs finger-tip preci-sion and flying speed. Each weigher picks up tiny lumps of rag which she drops into a hole – sometimes taking back a few shreds – until the exact weight is reached. A counter records her performance. The machines clatter all day from 7.30 a.m. to 4.30 p.m., except for a fifteen-minute breakfast break and an hour for lunch, recording all the time.

Failure in performance standard or speed leads to a warning, and downgrading to a lower 'proficiency pay rate'. Each minute, ten empty foil packs pass below the scale inside the machine's belly; one weighing per woman every six seconds.

It is rowdy and pacey here. But it is also good for a laugh, and that counts in factory life. Most of the younger women are in the machine weighing room. There are other young women in the smaller, quieter hand-packing rooms, and the distinction between the 'crowds' in each came up again and again:

Patti (from the machine weighing room): They take their work seriously, whereas we don't. If you go in there, you can't talk. *They* all keeps themselves to themselves, whereas *we* all mucks in together.

Upstairs in the stripping department, and downstairs in the spinning room, are concentrated the older women – the long-term workers, women with children, women with grandchildren.

Stripping can be done either by hand or by machine. Hand-stemming means stripping the tobacco leaf from the stem between forefinger and thumb. Fingers get cut, calloused and bent. The dust catches the back of the throat; but it isn't a noisy job. There is an intimacy of years of shared experience, with quiet talk or, sometimes, group discussion about children and families, news and personal experiences.

Machine-stripping makes a regular clacking noise. It looks like feeding washing through a mangle, as tobacco leaf is fed between two rollers operated by a foot pedal. A blade cuts out the stem, and the stripper carefully stacks the left and right halves of the leaf, avoiding tearing it, but always fighting time, and fighting to keep up to [the] proficiency standard.

In the spinning room, concentration was so intense that I was frankly told not to interfere by interviewing. There was no time to talk and keep up at the same time.

The air here is thick with oppressive fumes from the ovens which cook speciality tobacco. One woman describes it wrily as a 'slave camp'. In fact, work here is the most skilled task in the factory. You have to carry out the seemingly impossible feat of joining 'wrapper' leaves together, while twisting them round a 'filler' to produce a long roll of tobacco. But spinning wasn't paid at craftsman's rates.

Keeping up with the machines or the performance rates and coping with monotony – that was what factory work was about. Geoff, the training supervisor, thought he really 'knew' the 'girls' at Churchmans:

'They're quite happy. They're in a fool's paradise. They've got the money coming in. They've never had it so good.' And indeed it was the money that kept them there. It was very good – *for a woman*:

Patti: We get good wages. I think I'm lucky to be working here. We ought to be grateful for having jobs.

But 'good for a woman' did not mean it was a living wage:

Sandra: You know, I thought it was good wages in here. Well it is, I suppose, except for the price of flats and food and bus fares.

And the money didn't mean that they were not bored:

Patti: I'd like to see them here. I'd like to see the manager on a weighing machine for a week.
Mary: Not a week! An hour would be enough!

Finding escapes made factory life tolerable. You had to pretend it wasn't happening, or steal a break:

Val: You gets used to it, though. I think it's imagination a lot of the time.
Sue: Some girls'll sit up all day and weigh. But with me, well, I gets me hair off. I mucks about. I gets so fed up, I goes out the back.

Twice a day there is music. In the hand-packing room, there is an encyclopaedia under the supervisor's desk for quizzes. Some machine weighers read books while their hands continue 'on automatic'.

Most important of all, however, is companionship and collective life. As the women talked to me, it became clear that a 'good' factory was one where you found mates. The *work* could never be 'good':

Jenny: You've just got to be friends with everyone. Like it's terrible if some-one's not talking to you. But if you're talking to them, and friends with them, it's all right.

Mucking in together, and having a laugh, are what make a 'good' day. There are jokes, sing-songs, teasing. In the hand-stripping room sits Vi, almost 60, single, bent and quite deaf:

Pearl: Vi's got the nice voice, haven't you, Vi? Come on, Vi!
Vi (in a croaking voice, the others listening solemnly): We was waltzing together, and the stars began to fall...In this wonderful moment, something's happened to my heart, We was once changing partners till I'm in your arms and then...So we'll keep on changing partners till I hold you once more.
Pearl: (shouting): Look, Vi, over there, your boyfriend's coming.
Vera: (pointing to a chargehand in his glass cubicle): Ooh. Here's your boyfriend coming. Here's Jo coming. You'll have a kiss now, Ivy.
Pearl and Vera (calling): Jo! Jo! (then like doves) Joey! Joey!
Vera: Ah, he didn't hear, Vi. Never mind, eh.

Some of the best laughs are from turning the tables on supervisors, especially getting the upper hand with men:

Pearl: Vi, sing *Robinson Crusoe*! Come over here, Stan (calling over to the chargehand).
Vi (singing): He's a dirty old man, called Crusoe, He sat on the rock and played with his sock,
(roars of laughter among the women, Stan looking hot under the collar)
        Oh dear old Robinson Crusoe.

Higher management, who quite often visited the shop floor, were not exempt from older women's mockery. While a visiting party of salesmen comb their hair before a photograph next to a hogshead of tobacco, the hand-stemmers taunt them through a glass partition:

Stella: He's combing his hair! If we combed our hair in the factory, he'd go out of his mind.
Vera: Well, go and tell him, Stan, manager or no.

At this point the salesmen pose with their arms round each other:

All the women: Ah! Ah!
Vera: Wish they could hear us! AH! Everybody together. AH!
All the women (even louder): AH! AH!
Vera: I'm glad he had a sauna. He's slimming; Nicholson, he's on a diet.
Me: Which one is he?
Stella: The manager. With his hand here. He's always got his hand down his trousers.

Chargehands have to 'deal with' the build-up of boredom and frustration:

Val: I goes to sleep. I daydream. But when we don't talk for two hours, I start tormentin the others, pulling the rag about, muck about sort of thing. With the Irish, you know, I picks on them. About Ireland – take the soldiers back, the bombings, all that – only mucking about like I don't mean it. But then we has a little row, but we don't mean what we says. But I get so bored, I got to do something, or I start going out the back and have a fag. (Music comes on.) It's the best part of the day when the records come on.

Older women find the younger generation 'more defiant' than they used to be. 'Good thing, too, though sometimes it can go too far.' Shop-floor humour is aggressive, often sexual. 'Who were you in bed with last night?' – '*Me*? In bed with someone? Don't be disgusting.' There are quick-witted insults, jibes, competition. Sometimes there are uproarious sessions of jokes.
Once I was called over to a group helpless with splutters of laughter, red faces and watery eyes:

Cherry: What do you think of polo?
Me: Polo?
Cherry (shrieks up a pitch): Yes! The mint with the hole!
(Uproar.)
Ann: Want a banana? (shrieks)
Cherry: Oh yeh – a banana!
Ann: Can I have it peeled, please?

Then they turn on Cherry, who has a face burnt red by a sun lamp:

Rene: You've got radiation.
All: Radiation! Radiation! Radiation!
Rene: Only three weeks to live! Never mind, eh. What are you going to do?
Cherry: I don't want to be a virgin all my life. (A good minute's solid ribaldry.)
Rene: Ssh. Not so loud.
Me: What else are you going to do?
Cherry: Two weeks left? Must see the changing of the guards. Ooh aah.

72   Catherine Marsh

The Value of the Survey Method

The word ['survey'] has a long tradition in the English language, and developed from being the fact of viewing or inspecting something in detail (as in a land survey) to the act of doing so rigorously and comprehensively, and finally to the written results. The idea of the social survey started with this connotation of the collection of social facts, but has undergone an evolution such that nowadays the survey method is a way not just of collecting data but also of analysing the results.

A survey refers to an investigation where:

a systematic measurements are made over a series of cases yielding a rectangle of data;
b the variables in the matrix are analysed to see if they show any patterns;
c the subject matter is social.

In other words, surveys have a particular method of data collection, a particular method of data analysis and a particular substance.

The only restriction made on the survey as a method of collecting data is to insist that it be systematic, looking at more than one *case*, be it individuals, hospitals, countries or whatever, and measuring the same variables on each case, so that you end up with each case having one and only one code for each variable. The data could come from observation, from fixed-choice responses to a postal questionnaire, from content analysis of newspapers, or from postcoding tape-recorded depth interviews. The important thing is that there is more than one case and that variation between cases is considered systematically. 'Survey analysis' involves making causal inferences from some kind of passive observation programme. The word 'survey' *is* sometimes used to refer to such investigations as a split-ballot question-wording trial, where there has been an experimental manipulation, but I think it is clearer if we use the word 'experiment' to describe such investigations.

Surveys and experiments are the only two methods known to me to test a hypothesis about how the world works. The experimenter intervenes in the social world, does something to a set of subjects (and usually also refrains from doing that thing to a set of controls) and looks to see what effect *manipulating* variance in the independent variable has on the dependent variable. If the subjects have been assigned in some fashion to control and experimental groups, the experimenter can be sure that it is what she did to the independent variable that has produced any differences between the groups.

The survey researcher has only made a series of observations; to be sure, as we shall come on to argue, these cannot be seen as passive reflections of unproblematic reality, but they must be logically distinguished from the manipulation that the experimenter engages in. The only element of randomness in the survey design comes in random selection of cases; *random sampling does not achieve the same result as random allocation into control and experimental groups*. The survey researcher may have a theory which leads her to suspect that X is having a causal effect on Y. If she wants to test this, she has to measure X and Y on a variety of different subjects, and infer from the fact that X and Y covary that the original hypothesis was true. But unlike the experimenter, she cannot rule out the possibility *in principle* of there being a third variable prior to X and Y and causing the variance in both; the experimenter knows that the relationship is not spurious because she knows exactly what produced the variance in X – *she* did.

In other words, in survey research the process of testing causal hypotheses, central to any theory-building endeavour, is a very indirect process of drawing inferences from already existing variance in populations by a rigorous process of comparison. In practice, one of the major strategies of the survey researcher is to control for other variables that she thinks might realistically be held also to produce an effect, but she never gets round the purist's objection that she has not definitively established a causal relationship. Furthermore, although having panel data across time certainly helps with the practical resolution of the problem of how to decide which of one's variables are prior to which others, it does not solve the logical difficulty that, in principle, any relationship which one finds may be explained by the operation of another unmeasured factor.

Finally, the subject matter of the surveys that sociologists are interested in is always social. Many different disciplines collect systematic observational data and make inferences from it. Biologists looking at correlations between plant growth and different types of environment, psychologists coding films of mother–child interactions, or astronomers drawing inferences about the origins of the universe from measurements of light intensity taken now, are all performing activities whose logic is similar to that of the social survey analyst, but they would not describe their studies as 'surveys'. . . .

Surveys have a lot to offer the sociologist. Since experimentation cannot be used to investigate a wide range of macrosocial processes, there is often no alternative to considering variation across cases in a systematic fashion. Since the processes of determination in the social world are subjective in important ways, involving actors' meanings and intentions, the survey researcher has to face the task of measuring these subjective aspects. It is not easy. Perhaps the most misguided and damaging of all the criticisms that have been made of survey research was C. W. Mills's contention that their design and implementation involved no sociological imagination, but only the mechanical skills of techniques following time-honoured formulae. Nor are surveys cheap. Because of the ever-present danger of faulty inference from correlational data, measurements of all the possible confounding variables must be made, and the sample size must be large enough to ensure adequate representation of cases in the subcells created in analysis.

The survey method is a tool. Like any tool, it is open to misuse. It can be used in providing evidence for sociological arguments or, as in any aspect of sociology, it can be used for ideological constructions. Surveys are expensive, so it tends to be people with power and resources who have used them most heavily.

73   Joanna Mack and Stewart Lansley

Absolute and Relative Poverty in Britain: An Illustration of Survey Work

There has been a long tradition that has tried to define poverty narrowly in terms of health, aiming either for a universal standard or for a standard relative to a particular moment in time. There has been an equally long tradition that has seen a person's needs as being culturally and socially, as well as physically, determined. It is a view that recognizes that there is more to life than just existing. Two hundred years ago the economist Adam Smith wrote:

> By necessaries, I understand not only commodities which are indispensably necessary for the support of life but whatever the custom of the country renders it indecent for creditable people, even of the lowest order, to be without. A linen shirt, for example, is strictly speaking not a

necessity of life. The Greeks and Romans lived, I suppose, very comfortably though they had no linen. But in the present time ... a creditable day-labourer would be ashamed to appear in public without a linen shirt, the want of which would be supposed to denote that disgraceful state of poverty.

This theme was adopted and first used for a more practical purpose by Charles Booth in his pioneering surveys of poverty in London from the late 1880s to the turn of the century. He defined the very poor as those whose means were insufficient 'according to the normal standards of life in this country'. . . .

The essentially relative nature of poverty is immediately obvious when viewing people's standards of living in these broader terms. Purchases of consumer durables are specific to each generation, or even each decade, and activities involving social participation have no meaning outside the society in which people live. This has long been recognized; Karl Marx wrote in 1849: 'Our needs and enjoyments spring from society; we measure them, therefore, by society and not by the objects of their satisfaction. Because they are of a social nature, they are of a relative nature.'. . .

[Yet] a body of opinion has persisted that places emphasis only on 'absolute' poverty. The fact that the poor in Britain today are better off than the poor of the past, and than the poor of other countries today, is seen to devalue their problems. Dr Rhodes Boyson, as Minister for Social Security, gave his view of 'relative' poverty to the House of Commons in a debate on the rich and the poor called by the opposition:

> Those on the poverty line in the United States earn more than 50 times the average income of someone in India. That is what relative poverty is all about. . . . Apparently, the more people earn, the more they believe poverty exists, presumably so that they can be pleased about the fact that it is not themselves who are poor.

Others, in contrast, have argued that the facts of starvation in the poorest countries of the world and the intense deprivations suffered by the poor of the past are not relevant to the problems of the poor of the industrialized world today. Tony Crosland, for example, argued not just for the importance of a concept of 'primary' poverty but also that

> poverty is not, after all, an absolute, but a social or cultural concept. . . . This demands a relative, subjective view of poverty, since the unhappiness and injustice it creates, even when ill-health and malnutrition are avoided, lies in the enforced deprivation not of luxuries indeed, but of small comforts which others have and are seen to have, and which in the light of prevailing cultural standards are really 'conventional necessities'.

During the 1960s this view became widely accepted, as a result – at least in part – of the work of Professor Peter Townsend. For the last thirty years, Townsend has argued that poverty can only be viewed in terms of the concept of 'relative deprivation'. In his studies of poverty he has refined this concept, culminating in his 1969 survey of living standards. In his report of this comprehensive and influential study, Townsend defined poverty as follows:

> Individuals, families and groups in the population can be said to be in poverty when they lack the resources to obtain the types of diet, participate in the activities and have the living conditions and amenities which are customary, or are at least widely encouraged or approved, in the societies to which they belong.

Although something like this definition of poverty would now be widely accepted, there remains immense room for debate about what exactly it means.

The central brief given to MORI, the survey specialists commissioned by London Weekend Television to design and conduct the *Breadline Britain* survey, was as follows:

> The survey's first, and most important, aim is to try to discover whether there is a public consensus on what is an acceptable standard of living for Britain in 1983 and, if there is a consensus, who, if anyone, falls below that standard.
>
> The idea underlying this is that a person is in 'poverty' when their standard of living falls below the minimum deemed necessary by current public opinion. This minimum may cover not only the basic essentials for survival (such as food) but also access, or otherwise, to participating in society and being able to play a social role.

The survey established, for the first time ever, that a majority of people see the necessities of life in Britain in the 1980s as covering a wide range of goods and activities, and that people judge a minimum standard of living on socially established criteria and not just the criteria of survival or subsistence.

Table 1 lists the thirty-five items that were tested, ranked by the proportion of respondents identifying each item as a 'necessity'. This ranking shows that there is a considerable degree of social consensus. Over nine in ten people are agreed about the importance of the following basic living conditions in the home:

- heating;
- an indoor toilet (not shared);
- a damp-free home;
- a bath (not shared); and
- beds for everyone.

The right of everyone, regardless of income, to exactly these sorts of basic minima was a key objective of postwar housing policy until the recent sharp cutbacks in public-sector housing investment.

The survey also found a considerable degree of consensus about the importance of a wide range of other goods and activities. More than two-thirds of the respondents classed the following items as necessities:

- enough money for public transport;
- a warm waterproof coat;
- three meals a day for children;
- self-contained accommodation;
- two pairs of all-weather shoes;
- a bedroom for every child over 10 of different sex;
- a refrigerator;
- toys for children;
- carpets;
- celebrations on special occasions such as Christmas;
- a roast joint or its equivalent once a week; and
- a washing machine.

This widespread consensus on what are necessities clearly reflects the standards of today and not those of the past. In Rowntree's study of poverty in York in

Table 1 The public's perception of necessities

Standard-of-living items in rank order	% classing item as necessity	Standard-of-living items in rank order	% classing item as necessity
1 Heating to warm living areas of the home if it's cold	97	18 New, not second-hand, clothes	64
2 Indoor toilet (not shared with another household)	96	19 A hobby or leisure activity	64
3 Damp-free home	96	20 Two hot meals a day (for adults)	64
4 Bath (not shared with another household)	94	21 Meat or fish every other day	63
5 Beds for everyone in the household	94	22 Presents for friends or family once a year	63
6 Public transport for one's needs	88	23 A holiday away from home for one week a year, not with relatives	63
7 A warm waterproof coat	87	24 Leisure equipment for children e.g. sports equipment or a bicycle	57
8 Three meals a day for children	82	25 A garden	55
9 Self-contained accommodation	79	26 A television	51
10 Two pairs of all-weather shoes	78	27 A 'best outfit' for special occasions	48
11 Enough bedrooms for every child over 10 of different sex to have his/her own	77	28 A telephone	43
12 Refrigerator	77	29 An outing for children once a week	43
13 Toys for children	71	30 A dressing gown	40
14 Carpets in living rooms and bedrooms	70	31 Children's friends round for tea/a snack once a fortnight	37
15 Celebrations on special occasions such as Christmas	40	32 A night out once a fortnight (adults)	36
16 A roast meat joint or its equivalent once a week	67	33 Friends/family round for a meal once a month	32
17 A washing machine	67	34 A car	22
		35 A packet of cigarettes every other day	14

Average of all 35 items = 64.1

1899, for a family to be classed as poor 'they must never spend a penny on railway fare or omnibus'. In Britain in the 1980s, nearly nine in ten people think that such spending is not only justified but a necessity for living today.

74   John Heritage

Conversation Analysis

The inception and development of conversation analysis as a distinctive field of research is closely linked with problems surrounding the tendency for ordinary language descriptions to gloss or idealize the specifics of what they depict. This tendency is inherent in the use of type concepts in the social sciences irrespective of whether the types are produced by 'averaging' as recommended by Durkheim[1] or by explicit idealization as proposed by Weber in his various methodological writings. In an early paper, Sacks criticized the use of both of these categories of type concepts in sociology on the grounds that they necessarily blur the specific features of the events under investigation.[2] The result, he argued, is that sociological concepts and generalizations can have only a vague and indeterminate relationship with any specific set of events. This, in turn, inhibits the development of sociology as a cumulative body of knowledge because, given this indeterminacy, it can be difficult to decide whether a specific case in fact supports or undermines a given sociological generalization.

Sacks's response to this problem was a deliberate decision to develop a method of analysis which would keep a grip on the primary data of the social world – the raw material of specific, singular events of human conduct:

> When I started to do research in sociology I figured that sociology could not be an actual science unless it was able to handle the details of actual events, handle them formally, and in the first instance be informative about them in the direct ways in which primitive sciences tend to be informative, that is, that anyone else can go and see whether what was said is so. And that is a tremendous control on seeing whether one is learning anything. So the question was, could there be some way that sociology could hope to deal with the details of actual events, formally and informatively? . . . I wanted to locate some set of materials that would permit a test.[3]

Sacks's work on tape-recorded conversation was initiated in deliberate pursuit of this methodological aim:

> It was not from any large interest in language or from some theoretical formulation of what should be studied that I started with tape-recorded conversation, but simply because I could get my hands on it and I could study it again and again, and also, consequentially, because others could look at what I had studied and make of it what they could, if, for example, they wanted to be able to disagree with me.[4]

The contemporary methodology of conversation analysis has maintained Sacks's pioneering focus on the details of actual interactions and his effort to forestall the process of idealization. Its insistence on the use of data collected from naturally occurring occasions of everyday interaction is paralleled by a corresponding *avoidance of a range of other research methodologies as unsatis-*

factory sources of data. These include: (1) the use of interviewing techniques in which the verbal formulations of subjects are treated as an appropriate substitute for the observation of actual behaviour; (2) the use of observational methods in which data are recorded through field notes or with pre-coded schedules; (3) the use of native intuitions as a means of inventing examples of interactional behaviour; and (4) the use of experimental methodologies involving the direction or manipulation of behaviour. These techniques have been avoided because each of them involves processes in which the specific details of naturally situated interactional conduct are irretrievably lost and are replaced by idealizations about how interaction works.

A range of considerations inform this preference for the use of recorded data over subjects' reports, observers' notes or unaided intuition or recollection. Anyone who has examined conversational materials will be highly conscious of the deficiencies of such resources by comparison with the richness and diversity of empirically occurring interaction. For example, although the following sequence is by no means extraordinary, it is difficult to imagine its invention by a social scientist.

```
(1)   (NB:VII:2)⁵
      E:  = Oh honey that was a lovely luncheon I shoulda ca:lled you
          s:soo┌:ner but I:┐l:┌lo:ved it. It w's just deli:ghtfu┌:l. ┐
      M:        └((f)) Oh:::┘ └ (    )                          └Well┘ =
      M:  = I w's gla┌d    you ┐(came).┐
      E:             └'nd yer f:┘ friends┘'re so da:rli:ng,=
      M:  = Oh:::┌: it w'z:┐
      E:         └e-that P-┘a:t isn'she a do:┌:ll?┐
      M:                                      └iYe┘h isn't she pretty,
          (.)
      E:  Oh: she's a beautiful girl.=
      M:  = Yeh I think she's a pretty gir┌l.
      E:                                   └En' that Reinam'n::
          (.)
      E:  She SCA:RES me.=
```

Not only is it impossible to imagine the above being invented, it is similarly inconceivable that it could be recollected in such detail either by an ethnographer or by an actual participant. And, even if it could be recollected, it could not be heard again and again. Moreover, as Sacks notes, it can be difficult to treat invented or recollected sequences as fully persuasive evidence for analytic claims.⁶ And even if they are accepted, such inventions or recollections can tell us nothing about the frequency, range, variety or typicality of the conversational procedures within the fragment.

The intuitive invention of data is subject to an additional problem which has nothing to do with complexity, but everything to do with the way unaided intuition tends to typify the ways interaction happens. Consider (2) below:

```
(2)   A:  I have a fourteen-year-old-son.
      B:  Well that's alright.
      A:  I also have a dog.
      B:  Oh I'm sorry.
```

Although (2) is simple enough, it is not the way we imagine interaction happens. If it had been invented, it might have been used to show what is meant by incoherent interaction. But in fact (2) is taken from a conversation in which the would-be tenant of an apartment (A) is describing circumstances to the landlord (B) which might disqualify the rental and, viewed in this context, the datum is perfectly coherent and sensible. The myriad ways in which specific contexts (e.g. particular social identities, purposes and circumstances) are talked into being and oriented to in interaction vastly exceed the comparatively limited, and overwhelmingly typified, powers of imaginative intuition.

A similar range of issues arises in relation to experimentally produced data. The success of social-psychological experiments is strongly dependent on the experimenter's ability to identify, control and manipulate the relevant dependent and independent variables. Not only is this extremely difficult to accomplish without some form of experimenter contamination, but also it is unlikely that an experimenter will be able to identify the range of relevant variables without previous exposure to naturally occurring interaction. Moreover, without such exposure the experimenter will find it difficult to extrapolate from experimental findings to real situations of conduct, nor will it prove easy to determine which (if any) of the experimental findings are artefacts of the experimental situation, since such a determination can only be achieved by systematic comparison with naturally occurring data. In sum, the most straightforward procedure has been to work with naturally occurring materials from the outset. Naturally occurring interaction presents an immense range of interactional variations in terms of which systematic comparisons may be used both to check and to extend particular analyses.

Thus the use of recorded data is an essential corrective to the limitations of intuition and recollection. In enabling repeated and detailed examination of the events of interaction, the use of recordings extends the range and precision of the observations which can be made. It permits other researchers to have direct access to the data about which claims are being made, thus making analysis subject to detailed public scrutiny and helping to minimize the influence of personal preconceptions or analytical biases. Finally, it may be noted that because the data are available in 'raw' form they can be reused in a variety of investigations and can be re-examined in the context of new findings. All of these major advantages derive from the fact that the original data are neither idealized nor constrained by a specific research design or by reference to some particular theory or hypothesis.

Part 19

Theoretical Perspectives in Sociology

Many different theoretical outlooks exist in sociology, although they tend to converge on a similar range of basic problems and issues. Reading 75 provides a succinct description of the tenets of one of the most influential bodies of thought from the nineteenth century, that of Karl Marx and Friedrich Engels. Human social life, Marx argues, is organized above all in terms of the practical requirements whereby material production is carried on. Changes in the social frameworks of production have profound consequences for all the other major institutions of society.

Marx and Engels did not recognize a separate discipline of 'sociology'. Their writings span whole areas of what would now be recognized as distinct disciplines of sociology, economics, history and philosophy. They were specifically hostile to the work of Auguste Comte, who first coined the term 'sociology' and regarded himself as its prime founder. Emile Durkheim, by contrast, drew heavily upon Comte's work and sought to consolidate the establishment of sociology as a distinctive and specific social science. According to Durkheim (reading 76), sociology is the study of social facts: objectively given conditions of social life. Social facts, he declared in a famous statement, should be treated as 'things'. Established patterns of social life, in other words, have a solidity and a resistance to the individual will on a par with material objects in the natural world. We might think of ourselves as the creators of social institutions, but in fact the more enduring of such institutions predate our individual lives and are 'external' characteristics of the environments in which we move.

Max Weber, the third great classical influence upon modern sociology, took a different position again (reading 77). Weber rejected the type of viewpoint expressed by Durkheim, arguing instead that social activity has to be understood in terms of the meanings which social behaviour has for those involved. Unlike objects in nature, human beings are purposive, reasoning agents, whose activities are not governed by mechanical considerations. To know why a person acts as he or she does involves interpreting the meaning of the action for that individual. Although sociology in this sense is 'subjective', Weber stated, it none the less strives for clear and verifiable accounts of human social life.

The acknowledged founders of sociology were all male and none of them gave any particular attention to the position of women in society, or to questions of gender more generally. Such issues, however, were discussed in nineteenth-century social thought, as the selection from Harriet Taylor Mill demonstrates (reading 78). Together with her husband, John Stuart Mill, Harriet Mill took up the challenge of women's emancipation. Women, she argued – and this was certainly true at the time at which she wrote – are educated to accept one dominant aim: making a satisfactory marriage. Once they start to embrace a wider range of social objectives, however, and move out from the confines of the domestic setting, they have the capability radically to change modern civilization. If marriage were abolished, she suggested, women could be placed on an equal par with men and many other desirable social changes would follow.

The following three pieces all concern traditions of social theory which have become particularly influential in the twentieth century. George H. Mead (reading 79) is the originator of what has come to be called 'symbolic interactionism' (he himself did not use that term). Symbolic interactionism shares common elements with Weber's standpoint, accentuating as it does the meaningful qualities of social activity. According to this perspective, social interaction is symbolic in nature. In contrast to Weber, however, Mead wrote extensively upon the self, arguing that social interaction is vital to the emergence of self-consciousness in the human individual. The individual first of all experiences herself or himself not in an immediate way, but by means of the attitudes and reactions others assume.

Functionalism and structuralism rank as two of the most influential theoretical approaches in modern sociology. Durkheim's writings provided the prime inspiration for the emergence of functional analysis, although some aspects of his writings also became incorporated within structuralism. Dorothy Emmet (reading 80) offers a lucid description of the concept of function. Functional analysis, she declares, consists essentially in relating one element of a larger system to the overall workings of that system. Studying the function of an organ in the body, therefore, would mean showing what contribution that organ makes to the life of the organism as a whole. Analysing the function of a social item, such as a religious practice, means showing how such a practice contributes to the overall continuity of the social order.

Like functionalist analysis, structuralism (reading 81) distances itself from interpretation of human action in terms of intentions or reasons. As a theoretical tradition, structuralism has its origins in the study of language, particularly as pioneered by the linguist, Ferdinand de Saussure. Saussure argued that the structural components of language are not actually contained in specific instances of speech. Language (*langue*) consists of sets of rules and strategies which language users have to employ if they are to generate grammatical speech and to understand others.

Structuralists have suggested that the structural qualities of social systems can be understood in a parallel fashion. According to this view, the structural characteristics of human societies are not best represented, as in functionalism, as parts of a 'visible' social unity. Rather, 'structure' should be understood as the rules and conventions which 'stand behind' observed regularities in social activity.

This theme is further developed in the final selection in the volume (reading 82). Most of the above standpoints either stress that social phenomena are independent of the intentions and reasons individuals have for what they do, or emphasize such reasons and intentions to the exclusion of structural influences. We need to develop an outlook in sociological theory which acknowledges the structural features of social systems, yet gives full recognition to the significance of 'meaningful' action. Such a perspective implies a reassessment of the relation between sociology and commonsense beliefs, since such beliefs are core elements of the meaningful activities of social actors.

75 Karl Marx and Friedrich Engels

The Materialist Conception of History

In the social production of their life, men enter into definite relations that are indispensable and independent of their will, relations of production which correspond to a definite stage of development of their material productive forces. The sum total of these relations of production constitutes the economic structure of society, the real foundation, on which rises a legal and political superstructure and to which correspond definite forms of social consciousness. The mode of production of material life conditions the social, political and intellectual life process in general. It is not the consciousness of men that determines their being, but, on the contrary, their social being that determines their consciousness. At a certain stage of their development, the material productive forces of society come in conflict with the existing relations of production, or – what is but a legal expression for the same thing – with the property relations within which they have been at work hitherto. From forms of development of the productive forces these relations turn into their fetters. Then begins an epoch of social revolution. With the change of the economic foundation the entire immense superstructure is more or less rapidly transformed. In considering such transformations a distinction should always be made between the material transformation of the economic conditions of production, which can be determined with the precision of natural science, and the legal, political, religious, aesthetic or philosophic – in short, ideological forms in which men become conscious of this conflict and fight it out. Just as our opinion of an individual is not based on what he thinks of himself, so can we not judge of such a period of transformation by its own consciousness; on the contrary, this consciousness must be explained rather from the contradictions of material life, from the existing conflict between the social productive forces and the relations of production. No social order ever perishes before all the productive forces for which there is room in it have developed; and new, higher relations of production never appear before the material conditions of their existence have matured in the womb of the old society itself. Therefore mankind always sets itself only such tasks as it can solve; since, looking at the matter more closely, it will always be found that the task itself arises only when the material conditions for its solution already exist or are at least in the process of formation. In broad outlines Asiatic, ancient, feudal and modern bourgeois modes of production can be designated as progressive epochs in the economic formation of society. The bourgeois relations of production are the last antagonistic form of the social process of production – antagonistic not in the sense of individual antagonism, but of one arising from the social conditions of life of the individuals; at the same time the productive forces developing in the womb of bourgeois society create the material conditions for the solution of that antagonism. This social formation brings, therefore, the prehistory of human society to a close.

76   Emile Durkheim

The Field of Sociology

The proposition according to which social facts are to be treated as things – which is the very foundation of our method – is one which has stimulated great opposition. It has been considered paradoxical and scandalous for us to assimilate the realities of the social world to those of the external world. Such criticism involves a singular misunderstanding of the meaning and application of this assimilation: the object of this was not to reduce the higher to the lower forms of being, but on the contrary to claim for the higher forms a degree of reality at least equal to that which is readily granted to the lower. We do not say that social facts are material things, but that they are things by the same right as material things, although they differ from them in type.

Just what is a 'thing'? A thing differs from an idea in the same way as that which we know from without differs from that which we know from within. A thing is any object of knowledge which is not naturally controlled by the intellect, which cannot be adequately grasped by a simple process of mental activity. It can only be understood by the mind on condition that the mind goes outside itself by means of observations and experiments, which move progressively from the more external and immediately accessible characteristics to the less visible and more deep-lying. To treat the facts of a certain order as things thus is not to place them in a particular category of reality, but to assume a certain mental attitude toward them; it is to approach the study of them on the principle that we are absolutely ignorant of their nature, and that their characteristic properties, like the unknown causes on which they depend, cannot be discovered by even the most careful introspection.

With the terms thus defined, our proposition, far from being a paradox, could almost pass for a truism if it were not too often misunderstood in the human sciences and especially in sociology. Indeed, one might say in this sense that, with the possible exception of the case of mathematics, every object of science is a thing. In mathematics, since we proceed from simple to more complex concepts it is sufficient to depend upon mental processes which are purely internal in character. But in the case of 'facts' properly so called, these are, at the moment when we undertake to study them scientifically, necessarily unknown *things* of which we are ignorant; for the representations which we have been able to make of them in the course of our life, having been made uncritically and unmethodically, are devoid of scientific value, and must be discarded. The facts of individual psychology themselves have this character and must be seen in this way. For although they are by definition purely mental, our consciousness of them reveals to us neither their real nature nor their genesis. It allows us to know them up to a certain point, just as our sensory knowledge gives us a certain familiarity with heat or light, sound or electricity; it gives us confused, fleeting, subjective impressions of them, but no clear and scientific notions or explanatory concepts. It is precisely for this reason that there has been founded in the course of this century an objective psychology whose fundamental purpose is to study mental facts from the outside, that is to say as things.

This is all the more necessary in the case of social facts, for consciousness is even more helpless in knowing them than in knowing its own life. It might be objected that since social facts are our own creations, we have only to look into our own mind in order to know what we put into them and how we formed them. But, in the first place, the greater part of our social institutions was bequeathed to us already formed by previous generations. We ourselves took no part in their formation, and consequently we cannot by introspection discover the causes which brought them into being. Furthermore, when we have in fact collaborated in their genesis, we can only with difficulty obtain even a very confused and a very distorted perception of the true nature of our action and the causes which determined it. When it is merely a matter of our private acts we know very imperfectly the relatively simple motives that guide us. We believe ourselves disinterested when we act egoistically; we think we are motivated by hate when we are yielding to love, that we obey reason when we are the slaves of irrational prejudices, etc. How, then, should we be able to discern with greater clarity the much more complex causes from which collective acts proceed? For, at the very least, each one of us participates in them only as an infinitesimal unit; a huge number of others collaborate with us, and what takes place in these other minds escapes us.

Thus our principle implies no metaphysical conception, no speculation about the fundamental nature of being. What it demands is that the sociologist put himself in the same state of mind as physicists, chemists or physiologists, when they enquire into a hitherto unexplored region of the scientific domain. When he penetrates the social world, he must be aware that he is penetrating the unknown. He must feel himself in the presence of facts whose laws are as unsuspected as were those of life before the development of biology; he must be prepared for discoveries which will surprise and disconcert him.

77   Max Weber

Meaning and Interpretation in Sociology

The term 'sociology' is open to many different interpretations. In the context used here it shall mean that science which aims at the interpretative understanding of social behaviour in order to gain an explanation of its causes, its course and its effects. It will be called human 'behaviour' only in so far as the person or persons involved engage in some subjectively meaningful action. Such behaviour may be mental or external; it may consist in action or omission to act. The term 'social behaviour' will be reserved for activities whose intent is related by the individuals involved to the conduct of others and is oriented accordingly.

1   'Meaning' is used here in two different senses. First, there is actual conduct by a specific actor in a given historical situation or the rough approximation based on a given quantity of cases involving many actors; and, second, there is the conceptually 'ideal type' of subjective meaning attributed to a hypothetical actor in a given type of conduct. In neither sense can it be used as an objectively 'valid' or as a metaphysically fathomable 'true' meaning. Herein lies the distinction between the behavioural sciences, such as sociology and history, and the orthodox disciplines, such as jurisprudence, logic, ethics or aesthetics, whose purpose it is to determine the 'true' and 'valid' meaning of the objects of their analysis.

2   The line between meaningful and merely responsive (i.e. subjectively not meaningful) behaviour is extremely fluid. A significant part of all sociologically relevant behaviour, principally purely traditional behaviour (see below), fluctu-

ates between the two. Meaningful, i.e. subjectively understandable conduct does not figure at all in many cases of psychophysical processes, or, if it does, is recognizable only by the expert; mystical experiences which cannot be adequately communicated in words are never fully understandable for anyone who is not susceptible to such experiences. On the other hand, the ability to perform a similar action is not a precondition to understanding; it is not necessary 'to be Caesar in order to understand Caesar'. To be able to put one's self in the place of the actor is important for clearness of understanding but not an absolute precondition for meaningful interpretation. Understandable and non-understandable parts of a process are often inextricably intertwined.

3　All interpretation strives, as does science generally, for clarity and verifiable proof. Such proof of understanding will be either of a rational, i.e. logical or mathematical, or of an emotionally emphatic, artistically appreciative, character. Rational proof can be supplied in the sphere of behaviour by a clear intellectual grasp of everything within its intended context of meaning. Emphatic proof in the sphere of behaviour will be supplied by complete sympathetic emotional participation. Direct and unambiguous intelligibility is rational understanding of the highest order, especially in mathematically and logically related propositions. We understand plainly what it means when anyone uses the proposition $2 + 2 = 4$ or the Pythagorean theorem in reasoning or argument, or when a chain of reasoning is logically executed in accordance with accepted ways of thought. In the same way we understand the actions of a person who tries to achieve a certain goal by choosing appropriate means, if the facts of the situation on the basis of which he makes his choice are familiar to us. Any interpretation of such rationally purposeful action possesses – for an understanding of the means employed – the highest degree of proof. Not with the same accuracy, but still accurate enough for most purposes of explanation, it is possible to understand errors (including problem entanglements) to which we ourselves are susceptible or whose origin can be detected by sympathetic self-analysis. On the other hand, many ultimate *goals* or *values* toward which experience shows that human behaviour may be oriented often cannot be understood as such, though it is possible to grasp them intellectually. The more radically they vary from our own ultimate values, the more difficult it is for us to understand them through sympathetic participation. Depending upon the circumstances of a particular case, it must then suffice to achieve only a purely intellectual understanding of such values or, failing that, a simple acceptance of them as given data. As far as is possible, the conduct motivated by these values can then be understood on the basis of whatever opportunities appear to be available for a sympathetic emotional and/or intellectual interpretation at different stages of its development. Here belong many zealous acts of religion or piety which are quite incomprehensible to those not susceptible to such values; as well as the extreme rationalistic fanaticism typical of the exponents of the 'rights of man' theories which are abhorrent to those who, for their part, emphatically repudiate them.

As our susceptibility grows, the more readily are we able to experience such true passions as fear, anger, ambition, envy, jealousy, love, enthusiasm, pride, vengeance, pity, devotion and other desires of every kind, as well as the irrational behaviour issuing from them. Even when the degree of intensity in which these emotions are found far surpasses our own potentialities for experiential understanding, we can still interpret intellectually their impact on the direction taken by our behaviour as well as the choice of means used to implement it. For purposes of systematic scientific analysis it will be convenient to represent all irrational, emotionally conditioned elements of conduct as deviations from a conceptually pure type of goal-oriented behaviour. For example, an analysis of a crisis on the stock exchange would be most conveniently attempted in the following manner: first, a determination of how it would have run its course in the absence of irrational factors; second, using the foregoing as a hypothetical premise, the irrational components are then singled out as 'deviation' from the norm. In the same way, the determination of the rational course of a political or military campaign needs first to be made in the light of all known circumstances and known goals of the participants. Only then will it be possible to account for the causal significance of irrational factors as deviations from the ideal type.

The construction of a purely rational 'goal-oriented' course of conduct, because of its clear understandability and rational unambiguity, serves sociology as an 'ideal type'. Thus we are aided in our understanding of the way in which actual goal-oriented conduct is influenced by irrational factors of every kind (such as emotion, errors) and which then can be classified as deviations from the original hypothesized behaviour.

Only in this respect and because of methodological efficiency can the method of sociology be considered 'rationalistic'. Naturally, this procedure may not be interpreted as a rationalistic bias on the part of sociology, but simply as a methodological device. Neither can it be considered as evidence of the predominance of rationalism in human existence. To what extent the reality of rationalism does determine conduct is not to be considered here. That there is a danger of rationalistic interpretations in the wrong place will not be denied. Unfortunately, all experience confirms the existence of such a danger.

4   On the other hand, certain 'meaningless' (i.e. devoid of subjective meaning) processes and phenomena exist in all sciences of human behaviour. They act as stimuli, or effects, and they either encourage or inhibit human conduct. Such 'meaningless' behaviour should not be confused with inanimate or non-human behaviour. Every artefact (e.g. a machine) acquires meaning only to the extent that its production and use will serve to influence human behaviour; such meaning may be quite varied in its purposes. But without reference to such meaning the object remains completely unintelligible.

What makes this object intelligible, then, is its relation to human behaviour in its role of either means or end. It is this relationship of which the individual can claim to have awareness and to which his conduct has been oriented. Only in terms of such categories does an understanding of objects of this kind arise.

78   Harriet Taylor Mill

The Social Character of Gender

If I could be Providence for the world for a time, for the express purpose of raising the condition of women, I should come to you to know the *means* – the *purpose* would be to remove all interference with affection, or with anything which is, or which even might be supposed to be, demonstrative of affection. In the present state of women's mind, perfectly uneducated, and with whatever of timidity and dependence is natural to them increased a thousand fold by their habit of utter dependence, it would probably be mischievous to remove at once all restraints, they would buy themselves protectors at a dearer cost than even at present – but without raising their natures at all. It seems to me that once give women the desire to raise their social condition, and they have a power which in the present state of civilization and of men's characters, might be made of tremendous effect. Whether nature made a difference in the nature of men and women or not, it seems now that all men, with the exception of a few lofty minded, are sensualists more or less – women on the contrary are quite exempt from this trait, however it may appear otherwise in the cases of some. It seems strange that it should be so, unless it was meant to be a source of power in semi-civilized states such as the present – or it may not be so – it may be only that the habits of freedom and low indulgence on which boys grow up and the contrary notion of what is called purity in girls may have produced the appearance of different natures in the two sexes. As certain it is that there is equality in nothing now – all the pleasures such as they are being men's, and all the disagreeables and pains being women's, as that every pleasure would be infinitely heightened both in kind and degree by the perfect equality of the sexes. Women are educated for one single object, to gain their living by marrying – (some poor souls get it without the churchgoing. It's the same way – they do not seem to be a bit worse than their honoured sisters). To be married is the object of their existence and that object being gained they do really cease to exist as to anything worth calling life or any useful purpose. One observes very few marriages where there is any real sympathy or enjoyment or companionship between the parties. The woman knows what her power is and gains by it what she has been taught to consider 'proper' to her state. The woman who would gain power by such means is unfit for power, still they do lose this power for paltry advantages and I am astonished it has never occurred to them to gain some large purpose; but their minds are degenerated by habits of dependance. I should think that 500 years hence none of the follies of their ancestors will so excite wonder and contempt as the fact of legislative restraints as to matters of feeling – or rather in the expression of feeling. When once the law undertakes to say which demonstration of feeling shall be given to which, it seems quite consistent not to legislate for *all*, and to say how many shall be seen and how many heard, and what kind and degree of feeling allows of shaking hands. The Turks' is the only consistent mode. I have no doubt that when the whole community is really educated, though the present laws of marriage were to continue they would be perfectly disregarded, because no one would marry. The wisest and perhaps the quickest means to do away with its evils is to be found in promoting education – as it is the means of all good – but meanwhile it is hard that those who suffer most from its evils and who are always the best people, should be left without remedy. Would not the best plan be divorce which could be attained by any *without any reason assigned*, and at small expence, but which could only be finally pronounced after a long period? not *less* time than two years should elapse between suing for divorce and permission to contract again – but what the decision will be must be certain at the moment of asking for it – unless during that time the suit should be withdrawn.

(I feel like a lawyer in talking of it only! O how absurd and little it all is!)

In the present system of habits and opinions, girls enter into what is called a contract perfectly ignorant of the conditions of it, and that they should be so is considered absolutely essential to their fitness for it!

But after all the one argument of the matter which I think might be said so as to strike both high and low natures is – who would wish to have the person without inclination? Whoever would take the benefit of a law of divorce must be those whose inclination is to separate and who on earth would wish another to remain with them against their inclination – I should think no one – people sophisticate about the matter now and will not believe that one *'really would wish to go'!* Suppose instead of calling it a 'law of divorce' it were to be called 'proof of affection' – they would like it better then.

At this present time, in this state of civilization, what evil could be caused by, first placing women on the most entire equality with men, as to all rights and privileges, civil and political, and then doing away with all laws whatever relating to marriage? Then if a woman had children she must take charge of them, women could not then have children without considering how to maintain them. Women would have no more reason to barter person for bread, or for anything else, than have men. Public offices being open to them alike, all occupations would be divided between the sexes in their natural arrangements. Fathers would provide for their daughters in the same manner as for their sons.

All the difficulties about divorce seem to be in the consideration for the children – but on this plan it would be the women's *interest* not to have children – now it is thought to be the woman's interest to have children as so many ties to the man who feeds her.

Love in its true and finest meaning, seems to be the way in which is manifested all that is highest best and beautiful in the nature of human beings – none but poets have approached to the perception of the beauty of the material world – still less of the spiritual – and hence never yet existed a poet, except by inspiration of that feeling which is the perception of beauty in all forms and by all means which are given us, as well as by *sight*. Are we not born with the *five* senses, merely as a foundation for others which we may make by them – and who extends and refines those material senses to the highest – into infinity – best fulfils the end of creation – that is only saying, *who enjoys most is most* virtuous. It is for *you* – the most worthy to be the apostle of all the highest virtues to teach such as may be tought, that the higher the *kind* of enjoyment, the *greater* the *degree*, perhaps there is but one class to whom this *can* be *tought* – the poetic nature struggling with superstition: you are fitted to be the saviour of such.

79   George H. Mead

Self and Society

The self has a character which is different from that of the physiological organism proper. The self is something which has a development; it is not initially there, at birth, but arises in the process of social experience and activity, that is, develops in the given individual as a result of his relations to that process as a whole and to other individuals within that process. The intelligence of the lower forms of animal life, like a great deal of human intelligence, does not involve a self. In our habitual actions, for example, in our moving about in a world that is simply there and to which we are so adjusted that no thinking is involved, there is a certain amount of sensuous experience such as persons have when they are just waking up, a bare thereness of the world. Such characters about us may exist in experience without taking their place in relationship to the self. One must, of course, under those conditions, distinguish between the experience that immediately takes place and our own organization of it into the experience of the self. One says upon analysis that a certain item had its place in his experience, in the experience of his self. We do inevitably tend at a certain level of sophistication to organize all experience into that of a self. We do so intimately identify our experiences, especially our affective experiences, with the self that it takes a moment's abstraction to realize that pain and pleasure can be there without being the experience of the self. Similarly, we normally organize our memories upon the string of our self. If we date things we always date them from the point of view of our past experiences. We frequently have memories that we cannot date, that we cannot place. A picture comes before us suddenly and we are at a loss to explain when that experience originally took place. We remember perfectly distinctly the picture, but we do not have it definitely placed, and until we can place it in terms of our past experience we are not satisfied. Nevertheless, I think it is obvious when one comes to consider it that the self is not necessarily involved in the life of the organism, nor involved in what we term our sensous experience, that is, experience in a world about us for which we have habitual reactions.

We can distinguish very definitely between the self and the body. The body can be there and can operate in a very intelligent fashion without there being a self involved in the experience. The self has the characteristic that it is an object to itself, and that characteristic distinguishes it from other objects and from the body. It is perfectly true that the eye can see the foot, but it does not see the body as a whole. We cannot see our backs; we can feel certain portions of them, if we are agile, but we cannot get an experience of our whole body. There are, of course, experiences which are somewhat vague and difficult of location, but the bodily experiences are for us organized about a self. The foot and hand belong to the self. We can see our feet, especially if we look at them from the wrong end of an opera glass, as strange things which we have difficulty in recognizing as our own. The parts of the body are quite distinguishable from the self. We can lose parts of the body without any serious invasion of the self. The mere ability to experience different parts of the body is not different from the experience of a table. The table presents a different feel from what the hand does when one hand feels another, but it is an experience of something with which we come definitely into contact. The body does not experience itself as a whole, in the sense in which the self in some way enters into the experience of the self.

It is the characteristic of the self as an object to itself that I want to bring out. This characteristic is represented in the word 'self', which is a reflexive, and indicates that which can be both subject and object. This type of object is essentially different from other objects, and in the past it has been distinguished as conscious, a term which indicates an experience with, an experience of, one's self. It was assumed that consciousness in some way carried this capacity of being an object to itself. In giving a behaviouristic statement of consciousness we have to look for some sort of experience in which the physical organism can become an object to itself.

When one is running to get away from someone who is chasing him, he is entirely occupied in this action, and his experience may be swallowed up in the objects about him, so that he has, at the time being, no consciousness of self at all. We must be, of course, very completely occupied to have that take place, but we can, I think, recognize that sort of a possible experience in which the self does not enter. We can, perhaps, get some light on that situation through those experiences in which in very intense action there appear in the experience of the individual, back of this intense action, memories and anticipations. Tolstoi as an officer in the war gives an account of having pictures of his past experience in the midst of his most intense action. There are also the pictures that flash into a person's mind when he is drowning. In such instances there is a contrast between an experience that is absolutely wound up in outside activity in which the self as an object does not enter, and an activity of memory and imagination in which the self is the principal object. The self is then entirely distinguishable from an organism that is surrounded by things and acts with reference to things, including parts of its own body. These latter may be objects like other objects, but they are just objects out there in the field, and they do not involve a self that is an object to the organism. This is, I think, frequently overlooked. It is that fact which makes our anthropomorphic reconstructions of animal life so fallacious. How can an individual get outside himself (experientially) in such a way as to become an object to himself? This is the essential psychological problem of selfhood or of self-consciousness; and its solution is to be found by referring to the process of social conduct or activity in which the given person or individual is implicated. The apparatus of reason would not be complete unless it swept itself into its own analysis of the field of experience; or unless the individual brought himself into the same experiential field as that of the other individual selves in relation to whom he acts in any given social situation. Reason cannot become impersonal unless it takes an objective, non-affective attitude toward itself; otherwise we have just consciousness, not *self*-consciousness. And it is necessary to rational conduct that the individual should thus take an objective, impersonal attitude towards himself, that he should become an object to himself. For the individual organism is obviously an essential and important fact or constituent element of the empirical situation in which it acts; and without taking objective account of itself as such, it cannot act intelligently, or rationally.

The individual experiences himself as such, not directly, but only indirectly, from the particular standpoints of other individual members of the same social group, or from the generalized standpoint of the social group as a whole to which he belongs. For he enters his own experience as a self or individual, not directly or immediately, not by becoming a subject to himself, but only in so far as he first becomes an object to himself just as other individuals are objects to him or in his experience; and he becomes an object to himself only by taking the attitudes of other individuals towards himself within a social environment or context of experience and behaviour in which both he and they are involved.

80   Dorothy Emmet

The Notion of Function

Social theorists, as well as those concerned with describing social behaviour, are often guided, deliberately or implicitly, by some model of society. By 'model' is here meant a way of representing a complex of relationships the adoption of which affects how the subject is approached. The form of representation may contain an implicit analogy, and it is necessary to watch this to see that it is not carried to a point where it may mislead. One model of society, developed by Hobbes, compares it with an artefact. Those who have used this model have been thinking primarily of a deliberately and purposively contrived 'device of government' doing what it is intended to do. Another model has been that of society as an organism, but this, taken in the common-sense meaning of an organism, i.e. a body like a human or animal body with a unitary life process and probably a single centre of consciousness, is now generally regarded as misleading. There is, however, another kind of model of society which seems to be very much alive at present. This looks on a society as a single system of interrelated elements with mutual adjustments and corrections, and it examines the 'functions' of social institutions by trying to see how they contribute to maintaining this unity.

This kind of model uses a type of description which is not couched in terms of conscious purpose or intention. In some cases, whether we consider this as a type of teleological or as a type of mechanistic description may be largely a matter of words. Yet even when such an explanation is being presented as a form of mechanistic description, there is no doubt that the terminology of 'function' has certain teleological associations, if not implications, and it is well to be aware of what these are, and to be able to see in any particular instance how much is being built on them.

The notion of 'function' is applicable where

a   the object of study can be considered as forming a system taken as a unitary whole;
b   the unitary whole must be ordered as a differentiated complex, in which it is possible to talk about 'part–whole' relationships;
c   the parts will be elements which can be shown to contribute to fulfilling the purpose for which the ordered whole has been set up, or, if it has not been purposefully set up, to maintaining it in a persisting or enduring state.

(The word 'contribute' here need carry no connotation of intention, or even of effort. I have used it, because it suggests a part–whole relationship, and to avoid the clumsiness of saying the parts 'play a part'.) I have included (c) as a general requirement in addition to (b), because the notion of function does not seem able, so to speak, to stand on its own feet. This is clearly so in the cases where we can speak of some part performing a function in a given whole when the whole itself is thought of as having a purpose; for instance, the function of a bit of the mechanism of a piece of apparatus can be described in relation to the purpose for which the apparatus has been constructed. In this way, the notion of function might be said to be indirectly teleological, and is commonly so used, both where the complex whole has been designed for a purpose, and where the way in which the parts of the whole work together makes it look as if it were designed. But where the purpose is not specified, or where we are reluctant to ascribe deliberate purpose at all, as in the case of biological organisms, the unexpressed presumption is likely to be that the function of an element is to be considered as the way in which it helps the system to persist and maintain itself in some form of recognizable continuity.

Here it looks as if a value judgement was being made, and perhaps not clearly recognized. Is the maintenance and stability of the system being taken as *desirable*, so that functions of elements in contributing to it are taken as thereby commendable? If so, this would introduce a teleology of values as implicit in a functional description. Or are we simply saying that, *taking some system for granted* as a complex whole, some element does in fact help maintain it? If the latter is all that is being said, then the statement that some element has a certain function might be looked on as no more than a statement of fact; it might even be said that it could be translated into a plain statement of results, as if we were to say that the statement that the function of the heart is to circulate the blood need mean no more than that the result of the heart beating is that the blood circulates: a statement in terms of efficient causality with no teleological implications. But I do not think this will quite do, since to talk about a 'function', and not only about a 'result', will be to consider the process with reference to a

unitary system with a persistent structure. This assumption of an ordered context means that if we say that *x* has a function, we are in fact saying more than
that *x* has the consequence *y*. It has the consequence *y* within a system the
efficiency or maintenance of which depends (*inter alia*) on *y*.

81   John Sturrock

Saussure and the Origins of Structuralism

We can say ... that any word in a language is a sign, and that language functions
as a system of signs.

Saussure analysed the sign into its two components: a sound or acoustic
component which he called the *signifier* (*signifiant* in French), and a mental or
conceptual component which he called the *signified* (*signifié*). In this analysis, be
it noted, things themselves, for which linguistic signs can be asked to stand when
we want to refer to the world around us, are ignored. The signified is not a thing
but the notion of a thing, what comes into the mind of the speaker or hearer
when the appropriate signifier is uttered. The signifier thus constitutes the
material aspect of language: in the case of the spoken language a signifier is any
meaningful sound which is uttered or heard, in the case of the written language
it is a meaningful mark inscribed on the page. The signified is the mental aspect
of language which we often deem to be immaterial, even though it is certain that
within the brain a signified is also a neural event. Signifiers and signifieds can
be separated in this way only by the theorist of language; in practice they are
inseparable. A truly meaningless sound is not a signifier because it does not
signify – there can be no signifier without a signified; correspondingly, no
concept can be said to exist unless it has found expression, that is to say been
materialized, either inwardly as a thought or outwardly in speech – there can be
no signified without a signifier....

The distinction between signifier and signified ... can also be applied in situations other than the analysis of the constituent signs of natural language. We
have experience in our daily lives of a great many signs that are not verbal ones:
of pictures and diagrams, for instance. And it is a fact that any object whatso-
ever, be it natural or artificial, can become a sign provided that it is employed
to communicate a message, i.e. to *signify*. The flower that grows only to blush
unseen can never be a sign since there is no one present to turn it into one. But
within a culture flowers can be and are used as signs: when they are made into a
wreath and sent to a funeral, for example. In this instance, the wreath is the
signifier whose signified is, let us say, 'condolence'. (There can be no precise
signified for a wreath because the language of flowers is too loose, at any rate in
our culture; but equally there can be no wreath without a significance of some
kind.)

The nature of the message conveyed by signs such as wreaths of flowers is one
determined by the culture in which the sender and recipient live. Flowers have
no *natural* significance, only a cultural or conventional one.... When they are
employed as signs they enter into what is often referred to as a *code*, a channel
of communication linking the two parties to any such cultural transaction....
The study of signs in general, and of the operation of the vast number of codes
in any culture which enable us to interpret these signs satisfactorily, is now
practised under the name of semiology in France and other European countries,

and of semiotics in the United States. It was Saussure, again, who first called for the institution of such a general science of signs.

He also introduced two other pairs of contrasted terms which are important to any understanding of the style of thought we are faced with. In the study of language he distinguished first of all between what he called *langue* and *parole*, or 'language' and 'speech'. *Language* is the theoretical system or structure of a language, the corpus of linguistic rules which speakers of that language must obey if they are to communicate; *speech* is the actual day-to-day use made of that system by individual speakers. This distinction can usefully be compared to the rather better-known one popularized more recently by the American grammarian Noam Chomsky, who distinguishes between our linguistic *competence* and our linguistic *performance*, meaning respectively the theory of language we appear to be able to carry constantly in our heads and the practical applications we make of it. For Saussure the linguist's proper job was to study not speech but language, because it was only by doing so that he could grasp the principles on which language functions in practice. This same important distinction emerges, in the work examined in this book, as one between *structure* and *event*, that is to say between abstract systems of rules and the concrete, individual happenings produced within that system. The relation between one and the other, and the question of which should take precedence – do structures precede events, or events structures? – has been much debated.

A second and, for my purposes here, final Saussurian distinction is that between the *synchronic* and the *diachronic* axes of investigation. It is permissible to study language – to take Saussure's own subject – along two radically different axes: as a system functioning at a given moment in time, or as an institution which has evolved through time. Saussure himself advocated the synchronic study of language, by contrast with the diachronic studies of the linguists who were his predecessors in the nineteenth century. They had been preoccupied by the history of particular languages, by etymologies, phonetic change and the like, and had never stopped to try and work out the total structure of a language, freezing it at a set moment of its evolution the easier to comprehend the principles on which it functioned.

Synchronic, or structural, linguistics thus introduced a revolutionary shift in perspective. It would have recognized that a total study of language must combine both perspectives, but it was prepared to ignore the diachronic perspective in order to set linguistics on a sounder, more productive footing. Structuralism as a whole is necessarily synchronic; it is concerned to study particular systems or structures under artificial and ahistorical conditions, neglecting the systems or structures out of which they have emerged in the hope of explaining their present functioning. . . .

Another influence on structuralism to be traced to Saussure's linguistics is not a matter of vocabulary, but is the most profound – and also the most elusive – of all. A crucial premiss of Saussure's theory of language is that the linguistic sign is 'arbitrary'. It is so in two ways: the signifier is arbitrary inasmuch as there is no natural, only a conventional, link between it and the thing it signifies (not the signified in this case). There is no property common to all trees, for instance, which makes it logical or necessary that we should refer to them as 'trees'. That is what we, as anglophone persons, call them by agreement among ourselves; the French choose differently, they refer to them as *'arbres'*. But language is arbitrary at the level of the signified also, for each native language divides up in different ways the total field of what may be expressed in words, as one soon finds out in the act of translating from one language to another. One language has concepts that are absent from another. The example which linguists like to give of such arbitrariness is that of colour terms, which vary greatly from one language to another, even though the colours themselves form a continuum and, being determined naturally by their wave frequency, are universal.

The extremely important consequence which Saussure draws from this two-fold arbitrariness is that language is a system not of fixed, unalterable essences but of labile forms. It is a system of relations between its constituent units, and those units are themselves constituted by the differences that mark them off from other, related units. They cannot be said to have any existence within themselves, they are dependent for their identity on their fellows. It is the place which a particular unit, be it phonetic or semantic, occupies in the linguistic system which alone determines its value. Those values shift because there is nothing to hold them steady; the system is fundamentally arbitrary in respect of nature and what is arbitrary may be changed.

'Language is a form and not a substance' was Saussure's famous summation of this quite fundamental insight, an insight without which none of the work done by Lévi-Strauss, Barthes, and the others would have been feasible. Structuralism holds to this vital assumption, that it studies relations between mutually con-ditioned elements of a system and not between self-contained essences. It is easiest once more to instantiate this from linguistics. There is nothing essential or self-contained about a given word; the word 'rock', let us take. That occupies a certain space, both phonetically and semantically. Phonetically it can only be defined by establishing what the limits of that space are: where the boundaries lie if it crosses which it changes from being the word 'rock' to being a different sign of the language – 'ruck', for instance, or 'wreck', which abut on it acousti-cally. Semantically, we can only delimit the meaning of the signifier 'rock' by differentiating it from other signs which abut on it semantically, such as 'stone', 'boulder', 'cliff'.

In short, without difference there can be no meaning. A one-term language is an impossibility because its single term could be applied to everything and differentiate nothing; it requires at least one other term to give it definition. It would be possible, if rudimentary, to differentiate the entire contents of the universe by means of a two-term code or language, as being either *bing* or *bong* perhaps. But without the introduction of that small phonetic difference, between the two vowel sounds, we can have no viable language at all.

82 Anthony Giddens

Sociology and the Explanation of Human Behaviour

The 'sociological' direction of modern philosophy involves a recovery of the everyday or the mundane. Our day-to-day activities are not merely inconsequen-tial habits, of no interest to the student of more profound matters, but on the contrary are relevant to the explication of quite basic issues in philosophy and in social science. Common sense is thus not to be dismissed as merely the inertia of habit or as a set of semi-formulated ideas of no importance to social analysis. To develop this observation further, however, we have to enquire a little more deeply into what common sense is. We cannot necessarily understand the term 'common sense' in a common-sense way.

Although no doubt more finely honed distinctions could be made, I shall distinguish two basic meanings of 'common sense'. One of these I call 'mutual knowledge' and separate from what can simply be called 'common sense' understood generically. By mutual knowledge I refer to knowledge of convention which actors must possess in common in order to make sense of what both they and other actors do in the course of their day-to-day social lives. Meanings are produced and reproduced via the practical application and continued reformulation in practice of 'what everyone knows'. As I would understand it, the programme of ethnomethodology consists in the detailed study of the nature and variations of mutual knowledge. Mutual knowledge refers to the methods used by lay actors to generate the practices which are constitutive of the tissue of social life. It is in substantial part non-discursive. That is to say, to use Wittgenstein's phrase, it consists of the capability to 'go on' in the routines of social life.

Not having any place for a concept of mutual knowledge, naturalistic social science presumes that the descriptive terminology of social analysis can be developed solely within professionally articulated theories. But in order to generate valid descriptions of social life, the sociological observer must employ the same elements of mutual knowledge used by participants to 'bring off' what they do. To be able to generate veridical descriptions of social activity means in principle being able to 'go on' in that activity, knowing what its constituent actors know in order to accomplish what they do.... The implications of the point are rich. All social analysis has a 'hermeneutic' or 'ethnographic' moment, which was simply dissolved in traditional mainstream social science.

There is one way in which a grasp of the inescapably hermeneutic character of social science provides an answer to the question of its enlightening possibilities. That is to say, we might suppose ... that what is 'new' in social science concerns only descriptions of forms of life (either in unfamiliar settings in our own culture, or in other cultures). In the view of the naturalistic social scientist, of course, the claim that social analysis can be no more than ethnography is absurd ... But it is a proposition that deserves to be taken seriously. For there is a sense in which lay agents must always 'know what they are doing' in the course of their daily activities. Their knowledge of what they do is not just incidental but is constitutively involved in that doing. If they already not only do know, but in at least one sense *must* know what they are doing, it might seem that social science cannot deliver 'findings' with which the actors involved are not already familiar. At a minimum we must accept that the conditions under which the social sciences can deliver enlightenment to lay actors are more complex than was presumed in naturalistic social science.

What forms, then, might such enlightenment assume? The following considerations provide the basis of an answer.

1   It has to be accepted that the ethnographic tasks of social science are indeed fundamentally important. That is to say, all of us live within specific cultures which differ from other cultures distributed across the world, and from others 'recoverable' by historical analysis. In modern societies we also all live in specific contexts of larger cultural totalities. The 'news value' of the ethnographic description of culturally alien settings is certainly a significant element in social science.

2   Second, social science can 'display' – that is, give discursive form to – aspects of mutual knowledge which lay actors employ non-discursively in their conduct. The term 'mutual knowledge' covers a diversity of practical techniques of making sense of social activities, the study of which is a task of social science in its own right. As I have already mentioned, it can be construed as the task of

ethnomethodology to provide such a 'display' of the taken-for-granted practicalities of our conduct. We might also instance, however, the writings of Erving Goffman as of singular importance in this respect. Perhaps more than any other single writer, Goffman has made clear how complicated, how subtle – but how routinely managed – are the components of mutual knowledge. We might also remark that the whole of linguistics is concerned with the 'display' of mutual knowledge. Linguistics is about what the language user knows, and must know, to be able to speak whatever language is in question. However, most of what we 'know' in order to speak a language, we know non-discursively. Linguistics tells us what we already know, but in a discursive form quite distinct from the typical modes of expression of such knowledge.

3   A matter of very considerable significance – social science can investigate the unintended consequences of purposive action. Actors always know what they are doing (under some description or potential description), but the consequences of what they do characteristically escape what they intend. A nest of interesting problems and puzzles is to be found here, and I shall only discuss them briefly. Naturalistic versions of social science depend for their cogency upon the observation that many of the events and processes in social life are not intended by any of the participants involved. It is in the 'escape' of social institutions from the purposes of individual actors that the tasks of social science are discovered. In this respect we must in some part continue to defend the version of social science advanced by the 'mainstream' against more 'interpretative' conceptions. A characteristic failing of those traditions of thought which have done most to bring into focus the significance of mundane social practices is that they have ignored altogether the unintended consequences of social activity. But it would be futile to imagine that the issue was adequately handled in naturalistic social science. For the naturalistic sociologist, the unintended character of much social activity is wedded to the view that social life can be analysed in terms of the operation of factors of which social actors are ignorant. But it is one thing to argue that some of the main parameters of social activity are unintended by those who participate in that activity; it is quite another to presume that, consequently, individual agents are acted upon by 'social causes' which somehow determine the course of what they do. Far from reinforcing such a conclusion, a proper appreciation of the significance of the unintended consequences of action should lead us to emphasize the importance of a sophisticated treatment of the purposive nature of human conduct. What is unintentional cannot be even characterized unless we are clear about the nature of what is intentional; and this, I would argue, also presumes an account of agents' reasons.

There are several different types of inquiry that relate to the role of unintended consequences in human action. For example, we might be interested in asking why a singular event occurred in spite of no one's intending it to occur. Thus a historian might pose the question: why did the First World War break out, when none of the main parties involved intended [its] actions to produce such an outcome? However, the type of question with which naturalistic social scientists have traditionally been preoccupied concerns the conditions of social reproduction. That is to say, they have sought to demonstrate that social institutions have properties which extend beyond the specific contexts of interaction in which individuals are involved. The connection between functionalism and naturalism has specific application here. For the point of functional explanation has normally been to show that there are 'reasons' for the existence and continuance of social institutions that are quite distinct from the reasons actors might have for whatever they do.

In recent years, partly as a result of a renewed critical examination of functionalism, it has become apparent that an account of institutional reproduction need not, and should not, have recourse to functional interpretations at all. Human social systems do not have needs, except as counterfactually posited 'as if' properties. It is perfectly appropriate, and often necessary, to enquire what conditions are needed for the persistence of a given set of social institutions over a specified period of time. But such an enquiry invites analysis of the mechanics of social reproduction, it does not supply an explanation for them. All large-scale social reproduction occurs under conditions of 'mixed intentionality'. In other words, the perpetuation of social institutions involves some kind of mix of intended and unintended outcomes of action. What this mix is, however, has to be carefully analysed and is historically variable. There is a range of circumstances which separate 'highly monitored' conditions of system reproduction from those involving a feedback of unintended consequences. The monitoring of conditions of system reproduction is undoubtedly a phenomenon associated with the emergence of modern society and with the formation of modern organizations generally. However, the intersection between intended and unintended consequences in respect of institutional reproduction is variable and in all instances needs to be concretely studied. A double objection can be made to explaining social reproduction in terms of statements of the form 'the function of x is ... '. The first is, as already stated, that such a statement has no explanatory value, and can only be rendered intelligible when applied to social activity in the form of a counterfactual proposition. The second is that the statement is ambiguous in respect of intentionality. In conditions in which reproduction is 'highly monitored', the tie between purposes (of some agents) and the continuity of social institutions will be direct and pervasive. Where an unintended feedback operates, the mechanics of the reproduction process will be quite different. It is normally essential to distinguish the difference.

Notes

Introduction

1 A. Giddens, *Sociology* (Cambridge: Polity, 1989).

Reading 4 (Goffman)

1 M. D. Riemer, 'Abnormalities of the Gaze: A Classification', *Psychiatric Quarterly*, 29 (1955), pp. 659–72.
2 R. K. White, B. A. Wright and T. Dembo, 'Studies in Adjustment to Visible Injuries: Evaluation of Curiosity by the Injured', *Journal of Abnormal and Social Psychology*, 43 (1948), p. 22.
3 Ibid., pp. 16–17.
4 H. Viscardi, jun., *A Man's Stature* (New York: John Day, 1952), p. 70.
5 From Simmel's *Soziologie*, cited in R. E. Park and E. W. Burgess, *Introduction to the Science of Sociology*, 2nd edn (Chicago: University of Chicago Press, 1924), p. 358.
6 H. Melville, *White Jacket* (New York: Grove Press, n.d.), p. 276.

Reading 5 (Duck)

1 R. A. Hinde, 'The Bases of a Science of Interpersonal Relationships', in S. W. Duck and R. Gilmour (eds), *Personal Relationships, vol. 1: Studying Personal Relationships* (London: Academic Press, 1981).
2 P. Blumstein and P. Schmartz, *American Couples: Money, Work, Sex* (New York: William Morrow, 1983).
3 J. M. White, 'Perceived Similarity and Understanding in Married Couples', *Journal of Social and Personal Relationships*, 2 (1985), pp. 40–7.

Reading 6 (Young)

1 W. James, *The Principles of Psychology* (New York: Dover, 1950), vol. 1, pp. 121, 112.
2 T. H. Huxley, *Lessons in Elementary Physiology* (London: Macmillan, 1866). Quoted in James, *Principles of Psychology*, vol. 1.

3 A. Marwick, *Britain in the Century of Total War* (London: Bodley Head, 1968).
4 H. Maudsley, *The Physiology of Mind* (London: Macmillan, 1876), p. 154.
5 James, *Principles of Psychology*, vol. 1, p. 122.
6 J. S. Bruner, *On Knowing: Essays for the Left Hand* (Cambridge, Mass.: Harvard University Press, 1979), pp. 6–7.

Reading 7 (Scull)

1 P. Rock, *Deviant Behaviour* (London: Hutchinson, 1973), pp. 156–9.

Reading 9 (Auld, Dorn and South)

1 J. Helmer, *Drugs and Minority Oppression* (New York: Seabury, 1975), p. 12.
2 R. Hartnoll, R. Lewis and S. Bryer, 'Recent Trends in Drug Use in Britain', *Druglink*, 19 (Spring 1984), pp. 22–4.

Reading 15 (Mishkind)

1 S. L. Franzio and S. A. Shields, 'The Body Esteem Scale: Multidimensional Structure and Sex Differences in a College Population', *Journal of Personality Assessment*, 48 (1984).
2 M. Gerzon, *A Choice of Heroes: The Changing Faces of American Manhood* (Boston: Houghton Mifflin, 1982).
3 R. Lippa, 'Sex Typing and the Perception of Body Outlines', *Journal of Personality*, 51 (1983).

Reading 18 (Giddens)

1 K. Marx and F. Engels, *Manifesto of the Communist Party*, in *Selected Works* (London, 1968), p. 35.
2 K. Marx, *Capital*, vol. 3 (Moscow, 1959), pp. 582ff.
3 K. Marx and F. Engels, *The German Ideology* (London, 1965), p. 61.
4 M. Weber, *Economy and Society* (New York, 1968), vol. 2, pp. 926–40 and vol. 1, pp. 302–7.
5 Ibid., vol. 2, p. 928.
6 Ibid., p. 927.

Reading 19 (Abercrombie and Warde)

1 J. H. Goldthorpe, C. Llewellyn and C. Payne, *Social Mobility and Class Structure in Modern Britain* (Oxford: Oxford University Press, 1980).
2 A. Heath, *Social Mobility* (London: Collins, 1981).
3 A. Stewart, K. Prandy and R. M. Blackburn, *Social Stratification and Occupations* (London: Macmillan, 1980).

Reading 20 (Scott)

1 C. Erickson, *British Industrialists: Steel & Hosiery, 1850–1950* (Cambridge: Cambridge University Press, 1959).

Reading 22 (Leiulfsrud and Woodward)

1   J. Goldthorpe, 'Women and Class Analysis: In Defence of the Conventional View', *Sociology*, 17 (1983), p. 481.
2   Ibid., p. 465.
3   Ibid., p. 477.
4   R. Eriksson, 'Social Class of Men, Women and Families', *Sociology*, 18 (1984).
5   Goldthorpe, 'Women and Class Analysis', p. 470.
6   M. Stanworth, 'Women and Class Analysis: A Reply to John Goldthorpe', *Sociology*, 18 (1984), pp. 159–69.
7   S. McRae, *Cross-Class Families* (Oxford: Clarendon Press, 1986).
8   P. Stamp, 'Balance of Financial Power in Marriage: An Exploratory Study of Bread-winning Wives', *Sociological Review*, 33 (1985).
9   J. Pahl, 'The Allocation of Money and the Structuring of Inequality within Marriage', *Sociological Review*, 31 (1983).

Reading 24 (Esping-Andersen)

1   M. Duverger, *Political Parties* (London: Methuen, 1964).
2   R. Michels, *Political Parties* (New York: Collier, 1962).
3   A. Sturmthal, *The Tragedy of European Labor, 1918–39* (New York: Columbia University Press, 1943).
4   A. Przworski, 'Social Democracy as a Historical Phenomenon', *New Left Review*, 122 (1980), pp. 27–8.
5   E. Bernstein, *Evolutionary Socialism* (New York: Schocken, 1971 [1899]).
6   J. Schumpeter, *Capitalism, Socialism and Democracy* (London: Allen and Unwin, 1976); Przworski, 'Social Democracy'.
7   Przworski, 'Social Democracy', p. 28.

Reading 25 (Held)

1   R. A. Dahl, *A Preface to Economic Democracy* (Cambridge: Polity, 1985), pp. 59–60.
2   See J. Schumpeter, *Capitalism, Socialism and Democracy* (London: Allen and Unwin, 1976).
3   Dahl, *Preface to Economic Democracy*, p. 60.

Reading 28 (Jacoby)

1   F. Neumann, *Behemoth: The Structure and Practice of National Socialism* (New York and London, 1942), p. 368.
2   O. Hintze, 'Nationale und europäische Orientierung in der heutigen politischen Welt' in G. Ostreich (ed.), *Soziologie und Geschichte: Gesammelte Abhandlungen zur Soziologie, Politik und Theorie der Geschichte* (Göttingen, 1964).
3   W. von Humboldt, *The Limits of State Action* (Cambridge, 1969), p. 14.
4   J. Schumpeter, *Capitalism, Socialism and Democracy* (New York: 1976), pp. 266, 293.
5   Ibid., p. 206.

Reading 29 (Fine)

1 J. Haas, 'Binging: Educational Control among High Skill Workers', *American Behavioural Scientist*, 16 (1972).
2 G. A. Fine, 'Small Groups and Culture Creation: The Idioculture of Little League Baseball Teams', *American Sociological Review*, 44 (1979), p. 734.
3 R. F. Bales, *Personality and Interpersonal Behaviour* (New York: Holt, Rinehart and Winston, 1970), pp. 153–4.
4 M. Csikszentmihalyi, *Beyond Boredom and Anxiety* (San Francisco: Jossey-Bass, 1975).

Reading 30 (Coser)

1 G. Simmel, *Conflict and the Web of Group Affiliations* (New York: Free Press, 1955), p. 150.
2 E. Goffman, *Asylums* (Garden City, NY: Anchor, 1961), p. 4.
3 Ibid., pp. 5–6.
4 R. K. Merton, 'The Role-Set', *British Journal of Sociology*, 8 (June 1957).
5 R. C. Binkley, *Realism and Nationalism 1852–1871* (New York: Harper Torchbooks, 1963), p. 147.
6 M. Weber, *Economy and Society*, ed. Gunther Roth and Claus Wittich (Totowa, NJ: Bedminster, 1968), vol. 3, p. 994.

Reading 31 (Kaldor)

1 Quoted in V. Mastny, *Russia's Road to the Cold War: Diplomacy, Warfare and the Politics of Communism, 1941–45* (New York: Columbia University Press, 1979), p. 283.
2 J. L. Gaddis, 'The Long Peace', *International Security*, 10/4 (Spring 1986), p. 142.
3 D. Yergin, *Shattered Peace: The Origins of the Cold War and the National Security State* (Boston, Mass.: Houghton Mifflin, 1977).
4 J. L. Gaddis, *Strategies of Containment: Critical Appraisal of Postwar American Security Policy* (Oxford: Oxford University Press, 1982), p. 357.
5 G. F. Kennan, *Memoirs 1925–50* (London: Hutchinson, 1968), p. 403.

Reading 32 (Segal)

1 R. Hill, 'Foreword' in H. I. McCubbin, B. B. Dahl and E. J. Hunter (eds), *Families in the Military System* (Beverly Hills, Ca.: Sage, 1976), p. 13.
2 C. C. Moskos, 'Institutional and Occupational Trends in the Armed Forces: An Update', *Armed Forces and Society*, 12 (Spring 1986).
3 N. Shea, *The Army Wife*, revised by A. Smith (New York: Harper and Row, 1966), pp. 1, 55.

Reading 33 (Elshtain)

1 S. Saywell, *Women in War* (New York: Viking, 1985), p. 38, italics added.
2 Ibid.

3　K. J. Cottam, 'Soviet Women in Combat in World War II: The Ground Forces and the Navy', *International Journal of Women's Studies*, 3/14 (1980), pp. 345–57.

4　Saywell, *Women in War*, pp. 149, 132.

Reading 34 (Aboud)

1　C. A. Renninger and J. E. Williams, 'Black–White Color Connotations and Racial Awareness in Preschool Children', *Perceptual and Motor Skills*, 22 (1966), pp. 771–85; J. E. Williams and J. K. Morland, *Race, Color and the Young Child* (Chapel Hill, NC: University of North Carolina Press, 1976).

2　D. J. Fox and V. D. Jordan, *Racial Preference and Identification of Black, American Chinese, and White Children*, Genetic Psychology Monographs, 88 (1973), pp. 229–86.

3　G. M. Vaughan, 'Concept Formation and the Development of Ethnic Awareness', *Journal of Genetic Psychology*, 103 (1963), pp. 93–103.

4　P. A. Katz, M. Sohn and S. R. Zalk, 'Perceptual Concomitants of Racial Attitudes in Urban Grade School Children', *Developmental Psychology*, 11 (1975), pp. 135–44.

5　F. E. Aboud and F. G. Mitchell, 'Ethnic Role-taking: The Effects of Preference and Self-identification', *International Journal of Psychology*, 12 (1977), pp. 1–17.

6　N. B. Johnson, M. R. Middleton and H. Tajfel, 'The Relationship between Children's Preferences for and Knowledge about Other Nations', *British Journal of Social and Clinical Psychology*, 9 (1970), pp. 428–38.

7　M. R. Middleton, H. Tajfel and N. B. Johnson, 'Cognitive and Affective Aspects of Children's National Attitudes', *British Journal of Social and Clinical Psychology*, 9 (1970), pp. 122–34.

8　F. Genesee, G. R. Tucker and W. E. Lambert, 'The Development of Ethnic Identity and Ethnic Role-taking Skills in Children from Different School Settings', *International Journal of Psychology*, 13 (1978), pp. 39–57.

9　Vaughan, 'Concept Formation'.

10　N. J. H. Madge, 'Context of the Expressed Ethnic Preferences of Infant School Children', *Journal of Child Psychology and Psychiatry*, 17 (1976), pp. 337–44; A. G. Davey, *Learning to be Prejudiced: Growing up in Multi-ethnic Britain* (London: Edward Arnold, 1983).

11　F. E. Aboud, 'Social and Cognitive Bases of Ethnic Identity Constancy', *Journal of Genetic Psychology*, 184 (1984), pp. 217–30.

12　A. Clark, D. Hocevar and M. H. Dembo, 'The Role of Cognitive Development in Children's Explanations and Preferences for Skin Color', *Developmental Psychology*, 16 (1980), pp. 332–9.

Reading 35 (Gilroy)

1　The word 'diaspora', originally used to refer to Jewish culture, refers to a population dispersed from its place of origin, but retaining links with it.

2　I. Wallerstein, 'Class Formation in the Capitalist World Economy', in *The Capitalist World Economy* (Cambridge: Cambridge University Press, 1979).

3　I. Geiss, *The Pan-African Movement* (London: Methuen, 1974).

4　R. Ellison, *Shadow and Act* (New York: Random House, 1964), p. 263.

Reading 38 (Davis and Murch)

1 M. Rheinstein, *Marriage, Stability, Divorce and the Law* (Chicago: University of Chicago Press, 1972), p. 307.
2 Ibid., p. 274.
3 B. Berger and P. Berger, *The War over the Family* (London: Hutchinson, 1983), p. 166.
4 J. Bernard, *The Future of Marriage* (New York: Bantam, 1973), p. 52.
5 A study carried out by the authors between 1982 and 1984 upon which their discussion is based.
6 Berger and Berger, *War over the Family*, p. 166.

Reading 39 (Pahl)

1 J. Pahl, *Money and Marriage* (London: Macmillan, 1989).
2 G. Wilson, *Money in the Family* (Aldershot: Avebury, 1987).
3 J. E. Todd and L. M. Jones, *Matrimonial Property* (London: HMSO, 1972).

Reading 40 (Stanko)

1 S. Steinmetz, *The Cycle of Violence: Assertive, Aggressive, and Abusive Family Interaction* (New York: Praeger, 1977).
2 R. E. Dobash and R. Dobash, *Violence against Wives* (New York: Free Press, 1979), pp. 19–20.
3 D. E. H. Russell, *Rape in Marriage* (New York: Macmillan, 1982).
4 M. Straus, R. J. Gelles and S. Steinmetz, *Behind Closed Doors* (New York: Doubleday, 1980).
5 Russell, *Rape in Marriage*, p. 99.
6 I. H. Frieze, 'Investigating the Causes and Consequences of Marital Rape', *Signs*, 8/3 (1983), pp. 532–53.
7 P. Carlen, *Women's Imprisonment: A Study in Social Control* (London: Routledge and Kegan Paul, 1983), pp. 39–41.
8 Dobash and Dobash, *Violence against Wives*, p. 111.
9 L. Lovelace, *Ordeal* (New York: Berkeley Books, 1981), pp. 80–1.
10 Dobash and Dobash, *Violence against Wives*, p. 125.
11 Ibid.
12 Personal communication, May 1983.
13 P. Chesler, Women and Madness (London: Allen Lane, 1972), p. 42.
14 C. Gilligan, *In a Different Voice* (Cambridge, Mass: Harvard University Press), p. 67.
15 A. Rich, 'Compulsory Heterosexuality and Lesbian Existence', in C. R. Stimpson and E. S. Person (eds), *Women: Sex and Sexuality* (Chicago: University of Chicago Press, 1980), pp. 62–91.
16 V. Binney, G. Harkell and J. Nixon, *Leaving Violent Men* (London: Women's Aid Federation, England, 1981), p. 8.
17 Dobash and Dobash, *Violence against Wives*, p. 145.

Reading 41 (Stanworth)

1 R. Rowland, 'A Child at Any Price?', *Women's Studies International Forum*, 8/6 (1985), pp. 539–46.

2   J. Raymond, 'Preface', in G. Corea, R. Duelli Klein et al., *Man-Made Women: How New Reproductive Technologies Affect Women* (London: Hutchinson, 1985), p. 12.
3   M. O'Brien, *The Politics of Reproduction* (London: Routledge and Kegan Paul, 1983).
4   Andrea Dworkin *Right-Wing Women* (New York: Pedigree Books, 1983) sketched out the idea of the 'reproductive brothel', as a metaphor for the ways in which men attempt to exert standardized control over women's reproductive capacities.
5   R. Rowland, 'Motherhood, Patriarchal Power, Alienation and the Issue of "Choice" in Sex Preselection', in Corea, Klein et al., *Man-Made Women*, p. 75.
6   K. Luker, *Abortion and the Politics of Motherhood* (Berkeley: University of California Press, 1984), pp. 168–9.
7   R. Rapp, 'Feminists and Pharmacrats', *The Women's Review of Books*, 11/10 (July 1985), p. 4.

Reading 43 (Reid)

1   I. Reid, *Social Class Differences in Britain*, 2nd edn (Oxford: Blackwell, 1981).
2   *Education: A Framework for Expansion* (London: DES/HMSO, 1972).
3   K. R. Fogelman and H. Goldstein, 'Social Factors Associated with Changes in Attainment between 7 and 11 Years of Age', *Educational Studies*, 2/2 (1976), p. 177.
4   J. W. B. Douglas, *The Home and the School* (London: MacGibbon and Kee, 1964).
5   K. R. Fogelman, H. Goldstein, J. Essen and M. Ghodsian, 'Patterns of Attainment', *Educational Studies*, 4/1 (1978), p. 178.
6   P. Burnhill, 'The Relationship between Examination Performance and Social Class', *CES Collaborative Research Newsletter*, 8 (1981).
7   *General Household Survey 1982* (London: OPCS/HMSO, 1984).
8   *Statistics of Education 1961: Supplement* (London: MoE/HMSO, 1962).
9   J. W. B. Douglas, J. M. Ross and H. R. Simpson, *All Our Future* (London: Peter Davies, 1968).
10 M. Rutter, R. Maughan, P. Mortimore and J. Ouston, *Fifteen Thousand Hours* (London: Open Books, 1979).
11 *Higher Education (The Robbins Report)*, Cmnd 2154 (London: HMSO, 1963).

Reading 45 (Liebes and Katz)

1   J. Stolz, 'Les Algériens regardent "Dallas"', in *Les Nouvelles Chaines* (Paris/Geneva: Presses Universitaires de France/Université d'études du developpement, 1983).
2   T. McCormack, *Studies in Communication*, vol. 1 (London: JAI, 1982).
3   M. Tracey, 'The Poisoned Chalice: International Television and the Idea of Dominance', *Daedalus* (Fall 1985).
4   U. Eco, 'Innovation and Repetition: Between Modern and Postmodern Aesthetics', *Daedalus* (Fall 1985).

5   W. Iser, *The Act of Reading: A Theory of Aesthetic Response* (London: Routledge and Kegan Paul, 1978).

Reading 48 (Hadden)

1   C. W. Mills, *The Sociological Imagination* (Oxford: Oxford University Press, 1959).
2   R. N. Bellah, *Beyond Belief* (New York: Harper and Row, 1970), p. 237.
3   D. Martin, 'Towards Eliminating the Concept of Secularisation', in J. Gould (ed.), *Penguin Survey of the Social Sciences* (London: Penguin, 1965).
4   L. Schiner, 'The Concept of Secularization in Empirical Research', *Journal for the Scientific Study of Religion*, 6 (1967).
5   D. Martin, *A General Theory of Secularization* (New York: Harper and Row, 1978).
6   K. Dobbelaere, *Secularization: A Multi-dimensional Concept*, Current Sociology Series, 29 (Berkeley, Ca.: Sage, 1981).
7   K. Dobbelaere, 'Secularization Theories and Sociological Paradigms: Convergences and Divergences', *Social Compass*, 31 (1984).
8   C. Y. Glock, 'The Religious Revival in America?', in J. Zahn (ed.), *Religion and the Face of America* (Berkeley, Ca.: University of California Extension, 1965), p. 82.
9   N. J. Demerath III, 'Trends and Anti-trends in Religious Change' in R. Sheldon and W. E. Moore (eds), *Indicators of Social Change* (Berkeley, Ca.: Russell Sage, 1968).
10 Ibid., pp. 368–9.
11 G. Gallup, jun., '50 Years of Gallup Surveys on Religion', in *The Gallup Report: Report no. 236* (1985).
12 Demerath, 'Trends and Anti-trends in Religious Change', p. 368.
13 H. Wheeler, 'The Phenomenon of God', *The Center Magazine*, 4 (1971), p. 8.
14 R. Stark and W. S. Bainbridge, *The Future of Religion* (Berkeley, Ca.: University of California Press, 1985), p. 124.
15 Ibid., p. 454.
16 E. Durkheim, *The Elementary Forms of Religious Life* (New York: Collier Books 1961 [1912]), p. 474.
17 T. S. Kuhn, *The Structure of Scientific Revolutions*, 2nd edn (Chicago: University of Chicago Press, 1970).

Reading 49 (Sivan)

1   A. Jarisha, *Shari'at Allah Hakima* (Cairo, 1977), ch. 2.
2   A. 'Abd al-Mu'ti, 'Egyptian Broadcasting', *Dirasat 'Arabiyya* (October 1978), pp. 35–41.
3   *al-Da'wa*, April 1977, pp. 4, 42.

Reading 50 (Offe)

1   E. Lederer and J. Marschak, 'Die Klassen auf dem Arbeitsmarkt und ihre Organisation', *Grundriss der Sozialökonomik* (Tübingen), 9 (1927), p. 112.

2 K. Polanyi, *The Great Transformations* (Boston, Mass., 1944), pp. 94ff.
3 E. Preiser, 'Besitz und Macht in der Distributionstheorie', in E. Salin (ed.), *Synopsis: Festgabe für Alfred Weber* (Heidelberg, 1948), p. 346.

Reading 53 (Routledge)

1 R. Martin, *New Technology and Industrial Relations* in Fleet Street (Oxford: Oxford University Press, 1981), p. 255.
2 Ibid., p. 279.
3 *The Times*, 23 October 1980.

Reading 54 (Schoenberger)

1 M. Aglietta, *A Theory of Capitalist Regulation* (London: New Left Books, 1979), p. 117.
2 Ibid.
3 A. Lipietz, 'Towards Global Fordism?', *New Left Review*, 132 (1982).
4 M. Aglietta, 'World Capitalism in the Eighties', *New Left Review*, 136 (1982), p. 6.
5 A. Gramsci, 'Americanism and Fordism', in *Selections from the Prison Notebooks*, ed. Q. Hoare and G. Smith (London: Lawrence and Wishart, 1971), p. 311.

Reading 55 (Pearson)

1 D. Elson and R. Pearson, 'The Latest Phase of the Internationalisation of Capital and its Implications for Women in the Third World', IOS Discussion Paper no. 150 (University of Sussex, 1980).
2 W. Konig, *Towards an Evaluation of International Subcontracting Activities in Developing Countries*, Report on Maquiladoras, Mexico (Mexico City: UNECLA, 1975).
3 L. Lim, *Women Workers in Multinational Corporations in Developing Countries*, Women's Studies Program Occasional Paper no. 9 (Michigan: University of Michigan, 1978), p. 37.
4 M. P. Fernandez-Kelly, *For We are Sold, I and My People: Women and Industry in Mexico's Frontiers* (Albany, NY: SUNY, 1983).
5 Ibid., p. 51.
6 Ibid., p. 85.

Reading 56 (Lyon)

1 Information Technology Advisory Panel, *Learning to Live with IT* (London: HMSO, 1986).
2 B. Goudzwaard, *Aid for the Overdeveloped West* (Toronto: Wedge, 1975), p. 4.
3 H. Jonas, *The Imperative of Responsibility* (Chicago: University of Chicago Press, 1984).

Reading 57 (Worsley)

1 K. Clark, *From Savagery to Civilization* (London, 1959), p. 30.
2 H. F. MacNair (ed.), *Modern Chinese History* (Shanghai, 1927), pp. 1–11.
3 A. D. Waley, *The Opium War through Chinese Eyes* (London, 1958), p. 33.
4 A. M. Mote (ed.), *The Travels of Marco Polo* (1946), pp. 278–96.
5 G. R. Idell (ed.), *The Bernal Díaz Chronicles* (1967), pp. 148–9.
6 H. R. Hays, *From Ape to Angel*: An Informal History of Social Anthropology (London, 1959), p. 257.
7 L. V. de Camoens, *The Lusiads*, tr. W. C. Atkinson (London, 1973), vol. II, canto X, stanzas 10, 43.

Reading 58 (Hoogvelt)

1 UNCTAD, *Trade and Development Report* (Geneva: UNCTAD, 1982), p. 102.
2 R. Prebisch, *Towards a New Trade Policy of Development, Proceedings of UN Conference on Trade and Development*, vol. 2 (Geneva: UNCTAD, 1964).
3 F. Cardoso and E. Faletto, *Dependency and Development in Latin America* (Berkeley, Ca.: University of California Press, 1979).
4 *Survey of Duty-Free Export Zones in SPO Member Countries* (ASLON Productivity Center, 1975).

Reading 64 (Porter and Porter)

1 J. H. Turner (ed.), *The Rev. Oliver Heywood, 1630–1702* (Brighouse, Yorks, 1881–5), vol. 3, p. 207.
2 *Elizabeth Montagu, Her Correspondence from 1720 to 1761*, ed. E. J. Climenson (London, 1906), vol. 1, p. 33.
3 *The Diary of Ralph Josselin*, ed. A. Macfarlane (Oxford, 1976), p. 21.
4 *The Diary of Samuel Pepys*, ed. R. Latham and W. Matthews (London, 1971–), vol. 5, p. 10.
5 *Letters and Journals of Lord Byron*, ed. L. A. Marchand (London, 1982), vol. 2, p. 58.

Reading 65 (Hall)

1 Royal College of General Practitioners, *Trends in General Practice* (London: RCGP, 1977).
2 Quoted in S. Lohr, 'Free-market Health System: New Thatcher Goal for Britain', *New York Times*, 1 February 1989.

Reading 66 (Hartmann)

1 J. P. Grant, *The State of the World's Children, 1982–83* (New York: UNICEF, 1983), p. 7.

Reading 67 (Kimmel)

1   P. Zagorin, 'Prolegomena to a Comparative History of Revolution in Early Modern Europe', *Comparative Studies in Society and History*, 18/2 (1976), p. 151.
2   R. E. Park, *Society* (Glencoe, Ill.: Free Press, 1955), p. 36.
3   J. Baecheler, *Revolution* (New York: Harper and Row, 1975), p. 91.
4   S. Neumann, 'The International Civil War', *World Politics*, 1/3 (1949), p. 333n.
5   E. K. Trimberger, *Revolution from Above: Military Bureaucrats and Development in Japan, Turkey, Egypt and Peru* (New Brunswick, NJ: Transaction, 1978), p. 12.
6   C. J. Friedrich (ed.), *Revolution* (New York: Atherton, 1966), p. 5.
7   S. Huntington, *Political Order in Changing Societies* (New Haven, Conn.: Yale University Press, 1968), p. 264.
8   T. Skocpol, *States and Social Revolutions: A Comparative Analysis of France, Russia and China* (Cambridge: Cambridge University Press, 1979), p. 4.
9   P. Calvert, *Revolution* (London: Macmillan, 1970), p. 15.

Reading 69 (Boden)

1   J. Meyrowitz, *No Sense of Place: The Impact of Electronic Media on Social Behaviour* (New York: Oxford University Press, 1985), p. 20.
2   For example, P. Sorokin, *The Sociology of Revolution* (New York: Howard Fertig, 1967 [1925]), pp. 6–12.
3   T. Skocpol, *States and Social Revolutions: A Comparative Analysis of France, Russia and China* (Cambridge: Cambridge University Press, 1979), p. 4.
4   C. Johnson, *Revolutionary Change* (Stanford, Ca.: Stanford University Press, 1982), pp. 169–75.
5   For example, L. Hunt, *Politics, Culture, and Class in the French Revolution* (Berkeley, Ca.: University of California Press, 1984), pp. 218–24.
6   A. Giddens, *The Nation-State and Violence* (Cambridge: Polity Press, 1987); 'Nine Theses on the Future of Sociology', in A. Giddens (ed.), *Social Theory and Modern Sociology* (Stanford, Ca.: Stanford University Press, 1987).
7   For example, *Le Monde*, 'Les Radios, premières ambassadrices de la liberté d'émettre', 24 January 1990.
8   M. Kundera, 'The Tragedy of Central Europe', *New York Review of Books*, 26 April 1984, pp. 33.
9   M. Gorbachev, speech at Stanford University, 4 June 1990.
10 M. Foucault, *Language, Counter-Memory, Practice* (Ithaca, NY: Cornell University Press, 1977), pp. 154–7.

Reading 74 (Heritage)

1   E. Durkheim, *The Rules of Sociological Method* (London: Routledge and Kegan Paul, 1982 [1897]).
2   H. Sacks, 'Sociological Description', *Berkeley Journal of Sociology*, 8 (1963), pp. 1–16.

3 H. Sacks, unpublished lectures, transcribed and indexed by G. Jefferson (University of California at Irvine, 1964–72).

4 Ibid.

5 Transcription conventions: a single left bracket [indicates the point of overlap onset; a single right bracket] indicates the point at which an utterance or utterance part terminates *vis-à-vis* another; (.) indicates a tiny 'gap' within or between utterances...probably no more than one-tenth of a second; :: colons indicate prolongation of the immediately prior sound – the length of the colon row indicates length of the prolongation; WORD upper case indicates especially loud sound.

6 H. Sacks, 'Methodological Remarks', in J. M. Atkinson and J. C. Heritage (eds), *Structures of Social Action: Studies in Conversation Analysis* (Cambridge: Cambridge University Press, 1984).

Index